LEADING FACTS
OF HISTORY SERIES

By D. H. MONTGOMERY

BEGINNER'S AMERICAN HISTORY
(Biographies of Eminent Americans)

AN ELEMENTARY AMERICAN HISTORY

THE LEADING FACTS OF AMERICAN
HISTORY (Revised Edition)

THE STUDENT'S AMERICAN HISTORY
(Revised Edition)

THE LEADING FACTS OF ENGLISH
HISTORY (Revised Edition)

THE LEADING FACTS OF FRENCH
HISTORY

KING GEORGE V

The Leading Facts of History Series

THE LEADING FACTS OF ENGLISH HISTORY

BY

D. H. MONTGOMERY

"Nothing in the past is dead to the man who would learn how the present came to be what it is." — STUBBS, "Constitutional History of England"

REVISED EDITION

GINN AND COMPANY
BOSTON · NEW YORK · CHICAGO · LONDON

𝕿𝖍𝖊 𝕬𝖙𝖍𝖊𝖓𝖆𝖚𝖒 𝕻𝖗𝖊𝖘𝖘

GINN AND COMPANY · PRO-
PRIETORS · BOSTON · U.S.A.

I DEDICATE THIS BOOK
TO THE MEMORY OF MY FRIEND
J. J. M.
WHO GENEROUSLY GAVE TIME, LABOR
AND VALUABLE SUGGESTIONS
TOWARD THE PREPARATION OF THE FIRST EDITION
FOR THE PRESS

PREFACE

Most of the materials for this book were gathered by the writer during several years' residence in England.

The attempt is here made to present them in a manner that shall illustrate the great law of national growth, in the light thrown upon it by the foremost English historians. The present edition has been carefully revised throughout, and, to a considerable extent, rewritten.

The authorities for the different periods will be found in the Classified List of Books in the Appendix; but the author desires to particularly acknowledge his indebtedness to the works of Bright, Brewer, Gardiner, Guest, Green, Lingard, Oman, and Traill; to the source books of Lee and of Kendall; and to the constitutional histories of Stubbs, Hallam, May, and Taswell-Langmead.

The author's hearty thanks are due to the late Professor W. F. Allen, of The University of Wisconsin; Professor Philip Van Ness Myers, of College Hill, Ohio; Professor George W. Knight, of Ohio State University; and to a number of teachers and friends for many valuable suggestions which they have kindly made.

DAVID H. MONTGOMERY

CONTENTS

[1] Each of these six Periods is followed by a General Reference Summary of that period. See pp. 43, 71, 141, 174, 230, 316.

[2] For special Genealogical Tables see pp. 124, 140, 161, 172, 179, 207, 323.

LIST OF MAPS

ILLUSTRATIONS

SUGGESTIONS TO TEACHERS

The writer of this brief manual is convinced that no hard-and-fast rules can be laid down for the use of a textbook in history. He believes that every teacher will naturally pursue a system of his own, and that by so doing he will get better results than if he attempt to follow a rigid mechanical course which makes no allowance for individual judgment and gives no scope to originality of method.

The author would simply suggest that where time is limited it might be well to omit the General Reference Summaries (see, for instance, p. 43) and to read the text as a continuous narrative. Then the important points in each day's lesson might be talked over at the end of the recitation or on the following day.

On the other hand, where time permits a thorough course of study, all of the topics may be taken up and carefully examined, and the General Reference Summaries may be consulted by way of review and for additional information. The pupil can also be referred to one or more books (see the Classified List of Books in the Appendix) on the subjects under consideration.

Instead of the teacher's asking a prescribed set of routine questions, the pupil may be encouraged to ask his own. Thus in undertaking the examination of a given topic — say, the Battle of Hastings (§§ 69–75), the issue of the Great Charter (§§ 195–202), or " The Industrial Revolution " and Watt's invention of an improved Steam Engine (§ 563) - there are five inquiries which naturally arise and which practically co the whole ground.

These are : 1. *When did the event occur ?* 2. *Where did it o* 3. *How did it occur ?* 4. *What caused it ?* 5. *What came* It will be seen that these five questions call attention first to th nology of the event, secondly to its geography, thirdly to the na describing it, fourthly to its relations to preceding events, and fifth. its relations to subsequent events.

The pupil will find that while in some instances he can readily obtain answers for all of these inquiries, — for example, in the case of the Great

Charter, — in other instances he will have to content himself with the answer to only a part of the questions, perhaps, in fact, to only a single one; nevertheless the search will always prove instructive and stimulating. Such a method of study, or one akin to it, will teach the pupil to think and to examine for himself. It will lead him to see the inevitable limitations and the apparent contradictions of history. It will make him realize, as perhaps nothing else can, that the testimony of different writers must be taken like that of witnesses in a court of justice. He will see that while authorities seldom entirely agree respecting details, they will generally agree in regard to the main features of important events. Last of all, and best as well as last, these five questions will be found to open up new and broader fields of inquiry, and they may perhaps encourage the pupil to continue his work on some subject in which he becomes interested, beyond the limits of the textbook and the classroom.

Pursued in this way, the study of history will cease to be a dry delving for dead facts in the dust of a dead past. It will rouse thought, it will quicken the pulse of intellectual life, and it will end by making the pupil feel the full force of the great truth: that the present is an outgrowth of the past, and that it is only when we know what men have done, that we can hope to understand what they are now doing.   D. H. M.

LEADING DATES

(The most important constitutional dates are marked by an asterisk)

55 B.C. Cæsar lands in Britain (§ 18)
449 A.D. Coming of the Saxons (§ 36)
597. Coming of St. Augustine (§ 41)
878. Alfred's Treaty of Wedmore (§ 56)
1066. Battle of Hastings (§ 74)
*1100. Henry I's Charter of Liberties (§ 135)
*1164. Constitutions of Clarendon (§ 165)
*1190. Rise of Free Towns (§ 183)
1204. John's Loss of Normandy (§ 191)
*1215. John grants Magna Carta (§§ 198, 199)
*1265. De Montfort's Parliament (§ 213)
*1279. Statute of Mortmain (§ 226)
1282. Conquest of Wales (§ 218)
*1295. First Complete Parliament (§ 217)
*1297. Confirmation of the Charters (§ 220)
1336. Rise of Wool Manufacture (§ 236)
1338. The Hundred Years' War (§ 237)
1346. Battle of Crécy ; Cannon (§ 238)
*1350. Origin of Trial by Jury (§ 176)
1378. Wycliffe's Bible ; Lollards (§ 254)
1381. Revolt of the Labor Class (§ 251)
1390. Chaucer writes (§ 253)
*1393. Great Act of Præmunire (§ 243)
1455. Wars of the Roses (§§ 299, 316)
1477. Caxton introduces Printing (§ 306)
1485. Battle of Bosworth Field (§ 315)
1497. Cabot discovers America (§ 335)
1509. The New Learning (§ 339)
*1534. The Act of Supremacy (§ 349)
1536. The Monasteries destroyed (§ 352)
*1549. Protestantism established (§ 362)
*1554. Mary restores Catholicism (§ 370)
1558. Rise of the Puritans (§ 378)
1559. Act of Uniformity (§ 382)
1582, 1605. Bacon's New Philosophy (§ 393)
1587. Mary Queen of Scots executed (§ 397)
1588. Destruction of the Armada (§ 400)
1588. Rise of the English Navy (§§ 401, 408)
1589 (?). Shakespeare's First Play (§ 392)
1601. The First Poor Law (§§ 403, 607)
1604. The "Divine Right of Kings" (§ 419)
1607. Virginia permanently settled (§ 421)
1611. The "King James Bible" (§ 418)
1622. First Regular Newspaper (§ 422)
*1628. The Petition of Right (§ 433)
1642. The Great Civil War (§ 441)
*1649. Charles I beheaded ; the Commonwealth established (§§ 448, 450)
1651. Navigation Act (§ 459)
1660. Restoration of Monarchy (§ 467)
*1660. Abolition of Feudal Dues (§ 482)
1665. The Plague in London (§ 474)
1666. Great Fire of London (§ 474)
1670. Secret Treaty of Dover (§ 476)
1673. The Test Act (§ 477)
1678. The Disabling Act (§ 478)
*1678. Rise of Political Parties (§ 479)
*1679. Habeas Corpus Act (§ 482)
1684. Newton's Law of Gravitation (§ 481)
1685. Monmouth's Rebellion (§ 486)
1687. Declaration of Indulgence (§ 488)
1688. The Great Revolution (§ 491)
*1689. The Bill of Rights (§ 497)

*1689. Mutiny Act, Toleration Act (§ 496)
1690. Battle of the Boyne (§ 500)
1694. National Debt ; Bank of England (§ 503)
*1695. Liberty of the Press (§§ 498, 556)
1697. Peace of Ryswick (§ 502)
*1701. Act of Settlement (§ 497)
*1707. England and Scotland united (§ 513)
1713. Peace of Utrecht (§ 512)
1720. The South Sea Bubble (§ 536)
*1721. Rise of Cabinet Government (§ 534)
1738. Rise of the Methodists (§ 546)
1748. Treaty of Aix-la-Chapelle (§ 542)
1751–1757. English Conquests in India (§ 544)
*1759. The English take Quebec (§ 545)
*1776. American Independence (§ 552)
*1782. American Independence acknowledged (§ 553)
1784. Mail Coaches begin to run (§ 566)
1785. "Industrial Revolution" ; Canals ; Watt's Steam Engine (§ 563)
1796. Vaccination introduced (§ 537)
1799. First Savings Bank (§ 621)
*1800. Great Britain and Ireland united (§ 562)
1805. Battle of Trafalgar (§ 557)
1807. Steam Navigation begins (§ 565)
1812. War with America (§ 558)
1815. Battle of Waterloo (§ 559)
1819. The Six Acts (§ 571)
1829. Catholic Emancipation (§ 573)
1830. First Passenger Railway (§ 584)
*1832. Great Suffrage Reform (§ 582)
1834. Matches invented (§ 584)
1834. The New Poor Law (§ 607)
*1835. Municipal Reform (§ 599)
1837–1911. Colonial Expansion (§ 618)
*1838–1848. Rise of Chartists (§ 591)
1839. Postage Reform (§ 590)
1845. First Telegraph (§ 614)
1845. The Irish Famine (§ 593)
1846. Repeal of the Corn Laws (§ 594)
1857. Rebellion in India (§ 597)
1858. Jews enter Parliament (§ 599)
1859. Darwin's Evolution (§ 606)
1861. The *Trent* Affair (§ 598)
1866. Permanent Atlantic Cable (§ 595)
1867. Second Suffrage Reform (§ 600)
1869. Partial Woman Suffrage (§ 599)
1869. Free Trade established (§ 594)
1869. Irish Church disestablished (§ 601)
1870. The Education Act (§ 602)
*1870. Civil Service Reform (§ 609)
1870. Irish Land Act (§ 603)
1871–1906. Trades Unions Acts (§ 616)
1884. Third Suffrage Reform (§ 600)
*1888, 1894. Local Government Acts (§ 608)
1899. The Boer War (§ 623)
*1906. Labor enters Parliament (§ 628)
1908. Old-Age Pensions (§ 628)
1910. Imperial Federation (§ 625)
*1911. Parliament Act ; Salary Act (§ 631)
*1914. Irish Home Rule Bill (§ 633)
*1914. Great European War (§ 634)

xviii

THE LEADING FACTS OF
ENGLISH HISTORY

FIRST PERIOD[1]

" This fortress built by Nature for herself
Against infection and the hand of war ;
This happy breed of men, this little world,
This precious stone set in the silver sea,
Which serves it in the office of a wall,
Or as a moat defensive to a house,
Against the envy of less happier lands ;
This blessed plot, this earth, this realm, this England."
SHAKESPEARE, " Richard II "

BRITAIN BEFORE WRITTEN HISTORY BEGAN

1. The Earliest Inhabitants of England. England was inhabited
for many centuries before its written history began. The earliest
races that possessed the country were stunted, brutal savages.
They used pieces of rough flint for tools and weapons. From
flint too they produced fire. They lived by hunting and fishing,
and often had no homes but caves and rock shelters.

Following the Cave-Men came a race that had learned how to
grind and polish the stone of which they made their hatchets,
knives, and spears. This race cleared and cultivated the soil to
some extent, and kept cattle and other domestic animals.

2. The Britons. Finally, a large-limbed, fair-haired, fierce-eyed
people invaded and conquered the island. They came from the

---

[1] REFERENCE BOOKS on this Period will be found in the CLASSIFIED LIST OF
BOOKS in the Appendix. The pronunciation of names will be found in the Index.
The LEADING DATES stand unenclosed ; all others are in parentheses.

west of Europe. They made their axes, swords, and spears of bronze, — a metal obtained by melting and mingling copper and tin. These implements were far superior to any made of stone.

The new people were good farmers; they exported grain, cattle, and hides to Gaul (France), and mined and sold tin ore to merchants who came by sea from the eastern shores of the Mediterranean.

This strong and energetic race, known as Celts, eventually called themselves Britons. By the time they had adopted that name they had made a great step forward, for they had learned how to mine and manufacture iron, — the most useful metal known to man; from it they forged scythes, swords, and spears.

Such were the people Cæsar met when he invaded Britain, fifty-five years before the beginning of the Christian era. The great Roman general called the Britons "barbarians"; but they compelled him to respect them, for they were a race of hard fighters, who fearlessly faced even his veteran troops.

3. The Religion of the Britons; the Druids. The Britons held some dim faith in an overruling Power and in a life beyond the grave. They offered human sacrifices to that Power, and when they buried one of their warriors, they buried his spear with him so that he might fight as good a battle in the next world as he had fought in this one.

Furthermore, the Britons had a class of priests called Druids, who seem to have worshiped the heavenly bodies. These priests also acted as prophets, judges, and teachers. Cæsar tells us that the Druids instructed the youth about the stars and their motions, about the magnitude of the earth, the nature of things, and "the might and power of the immortal gods."

More than this, the Druids probably erected the massive stone columns of that strange structure, open to the sky, whose ruins may still be seen on the lonely expanse of Salisbury Plain. There, on one of the fallen blocks, Carlyle and Emerson sat, when they made their pilgrimage to Stonehenge [1] many years ago, and discussed the life after death, with other questions of Druid philosophy.

[1] Stonehenge: This remarkable structure is believed to be the remains of a prehistoric monument to the dead, which was, perhaps, used also as a place of worship. It stands on Salisbury Plain about nine miles northeast of the city of Salisbury. (See

TWO OF THE COLUMNS AT STONEHENGE

3

4. What we owe to Prehistoric Man. We have seen that the Romans called the Britons "barbarians" (§ 2). But we should bear in mind that all the progress which civilization has since made is built on the foundations which those primitive races slowly and painfully laid during unnumbered centuries of toil and strife.

To them we owe man's wonderful discovery of the power to produce fire. To them we are indebted for the invention of the first tools, the first weapons, and the first attempts at architecture and pictorial art. They too tamed the dog, the horse, and our other domestic animals. They also discovered how to till the soil and how to mine and manufacture metals. In fact those "barbarians" who lived in "the childhood of the world," and who never wrote a line of history, did some things equal to any which history records, for out of wild plants and trees they developed the grains and fruits which now form an indispensable part of "our daily bread."

Finally, through their incessant struggles with nature, and incessant wars among themselves, those rude tribes learned to establish forms of self-government for towns or larger districts. Many of their salutary customs — their unwritten laws — still make themselves felt in the world.[1] They help bind the English nation together. They do even more than that, for their influence can be traced in the history of the newer nations, which, like the American republic, have descended from the great mother-countries of Europe.

map facing p. 38.) It consists of a broken circle of huge upright stones, some of which are still connected at the top by blocks of flat stones. Within this circle, which is about one hundred feet in circumference, is a circle of smaller stones. The structure had no roof. The recent discovery of stains of bronze or copper on one of the great stones, seven feet below the surface, strengthens the theory that Stonehenge was constructed by the race who used bronze implements and who were later known as Britons (§ 2). Consult Professor C. Oman's "England before the Norman Conquest"; see also R. W. Emerson's "English Traits," and O. W. Holmes's fine poem on the "Broken Circle," suggested by a visit to Stonehenge.

[1] For example, parts of the "Common Law" can be traced back, through English "dooms" (decisions or laws), to prehistoric times. See E. A. Freeman in the Encyclopædia Britannica (10th edition, VIII, 276). The New England "Town Meeting" can be likewise traced back to the German ancestors of the Anglo-Saxons.

CARVED BONE, FLINT DAGGER, AND BRONZE SPEARHEAD

SECOND PERIOD[1]

"Father Neptune one day to Dame Freedom did say,
  'If ever I lived upon dry land,
  The spot I should hit on would be little Britain.'
Says Freedom, 'Why, that's my own island.'
O, 't is a snug little island,
  A right little, tight little island!
Search the world round, none can be found
  So happy as this little island."

T. DIBDIN

THE GEOGRAPHY OF ENGLAND IN RELATION TO ITS HISTORY[2]

5. Geographical Names given by the Britons and the Romans.
The steps of English history may be traced to a considerable
extent by geographical names. Thus the names of most of the
prominent natural features, the hills, and especially the streams,
originated with the Britons. They carry us back to the Bronze Age
(§ 2) and perhaps earlier. Familiar examples of this are found in
the name Malvern Hills, and in the word Avon ("the water"),
which occurs in Stratford-on-Avon, and is repeated many times in
England and Wales.

The Roman occupation of Britain is shown by the names ending
in "cester" or "chester" (a corruption of *castra*, a military camp).
Thus Leicester, Worcester, Dorchester, Colchester, Chester, indicate
that these places were walled towns and military stations.

6. Saxon and Danish Names. On the other hand, the names of
many of the great political divisions, especially in the south and

1 REFERENCE BOOKS on this Period will be found in the CLASSIFIED LIST OF
BOOKS in the Appendix. The pronunciation of names will be found in the Index.
The LEADING DATES stand unenclosed; all others are in parentheses.

2 As this Period necessarily contains references to certain events which occurred
in later history, it may be advantageously reviewed by the pupil after he has reached
an advanced stage in his course of study.

east of England, mark the Saxon settlements, such as Essex (the East Saxons), Sussex (the South Saxons), Middlesex (the Middle or Central Saxons). In the same way the settlement of the two divisions of the Angles on the coast is indicated by the names Norfolk (the North folk) and Suffolk (the South folk). (See map facing p. 24.)

The conquests and settlements of the Danes are readily traced by the Danish termination " by " (an abode or town), as in Derby, Rugby, Grimsby. They occur with scarcely an exception north of London. They date back to the time when King Alfred made the Treaty of Wedmore (§ 56), A.D. 878, by which the Danes agreed to confine themselves to the northern half of the country. (See map facing p. 32.)

7. Norman Names. The conquest of England by the Normans created but few new names. These, as in the case of Richmond and Beaumont, generally show where the invading race built a castle or an abbey, or where, as in Montgomeryshire, they conquered and held a district in Wales.

While each new invasion left its mark on the country, it will be seen that the greater part of the names of counties and towns are of Roman, Saxon, or Danish origin. With some few and comparatively unimportant exceptions, the map of England remains to-day in this respect what those races made it more than a thousand years ago.

8. Climate. With regard to the climate of England, — its insular form, geographical position, and its exposure to the warm currents of the Gulf Stream give it a temperature generally free from great extremes of heat or cold. On this account, it is favorable to the full and healthy development of both animal and vegetable life.

Nowhere is greater vigor or longevity found. Charles II said that he was convinced that there was not a country in the world, so far as he knew, where one could spend so much time out of doors comfortably as in England.

9. Industrial Division of England. From an industrial and historical point of view, the country falls into two divisions. Let a line be drawn from Hull, on the northeast coast, to Leicester, in the Midlands, and thence to Exmouth, on the southwest coast. (See map on p. 10.) On the upper or northwest side of that line will lie the coal and iron which constitute the greater part of the mineral wealth and form the basis of the manufacturing industry of England; here too are all the largest towns except London.

On the lower or southeast side of the line there will be a comparatively level surface of rich agricultural land, and most of the fine old cathedral cities with their historic associations; in a word, the England of the past as contrasted with modern and democratic England, that part which has grown up since the introduction of steam.

10. Eastern and Western Britain compared. As the southern and eastern coasts of Britain were in most direct communication with the Continent, and were first settled, they continued until modern times to be the wealthiest, most civilized, and progressive part of the island. Much of the western portion is a rough, wild country. To it the East Britons retreated, keeping their primitive customs and language, as in Wales and Cornwall.

In all the great movements of religious or political reform, up to the middle of the seventeenth century, we find that the people of the eastern half of the island were usually on the side of a larger measure of liberty; while those of the western half were generally in favor of increasing the power of the King and the Church.

11. Influence of the Island Form on the Roman Invasion. Geologists tell us that Great Britain was once connected with the mainland of western Europe. It was fortunate for Britain that this connection was severed and that it became an island. We see an illustration of this advantage in the case of the Roman invasion. It was easy for the Romans to march great armies into Gaul and take complete possession of that country, but it was with no little difficulty that they sent fleets across the tempestuous waters of the Channel. This may have been one reason why they never succeeded in permanently establishing their language and their laws in the island of Britain. It is true that they conquered and held it for several centuries, but they never destroyed its individuality, — they never Latinized it as they did France and Spain.

12. Influence of the Island Form on the Saxon Invasion. In like manner, when the northern tribes of Europe overran the Roman Empire, they found themselves, in some measure, shut out from Britain by its wall of sea. The Jutes, Saxons, and Angles could not enter it in countless hordes, but only in small numbers and by occasional attacks. Because of this, the invaders could only drive back the Britons by slow degrees, and they never entirely crushed them.

Again, the conquerors could not build up a strong, united kingdom, but they had to content themselves with establishing a number of petty kingdoms which were constantly at war with each other. Later, the whole of England became subject to a single sovereign. But the chief men of the separate kingdoms, which had now become simply shires or counties, retained a certain degree of control over the government. This prevented the royal power from becoming the unchecked will of an arbitrary ruler. Finally, it may be said that the isolation of England had much to do with the development of the strong individual character of its people.

13. Influence of the Island Form on the Danes and Normans. In the course of the ninth, tenth, and eleventh centuries the Danes invaded England, but the sea prevented their coming all at once and with overwhelming force. They got possession of the throne (§ 63) and permanently established themselves in the northern half of the country. The English, however, held their own so well that the Danes were eventually compelled to unite with them. Even when the Normans invaded England and conquered it (§§ 74, 107), they felt obliged to make many concessions to both the English and the Danes. The result was that every invasion of the island ended in a compromise, so that no one race got complete predominance. In time all the elements mingled and became one people.

14. Influence of the Channel in Later History. Furthermore, the immense protective value of the Channel to England may be traced down to our own day. In the great crisis when Simon de Montfort was fighting (1264) to secure parliamentary representation for the people (§ 213), King Henry III sought help from France. The French monarch got a fleet ready to send to England, but bad weather held it back, and Henry was obliged to concede De Montfort's demands for reform.[1]

Again, when the Spanish Armada swooped down upon England (1588) a terrible tempest dispersed a part of the enemy's fleet.

[1] W. Stubbs's " Select Charters," p. 401.

Many of the vessels were wrecked (§ 399) and only a few were left to creep back, crippled and disheartened, to the ports of Spain. When Queen Elizabeth publicly thanked the leaders of her valiant navy for what they had done to repel the Spanish forces, she also acknowledged how much England owed to the protective power of wind and wave.

The same elements taught Napoleon a lesson which he never forgot. He had carefully planned an expedition against England (§ 557), but violent and long-continued storms compelled him to abandon the hazardous undertaking (1804). The great French commander felt himself invincible on land, but he was obliged to confess that "a few leagues of salt water" had completely out-generaled him.

In fact, ever since England organized a regular navy (1512) the encircling arms of the ocean have been her closest and surest friend. They have exempted her from keeping up a large standing army and so preserved her from the danger of military despotism at home. They too have made her the greatest sea power,[1] and, at the same time, the greatest colonizing power[2] the world has yet seen. They have also made her the greatest commercial power on the globe.[3]

It is true that the use of steam for vessels of war has diminished the natural protective service of the Channel, since a hostile fleet can now move against England in almost any weather. Still, the "silver streak," as the English call that waterway, will always remain, in some degree, a defense against sudden invasion, except, of course, from a squadron of military airships.

15. England as a Commercial Center. In closing this period, the position of England, with respect to facilities for commerce, deserves particular attention. In the first place the country has many excellent harbors; next, it is situated in the ocean which is the great highway between the two continents having the highest civilization and the most constant intercourse. Finally, a glance at the

[1] The English navy far outranks that of any other nation in the number of its warships.

[2] The English colonial possessions and "spheres of influence" cover an area of more than 11,400,000 square miles. (See map between pp. 422, 423.)

[3] The total commerce of the United Kingdom in 1910 was nearly £912,000,000, and that of the British Empire exceeded £1,990,680,000.

maps on pages 185 and 420 will show that geographically England is located at about the center of the land masses of the globe.

It is evident that a large island so placed stands in the most favorable position for easy and rapid trade communication with every quarter of the world. For this reason England has been able to attain, and thus far to maintain, the highest rank among maritime and commercial powers. It is true that since the opening of the Suez Canal (1869) the trade with the Indies, China, and Japan has considerably changed. Many cargoes of teas, silks, spices, and other Eastern products, which formerly went to London, Liverpool, or Southampton, to be reshipped to different countries of Europe, now pass by other routes direct to the consumer. Furthermore, it is a question what effect the completion of the Panama Canal will have on English trade in parts of the Pacific. But for the present England retains her supremacy as the great carrier and distributor of the productions of the earth, — a fact which has had a very decided influence on her history, and on her relations with other nations, both in peace and war.

INDUSTRIAL MAP OF ENGLAND (§ 9)

THIRD PERIOD[1]

"Force and Right rule the world: Force, till Right is ready."
JOUBERT

ROMAN BRITAIN, 55 B.C.; 43–410 A.D.

A CIVILIZATION WHICH DID NOT CIVILIZE

16. Europe shortly before Cæsar's Invasion of Britain. Before considering the Roman invasion of Britain let us take a glance at the condition of Europe. We have seen that the tribes (§ 2) of Britain, like those of Gaul (France), were not mere savages. On the contrary, we know that they had taken more than one important step in the path of progress; still the advance should not be overrated, for north of the shores of the Mediterranean there was no real civilization.

17. Cæsar's Campaigns. Such was the state of Europe when Julius Cæsar, who was governor of Gaul, but who aspired to be ruler of the world, set out on his first campaign against the tribes north of the Alps (58 B.C.).

In undertaking the war he had three objects in view: First, he wished to crush the power of those restless hordes that threatened the safety of the Roman Republic. Next, he sought military fame in the hope that it would make him supreme ruler of that Republic. Lastly, he wanted money to maintain his army and to bribe the party leaders of Rome to help him carry out his political plans. To this end he compelled every tribe which he conquered to pay him tribute in cash or slaves.

18. Cæsar reaches Boulogne and crosses over to Britain, 55 B.C. In three years Cæsar had subjugated the enemy in a succession

---

[1] REFERENCE BOOKS on this Period will be found in the CLASSIFIED LIST OF BOOKS in the Appendix. The pronunciation of names will be found in the Index. The LEADING DATES stand unenclosed; all others are in parentheses.

of victories, and a great part of Europe lay helpless at his feet. Late in the summer of 55 B.C. he reached Boulogne on the coast of Gaul. Standing there, he could see the gleaming chalk cliffs of Britain, so vividly described in Shakespeare's "King Lear." [1]

While encamped on the shore he "resolved," he says, "to pass over into Britain, having had trustworthy information that in all

"THE WHITE WALLS OF ENGLAND." — THE SHAKESPEARE
CLIFF, DOVER

his wars with the Gauls the enemies of the Roman commonwealth had constantly received help from thence." [2]

Embarking with a force of between eight and ten thousand men [3] in eighty small vessels, Cæsar crossed the Channel and landed not far from Dover, where he overcame the Britons (§ 2), who made a desperate resistance. After a stay of a few weeks, during which he did not leave the coast, he returned to Gaul.

19. Cæsar's Second Invasion of Britain. The next year (54 B.C.), a little earlier in the season, Cæsar made a second invasion with a

1 Shakespeare's "King Lear," Act IV, scene vi.   2 Cæsar's "Gallic War," Book IV.
8 Cæsar probably sailed about the 25th of August, 55 B.C. His force consisted of two legions, the 7th and 10th. A legion varied at different times from 3000 foot and 200 horse soldiers to 6000 foot and 400 horse.

much larger force, and penetrated the country to a short distance north of the Thames. Before the September gales set in, he reëmbarked for the Continent, never to return.

The total results of his two expeditions were a number of natives carried as hostages to Rome, a long train of captives destined to be sold in the slave markets, and some promises of tribute which the Britons never fulfilled. Tacitus, the Roman historian, says Cæsar " did not conquer Britain ; he only showed it to the Romans."

20. The Third Invasion of Britain by the Romans, 43 A.D. For nearly a hundred years the Romans made no further attempt on Britain, but in 43 A.D. the Emperor Claudius invaded the island. After nine years' fighting, he overcame Caractacus, the leader of the Britons, and carried him in chains to Rome. The brave chief refused to beg for life or liberty. " Can it be possible," said he, as he was led through the streets, " that men who live in such palaces as these envy us our wretched hovels ! " " It was the dignity of the man, even in ruins," says the Roman historian, " which saved him." The Emperor, struck with his bearing and his speech, ordered him to be set free.

21. The Romans plant a Colony in Britain ; Llyn-din. Meanwhile the armies of the Empire had established a strong colony at Colchester in the southeast of Britain. (See map facing p. 14.) There they built a temple and set up the statue of the Emperor Claudius, which the soldiers worshiped, both as a protecting god and as the representative of the Roman Empire.

The army had also conquered other places. One of these was a little native settlement on a bend in the Thames where the river broadened slightly. It consisted of a few miserable huts and a row of intrenched cattle pens. It was called in the British tongue Llyn-din or the Fort-on-the-pool. This name, which was pronounced with difficulty by Roman lips, eventually became known wherever ships sail, trade reaches, or history is read, — London.

22. Expedition against the Druids. But in order to complete the conquest of the country, the Roman generals resolved to crush the power of the Druids (§ 3), since these priests exhorted the Britons to refuse to surrender. The island of Anglesey, off the northwest coast of Wales, was the stronghold to which the Druids had retreated. (See map facing p. 14.) As the Roman soldiers approached to attack them, they beheld the priests and women standing on the shore, with uplifted hands, uttering "dreadful prayers and imprecations."

For a moment the Roman troops hesitated; then they rushed upon the Druids, cut them to pieces, and cast their bodies into their own sacred fires. From this blow Druidism as an organized faith never recovered, though traces of its religious rites still survive in the use of the mistletoe at Christmas and in May-day festivals.

23. Revolt of Boadicea (61). Still the power of the Latin legions was only partly established, for while the Roman general was absent with his troops at Anglesey, a formidable revolt had broken out in the east. A British chief, in order to secure half of his property to his family at his death, left it to be equally divided between his daughters and the Emperor. The governor of the district, under the pretext that Boadicea, the widow of the dead chief, had concealed part of the property, seized the whole of it.

Boadicea protested. To punish her presumption, the Romans stripped and scourged her, and inflicted still more brutal and infamous treatment on her daughters. Maddened by these outrages, Boadicea appealed to her countrymen for vengeance. The enraged Britons fell upon London, and other places held by the Romans, burned them to the ground, and slaughtered many thousand inhabitants. But in the end the Roman forces gained the victory, and Boadicea took her own life rather than fall into the hands of her conqueror.

The "warrior queen" died, let us trust, as the poet has represented, animated by the prophecy of the Druid priest that, —

> " Rome shall perish — write that word
>   In the blood that she has spilt; —
> Perish, hopeless and abhorred,
>   Deep in ruin, as in guilt." [1]

24. Christianity introduced into Britain. Perhaps it was not long after this that Christianity made its way to Britain; if so, it crept in so silently that nothing certain can be learned of its advent. The first church, it is said, was built at Glastonbury, in the southeast

---

[1] Cowper's " Boadicea. "

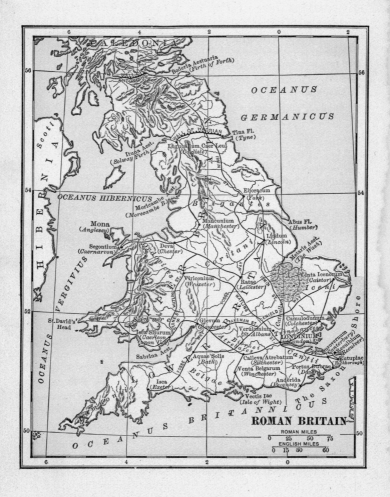

ROMAN BRITAIN

of the island. (See map facing p. 38.) It was a long, shedlike structure of wickerwork. "Here," says an old writer,[1] "the converts watched, fasted, preached, and prayed, having high meditations under a low roof and large hearts within narrow walls."

At first no notice was taken of the new religion. It was the faith of the poor and the obscure, and the Roman generals treated it with contempt; but as it continued to spread, it caused alarm.

The Roman Emperor was not only the head of the state, but the head of religion as well. He represented the power of God on earth: to him every knee must bow (§ 21). But the Christians refused this homage. They put Christ first; for that reason they were dangerous to the state, and were looked upon as traitors and rebels, or as men likely to become so.

25. Persecution of British Christians; St. Alban. Toward the last of the third century the Roman Emperor Diocletian resolved to root out this pernicious belief. The first British martyr was Alban. He refused to sacrifice to the Roman deities, and was beheaded.

But the ancient historian [2] says, with childlike simplicity, that the executioner who struck "the wicked stroke was not permitted to rejoice over the deed, for his eyes dropped out upon the ground together with the blessed martyr's head." Five hundred years later the magnificent abbey of St. Albans [3] rose on the spot to commemorate him who had fallen there.

26. Agricola builds a Line of Forts (78); Roman Agriculture. When Agricola, a wise and equitable Roman ruler, became governor of Britain he explored the coast, and first discovered Britain to be an island. He gradually extended the limits of the government, and, in order to prevent invasion from the north, he built a line of forts (completed by Antoninus) across Scotland, from the mouth of the river Forth to the Clyde. (See map facing p. 14.)

From this date the power of Rome was finally fixed. During the three hundred years which followed, the surface of the country underwent a great change. The Romans cut down forests, drained marshes, reclaimed waste land, and bridged rivers. Furthermore

---

[1] Thomas Fuller's " Church History of Britain. "
[2] Bede's " Ecclesiastical History of Britain," completed about the year 731.
[3] St. Albans : twenty miles northwest of London. (See map facing p. 16.)

they made the soil so productive that Britain became known in Rome as the most important grain-producing and grain-exporting province in the Empire.

27. Roman Cities; London; York. Where the Britons had once had a humble village enclosed by a ditch and protected by a stockade, the Romans built the cities of Chester, Lincoln, London, York, and other towns, protected by massive walls and towers of stone. These places have continued to be centers of population ever since.

London early became the Roman commercial metropolis, while the city of York in the north was made the military and civil capital of the country. (See map facing p. 14.) There the Sixth Legion was stationed. It was the most noted body of troops in the Roman army, and was called the "Victorious Legion." It remained there for upwards of three centuries. There, too, the governor resided and administered justice. For these reasons York got the name of "another Rome."

CARVED STONE FROM
ROMAN TEMPLE

The city had numerous temples and public buildings, such as befitted the Roman capital of Britain. There an event occurred in the fourth century which made an indelible mark on the history of mankind. Constantine, the subsequent founder of Constantinople, was proclaimed Emperor at York, and through his influence Christianity became the established religion of the entire Roman Empire.[1]

28. Roman System of Government; Roads. During the Roman possession of Britain the country was differently governed at different periods, but eventually it was divided into five provinces. These were intersected by a magnificent system of paved roads running in direct lines from city to city, and having London as a common center. (See map facing p. 14.)

Over these roads bodies of troops could march rapidly to any required point. By them, and by similar roads, leading through

---

[1] Constantine was the first Christian Emperor of Rome. The preceding emperors had generally persecuted the Christians.

France, Spain, and Italy, officers of state, mounted on relays of fleet horses, could pass from one end of the Empire to the other in a few days' time. (See map below, and that facing p. 14.)

So skillfully and substantially were these highways constructed, that modern engineers have been glad to adopt them as a basis for their work. The four chief Roman roads[1] continue to be the foundation, not only of numerous turnpikes in different parts of England, but also of several of the great railway lines, especially those from London to Chester and from London to York.

29. Roman Forts and Walls Defenses against Saxon Pirates. Next in importance to the roads were the fortifications. In addition to those which Agricola had built (§ 26), either Hadrian or Severus constructed a wall of solid masonry across the country from the shore of the North Sea to the Irish Sea. This wall, which was about seventy-five miles south of Agricola's work, was strengthened by a deep ditch and a rampart of earth. (See map facing p. 14.)

CHIEF ROMAN ROADS

It was further defended by square stone castles built at regular intervals of one mile. Between them were stone watchtowers, used as sentry boxes; while at every fourth mile there was a stone fort, covering several acres and occupied by a large body of troops.

But the northern tribes were not the only ones to be guarded against; bands of pirates prowled along the east and south coasts, burning, plundering, and kidnaping. These marauders came from Denmark and the adjacent countries (§ 37).

The Britons and Romans called them Saxons, a most significant name if it refers to the stout sharp knives which made them a terror to every land on which they set foot. To repel them, the Romans built a strong chain of forts along the coast, extending

[1] The four chief roads were: (1) Watling Street; (2) Icknield Street; (3) Irmin Street; and (4) The Fosse Way. (See map facing p. 14.)

from the Wash on the North Sea to the Isle of Wight on the south. (See map facing p. 14.)

The greater part of these Roman walls, fortifications, and cities have perished. But those which remain justify the statement that " outside of England no such monuments exist of the power and military genius of Rome."

30. Wherein Roman Civilization fell Short. But this splendid fabric of Roman power signally failed to win the support of the majority of the Britons. Civilization, like truth, cannot be forced on minds unwilling or unable to receive it. Least of all can it be forced by the sword's point and the taskmaster's lash.

In order to render his victories on the Continent (§ 17) secure, Cæsar butchered thousands of prisoners of war, or cut off the right hands of the entire population of large settlements to prevent them from rising in revolt.

The policy pursued in Britain, though very different, was equally heartless and equally fatal. There were rulers who endeavored to act justly, but such cases were rare. One of the leaders of the North Britons said, " The Romans give the lying name of Empire to robbery and slaughter; they make a desert and call it peace."

31. The Mass of the Native Population Slaves ; Roman Villas. It is true that the chief cities of Britain were exempt from oppression. They elected their own magistrates and made their own laws. But they enjoyed this liberty because their inhabitants were either Roman soldiers or their allies, or Romanized Britons.

Outside these cities the great mass of the native Britons were bound to the soil and could not leave it, while a large proportion were absolute slaves. Their work was in the brickyards, the quarries, the mines, or in the fields or forests.

The Roman masters of these people lived in stately villas adorned with pavements of different-colored marbles and beautifully painted walls. These country houses, often as large as palaces, were warmed in winter, like our modern dwellings, with currents of heated air. In summer they opened on terraces ornamented with vases and statuary, and on spacious gardens of fruits and flowers.[1] On the

---

[1] More than a hundred of these villas or country houses, chiefly in the south and southwest of England, have been exhumed. Some of them cover several acres.

other hand, the laborers on these great estates lived in wretched cabins plastered with mud and thatched with straw.

32. Roman Taxation and Cruelty. But if the condition of the British servile classes was hard, many who were free were but little better off, for nearly all that they could earn was swallowed up in taxes. The standing army of Britain, which the people of the country had to support, rarely numbered less than forty thousand. Great numbers of Britons were forced into the ranks, but most of them appear to have been sent away to serve abroad. Their life was one of perpetual exile. In order to meet the civil and military expenses entailed upon him, every farmer had to pay a third of all that his farm could produce, in taxes. Furthermore, he had to pay duty on every article that he sold; last of all, he was obliged to pay a duty or poll tax on his own head.

On the Continent there was a saying that it was better for a property owner to fall into the hands of savages than into those of the Roman assessors. When they went round, they counted not only every ox and sheep, but every plant, and registered them as well as the owners. " One heard nothing," says a writer of that time, speaking of the days when revenue was collected, " but the sound of flogging and all kinds of torture. The son was compelled to inform against his father, and the wife against her husband. If other means failed, men were forced to give evidence against themselves, and were assessed according to the confession they made to escape torment." [1]

So great was the misery of the land that sometimes parents destroyed their children, rather than let them grow up to a life of suffering. This vast system of organized oppression, like all tyranny, " was not so much an institution as a destitution," undermining and impoverishing the country. It lasted until time brought its revenge, and Rome, which had crushed so many nations of barbarians, was in her turn threatened with a like fate, by bands of northern barbarians stronger than herself.

---

[1] Lactantius, cited in Elton's " Origins of English History," p. 334. It should be noted, however, that Professor C. Oman in his " England before the Norman Conquest," pp. 175–176, takes a more favorable view of the condition of Britain under the Romans than that which most authorities maintain.

33. The Romans compelled to abandon Britain, 410. When Cæsar returned from his victorious campaigns in Gaul in the first century B.C., Cicero exultantly exclaimed, "Now let the Alps sink! the gods raised them to shelter Italy from the barbarians; they are no longer needed." For nearly five centuries that continued true; then the tribes of northern Europe could no longer be held back. When the Roman emperors saw that the crisis had arrived, they recalled their troops from Britain in 410. The rest of the Roman colonists soon followed.

At this time we find this brief but expressive entry in the "Anglo-Saxon Chronicle" (§§ 46, 99): "After this the Romans never ruled in Britain." A few years later this entry occurs: "418. This year the Romans collected all the treasures in Britain; some they hid in the earth, so that no one since has been able to find them, and some they carried with them into Gaul."

34. Remains of Roman Civilization. In the course of the next three generations the political and social elements of Roman civilization in Britain seem to have disappeared. A few words, such as "port" and "street," which may or may not have been derived from the Latin, have come down to us. But there was nothing left, of which we can speak with absolute certainty, save the material shell, — the walls, roads, forts, villas, arches, gateways, altars, and tombs, whose ruins are still seen scattered throughout the land.

The soil, also, is full of relics of the same kind. Twenty feet below the surface of the London of to-day lie the remains of the London of the Romans. In digging in the "City,"[1] the laborer's shovel every now and then brings to light pieces of carved stone with Latin inscriptions, bits of rusted armor, broken swords, fragments of statuary, and gold and silver ornaments.

So, likewise, several towns, long buried in the earth, and the foundations of upwards of a hundred country houses have been discovered; but these seem to be about all. If Rome left any traces of her literature, law, and methods of government, they are

---

[1] The "City": This is the name given to that part of central London, about a mile square, which was formerly enclosed by Roman walls. It contains the Bank of England, the Royal Exchange, and other very important business buildings. Its limit on the west is the site of Temple Bar; on the east, the Tower of London.

ROMAN WALL

At Cuddy's Crag, Northumberland

ROMAN ROAD

Salisbury Plain, Stonehenge, seen on the left, in the distance

21

so doubtful that they serve chiefly as subjects for antiquarians and historians to wrangle over.[1]

Were it not for the stubborn endurance of ivy-covered ruins like those of Pevensey[2] and York, and of that gigantic wall of Roman military masonry which still stretches across the bleak moors of Northumberland, we might well doubt whether there ever was a time when the Cæsars held Britain in their relentless grasp. (See map facing p. 14.)

35. Good Results of the Roman Conquest of Britain. Still, it would be an error to suppose that the Roman conquest and occupation of the island had no results for good.

Britain furnished Rome with abundant food supplies, and sent thousands of troops to serve in the Roman armies on the Continent. Britain also supported the numerous colonies which were constantly emigrating to her from Italy, and thus kept open the lines of communication with the mother country.

By so doing the island helped to maintain the circulation of the life currents in the remotest branches of the Roman Empire. Because of this, that Empire was able to resist the barbarians until the seeds of the old civilization had come to root themselves in France, Spain, and elsewhere. Those countries accepted more or less completely the Roman language, the Roman law, and the Roman idea of government. They also accepted that form of the Christian Church which the Emperor Constantine (§ 27) had established on a broad and permanent foundation.

In itself, then, though Britain gained perhaps comparatively little from the Roman occupation, yet through that occupation mankind was destined to gain much. During the four centuries in which the Latin legions held that remote portion of the Empire, the story of Britain was one which history often repeats, — a small outpost of Europe was sacrificed, for a time, in order that all the rest of western Europe might be saved.[3]

---

[1] Scarth, Pearson, Guest, Elton, and Coote believe that Roman civilization had a permanent influence; while Lappenburg, Stubbs, Freeman, Green, Wright, and Gardiner deny it.

[2] Pevensey, on the coast of Sussex: Here are the remains of a great Roman fortress. (See map facing p. 14.)

[3] Rome was plundered by the Goths in 410, and the Empire fell in 476.

FOURTH PERIOD[1]

"The happy ages of history are never the productive ones." — HEGEL

THE COMING OF THE SAXONS, OR ENGLISH
449 (?) A.D.

THE BATTLES OF THE TRIBES — BRITAIN BECOMES ENGLAND

36. The Britons beg for Help; Coming of the Jutes, 449 (?).
The Britons were in perilous condition after the Romans had left
the island (§ 33). They had lost their old spirit (§§ 2, 18).[2] They
were no longer brave in war or faithful in peace. The Picts and
Scots[3] attacked them on the northwest, and the Saxon pirates (§ 29)
assailed them on the southeast. These terrible foes cut down the
Britons, says an old writer, as "reapers cut down grain ready for
the harvest."

At length the chief men wrote to the Roman consul, begging
him to help them. They entitled their piteous and pusillanimous
appeal, "The Groans of the Britons." They said, "The savages
drive us to the sea, the sea casts us back upon the savages; between them we are either slaughtered or drowned." But the consul was busy fighting enemies at home, and he left the groaning
Britons to shift for themselves.

Finally, the courage of despair forced them to act. They seem
to have resolved to fight fire with fire. Acting on this resolution,
they accordingly invited a band of sea rovers to come and help

1 REFERENCE BOOKS on this Period will be found in the CLASSIFIED LIST OF
BOOKS in the Appendix. The pronunciation of names will be found in the Index.
The LEADING DATES stand unenclosed; all others are in parentheses.

2 Gildas, in Bohn's "Six Old English Chronicles"; but compare Professor
C. Oman's "England before the Norman Conquest," pp. 175-176.

3 The Picts and Scots were ancient savage tribes of Scotland.

23

them against the Picts and Scots. The chiefs of these Jutes[1] or Saxon pirates did not wait for a second invitation. Seizing their "rough-handled spears and bronze swords," they set sail for the shining chalk cliffs of Britain, 449 (?). They put an end to the ravages of the Picts and Scots. Then instead of going back to their own country, they took possession of the best lands of Kent and refused to give them up. (See map opposite.)

37. The Saxons and Angles conquer Britain. The success of the first band of sea robbers in Britain (§ 36) stimulated other bands to invade the island (477-541). They slaughtered multitudes of Britons and made slaves of many more. The conquerors named the parts of the country which they settled, from themselves. Each independent settlement was hostile to every other. Thus Sussex was the home of the South Saxons, Wessex of the West Saxons, Essex of the East Saxons. (See map opposite.) Finally, a band of Angles came from a little corner, south of the peninsula of Denmark, which still bears the name of Angeln. They took possession of all of eastern Britain not already appropriated. Eventually they came to control the greater part of the land, and from them, all the other tribes, when fused together, got the name of Angles or English (§ 50). (See map opposite.)

38. Resistance made by the Britons; King Arthur. Meanwhile the Britons had plucked up courage and made the best fight they could. They were naturally a brave people (§§ 2, 18). The fact that it took the Saxons more than a hundred years to get a firm grip on the island shows that fact. The legend of King Arthur's exploits also illustrates the valor of the race to which he belonged. According to tradition this British Prince, who had become a convert to Christianity (§ 25), met and checked the invaders in their insolent march of triumph. The battle, it is said, was fought at Mount Badon or Badbury in Dorsetshire. There, with his irresistible sword, "Excalibur," and his stanch British spearmen, Arthur

[1] The Jutes, Saxons, and Angles appear to have belonged to the same Teutonic or German race. They inhabited the seacoast and vicinity, from the mouth of the Elbe, northward along the coast of Denmark or Jutland. These tribes which conquered England, and settled there, remained for a long time hostile to each other, but eventually, they united and came to be known as Anglo-Saxons or English. (See map opposite.)

THE CONQUEST OF BRITAIN
BY THE LOW GERMAN TRIBES OF
SAXONS, JUTES, AND ANGLES (OR ENGLISH)

Home of the Norse
or Northmen

THULE
(Shetlands)

ORCADES
(Orkneys)

S C A N D I N A V I A

Picts

N O R T H

Jutes

Danes

Strathclyde

Northumberland

S E A

Angles

Angles

Scots

Angles

Angles

Angles

Jutes

Angles
or English

R. Elbe

HIBERNIA

B R I T A I N

East
Anglia

Angles

Saxons

Frisians
or
Franks

S a x o n s

R.
Weser

North Wales

Mercia

Essex

Saxons

Jutes

Wales

Wessex

Kent

Sussex

Saxons

(Afterwards)

NORMANDY

R.
Rhine

Welsh

(Afterwards)
BRITANNY

R. Seine

G A U L

(Afterwards called) F R A N C E

compelled his foes to acknowledge that he was not a myth but a man [1] able " to break the heathen and uphold the Christ."

39. The Saxons or English force the Britons to retreat. But though King Arthur may have checked the pagan Saxon invaders, he could not drive them out of the country. They had come to stay. On the other hand, many Britons were forced to take refuge among the hills of Wales. There they continued to abide. That ancient stock never lost its love of liberty. More than eleven centuries later their spirit helped to shape the destinies of the New World. Thomas Jefferson and several of the other signers of the Declaration of American Independence were either of Welsh birth or of direct Welsh descent.

40. Gregory and the English Slaves. The next period, of nearly eighty years, is a dreary record of constant battles and bloodshed. Out of this very barbarism a regenerating influence finally arose.

In their greed for gain, some of the English tribes did not hesitate to sell their own children into bondage. A number of these slaves, exposed in the market place in Rome, attracted the attention of a monk named Gregory.

Struck with the beauty of their clear, ruddy complexions and fair hair, he inquired from what country they came. " They are Angles " (§ 37), was the dealer's answer. " No, not Angles, but angels," answered the monk ; and he resolved that, when he could, he would send missionaries to convert a race of so much promise.[2]

41. Coming of Saint Augustine, 597. When Gregory (§ 40) became Pope he fulfilled his resolution, and sent Augustine with a band of forty monks to Britain. In 597 they landed on the very spot where the first Saxon war band had set foot on English soil nearly one hundred and fifty years before. Like Cæsar and his legions, Augustine and his monks brought with them the power of Rome. But this time that power did not come armed with the sword to force men to submit or die, but inspired with a persuasive voice to cheer them with new hope.

[1] See " Arthur " in the " Dictionary of National British Biography " ; and Professor Rowley in Low and Pulling's " Dictionary of English History," p. 434. See also Geoffrey of Monmouth's " History of the Britons " and Tennyson's " Idylls of the King."

[2] Bede's " Ecclesiastical History."

42. Augustine converts the King of Kent and his People (597).
The English at that time were wholly pagan, and had, in all probability, destroyed every vestige of the faith for which the British martyrs gave their lives (§ 25). But the King of Kent had married a French princess who was a devout Christian. Through the Queen's influence, the King was induced to receive Augustine. He was afraid, however, of some magical practice, so he insisted that their meeting should take place in the open air and on the island of Thanet. (See map facing p. 32.)

The historian Bede tells us that the monks, holding a tall silver cross and a picture of Christ in their hands, advanced and saluted the King. Augustine delivered his message, was well received, and invited to Canterbury, the capital of Kent. There the King became a convert to his preaching, and before the year had passed ten thousand of his subjects had received baptism; for to gain the King was to gain his tribe as well.

43. Augustine builds the First Monastery. At Canterbury Augustine became the first archbishop over the first cathedral. There, too, he established the first monastery in which to train missionaries to carry on the work which he had begun (§ 45). Part of the original monastery of St. Augustine is now used as a Church of England missionary college, and it continues to bear the name of the man who brought Christianity to that part of Britain. The example of the ruler of Kent was not without its effect on others.

44. Conversion of the North. The north of England, however, owed its conversion chiefly to the Irish monks of an earlier age. They had planted monasteries in Ireland and Scotland from which colonies went forth, one of which settled in Durham. Cuthbert, a Saxon monk of that monastery in the seventh century, traveled as a missionary throughout Northumbria, and was afterward recognized as the saint of the North. Through his influence that kingdom was induced to accept Christianity. Other missionaries went to other districts to carry the "good tidings of great joy."

In one case an aged chief arose in an assembly of warriors and said: "O king, as a bird flies through this hall in the winter night, coming out of the darkness and vanishing into it again, even such

THE COMING OF ST. AUGUSTINE

27

is our life. If these strangers can tell us aught of what is beyond, let us give heed to them."

But, as Bede informs us in his history of the English Church (§ 99), some of the converts were too cautious to commit themselves entirely to the new religion. One king, who had set up a large altar devoted to the worship of Christ, set up a smaller one at the other end of the hall to the old heathen deities, in order that he might make sure of the favor of both.

45. Christianity organized; Labors of the Monks. Gradually, however, the pagan faith was dropped. Christianity was largely organized by bands of monks and nuns, who had renounced the world in order to lead lives of self-sacrifice and service. They bound themselves by the three vows of obedience, poverty, and chastity, and the monastic law forbade them to marry. Monasteries existed or were now established in a number of places in England.[1]

These monasteries were educational as well as industrial centers. The monks spent part of each day in manual toil, for they held that " to labor is to pray." They cleared the land, drained the bogs, plowed, sowed, and reaped. Another part of the day they spent in religious exercises, and a third in writing, translating, and teaching.

Each monastery had a school attached to it, and each had, besides, its library of manuscript books and its room for the entertainment of travelers and pilgrims. In these libraries important charters granted by the King and important laws relating to the kingdom were preserved.

46. Literary Work of the Monks. It was at the monastery of Jarrow[2] that Bede wrote in rude Latin the Church history of England. It was at that in Whitby that the poet Cædmon composed his poem on the Creation, in which, a thousand years before Milton, he dealt with Milton's theme in Milton's spirit.

It was at the great monasteries of Peterborough and Canterbury that the " Anglo-Saxon Chronicle " was probably begun (§ 99). It

---

[1] For instance, at Lindisfarne, or Holy Island, off the coast of Northumberland (see Scott's " Marmion," Canto II, 9-10), at Wearmouth and Jarrow in Durham, at Whitby on the coast of Yorkshire, and at Peterborough in Northamptonshire. (See map facing p. 38.)

[2] Jarrow, Whitby, etc.; see note 1, above.

was the first history of England written in English, and the one from which we derive very important knowledge of the period extending from the beginning of the Christian era down to a time nearly a hundred years after the Norman conquest of the island. Furthermore we find that the history of the country was written by the monks in the form of independent narratives, some of which are of very great value as sources of information.[1]

47. Influence of Christianity on Society. But the power of Christianity for good was not confined to the monasteries; the priests took their part in it. Unlike the monks, they were not bound by monastic rules, though they were forbidden to marry. They lived in the world and worked for the world, and had an immense social influence. The Church, as a rule, in all forms of its activity took the side of the weak, the suffering, and the oppressed. Slavery was then the normal condition of a large class, but when the Church held slaves it protected them from ill usage. It secured Sunday for them as a day of rest, and it often labored effectually for their emancipation.

48. Political Influence of Christianity, 664. More than this, Christianity had a powerful political influence. A great synod or council was held at Whitby, on the coast of Yorkshire, 664, to decide when Easter should be observed. Delegates to that meeting were sent from different parts of the country. After a protracted discussion all the churches finally agreed to accept the Roman custom. This important decision encouraged a spirit of true religious unity. The bishops, monks, and priests who gathered at Whitby represented Saxon tribes which were often bitterly hostile to each other (§ 37), but their action on the Easter question united them in a certain way. It made them feel that they had a common interest, that they were members of the same Church, and that, in that Church, they were laboring for the same object. The fact that they bowed to one supreme spiritual authority had a political significance. It suggested that the time might be coming when all

---

[1] See six extracts from the "Anglo-Saxon Chronicle," in E. K. Kendall's "Source-Book of English History," chaps. ii and iii; also William of Malmesbury's "Conquered and Conquerors" (1066), and Matthew Paris's "England in 1257," in the same book, pp. 41 and 78. See also Bohn's "Six Old English Chronicles."

the conflicting tribes or petty kingdoms in Britain would acknowledge the authority of one King, and form one English nation.

49. Egbert becomes King of Wessex, and Overlord of the Whole Country, 829. Somewhat more than a hundred and sixty years later a great step was taken toward the accomplishment of the political union of the different sections of Britain. By the death of the King of Wessex (§ 37), Egbert, a descendant of Cerdic, the first chief and King of that country, succeeded to the crown. He had spent some time in France at the court of Charlemagne and had seen that great ruler make himself master of most of western Europe. Egbert was not content to remain simply King of Wessex. He resolved to make himself master of the whole country. He began a series of wars by which he, at length, compelled all the other Saxon Kings to acknowledge him as their Overlord. That title marks the beginning, in 829, of a new period in the history of the island.

50. How Britain got the Name of England. In making himself supreme ruler over the entire English population of Britain, Egbert laid the foundations of what was finally to become the " Kingdom of England." Several causes contributed to this change of name. We can trace the process step by step. First, the people of Kent and the great council held at Whitby (§§ 42, 48) laid the cornerstone of the National Church ; next, the people of Wessex furnished the National Overlord (§ 49) ; finally, the preponderance of the people called Angles (§ 37) furnished the National Name of Angle-Land or England.

It is a fact worthy of notice, in this connection, that from Egbert as a royal source every subsequent English sovereign (except the four Danish Kings, Harold II, and William the Conqueror) has directly or indirectly descended down to the present time. (See Table of Royal Descent in the Appendix, p. xlii.)

51. Alfred the Great. Of these sovereigns the most conspicuous during the period of which we are writing was Alfred. He was a grandson of Egbert (§ 49). He was rightly called Alfred the Great, since he was the embodiment of whatever was best and bravest in the English character. The keynote of his life may be found in the words which he spoke at the close of it, " So long as I have lived, I have striven to live worthily."

ENGLAND
in 626

PICTS

Alcluyd
(Dumbarton)
R. Forth
Eadwinesburgh
Bamborough
LINDISFARNE
Degsastan?
Strathclyde
I. OF MAN
Bernicia
NORTHUMBERLAND
Cumbria
Deira
York
Godmundingham
Elmet
Loidis
Heathfield
Lindiswara
R. Humber
Chester
Rotford
Lincoln
Bangor Iscoed
The Wash
Gwynedd
R. Trent
Masenfield
(Oswestry)
Mercians
Leicester
Elmham
East
Angles
Middle
English
Bedford
WALES
Magesetan
R. Stour
Gloucester
East
Colchester
Saxons
Caerwent
Hwiccan
Cirencester
Middle
London
Deorham
Dorchester
Saxons
Bath
R. Thames
Canterbury
Somerset
KENT
Winchester
West
Saxons
South
Dorset
Saxons
Exeter
I. OF WIGHT
West Wales

Christianity was introduced into North Humberland at this period (see § 44);
and for a short time Edwin, King of North Humberland, became, says the Chronicle, "lord over all Britain, save Kent alone."

52. Danish Invasion. When Alfred came to the throne (871) the Danes, or Northmen, as they were often called, were sweeping down upon the country. A few months before he became King; he had aided his brother in a desperate struggle with them. In the beginning, the object of the Danes was to plunder, later, to possess, and finally, to rule over the country. They had already overrun a large portion of England and had invaded Wessex or the country of the West Saxons. (See map facing p. 30.) Wherever their raven flag appeared, destruction and slaughter followed.

53. The Danes or Northmen destroy the Monasteries. These terrible pirates despised Christianity. They scorned it as the weak religion of a weak people. They hated the English monasteries most of all and made them the especial objects of their attacks (§§ 43, 45, 46). Many of these institutions had accumulated wealth, and some had gradually sunk into habits of laziness, luxury, and other evil courses of life. The Danes, who were full of the vigorous virtues of heathenism, liked nothing better than to scourge these effeminate vices of the cloisters.

From the thorough way in which they robbed, burned, and murdered, there can be no doubt that they enjoyed their work of destruction. In their helplessness and terror, the panic-stricken monks added to their usual prayers, this fervent petition: "From the fury of the Northmen, good Lord deliver us!" The power raised up to answer that supplication was Alfred the Great.

54. Alfred's Victories over the Danes; the White Horse. After repeated defeats Alfred finally drove back these savage hordes, who thought it a shame to earn by sweat what they could win by blood.

In these attacks Alfred led one half the army and his brother Ethelred led the other. They met the Danes at Ashdown Ridge in Berkshire. (See map facing p. 32.) While Ethelred stopped to pray for success, Alfred, under the banner of the "White Horse," — the common standard of the English at that time, — began the attack and won the day.

Tradition declares that after the victory he ordered his army to commemorate their triumph by carving that colossal figure of a horse on the side of a neighboring chalk hill, which still remains so conspicuous an object in the landscape. It was shortly after this that Alfred became "King of the West Saxons"; but the war, far from being ended, had in fact but just begun.

55. The Danes compel Alfred to retreat. The Danes, reënforced by other invaders, overcame Alfred's forces and compelled him to retreat. He fled to the wilds of Somersetshire, and was glad to take up his abode for a time, so the story runs, in a peasant's hut. Subsequently he succeeded in rallying part of his people, and built a stronghold on a piece of rising ground, in the midst of an almost impassable morass. There he remained during the winter.

56. Alfred's Great Victory; Treaty of Wedmore, 878. In the spring Alfred marched forth and again attacked the Danes. They were intrenched in a camp at Edington, Wiltshire. He surrounded them, and starved them into complete submission. They had to confess that Alfred's muscular Christians were more than a match for the most stalwart heathen. The Danish leader swore to maintain a peace, called the Peace or Treaty of Wedmore. (See maps facing p. 32 and p. 38.) More than this, the discomfited warrior sealed the oath with his baptism, — an admission that Alfred had not only beaten him but converted him as well.

By the Treaty of Wedmore, 878, the Danes bound themselves to remain north and east of a line drawn from London to Chester, following the old Roman road called Watling Street. All south of this line, including a district around London, was recognized as the dominions of Alfred, whose chief city, or capital, was Winchester. (See map facing p. 32.)

By this treaty the Danes got much the larger part of England (called the Danelaw), but they acknowledged Alfred as their Overlord. He thus became, in name at least, what his predecessor, Egbert (§ 49), had claimed to be, — supreme ruler of the whole country, though the highest title he ever assumed was "King of the Saxons or English."

57. Alfred's Laws; his Translations. Alfred proved himself to be more than mere ruler, for he was also a lawgiver and teacher as well. Through his efforts a written code was compiled, prefaced by the Ten Commandments and ending with the Golden Rule.

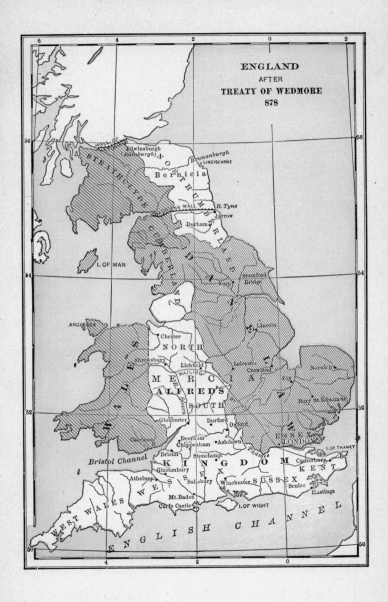

ENGLAND
AFTER
TREATY OF WEDMORE
878

Referring to this introduction, Alfred said, " He who keeps this shall not need any other law book."

Next, that learning might not utterly perish in the ashes of the abbeys and monasteries which the Danes had destroyed (§ 53), the King, though feeble and suffering, set himself to translate from the Latin the " Universal History of Orosius," and also Bede's valuable " Church History of England."

58. Alfred's Navy. Alfred, however, still had to fight against fresh invasion by the Danes, who continued to make descents upon the coast, and even sailed up the Thames to take London. The English King constructed a superior class of fast-sailing war vessels from designs made by himself. With this fleet, which may be regarded as the beginning of the English navy, he fought the enemy on their own element. He thus effectually checked a series of invasions which, if they had continued, might have reduced the country to barbarism.

59. Estimate of Alfred's Reign. Considered as a whole, Alfred's reign (871–901) is the most noteworthy of any in the annals of the early English sovereigns. It was marked throughout by intelligence and progress

His life speaks for itself. The best commentary on it is the fact that, in 1849, the people of Wantage, his native place, celebrated the thousandth anniversary of his birth, — another proof that " what is excellent, as God lives, is permanent." [1]

60. St. Dunstan's Three Great Reforms (960–988). Long after Alfred's death, St. Dunstan, then Archbishop of Canterbury and head of the English Church, set out to push forward the work begun by the great King. He labored to accomplish three things. First, he sought to establish a higher system of education; secondly, he desired to elevate the general standard of monastic life; finally, he tried to inaugurate a period of national peace and economic progress.

He began his first work when he had control of the abbey of Glastonbury, in the southwest of England. He succeeded in making the school connected with that abbey the most famous one in the whole kingdom (§ 45). He not only taught himself, but, by his enthusiasm, he inspired others to teach. He was determined

[1] R. W. Emerson's " Poems."

that from Glastonbury a spirit should go forth which should make the Church of England the real educator of the English people. Next, he devoted himself to helping the inmates of the monasteries in their efforts to reach a truer and stronger manhood. That, of course, was the original purpose for which those institutions had been founded (§ 45), but, in time, many of them had more or less degenerated. Every athlete and every earnest student knows how hard it is to keep up the course of training he has resolved upon. The strain sometimes becomes too great for him. Well, the monk in his cell had found out how difficult it was for him to be always faithful to his religious vows. St. Dunstan roused these men to begin their work anew. He re-created monasticism in England, making it stricter in discipline and purer in purpose.

Last of all, the Archbishop endeavored to secure greater freedom from strife. He saw that the continued wars of the English were killing off their young men — the real hope of the country — and were wasting the best powers of the nation. His influence with the reigning monarch was very great, and he was successful, for a time, in reconciling the Danes and the English (§§ 53, 56). It was said that he established " peace in the kingdom such as had not been known within the memory of man." At the same time the Archbishop, who was himself a skillful mechanic and worker in metals,[1] endeavored to encourage inventive industry and the exportation of products to the Continent. He did everything in his power to extend foreign trade, and it was largely through his efforts that " London rose to the commercial greatness it has held ever since." [2] Because of these things, one of the best known English historians,[3] speaking of that period, declares that Dunstan " stands forth as the leading man in both Church and State."

61. New Invasions ; Danegeld (992). With the close of Dunstan's career, a period of decline set in. The Northmen began to make fresh inroads (§ 53). The resistance to them became feeble

---

[1] The common people regarded his accomplishments in this direction with superstitious awe. Many stories of his skill were circulated, and it was even whispered that in a personal contest with the Evil One, it was the foul fiend and not the monk who got the worst of it, and fled from the saint's workshop, howling with dismay.

[2] R. Green's " English People."

[3] E. A. Freeman's " Norman Conquest," I, 65.

and faint-hearted. At last a royal tax, called Danegeld, or Dane money (992), was levied on all landed property in England in order to buy off the invaders. For a brief period this cowardly concession answered its purpose. But a time came when the Danes refused to be bribed to keep away.

62. The Northmen invade France. The Danish invasion of England was really a part of a great European movement. The same Northmen who had obtained so large a part of the island (§ 56) had, in the tenth century, established themselves in France.

There they were known as Normans, a softened form of the word "Northmen," and the district where they settled came to be called from them Normandy. They founded a line of dukes, or princes, who were destined, in the course of the next century, to give a new aspect to the events of English history.

63. Sweyn conquers England; Canute [1] (1017–1035). Early in the eleventh century Sweyn, the Dane, conquered England (1013), and "all the people," says the "Anglo-Saxon Chronicle" (§ 99), "held him for full king." He was succeeded by his son Canute (1017). He could hardly be called a foreigner, since he spoke a language and set up a government differing but little from that of the English.

After his first harsh measures were over he sought the friendship of both Church and people. He gave the country peace. Tradition reports that he rebuked the flattery of courtiers by showing them that the inrolling tide is no respecter of persons; he endeavored to rule justly, and his liking for the monks found expression in his song:

> " Merrily sang the monks of Ely
>   As Cnut the King was passing by."

64. Canute's Plan; the Four Earldoms. Canute's plan was to establish a great northern empire embracing Denmark, Norway, Sweden, and England. To facilitate the government of so large a realm, he divided England into four districts, — Wessex, Mercia, East Anglia, and Northumbria, — which, with their dependencies, embraced the entire country. (See map facing p. 38.)

---

[1] " Cnut," a shortened form of Canute.

Each of these districts was ruled by an earl [1] invested with almost royal power. For a time the arrangement worked well, but eventually discord sprang up and imperiled the unity of the kingdom. After Canute's death two of his sons divided England between themselves; both were bad rulers.

65. Restoration of the Saxon or English Kings; Edward the Confessor (1042–1066). On the accession of the Danish conqueror Sweyn (§ 63), Ethelred II, the English King, sent his French wife Emma back to Normandy for safety. She took her son, Prince Edward, then a lad of nine, with her. He remained at the French court nearly thirty years, and among other friends to whom he became greatly attached was his second cousin, William, Duke of Normandy.

The oppressive acts of Canute's sons (§ 64) excited insurrection (1042), and both Danes and English joined in the determination to restore the English line. They invited Prince Edward to accept the crown. He returned to England, obtained the throne, and pledged himself to restore the rights of which the people had been deprived. By birth King Edward was already half Norman; by education and tastes he was wholly so.

It is very doubtful whether he could speak a word of English, and it is certain that from the beginning he surrounded himself with French favorites, and filled the Church with French priests. Edward's piety and blameless life gained for him the title of "the Confessor," or, as we should say to-day, "the Christian."

He married the daughter of Godwin, Earl of Wessex, the most powerful noble in England. Godwin really ruled the country in the King's name until his death (1053), when his son Harold (§ 67) succeeded him as earl.

66. Edward the Confessor builds Westminster Abbey. During a large part of his reign the King was engaged in building an abbey or monastery at the west end of London, and hence called the Westminster.[2] He had just completed and consecrated this great

---

[1] Earl ("chief" or "leader"): a title of honor and of office. The four earldoms established by Canute remained nearly unchanged until the Norman Conquest, 1066.

[2] Minster: a name given originally to a monastery; next, to a church connected with a monastery; but now applied to several large English cathedrals.

SCENE OF ALFRED'S VICTORY, WHITE HORSE HILL, BERKSHIRE

work when he died, and was buried there. We may still see a part of the original building in the crypt or basement of the abbey, while the King's tomb above is the center of a circle of royal graves.

Multitudes made pilgrimages to King Edward's tomb, for the Pope had enrolled him among the saints. Even now a little band of devoted Catholics gather around his shrine every year. They go there to show their veneration for the virtues and the piety of a ruler who would have adorned a monastery, but had not breadth and vigor to fill a throne.

67. Harold becomes King (1066). On his deathbed, King Edward, who had no children, recommended Harold, Earl of Wessex, as his successor (§ 65). But the Normans in France declared Edward had promised that his cousin William, Duke of Normandy (§ 65), should reign after him. The Witan, or National Council of England (§ 81), chose Harold. That settled the question, for the Council alone had the right to decide who should rule over the English people. Harold was soon afterward crowned (January 16, 1066).

68. Duke William prepares to invade England (1066). William, Duke of Normandy, was getting ready for a hunting expedition when the news was brought to him of Harold's accession (§ 67). The old chronicler says that the Duke " stopped short in his preparations; he spoke to no man, and no man dared speak to him." Finally he resolved to appeal to the sword and take the English crown by force.

During the spring and summer of that year, he occupied himself in fitting out a fleet to invade England, and his smiths and armorers were busy making lances, swords, and coats of mail. The Pope favored the expedition and presented a banner blessed by himself, to be carried in the attack ; " mothers, too, sent their sons for the salvation of their souls."

69. The Expedition Sails (1066). William sailed on his great expedition in the autumn with a fleet of several hundred vessels and a large number of transports. The Duke's ship, with the consecrated banner at the masthead, led the fleet.

His army consisted of archers and cavalry. Its strength has been variously estimated at from 14,000 men up to 60,000. They

ENGLAND
AT THE TIME OF THE
NORMAN CONQUEST
1066

Showing the Four Great Earldoms of:
1. Wessex; 2. Mercia; 3. East Anglia;
4. Northumbria; with the dependent
kingdoms of North Wales, West
Wales, and the Isle of Man.

SCOTLAND

The Forth

R.Tweed

LOTHIANS

LINDISFARNE I.

Bamborough

STRATHCLYDE

GALLOWAY

NORTHUMBRIA

BERNICIA

CUMBERLAND

R. Tees

Whitby

Stamfordbridge

DEIRA

Beverley

R. Humber

R. Trent

Lincoln

Chester

Nottingham

R. Dee

Derby

Croyland

WATLING

Leicester Peterborough

NORTHFOLK

NORTH

MERCIA

EAST

Ely

ANGLIA

Thetford

WALES

OFFA'S

Worcester

Cambridge

SOUTHFOLK

Severn

R.

Bedford

Ipswich

R.Avon

Oxford

ESSEX

STREET

R. Thames

LONDON

Bristol

Chippenham

Wantage

Reading

Rochester

I. OF THANET

Ashdown

R. Avon

Bath

SURREY

KENT

Canterbury

Bristol Channel

Wedmore

Stonehenge

Winchester

Dover

Athelney

Glastonbury

SUSSEX

Senlac

Salisbury

Southampton Anderida

Hastings

WESSEX

MT. BADON

Pevensey

Exeter

Dorchester

WEST WALES

were partly his own subjects, and partly hired soldiers, or those who joined for the sake of plunder. William also carried a large force of smiths and carpenters, with timber ready cut and fitted to set up a wooden castle.

70. William lands at Pevensey. The next day the fleet anchored at Pevensey, on the south coast of England, under the walls of an old Roman fortress which had stood, a vacant ruin, since the Saxons stormed it nearly six hundred years before. (See map facing p. 38.) Tradition says that as William stepped on shore he stumbled and fell flat with his face downward. " God preserve us ! " cried one of his men ; " this is a bad sign." But the Duke, grasping the pebbles of the beach with both his outstretched hands, exclaimed, " Thus do I seize the land ! "

71. King Harold in the North. There was, in fact, no power to prevent him from establishing his camp, for King Harold (§ 67) was in the north quelling an invasion headed by the King of the Norwegians and his brother Tostig, who hoped to secure the throne for himself. Harold had just sat down to a victory feast, after the battle of Stamford Bridge, Yorkshire, when news was brought to him of the landing of William.

It was this fatal want of unity in England which made the Norman Conquest possible. If Harold's own brother, Tostig, had not turned traitorously against him, or if the north country had stood squarely by the south, Duke William might have found his fall on the beach an omen full of disaster.

72. What Duke William did after Landing. As there was no one to oppose him, William made a fort in a corner of the old Roman wall at Pevensey (§ 70), and then marched to Hastings, a few miles farther east, where he set up a wooden castle on that hill where the ruins of a later stone castle may still be seen. Having done this, he pillaged the country in every direction.

73. Harold marches to meet William. King Harold, having gathered what forces he could, marched to meet William at a place midway between Pevensey and Hastings, about five miles back from the coast. Harold had the advantage of a stockaded fort he had built ; William, that of a body of cavalry and archers, for the English fought on foot with javelins and battle-axes mainly.

The Saxons spent the night in feasting and song, the Normans in prayer and confession; both were eager to fight.

74. The Great Battle of Hastings, 1066. On the morning of the 14th of October the fight began. It lasted until dark, with heavy

THE BATTLE OF HASTINGS, 1066

From the Bayeux Tapestry. The Normans are on the left, the
Saxons on the right

loss on both sides. At length William's strategy carried the day, and Harold and his brave followers found to their cost that then, as now, it is "the thinking bayonet" which conquers. The English King was slain and every man of his chosen troops with him. A monk who wrote the history of the period of the Conquest, says that "the vices of the Saxons had made them effeminate and womanish, wherefore it came to pass that, running against Duke William, they lost themselves and their country with one, and that an easy and light, battle." Doubtless the English had fallen off in many ways from what they had been generations earlier; but the record at Hastings shows that they had lost neither strength, courage, nor endurance, and a harder battle was never fought on British soil.

75. Battle Abbey; Harold's Grave; the Bayeux Tapestry. A few years later, the Norman Conqueror built the Abbey of Battle on the spot to commemorate the victory by which he gained his crown. He directed that the monks of the abbey should chant perpetual prayers over the Norman soldiers who had fallen there. Here, also, tradition represents him as having buried Harold's body, just after the fight, under a heap of stones by the seashore. Some months later, it is said that the friends of the English King removed the remains to Waltham, near London, and buried them in the church which he had built and endowed there. Be that as it may, his grave, wherever it is, is the grave of the old England. Henceforth a new people (though not a new race, for the Normans originally came from the same Germanic stock as the English did) (§ 62) will appear in the history of the island.

Several contemporary accounts of the battle exist by both French and English writers, but one of the best histories of it is that which was wrought in colors by a woman's hand. It represents the scenes of the famous contest on a strip of canvas known as the Bayeux Tapestry (§ 155), a name derived from the French town where it is still preserved.

76. Close of the Period; what the Saxon Conquest of Britain had accomplished. The death of King Harold ends the Saxon or English period of history. Before entering upon the reign of William the Conqueror let us consider what that period had accomplished. We have seen that the Jutes, Saxons, and Angles (§§ 36, 37) invaded Britain at a critical period. Its original inhabitants had become cowed and enervated by the despotism and the worn-out civilization forced on them by the Romans (§§ 30–32).

The newcomers brought that healthy spirit of barbarism, that irrepressible love of personal liberty, which the country sorely needed. The conquerors were rough, ignorant, cruel; but they were vigorous, fearless, and determined.

These qualities were worth a thousand times more to Britain than the gilded corruption of Rome. But in the course of time the Saxons or English themselves lost spirit (§ 36). Their besetting sin was a stolidity which degenerated into animalism and sluggish content.

77. Fresh Elements contributed by the Danes or Northmen. Then came the Danes or Northmen (§§ 52, 63). They brought with them a new spirit of still more savage independence which found expression in their song, " I trust my sword, I trust my steed, but most I trust myself at need."

They conquered a large part of the island, and in conquering regenerated it. So strong was their love of independence, that even the lowest classes of farm laborers were quite generally free.

More small independent landholders were found among the Danish population than anywhere else; and it is said that the number now existing in the region which they settled in the northeast of England is still much larger than in the south. (See map facing p. 32.) Finally, the Danes and the English, both of whom sprang from the North German tribes (§ 36), mingled and became in all respects one people.

78. Summary: What the Anglo-Saxons accomplished. Thus Jutes, Saxons, Angles, and Danes, whom together we may call the Anglo-Saxons,[1] laid the corner stone of the English nation. However much that nation has changed since, it remains, nevertheless, in its solid and fundamental qualities, what those peoples made it.

They gave first the language, simple, strong, direct, and plain, — the familiar, everyday speech of the fireside and the street, the well-known words of both the newspaper and the Bible.

Next they established the government in its main outlines as it still exists ; that is, a king, a legislative body representing the people, and a judicial system embodying the germ, at least, of trial by jury (§ 89).

Last, and best, they furnished conservative patience, persistent effort, indomitable tenacity of purpose, and cool, determined

---

[1] Anglo-Saxons : Some authorities insist that this phrase means the Saxons of England in distinction from those of the Continent. It is used here, however, in the sense given by Professor Freeman, as a term describing the people formed in England by the union of the Germanic tribes which had settled in the island.

courage. These qualities have won glorious victories on both sides of the Atlantic, not only in the conflicts of war, but in the contests of peace, and who can doubt that they are destined to win still greater ones in the future?

GENERAL REFERENCE SUMMARY OF THE SAXON, OR EARLY ENGLISH, PERIOD (449–1066)

This section contains a summary of much of the preceding period, with considerable additional matter. It is believed that teachers and pupils may find it useful for reference on certain topics (e.g. feudalism, etc.) which could not be conveniently treated in detail in the history proper.

I. GOVERNMENT. II. RELIGION. III. MILITARY AFFAIRS. IV. LITERATURE, LEARNING, AND ART. V. GENERAL INDUSTRY AND COMMERCE. VI. MODE OF LIFE, MANNERS, AND CUSTOMS

I. GOVERNMENT

79. Beginning of the English Monarchy. During the greater part of the first four centuries after the Saxon conquest Britain was divided into a number of tribal settlements, or petty kingdoms, held by Jutes, Angles, and Saxons, constantly at war with each other. In the ninth century, the West Saxons, or inhabitants of Wessex, succeeded, under the leadership of Egbert, in practically conquering and uniting the country. Egbert now assumed the title of Overlord or Supreme Ruler of the English people. In time Britain came to be known, from the name of its largest tribe, the Angles, as Angle-Land, or England. Meanwhile the Danes had obtained possession of a large part of the country on the northeast, but they eventually united with the English and became one people.

80. The King and the Witan. The government of England was vested in an elective sovereign, assisted by the National Council of the Witan, or Wise Men. It is an open question whether every freeman had the right to attend this national council,[1] but, in practice, the right became confined to a small number of the nobles and clergy.

81. What the Witan could do. 1. The Witan elected the King (its choice being confined, as a rule, to the royal family). 2. In case of misgovernment, it deposed him. 3. It made or confirmed grants of public lands. 4. It acted as a supreme court of justice both in civil and criminal cases. (See the Constitutional Summary in the Appendix, p. ii, § 3.)

---

[1] Professors Stubbs and Freeman take opposite views on this point.

82. What the King and Witan could do. 1. They enacted the laws, both civil and ecclesiastical. (In most cases this meant nothing more than stating what the custom was, the common law being merely the common custom.) 2. They levied taxes. 3. They declared war and made peace. 4. They appointed the chief officers and bishops of the realm.

83. Land Tenure before the Conquest. Before they invaded Britain the Saxons and kindred tribes appear to have held their lands in common. Each head of a family had a permanent homestead, but that was all.[1] " No one," says Cæsar, " has a fixed quantity of land or boundaries to his property. The magistrates and chiefs assign every year to the families and communities who live together, as much land and in such spots as they think suitable. The following year they require them to take up another allotment.

" The chief glory of the tribes is to have their territory surrounded with as wide a belt as possible of waste land. They deem it not only a special mark of valor that every neighboring tribe should be driven to a distance, and that no stranger should dare to reside in their vicinity, but at the same time they regard it as a precautionary measure against sudden attacks." [2]

84. Folkland. Each tribe, in forming its settlement, seized more land than it actually needed. This excess was known as Folkland (the People's land),[3] and might be used by all alike for pasturing cattle or cutting wood. With the consent of the Witan, the King might grant portions of this Folkland as a reward for services done to himself or to the community. Such grants were usually conditional and could only be made for a time. Eventually they returned to the community.

Other grants, however, might be made in the same way, which conferred full ownership. Such grants were called Bocland (Book land), because conveyed by writing, or registered in a charter or book. In time the King obtained the power of making these grants without having to consult the Witan, and at last the whole of the Folkland came to be regarded as the absolute property of the Crown.

85. Duties of Freemen. Every freeman was obliged to do three things: 1. He must assist in the maintenance of roads and bridges. 2. He must aid in the repair of forts. 3. He must serve in case of war. Whoever neglected or refused to perform this last and most important of all duties was declared to be a " *nithing*," or infamous coward.[4]

---

[1] Tacitus (" Germania ") says that each house "was surrounded by a space of its own."   [2] Cæsar, " Gallic War," Book VI.

[3] But some recent authorities regard it as family land.

[4] Also written *Niding*. The English, as a rule, were more afraid of this name than of death itself.

86. The Feudal System (see, too, the Constitutional Summary in the Appendix, p. iii, § 5). The essential principle of the feudal system was the holding of land on condition of military or other service. It appears to have gradually grown up in England from grants made by the King. In addition to the Eorls (earls)[1] or nobles by birth, there gradually grew up a class known as Thanes (companions or servants of the King), who in time outranked those who were noble by birth. He would frequently have occasion to give rewards to the nobles and chief men for faithful service and for deeds of valor. As nearly all his wealth consisted in land, he would naturally give that. To this gift, however, he would attach a condition. On making such a grant the King required the receiver to agree to furnish a certain number of fully equipped soldiers to fight for him. These grants were originally made for life only, and on the death of the recipient they returned to the Crown.

Next, the nobles and other great landholders, following the example of the King, granted portions of their estates to tenants on similar conditions, and these again might grant portions to those below them in return for satisfactory military or other service.

In time it came to be an established principle, that every freeman below the rank of a noble must be attached to some superior whom he was bound to serve, and who, on the other hand, was his legal protector and responsible for his good behavior. The man who refused to acknowledge his duty to serve a lord or superior was looked upon as an outlaw, and might be seized like a robber. In that respect, therefore, he would be worse off than the slave, who had a master to whom he was accountable and who was accountable for him.

Eventually it became common for the small landholders, especially during the Danish invasions, to seek the protection of some neighboring lord who had a large band of followers at his command. In such cases the freeman gave up his land and received it again on certain conditions. The usual form was for him to kneel and, placing his hands within those of the lord, to swear an oath of homage, saying, "*I become your man* for the lands which I hold of you, and I will be faithful to you

---

[1] The Saxons, or Early English, were divided into three classes : Eorls (they must not be confounded with the Danish *jarls* or *earls*), who were noble by birth ; Ceorls (churls), or simple freemen; and slaves. The slaves were either the absolute property of the master, or were bound to the soil and sold with it. This latter class, under the Norman name of *villeins*, became numerous after the Norman Conquest in the eleventh century. The chieftains of the first Saxon settlers were called either Ealdormen (aldermen) or Heretogas, the first being civil or magisterial, the latter military officers. The Thanes were a later class, who, from serving the King or some powerful leader, became noble by military service.

against all men, saving only the service which I owe to my lord the King." On his side the lord solemnly promised to defend his tenant or vassal in the possession of his property, for which he was to perform some service to the lord.

In these two ways, first, by grant of lands from the King or a superior, and, secondly, by the act of homage (known as *commendation*) on the part of the recipient when he had given up lands on condition of protection and had received them back again, the feudal system (a name derived from *feodum*, meaning land or property) grew up in England. Its growth, however, was irregular and incomplete ; and it should be distinctly understood that it was not until after the Norman Conquest in the eleventh century that it became fully established. It should also be distinctly understood that William the Conqueror made a most important change in this system by requiring the tenants of all the great landholders, as well as their masters, to swear direct obedience to him (§ 121).

87. Advantages of Feudalism. This system had at that time many advantages. 1. The old method of holding land in common was a wasteful one, since the way in which the possessor of a field might cultivate it would perhaps spoil it for the one who received it at the next allotment. 2. In an age of constant warfare, feudalism protected all classes better than if they had stood apart, and it often enabled the King to raise a powerful and well-armed force in the easiest and quickest manner. 3. It cultivated two important virtues, — fidelity on the part of the vassal, protection on that of the lord. It had something of the spirit of the Golden Rule in it. Its corner stone was the faithfulness of man to man. Society has outgrown the outward forms of feudalism, which like every system had its drawbacks, but it would seem as though it could never wholly outgrow the feudal principle.

88. Political Divisions ; the Sheriff. Politically the kingdom was divided into townships, hundreds (districts furnishing a hundred warriors, or supporting a hundred families), and shires or counties, the shire having been originally, in some cases, the section settled by an independent tribe, as Sussex, Essex, etc.

In each shire the King had an officer, called a shire reeve or sheriff,[1] who represented him, collected the taxes due the Crown, and saw to the execution of the laws. In like manner, the town and the hundred had a headman of its own choosing to see to matters of general interest.

89. The Courts. As the nation had its assembly of wise men acting as a high court, so each shire, hundred, and town had its court, which

---

[1] Reeve : a man in authority, or having charge of something.

all freemen might attend. There, without any special judge, jury, or lawyers, cases of all kinds were tried and settled by the voice of the entire body, who were both judge and jury in themselves.

90. Methods of Procedure; Compurgation. In these courts there were two methods of procedure : first, the accused might clear himself of the charge brought against him by compurgation[1]; that is, by swearing that he was not guilty and getting a number of reputable neighbors to swear that they believed his oath.

If their oaths were not satisfactory, witnesses might be brought to swear to some particular fact. In every case the value of the oath was graduated according to the rank of the person, that of a man of high rank being worth as much as that of twelve common men.

91. The Ordeal. Secondly, if the accused could not clear himself in this way, he was obliged to submit to the ordeal.[2] This usually consisted in carrying a piece of hot iron a certain distance, or in plunging the arm up to the elbow in boiling water.

The person who underwent the ordeal appealed to God to prove his innocence by protecting him from harm. Rude as both these methods were, they were better than the old tribal method, which permitted every man or every man's family to be the avenger of his wrongs.

92. The Common Law. The laws by which these cases were tried were almost always ancient customs, few of which had been reduced to writing. They formed that body of Common Law[3] which is the foundation of the modern system of justice both in England and America.

93. Penalties. The penalties inflicted by these courts consisted chiefly of fines. Each man's life had a certain "*wergild*" or money value. The fine for the murder of a man of very high rank was 2400 shillings; that of a simple freeman was only one twelfth as much.

A slave could neither testify in court nor be punished by the court; for the man in that day who held no land had no rights. If a slave was convicted of crime, his master paid the fine, and then flogged him until he had got his money's worth out of him. Treason was punished with death, and common scolds were ducked in a pond until they were glad to hold their tongues. These methods of administering justice were crude, but they had the great merit of being effective. They aimed to do two very necessary things : first, to protect the community against dangerous criminals; secondly, to teach those criminals that "the way of the transgressor is hard."

---

[1] Compurgation : the act of wholly purifying or clearing a person from guilt.
[2] Ordeal : a severe test or judgment.
[3] So called, in distinction from the statute laws made by Parliament.

II. Religion

94. The Ancient Saxon Faith. Before their conversion to Christianity, the Saxons worshiped Woden and Thor, names preserved in Wednesday (Woden's day) and Thursday (Thor's day). The first appears to have been considered to be the creator and ruler of heaven and earth; the second was his son, the god of thunder, slayer of evil spirits, and friend of man.

The essential element of their religion was the deification of strength, courage, and fortitude. It was a faith well suited to a warlike people. It taught that there was a heaven for the brave and a hell for cowards.

95. What Christianity did. Christianity, on the contrary, laid emphasis on the virtues of self-sacrifice and sympathy. It took the side of the weak and the helpless. The Church itself held slaves, yet it labored for emancipation. It built monasteries and encouraged industry and education. The church edifice was a kind of open Bible.

Very few who entered the sacred building then could have spelled out a single word of either the Old or New Testament, even if they had then been translated from Latin into English; but all, from the poorest peasant or meanest slave up to the greatest noble, could read the meaning of the Scripture histories painted in brilliant colors on wall and window.

The church, furthermore, was a peculiarly sacred place. It was powerful to shield those who were in danger. If a criminal, or a person fleeing from vengeance, took refuge in it, he could not be seized until forty days had expired, during which time he had the privilege of leaving the kingdom and going into exile.

This "right of sanctuary" was often a needful protection in an age of violence. In time, however, the system became an intolerable abuse, since it enabled robbers and desperadoes of all kinds to defy the law. The right was modified at different times, but was not wholly abolished until 1624, in the reign of James I.

III. Military Affairs

96. The Army. The army consisted of a national militia, or "*fyrd*," and a feudal militia. From the earliest times all freemen were obliged to fight in the defense of the country. Under the feudal system, every large landholder had to furnish the King a stipulated number of men, fully equipped with armor and weapons. As this method was found more effective than the first, it gradually superseded it.

The Saxons always fought on foot. They wore helmets and rude, flexible armor, formed of iron rings, or of stout leather covered with small plates of iron and other substances. They carried oval-shaped shields. Their chief weapons were the spear, javelin, battle-ax, and sword. The wars of this period were those of the different tribes seeking to get the advantage over each other, or of the English with the Danes.

97. The Navy. Until Alfred's reign the English had no navy. From that period they maintained a fleet of small warships to protect the coast from invasion. Most of these vessels appear to have been furnished by certain ports on the south coast.

IV. LITERATURE, LEARNING, AND ART

98. Runes. The language of the Saxons was of Low-German origin. Many of the words resemble the German of the present day. When written, the characters were called *runes*, mysteries or secrets. The chief use of these runes was to mark a sword hilt, or some article of value, or to form a charm against evil and witchcraft.

It is supposed that one of the earliest runic inscriptions is the following, which dates from about 400 A.D. It is cut on a drinking horn,[1] and (reproduced in English characters) stands thus:

EK HLEWAGASTIR · HOLTINGAR · HORNA · TAWIDO

I, Hlewagastir, son of Holta, made the horn

With the introduction of Christianity the Latin alphabet, from which our modern English alphabet is derived, took the place of the runic characters, which bore some resemblance to Greek, and English literature began with the coming of the monks.

99. The First Books. One of the first English books of great value was the "Anglo-Saxon Chronicle," a history covering a period beginning 1 A.D. and ending in 1154. The work was probably written by the monks in Canterbury, Peterborough, and other monasteries. It may be considered as an annual register of important events. Thorpe says of it, "No other nation can produce any history written in its own vernacular, at all approaching the "Anglo-Saxon Chronicle" either in antiquity, truthfulness, or extent, the historical books of the Bible alone excepted."

---

[1] The golden horn of Gallehas, found on the Danish-German frontier.

Though written in prose, it contains various fragments of poetry, of which the following (rendered into modern English), on the death of Edward the Confessor (1066), may be quoted as an example:

" Then suddenly came
    Death the bitter
And that dear prince seized.
    Angels bore
His steadfast soul
    Into heaven's light.
But the wise King
    Bestowed his realm
On one grown great,

On Harold's self,
    A noble Earl!
Who in all times
    Faithfully hearkened
Unto his lord
    In word and deed,
Nor ever failed
    In aught the King
Had needed of him ! "

Other early books were Cædmon's poem of the Creation, also in English, and Bede's " Church History " of Britain, written in Latin, a work giving a full and most interesting account of the coming of Augustine and his first preaching in Kent. All of these books were written by the monks in different monasteries.

100. Art. The English were skillful workers in metal, especially in gold and silver, and also in the illumination of manuscripts.[1] Alfred's Jewel, a fine specimen of the blue-enameled gold of the ninth century, is preserved in the Ashmolean Museum, Oxford. It bears the inscription: "Alfred me heht gewurcan," *Alfred caused me to be worked* [*or made*].

The women of that period excelled in weaving fine linen and woolen cloth and in embroidering tapestry.

101. Architecture. In architecture no advance took place until very late. The small ancient church at Bradford-on-Avon in the south of England belongs to the Saxon period. The Saxon stonework exhibited in a few buildings like the church tower of Earl's Barton, Northamptonshire, is an attempt to imitate timber with stone, and has been called " stone carpentry." [2] Edward the Confessor's work in Westminster Abbey was not Saxon, but Norman, he having obtained his plans, and probably his builders, from Normandy.

V. General Industry and Commerce

102. Farms ; Slave Trade. The farming of this period, except on the Church lands, was of the rudest description. Grain was ground by the women and slaves in stone hand mills. Later, the mills were driven

[1] These illuminations get their name from the gold, silver, and bright colors used in the pictures, borders, and decorated letters with which the monks ornamented these books. For beautiful specimens of the work, see Silvestre's " Paléographie."

[2] See Parker's " Introduction to Gothic Architecture " for illustrations of this work.

by wind or water power. The principal commerce was in wool, lead,
tin, and slaves. A writer of that time says he used to see long trains
of young men and women tied together, offered for sale, "for men
were not ashamed," he adds, "to sell their nearest relatives, and even
their own children."

VI. Mode of Life, Manners, and Customs

103. The Town. The first Saxon settlements were quite generally
on the line of the old Roman roads. They were surrounded by a rampart of earth set with a thick hedge or with rows of sharp stakes. Outside this was a deep ditch. These places were called towns,[1] from
"*tun*," meaning a fence or hedge. The chief fortified towns were called
"*burghs*" or boroughs. Later on, this class of towns generally had a
corporate form of government, and eventually they sent representatives
to Parliament (§ 213).

104. The Hall. The buildings in these towns were of wood. Those
of the lords or chief men were called "halls," from the fact that they
consisted mainly of a hall, or large room, used as a sitting, eating, and
often as a sleeping room, — a bundle of straw or some skins thrown on
the floor serving for beds. There were no chimneys, but a hole in the
roof let out the smoke. If the owner was rich, the walls would be decorated with bright-colored tapestry, and with suits of armor and shields
hanging from pegs.

105. Life in the Hall. Here in the evening the master supped on
a raised platform at one end of the "hall," while his followers ate at a
lower table.

The Saxons were hard drinkers as well as hard fighters. After the
meal, while horns of ale and mead were circulating, the minstrels, taking
their harps, would sing songs of battle and ballads of wild adventure.

Outside the "hall" were the "bowers," or chambers for the master
and his family, and, perhaps, an upper chamber for a guest, called later
by the Normans a *sollar*, or sunny room.

If a stranger approached a town, he was obliged to blow a horn;
otherwise he might be slain as an outlaw.

Here in the midst of rude plenty the Saxons, or Early English, lived
a life of sturdy independence. They were rough, strong, outspoken, and
fearless. Theirs was not the nimble brain, for that was to come with
another people (the Normans), though a people originally of the same

---

[1] One or more houses might constitute a town. A single farmhouse is still so
called in Scotland.

race. The mission of the Saxons was to lay the foundation; or, in other words, to furnish the muscle, grit, and endurance, without which the nimble brain is of little permanent value.

106. Guilds. The inhabitants of the towns and cities had various associations called guilds (from *gild*, a payment or contribution). The object of these was mutual assistance. The most important were the Frith guilds or Peace guilds and the Merchant guilds. The former constituted a voluntary police force to preserve order and bring thieves to punishment.

Each member contributed a small sum to form a common fund which was used to make good any losses incurred by robbery or fire. The association held itself responsible for the good behavior of its members, and kept a sharp eye on strangers and stragglers, who had to give an account of themselves or leave the country.

The Merchant guilds were organized, apparently at a late period, to protect and extend trade. After the Norman Conquest they came to be very wealthy and influential. In addition to the above, there were social and religious guilds, which made provision for feasts, for maintenance of religious services, and for the relief of the poor and the sick.

SANCTUARY KNOCKER,
DURHAM CATHEDRAL
(§ 95)

FIFTH PERIOD[1]

"In other countries the struggle has been to gain liberty; in England, to preserve it." — ALISON

A GREAT YEAR IN ENGLAND'S HISTORY

THE NORMAN CONQUEST

THE KING AGAINST THE BARONS

BUILDING THE NORMAN SUPERSTRUCTURE — THE AGE OF FEUDALISM

NORMAN SOVEREIGNS

WILLIAM I, 1066–1087	HENRY I, 1100–1135
WILLIAM II, 1087–1100	STEPHEN (House of Blois), 1135–1154

107. William marches on London; he grants a Charter to the City. Soon after the great and decisive battle of Hastings (§ 74), William the Conqueror advanced on London and set fire to the Southwark suburbs. The Londoners, terrified by the flames, and later cut off from help from the north by the Conqueror's besieging army, opened their gates and surrendered without striking a blow. In return, William, shortly after his coronation, granted the city a charter, by which he guaranteed to the inhabitants the liberties which they had enjoyed under Edward the Confessor (§ 65).

That document may still be seen among the records in the Guildhall, in London.[2] It is a narrow strip of parchment not the length of a man's hand. It contains a few lines in English, to which

---

[1] REFERENCE BOOKS on this Period will be found in the CLASSIFIED LIST OF BOOKS in the Appendix. The pronunciation of names will be found in the Index. The LEADING DATES stand unenclosed; all others are in parentheses.

[2] See Constitutional Documents in the Appendix, p. xxxiii.

William's royal seal was appended. It has indeed been said on high authority that the King also signed the charter with a cross ; but no trace of it appears on the parchment. The truth seems to be that he who wielded the sword with such terrible efficiency disdained handling the pen (§ 154).

108. The Coronation ; William returns to Normandy. On the following Christmas Day (1066) William was anointed and crowned in Westminster Abbey. His accession to the throne marked the union of England and Normandy (§ 191). (See map facing p. 54.) He assumed the title of " King of the English," which had been used by Edward the Confessor and by Harold. The title " King of England " did not fully and finally come into use until John's

WILLIAM'S CHARTER TO LONDON. (Reduced copy)

accession, more than a hundred and thirty years later. William did not remain in London, but made Winchester, in the south of England, his capital. In the spring (1067) he sailed for Normandy, where he had left his queen, Matilda, to govern in his absence.

While on the Continent he intrusted England to the hands of two regents, one his half-brother Odo, Bishop of Bayeux, the other his friend William Fitz-Osbern ; the former he had made Earl of Kent, the latter Earl of Hereford.

During the next three years there were outbreaks and uprisings in the lowlands of Cambridgeshire and the moors of Yorkshire, besides incursions of both Danes and Scots.

109. William quells Rebellion in the North (1068). The oppressive rule of the regents (§ 108) soon caused a rebellion, and in December William returned to England to put it down. He found the task a hard one. The King of Denmark made it all the harder by sending over a powerful fleet to help the English. William bribed the Danish commanders and they " sailed away without striking a blow." Then, little by little, he brought the land to obedience. By

DOMINIONS OF
WILLIAM THE CONQUEROR,
about 1087.

Scale of Miles.
0   50   100   150

forced marches in midwinter, by roads cast up through bogs, and by sudden night attacks William accomplished the end he sought.

But (1068) news came of a fresh revolt in the north, accompanied by another invasion of foreign barbarians. Then William, roused by terrible anger, swore by the " splendor of God " that he would lay waste the land.

He made good his oath. For a hundred miles beyond the river Humber in Yorkshire he ravaged the country, burning villages, destroying houses, crops, and cattle, and reducing the wretched people to such destitution that many sold themselves for slaves to escape starvation. Having finished his work in the north, he turned toward the ancient Roman city of Chester, in the west, and captured it. (See map facing p. 38.)

110. Hereward (1091). Every part of the land was now in William's power except an island in the swamps of Ely, in the east of England. There the Englishman Hereward, with his resolute little band of fellow countrymen, continued to defy the power of the Conqueror. (See map facing p. 38.) " Had there been three more men like him in the island," said one of William's own soldiers, " the Normans would never have entered it." But as there were not three more, the Conquest was at length completed.

111. Necessity of William's Severity. The work of death had been fearful. But it was better that England should suffer from these pitiless measures than that it should sink into anarchy, or into subjection to hordes of Northmen (§ 53). For those fierce barbarians destroyed not because they desired to build something better, but because they hated civilization and all its works.

Whatever William's faults may have been, his great object was to build up a government better than any England had yet seen. Hence his severity, hence his castles and forts, by which he made sure of retaining his hold upon whatever he had gained.

112. William builds the Tower of London. We have seen that William gave London a charter (§ 107); but overlooking the place in which that charter was kept, he built the Tower of London to hold the turbulent city in wholesome restraint. That tower, as fortress, palace, and prison, stands as the dark background of most of the great events in English history.

It was the forerunner of a multitude of Norman castles. They rose on the banks of every river, and on the summit of every rocky height, from the west hill of Hastings to the peak of Derbyshire, and from the banks of the Thames to those of the Tweed.

PART OF THE TOWER OF LONDON

"The Great White Tower" built by William the Conqueror

Side by side with these strongholds there also rose a great number of monasteries, churches, and cathedrals.

113. William confiscates the Land; Classes of Society. Hand in hand with the progress of conquest, the confiscation of land went on. William had seized the lands belonging to Harold (§ 67) and those of the chief men associated with him, and had given them to his own followers in England. In this way, all the greatest estates and the most important offices passed into the hands of the Normans. The King made these royal grants on the express condition that those who received them should furnish him a certain number of armed men whenever he should demand them.

Two great classes of society now existed in England. First, the leading Norman conquerors, who, as chief tenants or landholders under the Crown, and as peers of the realm, had the title of barons. They numbered about fifteen hundred, and, as we have just seen, they were all pledged to draw their swords in behalf of the King. Secondly, the English who had been reduced to a subordinate state ; most of these now held their land as grants from the Norman barons on condition of some kind of service. A majority of these men were no longer entirely free, while some were actual slaves. The greater part of this servile class were villeins or farm laborers (§ 150). They were bound to the soil, and could be sold with it, but not, like the slaves, separately from it. They could be compelled to perform any menial labor, but usually held their plots of land and humble cottages on condition of plowing a certain number of acres or doing a certain number of days' work in each year. In time the villeins generally obtained the privilege of paying a fixed money rent, in place of labor, and their condition gradually improved.

114. How William distributed his Gifts. Yet it is noticeable that when William granted estates to his Norman followers (§ 113), he was careful not to give any baron too much land in any one county or shire. His experience in Normandy had taught him that it was better to divide than to concentrate the power of the great nobles, who were often only too ready to plot to get the crown for themselves.

Thus William developed and extended the feudal system of land tenure,[1] already in existence in outline among the Saxons (§ 86), until it covered every part of the realm. He, however, kept this system strictly subordinate to himself, and we shall see that before the close of his reign he held a great meeting by which he got absolute control over it (§ 121).

[1] See, too, the Constitutional Summary in the Appendix, p. v, § 6.

115. The Three Counties Palatine. The only exceptions which William made in these carefully restricted grants were the three Counties Palatine,[1] which he created. They bordered on Wales in the west, Scotland in the north, and the English Channel in the southeast. To the earls of these counties of Chester, Durham, and Kent, which were especially liable to attack from Wales, Scotland, or France, William thought it expedient to give almost royal power, which descended in their families, thus making the title hereditary. (See map facing p. 436.)

116. How William stopped Assassination; the Law of Englishry; Gregory VII. The hard rule of the Norman nobles caused many secret assassinations. To put a stop to these crimes, William enacted the Law of Englishry. It compelled the people of the district where a murder was perpetrated to pay a heavy fine for every Norman so slain; for it was assumed that every man found murdered was a Norman, unless proof could be brought to the contrary.

While these events were taking place in England, Hildebrand, the archdeacon who had urged the Pope to favor William's expedition against England (§ 68), ascended the papal throne, under the title of Gregory VII. He was the ablest, the most ambitious, and, in some respects, the most farsighted man who had been elected supreme head of the Catholic Church.

117. State of Europe; Gregory's Scheme of Reform. Europe was at that time in a condition little better than anarchy. A perpetual quarrel was going on between the feudal barons. The Church, too, as we have seen (§§ 53, 60), had temporarily lost much of its power for good. Pope Gregory conceived a scheme of reform which he intended should be both wide and deep.

Like Dunstan (§ 60), he determined to correct the abuses which had crept into the monasteries. He resolved to have a priesthood who should devote themselves body and soul to the interests of the Church; he resolved to bring all society into submission to that priesthood; finally, he resolved to make the priesthood itself

---

[1] Palatine (from *palatium*, palace): having rights equal with the King in his palace. The county of Chester is now Cheshire. Durham bordered on Northumberland, then opposed to William. Shropshire was practically a fourth County Palatine until Henry I. Later, Lancaster was added to the list.

acknowledge him as its sole master. His purpose in this gigantic scheme was a noble one; it was to establish the unity and peace of Europe.

118. The Pope and the Conqueror, 1076. Pope Gregory looked to William for help in this matter. The Conqueror, who was a zealous Catholic, was ready to give that help, but with limitations. He pledged himself to aid in reforming the English Church, which had enjoyed "an insular and barbaric independence." He undertook to remove inefficient men from its high places. The King also agreed to do something that had never been done before in England, namely, to establish separate courts (§ 151) for the trial of Church cases (§§ 164, 165). Finally, he agreed to pay the customary yearly tax to Rome, called "Peter's pence."

But Pope Gregory was not satisfied. He demanded that the Conqueror should do him homage for his crown, and should swear "to become his man" (§ 86). This William respectfully, but decidedly, refused to do, saying that as no "King of the English before him had ever become the Pope's man, so neither would he." In taking this action the King declared himself to be an obedient and affectionate son of the "Holy Catholic Church." But at the same time he laid down these three rules to show that he would not tolerate any interference with his power as an independent English sovereign:

1. That no Pope should be acknowledged in England, or letters from the Pope received there, without his sanction.

2. That no national synod or meeting of churchmen (§ 48) should enact any decrees binding the English Church, without his confirmation.

3. That no baron or officer of his should be expelled from the Church without his permission.[1]

It is noticeable that Pope Gregory never seems to have censured William for the position he took, — perhaps because one brave man always understands and respects another.

Yet a little later than this (1077), when Henry IV, Emperor of Germany, refused to comply with certain demands made by

[1] Taswell-Langmead's "English Constitutional History," p. 59; Professor W. Stubbs's "Constitutional History of England," I, 286.

Gregory VII, the German monarch had to submit. More than this, he was compelled to stand barefooted in the snow before the Pope's palace, waiting three days for permission to enter and beg forgiveness.

119. William a Stern but Just Ruler; the Jews; the New Forest. Considering his love of power and strength of will, the reign of William was conspicuous for its justice. He was harsh, but generally fair. He protected the Jewish traders who came over to England in his reign, for he saw that their commercial enterprise and their financial skill would be of immense value in developing the country. Then too, if the royal treasury should happen to run dry, he thought it might be convenient to coax or compel the Jews to lend him a round sum.

On the other hand, the King seized a tract of over sixty thousand acres in Hampshire for a hunting ground, which he named the New Forest.[1] It was said that William destroyed many churches and estates in order to form this forest, but these accounts appear to have been greatly exaggerated. The real grievance was not so much the appropriation of the land, which was sterile and of little value, but it was the enactment of the savage Forest Laws. These ordinances made the life of a stag of more value than that of a man, and decreed that any one found hunting the royal deer should have both eyes torn out (§ 205).

120. The Great Survey; Domesday Book, 1086. Not quite twenty years after his coronation William ordered a survey and valuation to be made of the whole realm outside of London. The only exceptions were certain border counties on the north where war had left little to record save heaps of ruins and ridges of grass-grown graves (§ 109).

The returns of that survey were known as Domesday or Doomsday Book. The English people said this name was given to it, because, like the Day of Doom, it spared no one. It recorded every piece of property and every particular concerning it. As the

[1] Forest: As here used, this does not mean a region covered with woods, but simply a section of country, partially wooded and suitable for game, set apart as a royal park or hunting ground. As William made his residence at Winchester, in Hampshire, in the south of England (see map facing p. 38), he naturally took land in that vicinity for the chase.

"Anglo-Saxon Chronicle" (§ 46) indignantly declared, "not a rood of land, not a peasant's hut, not an ox, cow, pig, or even a hive of bees escaped."

While the report showed the wealth of the country, it also showed the suffering it had passed through in the revolts against William. Many towns had fallen into decay. Some were nearly depopulated. In Edward the Confessor's reign (§ 65) York had 1607 houses; at the date of the survey it had but 967, while Oxford, which had had 721 houses, had then only 243.

This census and assessment proved of the highest importance to William and his successors. The people indeed said bitterly that the King kept the book constantly by him, in order "that he might be able to see at any time of how much more wool the English flock would bear fleecing." The object of the work, however, was not to extort money, but to present a full and exact report of the financial and military resources of the kingdom which might be directly available for revenue and defense.

121. The Great Meeting; the Oath of Allegiance to William, 1086. In the midsummer following the completion of Domesday Book, William summoned all the barons and chief landholders of the realm, with their principal vassals or tenants, to meet him on Salisbury Plain, Wiltshire.[1] It is said that the entire assemblage numbered sixty thousand. There was a logical connection between that summons and the great survey (§ 120). Each man's possessions and each man's responsibility were now known. Thus Domesday Book prepared the way for the assembly and for the action that was to be taken there.

The place chosen was historic ground. On that field William had once reviewed his victorious troops. Toward the north of the widespread plain rose the rugged columns of Stonehenge (§ 3), surrounded by the burial mounds of prehistoric peoples. On the south rose the fortified hill of Old Sarum, scarred by British and

---

[1] See map of England facing p. 436. Wiltshire is in the south of England. Alfred had established the seat of government at Winchester in Hampshire, but under Edward the Confessor and Harold it was transferred to Westminster (London); the honor was again restored to Winchester by William, who made it his principal residence. This was perhaps the reason why he chose Salisbury Plain (the nearest open region) for the great meeting. It was held where the modern city of Salisbury stands.

by Roman entrenchments. William probably made his headquarters in the Norman castle then standing on that hill. On the plain below were the encampments of all the chief landholders of England.

122. The Oath of Allegiance. There William the Conqueror finished his work. There not only every baron, but every baron's free vassal or tenant, from Cornwall to the Scottish borders, bowed before the King and swore to be "his man" (§ 86). By that act England was made one. By it, it was settled that every landholder in the realm, of whatever condition, was bound first of all to fight in behalf of the Crown, even if in so doing he had to fight against his own lord.[1] The barons broke this oath in the next reign (§ 130), but the moral obligation to keep it still remained binding.

123. What William had done. A score of years before, William had landed, seeking a throne to which no law had given him any claim whatever (§ 67).[2] But Nature had elected him to it when she endowed him with power to take, power to use, and power to hold. Under Harold, England was a kingdom divided against itself (§ 71). It was fortunate for the country that William came; for out of chaos, or affairs fast drifting to chaos, his strong hand, clear brain, and resolute purpose brought order, beauty, safety, and stability. We may say, therefore, with an eminent French historian, that "England owes her liberties to her having been conquered by the Normans."[3]

124. William's Death (1087). In less than a year from that time, William went to Normandy to quell an invasion led by his eldest son, Robert. As he rode down a steep street in Mantes, his horse stumbled and he received a fatal injury. He was carried to the priory of St. Gervase, just outside the city of Rouen.

Early in the morning he was awakened by the great cathedral bell. "It is the hour of praise," his attendant said to him, "when the priests give thanks for the new day." William lifted up his hands in prayer and expired.

---

[1] See §§ 86, 150; see also the Constitutional Summary in the Appendix, p. v, § 6. Even if men should disregard this oath of allegiance, they could not help feeling that the principle it represented had been acknowledged by them.

[2] "William, in short, had no kind of right to the crown, whether by birth, bequest, or election." (E. A. Freeman's "Short History of the Norman Conquest," p. 65.)

[3] Guizot; see also note 1 on page 64.

125. His Burial (1087). His remains were taken for interment to St. Stephen's church, which he had built in the city of Caen, Normandy. As they were preparing to let down the body into the grave, a man suddenly stepped forward and forbade the burial. William, he said, had taken the land, on which the church stood, from his father by violence. He demanded payment. The corpse was left on the bier, and inquiry instituted, and not until the debt was discharged was the body lowered to its last resting place.

" Thus," says the old chronicle, " he who had been a powerful king, and the lord of so many territories, possessed not then of all his lands more than seven feet of earth," and not even that until the cash was paid for it. But William's bones were not to rest when finally laid in the grave, for less than five centuries later (1532) the French Protestants dug them up and scattered them.

126. Summary (1066–1087). The results of the Norman Conquest may be thus summed up :

1. The Conquest was not the subjugation of the English by a different race, but rather a victory won for their advantage by a branch of their own race.[1]

2. It found England a divided country (§ 71); it made it a united kingdom. It also united England and Normandy (§§ 108, 191), and brought the new English kingdom into closer contact with the higher civilization of the Continent. This introduced fresh intellectual stimulus, and gave to the Anglo-Saxon a more progressive spirit.

3. It modified the English language by the influence of the Norman-French element, thus giving it greater flexibility, refinement, and elegance of expression.

4. It substituted for the fragile and decaying structures of wood generally built by the Saxons, Norman castles, abbeys, and cathedrals of stone.

5. It hastened influences, which were already at work, for the consolidation of the nation. It developed and completed the feudal form of land tenure, but it made that tenure strictly subordinate to the Crown, and so freed it, in great measure, from the evils of Continental feudalism (§§ 86, 150).

[1] It has already been shown that Norman, Saxon, and Dane were originally branches of the Teutonic or German race (§§ 36, 62).

6. It reorganized the English Church and defined the relation of the Crown to that Church and to the Pope (§ 118).

7. It abolished the four great earldoms (§ 64), which had been a constant source of weakness, danger, and division; it put an end to the Danish invasions; it brought the whole of England under a strong monarchical government, to which not only all the great nobles, but also their vassals or tenants, were compelled to swear allegiance (§§ 121, 122).

8. It made no radical changes in the English laws, but enforced impartial obedience to them among all classes.[1]

WILLIAM RUFUS [2] — 1087–1100

127. William the Conqueror's Bequest (1087). William the Conqueror left three sons, — Robert, William Rufus, and Henry. He also left a daughter, Adela, who married a powerful French nobleman, Stephen, Count of Blois. On his deathbed (§ 124) William bequeathed Normandy to Robert. He expressed a wish that William Rufus should become ruler over England, while to Henry he left five thousand pounds of silver, with the prediction that he would ultimately be the greatest of them all.

Before his eyes were closed, the two sons, who were with him, hurried away, — William Rufus to seize the realm of England, Henry to get possession of his treasure. Robert was not present. His recent rebellion (§ 124) would alone have been sufficient reason for allotting to him the lesser portion; but even had he deserved the scepter, William knew that it required a firmer hand than his to hold it.

128. Condition of England. France was simply an aggregation of independent and mutually hostile dukedoms. The ambition of the Norman leaders threatened to bring England into the same condition. During the twenty-one years of William the Conqueror's

---

[1] Professor E. A. Freeman, who is the highest authority on this subject (see especially his " Short History of the Norman Conquest "), holds the view that the coming of William was, on the whole, of the greatest advantage to England. Nearly all leading historians agree with him; for a different view consult Professor C. Oman's " England before the Norman Conquest," pp. 648–651.

[2] William Rufus: William the Red, a nickname probably derived from his red face.

reign, the Norman barons on the Continent had constantly tried to break loose from his restraining power. It was certain, then, that the news of his death would be the signal for still more desperate attempts.

129. Character of William Rufus. Rufus had his father's ability and resolution, but none of his father's conscience. As the historian of that time declared, " he feared God but little, man not at all." He had Cæsar's faith in destiny, and said to a boatman who hesitated to set off with him in a storm at his command, " Did you ever hear of a king's being drowned ? "

130. His Struggle with the Barons. The barons broke the solemn oath which they had taken in the previous reign (§ 122) to be faithful to the Crown. During the greater part of the thirteen years of the new King's reign they were fighting against him. On William's part it was a battle of centralization against disintegration. He rallied the country people to his help — those who fought with bows and spears. " Let every man," said the King, "who would not be branded infamous and a coward, whether he live in town or country, leave everything and come to me " (§ 85).

In answer to that appeal, the English people rallied around their Norman sovereign, and gained the day for him under the walls of Rochester Castle, Kent. Of the two evils, the tyranny of one or the tyranny of many, the first seemed to them preferable.

131. William's Method of raising Money; he defrauds the Church. If in some respects William the Conqueror had been a harsh ruler, his son was worse. His brother Robert had mortgaged Normandy to him in order to get money to join the first crusade (§ 182). William Rufus raised whatever funds he desired by the most oppressive and unscrupulous means.

William's most trusted counselor was Ranulf Flambard. Flambard had brains without principle. He devised a system of plundering both Church and people in the King's interest. Lanfranc, Archbishop of Canterbury, died three years after William's accession. Through Flambard's advice the King left the archbishopric vacant and appropriated its revenues to himself. He practiced the same course with respect to every office of the Church.

132. The King makes Anselm Archbishop (1093). While this process of systematized robbery was going on, the King suddenly fell ill. In his alarm lest death was at hand, he determined to make reparation to the defrauded and insulted priesthood. He invited Anselm, the abbot of a famous monastery in Normandy, to accept the archbishopric. Anselm, who was old and feeble, declined, saying that he and the King could not work together. " It would be," said he, " like yoking a sheep and a bull."

But the king would take no refusal. Calling Anselm to his bedside, he forced the staff of office into his hands. Anselm became the champion of the freedom of the Church. But when the King recovered, he resumed his old practices and treated the Archbishop with such insult that he left the country for a time.

133. William's Merit ; his Death. William II's one merit was that he kept England from being devoured piecemeal by the Norman barons, who regarded her as a pack of hounds in full chase regard the hare that is on the point of falling into their rapacious jaws.

Like his father, he insisted on keeping the English Church independent of the ever-growing power of Rome (§ 118). In both cases his motives were purely selfish, but the result to the country was good.

His power came suddenly to an end (1100). He had gone in the morning to hunt in the New Forest (§ 119) with his brother Henry. He was found lying dead among the bushes, pierced by an arrow shot by an unknown hand.

William's character speaks in his deeds. It was hard, cold, despotic, yet in judging it we should consider the words of that quaint old writer, Thomas Fuller, when he says, " No pen hath originally written the life of this King but what was made with a monkish penknife, and no wonder if his picture seems bad, which was thus drawn by his enemy."

134. Summary. Notwithstanding William's oppression of both Church and people, his reign checked the revolt of the baronage and prevented the kingdom from falling into anarchy like that existing in France.

HENRY I — 1100-1135

135. Henry's Charter of Liberties. Henry, third son of William the Conqueror, was the first of the Norman kings who was born and educated in England. Foreseeing a renewal of the contest with the barons (§ 130), he issued a Charter of Liberties on his accession, by which he bound himself to reform the abuses which had been practiced by his brother William Rufus. This charter guaranteed: (1) The rights of the Church (which William Rufus had constantly violated); (2) the rights of the nobles and landholders against extortionate demands by the Crown; (3) the right of all classes to the protection of the old English customs or laws.

The King sent a hundred copies of this important document to the leading abbots and bishops for preservation in their respective monasteries and cathedrals (§ 45).

As this charter was the earliest written and formal guarantee of good government ever given by the Crown to the nation, it marks an important epoch in English history. It may be compared to the statements of principles and pledges issued by our modern political parties. It was a virtual admission that the time had come when even a Norman sovereign could not dispense with the support of the country. It was therefore an admission of the truth that while a people can exist without a king, no king can exist without a people.

Furthermore, this charter established a precedent for those which were to follow, and which reached a final development in the Great Charter wrested from the unwilling hand of King John somewhat more than a century later (§ 198). Henry further strengthened his position with his English subjects by his marriage with Maud, niece of the Saxon Edgar, a direct descendant of King Alfred (§ 51).

136. The Appointment of Bishops settled. King Henry also recalled Anselm (§ 132) and reinstated him in his office. But the peace was of short duration. The Archbishop insisted, as did the Pope, that the power of appointment of bishops should be vested wholly in Rome. The King was equally determined that such appointments should spring from himself. Like William the Conqueror (§ 118), he declared: " No one shall remain in my land who will not do me homage " (§ 86).

The quarrel was eventually settled by compromise. The Pope was to invest the bishop with ring and crosier, or pastoral staff of office, as emblems of the spiritual power; the King, on the other hand, was to grant the lands from which the bishop drew his revenues, and in return was to receive his homage or oath of allegiance.

This acknowledgment of royal authority by the Church was of great importance, since it gave the King power as feudal lord to demand from each bishop his quota of fully equipped knights or cavalry soldiers (§§ 150, 152). This armed force would usually be commanded by the bishop in person (§ 140).

137. Henry's Quarrel with Robert; the "Lion of Justice." While this Church question was in dispute, Henry had still more pressing matters to attend to. His elder brother Robert (§§ 124, 127) had invaded England and demanded the crown. The greater part of the Norman nobles supported this claim, but the English people held to Henry. Finally, in consideration of a heavy money payment, Robert agreed to return to Normandy and leave his brother in full possession of the realm. On his departure, Henry resolved to drive out the prominent nobles who had aided Robert. Of these, the Earl of Shrewsbury, called "Robert the Devil," was the leader. With the aid of the English, who hated him for his cruelty, the earl was at last compelled to leave the country.

He fled to Normandy, and, in violation of a previous agreement, was received by Henry's brother Robert. Upon that, Henry declared war, and, crossing the Channel, fought (1106) the battle of Tinchebrai,[1] by which he conquered and held Normandy as completely as William, Duke of Normandy, had conquered England forty years before. The King carried his brother captive to Wales, and kept him in prison during his life in Cardiff Castle. This ended the contest with the nobles.

By his uprightness, his decision, his courage, and by his organization of better courts of law (§ 147), Henry fairly won the honorable title of the "Lion of Justice"; for the "Anglo-Saxon Chronicle" says, "No man durst misdo against another in his time."[2]

---

[1] Tinchebrai, Normandy, in the region west of Caen and Avranches. (See map facing p. 54.)

[2] See, too, the Summary of Constitutional History in the Appendix, p. vi, § 7.

138. Summary. The three leading points of Henry I's reign are : (1) the self-limitation of the royal power embodied in his Charter of Liberties ; (2) the settlement of old disputes between the King and the Church; (3) the banishment of the chief of the mutinous barons, and the victory of Tinchebrai, with its important results.

STEPHEN — 1135–1154　*Lee*

139. The Rival Candidates. With Henry I's death two candidates presented themselves for the throne, — Henry's daughter, Matilda (for he left no lawful son), and his nephew, Stephen. In France the custom of centuries had determined that the crown should never descend to a female. It was an age when the sovereign was expected to lead his army in person, and it certainly was not expedient that a woman should hold a position one of whose chief duties she could not discharge. This French custom had, of course, no force in England ; but the Norman nobles must have recognized its reasonableness ; or if not, the people did.[1]

Four years after Stephen's accession Matilda landed in England and claimed the crown. The east of England stood by Stephen, the west by Matilda. For the sake of promoting discord, and through discord their own private ends, part of the barons gave their support to Matilda, while the rest refused, as they said, to " hold their estates under a distaff." In the absence of the Witan or National Council (§ 80), London unanimously chose Stephen King (1135).

The fatal defect in the new King was the absence of executive ability. Following the example of Henry (§ 135), he issued two charters or pledges of good government ; but without power to carry them out, they proved simply waste paper.

140. The Battle of the Standard (1138). David I of Scotland, Matilda's uncle, espoused her cause and invaded England with a powerful force. He was met at North Allerton, in Yorkshire, by the party of Stephen, and the battle of the Standard was fought.

[1] Before Henry's death, the baronage had generally sworn to support Matilda (commonly called the Empress Matilda, or Maud, from her marriage to the Emperor Henry V of Germany ; later, she married Geoffrey of Anjou). But Stephen, with the help of London and the Church, declared himself "*elected King by the assent of the clergy and the people.*" Many of the barons now gave Stephen their support.

The leaders of the English were both churchmen, who showed that they could fight as vigorously as they could pray (§ 136). The standard consisted of four consecrated banners, surmounted by a cross. This was set up on a wagon, on which one of the bishops stood. The sight of this sacred standard made the English invincible. (See map facing page 436.)

After a fierce contest the Scots were driven from the field. It is said that this was the first battle in which the English peasants used the long bow ; they had taken the hint, perhaps, from the Norman archers at the battle of Hastings (§§ 73, 74). Many years later, their skill in foreign war made that weapon as famous as it was effective (§ 238).

141. Civil War (1138-1153). For fifteen years following, the country was torn by civil war. While it raged, fortified castles, which, under William the Conqueror, had been built and occupied by the King only, or by those whom he could trust, now arose on every side. These strongholds became, as the "Anglo-Saxon Chronicle" (§ 99) declares, "very nests of devils and dens of thieves." More than a thousand of these castles, it is said, were built. The armed bands who inhabited them levied tribute on the whole country around.

Not satisfied with that, these miscreants seized those who were suspected of having property, and, in the words of the "Chronicle," "tortured them with pains unspeakable ; for some they hung up by the feet and smoked with foul smoke ; others they crushed in a narrow chest with sharp stones. About the heads of others they bound knotted cords until they went into the brain." " Thousands died of hunger, the towns were burned, and the soil left untilled. By such deeds the land was ruined, and men said openly that Christ and his saints were asleep."

The sleep, however, was not always to last ; for in the next reign, Justice, in the person of Henry II, effectually vindicated her power. The strife for the crown continued till the last year of Stephen's reign. Then the Church came to the rescue, and through its powerful influence the Treaty of Wallingford (in Berkshire) was made. By that treaty it was agreed that Matilda's son Henry should succeed Stephen.

142. Summary. Stephen was the last of the Norman kings. Their reign had covered nearly a century. The period began in conquest and usurpation; it ended in gloom. We are not, however, to judge it by Stephen's reign alone, but as a whole.

Thus considered, it shows at least one point of advance over the preceding period, — the triumph of the moral power of the Church over feudal discord. But Stephen's reign was not all loss in other respects, for out of the " war, wickedness, and waste" of his misgovernment came a universal desire for peace through law. Thus indirectly this weak King's inefficiency prepared the way for future reforms.

GENERAL REFERENCE SUMMARY OF THE NORMAN PERIOD (1066–1154)

(See note in italics on page 43.)

I. Government. II. Religion. III. Military Affairs. IV. Literature, Learning, and Art. V. General Industry and Commerce. VI. Mode of Life, Manners, and Customs

I. Government

143. The King. We have seen that the Saxons, or Early English rulers, in the case of Egbert and his successors, styled themselves Kings of the West Saxons or of some other division of that race, and that finally they assumed the broader title of " Kings of the English," or leaders of the entire race or people (§ 49). The Norman sovereigns made no immediate change in this title, but as a matter of fact William, toward the close of his reign, claimed the whole of the country as his own by right of conquest.

For this reason he and his Norman successors might properly have called themselves " Kings of England," that is, supreme owners of the soil and rulers over it; but this title of territorial sovereignty was not formally assumed until about fifty years later, in John's reign.

144. The Great Council. Associated with the King in government was the Great or Central Council, made up of, first, the earls and barons; and secondly, of the archbishops, bishops, and abbots; that is, of all the great landholders holding directly from the Crown. The Great Council usually met three times a year, — at Christmas, Easter, and Whitsuntide. All laws were held to be made by the King, acting with the advice and consent of this Council, — which in the next century first came to be known as Parliament (1246, 1265, 1295), — but practically the King alone often enacted such laws as he saw fit (§§ 213, 217).

When a new sovereign came to the throne, it was with the consent or by the election of the Great Council, but their choice was generally limited to some one of the late King's sons, and unless there was good reason for making a different selection, the oldest was chosen. Finally the right of imposing taxes rested, theoretically at least, in the King and Council, but, in fact, the King himself frequently levied them. This action of the King was a cause of constant irritation and of frequent insurrection.

145. The Private or King's Council. There was also a second and permanent council, called the King's Council. The three leading officers of this were: first, the Chief Justice, who superintended the execution of the laws, represented the King, and ruled for him during his absence from the country; secondly, the Lord Chancellor (so called from *cancelli*, the screen behind which he sat with his clerks), who acted as the King's adviser and confidential secretary, and as keeper of the Great Seal, with which he stamped all important papers;[1] thirdly, the Lord High Treasurer, who took charge of the King's revenue, received all moneys due the Crown, and kept the King's treasure in the vaults at Winchester or Westminster.

146. Tallies. All accounts were kept by the Treasurer on tallies or small sticks, notched on the opposite sides to represent different sums. These were split lengthwise. One was given as a receipt to the sheriff, or other person paying in money to the treasury, while the duplicate of this tally was held by the Treasurer. This primitive method of keeping royal accounts remained legally in force until 1785, in the reign of George III.

147. The Curia Regis,[2] or the King's Court of Justice. The Chief Justice and Chancellor were generally chosen by the King from among the clergy; first, because the clergy were men of education, while the barons were not; and next, because it was not expedient to intrust too much power to the barons. These officials, with the other members of the Private Council, constituted the King's High Court of Justice.

---

[1] The Lord Chancellor was also the "Keeper of the King's Conscience," because intrusted with the duty of redressing those grievances of the King's subjects which required royal interference. The Court of Chancery (mentioned on page 73, note 1) grew out of this office.

[2] Curia Regis: This name was given, at different times, first, to the Great or National Council; secondly, to the King's Private Council; and lastly, to the High Court of Justice, consisting of members of the Private Council.

It followed the King as he moved from place to place, to hear and decide cases carried up by appeal from the county courts, together with other questions of importance.[1] In local government the country remained under the Normans essentially the same as it had been before the Conquest. The King continued to be represented in each county by an officer called the sheriff, who collected the taxes and enforced the laws.

148. Trial by Battle. In the administration of justice, Trial by Battle was introduced in addition to the Ordeal of the Saxons (§ 91). This was a duel in which each of the contestants appealed to Heaven to give him the victory, it being believed that the right would vanquish. Noblemen[2] fought on horseback in full armor, with sword, lance, and battle-ax; common people fought on foot with clubs.

In both cases the combat was in the presence of judges and might last from sunrise until the stars appeared. Priests and women had the privilege of being represented by champions, who fought for them. Trial by Battle was claimed and allowed by the court (though the combat did not come off) as late as 1817, in the reign of George III. This custom was finally abolished in 1819.[3]

149. Divisions of Society. The divisions of society remained after the Conquest nearly as before, but the Saxon orders of nobility, with a few very rare exceptions, were deprived of their rank and their estates given to the Normans.

It is important to notice here the marked difference between the new or Norman nobility and that of France.

In England a man was considered noble because, under William and his successors, he was a member of the Great or National Council (§ 80),

[1] The King's High Court of Justice (Curia Regis) was divided, about 1215, into three distinct courts: (1) the Exchequer Court (so called from the chequered cloth which covered the table of the court, and which was probably made useful in counting money), which dealt with cases of finance and revenue; (2) the Court of Common Pleas, which had jurisdiction in civil suits between subject and subject; (3) the Court of King's Bench, which transacted the remaining business, both civil and criminal, and had special jurisdiction over all inferior courts and civil corporations.

Later, a fourth court, that of Chancery (see § 145, and note 1), over which the Lord Chancellor presided, was established as a court of appeal and equity, to deal with cases where the common law gave no relief.

[2] See Shakespeare's "Richard II," Act I, scenes i and iii; also Scott's "Ivanhoe," Chapter XLIII.

[3] Trial by Battle might be demanded in cases of chivalry or honor, in criminal actions, and in civil suits. The last were fought not by the disputants themselves but by champions.

or, in the case of an earl, because he represented the King in the government of a county or earldom.

His position did not exempt him from taxation, nor did his rank descend to more than one of his children. In France, on the contrary, the aristocracy were noble by birth, not office; they were generally exempt from taxation, thus throwing the whole of that burden on the people, and their rank descended to all their children.

During the Norman period a change was going on among the slaves, whose condition gradually improved. On the other hand, many who had been free now sank into that state of villeinage (§ 150) which, as it bound them to the soil, was but one remove from actual slavery.

The small, free landholders who still existed were mostly in the old Danish territory north of Watling Street (see map facing p. 32), and in the county of Kent on the southeast coast of England.

150. Tenure of Land in the Norman Period ; Military Service, Feudal Dues, National Militia, Manors and Manor Houses. All land was held directly or indirectly from the King on condition of military or other service. The number of chief tenants who derived their title from the Crown, including ecclesiastical dignitaries, was probably about fifteen hundred. These constituted the Norman barons. The undertenants were about eight thousand, and consisted chiefly of the English who had been driven out from their estates.

Every holder of land was obliged to furnish the King a fully armed and mounted soldier, to serve for forty days during the year for each piece of land bringing £20 annually, or about $2000 in modern money [1] (the pound of that day probably representing twenty times that sum now). All the chief tenants were also bound to attend the King's Great or National Council three times a year, — at Christmas, Easter, and Whitsuntide.

Feudal Dues or Taxes. Every free tenant was obliged to pay a sum of money to the King or baron from whom he held his land, on three special occasions: (1) to ransom his lord from captivity in case he was made a prisoner of war; (2) to defray the expense of making his lord's eldest son a knight; (3) to provide a suitable marriage portion on the marriage of his lord's eldest daughter.

In addition to these taxes, or "aids," as they were called, there were other demands which the lord might make, such as: (1) a year's profits of the land from the heir, on his coming into possession of his father's

---

[1] This amount does not appear to have been fully settled until the period following the Norman kings, but the principle was recognized by William.

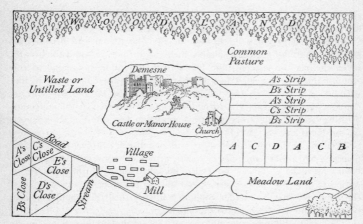

A MANOR OR TOWNSHIP HELD BY A LORD, NORMAN PERIOD

The building is Ludlow Castle, Shropshire. Manor houses proper, as distinct from castles, existed in England at least from the thirteenth century

(See Gibbins's " Industrial History of England " and Cheyney's " Industrial and Social England ")

The inhabitants of a manor, or the estate of a lord, were : (1) the lord himself, or his representative, who held his estate on condition of furnishing the King a certain number of armed men (§§ 113, 150); (2) the lord's personal followers, who lived with him, and usually a parish priest or a number of monks ; (3) the farm laborers, or villeins, bound to the soil, who could not leave the manor, were not subject to military duty, and who paid rent in labor or produce ; there might also be a few actual slaves, but this last class gradually rose to the partial freedom of villenage ; (4) certain free tenants or "sokemen," who paid a fixed rent either in money or service and were not bound to the soil as the villeins were.

Next to the manor house (where courts were also held) the most important buildings were the church (used sometimes for markets and town meetings) ; the lord's mill (if there was a stream), in which all tenants must grind their grain and pay for the grinding ; and finally, the cottages of the tenants, gathered in a village near the mill.

The land was divided as follows : (1) the "demesne" (or domain) surrounding the manor house ; this was strictly private — the lord's ground ; (2) the land outside the demesne, suitable for cultivation ; this was let in strips, usually of thirty acres, but was subject to certain rules in regard to methods of tillage and crops ; (3) a piece of land which was divided into fenced fields, called " closes " (because enclosed), and which tenants might hire and use as they saw fit ; (4) common pasture, open to all tenants to pasture their cattle on ; (5) waste or untilled land, where all tenants had the right to cut turf for fuel, or gather plants or shrubs for fodder ; (6) the forest or woodland, where all tenants had the right to turn their hogs out to feed on acorns, and where they might also collect a certain amount of small wood for fuel ; (7) meadow land on which tenants might hire the right to cut grass and make hay. On the above plan the fields of tenants — both those of villeins and of "sokemen," or tenants who paid a fixed rent in money or service — are marked by the letters A, B, C, etc.

If the village grew, the tenants might, in time, purchase from the lord the right to manage their own affairs in great measure, and so become a Free Town (§ 183).

estate; this was called a *relief;* (2) the income from the lands of orphan heirs not of age; (3) payment for privilege of disposing of land.[1]

In case of an orphan heiress not of age, the feudal lord became her guardian and might select a suitable husband for her. Should the heiress reject the person selected, she forfeited a sum of money equal to the amount the lord expected to receive by the proposed marriage. Thus we find one woman in Ipswich giving a large fee for the privilege of "not being married except to her own good liking." In the collection of these "aids" and "reliefs," great extortion was often practiced both by the King and the barons.

Besides the feudal troops there was a national militia, consisting of peasants and others not provided with armor, who fought on foot with bows and spears. These could also be called on as during the Saxon period (§ 96). In some cases where the barons were in revolt against the King, for instance, under William Rufus (§ 130), this national militia proved of immense service to the Crown.

The great landholders let out part of their estates to tenants on similar terms to those on which they held their own, and in this way the entire country was divided up. The lowest class of tenants were the common agricultural laborers called villeins, — a name derived from the Latin *villa*, meaning a country house or farm. These villeins, or serfs, held small pieces of land on condition of performing labor for it. They were bound to the soil and could be sold with it, but not, like slaves, apart from it. They were not wholly destitute of legal rights.

Under William I and his successors, all free tenants, of whatever grade, were bound to uphold the King,[2] and in case of insurrection or civil war to serve under him (§ 122). In this most important respect the great landholders of England differed from those of the Continent, where the lesser tenants were bound only to serve their own masters, and might, and in fact often did, take up arms against the King. William removed this serious defect. By doing so he did the country an incalculable service. He completed the organization of *feudal land tenure*, but he never established *the Continental system* of feudal government. (See, too, the Constitutional Summary in the Appendix, p. v, § 6.)

---

[1] The clergy, being a corporate and hence an ever-living body, were exempt from these last demands. Not satisfied with this, they were constantly endeavoring, with more or less success, to escape *all* feudal obligations, on the ground that they rendered the state divine service. In 1106, in the reign of Henry I, it was settled, for the time, that the bishops were to do homage to the King, i.e. furnish military service for the lands they received from him as their feudal lord (§ 136).

[2] See the Constitutional Summary in the Appendix, pp. iii–v, §§ 5, 6.

II. Religion

151. The Church. With respect to the organization of the Church, no changes were made under the Norman kings. They, however, generally deposed the English bishops and substituted Normans or foreigners, who, as a class, were superior in education to the English. William the Conqueror made it pretty clearly understood that he considered the Church subordinate to his will, and that in all cases of dispute about temporal matters, he, and not the Pope, was to decide (§ 118). During the Norman period great numbers of monasteries were built.

In one very important respect William the Conqueror greatly increased the power of the Church by establishing ecclesiastical courts in which all cases relating to the Church and the clergy were tried by the bishops according to laws of their own. Persons wearing the dress of a monk or priest, or those who could manage to spell out a verse of the Psalms, and so pass for ecclesiastics, would claim the right to be tried under the Church laws, and, as the punishments which the Church inflicted were notoriously mild, the consequence was that the majority of criminals escaped the penalty of their evil doings. So great was the abuse of this privilege, that, at a later period, Henry II made an attempt to reform it (§ 164); but it was not wholly and finally done away with until the beginning of the nineteenth century.

III. Military Affairs

152. The Army. The army consisted of cavalry, or knights, and foot soldiers. The former were almost wholly Normans. They wore armor similar to that used by the Saxons. It is represented in the pictures of the Bayeux Tapestry (§§ 75, 155), and appears to have consisted of leather or stout linen, on which pieces of bone, or scales, or rings of iron were securely sewed. Later, these rings of iron were set up edgewise, and interlinked, or the scales made to overlap. The helmet was pointed, and had a piece in front to protect the nose. The shield was long and kite-shaped.

The weapons of this class of soldiers consisted of a lance and a double-edged sword. The foot soldiers wore little or no armor and fought principally with long bows. In case of need, the King could probably muster about ten thousand knights, or armed horsemen, and a much larger force of foot soldiers. Under the Norman kings the principal wars were insurrections against William I, the various revolts of the barons, and the civil war under Stephen.

153. Knighthood.[1] Candidates for knighthood were usually obliged to pass through a long course of training under the care of some distinguished noble. The candidate served first as a page, or attendant in the house; then, as a squire or attendant, he followed his master to the wars. After seven years in this capacity, he prepared himself for receiving the honors of knighthood by spending several days in a church, engaged in solemn religious rites, fasting, and prayer.

The young man, in the presence of his friends and kindred, then made oath to be loyal to the King, to defend religion, and to be the champion of every lady in danger or distress. Next, a high-born dame or great warrior buckled on his spurs, and girded the sword, which the priest had blessed, to his side. This done, he knelt to the prince or noble who was to perform the final ceremony. The prince struck him lightly on the shoulder with the flat of the sword, saying: " In the name of God, St. Michael,[2] and St. George [the patron saint of England], I dub thee knight. Be brave, hardy, and loyal."

Then the young cavalier leaped into the saddle and galloped up and down, brandishing his weapon in token of strength and skill. In case a knight proved false to his oaths, he was publicly degraded. His spurs were taken from him, his shield was reversed, his armor broken to pieces, and a sermon preached upon him in the neighboring church, proclaiming him dead to the order.

IV. LITERATURE, LEARNING, AND ART

154. Education; Use of Seals or Stamps. The learning of this period was confined almost wholly to the clergy. Whatever schools existed were connected with the monasteries and nunneries. Oxford had begun to be regarded as a seat of learning (1120). The instruction was given by priests, though some noted Jewish scholars may have had pupils there. Very few books were written during this period. Generally speaking, the nobility considered fighting the great business of life and cared nothing for education. They thought that reading and writing were beneath their dignity, and left such accomplishments to monks, priests, and

---

[1] Knighthood: Originally the knight was a youth or attendant. Later, the word came to mean an armed horse soldier or cavalier who had received his weapons and title in a solemn manner. As a rule, only the wealthy and noble could afford the expense of a horse and armor; for this reason chivalry, or knighthood, came to be closely connected with the idea of aristocracy. In some cases soldiers were made knights on the battlefield as a reward for valor.

[2] St. Michael, as representative of the triumphant power of good over evil.

lawyers. For this reason seals or stamps having some device or signature engraved on them came to be used on all papers of importance.

155. Historical Works; the Bayeux Tapestry. The chief books written in England under the Norman kings were histories. Of these the most noteworthy were the continuation of the "Anglo-Saxon Chronicle" in English (§ 99) and the chronicles of William of Malmesbury and Henry of Huntingdon in Latin.[1] William's book and the "Saxon Chronicle" still continue to be of great importance to students of this period. Mention has already been made of the Bayeux Tapestry (§ 75), a history of the Norman Conquest worked in colored worsteds, on a long strip of narrow canvas.

It consists of a series of seventy-two scenes, or pictures, done about the time of William's accession. It was probably intended to decorate the cathedral of Bayeux, in Normandy, France, where it was originally placed. Some have supposed it to be the work of his Queen, Matilda. The entire length is two hundred and fourteen feet and the width about twenty inches. It represents events in English history from the last of Edward the Confessor's reign to the battle of Hastings. As a guide to a knowledge of the armor, weapons, and costume of the period, it is of very great value. The tapestry is preserved at Bayeux.

156. Architecture. Under the Norman sovereigns there was neither painting, statuary, nor poetry worthy of mention. The spirit that creates these arts found expression in architecture introduced from the Continent. The castle, cathedral, and minster, with here and there an exceptional structure like the Tower of London, London Bridge, and the Great Hall at Westminster, built by William Rufus, were some well-known Norman buildings which mark the time. All were of stone, a material which the Normans generally preferred to any other. Aside from Westminster Abbey, which, although the work of Edward the Confessor, was really Norman, a fortress or two, like Coningsborough in Yorkshire, and a few churches, like that at Bradford-on-Avon, the Saxons had erected little of note.

The characteristic of the Norman style of architecture was its massive grandeur. The churches were built in the form of a cross, with a square, central tower, the main entrance being at the west. The interior was divided into a nave, or central portion, with an aisle on each side for the passage of religious processions. The windows were narrow, and

[1] Geoffrey of Monmouth's "History of the Britons" belongs to this period. It abounds in romances about King Arthur. Tennyson based his "Idylls of the King" on it.

rounded at the top. The roof rested on round arches supported by heavy columns. The cathedrals of Peterborough, Ely, Durham, Norwich, the church of St. Bartholomew, London, and St. John's Chapel in the Tower of London are fine examples of Norman work.

The castles consisted of a square keep, or citadel, with walls of immense thickness, having a few slitlike windows in the lower story and somewhat larger ones above. In these buildings everything was made subordinate to strength and security. They were surrounded by a high stone wall and deep ditch, generally filled with water. The entrance to them was over a drawbridge through an archway protected by an iron grating, or portcullis, which could be raised and lowered at pleasure. The Tower of London, Rochester Castle, Norwich Castle, Castle Rising, Richmond Castle, Carisbrooke Keep, New Castle on the Tyne, and Tintagel Hold were built by William or his Norman successors.

The so-called Jews' houses at Lincoln and St. Edmundsbury are rare and excellent examples of Norman domestic architecture. Although in many cases the Norman castles are in ruins, yet these ruins bid fair to stand as long as the Pyramids. They were mostly the work of churchmen, who were the best architects of the day, and knew how to plan a fortress as well as to build a minster.

V. General Industry and Commerce

157. Trade. No very marked change took place in respect to agriculture or trade during the Norman period. Jews are mentioned in a few cases in Saxon records, but they apparently did not enter England in any number until after William the Conqueror's accession. They soon got control of much of the trade, and were the only capitalists of the time.

They were protected by the Kings in money lending at exorbitant rates of interest. In turn, the Kings extorted immense sums from them.

The guilds (§ 106), or associations for mutual protection among merchants and manufacturers, now became prominent, and in time they acquired great political influence.

VI. Mode of Life, Manners, and Customs

158. Dress. The Normans were more temperate and refined in their mode of living than the Saxons. In dress they made great display. In Henry I's reign it became the custom for the nobility to wear their hair very long, so that their curls resembled those of women. The clergy thundered against this effeminate fashion, but with no effect. At last, a priest preaching before the King on Easter Sunday, ended his sermon by taking out a pair of shears and cropping the entire congregation, King and all.

By the regulation called the curfew, a bell rang at sunset in summer and at eight in winter, which was the government signal for putting out lights and covering up fires. This law, which was especially hated by the English, as a Norman innovation and act of tyranny, was a necessary precaution against fire, at a time when London and other cities were masses of wooden hovels.

Surnames came in with the Normans. Previous to the Conquest, Englishmen had but one name; and when, for convenience, another was needed, they were called by their occupation or from some personal peculiarity, as Edward the Carpenter, Harold the Dauntless. Among the Normans the lack of a second, or family, name had come to be looked upon as a sign of low birth, and the daughter of a great lord (Fitz-Haman) refused to marry a nobleman who had but one, saying, " My father and my grandfather had each two names, and it were a great shame to me to take a husband who has less."

The principal amusements were hunting, and hawking (catching birds and other small game by the use of trained hawks).

The Church introduced theatrical plays, written and acted by the monks. These represented scenes in Scripture history, and, later, the careers of the Vices and the Virtues were personified.

Jousts and tournaments, or mock combats between knights, were not encouraged by William I or his immediate successors, but became common in the period following the Norman Kings. On some occasions they were fought in earnest, and resulted in the death of one, or more, of the combatants.

HAWKING SCENE (§ 158)
From an old manuscript

SIXTH PERIOD[1]

" Man bears within him certain ideas of order, of justice, of reason, with a constant desire to bring them into play . . . ; for this he labors unceasingly." — GUIZOT, "History of Civilization."

THE ANGEVINS, OR PLANTAGENETS, 1154–1399

THE BARONS *VERSUS* THE CROWN

CONSOLIDATION OF NORMAN AND SAXON INTERESTS — RISE OF THE NEW ENGLISH NATION

HENRY II,	1154–1189	EDWARD I,	1272–1307
RICHARD I,	1189–1199	EDWARD II,	1307–1327
JOHN,	1199–1216	EDWARD III,	1327–1377
HENRY III,	1216–1272	RICHARD II,	1377–1399

159. Accession and Dominions of Henry II. Henry was just of age when the death of Stephen (§ 141) called him to the throne.

From his father, Count Geoffrey of Anjou, a province of France, came the title of Angevin. The name Plantagenet, by which the family came to be known later, was derived from the count's habit of wearing a sprig of the golden-blossomed broom plant, or Plante-genêt, as the French called it, in his helmet.

Henry received from his father the dukedoms of Anjou and Maine, from his mother Normandy and the dependent province of Brittany, while through his marriage with Eleanor, the divorced Queen of France, he acquired the great southern dukedom of Aquitaine.

Thus on his accession he became ruler over all England, and over more than half of France besides, his realms extending from

---

[1] REFERENCE BOOKS on this Period will be found in the CLASSIFIED LIST OF BOOKS in the Appendix. The pronunciation of names will be found in the Index. The LEADING DATES stand unenclosed; all others are in parentheses.

the borders of Scotland to the base of the Pyrenees. (See map facing p. 84.)

To these extensive possessions Henry added the eastern half of Ireland.[1] The country was but partially conquered and never justly ruled. The English power there remained "like a spear-point embedded in a living body," inflaming all around it.[2]

160. Henry II's Charter and Reforms. On his mother's side Henry was a descendant of Alfred the Great (§ 51); for this reason he was hailed with enthusiasm by the native English. He at once began a system of reforms worthy of his illustrious ancestor. His first act was to issue a charter confirming the Charter of Liberties or pledges of good government which his grandfather, Henry I, had made (§ 135). His next was to begin leveling to the ground the castles unlawfully built in Stephen's reign, which had caused such widespread misery to the country[3] (§ 141). He continued the work of demolition until it is said he destroyed no less than eleven hundred of these strongholds of oppression.

The King next turned his attention to the coinage. During the civil war (§ 141) the barons had issued money debased in quality and deficient in weight. Henry abolished this dishonest currency and issued silver pieces of full weight and value.

---

[1] Ireland : The population of Ireland at this time consisted mainly of descendants of the Celtic and other prehistoric races which inhabited Britain at the period of the Roman invasion. Later, the Danes formed some settlements in the vicinity of Dublin.

The conquest of England by the Normans was practically a victory gained by one branch of a German race over another (Saxons, Normans, and Danes having originally sprung from the same Teutonic stock or from one closely akin to it, and the three soon mingled); but the partial conquest of Ireland by the English was a radically different thing. They and the Irish had really nothing in common. The latter refused to accept the feudal system, and continued to split up into savage tribes or clans under the rule of petty chiefs always at war with each other. The English established a Parliament in Ireland (1295); but its authority did not really extend beyond their colony. Later, many of the English colonists married Irish women, and adopted Irish customs and the Irish language. This, of course, affected their Parliamentary legislation. In 1494 the Crown secured the passage of Poynings's Act; it put the English Council above the Irish Parliament. The measure was not favorable to peace, and Ireland remained, partly through the battles of the clans and partly through English aggression, in a state of unrest which prevented all true national growth.

[2] W. E. H. Lecky's "England in the XVIIIth Century," II, 102.

[3] Under William the Conqueror and his immediate successors no one was allowed to erect a castle without a royal license. During Stephen's time the great barons constantly violated this salutary regulation.

161. War with France; Scutage (1160). Having completed these reforms, the King turned his attention to his Continental possessions. Through his wife, Henry claimed the county of Toulouse in southern France. To enforce this claim he declared war.

Henry's barons, however, refused to furnish troops to fight outside of England. The King wisely compromised the matter by offering to accept from each knight a sum of money in lieu of service, called scutage, or shield money.[1] The proposal was agreed to (1160), and in this way the knights furnished the King the means to hire soldiers for foreign wars.

Later in his reign Henry supplemented this tax by the passage of the Assize of Arms, a law which revived the national militia (§§ 96, 150) and placed it at his command for home service. By these two measures the King made himself practically independent of the barons, and thus gained a greater degree of power than any previous ruler had possessed.

162. Thomas Becket. There was, however, one man in Henry's kingdom — his Lord Chancellor (§ 145), Thomas Becket — who was always ready to serve him. At his own expense the Chancellor now equipped seven hundred knights, and, crossing the Channel, fought valiantly for the suppression of the rebellion in Toulouse (§ 161) in the south of France. (See map facing p. 84.)

Shortly after Becket's return from the Continent Henry resolved to appoint him Archbishop of Canterbury. Becket knew that the King purposed beginning certain Church reforms with which he was not in sympathy, and declined the office. But Henry would take no denial. At last Becket consented, but he warned the King that he should uphold the rights of the clergy. He now became the head of the Catholic Church in England. He was the first man of English birth called to that exalted position since the Norman Conquest.

This promotion made a decided change in Becket's relation to the King. So long as he was Chancellor he was bound to do

---

[1] Scutage: from the Latin *scutum*, a shield; the understanding being that he who would not take his shield and do battle for the King should pay enough to hire one who would. The scutage was assessed at two marks. Later, the assessment varied. The mark was two thirds of a pound of silver by weight, or thirteen shillings and fourpence ($3.20). Reckoned in modern money, the tax was probably at least twenty times two marks, or about $128.

THE DOMINIONS
of the
PLANTAGENETS
in the time of
HENRY II.

Scale of Miles.

0   50   100   150   200

NORTH   SEA

Irish Channel

ULSTER
Armagh
CONNAUGHT
R. Shannon
LEINSTER
Dublin
Wexford
MUNSTER
Limerick
Waterford

Anglesey
WALES
Milford
R. Severn
Bristol
Exeter

Stirling
Edinburgh
R. Forth
R. Tweed
R. Tyne Newcastle
Durham
Solway Firth
Carlisle
R. Eden
R. Ouse
York
R. Humber
The Wash
R. Dee
R. Mersey
Chester
R. Trent
Leicester
THE PLANTAGENET
Oxford
Runnymede
Clarendon
Salisbury
Winchester
Southampton
London
R. Thames
Canterbury
Dover
Hastings
Calais
Boulogne
Bruges
Flanders

English Channel

Cherbourg
Havre
Caen
NORMANDY
Rouen
R. Seine
PARIS
R. Marne
Champagne
Troyes
Ecos
Verdun
THE EMPIRE
R. Rhine

Brest
BRITTANY
Rennes
MAINE
Le Mans
ANJOU
Angers
Nantes
R. Loire
Tours
Fontevrault
Chinon
Blois
Orleans
Berry
Burgundy
R. Saone
R. Yonne

BAY   OF

Poitou

BISCAY

R. Garonne
Marche
Limoges
Auvergne
Lyons
R. Rhone
R. Isere

AQUITAIN
(GUIENNE)
Bordeaux

DOMINIONS

GASCONY
R. Adour
Toulouse
LANGUEDOC
Avignon
Arles
Provence
Marseille

M.-N. ENG., BUFFALO.

what the King ordered, but as soon as he was made Archbishop he became the servant of the Church. Again, on his assumption of this sacred office Becket underwent a remarkable change of character. He had been a man of the world, fond of pomp and pleasure. He now gave up all luxury and show. He put on sackcloth, lived on bread and water, and spent his nights in prayer, tearing his flesh with a scourge.

163. Becket's First Quarrel with the King. The new Archbishop's presentiment of trouble soon proved true. Becket had hardly taken his seat when a quarrel broke out between him and the King. In his need for money Henry levied a tax on all lands, whether belonging to the barons or to churchmen. Becket opposed this tax.[1] He was willing, he said, that the clergy should contribute, if they desired to do so, but not that they should be compelled to pay the tax.

The King declared with an oath that all should pay alike; the Archbishop vowed with equal determination that not a single penny should be collected from the Church. From that time the King and Becket never met again as friends.

164. The Second Quarrel. Shortly afterward, a much more serious quarrel broke out between the King and the Archbishop. Under the law made by William the Conqueror, the Church had the right to try in its own courts all offenses committed by monks and priests (§ 118). This privilege, in time, led to great abuses, since even in cases of the commission of the gravest crimes the Church had no direct power to inflict the penalty of death. On the contrary, the heaviest sentence it could give was imprisonment in a monastery, with degradation from the clerical office; while in less serious cases the offenders generally got off with fasting and flogging.

On this account some criminals who deserved to be hanged escaped with a comparatively slight penalty. Such a case now occurred. In one instance a priest had committed an unprovoked murder. Henry commanded him to be brought before the King's court; Becket interfered, and ordered the case to be tried by the bishop of the diocese. The bishop simply sentenced the murderer to lose his place for two years.

---

[1] See page 76, note 1, on Clergy.

165. The Constitutions of Clarendon, 1164. The King determined that such flagrant disregard of justice should no longer go on. He called a council of his chief men at Clarendon, near Salisbury, in Wiltshire, and laid the case before them. He demanded that in future the state or civil courts should be supreme, and that in every instance their judges should decide whether a criminal should be tried by the common law of the land or handed over to the Church courts.

He furthermore required that the clergy should be held strictly responsible to the Crown, so that in case of dispute the final appeal should be neither to the Archbishop nor to the Pope, but to himself. In this respect he went even farther than William the Conqueror had done (§ 118). After protracted debate the council, composed of a committee of bishops and barons, passed the measures which the King demanded. The new laws were entitled the Constitutions of Clarendon. They consisted of sixteen articles which clearly defined the powers and jurisdiction of the King's courts and the Church courts. Their great object was to secure a more uniform administration of justice for all classes of men. (See the Constitutional Summary in the Appendix, pp. viii and xxxii.)

Becket, though bitterly opposed to the new laws, finally assented, and swore to obey them. Afterward, feeling that he had conceded too much, he retracted his oath and refused to be bound by the Constitutions. The other Church dignitaries became alarmed at the prospect, and left Becket to settle with the King as best he might. Henceforth it was a battle between the King and the Archbishop, and each resolved that he would never give up until he had won the final victory (§ 170).

166. The King enforces the New Laws; Becket leaves the Country. Henry at once proceeded to put the Constitutions of Clarendon into execution without fear or favor. A champion of the Church of that day says, " Then was seen the mournful spectacle of priests and deacons who had committed murder, manslaughter, robbery, theft, and other crimes, carried in carts before the commissioners and punished as though they were ordinary men." [1]

Furthermore, the King seems now to have resolved to ruin Becket or drive him from the kingdom. He accordingly summoned

[1] William of Newburgh s " Chronicle."

the Archbishop before a royal council at Northampton to answer to certain charges made against him. Becket answered the summons, but he refused to acknowledge the jurisdiction of the council, and appealed to the Pope. " Traitor ! " cried a courtier, as he picked up a bunch of muddy rushes from the floor and flung them at the Archbishop's head. Becket turned and, looking him sternly in the face, said, " Were I not a churchman, I would make you repent that word." Realizing, however, that he was now in serious danger, he soon after left Northampton and fled to France.

167. Banishment *versus* Excommunication (1164). Finding Becket beyond his reach, Henry next proceeded to banish the Archbishop's kinsmen and friends, without regard to age or sex, to the number of nearly four hundred. These miserable exiles, many of whom were nearly destitute, were forced to leave the country in midwinter, and excited the pity of all who saw them.

Becket indignantly retaliated. He hurled at the King's counselors the awful sentence of excommunication or expulsion from the Church (§ 194). It declared the King accursed of God and man, deprived of help in this world, and shut out from hope in the world to come. In this manner the quarrel went on with ever-increasing bitterness for the space of six years.

168. Prince Henry crowned ; Reconciliation (1170). Henry, who had long wished to associate his son, Prince Henry, with him in the government, had him crowned at Westminster by the Archbishop of York, the bishops of London and Salisbury taking part.

By custom, if not indeed by law, Becket alone, as Archbishop of Canterbury, had the right to perform this ceremony.

When Becket heard of the coronation, he declared it an outrage both against Christianity and the Church. So great an outcry now arose that Henry believed it expedient to recall the absent Archbishop, especially as the King of France was urging the Pope to take up the matter. Henry accordingly went over to the Continent, met Becket, and persuaded him to return.

169. Renewal of the Quarrel ; Murder of Becket (1170). But though the Archbishop and the King had given each other the " kiss of peace," yet the reconciliation was on the surface only ; underneath, the old hatred smoldered, ready to burst forth into flame. As soon as he reached England, Becket invoked the thunders of the Church against those who had officiated at the coronation of Prince Henry. He excommunicated the Archbishop of York with his assistant bishops.

The King took their part, and in an outburst of passion against Becket he exclaimed, " Will none of the cowards who eat my bread rid me of that turbulent priest?" In answer to his angry cry for relief, four knights set out without Henry's knowledge for Canterbury, and brutally murdered the Archbishop within the walls of his own cathedral.

170. Results of the Murder. The crime sent a thrill of horror throughout the realm. The Pope proclaimed Becket a saint with the title of Saint Thomas. The mass of the English people looked upon the dead ecclesiastic as a martyr who had died in the defense of the Church, and of all those — but especially the laboring classes and the poor — around whom the Church cast its protecting power.

The great cathedral of Canterbury was hung in mourning; Becket's shrine became the most famous in England. The stone pavement, and the steps leading to it, still show by their deep-worn hollows where thousands of pilgrims coming from all parts of the kingdom, and from the Continent even, used to creep on their knees to the saint's tomb to pray for his intercession.

Henry himself was so far vanquished by the reaction in Becket's favor, that he gave up any further attempt to formally enforce the Constitutions of Clarendon (§ 165), by which he had hoped to establish a uniform system of administration of justice. But the attempt, though baffled, was not wholly lost; like seed buried in the soil, it sprang up and bore good fruit in later generations. However, it was not until near the close of the reign of George III (1813) that the civil courts fully and finally prevailed.

171. The King makes his Will; Civil War. Some years after the murder, the King bequeathed England and Normandy (§§ 108, 159) to Prince Henry.[1] He at the same time provided for his sons Geoffrey and Richard. To John, the youngest of the brothers,

---

1 After his coronation Prince Henry had the title of Henry III; but as he died before his father, he never properly became king in his own right.

he gave no territory, but requested Henry to grant him several castles, which the latter refused to do. "It is our fate," said one of the sons, "that none should love the rest; that is the only inheritance which will never be taken from us."

It may be that that legacy of hatred was the result of Henry's unwise marriage with Eleanor, an able but perverse woman, or it may have sprung from her jealousy of "Fair Rosamond" and other favorites of the King.[1] Eventually this feeling burst out into civil war. Brother fought against brother, and Eleanor, conspiring with the King of France, turned against her husband.

172. The King's Penance (1173). The revolt against Henry's power began in Normandy (1173). While he was engaged in quelling it, he received intelligence that Earl Bigod of Norfolk[2] and the bishop of Durham, both of whom hated the King's reforms, since they curtailed their authority, had risen against him.

Believing that this new trouble was a judgment of Heaven for Becket's murder, Henry resolved to do penance at his tomb. Leaving the Continent with two prisoners in his charge, — one his son Henry's queen, the other his own, — he traveled with all speed to Canterbury. There, kneeling abjectly before the grave of his former chancellor and friend, the King submitted to be beaten with rods by the priests, in expiation of his sin.

173. End of the Struggle of the Barons against the Crown. Henry then moved against the rebels in the north (§ 171). Convinced of the hopelessness of holding out against his forces, they submitted. With their submission the long struggle of the barons

---

[1] "Fair Rosamond" [*Rosa mundi*, the Rose of the world (as *then* interpreted)] was the daughter of Lord Clifford. According to tradition the King formed an attachment for this lady before his unfortunate marriage with Eleanor, and constructed a place of concealment for her in a forest in Woodstock, near Oxford. Some accounts report that Queen Eleanor discovered her rival and put her to death. She was buried in the nunnery of Godstow near by. When Henry's son John became King, he raised a monument to her memory with the inscription in Latin:

> "This tomb doth here enclose
> The world's most beauteous Rose —
> Rose passing sweet erewhile,
> Now naught but odor vile."

[2] Hugh Bigod: The Bigods were among the most prominent and also the most turbulent of the Norman barons.

against the Crown came to an end (§§ 124, 130). It had lasted nearly a hundred years (1087–1174).

The King's victory in this contest was of the greatest importance. It settled the question, once for all, that England was not, like the rest of Europe, to be managed in the interest of a body of great baronial landholders always at war with each other ; but was henceforth to be governed by one central power, restrained but not overridden by that of the nobles and the Church.

174. The King again begins his Reforms (1176). As soon as order was restored, Henry once more set about completing his legal and judicial reforms (§ 165). His great object was to secure a uniform system of administering justice which should be effective and impartial.

Henry I had undertaken to divide the kingdom into districts or circuits, which were assigned to a certain number of judges, who traveled through them at stated times collecting the royal revenue and administering the law (§§ 137, 147). Henry II revised and perfected this plan.[1]

In addition to the private courts which, under feudal law, the barons had set up on their estates (§ 150), they had in many cases got the entire control of the town and other local courts. There they dealt out such justice or injustice as they pleased. The King's judges now assumed control of these tribunals, and so brought the common law of the realm to every man's door.

175. Grand Juries. The Norman method of settling disputes was by Trial by Battle, in which the contestants or their champions fought the matter out either with swords or cudgels (§ 148). There were those who objected to this club law. To them the King offered the privilege of leaving the case to the decision of twelve knights, chosen from the neighborhood, who were supposed to know the facts. (See the Constitutional Summary in the Appendix, p. vi, § 8.)

In like manner, when the judges passed through a circuit, a grand jury of not less than sixteen was to report to them the criminals of

[1] This was accomplished by means of the two laws called the Grand Assize and the Assize of Clarendon (not to be confounded with the Constitutions of Clarendon). The Assize of Clarendon was the first true code of national law ; it was later expanded and made permanent under the name of the Assize of Northampton. (See the Constitutional Summary in the Appendix, p. vii, § 8.)

each district. These the judges forthwith sent to the Church to be examined by the Ordeal (§ 91). If convicted, they were punished; if not, the judges considered them to be suspicious characters, and ordered them to leave the country within eight days. In that way the rascals of that generation were summarily disposed of.

Henry II may rightfully be regarded as having taken the first step toward founding the system of Trial by Jury, which England, and England alone, fully matured. That method has since been adopted by every civilized country of the globe. (See the Constitutional Summary in the Appendix, p. vii, § 8.)

176. Origin of the Modern Trial by Jury, 1350. In the reign of Henry's son John, the Church abolished the Ordeal (§ 91) throughout Christendom (1215). It then became the custom in England to choose a petty jury, acquainted with the facts, who confirmed or denied the accusations brought by the grand jury. When this petty jury could not agree, the decision of a majority was sometimes accepted.

The difficulty of securing justice by this method led to the custom of summoning witnesses. These witnesses appeared before the petty jury and testified for or against the party accused. In this way it became possible to obtain a unanimous verdict.

The first mention of this change occurs more than a hundred and thirty years later, in the reign of Edward III (1350); and from that time, perhaps, may be dated the true beginning of our modern method, by which the jury bring in a verdict, not from what they personally know, but from evidence sworn to by those who do.

177. The King's Last Days. Henry's last days were full of bitterness. Ever since his memorable return from the Continent (§ 172), he had been obliged to hold the Queen a prisoner lest she should undermine his power (§ 171). His sons were discontented and rebellious. Toward the close of his reign they again plotted against him with King Philip of France. Henry then declared war against that country.

When peace was made, Henry, who was lying ill, asked to see a list of those who had conspired against him. At the head of it stood the name of his youngest son, John, whom he trusted. At the sight of it the old man turned his face to the wall, saying, " I have nothing left to care for ; let all things go their way." Two days afterward he died of a broken heart.

178. Summary. Henry II left his work only half done ; yet that half was permanent, and its beneficent mark may be seen on the English law and the English constitution at the present time.

When he ascended the throne he found a people who had long been suffering the miseries of a protracted civil war. He established a stable government. He redressed the wrongs of his people. He punished the mutinous barons.

He compelled the Church, at least in some degree, to acknowledge the supremacy of the State. He reformed the administration of law ; established methods of judicial inquiry which gradually developed into our modern Trial by Jury ; and he made all men feel that a king sat on the throne who believed in a uniform system of justice and who endeavored to make it respected.

RICHARD I (CŒUR DE LION) [1] — 1189–1199

179. Accession and Character of Richard I. Henry II was succeeded by his second son, Richard, his first having died during the civil war (1183) in which he and his brother Geoffrey had fought against Prince Richard and their father (§ 171). Richard was born at Oxford, but he spent his youth in France.

The only English sentence that he was ever known to speak was when he was in a raging passion. He then vented his wrath against an impertinent Frenchman, in some broken but decidedly strong expressions of his native tongue. Richard has been called " a splendid savage," having most of the faults and most of the virtues of such a savage.

The King's bravery in battle and his daring exploits gained for him the flattering surname of Cœur de Lion. He had a right to it, for he certainly possessed the heart of a lion, and he never

[1] Richard Cœur de Lion : Richard the Lion-Hearted. An old chronicler says the King got the name from his adventure with a lion. The beast attacked him, and as the King had no weapons, he thrust his hand down his throat and "tore out his heart." This story is not without value, since it illustrates how marvelous legends grow up around the lives of remarkable men.

failed to try to get the lion's share. He might, however, have been called, with equal truth, Richard the Absentee, since out of a nominal reign of ten years he spent but a few months in England, the remaining time being consumed in wars abroad.

180. Condition of Society. Perhaps no better general picture of society in England during this period can be found than that presented by Sir Walter Scott's novel, " Ivanhoe." There every class appears. One sees the Saxon serf and swineherd wearing the brazen collar of his master Cedric ; the pilgrim wandering from shrine to shrine, with the palm branch in his cap to show that he has visited the Holy Land ; the outlaw, Robin Hood, lying in wait to strip rich churchmen and other travelers who were on their way through Sherwood Forest. He sees, too, the Norman baron in his castle torturing the aged Jew to extort his hidden gold ; and the steel-clad knights, with Ivanhoe at their head, splintering lances in the tournament, presided over by Richard's brother, the traitorous Prince John (§ 177).

181. Richard's Coronation. Richard was on the Continent at the time of his father's death. His first act was to liberate his mother from her long imprisonment at Winchester (§ 177) ; his next, to place her at the head of the English government until his arrival from Normandy. Unlike Henry II, Richard did not issue a charter, or pledge of good government (§ 160). He, however, took the usual coronation oath to defend the Church, maintain justice, make salutary laws, and abolish evil customs ; such an oath might well be considered a charter in itself.

182. The Crusades (1190); how Richard raised Money. At that period all western Europe was engaged in the series of wars known as the Crusades. The object of this long contest, which began in 1096 and ended in 1270, was to compel the Saracens or Mohammedans to give up possession of the Holy Land to the Christians (§ 186). Immediately after his coronation, Richard resolved to join the King of France and the Emperor of Germany in the Third Crusade. To get money for the expedition, the King extorted loans from the Jews (§ 119), who were the creditors of half England and had almost complete control of the capital and commerce of every country in Europe.

The English nobles who joined Richard also borrowed largely from the same source; and then, suddenly turning on the hated lenders, they tried to extinguish the debt by extinguishing the Jews. A pretext against the unfortunate race was easily found. Riots broke out in London, York, and elsewhere, and hundreds of Israelites were brutally massacred.

Richard's next move to obtain funds was to impose a heavy tax; his next, to dispose of titles of rank and offices in both Church and State, to all who wished to buy them. Thus, to the aged and covetous bishop of Durham he sold the earldom of Northumberland for life, saying, as he concluded the bargain, "Out of an old bishop I have made a new earl."

He sold, also, the office of chief justice to the same prelate for an additional thousand marks (§ 161, note 1), while the King of Scotland purchased freedom from subjection to the English King for ten thousand marks.

Last of all, Richard sold cities and towns, and he also sold charters to towns. One of his courtiers remonstrated with him for his greed for gain. The King replied, "I would sell London itself could I find a purchaser rich enough to buy it."

183. The Rise of the Free Towns. Of all these devices for raising money, that of selling charters to towns had the most important results. From the time of the Norman Conquest the large towns of England, with few exceptions, were considered part of the King's property; the smaller places generally belonged to the great barons.

The citizens of these towns were obliged to pay rent and taxes of various kinds to the King or lord who owned them. These dues were collected by an officer appointed by the King or lord (usually the sheriff), who was bound to obtain a certain sum, whatever more he could get being his own profit. For this reason it was for his interest to exact from every citizen the uttermost penny. London, as we have seen, had secured a considerable degree of liberty through the charter granted to it by William the Conqueror (§ 107). Every town was now anxious to obtain a similar charter.

The three great objects which the citizens of the towns sought were:

(1) To get the right of paying their taxes directly to the King.

(2) To elect their own magistrates.

(3) To administer justice in their own courts in accordance with laws made by themselves.

The only way to gain these privileges was to pay for them. Many of the towns were rich, and, if the King or lord needed money, they bargained with him for the favors they desired. When the agreement was made, it was drawn up in Latin and stamped with the King's seal (§ 154). Then the citizens took it home in triumph and locked it up as the safeguard of their liberties, or at least of some part of them.

Thus, the people of Leicester, in the next reign, purchased from the Earl of Leicester, their feudal lord, the right to decide their own disputes. For this they paid a yearly tax of threepence on every house having a gable on the main street. These concessions may seem small, but they prepared the way for greater ones.

What was still more important, these charters educated the citizens of that day in a knowledge of self-government. The tradesmen and shopkeepers of these towns did much to preserve free speech and equal justice. Richard granted a large number of these town charters, and thus unintentionally made himself a benefactor to the nation.[1]

184. Failure of the Third Crusade. The object of the Third Crusade (§ 182) was to drive the Mohammedans from Jerusalem. In this it failed. Richard got as near Jerusalem as the Mount of Olives. When he had climbed to the top, he was told that he could have a full view of the place; but he covered his face with his mantle, saying, "Blessed Lord, let me not see thy holy city, since I may not deliver it from the hands of thine enemies!"

185. Richard taken Prisoner; his Ransom (1194). On his way home the King fell into the hands of the German Emperor, who held him captive. His brother John (§ 177), who had remained in England, plotted with Philip of France to keep Richard in prison while he got possession of the throne. It is not certainly known how the news of Richard's captivity reached England. One account

---

[1] Rise of Free Towns: By 1216 the most advanced of the English towns had become to a very considerable extent self-governing. See W. Stubbs's "Constitutional History of England."

relates that it was carried by Blondel, a minstrel who had accompanied the King to Palestine. He, it is said, wandered through Germany in search of his master, singing a song, which he and Richard had composed together, at every castle he came to. One day, as he was thus singing at the foot of a tower, he heard the well-known voice of the King take up the next verse in reply.

Finally, Richard regained his liberty (1194), but to do it he had to raise an enormous ransom. Every Englishman, it was said, was obliged to give a fourth of his personal property, and the priests were forced to strip the churches of their jewels and silver plate.

When the King of France heard that the ransom money had at length been raised, he wrote to John, telling him that his brother was free. " Look out for yourself," said he ; " the devil has broken loose." Richard generously pardoned his treacherous brother ; and when the King was killed in a war in France (1199) John gained the throne he coveted, but gained it only to disgrace it.

186. Purpose of the Crusades. Up to the time of the Crusades, the English, when they entered upon Continental wars, had been actuated either by ambition for military glory or desire for conquest. But they undertook the Crusades from motives of religious enthusiasm.

Those who engaged in them fought for an idea. They considered themselves soldiers of the cross. Moved by this feeling, " all Christian believers seemed ready to precipitate themselves in one united body upon Asia " (§ 182). Thus the Crusades were " the first European event." [1] They gave men something noble to battle for, not only outside their country, but outside their own selfish interests.

Richard, as we have seen, was the first English King who took part in them. Before that period England had stood aloof, — " a world by itself." The country was engaged in its own affairs or in its contests with France. Richard's expedition to the Holy Land brought England into the main current of history, so that it was now moved by the same feeling which animated the Continent.

187. The Results of the Crusades : Educational, Social, Political. From a purely military point of view, the Crusades ended in disastrous failure, for they left the Mohammedans in absolute possession

---

[1] Guizot's " History of Civilization."

of the Holy Land. Although this is the twentieth century since the birth of Christ, the Mohammedans still continue in that possession. But in spite of their failure these wars brought great good to England. In many respects the civilization of the East was far in advance of the West. One result of the Crusades was to open the eyes of Europe to this fact. When Richard and his followers set out, they looked upon the Mohammedans as barbarians; before they returned, many were ready to acknowledge that the barbarians were chiefly among themselves.

At that time England had few Latin and no Greek scholars. The Saracens or Mohammedans, however, had long been familiar with the classics, and had translated them into their own tongue. Not only did England gain its first knowledge of the philosophy of Plato and Aristotle from Mohammedan teachers, but it also received from them the elements of arithmetic, algebra, geometry, and astronomy.

This new knowledge gave a gre t impulse to education, and had a most important influence on th growth of the universities of Cambridge and Oxford, though these institutions did not become prominent until more than a century later.

Had these been the only results, they would still, perhaps, have been worth all the blood and treasure spent by the crusaders in their vain attempts to recover the permanent possession of the sepulcher of Christ; but these were by no means all. The Crusades brought about a social and political revolution. They conferred benefits and removed evils. When they began, the greater part of the inhabitants of western Europe, including England, were farm laborers, who, under the name of serfs or villeins, were chained to the soil (§ 150). They had neither freedom, property, nor knowledge.

There were in fact but three classes, who really deserved the name of citizens and freemen; these were the churchmen (comprising the clergy, monks, and other ecclesiastics), the nobles, and the inhabitants of certain favored towns. The effect of the Crusades was to increase the number of this last class. We have seen that Richard was compelled, by his need of money, to grant charters conferring local self-government on many towns (§§ 182, 183).

For a similar reason the great nobles often granted the same powers to towns which they controlled. The result was that their immense estates were broken up in some measure. It was from this period, says the historian Gibbon, that the common people (living in these chartered towns) began to acquire political rights, and, what is more, to defend them.

188. Summary. We may say in closing that the central fact in Richard's reign was his embarking in the Crusades. From them, directly or indirectly, England gained two important advantages: first, a greater degree of political liberty, especially in the case of the towns; secondly, a new intellectual and educational impulse.

JOHN — 1199–1216

189. John Lackland ; the King's Quarrels. When Henry II in dividing his realm left his youngest son, John, dependent on the generosity of his brothers, he jestingly gave him the surname of "Lackland" (§ 171). The nickname continued to cling to him even after he had become King of England and had also secured Normandy and several adjacent provinces in France.

The reign of the new King was taken up mainly with three momentous quarrels: first, with France; next, with the Pope; lastly, with the barons. By his quarrel with France he lost Normandy and the greater part of the adjoining provinces, thus becoming in a new sense John Lackland. By his quarrel with the Pope he was humbled to the earth. By his quarrel with the barons he was forced to grant England the Great Charter.

190. Murder of Prince Arthur. Shortly after John's accession the nobles occupying a part of the English possessions in France expressed their desire that John's nephew, Arthur, a boy of twelve, should become their ruler. John refused to grant their request.

War ensued, and Arthur fell into the hands of his uncle John, who imprisoned him in the castle of Rouen, the capital of Normandy. A number of those who had been captured with the young prince were starved to death in the dungeons of the same castle, and not long after Arthur himself mysteriously disappeared. Shakespeare represents John as ordering the keeper of the castle to put out the lad's eyes, and then tells us that he was killed in an attempt to escape.[1] The general belief, however, was that the King murdered him.

191. John's Loss of Normandy (1204). Philip, King of France, accused John of the crime, and ordered him as Duke of Normandy, and hence as his feudal dependant (§ 86), to appear at Paris for trial. John refused. The court met, declared him a traitor, and sentenced him to forfeit all his lands on the Continent.

John's late brother, Richard Cœur de Lion (§ 185), had built a famous stronghold on the Seine to hold Rouen and Normandy. He named it " Saucy Castle." King Philip vowed in Richard's lifetime that he would make himself master of it. " I would take it," said the French King, " were its walls of iron." " I would hold it," retorted Richard, " were its walls of butter." Richard made his word good, and kept the castle as long as he lived ; but his successor, John, was of poorer and meaner stuff. He left his Norman nobles to carry on the war against Philip as best they could. At last, after much territory had been lost, the English King made an attempt to regain

" SAUCY CASTLE "

(Château Gaillard)

it. But it was too late, and " Saucy Castle " fell. Then the end speedily came. Philip seized all Normandy and followed up the victory by depriving John of his entire possessions north of the river Loire. (See map facing p. 84.)

192. Good Results of the Loss of Normandy. Thus after a union of nearly a hundred and forty years Normandy was finally separated from England (§ 108). From that time the Norman nobles were

---

[1] Shakespeare's " King John," Act IV, scenes i and iii.

compelled to choose between the island of England and the Continent for their home. Before that time the Norman's contempt for the Saxon was so great, that his most indignant exclamation was, " Do you take me for an Englishman ? "

Now, however, shut in by the sea, with the people he had hitherto oppressed and despised, the Norman came to regard England as his country, and Englishmen as his countrymen. Thus the two races, who were closely akin to each other in their origin (§ 126), found at last that they had common interests and common enemies,[1] and henceforth they made the welfare of England their main thought.

193. The King's Despotism. Hitherto our sympathies have been mainly with the kings. We have watched them struggling against the lawless nobles (§ 173), and every gain which they have made in power we have felt was so much won for the cause of good government. But we are coming to a period when our sympathies will be the other way. Henceforth the welfare of the nation will depend largely on the resistance of these very barons to the despotic encroachments of the Crown.[2]

194. Quarrel of the King with the Church (1208). Shortly after his defeat in France (§ 191), John entered upon his second quarrel. Pope Innocent III had commanded a delegation of the monks of Canterbury to choose Stephen Langton archbishop in place of a person whom the King had compelled them to elect. When the news reached John, he forbade Langton's landing in England, although it was his native country.

The Pope forthwith declared the kingdom under an interdict, or suspension of religious services. For two years the churches were hung in mourning, the bells ceased to ring, the doors were shut fast. For two years the priests denied the sacraments to the living and funeral prayers for the dead. At the end of that time the Pope, by a bull of excommunication (§ 167), cut off the King as a withered branch from the Church. John laughed at the interdict, and met the decree of excommunication with such cruel treatment of the priests that they fled terrified from the land.

---

[1] Macaulay's " England " ; also W. Stubbs's " Early Plantagenets," p. 136.
[2] Ransome's " Constitutional History of England."

The Pope now took a third and final step; he deposed John and ordered Philip, King of France, to seize the English Crown. Then John, knowing that he stood alone, made a virtue of necessity. He knelt at the feet of the Pope's legate, or representative, accepted Stephen Langton as Archbishop of Canterbury, and promised to pay a yearly tax to Rome of one thousand marks (about $64,000 in modern money) for permission to keep his crown. The Pope was satisfied with the victory he had gained over his ignoble foe, and peace was made.

195. The Great Charter. But peace in one direction did not mean peace in all. John's tyranny, brutality, and disregard of his subjects' welfare had gone too far. He had refused the Church the right to fill its offices and to enjoy its revenues. He had extorted exorbitant sums from the barons. He had violated the charters of London and other cities. He had compelled merchants to pay large sums for the privilege of carrying on their business unmolested. He had imprisoned men on false or frivolous charges, and refused to bring them to trial. He had unjustly claimed heavy sums from villeins, or farm laborers (§ 113), and other poor men; and when they could not pay, had seized their carts and tools, thus depriving them of their means of livelihood.

Those who had suffered these and greater wrongs were determined to have reformation, and to have it in the form of a written charter or pledge bearing the King's seal. Stephen Langton, the new archbishop, was likewise determined. He no sooner landed in England than he demanded of the King that he should swear to observe the laws of Edward the Confessor (§ 65), a phrase [1] in which the whole of the national liberties was summed up.

196. Preliminary Meeting at St. Albans (1213). In the summer (1213) a council was held at St. Albans, near London, composed of representatives from all parts of the kingdom. It was the first assembly of the kind on record. It convened to consider what claims should be made on the King in the interest of the nobles, the clergy, and the people at large. A few weeks later they met again, at St. Paul's in London.

---

[1] Not necessarily the laws made by that King, but rather the customs and rights enjoyed by the people during his reign.

The deliberations of the assembly took shape probably under Archbishop Langton's guiding hand. He had obtained a copy of the charter granted by Henry I (§ 135). This was used as a model for drawing up a new one of similar character, but in every respect fuller and stronger in its provisions.

197. Battle of Bouvines ; Second Meeting of the Barons (1214). John foolishly set out for the Continent, to fight the French at the same time that the English barons were preparing to bring him to terms. He was defeated in the decisive battle of Bouvines, in the north of France, and returned to England crestfallen (1214), and in no condition to resist demands at home. Late in the autumn the barons met in the abbey church of Bury St. Edmunds, in Suffolk, under their leader, Robert Fitz-Walter, of London. Advancing one by one up the church to the high altar, they solemnly swore that they would oblige John to grant the new charter, or they would declare war against him.

198. The King grants the Charter, 1215. At Easter (1215) the same barons, attended by two thousand armed knights, met the King at Oxford and made known their demands. John tried to evade giving a direct answer. Seeing that was impossible, and finding that the people of London were on the side of the barons, he yielded and requested them to name the day and place for the ratification of the charter.

" Let the day be the 15th of June, the place Runnymede," [1] was the reply. In accordance therewith, we read at the foot of the shriveled parchment preserved in the British Museum, " Given under our hand . . . in the meadow called Runnymede, between Windsor and Staines, on the 15th of June, in the seventeenth year of our reign."

199. Terms and Value of the Charter, 1215 ; England leads in Constitutional Government. This memorable document was henceforth known as Magna Carta,[2] or the Great Charter, — a term used to emphatically distinguish it from all previous and partial charters.

---

[1] Runnymede : about twenty miles southwest of London, on the south bank of the Thames, in Surrey.

[2] Magna Carta : *Carta* is the spelling in the medieval Latin of this and the preceding charters. (See the Constitutional Documents in the Appendix, p. xxix.)

KING JOHN GRANTS MAGNA CARTA

It stipulated that the following grievances should be redressed : First, those of the Church ; secondly, those of the barons and their vassals or tenants ; thirdly, those of citizens and tradesmen ; fourthly, those of freemen and villeins or serfs (§§ 113, 150).

Such was the first agreement entered into between the King and all classes of his people. Of the sixty-three articles which constitute it, the greater part, owing to the changes of time, are now obsolete ; but three possess imperishable value. These provide :

(1) *That no free man shall be imprisoned or proceeded against except by his peers,*[1] *or the law of the land.*

(2) *That justice shall neither be sold, denied, nor delayed.*

(3) *That all dues from the people to the King, unless otherwise distinctly specified, shall be imposed only with the consent of the National Council* (§ 144).

This last provision "converted the power of taxation into the shield of liberty."[2]

Thus, for the first time, the interests of all classes were protected, and for the first time the English people appear in the constitutional history of the country as a united body. So highly was this charter esteemed, that in the course of the next two centuries it was confirmed no less than thirty-seven times ; and the very day that Charles II entered London, after the civil wars of the seventeenth century, the House of Commons asked him to confirm it again (1660). Magna Carta was the first great step in that development of constitutional government in which England has taken the lead.

200. John's Efforts to break the Charter (1215).   But John had no sooner set his hand to this document than he determined to repudiate it. He hired bands of soldiers on the Continent to come to his aid. The charter had been obtained by armed revolt ; for this reason the Pope opposed it. He suspended Archbishop Langton (§ 196), and threatened the barons with excommunication (§ 167), if they persisted in enforcing the provisions of the charter.

---

[1] Peers (from Latin *pares*) : equals ; this clause secures a fair and open trial.

[2] Sir J. Mackintosh's "History of England." This provision was dropped in the next reign (see W. Stubbs's "Constitutional History of England") ; but after the great civil war of the seventeenth century the principle it laid down was firmly reëstablished.

201. The Barons invite Louis of France to aid them (1215). In their desperation, — for the King's hired foreign soldiers were now ravaging the country, — the barons despatched a messenger to John's sworn enemy, Philip, King of France. They invited him to send over his son, Prince Louis, to free them from tyranny, and become ruler of the kingdom. He came with all speed, and soon made himself master of the southern counties.

202. King John's Death (1216). John was the first sovereign who had styled himself, on his great seal, "King of England," [1] thus formally claiming the actual ownership of the realm. He was now to find that the sovereign who has no place in his subjects' hearts has small hold of their possessions.

The rest of his ignominious reign was spent in war against the barons and Prince Louis of France. "They have placed twenty-five kings over me!" he shouted, in his fury, referring to the twenty-five leading men who had been appointed to see that the Great Charter did not become a dead letter. But the twenty-five did their duty, and the war went on.

In the midst of it John suddenly died. The old record said of him — and said rightly — that he was "a knight without truth, a king without justice, a Christian without faith." [2] The Church returned good for evil, and permitted him to be buried in front of the high altar of Worcester cathedral.

203. Summary. John's reign may be regarded as a turning point in English history.

1. Through the loss of Normandy, the Norman nobility found it for their interest to make the welfare of England and of the English race one with their own. Thus the two peoples became more and more united, until finally all differences ceased.

---

[1] The late Professor E. A. Freeman, in his "Norman Conquest," I, 85, note, says that though Richard Cœur de Lion had used this title in issuing charters, yet John was the first king who put this inscription on the great seal.

[2] The late Professor W. Stubbs, of Oxford, says, in his "Early Plantagenets," p. 152: "John ended thus a life of ignominy in which he has no rival in the whole long list of our sovereigns. . . . He was in every way the worst of the whole list: the most vicious, the most profane, the most tyrannical, the most false, the most short-sighted, the most unscrupulous." A more recent writer (Professor Charles Oman, of the University of Oxford), says of John, "No man had a good word to say for him . . .; he was loathed by every one who knew him."

2. In demanding and obtaining the Great Charter, the Church and the nobility made common cause with all classes of the people. That document represents the victory of the entire nation. We shall see that the next eighty years will be mainly taken up with the efforts of the nation to hold fast what it had gained.

HENRY III — 1216–1272

204. Accession and Character. John's eldest son, Henry, was crowned at the age of nine. During his long and feeble reign of fifty-six years England's motto might well have been the warning words of Scripture, " Woe to thee, O land, when thy king is a child ! " since a child he remained to the last ; for if John's heart was of millstone, Henry's was of wax.

Dante in one of his poems, written perhaps not long after Henry's death, represents him as he sees him in imagination just on the borderland of purgatory. The King is not in suffering, for as he has done no particular good, so he has done no great harm. He appears " as a man of simple life, spending his time singing psalms in a narrow valley."

That shows one side of his negative character ; the other was his love of extravagance, vain display, and instability of purpose. Much of the time he drifted about like a ship without compass or rudder.

205. Reissue of the Great Charter. Louis, the French prince who had come to England in John's reign as an armed claimant to the throne (§ 201), finding that both the barons and the Church preferred an English to a foreign king, now retired. During his minority Henry's guardians twice reissued the Great Charter (§ 199) : first, with the omission of the article which reserved the power of taxation to the National Council (§ 199, No. 3) ; and, secondly, with an addition declaring that no man should lose life or limb for hunting in the royal forests (§ 119).

On the last occasion the Council granted the King in return a fifteenth of their movable or personal property. This tax reached a large class of people, like merchants in towns, who were not landholders. On this account it had a decided influence in making them desire to have a voice in the National Council, or Parliament, as it began to be called in this reign (1246). It thus helped, as we shall see later on, to prepare the way for a very important change in that body.[1]

206. Henry's Extravagance. When Henry became of age he entered upon a course of extravagant expenditure. This, with unwise and unsuccessful wars, finally piled up debts to the amount of nearly a million of marks, or, in modern money, upwards of £13,000,000. To satisfy the clamors of his creditors, he mortgaged the Jews (§ 119), or rather the right of extorting money from them, to his brother Richard.

He also violated charters and treaties in order to compel those who benefited by them to purchase their reissue. On the birth of his first son, Prince Edward, he showed himself so eager for congratulatory gifts, that one of the nobles present at court said, " Heaven gave us this child, but the King sells him to us."

207. His Church Building. Still, not all of the King's extravagance was money thrown away. Everywhere on the Continent magnificent churches were rising. The heavy and somber Norman architecture, with its round arches and square, massive towers, was giving place to the more graceful Gothic style, with its pointed arch and lofty, tapering spire.

The King shared the religious enthusiasm of those who built the grand cathedrals of Salisbury and Lincoln. He himself rebuilt the greater part of Westminster Abbey (§ 66) as it now stands. A monument so glorious ought to make us willing to overlook some faults in the builder. Yet the expense and taxation incurred in erecting the great minster must be reckoned among the causes that bred discontent and led to civil war (§ 212).

208. Religious Reformation ; the Friars, 1221 ; Roger Bacon. While this movement, which covered the land with religious edifices, was in progress, religion itself was undergoing a change. The old monastic orders had grown rich, indolent, and corrupt.

---

[1] The first tax on movable or personal property appears to have been levied by Henry II, in 1188, for the support of the Crusades. Under Henry III the idea began to become general that no class should be taxed without their consent ; out of this grew the representation of townspeople in Parliament.

The priests had well-nigh ceased to do missionary work. At this period a reform sprang up within the Church itself. On the Continent two new religious orders arose, calling themselves Friars, or Brothers. They first came to England in 1221. These Brothers bound themselves to a life of self-denial and good works. Some labored in the outskirts of towns among the poor and the sick and called them to hear the glad tidings of the teachings of Christ. From their living on charity they came to be known as "Begging Friars."

Others, like Roger Bacon at Oxford, took an important part in education, and endeavored to rouse the sluggish monks to make efforts in the same direction. Bacon's experiments in physical science, which was then neglected and despised, got him the reputation of being a magician. He was driven into exile, imprisoned for many years, and deprived of books and writing materials.

But, as nothing could check the religious fervor of his mendicant brothers, so no hardship or suffering could daunt the intellectual enthusiasm of Bacon. When he emerged from captivity he issued his great book entitled an "Inquiry into the Roots of Knowledge."[1] It was especially devoted to mathematics and the sciences, and deserves the name of the encyclopedia of the thirteenth century.

209. The "Mad Parliament"; the Provisions of Oxford (1258). But the prodigal expenditure and mismanagement of Henry kept on increasing. At last the burden of taxation became too great to bear. Bad harvests had caused a famine, and multitudes perished even in London. Confronted by these evils, Parliament (§ 205) met in the Great Hall at Westminster. Many of the barons were in complete armor. As the King entered there was an ominous clatter of swords. Henry, looking around, asked timidly, "Am I a prisoner?"

"No, sire," answered Earl Bigod (§ 172); "but we must have reform." The King agreed to summon a Parliament to meet at Oxford and consider what should be done. The enemies of this

---

[1] Bacon designated this book by the name of "Opus Majus," or "Greater Work," to distinguish it from a later summary which he called his "Opus Minus," or "Smaller Work."

assembly nicknamed it the "Mad Parliament" (1258); but there was method and determination in its madness, for which the country was grateful.

With Simon de Montfort, the King's brother-in-law, at their head, they drew up a set of articles, called the Provisions of Oxford, to which Henry gave an unwilling assent. These Provisions practically took the government out of the King's inefficient hands and vested it in the control of three committees, or councils. (See Summary of Constitutional History in the Appendix, p. x, § 11.)

210. Renewal of the Great Charter (1253). Meanwhile the King had been compelled to reaffirm that Great Charter which his father had unwillingly granted at Runnymede (§ 198). Standing in St. Catherine's Chapel within the partially finished church of Westminster Abbey (§ 207), Henry, holding a lighted taper in his hand, in company with the chief men of the realm, swore to observe the provisions of the covenant.

At the close he exclaimed, as he dashed the taper on the pavement, while all present repeated the words and the action, "So go out with smoke and stench the accursed souls of those who break or pervert this charter."

There is no evidence that the King was insincere in his oath; but unfortunately his piety was that of impulse, not of principle. The compact was soon broken, and the land was again compelled to bear the burden of exorbitant taxes. These were extorted by violence, partly to cover Henry's own extravagance, but also to swell the coffers of the Pope, who had promised to make Henry's son, Prince Edward, ruler over Sicily.

211. Growing Feeling of Discontent. During this time the barons were daily growing more mutinous and defiant, saying that they would rather die than be ruined by the "Romans," as they called the papal power. To a fresh demand for money Earl Bigod (§ 209) gave a flat refusal. "Then I will send reapers and reap your fields for you," cried the King to him. "And I will send you back the heads of your reapers," retorted the angry Earl.

It was evident that the nobles would make no concession. The same spirit was abroad which, at an earlier date (1236), made the Parliament of Merton declare, when asked to alter the customs or

laws of the country to suit the ordinances of the Church of Rome,
"We will not change the laws of England." So now they were
equally resolved not to pay the Pope money in behalf of the
King's son.

212. Civil War; Battle of Lewes (1264). The crisis was soon
reached. War broke out between the King and his brother-in-law,
Simon de Montfort, Earl of Leicester (§ 209), better known by
his popular name of Sir Simon the Righteous.

With fifteen thousand Londoners and a number of the barons,
he met Henry, who had a stronger force, on the heights above
the town of Lewes, in Sussex. (See map facing p. 436.) The result
of the great battle fought there was as decisive as that fought two
centuries before by William the Conqueror (§ 74), not many miles
distant on the same coast.

213. De Montfort's Parliament; the House of Commons, 1265.
Bracton, the foremost jurist of that day, said in his comments on the
dangerous state of the times, "If the King were without a bridle,
— that is, the law, — his subjects ought to put a bridle on him."

Earl Simon (§ 209) had that "bridle" ready, or rather he saw
clearly where to get it. The battle of Lewes had gone against
Henry, who had fallen captive to De Montfort. By virtue of the
power he now possessed, the Earl summoned a Parliament. It
differed from all previous Parliaments in the fact that now, for
the first time, representatives of the boroughs or principal towns
(§ 103) were called to London to join the earls, barons, and clergy
in their deliberations.

Thus, in the winter of 1265, that House of Commons, or legislative assembly of the people, as distinguished from the House of
Lords, originated. After it was fully and finally established in the
next reign (§ 217), it sat for more than three hundred years in
the chapter house [1] of Westminster Abbey. It showed that at last
those who had neither land nor rank, but who paid taxes on personal property only, had obtained at least temporary representation
in Parliament.

When that principle should be fully recognized, the King would
have a "bridle" which he could not shake off. Henceforth Magna

---

1 The building where the governing body of an abbey transacts business.

Carta (§ 199) would be no longer a dead parchment promise of reform, rolled up and hidden away, but would become a living, ever-present, effective truth. (See §§ 261, 262, and Constitutional Summary in the Appendix, p. x, § 11.)

From this date the Great Council or Parliament of England (§ 144) commenced to lose its exclusive character of a single House consisting of the upper classes only. Now, it gave promise of becoming a true representative body standing for the whole nation. Thus De Montfort began — or at least tried to begin — what President Lincoln called "government of the people, by the people, for the people." But it should be distinctly understood that his work had the defects of a first attempt, and that it did not last. For, in the first place, De Montfort failed to summon all who were entitled to have seats in such a body ; and secondly, he summoned only those who favored his policy. We shall see that the honor of calling the first full and free Parliament was reserved for Edward I. Thirty years later, he summoned that body, which be-

BELL TOWER OF EVESHAM
ABBEY (1265)

came the final model of every such assembly which now meets, whether in the Old World or the New (§ 217).

214. Earl Simon's Death (1265). But De Montfort's great effort soon met with a fatal reaction. The barons, jealous of his power, fell away from him. Prince Edward, the King's eldest son, gathered them round the royal standard to attack and crush the man who had humiliated his father. De Montfort was at Evesham, Worcestershire (see map facing p. 436); from the top of the Bell Tower of the Abbey he saw the Prince approaching. "Commend

your souls to God," he said to the faithful few who stood by him;
" for our bodies are the foes'!" There he fell. He was buried in
Evesham Abbey, but no trace of his grave exists.

In the north aisle of Westminster Abbey, not far from Henry
III's tomb, may be seen the emblazoned arms of the brave Earl
Simon. But England, so rich in effigies of her great men, so faithful, too, in her remembrance of them, has not yet set up in the
vestibule of the House of Commons, among the statues of her
statesmen, the image of him who took the first actual step toward
founding that House in its present form.

215. Summary. Henry III's reign lasted over half a century.
During that period England, as we have seen, was not standing
still. It was an age of reform. In religion the " Begging Friars "
were exhorting men to better lives. In education Roger Bacon
and other devoted scholars were laboring to broaden knowledge
and deepen thought.

In political affairs the people now first obtained a place in
Parliament. Their victory was not permanent then, but it was
the precursor of the establishment of a permanent House of
Commons which was to come in the next reign.

EDWARD I — 1272-1307

216. Edward I and the Crusades. Henry's son, Prince Edward,
was in the East, fighting the battles of the Crusades (§ 182), at the
time of his father's death. According to an account given in an
old Spanish chronicle, an enemy attacked him with a poisoned
dagger. His wife, Eleanor, saved his life by heroically sucking the
poison from the wound (§ 223).

217. Edward's First " Complete or Model Parliament," 1295.
Many years after his return to England, Edward convened a Parliament, 1295, to which representatives of all classes of freemen
were summoned, and from this time they regularly met (§ 213).
Parliament henceforth consisted of two Houses.[1] The first included
the Lords and Clergy. The second comprised the Commons (or

---

[1] But during the period of the Commonwealth and Protectorate (1648–1660) the
House of Lords did not meet (§ 450).

representation of the common people). It thus became "a complete image of the nation," "assembled for purposes of taxation, legislation, and united political action."[1] This body declared that all previous laws should be impartially executed, and that there should be no interference with elections.[2] By this action King Edward showed that he had the wisdom to adopt and perfect the example his father's conqueror had left him (§ 213). Thus it will be seen that though Earl Simon the Righteous (§§ 212, 213, 214) was dead, his reform went on. It was an illustration of the truth that while "God buries his workers, he carries on his work."

218. Conquest of Wales, 1282 ; Birth of the First Prince of Wales. Henry II had labored to secure unity of law for England. Edward I's aim was to bring the whole island of Britain under one ruler. On the west, Wales only half acknowledged the power of the English King, while on the north, Scotland was practically an independent sovereignty. The new King determined to begin by annexing Wales to the Crown.

He accordingly led an army thither, and after several victorious battles, considered that he had gained his end. To make sure of his new possessions, he erected along the coast the magnificent castles of Conway, Beaumaris, Harlech, and Carnarvon, all of which he garrisoned with bodies of troops ready to check revolt.

In the last-named stronghold, tradition still points out a little dark chamber in the Eagle Tower, more like a state-prison cell than a royal apartment, where Edward's second son was born (1284). Years afterward the King created him the first Prince of Wales (1301). The Welsh had vowed that they would never accept an Englishman as King; but the young Prince was a native of their soil, and certainly in his cradle, at least, spoke as good Welsh as their own children of the same age. No objection, therefore, could be made to him ; by this happy compromise, it is said, Wales became a principality joined to the English Crown.[3]

---

[1] Stubbs's " Early Plantagenets " (Edward I). See also the Summary of Constitutional History in the Appendix, p. xi, § 12.

[2] The First Statute of Westminster.

[3] Wales was not wholly incorporated with England until more than two centuries later, namely in 1536, in the reign of Henry VIII. It then obtained local self-government and representation in Parliament.

219. Conquest of Scotland (1290–1296); the Stone of Scone. An opportunity now presented itself for Edward to assert his power in Scotland. Two claimants, both of Norman descent, had come forward demanding the crown.[1] One was John Baliol; the other, Robert Bruce, an ancestor of the famous Scottish King and general of that name, who will come prominently forward in the next reign. Edward was invited by the contestants to settle the dispute. He decided in Baliol's favor, but insisted, before doing so, that the latter should acknowledge the overlordship of England, as the King of Scotland had done to William I.

Baliol made a virtue of necessity, and agreed to the terms; but shortly after formed a secret alliance with France against Edward, which was renewed from time to time, and kept up between the two countries for three hundred years. It is the key to most of the wars in which England was involved during that period. Having made this treaty, Baliol now openly renounced his allegiance to the English King. Edward at once organized a force, attacked Baliol, and at the battle of Dunbar (1296) compelled the Scottish nobleman to acknowledge him as ruler.

At the Abbey of Scone, near Perth, the English seized the famous " Stone of Destiny," the palladium of Scotland, on which her Kings were crowned. (See map facing p. 120.) Carrying the trophy to Westminster Abbey, Edward enclosed it in that ancient coronation chair which has been used by every sovereign since, from his son's accession (1307) down to the present day.

220. Confirmation of the Charters, 1297. Edward next prepared to attack France. In great need of money, he demanded

[1] Scotland: At the time of the Roman conquest of Britain, Scotland was inhabited by a Celtic race nearly akin to the primitive Irish, and more distantly so to the Britons. In time, the Saxons from the Continent invaded the country, and settled on the lowlands of the east, driving back the Celts to the western highlands. Later, many English emigrated to Scotland, especially at the time of the Norman Conquest, where they found a hearty welcome.

In 1072 William the Conqueror compelled the Scottish King to acknowledge him as Overlord, and eventually so many Norman nobles established themselves in Scotland that they constituted the chief landed aristocracy of the country. The modern Scottish nation, though it keeps its Celtic name (Scotland), is made up in great measure of inhabitants of English descent, the pure Scotch being confined mostly to the Highlands, and ranking in population only as about one to three of the former.

a large sum from the clergy, and seized a quantity of wool in the hands of the merchants. The barons, alarmed at these arbitrary measures, insisted on the King's confirming all previous charters of liberties, including the Great Charter (§§ 135, 160, 199). This confirmation expressly forbade that the Crown should take the people's money or goods except by the consent of Parliament. Thus out of the war England gained the one thing it needed to give the finishing touch to the building up of Parliamentary power (§§ 213, 217); namely, a solemn acknowledgment by the King that the nation alone had the right to levy taxes.[1] (See Summary of Constitutional History in the Appendix, p. xi, § 12.)

221. Revolt and Death of Wallace (1303). A new revolt now broke out in Scotland (§ 219). The patriot, William Wallace, rose and led his countrymen against the English, — led them with that impetuous valor which breathes in Burns's lines :

> " Scots, wha hae wi' Wallace bled."

Fate, however, was against him. After eight years of desperate fighting, the valiant soldier was captured, executed on Tower Hill in London as a traitor, and his head, crowned in mockery with a wreath of laurel, was set on a pike on London Bridge.

But though the hero who perished on the scaffold could not prevent his country from becoming one day a part of England, he did hinder its becoming so on unfair and tyrannical terms. " Scotland," says Carlyle, " is not Ireland. No ; because brave men arose there, and said, ' Behold, ye must not tread us down like slaves, — and ye shall not, — and ye cannot ! ' " But Ireland failed, not for any lack of brave men, but for lack of unity among them.

222. Expulsion of the Jews, 1290. The darkest stain on Edward's reign was his treatment of the Jews (§ 119). Up to this period that unfortunate race had been protected by the Kings of England as men protect the cattle which they fatten for slaughter.

---

[1] Professor Stubbs says in his works (i.e. " Constitutional History of England," and " Select Charters "), that the Confirmation of the Charters " established the principle that for all taxation, direct and indirect, the consent of the nation must be asked, and made it clear that all transgressions of that principle, whether within the letter of the law or beyond it, were evasions of the spirit of the Constitution." See also J. Rowley's " Rise of the English People."

So long as they accumulated money, and so long as the sovereign could extort from them whatever portion of their accumulations he saw fit to demand, they were worth guarding. A time had now come when the populace clamored for their expulsion from the island, on the ground that their usury and rapacity were ruining the country.

Edward yielded to the clamor, and first stripping the Jews of their possessions, he prepared to drive them into exile. It is said

A QUEEN ELEANOR CROSS

that even their books were taken from them and given to the libraries of Oxford. Thus pillaged, they were forced to leave the realm, — a miserable procession, numbering some sixteen thousand. Many perished on the way, and so few ventured to return that for three centuries and a half, until Cromwell came to power, they disappear from English history (§ 458).

223. Death of Queen Eleanor. Shortly after this event, Queen Eleanor died (§ 216). The King showed the devoted love he bore her in the beautiful crosses of carved stone that he raised to her memory, three of which still stand.[1] These were erected at the places where her coffin was set down, in its transit from Grantham,

in Lincolnshire, where she died, to the little village of Charing (now Charing Cross, the geographical center of London). This was the last station before her body reached its final resting place, in that abbey at Westminster which holds such wealth of historic dust. Around Queen Eleanor's tomb wax lights were kept constantly burning, until the Protestant Reformation extinguished them, nearly three hundred years later.

---

[1] Originally there were thirteen of these crosses. Of these, three remain : namely, at Northampton, at Geddington, near by, and at Waltham, about twelve miles northeast of London.

224. Edward's Reforms ; Statute of Winchester (1285). The condition of England when Edward came to the throne was far from settled. The country was overrun with marauders. To suppress these, the Statute of Winchester made the inhabitants of every district punishable by fines for crimes committed within their limits. Every walled town had to close its gates at sunset, and no stranger could be admitted during the night unless some citizen would be responsible for him.

In addition, both sides of the main roads were cleared of bushes in order that desperadoes might not lie in wait for travelers. Furthermore, every citizen was required to keep arms and armor, according to his condition in life, and to join in the pursuit and arrest of criminals.

225. Land Legislation, 1285, 1290. Two very important statutes were passed during this reign, respecting the free sale or transfer of land.[1]

The effect of these statutes was to confine the great estates to the hands of their owners and direct descendants, or, when land changed hands, to keep alive the claims of the great lords or the Crown upon it. These laws rendered it difficult for landholders to evade their feudal duties to the King (§ 150) by the sale or subletting of estates. Hence, while they often built up the strength of the great families, they also operated to increase the power of the Crown at the very time when the growing influence of Parliament and the people was beginning to act as a check upon the royal authority.

226. Legislation respecting the Church ; Statute of Mortmain, 1279. A third enactment checked the undue increase of Church property. Through gifts and bequests the clergy had become owners of a very large part of the most fertile soil of the realm. No farms, herds of cattle, or flocks of sheep compared with theirs. These lands were said to be in mortmain, or " dead hands " ; since the Church, being a corporation, never let go its hold, but kept its property with the tenacity of a dead man's grasp.

---

[1] These laws may be regarded as the foundation of the English system of landed property ; they completed the feudal claim to the soil established by William the Conqueror. They are known as the Second Statute of Westminster (De Donis, or Entail, 1285) and the Third Statute of Westminster (Quia Emptores, 1290). See § 264 and Summary of Constitutional History in the Appendix, p. xi, § 11.

The clergy constantly strove to get these Church lands exempted from furnishing soldiers, or paying taxes to the King (§ 136). Instead of men or money they offered prayers. Practically, the Crown succeeded from time to time in compelling them to do considerably more than this, but seldom without a violent struggle, as in the case of Henry II and Becket (§ 165).

On account of these exemptions it had become the practice with many persons who wished to escape bearing their just share of the support of the King, to give their lands to the Church, and then receive them again as tenants of some abbot or bishop. In this way they evaded their military and pecuniary obligations to the Crown. To put a stop to this practice, and so make all landed proprietors do their part, the Statute of Mortmain was passed, 1279. It required the donor of an estate to the Church to obtain a royal license, which, it is perhaps needless to say, was not readily granted.[1]

227. Death of Edward I. Edward died while endeavoring to subdue a revolt in Scotland, in which Robert Bruce, grandson of the first of that name (§ 219), had seized the throne. His last request was that his son Edward should continue the war. "Carry my bones before you on your march," said the dying King, "for the rebels will not be able to endure the sight of me, alive or dead!"

Not far from the beautiful effigy of Queen Eleanor in Westminster Abbey (§ 223), "her husband rests in a severely simple tomb. Pass it not by for its simplicity; few tombs hold nobler dust."[2]

228. Summary. During Edward I's reign the following changes took place:

1. Wales and Scotland were conquered, and the first remained permanently a part of the English kingdom.

2. The landed proprietors of the whole country were made more directly responsible to the Crown.

3. The excessive growth of Church property was checked.

4. Laws for the better suppression of acts of violence were enacted and rigorously enforced.

---

[1] See p. 76, note 1, on Clergy; and see Summary of Constitutional History in the Appendix, p. xi, § 11.

[2] Goldwin Smith's " History of the United Kingdom."

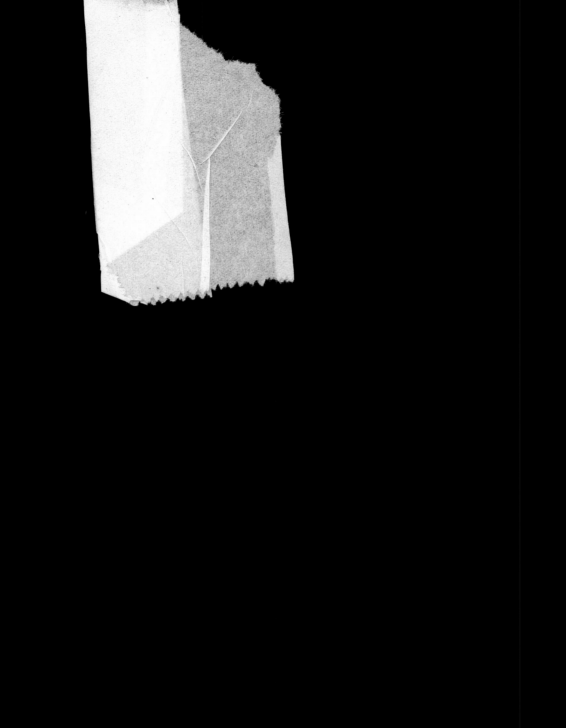

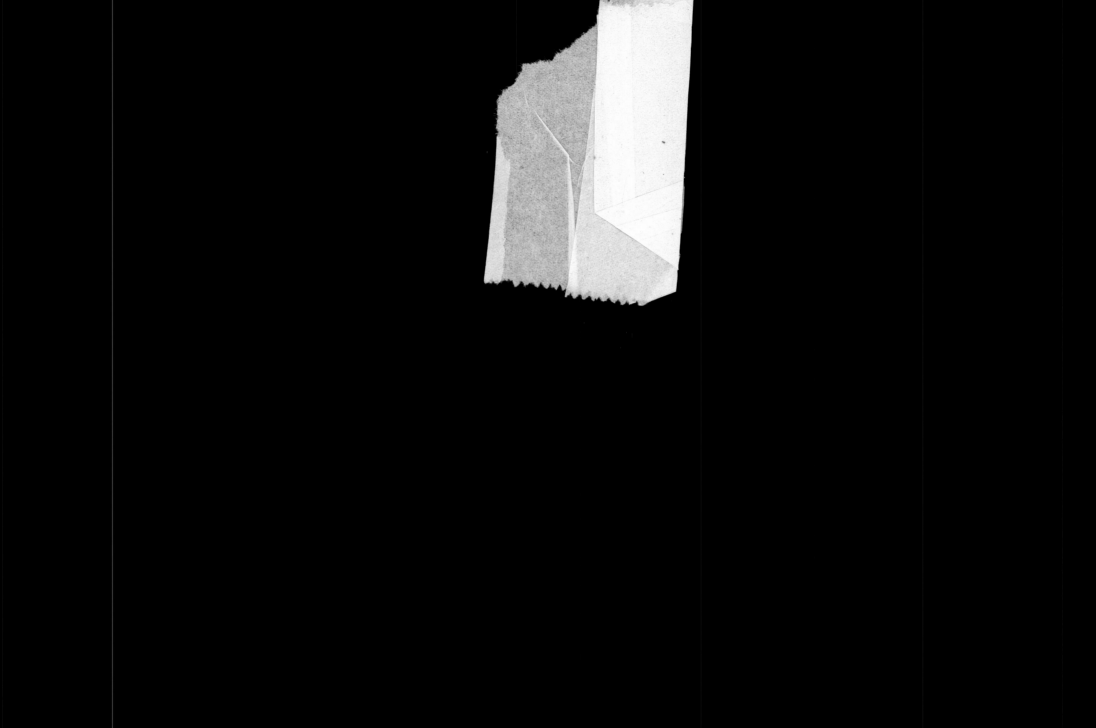

5. The Great Charter, with additional articles for the protection of the people, was confirmed by the King, and the power of taxation expressly acknowledged to reside in Parliament only.

6. Parliament, a legislative body now representing all classes of the nation, was permanently organized, and for the first time regularly and frequently summoned by the King.[1]

EDWARD II — 1307–1327

229. Accession and Character. The son to whom Edward I left his power was in every respect his opposite. The old definition of the word " king " was " the man who *can*," or the able man. The modern explanation usually makes him " the chief or head of a people." Edward II would satisfy neither of these definitions. He lacked all disposition to do anything himself ; he equally lacked power to incite others to do. By nature he was a jester, trifler, and waster of time.

Being such, it is hardly necessary to say that he did not push the war with Scotland. Robert Bruce (§ 227) did not expect that he would ; that valiant fighter, indeed, held the new English sovereign in utter contempt, saying that he feared the dead father, Edward I, much more than the living son.

230. Piers Gaveston ; the Lords Ordainers ; Articles of Reform. During the first five years of his reign, Edward II did little more than lavish wealth and honors on his chief favorite and adviser, Piers Gaveston, a Frenchman who had been his companion and playfellow from childhood. While Edward I was living, Parliament had with his sanction banished Gaveston from the kingdom, as a man of corrupt practices ; but Edward II was no sooner crowned than he recalled him, and gave him the government of the realm during his absence in France, on the occasion of his marriage.

On Edward's return, the barons protested against the monopoly of privileges by a foreigner, and the King was obliged to consent to

[1] It will be remembered that De Montfort's Parliament in 1265 (§ 213) was not regularly and legally summoned, since the King (Henry III) was at that time a captive. The first Parliament (consisting of a House of Commons and House of Lords, including the upper Clergy), convened by the Crown, was that called by Edward I in 1295 (§ 217).

Gaveston's banishment. He soon came back, however, and matters went on from bad to worse. Finally, the indignation of the nobles rose to such a pitch that at a council held at Westminster the government was virtually taken from the King's hands and vested in a body of barons and bishops.

The head of this committee was the King's cousin, the Earl of Lancaster ; and from the Ordinances or Articles of Reform which the committee drew up for the management of affairs they got the name of the Lords Ordainers. Gaveston was now sent out of the country for a third time ; but the King persuaded him to return, and gave him the office of Secretary of State. This last insult — for so the Lords Ordainers regarded it — was too much for the nobility to bear.

They resolved to exile the hated favorite once more, but this time to send him to that " undiscovered country " from which " no traveler returns." Edward, taking the alarm, placed Gaveston in Scarborough Castle, on the coast of Yorkshire, thinking that he would be safe there. The barons besieged the castle, starved Gaveston into surrender, and beheaded him forthwith. Thus ended the first favorite.

231. Scotland regains its Independence ; Bannockburn, 1314.
Seeing Edward's lack of manly fiber, Robert Bruce (§ 229), who had been crowned King of the Scots, determined to make himself ruler in fact as well as in name. He had suffered many defeats ; he had wandered a fugitive in forests and glens ; he had been hunted with bloodhounds like a wild beast ; but he had never lost courage or hope. On the field of Bannockburn, northwest of Edinburgh (1314), he once again met the English, and in a bloody and decisive battle drove them back like frightened sheep into their own country. (See map facing p. 120.) By this victory, Bruce reëstablished the independence of Scotland, — an independence which continued until the rival kingdoms were peacefully united under one crown, by the accession of the Scottish King, James, to the English throne (1603).

232. The New Favorites ; the King made Prisoner (1314–1326).
For the next seven years the Earl of Lancaster (§ 230) had his own way in England. During this time Edward, whose weak

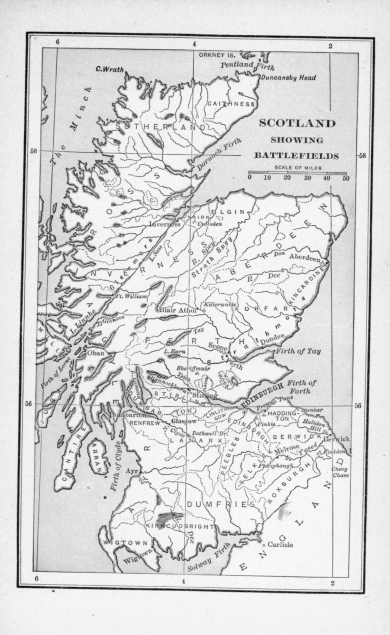

SCOTLAND
SHOWING
BATTLEFIELDS

SCALE OF MILES

0   10   20   30   40   50

nature needed some one to lean on, had got two new favorites, — Hugh Despenser and his son. They were men of more character than Gaveston (§ 230), but as they cared chiefly for their own interests, they incurred the hatred of the baronage.

The King's wife, Isabelle of France, now turned against him. She had formerly acted as a peacemaker, but from this time she did all in her power to make trouble. Roger Mortimer, one of the leaders of the barons, was the sworn enemy of the Despensers. The Queen had formed a guilty attachment for him. The reign of Mortimer and Isabelle was "a reign of terror." Together they plotted the ruin of Edward and his favorites. They raised a force, seized and executed the Despensers (1326), and then took the King prisoner.

233. Deposition and Murder of the King (1327). Having locked up Edward in Kenilworth Castle, Warwickshire, the barons now resolved to remove him from the throne. Parliament drew up articles of deposition against him, and appointed commissioners to demand his resignation of the crown.

When they went to the castle, Edward appeared before them clad in deep mourning. Presently he sank fainting to the floor. On his recovery he burst into a fit of weeping. But, checking himself, he thanked Parliament through the commissioners for having chosen his eldest son Edward, a boy of fourteen, to rule over the nation.

Sir William Trussel then stepped forward and said: "Unto thee, O King, I, William Trussel, in the name of all men of this land of England and Speaker of this Parliament, renounce to you, Edward, the homage [oath of allegiance] that was made to you some time; and from this time forth I defy thee and deprive thee of all royal power, and I shall never be attendant on thee as King from this time."

Then Sir Thomas Blount, steward of the King's household, advanced, broke his staff of office before the King's face, and proclaimed the royal household dissolved.

Edward was soon after committed to Berkeley Castle,[1] in Gloucestershire. There, by the order of Mortimer, with the connivance

---

[1] Berkeley Castle is considered one of the finest examples of feudal architecture now remaining in England. Over the stately structure still floats the standard borne in the Crusades by an ancestor of the present Lord Berkeley.

of Queen Isabelle, the " she-wolf of France," who acted as his companion in iniquity (§ 232), the King was secretly and horribly murdered.

234. Summary. The lesson of Edward II's career is found in its culmination. Other sovereigns had been guilty of misgovernment, others had put unworthy and grasping favorites in power, but he was the first King whom Parliament had deposed.

By that act it became evident that great as was the power of the King, there had now come into existence a greater still, which could not only make but unmake him who sat on the throne.

EDWARD III — 1327-1377

235. Edward's Accession ; Execution of Mortimer. Edward III, son of Edward II, was crowned at fourteen. Until he became of age, the government was nominally in the hands of a council, but really in the control of Queen Isabelle and her " gentle Mortimer," the two murderers of his father (§ 233).

Early in his reign Edward attempted to reconquer Scotland (§ 219), but failing in his efforts, made a peace acknowledging the independence of that country. At home, however, he now gained a victory which compensated him for his disappointment in not subduing the Scots.

Mortimer was staying with Queen Isabelle at Nottingham Castle. Edward obtained entrance by a secret passage, carried him off captive, and soon after brought him to the gallows. He next seized his mother, the Queen, and kept her in confinement for the rest of her life in Castle Rising, Norfolk.

236. The Rise of English Commerce ; Wool Manufacture, 1336. The reign of Edward III is directly connected with the rise of a flourishing commerce with the Continent. In the early ages of its history England was almost wholly an agricultural country. At length the farmers in the eastern counties began to turn their attention to wool growing. They exported the fleeces, which were considered the finest in the world, to the Flemish cities of Ghent and Bruges. There they were woven into cloth and returned to be sold in the English market ; for, as an old writer quaintly remarks,

" The English people at that time knew no more what to do with the wool than the sheep on whose backs it grew." [1]

Edward's wife, Queen Philippa, was a native of a French province adjoining Flanders, which was also engaged in the production of cloth. (See map facing p. 128.) She used her influence in behalf of the establishment of woolen factories at Norwich, and other towns in the east of England, in 1336. Skilled Flemish workmen were induced to come over, and by their help England successfully laid the foundation of one of her greatest and most lucrative industries.

From that time wool was considered a chief source of the national wealth. Later, that the fact might be kept constantly in mind, a square crimson bag filled with it — the " Woolsack " — became, and still continues to be, the seat of the Lord Chancellor in the House of Lords.

237. The Beginning of the Hundred Years' War, 1338. Indirectly, this trade between England and Flanders helped to bring on a war of such duration that it received the name of the Hundred Years' War.

Flanders was at that time a dependency of France (see map facing p. 128), but its great commercial towns were rapidly rising in power, and were restive and rebellious under the exactions and extortion of their feudal master, Count Louis. Their business interests bound them strongly to England; and they were anxious to form an alliance with Edward against Philip VI of France, who was determined to bring the Flemish cities into absolute subjection.

Philip was by no means unwilling to begin hostilities with England. He had long looked with a greedy eye on the tract of country south of the Loire,[2] which remained in possession of the English kings, and only wanted a pretext for annexing it. Through his alliance with Scotland, he threatened to attack Edward's kingdom on the north. Again, Philip's war vessels had been seizing English ships laden with wool, so that intercourse with Flanders was maintained with difficulty and peril.

---

[1] Thomas Fuller. This remark applies to the production of fine woolens only. The English had long manufactured common grades of woolen cloth to some extent.

[2] Namely Aquitaine (with the exception of Poitou). At a later period the province got the name of Guienne, which was a part of it. (See map facing p. 128.)

Edward remonstrated in vain against these outrages. At length, having concluded an alliance with Ghent, the chief Flemish city, he boldly claimed the crown of France as his lawful right,[1] and followed the demand with a declaration of war. Edward based his claim on the fact that through his mother Isabelle he was nephew to the late French King, Charles IV, whereas the reigning monarch was only cousin of that monarch. To this the French replied that since their law excluded women from the throne, Edward's claim was worthless, because he could not inherit the crown of France from one who could not herself have worn it.

238. Battle of Crécy; the "Black Prince," 1346. For the next eight years, fighting between the two countries was going on pretty constantly on both land and sea, but without decisive results. Edward was pressed for money and had to resort to all sorts of expedients to get it, even to pawning his own and the Queen's crown, to raise enough to pay his troops. At last he succeeded in equipping a strong force, and with his son, Prince Edward, a lad of fifteen, invaded Normandy.

His plan seems to have been to attack the French army in the south of France; but after landing he changed his mind, and determined to ravage Normandy, and then march north to meet his Flemish allies, who were advancing to join him. King Edward halted on a little rise of ground not far from Crécy (or Cressy), near the coast, on the way to Calais. There a desperate battle took place. (See map facing p. 128.)

[1] CLAIM OF EDWARD III TO THE FRENCH CROWN

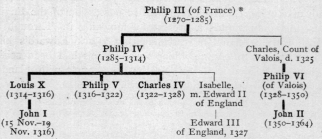

* The heavy lines indicate the direct succession.

THE BATTLE OF CRÉCY, 1346

125

The French had the larger force, but Edward the better position. Philip's army included a number of hired Genoese crossbowmen, on whom he placed great dependence; but a thunderstorm had wet their bowstrings, which rendered them nearly useless, and, as they advanced toward the English, the afternoon sun shone so brightly in their eyes that they could not take accurate aim. The English archers, on the other hand, had kept their long bows in their cases, so that the strings were dry and ready for action (§ 270).

In the midst of the fight, the Earl of Warwick, who was hard pressed by the enemy, became alarmed for the safety of young Prince Edward. He sent to the King, asking reënforcements. "Is my son killed?" asked the King. "No, sire, please God!" "Is he wounded?" "No, sire." "Is he thrown to the ground?" "No, sire; but he is in great danger." "Then," said the King, "I shall send no aid. Let the boy win his spurs [1]; for I wish, if God so order it, that the honor of the victory shall be his." The father's wish was gratified. From that time the "Black Prince," as the French called Prince Edward, from the color of his armor, became a name renowned throughout Europe.

The battle, however, was gained, not by his bravery, or that of the nobles who supported him, but by the sturdy English yeomen armed with their long bows. With these weapons they shot their keen white arrows so thick and fast, and with such deadly aim, that a writer who was present on the field compared them to a shower of snow. It was that fatal snowstorm which won the day.[2] We shall see presently (§ 240) that the great importance of this victory to the English turned on the fact that by it King Edward was able to move on Calais and secure possession of that port.

---

[1] Spurs were the especial badge of knighthood. It was expected of every one who attained that honor that he should do some deed of valor; this was called "winning his spurs."

[2] The English yeomen, or country people, excelled in the use of the long bow. They probably learned its value from their Norman conquerors, who employed it with great effect at the battle of Hastings. Writing at a much later period, Bishop Latimer said: "In my tyme my poore father was as diligent to teach me to shote as to learne anye other thynge. . . . He taught me how to drawe, how to laye my bodye in my bowe, and not to drawe wyth strength of armes as other nacions do, but wyth strength of the bodye. I had bowes boughte me accordyng to my age and

239. Use of Cannon, 1346 ; Chivalry. At Crécy (§ 238) small cannon appear to have been used for the first time in field warfare, though gunpowder was probably known to the English friar, Roger Bacon (§ 208), a hundred years before. The object of the cannon was to frighten and annoy the horses of the French cavalry. They were laughed at as ingenious toys ; but in the course of the next two centuries those toys revolutionized warfare (§ 270) and made the steel-clad knight little more than a tradition and a name.

In its day, however, knighthood (§ 153) did the world good service. Chivalry aimed to make the profession of arms a noble instead of a brutal calling. It gave it somewhat of a religious character.

It taught the warrior the worth of honor, truthfulness, and courtesy, as well as valor, — qualities which still survive in the best type of the modern gentleman. We owe, therefore, no small debt to that military brotherhood of the past, and may join the English poet in his epitaph on the order :

> " The Knights are dust,
>   Their good swords rust ;
>   Their souls are with the saints, we trust." [1]

240. Edward III takes Calais, 1347. King Edward now marched against Calais. He was particularly anxious to take the place : first, because it was a favorite resort of desperate pirates ; secondly, because such a fortified port on the Strait of Dover, within sight of the chalk cliffs of England, would give him at all times " an open doorway into France."

After besieging it for nearly a year, the garrison was starved into submission and prepared to open the gates. Edward was so

strength ; as I encreased in them, so my bowes were made bigger, and bigger, for men shal neuer shot well, excepte they be broughte up in it." The advantage of this weapon over the steel crossbow (used by the Genoese) lay in the fact that it could be discharged much more rapidly, the latter being a cumbrous affair, which had to be wound up with a crank for each shot. Hence the English long bow was to that age what the revolver is to ours. It sent an arrow with such force that only the best armor could withstand it. The French peasantry at that period had no skill with this weapon, and about the only part they took in a battle was to stab horses and despatch wounded men.

Scott, in the Archery Contest in " Ivanhoe " (Chapter XIII), has given an excellent picture of the English bowman.

[1] Coleridge ; see Scott's " Ivanhoe."

exasperated with the stubborn resistance the town had made, that he resolved to put the entire population to the sword. But at last he consented to spare them, on condition that six of the chief men should give themselves up to be hanged. A meeting was called, and St. Pierre, the wealthiest citizen of the place, volunteered, with five others, to go forth and die. Bareheaded, barefooted, with halters round their necks, they silently went out, carrying the keys of the city. When they appeared before the English King, he ordered the executioner, who was standing by, to seize them and carry out the sentence forthwith. But Queen Philippa (§ 236), who had accompanied her husband, now fell on her knees before him, and with tears begged that they might be forgiven. For a long time Edward was inexorable, but finally, unable to resist her entreaties, he granted her request, and the men who had dared to face death for others found life both for themselves and their fellow citizens.[1] Calais now became an English town and the English kept it for more than two hundred years (§ 373). This gave them the power to invade France whenever it seemed for their interest to do so.

241. Victory of Poitiers (1356). After a long truce, war again broke out. Philip VI had died, and his son, John II, now sat on the French throne. Edward, during this campaign, ravaged northern France. The next year his son, the Black Prince (§ 238), marched from Bordeaux into the heart of the country.

Reaching Poitiers with a force of ten thousand men, he found himself nearly surrounded by a French army of sixty thousand. The Prince so placed his troops amidst the narrow lanes and vineyards, that the enemy could not attack him with their full strength. Again the English archers gained the day (§ 238), and King John himself was taken prisoner and carried in triumph to England. (See map facing p. 128.)

242. Peace of Brétigny, 1360. The victory of Poitiers was followed by another truce; then war began again. Edward intended besieging Paris, but was forced to retire to obtain provisions for his troops. Negotiations were now opened by the French. While these negotiations were going on, a terrible thunderstorm destroyed great numbers of men and horses in Edward's camp.

[1] Froissart's " Chronicles."

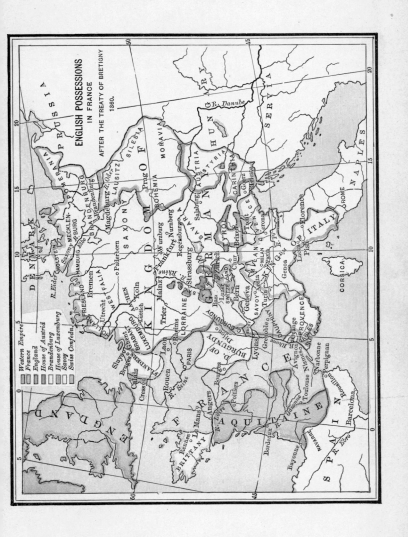

ENGLISH POSSESSIONS
IN FRANCE

AFTER THE TREATY OF BRETIGNY
1360.

Western Empire
France
England
House of Austria
Brandenburg
House of Luxemburg
Savoy
Swiss Confedn.

Edward, believing it a sign of the displeasure of Heaven against his expedition, fell on his knees, and within sight of the Cathedral of Chartres vowed to make peace. A treaty was accordingly signed at Brétigny near by. By it, Edward renounced his claim to Normandy and the French crown. But notwithstanding that fact, all English sovereigns insisted on retaining the title of " King of France " down to a late period of the reign of George III. France, on the other hand, acknowledged the right of England, in full sovereignty, to the country south of the Loire, together with Calais, and agreed to pay an enormous ransom in gold for the restoration of King John.

243. Effects of the French Wars in England. The great gain to England from these wars was not in the territory conquered, but in the new feeling of unity they aroused among all classes. The memory of the brave deeds achieved in those fierce contests on a foreign soil never faded out. The glory of the Black Prince (§§ 238, 241), whose rusty helmet and dented shield still hang above his tomb in Canterbury Cathedral,[1] became one with the glory of the plain bowmen, whose names are found only in country churchyards.

Henceforth, whatever lingering feeling of jealousy and hatred had remained in England, between the Norman and the Englishman (§ 192), now gradually melted away. An honest, patriotic pride made both feel that at last they had become a united and homogeneous people.

The second effect of the wars was political. In order to carry them on, the King had to apply constantly to Parliament for money (§§ 217, 220). Each time that body granted a supply, they insisted on some reform which increased their strength, and brought the Crown more and more under the influence of the nation. (See Summary of Constitutional History in the Appendix, p. xii, § 13.)

Thus it came to be clearly understood that though the King held the sword, the people held the purse; and that the ruler who made the greatest concessions got the largest grants.

It was also in this reign that the House of Commons (§§ 213, 217, 262), which now sat as a separate body, obtained the important power of impeaching, or bringing to trial before the upper House,

---

[1] This is probably the oldest armor of the kind in Great Britain. See Stothard's " Monumental Effigies."

any of the King's ministers or council who should be accused of misgovernment (1376). (See § 247, and Summary of Constitutional History in the Appendix, p. xii, § 13.)

About this time, also, statutes were passed which forbade appeals from the King's courts of justice to that of the Pope,[1] who was then a Frenchman, and was believed to be under French political influence. Furthermore, all foreign Church officials were prohibited from asking or taking money from the English Church, or interfering in any way with its management.[2]

244. The Black Death, or Plague, 1349. Shortly after the first campaign in France, a frightful pestilence broke out in London, which swept over the country, destroying upwards of half the population. The disease, which was known as the Black Death, had already traversed Europe, where it had proved equally fatal.

"How many amiable young persons," said a noted writer of that period, "breakfasted with their friends in the morning, who, when evening came, supped with their ancestors!" In Bristol and some other English cities, the mortality was so great that the living were hardly able to bury the dead; so that all business, and for a time even war, came to a standstill.

245. Effect of the Plague on Labor, 1349. After the pestilence had subsided, it was impossible to find laborers enough to till the soil and shear the sheep. Those who were free now demanded higher wages, while the villeins, or serfs (§ 113), and slaves left their masters and roamed about the country asking pay for their work, like freemen.

It was a general agricultural strike, which lasted over thirty years. It marks the beginning of that contest between capital and labor which had such an important influence in the next reign, and which, after a lapse of more than five hundred years, is not yet satisfactorily adjusted.

Parliament endeavored to restore order. It passed laws forbidding any freeman to ask more for a day's work than before the

[1] First Statute of Provisors (1351) and of Præmunire (1353) (§ 265). The first Statute of Præmunire did not mention the Pope or the Court of Rome by name; the second, or Great Statute of Præmunire of 1393, expressly mentioned them in the strongest terms. See Constitutional Documents in the Appendix, p. xxxii.

[2] Statute of Provisors (1351), and see § 265.

THE TOMB OF THE BLACK PRINCE IN CANTERBURY CATHEDRAL

Part of the Prince's armor is seen above the tomb

plague. It gave the master the right to punish a serf who persisted in running away, by branding him on the forehead with the letter F, for "fugitive." But legislation was in vain; the movement had begun, and statutes of Parliament could no more stop it than they could stop the rolling in of the ocean tide. It continued to go on until it reached its climax in the peasant insurrection led by Wat Tyler, under Edward's successor, Richard II (§ 251).

246. Beginning of English Literature, 1369-1377. During Edward's reign the first work in English prose may have been written. It was a volume of travels by Sir John Mandeville, who had journeyed in the East for over thirty years. On his return he wrote an account of what he had heard and seen, first in Latin, that the learned might read it; next in French, that the nobles might read it; and lastly he, or some unknown person, translated it into English for the common people. He dedicated the work to the King.

Perhaps the most interesting and wonderful thing in it was the statement of his belief that the world is a globe, and that a ship may sail round it "above and beneath," — an assertion which probably seemed to many who read it then as less credible than any of the marvelous stories in which his book abounds.

William Langland was writing rude verses (1369) about his " vision of Piers the Plowman," contrasting " the wealth and woe " of the world, and so helping forward that democratic outbreak which was soon to take place among those who knew the woe and wanted the wealth. John Wycliffe (§ 254), a lecturer at Oxford, attacked the rich and indolent churchmen in a series of tracts and sermons, while Chaucer, who had fought on the fields of France, was preparing to bring forth the first great poem in our language (§ 253).

247. The " Good Parliament " (1376); Edward's Death. The " Good Parliament " (1376) attempted to carry through important reforms. It impeached (for the first time in English history)[1] certain prominent men for fraud (§ 243). But in the end its work failed for want of a leader. The King's last days were far from happy. His son, the Black Prince (§ 238), had died, and Edward fell entirely into the hands of selfish favorites and ambitious schemers like John

[1] See Summary of Constitutional History in the Appendix, p. xii, § 13.

of Gaunt, Duke of Lancaster. Perhaps the worst one of this corrupt "ring" was a woman named Alice Perrers, who, after Queen Philippa was no more (§ 240), got almost absolute control of the King. She stayed with him until his last sickness. When his eyes began to glaze in death, she plucked the rings from his unresisting hands, and fled from the palace.

248. Summary. During this reign the following events deserve especial notice :

1. The acknowledgment of the independence of Scotland.

2. The establishment of the manufacture of fine woolens in England.

3. The beginning of the Hundred Years' War, with the victories of Crécy and Poitiers, the Peace of Brétigny, and their social and political results in England.

4. The Black Death and its results on labor.

5. Parliament enacts important laws for securing greater independence to the English Church.

6. The rise of modern literature, represented by the works of Mandeville, Langland, and the early writings of Wycliffe and Chaucer.

RICHARD II — 1377–1399

249. England at Richard's Accession. The death of the Black Prince (§§ 238, 241, 247) left his son Richard heir to the crown. As he was but eleven years old, Parliament provided that the government during his minority should be carried on by a council ; but John of Gaunt, Duke of Lancaster (§ 247), speedily got the control of affairs.

He was an unprincipled man, who wasted the nation's money, opposed reform, and was especially hated by the laboring classes. The times were critical. War had again broken out with both Scotland and France, the French fleet was raiding the English coast, the national treasury had no money to pay its troops, and the government debt was rapidly accumulating.

250. The New Tax ; the Tyler and Ball Insurrection (1381). In order to raise money, the government resolved to levy a new form of tax, — a poll or head tax, — which had first been tried on a small scale during the last year of the previous reign. The attempt had been made to assess it on all classes, from laborers to lords.

This imposition was now renewed in a much more oppressive form. Not only every laborer, but every member of a laborer's family above the age of fifteen, was required to pay what would be equal to the wages of an able-bodied man for at least several days' work.[1]

We have already seen that, owing to the ravages of the Black Death, and the strikes which followed, the country was on the verge of revolt (§§ 244, 245). This new tax was the spark that caused the explosion. The money was roughly demanded in every poor man's cottage, and its collection caused the greatest distress. In attempting to enforce payment, a brutal collector shamefully insulted the young daughter of a workman named Wat Tyler. The indignant father, hearing the girl's cry for help, snatched up a hammer, and rushing in, struck the ruffian dead on the spot.

Tyler then collected a multitude of discontented laborers on Blackheath Common, near London, with the determination of attacking the city and overthrowing the government.

John Ball, a fanatical priest, harangued the gathering, now sixty thousand strong, using by way of a text lines which were at that time familiar to every workingman:

> " When Adam delved and Eve span,
> Who was then the gentleman ? "

" Good people," he cried, " things will never go well in England so long as goods be not in common, and so long as there be villeins (§ 113) and gentlemen. They call us slaves, and beat us if we are slow to do their bidding, but God has now given us the day to shake off our bondage."

251. The Great Uprising of the Laboring Class, 1381. Twenty years before, there had been similar outbreaks in Flanders and in France. This, therefore, was not an isolated instance of insurrection,

---

[1] The tax on laborers and their families varied from four to twelve pence each, the assessor having instructions to collect the latter sum, if possible. The wages of a day laborer were then about a penny, so that the smallest tax for a family of three would represent the entire pay for nearly a fortnight's labor. See Pearson's "England in the Fourteenth Century."

but rather part of a general uprising. The rebellion begun by Tyler and Ball (§ 250) spread through the southern and eastern counties of England, taking different forms in different districts. It was violent in St. Albans, where the peasants, and farm laborers generally, rose against the exactions of the abbot, but it reached its greatest height in London.

For three weeks the mob held possession of the capital. They pillaged and then burned John of Gaunt's palace (§§ 247, 249). They seized and beheaded the Lord Chancellor and the chief collector of the odious poll tax (§ 250). They destroyed all the law papers they could lay hands on, and ended by murdering a number of lawyers; for the rioters believed that the members of that profession spent their time forging the chains which held the laboring class in subjection.

252. Demands of the Rebels; End of the Rebellion. The insurrectionists demanded of the King that villeinage (§ 113) should be abolished, and that the rent of agricultural lands should be fixed by Parliament at a uniform rate in money. They also insisted that trade should be free, and that a general unconditional pardon should be granted to all who had taken part in the rebellion.

Richard promised redress; but while negotiations were going on, Walworth, mayor of London, struck down Wat Tyler with his dagger, and with his death the whole movement collapsed almost as suddenly as it arose. Parliament now began a series of merciless executions, and refused to consider any of the claims to which Richard had shown a disposition to listen. In their punishment of the rebels, the House of Commons vied with the Lords in severity, few showing any sympathy with the efforts of the peasants to obtain their freedom from feudal bondage.

The uprising, however, was not in vain, for by it the old restrictions were in some degree loosened, so that in the course of the next century and a half, villeinage (§ 113) was gradually abolished, and the English laborer acquired that greatest yet most perilous of all rights, the complete ownership of himself.[1]

[1] In Scotland, villeinage lasted much longer, and as late as 1774, in the reign of George III, men working in coal and salt mines were held in a species of slavery, which was finally abolished the following year.

So long as he was a serf, the peasant could claim assistance from his master in sickness and old age; in attaining independence he had to risk the danger of pauperism, which began with it, — this possibility being part of the price which man must everywhere pay for the inestimable privilege of freedom.

253. The New Movement in Literature, 1390 (?). The same spirit which demanded emancipation on the part of the working classes showed itself in literature. We have already seen (§ 246) how, in the previous reign, Langland, in his poem of "Piers Plowman," gave bold utterance to the growing discontent of the times in his declaration that the rich and great destroyed the poor.

In a different spirit, Chaucer, "the morning star of English song," now began (1390?) to write his "Canterbury Tales," a series of stories in verse, supposed to be told by a merry band of pilgrims on their way from the Tabard Inn in Southwark, London, to the shrine of St. Thomas Becket in Canterbury (§ 170).

There is little of Langland's complaint in Chaucer, for he was generally a favorite at court, seeing mainly the bright side of life, and sure of his yearly allowance of money and daily pitcher of wine from the royal bounty. Yet, with all his mirth, there is a vein of playful satire in his description of men and things. His pictures of jolly monks and easy-going churchmen, with his lines addressed to his purse as his "saviour, as down in this world here," show that he saw beneath the surface of things. He too was thinking, at least at times, of the manifold evils of poverty and of that danger springing from religious indifference which poor Langland had taken so much to heart.

254. Wycliffe; the First Complete English Bible, 1378. But the real reformer of that day was John Wycliffe, rector of Lutterworth in Leicestershire and lecturer at Oxford (§ 246). He boldly attacked the religious and the political corruption of the age. The "Begging Friars," who had once done such good work (§ 208), had now grown too rich and lazy to be of further use.

Wycliffe, whose emaciated form concealed an unconquerable energy and dauntless courage, organized a new band of brothers known as "Poor Priests." They took up and pushed forward the reforms the friars had dropped. Clothed in red sackcloth cloaks, barefooted, with staff in hand, they went about from town to town [1] preaching "God's law," and demanding that Church and State bring themselves into harmony with it.

The only complete Bible then in use was the Latin version. The people could not read a line of it, and many priests were almost as ignorant of its contents. To carry on the revival which he had begun, Wycliffe now began to translate the entire Scriptures into English, 1378. When the great work was finished it was copied and circulated by the "Poor Priests."

But the cost of such a book in manuscript — for the printing press had not yet come into existence — was so high that only the rich could buy the complete volume. Many, however, who had no money would give a load of farm produce for a few favorite chapters.

In this way Wycliffe's Bible was spread throughout the country among all classes. Later, when persecution began, men hid these precious copies and read them with locked doors at night, or met in the forests to hear them expounded by preachers who went about at the peril of their lives. These things led Wycliffe's enemies to complain "that common men and women who could read were better acquainted with the Scriptures than the most learned and intelligent of the clergy."

255. The Lollards ; Wycliffe's Remains burned. The followers of Wycliffe were nicknamed Lollards, a word of uncertain meaning but apparently used as an expression of contempt. From having been religious reformers denouncing the wealth and greed of a corrupt Church, they seem, in some cases, to have degenerated into socialists or communists. This latter class demanded, like John Ball (§ 250), — who may have been one of their number, — that all property should be equally divided, and that all rank should be abolished.

This fact should be borne in mind with reference to the subsequent efforts made by the government to suppress the movement. In the eyes of the Church, the Lollards were heretics ; in

---

[1] Compare Chaucer's

> "A good man ther was of religioun,
>   That was a poure persone [parson] of a town."

Prologue to the "Canterbury Tales" (479)

the judgment of many moderate men, they were destructionists and anarchists, as unreasonable and as dangerous as the "dynamiters" of to-day.

More than forty years after Wycliffe's death (1384), a decree of the Church council of Constance [1] ordered the reformer's body to be dug up and burned (1428). But his influence had not only permeated England, but had passed to the Continent, and was preparing the way for that greater movement which Luther was to inaugurate in the sixteenth century.

Tradition says that the ashes of his corpse were thrown into a brook flowing near the parsonage of Lutterworth, the object being to utterly destroy and obliterate the remains of the arch-heretic. Fuller says : "This brook did convey his ashes into the Avon, Avon into Severn, Severn into the narrow sea, and that into the wide ocean. And so the ashes of Wycliffe are the emblem of his doctrine, which is now dispersed all the world over." [2]

256. Richard's Misgovernment ; the "Merciless Parliament." Richard had the spirit of a tyrant. He declared "that he alone could change and frame the laws of the kingdom." [3] His reign was unpopular with all classes. The people hated him for his extravagance ; the clergy, for his failing to put down the Wycliffites (§§ 254, 255), with the doctrines of whose founder he was believed to sympathize ; while the nobles disliked his injustice and favoritism.

In the "Merciless Parliament" (1388) the "Lords Appellant," that is, the noblemen who accused Richard's counselors of treason, put to death all of the King's ministers that they could lay hands on. Later, that Parliament attempted some political reforms, which were partially successful. But the King soon regained his power, and took summary vengeance (1397) on the "Lords Appellant."

---

[1] Constance, in southern Germany. This council (1415) sentenced John Huss and Jerome of Prague, both of whom may be considered Wycliffites, to the stake.

[2] Thomas Fuller's "Church History of Britain." Compare also Wordsworth's "Sonnet to Wycliffe," and the lines, attributed to an unknown writer of Wycliffe's time :

> "The Avon to the Severn runs,
> The Severn to the sea ;
> And Wycliffe's dust shall spread abroad,
> Wide as the waters be."

[3] W. Stubbs's "Constitutional History of England," II, 505.

Two influential men were left, Thomas Mowbray, Duke of Norfolk, and Henry Bolingbroke, Duke of Hereford, whom he had found no opportunity to punish. After a time they openly quarreled, and accused each other of treason.

A challenge passed between them, and they prepared to fight the matter out in the King's presence ; but when the day arrived, the King banished both of them from England (1398). Shortly after they had left the country Bolingbroke's father, John of Gaunt, Duke of Lancaster, died. Contrary to all law, Richard now seized and appropriated the estate, which belonged by right to the banished nobleman.

257. Richard deposed and murdered (1399). When Bolingbroke, now by his father's death Duke of Lancaster, heard of the outrage, he raised a small force and returned to England, demanding the restitution of his lands.

Finding that the powerful family of the Percies were willing to aid him, and that many of the common people desired a change of government, the Duke boldly claimed the crown, on the ground that Richard had forfeited it by his tyranny, and that he stood next in succession through his descent from Henry III. But in reality Henry Bolingbroke had no claim save that given by right of conquest, since the boy Edmund Mortimer held the direct title to the crown.[1]

The King now fell into Henry's hands, and events moved rapidly to a crisis. Richard had rebuilt Westminster Hall (§ 156). The first Parliament which assembled there deposed him on the ground that he was "altogether insufficient and unworthy," and they gave the throne to the victorious Duke of Lancaster. Shakespeare represents the fallen monarch saying in his humiliation :

> "With mine own tears I wash away my balm,[2]
> With mine own hand I give away my crown."

After his deposition Richard was confined in Pontefract Castle, Yorkshire, where he found, like his unfortunate ancestor, Edward II

---

[1] See Genealogical Table, under No. 3 and 4, p. 140.
[2] "Richard II," Act IV, scene i. The balm was the sacred oil used in anointing the King at his coronation.

(§ 233), " that in the case of princes there is but a step from the prison to the grave." His death did not take place, however, until after Henry's accession.[1] Most historians condemn Richard as an unscrupulous tyrant. Froissart, who wrote in his time, says that he ruled " fiercely," and that no one in England dared " speak against anything the King did." A recent writer thinks he may have been insane, and declares that whether he " was mad or not, he at all events acted like a madman." But another authority defends him, saying that Richard was not a despot at heart, but used despotic means hoping to effect much-needed reforms.[2]

258. Summary. Richard II's reign comprised :

1. The peasant revolt under Wat Tyler, which led eventually to the emancipation of the villeins, or farm laborers.

2. Wycliffe's reformation movement and his complete translation of the Latin Bible, with the rise of the Lollards.

3. The publication of Chaucer's " Canterbury Tales," the first great English poem.

4. The deposition of the King, and the transfer of the crown by Parliament to Henry, Duke of Lancaster.

[1] Henry of Lancaster was the son of John of Gaunt, who was the fourth son of Edward III ; but there were descendants of that King's *third* son (Lionel, Duke of Clarence) living, who, of course, had a prior claim, as the following table shows :

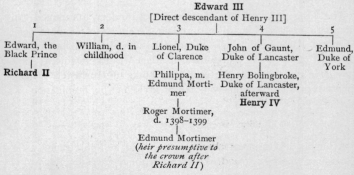

Edward III
[Direct descendant of Henry III]

1	2	3	4	5
Edward, the Black Prince	William, d. in childhood	Lionel, Duke of Clarence	John of Gaunt, Duke of Lancaster	Edmund, Duke of York
Richard II		Philippa, m. Edmund Mortimer	Henry Bolingbroke, Duke of Lancaster, afterward **Henry IV**	
		Roger Mortimer, d. 1398–1399		
		Edmund Mortimer (*heir presumptive to the crown after Richard II*)		

This disregard of the strict order of succession furnished a pretext for the Civil Wars of the Roses, which broke out sixty years later. See § 299.

[2] See Gardiner, Stubbs, and the " Dictionary of English History."

GENERAL REFERENCE SUMMARY OF THE ANGEVIN, OR PLANTAGENET, PERIOD (1154–1399)

(See note in italics on page 43.)

I. GOVERNMENT. II. RELIGION. III. MILITARY AFFAIRS. IV. LITERA-TURE, LEARNING, AND ART. V. GENERAL INDUSTRY AND COMMERCE. VI. MODE OF LIFE, MANNERS, AND CUSTOMS

I. GOVERNMENT

259. Judicial Reforms. In 1164 Henry II undertook, by a series of statutes called the Constitutions of Clarendon, to bring the Church under the common law of the land, but was only temporarily successful. By subsequent statutes he reorganized the administration of justice, and laid the foundation of trial by jury.

260. Town Charters. Under Richard I many towns secured charters giving them the control of their own affairs in great measure. In this way municipal self-government arose, and a prosperous and intelligent class of merchants and artisans grew up who eventually obtained important political influence in the management of national affairs.

261. Magna Carta, or the Great National Charter. This pledge, extorted from King John in 1215, put a check to the arbitrary power of the sovereign, and guaranteed the rights of all classes, from the serf and the townsman to the bishop and baron (§ 199). It consisted originally of sixty-three articles, founded mainly on the first royal charter (that of Henry I), given in 1100 (§ 135).

Magna Carta was not a statement of principles, but a series of specific remedies for specific abuses, which may be summarized as follows:

(1) The Church to be free from royal interference, especially in the election of bishops.

(2) No taxes except the regular feudal dues (§ 150) to be levied, except by the consent of the Great Council, or Parliament.

(3) The Court of Common Pleas (see p. 73, note 1) not to follow the King, but to remain stationary at Westminster. Justice to be neither sold, denied, nor delayed. No man to be imprisoned, outlawed, punished, or otherwise molested, save by the judgment of his equals or by the law of the land. The necessary implements of all freemen, and the farming tools of villeins, or farm laborers (§ 113), to be exempt from seizure.

(4) Weights and measures to be kept uniform throughout the realm. All merchants to have the right to enter and leave the kingdom without paying exorbitant tolls for the privilege.

(5) Forest laws to be justly enforced.

(6) The charter to be carried out by twenty-five barons together with the mayor of London.

This document marks the beginning of a written constitution, and it proved of the highest value henceforth in securing good government. It was confirmed thirty-seven times by subsequent kings and parliaments, the confirmation of this and previous charters by Edward I in 1297 being of especial importance.

262. Rise of the House of Commons. In 1265, under Henry III, through the influence of Simon de Montfort, two representatives from each city and borough, or town, together with two knights of the shire, or country gentlemen, were summoned to meet with the Lords and Clergy in the Great Council, or Parliament; but the House of Commons did not become a permanent body until the Model Parliament of 1295 was summoned. From that time the body of the people began to have a permanent voice in making the laws.

Later in the period the knights of the shire joined the representatives from the towns in forming a distinct body in Parliament, sitting by themselves under the name of the House of Commons. They asserted their right to assent to legislation, and (1376) they exercised the right of impeaching before the House of Lords government officers guilty of misuse of power. Somewhat later (1407) they obtained the sole right to originate " Money Bills," that is, grants or appropriations of money for public purposes or for the King's use.

263. New Class of Barons. Under Henry III other influential men of the realm, aside from the barons, who were tenants in chief, began to be summoned to the King's council. These were called "barons by writ." Later (under Richard II), barons were created by open letters bearing the royal seal, and were called "barons by patent."[1]

264. Land Laws. During this period important laws (De Donis, or Entail, and Quia Emptores) respecting land were passed, which had the effect of keeping estates in families, and also of preventing their possessors from evading their feudal duties to the King. At the same time the Statute of Mortmain (a restriction on the acquisition of land by the Church, which was exempt from paying certain feudal dues) was imposed to prevent the King's revenue from being diminished.

---

[1] This is the modern method of raising a subject (e.g. the poet, Alfred Tennyson) to the peerage. It marks the fact that from the thirteenth century the ownership of land was no longer considered a necessary condition of nobility; and that the peerage was gradually developing into the five degrees, which were completed in 1440, in the following ascending order: barons, viscounts, earls, marquises, dukes.

II. Religion

265. Restriction of the Papal Power. During the Angevin period the popes endeavored to introduce the canon law (a body of ordinances consisting mainly of the decisions of Church councils and popes) into England, with the view of making it supreme; but the Parliament of Merton refused to accept it, saying, "We will not change the laws of England."

The Statute of Mortmain was also passed (§§ 226, 264) and other measures (Statute of Provisors and Statute of Præmunire) (§ 243), which forbade the Pope from taking the appointment of bishops and other ecclesiastics out of the hands of the clergy; and which prohibited any appeal from the King's Court to the Papal Court. Furthermore, many hundreds of parishes, formerly filled by foreigners who could not speak English, were now given to native priests, and the sending of money out of the country to support foreign ecclesiastics was in great measure stopped.

During the Crusades two religious military orders had been established, called the Knights Hospitalers and the Knights Templars. The object of the former was, originally, to provide entertainment for pilgrims going to Jerusalem; that of the latter, to protect them. Both had extensive possessions in England. In 1312 the order of Templars was broken up on a charge of heresy and evil life, and their property in England given to the Knights Hospitalers, who were also called Knights of St. John.

266. Reform. The Mendicant or "Begging Friars" began a reformatory movement in the Church and accomplished much good. This was followed by Wycliffe's attack on religious abuses, by his complete translation of the Bible, with the revival carried on by the "Poor Priests," and by the rise of the Lollards. Eventually severe laws were passed against the Lollards, partly because of their heretical opinions, and partly because they became in a measure identified with socialistic and communistic efforts to destroy rank and equalize property.

III. Military Affairs

267. Scutage. By a tax called scutage, or shield money, levied on all knights who refused to serve the King in foreign wars, Henry II obtained the means to hire soldiers. By a law reviving the national militia, composed of freemen below the rank of knights, the King made himself in considerable measure independent of the barons with respect to raising troops.

268. Armor; Heraldry. The linked or mail armor now began to be superseded by that made of pieces of steel joined together so as to fit the body. This, when it was finally perfected, was called plate armor, and was both heavier and stronger than mail.

With the introduction of plate armor and the closed helmet it became the custom for each knight to wear a device, called a crest, on his helmet, and also to have one called a coat of arms (because originally worn on a loose coat over the armor).

The coat of arms served to distinguish the wearer from others, and was of practical use not only to the followers of a great lord, who thus knew him at a glance, but it served in time of battle to prevent the confusion of friend and foe. Eventually, coats of arms became hereditary, and the descent, and to some extent the history, of a family can be traced by them. In this way heraldry may often prove helpful in gaining knowledge of men and events.

269. Chivalry; Tournaments. The profession of arms was regulated by certain rules, by which each knight solemnly bound himself to serve the cause of religion and the King, and to be true, brave, and courteous to those of his own rank, to protect ladies (women of gentle birth), and succor all persons in distress. Under Edward III the system of knighthood or chivalry reached its culmination and began to decline.

One of the grotesque features of the attack on France was an expedition of English knights with one eye bandaged; this half-blind company having vowed to partially renounce their sight until they did some glorious deed. The chief amusement of the nobles and knights was the tournament, a mock combat fought on horseback, in full armor, which sometimes ended in a real battle. At these entertainments a lady was chosen queen, who gave prizes to the victors.

270. The Use of the Long Bow; Introduction of Cannon; Wars. The common weapon of the yeomen, or foot soldiers, was the long bow. It was made of yew-tree wood, and was of the height of the user. Armed with this weapon, the English soldiers proved themselves irresistible in the French wars, the French having no native archers of any account.

Roger Bacon is supposed to have known the properties of gunpowder as early as 1250, but no practical use was made of the discovery until the battle of Crécy, 1346, when a few very small cannon are said to have been employed by the English against the enemy's cavalry. Later, cannon were used to throw heavy stones in besieging castles. Still later, rude handguns came slowly into use. From this period kings gradually began to realize the full meaning of the harmless-looking black grains, with whose flash and noise the Oxford monk had amused himself.

The chief wars of the time were the contests between the kings and the barons, Richard I's Crusade, John's war with France, resulting in the loss of Normandy, Edward I's conquest of Wales and temporary subjugation of Scotland, and the beginning of the Hundred Years' War with France under Edward III.

The navy of this period was made up of small, one-masted vessels, seldom carrying more than a hundred and fifty fighting men. As the mariner's compass had now come into general use, these vessels could, if occasion required, make voyages of considerable length.

IV. LITERATURE, LEARNING, AND ART

271. Education. In 1264 Walter de Merton founded the first college at Oxford, an institution which has ever since borne his name, and which really originated the English college system. During the reign of Edward III, William of Wykeham, Bishop of Winchester, gave a decided impulse to higher education by the establishment, at his own expense, of Winchester College, the first great public school founded in England. Later, he built and endowed New College at Oxford to supplement it.

In Merton's and Wykeham's institutions young men of small means were instructed, and in great measure supported, without charge. They were brought together under one roof, required to conform to proper discipline, and taught by the best teachers of the day. In this way a general feeling of emulation was roused, and at the same time a fraternal spirit cultivated, which had a strong influence in favor of a broader and deeper intellectual culture than the monastic schools at Oxford and elsewhere had encouraged.

272. Literature. The most prominent historical work was that by Matthew Paris, a monk of St. Alban's, written in Latin, based largely on earlier chronicles, and covering the period from the Norman Conquest, 1066, to his death, in 1259. It is a work of much value, and was continued by writers of the same abbey.

The first English prose work was a volume of travels by Sir John Mandeville, dedicated to Edward III. It was followed by Wycliffe's translation of the Bible into English from the Latin version, and by Chaucer's "Canterbury Tales," the first great English poem.

273. Architecture. Edward I and his successors began to build structures combining the palace with the stronghold.[1] Conway and

---

[1] The characteristic features of the Edwardian castles are double surrounding walls, with numerous protecting towers, and the omission of the square Norman keep.

Carnarvon Castles in Wales, Warwick Castle, Warwickshire, and a great part of Windsor Castle on the Thames, twenty-three miles west of London, are magnificent examples; the last is still occupied as a royal residence.

In churches, the massive architecture of the Normans, with its heavy columns and round arches, was followed by the Early English style or the first period of the Gothic, with pointed arches, slender, clustered columns, and tapering spires. Salisbury Cathedral is the grandest example of the Early English style.

Later, the Decorated style was adopted. It was characterized by broader windows, highly ornamented to correspond with the elaborate decoration within, which gave this style its name; this is seen to advantage in Exeter Cathedral, York Minster, and Merton College Chapel at Oxford.

V. General Industry and Commerce

274. Fairs; Guilds. The domestic trade of the country was largely carried on during this period by great fairs held at stated times by royal license. Bunyan, in " Pilgrim's Progress," gives a vivid picture of one of these centers of trade and dissipation, under the name of " Vanity Fair." Though it represents the great fair of Sturbridge, near Cambridge, as he saw it in the seventeenth century, yet it undoubtedly describes similar gatherings in the time of the Plantagenets.

In all large towns the merchants had formed associations for mutual protection and the advancement of trade, called merchant guilds. Artisans now instituted similar societies, under the name of craft guilds. For a long time the merchant guilds endeavored to shut out the craft guilds, — the men, as they said, " with dirty hands and blue nails," — from having any part in the government of the towns. But eventually the latter got their full share, and in some cases, as in London, became the more influential party of the two. There they still survive under the name of the " City Companies."

275. The Wool Trade. Under Edward III a flourishing trade in wool grew up between England and Flanders. The manufacture of fine woolen goods was also greatly extended in England. All commerce at this period was limited to certain market towns called " staples."

To these places produce and all other goods for export had to be carried in order that the government might collect duty on them before they were sent out of the country. If an Englishman carried goods abroad and sold them in the open market without first paying a tax to the Crown, he was liable to the punishment of death. Imports also paid duties.

276. The Great Strike. The scarcity of laborers caused by the ravages of the Black Death caused a general strike for higher wages on the part of free workingmen, and also induced thousands of villeins to run away from their masters, in order to get work on their own account. The general uprising which a heavy poll tax caused among the villeins (§ 150), or farm laborers, and other workingmen, though suppressed at the time, led to the ultimate emancipation of the villeins by a gradual process extending through many generations.

VI. Mode of Life, Manners, and Customs

277. Dress; Furniture. During most of this period great luxury in dress prevailed among the rich and noble. Silks, velvets, scarlet cloth, and cloth of gold were worn by both men and women. At one time the lords and gallants at court wore shoes with points curled up like rams' horns and fastened to the knee with silver chains.

Attempts were made by the government to abolish this and other ridiculous fashions, and also to regulate the cost of dress according to the rank and means of the wearer; but the effort met with small success. Even the rich at this time had but little furniture in their houses, and chairs were almost unknown. The floors of houses were strewn with rushes, which, as they were rarely changed, became horribly filthy, and were a prolific cause of sickness.

278. The Streets; Amusements; Profanity. The streets of London and other cities were rarely more than twelve or fifteen feet wide. They were neither paved nor lighted. Pools of stagnant water and heaps of refuse abounded. There was no sewerage. The only scavengers were the crows. The houses were of timber and plaster, with projecting stories, and destructive fires were common. The chief amusements were hunting and hawking, contests at archery, and tournaments. Plays were acted by amateur companies on stages on wheels, which could be moved from street to street.

The subjects continued to be drawn in large measure from the Bible and from legends of the saints. They served to instruct men in Scripture history, in an age when few could read. The instruction was not, however, always taken to heart, as profane swearing was so common that an Englishman was called on the Continent by his favorite oath, which the French regarded as a sort of national name before that of " John Bull " came into use.

Test.

SEVENTH PERIOD[1]

> " God's most dreaded instrument,
>   In working out a pure intent,
>   Is man — arrayed for mutual slaughter."
>
> WORDSWORTH

THE SELF–DESTRUCTION OF FEUDALISM

BARON AGAINST BARON

THE HOUSES OF LANCASTER AND YORK (1399–1485)

HOUSE OF LANCASTER (the Red Rose) HOUSE OF YORK (the White Rose)

HENRY IV, 1399–1413	EDWARD IV, 1461–1483
HENRY V, 1413–1422	†EDWARD V, 1483
*HENRY VI, 1422–1461	RICHARD III, 1483–1485

279. Henry IV's Accession. Richard II left no children. The nearest heir to the kingdom by right of birth was the boy Edmund Mortimer, a descendant of Richard's uncle Lionel, Duke of Clarence.[2] Henry ignored Mortimer's claim, and standing before Richard's empty throne in Westminster Hall (§ 257), boldly demanded the crown for himself.[3]

The nation had suffered so much from the misgovernment of those who had ruled during the minority of Richard, and later

---

[1] REFERENCE BOOKS on this Period will be found in the CLASSIFIED LIST OF BOOKS in the Appendix. The pronunciation of names will be found in the Index. The LEADING DATES stand unenclosed; all others are in parentheses.

* Henry VI, deposed 1461 ; reinstated for a short time in 1470.

† Edward V, never crowned.

[2] See Genealogical Table on page 140.

[3] " In the name of the Father, Son, and Holy Ghost, I, Henry of Lancaster, challenge this realm of England and the Crown, with all the members and the appurtenances, as that I am descended by right line of blood, coming from the good King Henry III, and through that right that God of his grace hath sent me, with help of kin and of all my friends to recover it, the which realm was in point to be undone by default of government and undoing of the good laws."

by Richard himself, that they wanted no more boy kings. Parliament, therefore, set aside the direct line of descent and accepted Henry. But the air was full of tumultuous passion. The Lords were divided in their allegiance, some stood by the former King, others by the new one. No less than forty noblemen challenged each other to fight, and civil war seemed imminent.[1]

280. Conspiracy in Favor of Richard. The new King had hardly seated himself on the throne when a conspiracy was discovered, having for its object the release and restoration of Richard, still a prisoner in Pontefract Castle. The plot was easily crushed. A month later Richard was found dead (§ 257).

Henry had his body brought up to London and exposed to public view in St. Paul's Cathedral, in order that not only the people, but all would-be conspirators might now see that Richard's hands could never again wield the scepter.

There was, however, one man at least who refused to be convinced. Owen Glendower, a Welshman, whom the late King had befriended, declared that Richard was still living, and that the corpse exhibited was not his body. Glendower prepared to maintain his belief by arms. King Henry mustered a force with the intention of invading Wales and crushing the rebel on his own ground; but a succession of terrible tempests ensued.

The English soldiers got the idea that Glendower raised these storms, for as an old chronicle declares : " Through art magike he [Glendower] caused such foule weather of winds, tempest, raine, snow, and haile to be raised for the annoiance of the King's armie, that the like had not beene heard of." [2] For this reason the troops became disheartened, and the King was obliged to postpone the expedition.

281. Revolt of the Percies ; Bold Step of the House of Commons, 1407. The powerful Percy family had been active in helping Henry to obtain the throne,[3] and had spent large sums in defending the North against invasions from Scotland.[4] They

---

[1] J. F. Bright's " History of England," I, 276.

[2] Holinshed's " Chronicle."

[3] Thomas Percy, Earl of Worcester, with Henry Percy, Earl of Northumberland, and his son, Sir Henry Percy, or " Hotspur " (§ 257).

[4] See the " Ballad of Chevy Chase."

expected a royal reward for these services, and were sorely disappointed because they did not get it. As young Henry Percy
said of the King:

> " My father, and my uncle, and myself,
>   Did give him that same royalty he wears;
>   And, — when he was not six-and-twenty strong,
>   Sick in the world's regard, wretched and low,
>   A poor, unminded outlaw sneaking home, —
>   My father gave him welcome to the shore:
>   .   .   .   .
>   Swore him assistance and perform'd it too." [1]

But the truth is, King Henry had little to give except promises.
Parliament voted money cautiously, limiting its supplies to specific
purposes. Men of wealth, feeling anxious about the issue of the
King's usurpation, — for such many regarded it, — were afraid to
lend him what he required.

In 1407 the House of Commons (§§ 213, 217) took a very decisive step. It demanded and obtained first, the exclusive right
of originating all "Money Bills," or in other words, of making all
grants of money which the King asked for. This practically gave
the people the control of the nation's purse.[2] Secondly, the Commons demanded and obtained from the King that he should not
in any way interfere with their right to deliberate what action they
should take in regard to making such grants of money. Besides
being held in check by the House of Commons, the King was hampered by a council whose advice he had pledged himself to follow.
For these reasons Henry's position was in every way precarious.

He had no clear title to the throne, and he had no means to buy
military support. In addition to these difficulties, he had made an
enemy of Sir Henry Percy. He had refused to ransom his brother-
in-law, a Mortimer,[3] whom Glendower had captured, but whom the
King wished well out of the way with all others of that name.

---

[1] Shakespeare's "Henry IV," Part I, Act IV, scene iii.

[2] This right of originating "Money Bills" had been claimed as early as the reign
of Richard II, but it was not fully and formally recognized until 1407. See Taswell-
Langmead's "English Constitutional History," p. 260, and Summary of Constitutional History in the Appendix, p. xii, § 13.

[3] Sir Edmund Mortimer: He was uncle to the Edmund Mortimer, Earl of March,
who was heir to the crown. See Bailey's "Succession to the English Crown."

Young Percy proved a dangerous foe. His hot temper and impetuous daring had got for him the title of the "Hotspur of the North." He was so fond of fighting that Shakespeare speaks of him as "he that kills me some six or seven dozen of Scots at a breakfast, washes his hands, and says to his wife, *Fie upon this quiet life! I want work*."[1] This "fire eater," with his father, his uncle (the Earl of Worcester), the Scotch Earl of Douglas, and, last of all, Owen Glendower, now formed an alliance to force Henry to give up the throne.

282. Battle of Shrewsbury (1403). At Shrewsbury, on the edge of Wales, the armies of the King and of the revolutionists met. A number of Henry's enemies had sworn to single him out in battle. The plot was divulged, and it is said that thirteen knights arrayed themselves in armor resembling the King's in order to mislead the assailants. The whole thirteen perished on that bloody field, where fat Sir John Falstaff vowed he fought on Henry's behalf "a long hour by Shrewsbury clock."[2]

The insurgents were utterly defeated. Douglas was taken prisoner, "Hotspur" was killed, and several of his companions were beheaded after the battle. But new insurrections arose, and the country was far from enjoying any permanent peace.

283. Persecution of the Lollards; Statute of Heresy; the First Martyr (1401). Thus far Henry had spent much time in crushing rebels, but he had also given part of it to burning heretics. To gain the favor of the clergy, and so render his throne more secure, the King favored the passage of a Statute of Heresy. The Lords and bishops passed such a law (to which the House of Commons seems to have assented).[3] It punished the Lollards (§ 255) and also all others who dissented from the essential doctrines of Rome with death.

William Sawtrey, a London clergyman, was the first victim under the new law (1401). He had declared that he would not worship "the cross on which Christ suffered, but only Christ himself who had suffered on the cross." He had also openly denied the doctrine

---

1 Shakespeare's "Henry IV," Part I, Act II, scene iv.
2 Shakespeare's "Henry IV," Part I, Act V, scene iv.
3 See Stubbs's "Constitutional History of England," III, 32.

of transubstantiation, which teaches that the sacramental bread is miraculously changed into the actual body of the Saviour. For these and minor heresies he was burned at Smithfield, in London, in the presence of a great multitude.

Some years later a second martyrdom took place. But as the English people would not allow torture to be used in the case of the Knights Templars in the reign of Edward II (§ 265), so but very few of them seem to have believed that by committing the body to the flames they could burn error out of the soul.

The Lollards, indeed, were still cast into prison, as some of the extreme and communistic part of them doubtless deserved to be (§ 255), but we hear of no more being put to cruel deaths during Henry's reign, though later, the utmost rigor of the law was again to some extent enforced.

284. Henry's Last Days. Toward the close of his life the King seems to have thought of reviving the Crusades for the conquest of Jerusalem (§ 182), where, according to tradition, an old prediction declared that he should die. But his Jerusalem was nearer than that of Palestine. While praying at the tomb of Edward the Confessor in Westminster Abbey (§ 66), he was seized with mortal illness. His attendants carried him into a room near by.

When he recovered consciousness, and inquired where he was, he was told that the apartment was called the Jerusalem Chamber. "Praise be to God," he exclaimed, "then here I die!" There he breathed his last, saying to his son, young Prince Henry:

> "God knows, my son,
> By what by-paths and indirect crook'd ways,
> I met this crown; and I myself know well
> How troublesome it sat upon my head;
> To thee it shall descend with better quiet,
> Better opinion, better confirmation;
> For all the soil of the achievement[1] goes
> With me into the earth."

285. Summary. At the outset of his reign Parliament showed its power by changing the succession and making Henry King

[1] "Soil of the achievement": stain or blame by which the crown was won. Shakespeare's "Henry IV," Part II, Act IV, scene iv.

instead of young Edmund Mortimer, the direct hereditary heir to the crown. Though successful in crushing rebellion, Henry was obliged to submit to the guidance of a council.

Furthermore, he was made more entirely dependent on Parliament, especially in the matter of supplies, than any previous King, for the House of Commons now got and held control of the nation's purse. For the first time in English history heresy was made punishable by death; yet such was the restraining influence of the people, that but two executions took place in Henry IV's reign.

HENRY V — 1413–1422

286. Lollard Outbreak at Henry's Accession. Henry's youth had been wild and dissolute, but the weight of the crown sobered him. He cast off poor old "Jack Falstaff"[1] (§ 282) and his other roistering companions, and began his new duties in earnest.

Sir John Oldcastle, or Lord Cobham, was at this time the most influential man among the Lollards (§§ 255, 283). He was brought to trial and convicted of heresy. The penalty was death; but the King granted him a respite, in the hope that he might recant, and Oldcastle managed to escape from prison (1414).

Immediately after, a conspiracy was detected among the Lollards for seizing the government, destroying the chief monasteries in and about London, and raising Oldcastle to power. Henry attacked the rebels unawares, killed many, and took a large number of prisoners, who were executed on a double charge of heresy and treason. Several years afterwards Oldcastle was burned as a heretic.

287. Report that Richard II was alive. A strange report now began to circulate. It was said that Richard II (§ 257) had been seen in Scotland, and that he was preparing to claim the throne which Henry's father had taken from him. To silence this seditious rumor, the King, it is said, exhumed Richard's body from its grave in the little village of Langley, Hertfordshire. At any rate, a dead body, reputed to be Richard's, was brought to London and propped up in a chair, so that all might see it.

---

[1] Shakespeare's "Henry IV," Part II, Act V, scene v, beginning, "I know thee not, old man."

In this manner the King and his court escorted the corpse in solemn procession to Westminster Abbey, where it was reinterred among the tombs of the English sovereigns. With it he buried once for all the troublesome falsehood which had kept up insurrection, and had made the deposed King more feared after death than he had ever been during life.

288. War with France (1415). To divert the attention of the nation from dangerous home questions likely to cause new plots and fresh revolts (§§ 286, 287), Henry now determined to act on his father's dying counsel and pick a foreign quarrel. The old grudge against France, which began with the feuds of Duke William of Normandy before he conquered England, made a war with that country always popular. At this period the French were divided into fierce parties that hated each other even more, if possible, than they hated the English. This, of course, greatly increased the chances of Henry's success, as he might form an alliance with one of these factions.

The King believed it a good opportunity to get three things he wanted, — a wife, a fortune, and the French crown. The King of France and his most powerful rival, the Duke of Burgundy, had each a daughter. To make sure of one of them, Henry secretly proposed to both. After long and fruitless negotiations the French King declined to grant the enormous dowry which the English King demanded. The latter gladly interpreted this refusal as equivalent to a declaration of war.

289. The Great Battle of Agincourt, 1415. Henry set to work with vigor, raised an army, and invaded France. He besieged Harfleur, near the mouth of the Seine, and took it; but his army suffered so much from sickness that, after leaving a garrison in the place, he resolved to move north, to the walled city of Calais. It will be remembered that the English had captured that city nearly seventy years before (§ 240), and Henry intended to wait there for reënforcements. (See map facing p. 128.)

After a long and perilous march he reached a little village about midway between Crécy and Calais. There he encountered the enemy in great force. Both sides prepared for battle. The French had fifty thousand troops to Henry's seven or eight thousand;

but the latter had that determination which wins victories. He said to one of his nobles who regretted that he had not a larger force :

> " No, my fair cousin ;
> If we are marked to die, we are enough
> To do our country loss ; and if we live,
> The fewer men, the greater share of honor." [1]

A heavy rain had fallen during the night, and the plowed land over which the French must cross was so wet and miry that their heavily armed horsemen sank deep at every step. The English bowmen, on the other hand, being on foot, could move with ease. Henry ordered every archer to drive a stake, sharpened at both ends, into the ground before him. This was a substitute for the modern bayonet, and presented an almost impassable barrier to the French cavalry.

As at Crécy and Poitiers, the English bowmen gained the day (§§ 238, 241). The sharp stakes stopped the enemy's horses, and the blinding showers of arrows threw the splendidly armed knights into wild confusion. With a ringing cheer Henry's troops rushed forward.

> " When down their bows they threw,
> And forth their swords they drew,
> And on the French they flew :
>   No man was tardy.
> Arms from the shoulder sent ;
> Scalps to the teeth they rent ;
> Down the French peasants went :
>   These were men hardy." [2]

When the fight was over, the King asked, " What is the name of that castle yonder ? " He was told it was called Agincourt. " Then," said he, " from henceforth this shall be known as the battle of Agincourt." This decisive victory made the winner feel sure that he could now hold his throne in spite of all plots against him (§ 288).

290. Treaty of Troyes, 1420 ; Henry's Death. Henry went back in triumph to England. Two years later, he again invaded

---

[1] Shakespeare's " Henry V," Act IV, scene iii.

[2] These vigorous lines, from Drayton's " Ballad of Agincourt " (1606), if not quite true to the letter of history (since it is doubtful whether any French peasants were on the field), are wholly true to its spirit.

France. His victorious course continued. By the Treaty of Troyes (1420) he gained all that he had planned to get. He obtained large sums of money, the French Princess Catharine in marriage, and the promise of the crown of France on the death of her father, Charles VI, who was then insane and feeble. Meantime Henry was to govern the French kingdom as regent.

Henry returned to England with the bride he had won by the sword, but he was soon recalled to France by a revolt against his power. He died there, leaving an infant son, Henry. Two months afterward Charles VI died, so that by the terms of the treaty Henry's son now inherited the French crown.

291. Summary. The one great event with which Henry V's name is connected is the conquest of France. It was hailed at the time as a glorious achievement. In honor of it his tomb in Westminster Abbey was surmounted by a statue of the King, having a head of solid silver. Eventually the head was stolen and never recovered; the wooden statue still remains. The theft was typical of Henry's short-lived victories abroad, for all the territory he had gained was soon destined to be hopelessly lost.

HENRY VI (House of Lancaster, Red Rose) — 1422–1461

292. Accession of Henry; Renewal of the French War. The heir to all the vast dominions left by Henry V was proclaimed King of England and France when in his cradle, and crowned, while still a child, first in Westminster Abbey and then at Paris.

But the accession to the French possessions was merely an empty form, for as Prince Charles, the son of the late Charles VI of France, refused to abide by the Treaty of Troyes (§ 290) and give up the throne, war again broke out.

293. Siege of Orleans. The Duke of Bedford [1] fought vigorously in Henry's behalf. In five years the English had got possession of most of the country north of the Loire. They now determined to make an effort to drive the French Prince south of that river. To accomplish this they must take the strongly

---

[1] During Henry's minority, John, Duke of Bedford, was Protector of the realm. When absent in France, Humphrey, Duke of Gloucester, acted for him.

fortified town of Orleans, which was situated on its banks. (See map facing p. 84.)

Forts were accordingly built around the place, and cannon planted to batter down its walls (§ 239). Six months later, so much progress had been made in the siege, that it was plain the city could not hold out much longer. The fortunes of Prince Charles seemed to depend on the fate of Orleans. If it fell, nothing, apparently, could save France from yielding to her conqueror.

294. Joan of Arc, 1429–1431. At this juncture Joan of Arc, a peasant girl of eighteen, came forward to inspire her despairing countrymen with fresh courage. She believed that Heaven had called her to drive the English from the land. The troops rallied round her. Clad in white armor, mounted on a white war horse, she saved Orleans ; then she led the troops from victory to victory, until she saw Prince Charles triumphantly crowned in the Cathedral of Rheims. (See map facing p. 128.)

Her fortunes soon changed. Her own people basely abandoned her. The unworthy King Charles made no attempt to protect the " Maid of Orleans," and she fell into the hands of the infuriated English, who believed she was in league with the devil. In accordance with this belief Joan was tried for witchcraft and heresy at Rouen, and sentenced to the flames. She died (1431) as bravely as she had lived, saying in her last agonies that her celestial voices had not deceived her, and that through them she had saved France.

" God forgive us," exclaimed one of Henry's courtiers who was present, " we are lost ! We have burned a saint ! " It was the truth ; and from the martyred girl's ashes a new spirit seemed to go forth to bless her ungrateful country. The heart of the French people was touched ; they rose and drove the English invaders from the soil of France.

Before Henry VI reached his thirtieth year the Hundred Years' War with France, which Edward III had begun (§ 237), was ended (1453), and England had lost all of her possessions on the Continent, except a bare foothold at Calais, and that was destined to be lost a few generations later (§ 373).

295. Henry VI's Character and Marriage. When Henry became of age he proved to be but the shadow of a King. His health and character were alike feeble. At twenty-five he married the beautiful and unfortunate French Princess, Margaret of Anjou, who was by far the better man of the two. When years of disaster came, this dauntless " Queen of tears " headed councils, led armies, and ruled both King and kingdom.

296. Poverty of the Crown and Wealth of the Nobles. One cause of the weakness of the government was its poverty. The revenues of the Crown had been greatly diminished by gifts and grants to favorites. The King was obliged to pawn his jewels and the silver plate from his table to pay his wedding expenses ; and it is said on high authority [1] that the royal couple were sometimes in actual want of a dinner.

On the other hand, the Earl of Warwick and other great lords had made fortunes out of the French wars,[2] and lived in regal splendor. The Earl, it is said, had at his different castles and his city mansion in London upwards of thirty thousand men in his service. Their livery, or uniform, a bright red jacket with the Warwick arms — a bear erect holding a ragged staff — embroidered on it in white, was seen, known, and feared throughout the country.

Backed by such forces it was easy for the Earl and other powerful lords to overawe kings, parliaments, and courts. Between the heads of the great houses quarrels were constantly breaking out. The safety of the people was endangered by these feuds, which became more and more violent, and often ended in bloodshed and murder.

297. Disfranchisement of the Common People, 1430. With the growth of power on the part of the nobles, there was also imposed for the first time a restriction on the right of the people to vote for members of Parliament. Up to this period all freemen might take part in the election of representatives chosen by the counties to sit in the House of Commons.

A law was now passed forbidding any one to vote at these elections unless he was a resident of the county and possessed

---

[1] Fortescue, on the " Governance of England " (Plummer).

[2] First, by furnishing troops to the government, the feudal system having now so far decayed that many soldiers had to be hired ; secondly, by the plunder of French cities ; thirdly, by ransoms obtained from noblemen taken prisoners.

of landed property yielding an annual income of forty shillings
($200).[1] Subsequently it was further enacted that no county can-
didate should be eligible unless he was a man of means and
social standing.

These two measures were blows against the free self-government
of the nation, since their manifest tendency was to make the House
of Commons represent the property rather than the people of the
country (§ 319). (See, too, Summary of Constitutional History in
the Appendix, p. xiii, § 14.)

298. Cade's Rebellion (1450). A formidable rebellion broke out
in Kent (1450), then, as now, one of the most independent and
democratic counties in England. The leader was Jack Cade, who
called himself by the popular name of Mortimer (§ 257, note 1,
and § 279). He claimed to be cousin to Richard, Duke of York,
a nephew of that Edmund Mortimer, now dead, whom Henry IV
had unjustly deprived of his succession to the crown.

Cade, who was a mere adventurer, was quite likely used as a
tool by plotters much higher than himself. By putting him forward
they could judge whether the country was ready for a revolution
and change of sovereigns.

Wat Tyler's rebellion, seventy years before (§ 250), was almost
purely social in its character, having for its object the emancipation
of the enslaved laboring classes. Cade's insurrection was, on the
contrary, almost wholly political. His chief complaint was that
the people were not allowed their free choice in the election of
representatives, but were forced by the nobility to choose candidates they did not want. Other grievances for which reform was
demanded were excessive taxation and the rapacity of the evil
counselors who controlled the King.

Cade entered London with a body of twenty thousand men
under strict discipline. Many of the citizens sympathized with
Cade's projects of reform, and were ready to give him a welcome.
He took formal possession of the place by striking his sword on
London Stone, — a Roman monument still standing, which then

---

[1] The income required by the statute was forty shillings, which, says Freeman,
we may fairly call forty pounds of our present money. See E. A. Freeman's "Growth
of the English Constitution," p. 97.

marked the center of the ancient capital, — saying, as Shakespeare reports him, " Now is Mortimer lord of this city." [1]

After three days of riot and the murder of the King's treasurer, the rebellion came to an end through a general pardon. Cade, however, endeavored to raise a new insurrection in the south, but was shortly after captured, and died of his wounds.

299. Wars of the Roses, 1455–1485. The real significance of Cade's insurrection is that it showed the widespread feeling of discontent caused by misgovernment, and that it served as an introduction to the long and dreary period of civil strife known as the Wars of the Roses.

So long as the English nobles had France for a fighting ground, French cities to plunder, and French captives to hold for heavy ransoms, they were content to let matters go on quietly at home. But that day was over. Through the bad management, if not through the positive treachery, of Edmund, Duke of Somerset, the French conquests had been lost. Henry VI, a weak king, at times insane, sat on the English throne (§ 295), while Richard, Duke of York, a really able man and a descendant of the Mortimers (see table, p. 161), was, as many believed, unlawfully excluded from it.

This fact in itself would have furnished a plausible pretext for hostilities, even as far back as Cade's rising. But the birth of a son [2] to Henry (1453) probably gave the signal for the outbreak, since it cut off all hopes which Richard's friends may have had of his peaceful succession.

300. The Scene in the Temple Garden. Shakespeare represents the smoldering feud between the rival houses of Lancaster and

---

[1] " Now is Mortimer lord of this city, and here, sitting upon London Stone, I charge and command that, at the city's cost, this conduit runs nothing but claret wine this first year of our reign ; and now it shall be treason for any man to call me other than Lord Mortimer." — Shakespeare's " Henry VI," Part II, Act IV, scene vi.

It is noticeable that the great dramatist expresses no sympathy in this play with the cause of the people. In fact he ridicules Cade and his movement. In the same spirit he does not mention the Great Charter in his " King John," while in his " Richard II " he passes over Wat Tyler without a word. Perhaps the explanation may be found in the fact that Shakespeare lived in an age when England was threatened by both open and secret enemies. The need of his time was a strong, steady hand at the helm ; it was no season for reform or change of any sort ; on this account he may have thought it his duty to be silent in regard to democratic risings and demands in the past (§ 313, note 2).

[2] Prince Edward. See Genealogical Table, p. 161, under Henry VI.

York (both of whom it should be remembered were descendants of Edward III)[1] as breaking into an angry quarrel in the Temple Garden, London, when Richard, Duke of York, says:

> " Let him that is a true-born gentleman,
> And stands upon the honor of his birth,
> If he suppose that I have pleaded truth,
> From off this brier pluck a white rose with me." [2]

To this challenge John Beaufort, Duke of Somerset,[3] a descendant of the house of Lancaster, who has just accused Richard of being the dishonored son of a traitor, replies:

> " Let him that is no coward, nor no flatterer,
> But dare maintain the party of the truth,
> Pluck a red rose from off this thorn with me."

[1] Table showing the descendants of Edward III, with reference to the claims of Lancaster and York to the crown:

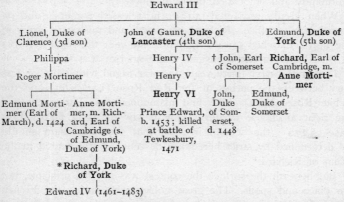

Edward III

| Lionel, Duke of Clarence (3d son) | John of Gaunt, **Duke of Lancaster** (4th son) | Edmund, **Duke of York** (5th son) |

Philippa — Henry IV — † John, Earl of Somerset   **Richard**, Earl of Cambridge, m. **Anne Morti-mer**

Roger Mortimer — Henry V

Edmund Morti-mer (Earl of March), d. 1424 — Anne Morti-mer, m. Rich-ard, Earl of Cambridge (s. of Edmund, Duke of York) — **Henry VI**, Prince Edward, b. 1453; killed at battle of Tewkesbury, 1471 — John, Duke of Som-erset, d. 1448 — Edmund, Duke of Somerset

*Richard, Duke of York

Edward IV (1461–1483)

* Inherited the title of Duke of York from his father's brother, Edward, Duke of York, who died without issue. Richard's father, the Earl of Cambridge, had forfeited his title and estates by treason, but Parliament had so far limited the sentence that his son was not thereby debarred from inheriting his uncle's rank and fortune. Richard, Duke of York, now represented the direct hereditary line of succession to the crown, while Henry VI and his son represented that established by Parliament through acceptance of Henry IV (§ 279).

† John, Earl of Somerset, was an illegitimate half brother of Henry IV's, but was, in 1397, declared legitimate by act of Parliament and a papal decree.

[2] Shakespeare's " Henry VI," Part I, Act II, scene iv.

[3] John, Duke of Somerset, died 1448. He was brother of Edmund, Duke of Somerset, who was slain at St. Albans, 1455.

A little later on the Earl of Warwick rejoins:

> " This brawl to-day,
> Grown to this faction in the Temple-garden,
> Shall send, between the red rose and the white,
> A thousand souls to death and deadly night." [1]

301. The Real Object of the Wars of the Roses. The wars, however, did not directly originate in this quarrel, but rather in the strife for power between Edmund, Duke of Somerset (John's brother), and Richard, Duke of York. Each desired to get the control of the government, though at first neither appears to have openly aimed at the crown.

During King Henry's attack of insanity (1453) Richard was appointed Protector of the realm, and shortly afterward the Duke of Somerset, the King's particular favorite and chief adviser, was cast into prison on the double charge of having culpably lost Normandy and embezzled public moneys.

When Henry recovered (1455), he released Somerset and restored him to office. Richard protested, and raising an army in the north, marched toward London. He met the royalist forces at St. Albans; a battle ensued, and Somerset was slain.

During the next thirty years the war raged with more or less fury between the parties of the Red Rose (Lancaster) and the White Rose (York). The first maintained that Parliament had the right to choose whatever king it saw fit, as in Henry IV's case (§ 279); the second insisted that the succession should be determined by strict hereditary descent, as represented in the claim of Richard. [2]

But beneath the surface the contest was not for principle, but for place and spoils. The great nobles, who during the French wars (§ 288) had pillaged abroad, now pillaged each other; and as England was neither big enough nor rich enough to satisfy the greed of all of them, the struggle gradually became a war of mutual extermination.

It was, to a certain extent, a sectional war. Eastern England, then the wealthiest and most progressive part of the country,

---

[1] Shakespeare's " Henry VI," Part I, Act II, scene iv.
[2] See Genealogical Table, p. 161.

had strongly supported Wycliffe in his reforms (§ 254). It now espoused the side of Richard, Duke of York, who was believed to be friendly to religious liberty, while the western counties fought for the cause of Lancaster and the Church.

302. The First Battles (1455–1460). We have already seen (§ 301) that the first blood was shed at St. Albans (1455), where the Yorkists, after half an hour's fighting, gained a complete victory. A similar result followed at Bloreheath, Staffordshire (1459). In a third battle, at Northampton, the Yorkists were again successful (1460). Henry was taken prisoner, and Queen Margaret fled with the young Prince Edward to Scotland. Richard now demanded the crown. (See map facing p. 172.)

Henry answered with unexpected spirit : " My father was King, his father also was King. I have worn the crown forty years from my cradle ; you have all sworn fealty to me as your sovereign, and your fathers did the like to my fathers. How, then, can my claim be disputed ?" After a long controversy, a compromise was effected. Henry agreed that if he were left in peaceable possession of the throne during his life, Richard or his heirs should succeed him.

303. Battles of Wakefield and Towton (1460–1461). But Queen Margaret refused to see her son, Prince Edward, thus tamely set aside. She raised an army and attacked the Yorkists. Richard, Duke of York, whose forces were inferior to hers, had entrenched himself in Sandal Castle near Wakefield, Yorkshire. Day after day Margaret went up under the walls and dared him to come out.

At length, stung by her taunts, the Duke sallied from his stronghold, and the battle of Wakefield was fought (1460). Margaret was victorious. Richard was slain, and the Queen, in mockery of his claims to sovereignty, cut off his head, decked it with a paper crown, and set it up over the chief gate of the city of York. Fortune now changed. The next year (1461) the Lancastrians were defeated with great slaughter at Towton, Yorkshire. The light spring snow was crimsoned with the blood of thirty thousand slain, and the way strewn with corpses for ten miles up to the walls of York.

The Earl of Warwick (§ 296), henceforth popularly known as the " King Maker," now placed Edward, eldest son of the late

Duke of York, on the throne, with the title of Edward IV (§ 300, table). Henry and Margaret fled to Scotland. The new government summoned them to appear, and as they failed to answer, proclaimed them traitors.

Four years later Henry was taken prisoner and sent to the Tower of London (§ 305). He may have been happier there than battling for his throne. He was not born to reign, but rather, as Shakespeare makes him say, to lead a shepherd's life, watching his flocks, until the peacefully flowing years should —

> " Bring white hairs unto a quiet grave." [1]

304. Summary. The history of the period is one of loss to England. The brilliant French conquests of Henry V (§§ 289, 290) slipped from the nerveless hands of his son, leaving France practically independent. The people's power to vote had been restricted (§ 297). The House of Commons had ceased to be democratic even in a moderate degree. Its members were all property holders elected by property holders (§ 297). Cade's rebellion was the sign of political discontent and the forerunner of civil war (§ 298).

The contests of the parties of the Red and the White Roses drenched England's fair fields with the best blood of her own sons. The reign ends with King Henry in prison, Queen Margaret and Prince Edward fugitives, and the Yorkist, Edward IV, placed on the throne by the help of the powerful Earl of Warwick (§ 296).

EDWARD IV (House of York, White Rose) — 1461–1483

305. Continuation of the War ; Barnet ; Death of Henry ; Tewkesbury (1471). During the whole of Edward IV's reign (§ 303) the war went on with varying success, but unvarying ferocity, until at last neither side would ask or give quarter. Some years after the accession of the new sovereign, the Earl of Warwick (§ 296)

---

[1] See Henry's soliloquy on the field of Towton, beginning,

> " O God ! methinks it were a happy life
> To be no better than a homely swain."

SHAKESPEARE'S " Henry VI," Part III,
Act II, scene v

quarreled with him, thrust him from the throne, and restored Henry VI (§ 303).

But a few months later, at the battle of Barnet, near London (1471), Warwick, who was "the last of the great barons," was killed, and Henry, who had been led back to the Tower of London again (§ 303), died one of those "conveniently sudden deaths" which were then so common.

The heroic Queen Margaret (§§ 295, 303), however, would not give up the contest in behalf of her son's claim to the crown. But fate was against her. A few weeks after the battle of Barnet her army was utterly defeated at Tewkesbury (1471), her son Edward slain, and the Queen herself taken prisoner. (See map facing p. 172.)

She was eventually released on the payment of a large ransom, and returned to France, where she died broken-hearted in her native Anjou, prophesying that the contest would go on until the Red Rose, representing her party, should get a still deeper dye from the blood of her enemies.

306. The Introduction of Printing, 1477. But an event was at hand of greater importance than any question of crowns or parties, though then none was wise enough to see its real significance. William Caxton, a London merchant, had learned the new art of printing with movable type[1] at Bruges in Flanders (now Belgium). When he returned to his native country, he set up a small press within the grounds of Westminster Abbey.

There, at the sign of a shield bearing a red "pale," or band, he advertised his wares as "good chepe." He was not only printer, but translator and editor. King Edward gave him some royal patronage. His Majesty was willing to pay liberally for work which not long before the clergy in France had condemned as a black art emanating from the devil. Many, too, of the English clergy regarded it with no very friendly eye, since it threatened to destroy the copying trade, of which the monks had well-nigh a monopoly (§ 154).

The first printed book which Caxton is known to have published in England was a small volume entitled " The Sayings of the

---

[1] The first printing in Europe was done in the early part of the fifteenth century from wooden blocks on which the words were cut. Movable types were invented about 1450.

Philosophers," 1477.[1] This venture was followed in due time by Chaucer's "Canterbury Tales" (§ 253), and whatever other poetry, history, or classics seemed worthy of preservation; making in all nearly a hundred distinct works comprising more than eighteen thousand volumes.

Up to this time a book of any kind was a luxury, laboriously "written by the few for the few"; but from this date literature of

CAXTON SHOWING THE KING A PRINTED PAGE

all sorts was destined to multiply and fill the earth with many leaves and some good fruit.

Caxton's patrons, though few, were choice, and when one of them, the Earl of Worcester, was beheaded in the wars, Caxton said, "The ax did then cut off more learning than was left in all the heads of the surviving lords." Towards the close of the nineteenth

---

[1] "The dictes or sayengis of the philosophres, enprynted by me william Caxton at westmestre, the year of our lord MCCCCLxxvii."

It has no title-page, but ends as above. A copy is preserved in the British Museum. The "Game and Play of the Chess" is supposed by some to have been published a year or two earlier, but as the book has neither printer's name, place of publication, nor date, the time of its issue remains wholly conjectural.

century a memorial window was placed in St. Margaret's Church within the abbey grounds, as a tribute to the man who, while England was red with slaughter, introduced "the art preservative of all arts," and preservative of liberty no less [1] (§ 322).

307. King Edward's Character. The King, however, cared more for his pleasures than for literature or the welfare of the nation. His chief aim was to beg, borrow, or extort money to waste in dissipation. The loans which he forced his subjects to grant, and which were seldom, if ever, repaid, went under the name of "benevolences." But it is safe to say that those who furnished them were in no very benevolent frame of mind at the time.

Exception may perhaps be made of the rich and elderly widow, who was so pleased with the King's handsome face that she willingly handed him £20 (a large sum in those days); and when the jovial monarch gallantly kissed her out of gratitude for her generosity, she at once, like a true and loyal subject, doubled the donation. Edward's course of life was not conducive to length of days, even if the times had favored a long reign. He died early, leaving a son, Prince Edward, to succeed him.

308. Summary. The reign was marked by the continuation of the Wars of the Roses, the death of King Henry VI and of his son, with the return of Queen Margaret to France. The most important event outside of the war was the introduction of the printing press into England by William Caxton.

EDWARD V (House of York, White Rose) — 1483

309. Gloucester appointed Protector. Prince Edward, heir to the throne, was a lad of twelve (§ 307). His position was naturally full of peril. It became much more so, from the fact that his ambitious and unscrupulous uncle, Richard, Duke of Gloucester, had been appointed Lord Protector of the realm until the boy

---

[1] "Lord! taught by thee, when Caxton bade
   His silent words forever speak;
   A grave for tyrants then was made,
   Then crack'd the chain which yet shall break."

EBENEZER ELLIOTT, "Hymn for the Printers'
Gathering at Sheffield," 1833

should become of age. Richard protected his young nephew as a wolf would protect a lamb.

He met the Prince coming up to London from Ludlow Castle, Shropshire, attended by his half brother, Sir Richard Grey, and his uncle, Lord Rivers. Under the pretext that Edward would be safer in the Tower of London than at Westminster Palace, Richard sent the Prince there, and soon found means for having his kinsmen, Grey and Rivers, executed.

310. Murder of Lord Hastings and the Two Princes. Richard shortly after showed his object. Lord Hastings was one of the council who had voted to make him Lord Protector, but he was unwilling to help him in his plot to seize the crown. While at the council table in the Tower of London Richard suddenly started up and accused Hastings of treason, saying, " By St. Paul, I will not to dinner till I see thy head off ! " Hastings was dragged out of the room, and without either trial or examination was beheaded on a stick of timber on the Tower green.

The way was now clear for the accomplishment of the Duke's purpose. The Queen Mother (Elizabeth Woodville, widow of Edward IV) (§ 305) took her younger son and his sisters, one of whom was the Princess Elizabeth of York, and fled for protection to the sanctuary (§ 95) of Westminster Abbey, where, refusing all comfort, " she sat alone, on the rush-covered stone floor." Finally, Richard half persuaded and half forced the unhappy woman to give up her second son to his tender care.

With bitter weeping and dread presentiments of evil she parted from him, saying : " Farewell, mine own sweet son ! God send you good keeping ! Let me kiss you once ere you go, for God knoweth when we shall kiss together again." That was the last time she saw the lad. He and Edward, his elder brother, were soon after murdered in the Tower, and Richard rose by that double crime to the height he coveted.

311. Summary. Edward V's nominal reign of less than three months must be regarded simply as the time during which his uncle, the Duke of Gloucester, perfected his plot for seizing the crown by the successive murders of Rivers, Grey, Hastings, and the two young Princes.

RICHARD III (House of York, White Rose) — 1483–1485

312. Richard's Accession ; he promises Financial Reform.
Richard used the preparations which had been made for the
murdered Prince Edward's coronation for his own (§ 310). He
probably gained over an influential party by promises of financial reform. In their address to him at his accession, Parliament
said, "Certainly we be determined rather to adventure and commit
us to the peril of our lives . . . than to live in such thraldom and
bondage as we have lived long time heretofore, oppressed and injured by extortions and new impositions, against the laws of God
and man, and the liberty, old policy and laws of this realm, wherein
every Englishman is inherited." [1]

313. Richard III's Character. Several attempts have been
made of late years to defend the King against the odium heaped
upon him by the older historians. But these well-meant efforts
to prove him less black than tradition painted him are answered
by the fact that his memory was thoroughly hated by those who
knew him best. No one of the age when he lived thought of
vindicating his character. He was called a "hypocrite" and a
"hunchback."

We must believe then, until it is clearly proved to the contrary, that the last of the Yorkist kings was what common report
and Shakespeare have together represented him,[2] — distorted in
figure, and with ambition so unrestrained that the words the great

---

[1] Taswell-Langmead's "Constitutional History of England."

[2] In this connection it may be well to say a word in regard to the historical value
of Shakespeare's utterances, which have been freely quoted in this book. He generally followed the Chronicles of Hall and Holinshed, which constitute two important sources of information on the periods of which they treat ; and he sometimes
followed them so closely that he simply turned their prose into verse. Mr. James
Gairdner, who is a high authority on the Wars of the Roses, calls Shakespeare "an
unrivaled interpreter" of that long and terrible conflict. (See the preface to his
"Houses of Lancaster and York.") In the preface to his "Richard III" Mr. Gairdner is still more explicit. He says : "A minute study of the facts of Richard's life
has tended more and more to convince me of the general fidelity of the portrait
with which we have been made familiar by Shakespeare and Sir Thomas More." On
Shakespeare's faithful presentation of history see also A. G. S. Canning's "Thoughts
on Shakespeare," p. 295 ; the Dictionary of National (British) Biography under
"Holinshed" ; Garnett and Gosse's "English Literature," Vol. II, p. 68 ; and H. N.
Hudson's "Shakespeare's Life and Characters," Vol. II, pp. 5–8. See, too, § 298, note 1.

English poet has seen fit to put into his mouth may have really expressed Richard's own thought:

> " Then, since the heavens have shap'd my body so,
>   Let hell make crookt my mind to answer it." [1]

Personally he was as brave as he was cruel and unscrupulous. He promoted some reforms; he encouraged Caxton in his great work (§ 306), and he abolished the forced loans ironically called " benevolences " (§ 307), at least for a time.

314. Revolts; Buckingham; Henry Tudor. During his short reign of two years, several revolts broke out, but came to nothing. The Duke of Buckingham, who had helped Richard III to the throne, turned against him because he did not get the rewards he expected. He headed a revolt; but as his men deserted him, he fell into the King's hands, and the executioner speedily did the rest.

Finally, a more formidable enemy arose. Before he gained the crown Richard had cajoled or compelled the unfortunate Anne Neville, widow of that Prince Edward, son of Henry VI, who was slain at Tewkesbury (§ 305), into becoming his wife. She might have said with truth, " Small joy have I in being England's Queen." The King intended that his son should marry Elizabeth of York, sister to the two Princes he had murdered in the Tower (§ 310). By so doing he would strengthen his position and secure the succession to the throne to his own family. But Richard's son shortly after died, and the King, having mysteriously got rid of his wife, now made up his mind to marry Elizabeth himself.

The Princess, however, was already betrothed to Henry Tudor, Earl of Richmond, the engagement having been effected during that sad winter which she and her mother spent in sanctuary (§ 95) at Westminster Abbey, watched by Richard's soldiers to prevent their escape (§ 310). The Earl of Richmond, who was an illegitimate descendant of the House of Lancaster (see Genealogical Table, p. 172), had long been waiting on the Continent for an opportunity to invade England and claim the crown.

Owing to the enmity of Edward IV and Richard toward him, the Earl had been, as he himself said, " either a fugitive or a captive

---

[1] Shakespeare's " Henry VI," Part III, Act V, scene vi.

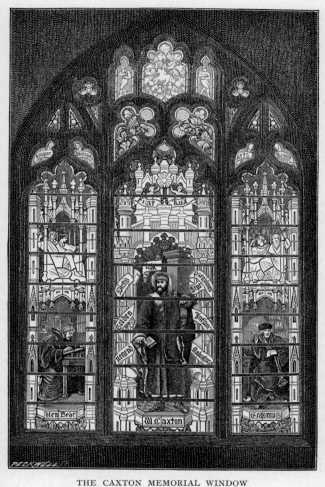

THE CAXTON MEMORIAL WINDOW

St. Margaret's Church, London; it almost touches Westminster Abbey

since he was five years old." He now determined to remain so
no longer. He landed (1485) with a force at Milford Haven,
in Wales, where he felt sure of a welcome, since his paternal
ancestors were Welsh.[1]

Advancing through Shrewsbury, he met Richard on Bosworth
Field, in Leicestershire.

315. Battle of Bosworth Field, 1485. There the decisive battle
was fought between the great rival houses of York and Lancaster
(§ 300). Richard represented the first, and Henry Tudor, Earl of
Richmond, the second. The King went out the evening before to
look over the ground. He found one of his sentinels slumbering at
his post. Drawing his sword, he stabbed him to the heart, saying,
" I found him asleep and I leave him asleep." Going back to his
tent, he passed a restless night. The ghosts of all his murdered
victims seemed to pass in procession before him. Such a sight
may well, as Shakespeare says, have "struck terror to the soul
of Richard." [2]

At sunrise the battle began. Before the attack, Richard, it is
said, confessed to his troops the murder of his two nephews
(§ 310), but pleaded that he had atoned for the crime with "many
salt tears and long penance." It is probable that had it not been
for the treachery of some of his adherents the King would have
won the day.

When he saw that he was deserted by those on whose help he
had counted, he uttered the cry of " Treason ! treason !" and
dashed forward into the thick of the fight. With the fury of
despair he hewed his way into the very presence of Henry
Tudor, and killing the standard bearer, flung the Lancastrian

---

[1] Descent of Henry Tudor, Earl of Richmond :

Henry V (House of Lancaster) married Catharine of France, who after his
| death married **Owen Tudor,** a Welshman of Anglesey
Henry VI |
                    Edmund Tudor (Earl of Richmond) married
                 Margaret Beaufort, a descendant of John of Gaunt,
                 Duke of Lancaster [she was granddaughter of
                 John, Earl of Somerset ; see p. 161]
                                    |
                    Henry Tudor, Earl of Richmond (also
                         called Henry of Lancaster)

[2] Shakespeare's " Richard III," Act V, scene iii.

ENGLAND
AND
WALES
1066-1485

banner to the ground. But he could go no further. Numbers overpowered him, and he fell.

During the battle Richard had worn his crown. After all was over, it was found hanging on a hawthorn bush[1] and handed to the victor, who placed it on his own head. The army then gathered round Henry Tudor thus crowned, and moved by one impulse joined in the exultant hymn of the Te Deum.[2] Thus ended the last of the Plantagenet line (§ 159). "Whatever their faults or crimes, there was not a coward among them."[3]

316. End of the Wars of the Roses (1485); their Effects. With Bosworth Field the Wars of the Roses ceased (§§ 299, 300). During the thirty years they had continued, fourteen pitched battles had been fought, in a single one of which (Towton) (§ 303) more Englishmen lost their lives than in the whole course of the wars with France during the preceding forty years. In all, eighty princes of the blood royal and more than half of the nobility of the realm perished.

Of those who escaped death by the sword, many died on the scaffold. The remnant who were saved had hardly a better fate. They left their homes only to suffer in foreign lands. A writer of that day[4] says, "I, myself, saw the Duke of Exeter, the King of England's brother-in-law, walking barefoot in the Duke of Burgundy's train, and begging his bread from door to door."

Every individual of two families of the great houses of Somerset and Warwick (§§ 296, 300) fell either on the field or under the executioner's ax. In tracing family pedigrees it is startling to see how often the record reads, "killed at St. Albans," "slain at Towton," "beheaded after the battle of Wakefield," and the like.[5]

When the contest closed, the feudal baronage was broken up (§§ 113, 114, 150). In a majority of cases the estates of the nobles either fell to the Crown for lack of heirs, or they were

---

[1] An ancient stained-glass window in the east end of Henry VII's Chapel (Westminster Abbey) commemorates this incident.

[2] "Te Deum laudamus" (We praise thee, O God): a Roman Catholic hymn of thanksgiving, now sung in English in the Episcopal and other churches.

[3] W. Stubbs's "Constitutional History of England."

[4] See the "Paston Letters."

[5] Guest's "Lectures on English History."

fraudulently seized by the King's officers. Thus the greater part of the wealthiest and most powerful aristocracy in the world disappeared so completely that they ceased to have either a local habitation or a name.

But the elements of civil discord at last exhausted themselves. Bosworth Field was a turning point in English history. When the sun went down, it saw the termination of the desperate struggle between the White Rose of York and the Red Rose of Lancaster; when it ushered in a new day, it shone also on a new King, Henry VII, who introduced a new social and political period.

317. Summary. The importance of Richard's reign is that it marks the close of the Wars of the Roses. Those thirty years of civil strife destroyed the predominating influence of the feudal barons. Henry Tudor (§ 314) now becomes the central figure, and will ascend the throne as Henry VII.

GENERAL REFERENCE SUMMARY OF THE LANCAS-TRIAN AND YORKIST PERIOD (1399-1485)

(See note in italics on page 43.)

I. GOVERNMENT. II. RELIGION. III. MILITARY AFFAIRS. IV. LITERATURE, LEARNING, AND ART. V. GENERAL INDUSTRY AND COMMERCE. VI. MODE OF LIFE, MANNERS, AND CUSTOMS

I. GOVERNMENT

318. Parliament and the Royal Succession. The period began with the parliamentary recognition of the claim to the crown of Henry, Duke of Lancaster, son of John of Gaunt, Duke of Lancaster, fourth son of Edward III. By this act the claim of Edmund Mortimer, a descendant of Edward III by his third son, Lionel, Duke of Clarence, was deliberately set aside, and this change in the order of succession eventually furnished an excuse for civil war.[1]

---

[1] Before the accession of Henry III, Parliament made choice of any one of the King's sons whom it considered best fitted to rule. After that time it was understood that the King's eldest son should be chosen to succeed him; or in case of his death during the lifetime of his father, the eldest son of the eldest son; and so forward in that line. The action taken by Parliament in favor of Henry IV was a departure from that principle, and a reassertion of its ancient right to choose any descendant of the royal family it deemed best. (See Genealogical Table, p. 140.)

319. Disfranchisement of Electors ; Benevolences. Under Henry VI a property qualification was established by act of Parliament which cut off all persons from voting for county members of the House of Commons who did not have an income of forty shillings (say £40, or $200, in modern money) from freehold land. County elections, the statute said, had "of late been made by a very great, outrageous, and excessive number of people . . . of which the most part were people of small substance and of no value."

Later, candidates for the House of Commons from the counties were required to be gentlemen by birth, and to have an income of not less than £20 (or say £400, or $2000, in modern money). Though the tendency of such laws was to make the House of Commons represent property holders rather than the freemen as a body, yet no apparent change seems to have taken place in the class of county members chosen.

Eventually, however, these and other interferences with free elections caused the rebellion of Jack Cade, in which the insurgents demanded the right to choose such representatives as they saw fit. But the movement appears to have had no practical result. During the civil war which ensued, King Edward IV compelled wealthy subjects to lend him large sums (seldom, if ever, repaid) called "benevolences." Richard III abolished this obnoxious system, but afterward revived it, and it became conspicuously hateful under his successor in the next period.

Another great grievance was Purveyance. By it the King's purveyors had the right to seize provisions and means of transportation for the King and his hundreds of attendants whenever they journeyed through the country on a "royal progress." The price offered by the purveyors was always much below the real value of what was taken, and frequently even that was not paid. Purveyance, which had existed from the earliest times, was not finally abolished until 1660.

II. Religion

320. Suppression of Heresy. Under Henry IV the first act was passed by Lords and clergy, apparently with the assent of the House of Commons, for punishing heretics by burning at the stake, and the first martyr suffered in that reign. Later, the Lollards, or followers of Wycliffe, who appear in many cases to have been socialists as well as religious reformers, were punished by imprisonment, and occasionally with death. The whole number of martyrs, however, was small.

III. Military Affairs

321. Armor and Arms. The armor of the period was made of steel plate, fitting and completely covering the body. It was often inlaid with gold and elegantly ornamented. Firearms had not yet superseded the old weapons. Cannon were in use, to some degree, and also clumsy handguns fired with a match.

The long bow continued to be the chief arm of the foot soldiers, and was used with great dexterity and fatal effect. Targets were set up by law in every parish, and the yeomen were required to practice frequently at contests in archery. The principal wars were the civil wars and those with France.

IV. Literature, Learning, and Art

322. Introduction of Printing ; Books. The art of printing was introduced into England about 1477 by Caxton, a London merchant. Up to that time all books had been written on either parchment or paper, at an average rate of about fifty cents per page in modern money. The age was not favorable to literature, and produced no great writers; but Caxton edited and published a large number of works, many of which he translated from the French and Latin.

The two books which throw most light on the history of the times are the " Sir John Paston Letters " (1424–1506), and a work by Chief Justice Fortescue on government, intended for the use of Prince Edward (slain at Tewkesbury). The latter work is remarkable for its bold declaration that the King " has the delegation of power from the people, and he has no just claims to any other power than this." The chief justice also praises the courage of his countrymen, and declares with honest pride that " more Englishmen are hanged in England in one year for robbery and manslaughter than are hanged in France in seven years."

323. Education. Henry VI took a deep interest in education, and founded the great public school of Eton, which ranks next in age to that of Winchester. The money for its endowment was obtained by the appropriation of the revenues of alien or foreign monasteries which had been erected in England, and which were confiscated by Henry V. The King watched the progress of the building from the windows of Windsor Castle, and to supplement the course of education to be given there, he furthermore erected and endowed the magnificent King's College, Cambridge.

324. Architecture. There was a new development of Gothic architecture in this period, the Decorated giving place to the Perpendicular.

The latter derives its name from the perpendicular divisions of the lights in the arches of the windows. It marks the final period of the Gothic or Pointed style, and is noted for the exquisite carved work of its ceilings. King's College Chapel, Cambridge, St. George's Chapel, Windsor, and Henry VII's Chapel (built in the next reign), connected with Westminster Abbey, are among the most celebrated examples of this style of architecture, which is peculiar to England.

The mansions of the nobility at this period exhibited great elegance. Crosby Hall, London, at one time the residence of Richard III, was one of the best examples of the " Inns " of the great families and wealthy knights. The Hall was pulled down in 1903, but it has been reërected on the Chelsea Embankment, on the Thames.

V. General Industry and Commerce

325. Agriculture and Trade. Notwithstanding the Civil Wars of the Roses, agriculture was prosperous and foreign trade largely increased. The latter was well represented by Sir Richard Whittington, thrice mayor of London, who, according to tradition, lent Henry V large sums of money, and then at an entertainment which he gave to the King and Queen in his city mansion, generously canceled the debt by throwing the bonds into the open sandalwood fire. There is a fine fresco, representing this scene, in the Royal Exchange, London.

Goldsmiths from Lombardy had now settled in London in such numbers as to give the name of Lombard Street to the quarter they occupied. They succeeded the Jews in the business of money lending and banking, and Lombard Street still remains famous for its bankers and brokers.

VI. Mode of Life, Manners, and Customs

326. Dress. Great sums were spent on dress by both sexes, and the courtiers' doublets, or jackets, were of the most costly silks and velvets, elaborately puffed and slashed. During the latter part of the period the pointed shoes, which had formerly been of prodigious length, suddenly began to grow broad, with such rapidity that Parliament passed a law limiting the width of the toes to six inches.

At the same time the court ladies adopted the fashion of wearing horns as huge in proportion as the noblemen's shoes. The government tried legislating them down, and the clergy fulminated a solemn curse against them; but fashion was more powerful than Church and Parliament combined, and horns and hoofs came out triumphant.

✓

EIGHTH PERIOD [1]

"One half her soil has walked the rest
In poets, heroes, martyrs, sages!"

O. W. HOLMES

POLITICAL REACTION — ABSOLUTISM OF THE CROWN — THE ENGLISH REFORMATION AND THE NEW LEARNING

CROWN OR POPE?

HOUSE OF TUDOR (1485–1603)

HENRY VII, 1485–1509	EDWARD VI, 1547–1553
HENRY VIII, 1509–1547	MARY, 1553–1558
ELIZABETH, 1558–1603	

327. Union of the Houses of Lancaster and York. Before leaving the Continent Henry Tudor (§ 314) had promised the Yorkist party that he would marry Elizabeth, eldest daughter of Edward IV (see Genealogical Table, p. 179), and sister to the young Princes murdered by Richard III (§ 310). Such a marriage would unite the rival houses of Lancaster and York, and put an end to the civil war.

A few months after the new King's accession the wedding was duly celebrated, and in the beautiful east window of stained glass in Henry VII's Chapel, Westminster Abbey, the Roses are seen joined; so that, as the quaint verse of that day says:

"Both roses flourish — red and white —
In love and sisterly delight;
The two that were at strife are blended,
And all old troubles now are ended."

[1] REFERENCE BOOKS on this period will be found in the CLASSIFIED LIST OF BOOKS in the Appendix. The pronunciation of names will be found in the Index. THE LEADING DATES stand unenclosed; all others are in parentheses.

Peace came from the union, but it was peace interrupted by insurrections which lasted for several years.

328. Condition of the Country ; Power of the Crown. Henry, it is said, had his claim to the throne printed by Caxton, and distributed broadcast over the country (§ 306). It was the first political appeal to the people made through the press, and was a sign of the new period upon which English history had entered. Since Caxton began his great work, the kingdom had undergone a most momentous change.

The leading nobles, like the Earl of Warwick (§§ 296, 303), were, with few exceptions, dead. Their estates were confiscated, their thousands of followers either buried on the battlefield or dispersed throughout the land (§ 316). The small number of titled families remaining was no longer to be feared. The nation itself, though it had taken comparatively little part in the war, was weary of bloodshed, and ready for peace on any terms.

The accession of the Welsh house of Tudor (§ 39) marks the beginning of a long period of almost absolute royal power. The nobility were too weak to place any check on the King.

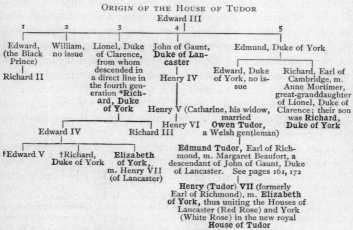

ORIGIN OF THE HOUSE OF TUDOR

* Inherited the title Duke of York from his uncle Edward. See No. 5.
† The Princes murdered by Richard III.

The clergy, who had not recovered from their dread of Lollardism (§§ 255, 283) and its attacks on their wealth and influence, were anxious for a strong conservative government such as Henry promised. The House of Commons had no clear united policy, and though the first Parliament put certain restraints on the Crown, yet they were never really enforced.[1] The truth is, that the new King was both too prudent and too crafty to give them an opportunity. By avoiding foreign wars he dispensed with the necessity of summoning frequent Parliaments, and with demanding large sums of money from them.

By thus ruling alone for a large part of the time, Henry got the management of affairs into his own hands, and transmitted the power to those who came after him. In this way the Tudors with their successors, the Stuarts, built up a system of " personal sovereignty " — or " one-man power " — unchecked by constitutional restraints. It continued for a hundred and fifty years, when the outbreak of the great Civil War brought it to an end forever.

329. Growth of a Stronger Feeling of Nationality. It would be an error, however, to consider this absolutism of the Crown as an unmitigated evil. On the contrary, it was in one important direction an advantage. There are times when the great need of a people is not more individual liberty, but greater national unity. Spain and France were two countries consisting of a collection of petty feudal states. Their nobility were always trying to steal each other's possessions and cut each other's throats.

But the rise in each country of a royal despotism forced the turbulent barons to make peace, and to obey a common central law. By this means both realms ultimately developed into great and powerful kingdoms.

When the Tudors came to the throne, England was still full of the rankling hate engendered by the Wars of the Roses (§ 299). Held down by the heavy hand of Henry VII, and later, by the

---

[1] At the accession of Henry VII, Parliament imposed the following checks on the power of the King: (1) No new tax to be levied without consent of Parliament; (2) No new law to be made without the same consent; (3) No committal to prison without a warrant specifying the offense, and the trial to be speedy; (4) Criminal charges and questions of fact in civil cases to be decided by jury; (5) The King's officers to be held responsible to the nation.

still heavier one of Henry VIII, the country learned the same
salutary lesson of growth under repression which had benefited
Spain and France. Henceforth Englishmen no longer boasted that
they belonged to the Yorkist or the Lancastrian faction (§ 300), but
began to pride themselves on their loyalty to Crown and country,
and on their readiness to draw their swords to defend both. Furthermore, English rule in Ireland was strengthened (§ 159).[1]

**330. Henry's Methods of raising Money ; the Court of Star
Chamber.** Henry's reign was in the interest of the middle classes,
— the farmers, tradesmen, and mechanics. His policy was to avoid
heavy taxation, to exempt the poor from the burdens of state, and
so ingratiate himself with a large body of the people.

In order to accomplish this, he revived " benevolences " (§§ 307,
313), and by a device suggested by his chief minister, Cardinal
Morton, and hence known and dreaded as " Morton's Fork," he
extorted large sums from the rich and well-to-do.[2]

The Cardinal's agents made it their business to learn every man's
income, and visit him accordingly. If a person lived handsomely,
the Cardinal would insist on a correspondingly liberal gift ; if, however, a citizen lived very plainly, the King's minister insisted none
the less, telling the unfortunate man that by his economy he must
surely have accumulated enough to bestow the required " benevolence." [3] Thus on one prong or the other of his terrible " fork "
the shrewd Cardinal impaled his writhing victims, and speedily filled
the royal treasury as it had never been filled before.[4]

But Henry VII had other methods for raising money. He sold
offices in Church and State, and took bribes for pardoning rebels.

---

[1] This was done by the passage of Poynings's Act (1494) in Ireland. It prohibited
the Irish Parliament from passing any law which did not receive the sanction of the
English Council. (See note 1, p. 83.) This act was repealed in 1782.

[2] Those whose income from land was less than £2, or whose movable property
did not exceed £15 (say $150 and $1125 now), were exempt. The lowest rate of assessment for the " benevolences " was fixed at twenty pence on the pound on land,
and half that rate on other property.

[3] Richard Reed, a London alderman, refused to contribute a " benevolence." He
was sent to serve as a soldier in the Scotch wars at his own expense, and the general
was ordered to " use him in all things according to sharp military discipline." The
effect was such that few after that ventured to deny the King what he asked.

[4] Henry is said to have accumulated a fortune of nearly two millions sterling, an
amount which would perhaps represent upwards of $90,000,000 now.

When he summoned a Parliament he obtained grants for putting down some real or pretended insurrection, or to defray the expenses of a threatened attack from abroad, and then quietly pocketed the appropriation, — a device not altogether unknown to modern government officials.

A third and last method for getting funds was invented in Henry's behalf by two lawyers, Empson and Dudley, who were so rapacious and cut so close that they were commonly known as " the King's skin shearers." They went about the country enforcing old and forgotten laws, by which they reaped a rich harvest.

Their chief instrument for gain, however, was a revival of the Statute of Liveries. This law imposed enormous fines on those noblemen who dared to equip their followers in military garb, or designate them by a badge equivalent to it, as had been their custom during the late civil wars (§ 296).

In order to thoroughly enforce the Statute of Liveries, Henry organized the Court of Star Chamber, so called from the starred ceiling where the tribunal met. This court had for its object the punishment of such crimes committed by the great families, or their adherents, as the ordinary law courts could not, or through intimidation dared not, deal with. It had no power to inflict death, but might impose long terms of imprisonment and ruinous fines. It, too, first made use of torture in England to extort confessions of guilt.

Henry seemed to have enforced the Law of Livery against friend and foe alike. Said the King to the Earl of Oxford, as he left his castle, where a large number of retainers in uniform were drawn up to do him honor, " My lord, I thank you for your entertainment, but my attorney must speak to you." The attorney, who was the notorious Empson, brought suit in the Star Chamber against the Earl, who was fined fifteen thousand marks, or something like $750,000, for the incautious display he had made.

331. The Introduction of Artillery strengthens the Power of the King. It was easier for Henry to pursue this arbitrary course because the introduction of artillery had changed the art of war. Throughout the Middle Ages the call of a great baron had, as Macaulay says, been sufficient to raise a formidable revolt. Countrymen and followers took down their tough yew long bows from the chimney corner, knights buckled on their steel armor, mounted their horses, and in a few days an army threatened the holder of the throne, who had no troops save those furnished by loyal subjects.

But since then, men had " digged villainous saltpeter out of the bowels of the harmless earth " to manufacture powder, and others had invented cannon (§ 239), " those devilish iron engines," as the poet Spenser called them, " ordained to kill." Without artillery, the old feudal army, with its bows, swords, and battle-axes, could do little against a king like Henry, who had it. For this reason the whole kingdom lay at his mercy ; and though the nobles and the rich might groan, they saw that it was useless to fight.

332. The Pretenders Symnel and Warbeck. During Henry's reign, two pretenders laid claim to the crown : Lambert Symnel, who represented himself to be Edward Plantagenet, nephew of the late King; and Perkin Warbeck, who asserted that he was Richard, Duke of York (§ 310), who had been murdered in the Tower by his uncle, Richard III. Symnel's attempt was easily suppressed, and he commuted his claim to the crown for the position of scullion in the King's kitchen.

Warbeck kept the kingdom in a turmoil for more than five years, during which time one hundred and fifty of his adherents were executed, and their bodies exposed on gibbets along the south coast of England to deter their master's French supporters from landing. At length Warbeck was captured, imprisoned, and finally hanged at Tyburn.

333. Henry's Politic Marriages. Henry accomplished more by the marriages of his children and by diplomacy than other monarchs had by their wars. He gave his daughter Margaret to King James IV of Scotland, and thus prepared the way for the union of the two kingdoms in 1603. He married his eldest son, Prince Arthur, to Catharine of Aragon, daughter of the King of Spain, by which he secured a very large marriage portion for the Prince, and, what was of equal importance, the alliance of Spain against France.

Arthur died soon afterward, and the King got a dispensation from the Pope, granting him permission to marry his younger son Henry to Arthur's widow. It was this Prince who eventually became King of England, with the title of Henry VIII, and we shall hereafter see that this marriage was destined by its results to change the whole course of the country's history.

334. The World as known at Henry's Accession (1485). The King also took some small part in certain other events, which seemed to him, at the time, of less consequence than these matrimonial alliances. But history has regarded them in a different light from that in which the cunning and cautious monarch considered them.

A glance at the map (opposite) will show how different our world is from that with which the English were acquainted when Henry was crowned. Then the earth was generally supposed to be a flat body surrounded by the ocean. The only countries of which anything was certainly known, with the exception of Europe, were parts of western Asia, together with a narrow strip of the northern, eastern, and western coasts of Africa. The knowledge which had once existed of India, China, and Japan appears to have died out in great measure with the travelers and merchants of earlier times who had brought it. The land farthest west of which anything was then known was Iceland.

335. First Voyages of Exploration; the Cabots, 1497. About the time of Henry's accession a new spirit of exploration sprang up. The Portuguese had coasted along the western shores of Africa as far as the Gulf of Guinea, and had established trading posts there. Later, they reached and doubled the Cape of Good Hope (1487). Stimulated by what they had done, Columbus, who believed the earth to be round, determined to sail westward in the hope of reaching the Indies. In 1492 he made his first voyage, and discovered a number of the West India Islands.

Five years afterward John Cabot, a Venetian residing in Bristol, England, with his son Sebastian, persuaded the King to aid them in a similar undertaking. They sailed from that port. On a map drawn by the father after his return we read the following lines : " In the year of our Lord 1497, John Cabot and his son Sebastian discovered that country which no one before his time had ventured to approach, on the 24th June, about 5 o'clock in the morning." That entry is supposed to record the discovery of Cape Breton

THE WORLD SHORTLY AFTER THE ACCESSION OF HENRY VII

Light arrows show voyages southward made up to 1492. Light track, Da Gama's voyage, 1497. Dark arrows, voyages of Columbus and Cabot. White crosses, countries of which something was known before 1492. White area, including western coast of Africa, the world as known shortly after Henry VII's accession

Island; a few days later they set foot on the mainland. This made the Cabots the first discoverers of the American *Continent*.

As an offset to that record we have the following, taken from the King's private account book: "10. Aug. 1497, To him that found the new isle £10."

Such was the humble beginning of a series of explorations which gave England possession of the largest part of North America.

336. Henry VII's Reign the Beginning of a New Epoch. A few years after Cabot's return Henry laid the corner stone of that "solemn and sumptuous chapel" which bears his own name, and which joins Westminster Abbey on the east. There he gave orders that his tomb should be erected, and that prayers should be said over it "as long as the world lasted."

Emerson remarks in his "English Traits" that when the visitor to the Abbey mounts the flight of twelve black marble steps which lead from it to the edifice where Henry lies buried, he passes from the medieval to the beginning of the modern age, — a change which the different style of architecture distinctly marks (§ 324).

The true significance of Henry's reign is, that it, in like manner, stands for a new epoch, — new in modes of government, in law, in geographical discovery, in letters, art, and religion.

The century just closing was indeed one of the most remarkable in history, not only in what it had actually accomplished, but still more in the seed it was sowing for the future. The celebrated German artist Kaulbach, in his fresco of "The Age of the Reformation," has summed up all that it was, and all that it was destined to become in its full development.

Therein we see it as the period which witnessed the introduction of firearms, and the consequent overthrow of feudal warfare and feudal institutions; the growth of the power of royalty and of nationality through royalty; the sailing of Columbus and of Cabot; the revival of classical learning; the publication of the first printed book; and finally, the birth of Martin Luther, the monk who broke away from the Catholic Church, and persuaded many people to become Protestants.

337. Summary. Looking back, we find that with Henry VII the absolutism of the Crown, or "personal monarchy," began in

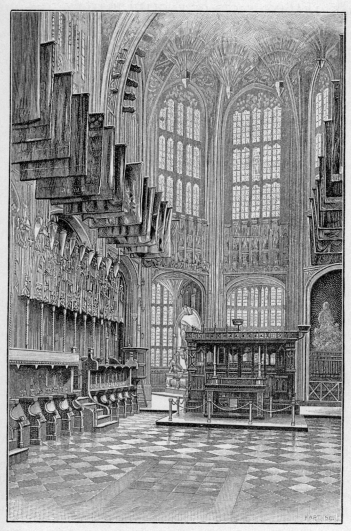

HENRY VII'S CHAPEL

Westminster Abbey

187

England. Yet the repressive power of that "personal monarchy" procured a prolonged peace for the English people and, despite "benevolences" and other exactions, they grew into stronger national unity.

Simultaneously with this increase of royal authority came the discovery of a "New World," in which England and her colonies were to have the chief part. A century will elapse before those discoveries begin to bear fruit. After that, our attention will no longer be confined to the British Islands, but will be fixed as well on that western continent where English enterprise and English love of liberty were destined to find a new and broader field of activity.

HENRY VIII — 1509-1547

338. Henry's Advantages. Henry VIII was not quite eighteen when he came to the throne. The country was at peace, was fairly prosperous, and the young King had everything in his favor. He was handsome, well educated, and fond of athletic sports. His frank disposition won friends everywhere, and he had inherited from his father the largest private fortune that had ever descended to an English sovereign. Intellectually, he was in hearty sympathy with the revival of learning, then in progress both on the Continent and in England.

339. The New Learning; Colet, Erasmus, More. During the greater part of the Middle Ages the chief object of education was to make men monks, and originally the schools established at Oxford and Cambridge were exclusively for that purpose. In their day they did excellent work; but a time came when men ceased to found monasteries, and began to erect colleges and hospitals instead.[1]

In the course of the fourteenth and fifteenth centuries William of Wykeham and King Henry VI built and endowed colleges which were specially designed to fit their pupils to live in the world and serve the state, instead of withdrawing from it to seek their own salvation.

---

[1] In the twelfth century four hundred and eighteen monasteries were founded in England; in the next century, only about a third as many; in the fourteenth, only twenty-three; after that date their establishment may be said to cease.

These new institutions encouraged a broader range of studies, and in Henry VI's time particular attention was given to the Latin classics, hitherto but little known. The geographical discoveries of Henry VII's reign, made by Columbus, Cabot, and others (§ 335), began to stimulate scientific thought. It was evident that the day was not far distant when questions about the earth and the stars would no longer be settled by a text from Scripture which forbade further inquiry.

With the accession of Henry VIII education received a still further impulse. A few zealous English scholars had just returned from Italy to Oxford, full of ardor for a new study, — that of Greek. Among them was a young clergyman named John Colet. He saw that by means of that language, of which the alphabet was as yet hardly known in England, men might put themselves in direct communication with the greatest thinkers and writers of the past.

Better still, they might acquire the power of reading the Gospels and the writings of St. Paul in the original, and thus reach their true meaning and feel their full influence. Colet's intimate friend and fellow worker, the Dutch scholar Erasmus, had the same enthusiasm. When in sore need of everything, he wrote in one of his letters, "As soon as I get some money I shall buy Greek books, and then I may buy some clothes." The third young man, who, with Erasmus and Colet, devoted himself to the study of Greek and to the advancement of learning, was Thomas More, who later became Lord Chancellor (§§ 145, 351).

The three looked to King Henry for encouragement in the work they had undertaken; nor did they look in vain. Colet, who had become a doctor of divinity and a dean of St. Paul's Cathedral, London, encountered a furious storm of opposition on account of his devotion to the "New Learning," as it was sneeringly called. His attempts at educational reform met the same resistance.

But Henry liked the man's resolute spirit, and said, "Let others have what doctors they will; this is the doctor for me." The King also took a lively interest in Erasmus, who was appointed professor of Greek at Cambridge, where he began his great work of preparing an edition of the Greek Testament with a Latin translation in parallel columns.

Up to this time the Greek Testament had existed in scattered manuscripts only. The publication of the work in printed form gave an additional impetus to the study of the Scriptures, helped forward the Reformation, and in a measure laid the foundation for a revised English translation of the Bible far superior to Wycliffe's (§ 254). In the same spirit of genuine love of learning, Henry founded Trinity College, Cambridge, and at a later date confirmed and extended Cardinal Wolsey's endowment of Christ Church College, Oxford.

340. Henry against Luther. The King continued, however, to be a stanch Catholic, and certainly had no thought at this period of doing anything which should tend to undermine the authority of that ancient form of worship. In Germany, Martin Luther was making ready to begin his tremendous battle against the power and teachings of the Papacy. In 1517 he nailed to the door of the church of Wittenberg that famous series of denunciations which started the movement that ultimately protested against the authority of Rome, and gave the name of Protestant to all who joined it.

A few years later Henry published a reply to one of Luther's books, and sent a copy bound in cloth of gold to the Pope. The Pope was so delighted with what he termed Henry's "angelic spirit" that he forthwith conferred on him the title of "Defender of the Faith." The English sovereigns have persisted in retaining this title to the present time, though for what reason, and with what right, even a royal intellect might be somewhat puzzled to explain.

With this new and flattering title the Pope also sent the King a costly two-handed sword, intended to represent Henry's zeal in smiting the enemies of Rome. But it was destined by fate to become the symbol of the King's final separation from the power that bestowed it (§ 349).

341. Victory of Flodden (1513); "Field of the Cloth of Gold"[1] (1520). Politically, Henry was equally fortunate. The Scotch had ventured to attack the kingdom during the King's absence on the Continent. At Flodden, on the borders of Scotland and England, they were defeated by the Earl of Surrey, with great slaughter. (See map facing p. 120.) This victory placed Scotland at Henry's feet.

[1] See Scott's "Marmion."

The King of France and the Emperor Charles V of Germany now vied with each other in seeking Henry's alliance. The Emperor visited England in order to meet the English sovereign, while the King of France arranged an interview in his own dominions, known, from the magnificence of its appointments, as the "Field of the Cloth of Gold." Henry held the balance of power by which he could make France or Germany predominate as he

A TOURNAMENT, "FIELD OF THE CLOTH OF GOLD"

saw fit. It was owing to his able diplomatic policy, or to that of Cardinal Wolsey, his chief counsellor, that England reaped advantages from both sides, and advanced from a comparatively low position to one that was fully abreast of the foremost nations of Europe.

342. Henry's Marriage with his Brother's Widow. Such was the King at the outset. In less than twenty years he had become another man. At the age of twelve he had married at his father's command, and solely for political and mercenary reasons, Catharine of Aragon, his brother Arthur's widow (§ 333), who was six years his senior. Such a marriage was forbidden, except in certain cases, by the Old Testament and by the ordinances of the Roman Catholic Church.

The Pope, however, had granted his permission, and when Henry ascended the throne, the ceremony was performed a second time. Several children were the fruit of this union, all of whom died in infancy, except one daughter, Mary, unhappily fated to figure as the " Bloody Mary " of later history (§ 374).

343. The King's Anxiety for a Successor ; Anne Boleyn. No woman had yet ruled in her own right, either in England or in any prominent kingdom of Europe, and Henry was anxious to have a son to succeed him. He could not bear the thought of being disappointed ; in fact he sent the Duke of Buckingham to the block for casually saying, that if the King died without issue, he should consider himself entitled to receive the crown.

It was while meditating this question of the succession, that Henry became attached to Anne Boleyn, one of the Queen's maids of honor ; she was a sprightly brunette of nineteen, with long black hair and strikingly beautiful eyes.

The light that shone in those eyes, though hardly that " Gospel light " which the poet calls it,[1] was yet bright enough to effectually clear up all difficulties in the royal mind. The King now declared that he felt conscientiously moved to obtain a divorce from his old wife, and to marry a new one. In that determination lay most momentous consequences, since it finally separated England from the jurisdiction of the Church of Rome.

344. Wolsey favors the Divorce from Catharine. Cardinal Wolsey, Henry's chief counselor, — the man who thought that he ruled both King and Kingdom,[2] — lent his powerful aid to bring about the divorce, but with the expectation that the King would marry a princess of France, and thus form an alliance with that

---

[1] " When love could teach a monarch to be wise,
    And Gospel light first dawned from Bullen's [Boleyn's] eyes." — GRAY.

[2] The Venetian ambassador in a despatch to his government, wrote of Cardinal Wolsey : " It is he who rules both the King and the entire Kingdom. At first the Cardinal used to say, ' *His Majesty will do so and so* ' ; subsequently he went on, forgetting himself, and commenced saying, ' *We shall do so and so* ' ; at present (1519) he has reached such a pitch that he says, ' *I shall do so and so.* ' "

country. If so, his own ambitious schemes would be forwarded, since the united influence of the two kingdoms might elevate him to the Papacy.

When Wolsey learned that the King's choice was Anne Boleyn (§ 343), he fell on his knees, and begged him not to persist in his purpose; but his entreaties had no effect, and the Cardinal was obliged to continue what he had begun.

345. The Court at Blackfriars (1529). The King had applied to the Pope to annul the marriage with Catharine (§ 342) on the ground of illegality; but the Emperor Charles V, who was the Queen's nephew, used his influence in her behalf. Vexatious delays now became the order of the day. At last, a court composed of Cardinal Wolsey and Cardinal Campeggio, an Italian, as papal legates, or representatives, was convened at Blackfriars, London, to test the validity of the marriage.

Henry and Catharine were summoned. The first appeared and answered to his name. When the Queen was called she declined to answer, but throwing herself at Henry's feet, begged him with tears and sobs not to put her away without cause. Finding him inflexible, she left the court, and refused to attend again, appealing to Rome for justice.

This was in the spring (1529). Nothing was done that summer, and in the autumn, the court, instead of reaching a decision, dissolved. Campeggio, the Italian legate, returned to Italy, and Henry, to his disappointment and rage, received an order from Rome to carry the question to the Pope for settlement.

346. Fall of Wolsey (1529). Both the King and Anne Boleyn believed that Wolsey had played false with them. They now resolved upon his destruction. The Cardinal had a presentiment of his impending doom. The French ambassador, who saw him at this juncture, said that his face had shrunk to half its size. But his fortunes were destined to shrink even more than his face.

By a law of Richard II no representative of the Pope had any rightful authority in England[1] (§ 265). Though the King had given his consent to Wolsey's holding the office of legate, yet now

---

[1] Act of Præmunire. See § 243 and Summary of Constitutional History in the Appendix, p. xiii, § 14, and p. xxxii.

that a contrary result to what he expected had been reached, he proceeded to prosecute him to the full extent of the law.

It was an easy matter for him to crush the Cardinal. Erasmus said of him, " He was feared by all, he was loved by few — I may say by nobody." His arrogance and extravagant ostentation had excited the jealous hate of the nobility; his constant demands for money in behalf of the King had set Parliament against him; and his exactions from the common people had, as the chronicle of the time tells us, made them weep, beg, and " speak cursedly."

Wolsey bowed to the storm, and to save himself gave up everything; his riches, pomp, power, all vanished as suddenly as they had come. It was Henry's hand that stripped him, but it was Anne Boleyn who moved that hand. Well might the humbled favorite say of her:

> " There was the weight that pulled me down.
> . . . all my glories
> In that one woman I have lost forever." [1]

Thus deprived of well-nigh everything but life, the Cardinal was permitted to go into retirement in the north; less than a twelve-month later he was arrested on a charge of high treason. Through the irony of fate, the warrant was served by a former lover of Anne Boleyn's, whom Wolsey, it is said, had separated from her in order that she might consummate her unhappy marriage with royalty. On the way to London Wolsey fell mortally ill, and turned aside at Leicester to die in the abbey there, with the words:

> " . . . O, Father Abbot,
> An old man, broken with the storms of state,
> Is come to lay his weary bones among ye:
> Give him a little earth for charity ! " [2]

347. Appeal to the Universities. Before Wolsey's death, Dr. Thomas Cranmer, of Cambridge, suggested that the King lay the divorce question before the universities of Europe. Henry caught eagerly at this proposition, and exclaimed, " Cranmer has the right pig by the ear." The scheme was at once adopted.

---

1 Shakespeare's " Henry VIII," Act III, scene ii.
2 Shakespeare's " Henry VIII," Act IV, scene ii.

Several universities returned favorable answers. In a few instances, as at Oxford and Cambridge, where the authorities hesitated, a judicious use of bribes or threats soon brought them to see the matter in a proper light.

348. The Clergy declare Henry Head of the Church, 1531. Armed with these decisions in his favor, Henry now charged the whole body of the English Church with being guilty of the same crime of which Wolsey had been accused (§ 346). The clergy, in their terror, made haste to buy a pardon at a cost reckoned at nearly $5,000,000 at the present value of money.

They furthermore declared Henry to be the supreme head on earth of the Church of England, adroitly adding, " in so far as is permitted by the law of Christ." Thus the Reformation came into England " by a side door, as it were." Nevertheless, it came.

349. Henry marries Anne Boleyn ; Act of Supremacy, 1534. Events now moved rapidly toward a crisis. In 1533, after having waited over five years, Henry privately married Anne Boleyn (§ 343), and she was soon after crowned in Westminster Abbey. When the Pope was informed of this, he ordered the King, under pain of excommunication (§ 194), to put her away, and to take back Queen Catharine (§ 345).

Parliament met that demand by passing the Act of Supremacy, 1534, which declared Henry to be without reservation the sole head of the Church, making denial thereof high treason.[1] As he signed the act, the King with one stroke of his pen overturned the traditions of a thousand years, and England stood boldly forth with a National Church independent of the Pope.[2]

[1] Henry's full title was now " Henry VIII, by the Grace of God, King of England, France, and Ireland, Defender of the Faith and of the Church of England, and also of Ireland, on earth the Supreme Head."

[2] Attention is called to the fact that a controversy, more or less serious in its character, had been going on, at intervals for nearly five hundred years, between the English sovereigns (or the barons) and the popes. It began with William the Conqueror in 1076 (§ 118). It was continued by Henry I (§ 136), by Henry II (§§ 163–170), by John (§ 194), by the barons under Henry III (§ 211), by Edward I (§ 226), and it may be said to have practically culminated under Henry VIII in the Act of Supremacy of 1534 (§ 349). But after the formal establishment of Protestantism by Edward VI in 1549 (§ 362) we find the Act of Supremacy reaffirmed, in slightly different form, by Queen Elizabeth in 1559 (§ 382). Finally, the Revolution of 1688 settled the question (§ 497).

350. Subserviency of Parliament. But as Luther said, Henry had a pope within him. The King now proceeded to prove the truth of Luther's declaration. We have already seen (§ 328) that since the Wars of the Roses had destroyed the power of the barons, there was no effectual check on the despotic will of the sovereign. The new nobility were the creatures of the Crown, hence bound to support it; the clergy were timid, the Commons anything but bold, so that Parliament gradually became the servile echo and ready instrument of the throne.

That body twice released the King from the discharge of his just debts. It even exempted him from paying certain forced loans which he had extorted from his people. Parliament also repeatedly changed the laws of succession to the Crown to please him. Moreover it promptly attainted and destroyed such victims as he desired to put out of the way (§ 351). Later (1539) it declared that proclamations, concerning religious doctrines, when made by the King and Council, should have the force of acts of Parliament. This new power enabled Henry to pronounce heretical many opinions which he disliked and to punish them with death.

351. Execution of More and Fisher (1535). Thomas Cromwell had been Cardinal Wolsey's private secretary; but he had now become chief counselor to the King, and in his crooked and cruel policy reduced bloodshed to a science. He first introduced the practice of condemning an accused prisoner without any form of trial (by Act of Attainder), and sending him to the block [1] without allowing him to speak in his own defense (§ 356). No one was now safe who did not openly side with the King.

Sir Thomas More, who had been Lord Chancellor (§ 339), and the aged Bishop Fisher were executed because they could not affirm that they conscientiously believed that Henry was morally and spiritually entitled to be the head of the English Church (§ 349).

Both died with Christian fortitude. More said to the governor of the Tower with a flash of his old humor, as the steps leading to the scaffold shook while he was mounting them, "Do you see me safe up, and I will make shift to get down by myself."

[1] Act of Attainder. See Constitutional Documents in Appendix, p. xxxii.

352. Destruction of the Monasteries ; Seizure of their Property, 1536–1539. When the intelligence of the judicial murder of the venerable ex-chancellor reached Rome, the Pope issued a bull of excommunication and deposition against Henry (§ 194). It delivered his soul to Satan, and his kingdom to the first invader.

The King retaliated by the suppression of the monasteries. In doing so, he simply hastened a process which had already begun. Years before, Cardinal Wolsey had not scrupled to shut up several, and take their revenues to found Christ Church College at Oxford. The truth was, that, in most cases, monasticism "was dead long before the Reformation came to bury it" (§ 339, note 1). It was dead because it had done its work, — in many respects a great and good work, which the world could ill have spared (§§ 43, 45, 46, 60). The monasteries simply shared the fate of all human institutions, however excellent they may be.

> "Our little systems have their day ;
> They have their day and cease to be :
> They are but broken lights of Thee,
> And Thou, O Lord, art more than they."[1]

Henry, however, had no such worthy object as Wolsey had. His pretext was that these institutions had sunk into a state of ignorance, drunkenness, and profligacy. This may have been true of some of the smaller monasteries, though not of the large ones. But the vices of the monasteries the King had already made his own. It was their wealth which he now coveted. The smaller religious houses were speedily swept out of existence (1536). This caused a furious insurrection in the North, called the "Pilgrimage of Grace" (1537); but the revolt was soon put down.

Though Parliament had readily given its sanction to the extinction of the smaller monasteries, it hesitated about abolishing the greater ones. Henry, it is reported, sent for a leading member of the House of Commons, and, laying his hand on the head of the kneeling representative, said, "Get my bill passed by to-morrow, little man, or else to-morrow this head of yours will come off." The next day the bill passed, and the work of destruction began

[1] Tennyson's "In Memoriam."

anew (1539). Property worth millions of pounds was confiscated, and abbots like those of Glastonbury and Charter House, who dared to resist, were speedily hanged.[1]

The magnificent monastic buildings throughout England were now stripped of everything of value, and left as ruins. (See map opposite.) The beautiful windows of stained glass were wantonly broken; the images of the saints were cast down from their niches; the chimes of bells were melted and cast into cannon; while the valuable libraries were torn up and sold to grocers and soap boilers for wrapping paper.

At Canterbury, Becket's tomb (§ 170) was broken open, and after he had been nearly four centuries in his grave, the saint was summoned to answer a charge of rebellion and treason. The case was tried at Westminster Abbey, the martyr's bones were sentenced to be burned, and the jewels and rich offerings of his shrine were seized by the King.

Among the few monastic buildings which escaped was the beautiful abbey church, now the cathedral of Peterborough, where Catharine of Aragon (§ 345), who died soon after the King's marriage with her rival, was buried. Henry had the grace to give orders that on her account it should be spared, saying that he would leave to her memory "one of the goodliest monuments in Christendom."

The great estates thus suddenly acquired by the Crown were granted to favorites or thrown away at the gambling table. "It is from this date," says Hallam, "that the leading families of England, both within and without the peerage, became conspicuous through having obtained possession of the monastery lands." These were estimated to comprise about one fourth of the whole area of the kingdom.

353. Effects of the Destruction of the Monasteries. The sweeping character of this act had a twofold effect. First, it made the King more absolute than before, for, since it removed the abbots, who had held seats in the House of Lords, that body was made just so much smaller and less able to resist the royal will.

---

[1] The total number of religious houses destroyed was 645 monasteries, 2374 chapels, 90 collegiate churches, and 110 charitable institutions. Among the most famous of these ruins are Glastonbury, Kirkstall, Furness, Netley, Tintern, and Fountains abbeys.

PRINCIPAL MONASTERIES DESTROYED BY HENRY VIII

Next, the abolition of so many religious institutions necessarily caused much misery, for the greater part of the monks and all of the nuns were turned out upon the world destitute of means. In the end, however, no permanent injury was done, since the monasteries, by their profuse and indiscriminate charity, had undoubtedly encouraged much of the very pauperism which they had relieved.

354. Distress among the Laboring Classes. An industrial revolution was also in progress at this time, which was productive of widespread suffering. It had begun early in Henry's reign through the great numbers of discharged soldiers, who could not readily find work.

Sir Thomas More had given a striking picture of their miserable condition in his " Utopia," a book in which he urged the government to consider measures for their relief; but the evil had since become much worse. Farmers, having discovered that wool growing was more profitable than the raising of grain, had turned their fields into sheep pastures; so that a shepherd with his dog now took the place of several families of laborers.

This change brought multitudes of poor people to the verge of starvation; and as the monasteries no longer existed to hold out a helping hand, the whole realm was overrun with beggars and thieves. Bishop Latimer, a noted preacher of that day, declared that if every farmer should raise two acres of hemp, it would not make rope enough to hang them all. Henry, however, set to work with characteristic vigor and made away, it is said, with great numbers, but without materially abating the evil (§ 403).

355. Execution of Anne Boleyn; Marriage with Jane Seymour (1536). Less than three years after her coronation, the new Queen, Anne Boleyn (§§ 343, 349), for whom Henry had " turned England and Europe upside down," was accused of unfaithfulness. She was sent a prisoner to the Tower. A short time after, her head rolled in the dust, the light of its beauty gone out forever.

The next morning Henry married Jane Seymour, Anne's maid of honor. Parliament passed an act of approval, declaring that it was all done " of the King's most excellent goodness." It also declared Henry's two previous marriages, with Catharine and with Anne Boleyn, void, and affirmed that their children, the Princesses

Mary and Elizabeth, were not lawfully the King's daughters. A later act of Parliament gave Henry the extraordinary power of naming his successor to the crown.[1] A year afterwards Henry's new Queen died, leaving an infant son, Edward. She was no sooner gone than the King began looking about for some one to take her place.

356. More Marriages (1540). Thomas Cromwell, the King's trusted adviser (§ 351), succeeded in persuading his master to agree to marry Anne of Cleves, a German Protestant Princess. Henry had never seen her, but her portrait represented her as a woman of surpassing beauty.

When Anne reached England, Henry hurried to meet her with all a lover's ardor. To his dismay, he found that not only was she ridiculously ugly, but that she could speak — so he said — "nothing but Dutch," of which he did not understand a word. Matters, however, had gone too far to retract, and the marriage was duly solemnized (1540). The King obtained a divorce within six months, and then took his revenge by cutting off Cromwell's head. What is more, he cut it off by virtue of that very Act of Attainder which Cromwell had used so unscrupulously in Henry's behalf (§ 351).

The same year (1540) Henry married Catharine Howard, a fascinating girl still in her teens, whose charms so moved the King that it is said he was tempted to have a special thanksgiving service prepared to commemorate the day he found her.

Unfortunately, Catharine was accused of having been guilty of misconduct before her marriage. She confessed her fault, but for such cases Henry had no mercy. The Queen was tried for high treason, and soon walked that fatal road in which Anne Boleyn had preceded her (§ 355).

Not to be baffled in his matrimonial experiments, the King took Catherine Parr for his sixth and last wife (1543). She was inclined to be a zealous Protestant, and she too might have gone to the

---

[1] By his last will he made Mary and Elizabeth heirs to the crown in case all male and female issue by himself or his son Edward failed (§ 361). Henry's eldest sister, Margaret (see No. 3 in Genealogical Table on page 207), was passed by entirely. But long after Henry's death, Parliament set his will aside (1603) and made James I (a descendant of Margaret) King of England.

block, on a charge of heresy, but her quick wit came to her rescue. She flattered the King's self-conceit as a profound theologian and the compliment saved her life.

357. Henry's Action respecting Religion. Though occupied with these rather numerous domestic infelicities, Henry was not idle in other directions. By an act known as the Six Articles, or, as the Protestants called it, the " Bloody Act," or the " Whip with Six Lashes " (1539), the King established a new and peculiar form of religion. In words, at least, it seemed to be practically the same as that upheld by the Pope, but with the Pope left out.[1]

Geographically, the country was about equally divided between Catholicism and Protestantism. The northwestern half clung to the ancient faith; the southeastern half, including most of the large cities where Wycliffe's doctrines had formerly prevailed, was favorable to the Reformation.

On the one hand, Henry prohibited the Lutheran or Protestant doctrine (§ 340); on the other, he caused the Bible to be translated (§§ 254, 339), and ordered a copy to be chained to a desk in every parish church in England (1538); but though all persons might now freely read the Scriptures, no one but the clergy was allowed to interpret them. Later in his reign, the King became alarmed at the spread of discussion about religious subjects, and prohibited the reading of the Bible by the " lower sort of people."

358. Heresy *versus* Treason. Men now found themselves in a strange and cruel dilemma. If it was dangerous to believe too much, it was equally dangerous to believe too little. Traitor and heretic were dragged to execution on the same hurdle ; for Henry burned as heretics those who declared their belief in Protestantism, and hanged or beheaded, as traitors, those who acknowledged the authority of the Pope and denied the supremacy of the King (§ 349).

Thus Anne Askew, a young and beautiful woman, was nearly wrenched asunder on the rack, in the hope of making her implicate the Queen in her heresy. She was afterward burned because

[1] The Six Articles : The chief article ordered that all persons who denied the Catholic doctrine of transubstantiation should be burned at the stake as heretics and that all their possessions should be forfeited to the Crown. The remaining five articles affirmed the obligation of all persons to accept and obey certain other Catholic doctrines under pain of punishment for felony, if they refused.

she insisted that the bread and wine used in the communion service seemed to her to be simply bread and wine, and not in any
sense the actual body and blood of Christ, as the King's statute
of the Six Articles (§ 357) solemnly declared.

On the other hand, the aged Countess of Salisbury suffered for
treason ; but with a spirit matching the King's, she refused to
kneel at the block, and told the executioner he must get her gray
head off as best he could.

359. Henry's Death. But the time was at hand when Henry
was to cease his hangings, beheadings, and marriages. Worn out
with debauchery, he died at the age of fifty-six, a loathsome, unwieldy, and helpless mass of corruption. In his will he left a large
sum of money to pay for perpetual prayers for the repose of his
soul. Sir Walter Raleigh said of him, "If all the pictures and
patterns of a merciless prince were lost in the world, they might
all again be painted to the life out of the story of this king."

It may be well to remember this, and along with it this other
saying of one of the ablest writers on English constitutional history, that "the world owes some of its greatest debts to men from
whose memory it recoils." [1] The obligation it is under to Henry
VIII is that through his influence — no matter what the motive —
England was lifted up out of the old medieval ruts, and placed
squarely and securely on the new highway of national progress.

360. Summary. In this reign we find that though England
lost much of her former political freedom, yet she gained that
order and peace which came from the iron hand of absolute power.
Next, from the destruction of the monasteries, and the sale or gift
of their lands to favorites of the King, three results ensued :

1. A new nobility was in great measure created, dependent on
the Crown.

2. The House of Lords was made less powerful by the removal
of the abbots who had had seats in it.

3. Pauperism and distress were temporarily increased.

4. Finally, England completely severed her connection with the
Pope, and established for the first time an independent National
Church, having the King as its head.

[1] W. Stubbs's "Constitutional History of England."

361. Bad Government; Seizure of Unenclosed Lands; High Rents; Latimer's Sermon. Edward, son of Henry VIII by Jane Seymour (§ 355), died at sixteen. In the first part of his reign of six years the government was managed by his uncle, the Duke of Somerset, an extreme Protestant, whose intentions were good, but who lacked practical judgment. During the latter part of his life Edward fell under the control of the Duke of Northumberland, who was the head of a band of scheming and profligate men.

They, with other nobles, seized the unenclosed lands of the country and fenced them in for sheep pastures, thus driving into beggary many who had formerly got a good part of their living from these commons. At the same time farm rents rose in some cases ten and even twenty fold,[1] depriving thousands of the means of subsistence, and reducing to poverty many who had been in comfortable circumstances.

The bitter complaints of the sufferers found expression in Bishop Latimer's outspoken sermon, preached before King Edward, in which he said : " My father was a yeoman [small farmer], and had no lands of his own, only he had a farm of three or four pounds [rent] by year, and hereupon tilled so much as kept half a dozen men ; he had walk [pasture] for a hundred sheep, and my mother milked thirty kine.

" He was able and did find the King a harness [suit of armor] with himself and his horse, until he came to the place where he should receive the King's wages. I can remember that I buckled his harness when he went into Blackheath Field. He kept me to school, or else I had not been able to have preached before the King's majesty now. He married my sisters with five pounds [dower] . . . apiece. He kept hospitality for his poor neighbors, and some alms he gave to the poor.

" And all this he did off the said farm, where he that now hath it payeth sixteen pounds a year or more, and is not able to do anything for his prince, for himself, nor for his children, or give a cup of drink

---

[1] This was owing to the greed for land on the part of the mercantile classes, who had now acquired wealth, and wished to become landed proprietors. See Froude's " England."

to the poor." But as Latimer pathetically said, " Let the preacher preach till his tongue be worn to the stumps, nothing is amended." [1]

362. Edward establishes Protestantism, 1549. Henry VIII had made the Church of England independent of the Pope (§ 349). His son took the next great step, and made it practically Protestant in doctrine. At his desire, Archbishop Cranmer compiled a book of Common Prayer in English. It was taken largely from the Roman Catholic Prayer Book, which was in Latin (1549). The first Act of Uniformity, 1549 (reënacted 1552), obliged all churches to use the new English Prayer Book, thereby (for the time) establishing a modified form of Protestantism throughout England (§ 405).[2]

Edward's sister, the Princess Mary, was a most devout Catholic. She refused to adopt the new service, saying to Bishop Ridley, who urged her to accept it as God's word, " I cannot tell what you call God's word, for that is not God's word now which was God's word in my father's time." It was at this period (1552) that the Articles of Religion of the Church of England were first drawn up ; but they did not take their final form until the reign of Elizabeth (§ 383).

363. King Edward and Mary Stuart. Henry VIII had attempted to marry his son Edward to young Queen Mary Stuart, daughter of the King of Scotland, but the match had been broken off. Edward's guardian now insisted that it should be carried out. He invaded Scotland with an army, and attempted to effect the marriage by force of arms, at the battle of Pinkie (1547).

The English gained a decided victory, but the youthful Queen, instead of giving her hand to young King Edward, left the country and married the son of the King of France. She will appear with melancholy prominence in the reign of Elizabeth. Had Mary Queen of Scots married Edward, we should perhaps have been spared that tragedy in which she was called to play both the leading and the losing part (§§ 394–397).

364. Renewed Confiscation of Church Property; Schools founded. The confiscation of such Roman Catholic church property as had been spared was now renewed (§ 352). The result of this confiscation and of the abandonment of Catholicism as the established form of

---

[1] Latimer's first sermon before King Edward VI, 8th of March, 1549.
[2] On the Church of England, see Macaulay's " England," I, 40–42.

worship was in certain respects disastrous to the country. In the general break-up, many who had been held in restraint by the old form of faith now went to the other extreme, and rejected all religion.

Part of the money obtained from the sale of church property was devoted, mainly through Edward's influence, to the endowment of upwards of forty grammar schools, besides a number of hospitals, in different sections of the country. But for a long time the destruction of the monastic schools (§§ 45, 60), poor as many of them had become, was a serious blow to the education of the common people.

365. Edward's London Charities ; Christ's Hospital. Just before his death Edward established Christ's Hospital, or home for the support and education of fatherless children, and refounded and renewed the St. Thomas and St. Bartholomew hospitals for the sick in London. Thus " he was the founder," says Burnet, "of those houses which, by many great additions since that time, have risen to be amongst the noblest of Europe."

Christ's Hospital was, perhaps, the first Protestant charity school opened in England; many more were patterned on it. It, and others like it, are known as " Blue-Coat Schools," from the costume of the boys, — a relic of the days of Edward VI. This consists of a long, blue coat, like a monk's gown, reaching to the ankles, girded with a broad leather belt, long, bright yellow stockings, and buckle shoes. Most of the boys go bareheaded winter and summer.

An exciting game of football, played in the schoolyard in this peculiar medieval dress, used to seem strangely in contrast with the sights of modern London streets. It was as through the spectator, by passing through a gateway, had gone back over three centuries of time. Coleridge, Lamb, and other noted men of letters were educated there, and have left most interesting reminiscences of their school life, especially Lamb, in his delightful " Essays of Elia." Late in the nineteenth century this famous institution was removed to the country, and part of the site of the ancient school is now covered with a great business structure.

366. Effect of Catholicism *versus* Protestantism. Speaking of the Protestant Reformation, of which Edward VI may be taken as a representative, Macaulay remarks that " it is difficult to say whether England received most advantage from the Roman Catholic religion or from the Reformation. " For the union of the Saxon and Norman races, and the abolition of slavery, she is chiefly indebted to the influence which the priesthood in the Middle Ages exercised over the people " (§ 47); " for political and intellectual freedom, and for all the blessings which they have brought in their train, she owes most to the great rebellion of the people against the priesthood."

367. Summary. The establishment of the Protestant faith in England, and of a large number of Protestant charity schools known as Edward VI's or " Blue-Coat Schools " may be regarded as the leading events of Edward's brief reign of six years.

MARY—1553–1558

368. Lady Jane Grey claims the Crown. On the death of King Edward, Lady Jane Grey, a descendant of Henry VII, and a relative of Edward VI, was persuaded by her father-in-law, the Duke of Northumberland, to assume the crown, which had been left to her by the will of the late King.

Edward's object in naming Lady Jane was to secure a Protestant successor, since his elder sister, Mary, was a zealous Catholic, while from his younger sister, Elizabeth, he seems to have been estranged. By birth, though not directly by Henry VIII's will, Mary was without doubt the rightful heir.[1] Queen Mary received

[1] Table showing the respective claims of Queen Mary and Lady Jane Grey to the crown. By his last will Henry VIII left the crown to Edward VI, and (in case he had no issue) to his daughters, Mary and Elizabeth, followed by the issue of his sister Mary. Edward VI's will undertook to change this order of succession.

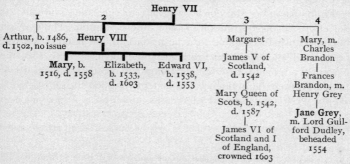

Henry VII

1	2	3	4
Arthur, b. 1486, d. 1502, no issue	Henry VIII	Margaret	Mary, m. Charles Brandon
	Mary, b. 1516, d. 1558 / Elizabeth, b. 1533, d. 1603 / Edward VI, b. 1538, d. 1553	James V of Scotland, d. 1542	Frances Brandon, m. Henry Grey
		Mary Queen of Scots, b. 1542, d. 1587	Jane Grey, m. Lord Guilford Dudley, beheaded 1554
		James VI of Scotland and I of England, crowned 1603	

the support of the country, and Lady Jane Grey and her husband, Lord Dudley, were arrested and sent to the Tower of London.

369. Question of Mary's Marriage; Wyatt's Rebellion (1554). While they were confined there, the question of the Queen's marriage came up. Out of several candidates for her hand, Mary gave preference to her cousin, Philip II of Spain. Her choice was very unpopular, for it was known in England that Philip was a selfish and gloomy fanatic, who cared for nothing but the advancement of the Roman Catholic faith.

An insurrection now broke out, led by Sir Thomas Wyatt, the object of which was to place the Princess Elizabeth on the throne, and thus secure the crown to Protestantism. Lady Jane Grey's father was implicated in the rebellion. The movement ended in failure, the leaders were executed, and Mary ordered her sister Elizabeth, who was thought to be in the plot, to be seized and imprisoned in the Tower (1554).

A little later, Lady Jane Grey and her husband perished on the scaffold. The name JANE, deeply cut in the stone wall of the Beauchamp Tower,[1] remains as a memorial of the nine days' Queen. She died at the age of seventeen, an innocent victim of the greatness which had been thrust upon her.

370. Mary marries Philip II of Spain (1554); Efforts to restore Catholicism. A few months afterward the royal marriage was celebrated, but Philip soon found that the air of England had too much freedom in it to suit his delicate constitution, and he returned to the more congenial climate of Spain.

From that time Mary, who was left to rule alone, directed all her efforts to the restoration of the Catholic Church. Hallam says her policy was acceptable to a large part of the nation.[2] On the other hand, the leaders in Scotland bound themselves by a solemn Covenant (1557) to crush out all attempts to reëstablish the Catholic faith. Through her influence Parliament repealed the legislation of Henry VIII's and Edward VI's reigns, in so far as it gave support

---

[1] The Beauchamp Tower is part of the Tower of London. On its walls are scores of names cut by those who were imprisoned in it.

[2] See A. H. Hallam's "Constitutional History of England," and compare J. Lingard's excellent "History of England," to the same effect.

to Protestantism. She revived the persecuting statutes against heretics (§ 283). The old relations with the Pope were resumed but the monastic lands were left in the hands of their new owners (§ 352). To accomplish her object in supporting her religion, the Queen resorted to the arguments of the dungeon, the rack, and the fagot, and when Bishops Bonner and Gardiner slackened their work of persecution and death, Mary, half crazed by Philip's desertion, urged them not to stay their hands.

371. Devices for reading the Bible. The penalty for reading the English Scriptures, or for offering Protestant prayers, was death. In his autobiography, Benjamin Franklin says that one of his ancestors, who lived in England in Mary's reign, adopted the following expedient for giving his family religious instruction. He fastened an open Bible with strips of tape on the under side of a stool. When he wished to read it aloud he placed the stool upside down on his knees, and turned the pages under the tape as he read them. One of the children stood watching at the door to give the alarm if any one approached; in that case, the stool was set quickly on its feet again on the floor, so that nothing could be seen.

372. Religious Toleration unknown in Mary's Age. Mary would doubtless have bravely endured for her faith the full measure of suffering which she inflicted. Her state of mind was that of all who then held strong convictions. Each party believed it a duty to convert or exterminate the other, and the alternative offered to the heretic was to " turn or burn."

Sir Thomas More, who gave his life as a sacrifice to conscience in Henry's reign (§ 351), was eager to put Tyndale to the torture for translating the Bible. Cranmer (§ 362), who perished at Oxford (1556), had been zealous in sending to the flames those who differed from him. Even Latimer (§ 361), who died bravely at the stake, exhorting his companion Ridley (1555) " to be of good cheer and play the man, since they would light such a candle in England that day as in God's grace should not be put out," had abetted the kindling of slow fires under men as honest and determined as himself but on the opposite side.

In like spirit Queen Mary kept Smithfield, London, ablaze with martyrs, whose blood was the seed of Protestantism. Yet persecution under Mary never reached the proportions that it did on the Continent. At the most, but a few hundred died in England for the sake of their religion, while Mary's husband, Philip II, during the last of his reign, covered Holland with the graves of Protestants, who had been tortured and put to cruel deaths, or buried alive, by tens of thousands.

373. Mary's Death (1558). But Mary's career was short. She died (1558) near the close of an inglorious war with France, which ended in the fall of Calais, the last English possession on the Continent (§ 240). It was a great blow to her pride, and a serious humiliation to the country. "After my death," she said, "you will find Calais written on my heart." Could she have foreseen the future, her grief would have been greater still. For with the end of her reign the Pope lost all power in England, never to regain it.

374. Mary deserving of Pity rather than Hatred. Mary's name has come down to us associated with an epithet expressive of the utmost abhorrence (§ 342); but she deserves pity rather than detestation. Froude justly says, "If any person may be excused for hating the Reformation, it was Mary."

Separated from her mother, the unfortunate Catharine of Aragon, when she was only sixteen, Mary was ill-treated by Henry's new Queen, Anne Boleyn, and hated by her father. Thus the springtime of her youth was blighted.

Her marriage brought her no happiness; sickly, ill-favored, childless, unloved, the poor woman spent herself for naught. Her first great mistake was that she resolutely turned her face toward the past; her second, that she loved Philip II of Spain (§ 369) with all her heart, soul, and strength; and so, out of devotion to a bigot, did a bigot's work, and earned that execration which never fails to be a bigot's reward. But the Queen's cruelty was the cruelty of sincerity, and never, like her father's hangings, beheadings, and burnings (§ 358), the result of tyranny, indifference, or caprice. A little book of prayers which she left, soiled by constant use and stained with many tears, tells the story of her broken and disappointed life.

375. Summary. This reign should be looked upon as a period of reaction. The temporary check which Mary gave to

Protestantism deepened and strengthened it. Nothing builds up a religious faith like martyrdom, and the next reign showed that every heretic that Mary had burned helped to make at least a hundred more.

ELIZABETH — 1558–1603

376. Accession of Elizabeth. Elizabeth, the last of the Tudor family, was the daughter of Henry VIII and Anne Boleyn (§ 349). At the time of Mary's death she was living in seclusion in Hatfield House, near London, spending most of her time in studying Greek and Latin authors. When the news was brought to her, she was deeply moved, and exclaimed, " It is the Lord's doings ; it is marvelous in our eyes." Five days afterwards she went up to London by that road over which the last time she had traveled it she was being carried a prisoner to the Tower (§ 369).

377. Difficulty of Elizabeth's Position. An act of Parliament declared Elizabeth to be the true and lawful heir to the crown [1] (§ 355); but her position was full of difficulty, if not absolute peril. Mary Stuart of Scotland, now by marriage Queen of France (§ 363),[2] claimed the English crown through descent from Henry VII. She based her claim on the ground that Elizabeth, the daughter of Henry VIII and Anne Boleyn, was not lawfully entitled to the throne, because the Pope had refused to recognize Henry's second marriage (§ 349). Both France and Rome supported Mary Stuart's claim.

On the other hand, Philip II of Spain (§§ 370, 374) favored Elizabeth, but solely because he hoped to marry her and annex her kingdom to his dominions. Scotland was divided between two religious factions, the Catholics and the Protestants, and its attitude as an independent kingdom could hardly be called friendly. The Catholics in the greater part of Ireland were in a state bordering on rebellion, and were ready to join in any attack on an English sovereign.

378. The Religious Problem. But the religious problem was more dangerous than any other, for England itself was divided in

---

[1] See Genealogical Table, p. 207.
[2] After Elizabeth, Mary Stuart, Queen of Scots, stood next in order of hereditary succession. See Table, p. 207.

its faith. In the north, many noble families stood by the Catholic faith, and hoped to see the Pope's authority fully and permanently restored (§ 352). In the towns of the southeast, a majority favored the Church of England as it had been organized under the Protestant influence of Edward VI (§ 362).[1]

Within these two great parties there were two more, who made up in zeal and determination what they lacked in numbers. One was the Jesuits; the other, the Puritans. The Jesuits were a new Roman Catholic order (1540), banded together by a solemn oath to restore the complete power of the Church and to extend it throughout the world. Openly or secretly their agents penetrated every country, and their opponents declared that they hesitated at nothing to gain their ends.

The Puritans were the extreme Protestants who, like John Calvin of Geneva and John Knox of Edinburgh, were bent on cleansing or "*purifying*" the reformed faith from every vestige of Catholicism. Many of them were what the rack and the stake had naturally made them, — hard, fearless, narrow, bitter.

In Scotland the Puritans had got possession of the government, while in England they were steadily gaining ground. They were ready to recognize the Queen as head of the Church of England, they even wished that all persons should be compelled to worship as the government prescribed, but they protested against what they considered the halfway form of Church which Elizabeth and the bishops seemed inclined to maintain.

379. The Queen's Choice of Counselors. Elizabeth's policy from the beginning was one of compromise. In order to conciliate the Catholic party, she retained eleven of her sister Mary's counselors. But she added to them Sir William Cecil (Lord Burghley), who was her chief adviser,[2] Sir Nicholas Bacon, and, later, Sir Francis Walsingham, with others who were favorable to the Protestant faith.

On his appointment, Elizabeth said to Cecil, "This judgment I have of you, that you will not be corrupted with any gifts, that you will be faithful to the State, and that without respect to my private will you will give me that counsel which you think best." Cecil served the Queen until his death, forty years afterward.

[1] See Goldwin Smith's "England."   [2] See Macaulay's essay on "Lord Burghley."

The almost implicit obedience with which Elizabeth followed his advice sufficiently proves that Cecil was the real power not only behind, but generally above, the throne.

380. The Coronation (1559). The bishops were Roman Catholics, and Elizabeth found it difficult to get one to perform the coronation services. At length one consented, but only on condition that the Queen should take the ancient form of coronation oath, by which she virtually bound herself to support the Roman Catholic Church.[1] To this Elizabeth consented, and having consulted an astrologer, Dr. Dee, he named a lucky day for the ceremony, and she was crowned (1559).

381. Changes in the Church Service (1559). The late Queen Mary (§ 373), besides having repealed the legislation of the two preceding reigns, in so far as it was opposed to her own strong religious convictions (§ 370), had restored the Roman Catholic Latin Prayer Book (§ 362). At Elizabeth's coronation a petition was presented stating that it was the custom to release a certain number of prisoners on such occasions. The petitioners, therefore, begged her Majesty to set at liberty the four evangelists, Matthew, Mark, Luke, and John, and also the apostle Paul, who had been for some time shut up in a strange language. The English Book of Common Prayer (§ 362), with some slight changes, was accordingly reinstated, Parliament repealed the laws by which the late Queen Mary had practically restored the Roman Catholic religion, and it authorized the publication of a new and revised edition of the English Bible (§ 357).

382. New Act of Supremacy; Act of Uniformity; High Commission Court, 1559. No sooner was the Queen's accession announced to the Pope than he declared her illegitimate (§§ 349, 355), and ordered her to lay aside her crown and submit herself to his guidance. Such a demand was a signal for battle. However much attached a

---

[1] By this oath every English sovereign from William the Conqueror to Elizabeth, inclusive, and even as late as James II, with the single exception of Edward VI, swore "to preserve religion in the same state as did Edward the Confessor." The form of the coronation oath was changed to support Protestantism by the Revolution of 1688. Finally, under George V, in 1910, the phraseology of the oath was modified by Act of Parliament in order to make it less objectionable not only to English Catholics, but to a large majority of the people of the nation.

large part of the nation, especially the country people, may have been to the Catholic religion of their fathers (§ 370), yet the majority of them were loyal to the Queen and intended to stand by her.

The temper of Parliament manifested itself in the immediate reënactment of the Act of Supremacy. It was essentially the same, " though with its edge a little blunted," as that by which Henry VIII had freed England from the dominion of the Pope (§ 349). It declared Elizabeth not " supreme head" but "supreme governor" of the Church. Later, the act was made more stringent (1563).

To this act, every member of the House of Commons was obliged to subscribe ; thus all Catholics were excluded from that body. The Lords, however, not being an elective body, were excused from the obligation at that time (§ 478).

In order to enforce the Act of Supremacy, Parliament passed a new Act of Uniformity (§ 362), which ordered the minister of every congregation in England, whether Catholic or Protestant, to use the services laid down in the recently established Book of Common Prayer, and to use no other. In fact the law forbade the holding of any other service, even in a room with closed doors. In case he failed to obey this law he would be severely punished, and for a third offense would be imprisoned for life. The same act imposed a heavy fine on all persons who failed to attend the Established Church of England on Sundays and holidays.

The reason for these stringent measures was that in that age Church and State were everywhere considered to be inseparable. No country in Europe — not even Protestant Germany — could then conceive the idea of their existing independently of each other. Whoever refused to support the established form of worship, whatever that might be, was looked upon as a " rebel" against the government.

In order to try such " rebels" Parliament now gave Queen Elizabeth power to organize the High Commission Court.[1] By that Court many Catholics were imprisoned and tortured for refusing to comply with the new Acts of Supremacy and Uniformity, and

---

[1] High Commission Court : so called because originally certain church dignitaries were appointed commissioners to inquire into heresies and kindred matters. See, too, Summary of Constitutional History in the Appendix, p. xiv, § 15.

later on about two hundred priests and Jesuits were put to death on charges of treason. A number of Puritans, also, were executed for publishing books or pamphlets which attacked the government, and others were cast into prison or banished from the realm.

383. The Thirty-Nine Articles (1563); the Queen's Religion. Four years later, the religious belief of the English Church, which had been first formulated under Edward VI (§ 362), was revised and reduced to the Thirty-Nine Articles which constitute it at the present time.[1] But the real value of the religious revolution which was taking place did not lie in the substitution of one creed for another, but in the new spirit of inquiry, and the new freedom of thought, which that change awakened.

As for Elizabeth herself, she seems to have had no deep and abiding convictions on these matters. Her political interests practically compelled her to favor Protestantism, but to the end of her life she kept up some Catholic forms. Though she upheld the service of the Church of England, yet she shocked the Puritans by keeping a crucifix, with lighted candles in front of it, hung in her private chapel, before which she prayed to the Virgin as fervently as her sister Mary had ever done.

384. The Nation halting between Two Opinions. In this double course she represented a large part of the nation, which hesitated about committing itself fully to either side. Men were not wanting who were ready to lay down their lives for conscience' sake, but they do not appear to have been numerous.

Some sympathized at heart with the notorious Vicar of Bray, who kept his pulpit under the whole or some part of the successive reigns of Henry VIII, Edward VI, Mary, and Elizabeth, changing his theology with each change of rule. When taunted as a turncoat, he replied, " Not so, for I have always been true to my principles, which are to live and die Vicar of Bray." [2]

[1] But the Clerical Subscription Act (1866) simply requires the clergy of the Church of England to make a general declaration of assent to the Thirty-Nine Articles and the Prayer Book.

[2] " For this as law I will maintain
Until my dying day, sir,
That whatsoever king shall reign,
I 'll be Vicar of Bray, sir."

Though there was nothing morally noble in 'such halting between two opinions, and facing both ways, yet it saved England for the time from that worst of all calamities, a religious civil war. Such a conflict rent France in pieces, drenched her fair fields with the blood of Catholics and Protestants, split Germany and Italy into petty states, and ended in Spain in the triumph of the Inquisition and of intellectual death.[1]

385. The Question of the Queen's Marriage. Elizabeth showed the same tact with regard to marriage that she did with regard to religion. Her first Parliament, realizing that the welfare of the country depended largely on whom the Queen should marry, begged her to consider the question of taking a husband. Her reply was that she had resolved to live and die a maiden queen. When further pressed, she returned answers that, like the ancient Greek oracles, might be interpreted either way.

The truth was that Elizabeth saw the difficulty of her position better than any one else. The choice of her heart at that time would probably have been Robert Dudley, her "sweet Robin," the handsome but unscrupulous Earl of Leicester; but, as he called himself a Protestant, she knew that to take him as consort would be to incur the enmity of the Catholic powers of Europe. On the other hand, if she accepted a Catholic, she would inevitably alienate a large and influential number of her own subjects.

In this dilemma she resolved to keep both sides in a state of hopeful expectation. Philip II of Spain, who had married her sister Mary (§ 370), made overtures to Elizabeth. She kept him waiting in uncertainty until at last his ambassador lost all patience, and declared that the Queen "was possessed with ten thousand demons."

Later, the Duke of Anjou, a son of Henry II of France, proposed. He was favorably received, but the country became so alarmed at the prospect of having a Catholic King, that Stubbs, a Puritan lawyer, published a coarse and violent pamphlet denouncing the marriage.[2] For this attack his right hand was cut off; as

---

[1] S. R. Gardiner's "History of England"; consult also J. F. Bright's "History of England" and L. Von Ranke's "History of England."

[2] Stubbs's pamphlet was entitled "The Discovery of the Gaping Gulf, wherein England is likely to be swallowed up by another French marriage, unless the Lords forbid the bans by letting her see the sin and punishment thereof."

it fell, says an eyewitness,[1] he seized his hat with the other hand, and waved it, shouting, "God save Queen Elizabeth!" That act was an index to the popular feeling. A majority of the people, whether Catholics or Protestants, stood by the Crown even when they condemned its policy, determined, at all hazards, to preserve the unity of the nation. That spirit of intense loyalty and love of country without regard to creed or calling found perfect expression in Shakespeare's utterance:

> "This England never did, nor never shall,
> Lie at the proud foot of a conqueror.
> .   .   .   .
> Come the three corners of the world in arms,
> And we shall shock them: nought shall make us rue,
> If England to itself do rest but true."[2]

We shall see that this feeling showed itself still more unmistakably, when, years later, men of all classes and of widely different religious views rose to destroy the Armada, — that great fleet which Spain sent to subjugate the English realm (§§ 398–401).

386. The Queen a Coquette. During all this time the court buzzed with whispered scandals. Elizabeth was by nature an incorrigible coquette. Robert Dudley, Earl of Leicester, the Earl of Essex, and Sir Walter Raleigh were by turns her favorites. Over her relations with Dudley there hangs the terrible shadow of the suspected murder of his wife, the beautiful Amy Robsart.[3]

Elizabeth's vanity was as insatiable as it was ludicrous. She issued a proclamation forbidding any one to sell her picture, lest it should fail to do her justice. She was greedy of flattery even when long past sixty, and there was a sting of truth in the letter which Mary Queen of Scots wrote her, saying, "Your aversion to marriage proceeds from your not wishing to lose the liberty of compelling people to make love to you."

387. Violence of Temper; Crooked Policy. In temper Elizabeth was arbitrary, fickle, and passionate. When her blood was up, she would swear like a trooper, spit on a courtier's new velvet

---

[1] Camden's "Annals," 1581.

[2] Shakespeare's "King John," Act V, scene vii; written after the defeat of the Armada.

[3] See the "De Quadra Letter" in Froude's "England."

suit, beat her maids of honor, and box Essex's ears. She wrote abusive and even profane letters to high Church dignitaries,[1] and she openly insulted the wife of Archbishop Parker, because she did not believe in a married clergy.

The age in which Elizabeth reigned was preëminently one of craft and intrigue. The Kings of that day endeavored to get by fraud what their less polished predecessors got by force. At this game of double dealing Elizabeth had few equals and no superior. So profound was her dissimulation that her most confidential advisers never felt quite sure that she was not deceiving them. In her diplomatic relations she never hesitated at an untruth if it would serve her purpose, and when the falsehood was discovered, she always had another and more plausible one ready to take its place. In all this her devotion to England stands out unquestioned and justifies the saying, " She lived and lied for her country."

388. Her Knowledge of Men ; the Monopolies. The Queen's real ability lay in her instinctive perception of the needs of the age, and in her power of self-adjustment to them. Elizabeth never made public opinion, but watched it and followed it. She knew an able man at sight, and had the happy faculty of attaching such men to her service. By nature she was both irresolute and impulsive ; but her sense was good and her judgment clear. She could tell when she was well advised, and although she fumed and blustered, she yielded.

It has been said that the next best thing to having a good rule is to know when to break it. Elizabeth always knew when to change her policy. No matter how obstinate she was, she saw the point where obstinacy became dangerous. In order to enrich Raleigh and her numerous other favorites, she granted them the exclusive right to deal in certain articles. These privileges were called " monopolies."

They finally came to comprise almost everything that could be bought or sold, from French wines to secondhand shoes. The effect was to raise prices so as to make even the common necessaries of

---

[1] For the famous letter to the bishop of Ely attributed to Elizabeth, see Hallam's " Constitutional History of England," Froude, or Creighton ; but the " Dictionary of National Biography " (" Elizabeth ") calls it a forgery.

life excessively dear. A great outcry finally arose; Parliament requested the Queen to abolish the " monopolies "; she hesitated, but when she saw their determined attitude she gracefully granted the petition (§ 433).

389. The Adulation of the Court. No English sovereign was so popular or so praised. The great writers and the great men of that day vied with each other in their compliments to Elizabeth's beauty, wisdom, and wit. She lived in an atmosphere of splendor, of pleasure, and of adulation. Her reign was full of pageants, progresses, or journeys made with great pomp and splendor, and feasts, like those which Scott describes in his delightful novel, " Kenilworth."

Spenser composed his poem, the " Faërie Queen," as he said, to extol " the glorious person of our sovereign Queen." Shakespeare is reported to have written the " Merry Wives of Windsor " for her amusement, and in his " Midsummer Night's Dream " he addresses her as the " fair vestal in the West." The translators of the Bible spoke of her as " that bright *Occidental Star*," and the common people loved to sing and shout the praises of their " good Queen Bess." After her death at Richmond, when her body was being conveyed down the Thames to Westminster, one extravagant eulogist declared that the very fishes that followed the funeral barge " wept out their eyes and swam blind after ! "

390. Grandeur of the Age; More's " Utopia." The reign of Elizabeth was, in fact, Europe's grandest age. It was a time when everything was bursting into life and color. The world had suddenly grown larger; it had opened toward the east in the revival of classical learning; it had opened toward the west, and disclosed a continent of unknown extent and unimaginable resources.

About twenty years after Cabot had discovered the mainland of America (§ 335), Sir Thomas More (§§ 339, 351) wrote a remarkable work of fiction, in Latin (1516), called " Utopia " (the Land of Nowhere). In it he pictured an ideal commonwealth, where all men were equal; where none were poor; where perpetual peace prevailed; where there was absolute freedom of thought; where all were contented and happy. It was, in fact, the Golden Age come back to earth again.

More's book, now translated into English (1551), suited such a time, for Elizabeth's reign was one of adventure, of poetry, of luxury, of rapidly increasing wealth. When men looked across the Atlantic, their imaginations were stimulated, and the most extravagant hopes did not appear too good to be true. Courtiers and adventurers dreamed of fountains of youth in Florida, of silver mines in Brazil, of rivers in Virginia, whose pebbles were precious stones.[1] Thus all were dazzled with visions of sudden riches and of renewed life.

391. Change in Mode of Life. England, too, was undergoing transformation. Once, a nobleman's residence had been simply a square stone fortress, built for safety only ; but now that the Wars of the Roses had destroyed the old feudal barons (§§ 299, 316), there was no need of such precaution. Men were no longer content to live shut up in somber strongholds, surrounded with moats of stagnant water, or in meanly built houses, where the smoke curled around the rafters for want of chimneys by which to escape, while the wind whistled through the unglazed latticed windows.

Mansions and stately manor houses like Hatfield, Knowle, parts of Haddon Hall, and the " Bracebridge Hall " of Washington Irving,[2] rose instead of castles, and hospitality, not exclusion, became the prevailing custom. The introduction of chimneys brought the cheery comfort of the English fireside, while among the wealthy, carpets, tapestry, and silver plate took the place of floors strewed with rushes, of bare walls, and of tables covered with pewter or wooden dishes.

An old writer, lamenting these innovations, says : " When our houses were built of willow, then we had oaken men ; but, now that our houses are made of oak, our men have not only become willow, but many are altogether of straw, which is a sore affliction."

392. An Age of Adventure and of Daring. But they were not all of straw, for that was a period of daring enterprise, of explorers,

---

[1] " Why, man, all their dripping-pans [in Virginia] are pure gould ; . . . all the prisoners they take are feterd in gold ; and for rubies and diamonds, they goe forth on holydayes and gather 'hem by the sea-shore, to hang on their children's coates." — " Eastward Hoe," a play by John Marston and others, " as it was playd in the Blackfriers [Theatre] by the Children of her Maiesties Revels." (1603 ?)

[2] Aston Hall, Birmingham, is the original of Irving's " Bracebridge Hall." It came a little later than Elizabeth's time, but is Elizabethan in style.

STRATFORD-ON-AVON

Showing the church where Shakespeare is buried

sea rovers, and freebooters. Sir Walter Raleigh planted the first English colony in America, which the maiden Queen named Virginia, in honor of herself. It proved unsuccessful, but he said, " I shall live to see it an English nation yet "; and he did.

Frobisher explored the coasts of Labrador and Greenland. Sir Francis Drake, who plundered the treasure ships of Spain wherever he found them, sailed into the Pacific, spent a winter in or near the harbor of San Francisco, and ended his voyage by circumnavigating the globe. (See map facing p. 222.) In the Far East,

London merchants had established the East India Company, the beginning of English dominion in Asia; while in Holland, Sir Philip Sydney gave his lifeblood for the cause of Protestantism.

393. Literature and Natural Philosophy. It was an age, too, not only of brave deeds but of high thoughts. Shakespeare, Spenser, and Jonson were making English literature the noblest of all literatures. Furthermore, Shakespeare had no equal as a teacher of English history. His historical plays appealed then, as they do now, to every heart. At his touch the dullest and driest records of the past are transformed and glow with color, life, movement, and meaning.[1]

On the other hand, Francis Bacon, son of Sir Nicholas Bacon, of Elizabeth's council, was giving a wholly different direction to education. In his new system of philosophy,[2] he taught men that in order to use the forces of nature they must learn by observation and experiment to know nature herself; "for," said he, "knowledge is power."

394. Mary Queen of Scots claims the Crown (1561). For England it was also an age of great and constant peril. Elizabeth's entire reign was undermined with plots against her life and against the life of the Protestant faith. No sooner was one conspiracy detected and suppressed than a new one sprang up. Perhaps the most formidable of these was the effort which Mary Stuart, Queen of Scots, made to supplant her English rival. Shortly after Elizabeth's accession, Mary's husband, the King of France, died. She returned to Scotland (1561) and there assumed the Scottish crown, at the same time asserting her right to the English throne.[3]

[1] On the value of Shakespeare's Historical Plays, see § 298, note 1; § 313, note 2; and § 410. [2] In his tract on "The Greatest Birth of Time," in 1582.

[3] See Genealogical Table (p. 207). Mary's claim was based on the fact that the Pope had never recognized Henry VIII's marriage to Anne Boleyn, Elizabeth's mother, as lawful, while she, herself, as the direct descendant of Henry's sister, Margaret, stood next in succession.

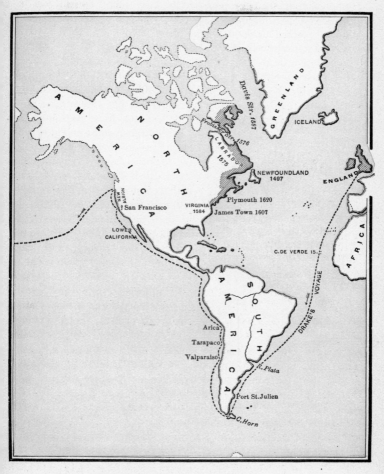

Showing the English discoveries in America in the 15th, 16th, and 17th centuries, with a part of Drake's voyage round the globe in 1577–1579.

395. Mary marries Darnley; his Murder. A few years later Mary married Lord Darnley. He became jealous of Rizzio, her private secretary, and, with the aid of accomplices, seized him in her presence, dragged him into an antechamber, and there stabbed him. The next year Darnley was murdered. It was believed that Mary and the Earl of Bothwell, whom she soon married, were guilty of the crime. The people rose and cast her into prison, and forced her to abdicate in favor of her infant son, James VI, who eventually became King of England and Scotland (1603).

396. Mary escapes to England (1568); plots against Elizabeth and Protestantism. Mary escaped and fled to England. Elizabeth, fearing she might pass over to France and stir up war, confined her in Bolton Castle, Yorkshire. During her imprisonment in another stronghold, to which she had been transferred, she was accused of being implicated in a plot for assassinating the English Queen and seizing the reins of government in behalf of herself and the Jesuits (§ 378).

It was, in fact, a time when the Protestant faith seemed everywhere marked for destruction. In France evil counselors had induced the King to order a massacre of the Reformers, and on St. Bartholomew's Day thousands were slain. The Pope, misinformed in the matter, ordered a solemn thanksgiving for the slaughter, and struck a gold medal to commemorate it. Philip II of Spain, whose cold, impassive face scarcely ever relaxed into a smile, now laughed outright. Still more recently, William the Silent, who had driven out the Catholics from a part of the Netherlands, had been assassinated by a Jesuit fanatic. Meanwhile the Pope had excommunicated Queen Elizabeth (1570) and had released her subjects from their allegiance to her. A fanatic nailed this bull of excommunication to the door of the Bishop of London's palace. This bold act, for which the offender suffered death, brought matters to a crisis.

Englishmen felt that they could no longer remain halting between two opinions. They realized that now they must resolve to take their stand by the Queen or else by the Pope. Parliament at once retaliated against the Pope by passing two stringent measures which declared it high treason for any one to deny the Queen's right to the crown, to name her successor, to denounce her as a heretic, or to say or do anything which should "alienate the hearts and minds of her Majesty's subjects from their dutiful obedience" to her. Later, the "Association," a vigilance committee, was formed by a large number of the principal people of the realm to protect Elizabeth against assassination. Not only prominent Protestants but many Catholic noblemen joined the organization to defend the Queen at all hazards.

397. Elizabeth beheads Mary, 1587. The ominous significance of these events had their full effect on the English Queen. Aroused to a sense of her danger, she signed the Scottish Queen's death warrant, and Mary, after nineteen years' imprisonment, was beheaded at Fotheringay Castle.[1]

As soon as the news of her execution was brought to Elizabeth, she became alarmed at the political consequences the act might have in Europe. With her usual duplicity she bitterly upbraided the minister who had advised it, and throwing Davidson, her secretary, into the Tower, fined him £10,000, the payment of which reduced him to beggary.

Not satisfied with this, Elizabeth even had the effrontery to write a letter of condolence to Mary's son, James VI, declaring that his mother had been beheaded by mistake! Yet facts prove that Elizabeth had not only determined to put Mary to death, but that she had urged those who held Mary prisoner to kill her privately.[2]

398. The Spanish Armada. Mary was hardly under ground when a new and greater danger threatened the country. At her death, the Scottish Queen, disgusted with her mean-spirited son James,[3] bequeathed her dominions, including her claim to the English throne, to Philip II of Spain (§ 370). He was then the most powerful sovereign in Europe, ruling over a territory equal to that of the Roman Empire in its greatest extent.

Philip II, with the encouragement of the Pope, and with the further help of the promise of a very large sum of money from him, resolved to invade England, conquer it, annex it to his possessions,

---

1 Fotheringay Castle, Northamptonshire, demolished by James I.
2 See "Elizabeth" in the "National Dictionary of (British) Biography."
3 James had deserted his mother and accepted a pension from Elizabeth.

and restore the religion of Rome. To accomplish this, he began fitting out the " Invincible Armada," an immense fleet of warships, intended to carry twenty thousand soldiers, and to receive on its way reënforcements of thirty thousand more from the Spanish army in the Netherlands.

399. Drake's Expedition ; Sailing of the Armada (1588). Sir Francis Drake (§ 392) determined to check Philip's preparations. He heard that the enemy's fleet was gathered at Cadiz. He sailed there, and in spite of all opposition effectually " singed the Spanish King's beard," as he said, by burning and otherwise destroying more than a hundred ships.

This so crippled the expedition that it had to be given up for that year, but the next summer a vast armament set sail. Motley[1] says it consisted of ten squadrons, of more than one hundred and thirty ships, carrying upwards of three thousand cannon.

The impending peril thoroughly roused England. Both Catholics and Protestants rose to defend their country and their Queen.

400. The Battle, 1588. The English sea forces under Lord High Admiral Howard, of Effingham, a zealous patriot, with Sir Francis Drake, who ranked second in command, were assembled at Plymouth, watching for the enemy. When the long-looked-for Spanish fleet came in sight, beacon fires were lighted on the hills to give the alarm.

> " For swift to east and swift to west the ghastly war flame spread ;
>   High on St. Michael's Mount it shone : it shone on Beachy Head.
>   Far on the deep the Spaniard saw, along each southern shire,
>   Cape beyond cape, in endless range, those twinkling points of fire."[2]

The enemy's ships moved steadily toward the coast in the form of a crescent seven miles across ; but Howard, Drake, Hawkins, Raleigh, and other noted captains, were ready to receive them. With their fast-sailing cruisers they sailed around the unwieldy Spanish warships, firing four shots to the enemy's one, and " harassing them as a swarm of wasps worry a bear." Several of the Spanish vessels were captured and one blown up. At last the

---

[1] Motley's " United Netherlands," II, 465 ; compare Froude's " England," XII, 466, and Laughton's " Armada " (State Papers), pp. xl-lvii.

[2] Macaulay's " Armada."

commander sailed for Calais to repair damages and take a fresh start. The English followed. When night came on, Drake sent eight blazing fire ships to drift down among the Armada as it lay at anchor. Thoroughly alarmed at the prospect of being burned where they lay, the Spaniards cut their cables and made sail for the north.

401. Destruction of the Armada, 1588 ; Elizabeth at Tilbury and at St. Paul's. They were hotly pursued by the English, who, having lost but a single vessel in the fight, might have cut them to pieces, had not Elizabeth's suicidal economy stinted them in both powder and provisions. Meanwhile the Spanish fleet kept moving northward. The wind increased to a gale, the gale to a furious storm. The commander of the Armada attempted to go around Scotland and return home that way ; but ship after ship was driven ashore and wrecked on the wild and rocky coast of western Ireland. On one strand, less than five miles long, over a thousand corpses were counted. Those who escaped the waves met death by the hands of the inhabitants. Of the magnificent fleet which had sailed so proudly from Spain only fifty-three vessels returned, and they were but half manned by exhausted crews stricken by pestilence and death. Thus ended Philip II's boasted attack on England.

When all danger was past, Elizabeth went to Tilbury, on the Thames below London, to review the troops collected there to defend the capital. " I know," said she, " that I have but the feeble body of a woman, but I have the heart of a king, and of a king of England too." Unhappily the niggardly Queen had half starved her brave sailors, and many of them came home only to die. None the less Elizabeth went with solemn pomp to St. Paul's Cathedral to offer thanks for the great victory, which was commemorated by a medal bearing this inscription : " God blew with his winds, and they were scattered." The date of the defeat of the Armada, 1588, was a turning point in English history. From that time England gradually rose, under the leadership of such illustrious commanders as Drake, Blake, and Nelson, until she became what she has ever since remained — the greatest sea power in the world (§§ 459, 557).

402. Insurrection in Ireland (1595). A few years later a terrible rebellion broke out in Ireland. From its partial conquest in the time of Henry II (§ 159), the condition of that island

THE SPANISH ARMADA

continued to be deplorable. First, the chiefs of the native tribes fought constantly among themselves; next, the English attempted to force the Protestant religion upon a people who detested it; lastly, the greed and misgovernment of the rulers put a climax to these miseries. Sir Walter Raleigh said, " The country was a commonwealth of common woe." What made this state of things still more dangerous was the fact that the Catholic rulers of Spain considered the Irish as their natural allies, and were plotting to send troops to that island in order to strike England a deadly side blow when she least expected it.

Elizabeth's government began a war, the object of which was " not to subdue but to destroy." The extermination was so merciless that the Queen herself declared that if the work of destruction went on much longer, " she should have nothing left but ashes and corpses to rule over." Then, but not till then, the starving remnant of the Irish people submitted, and England gained a barren victory which has ever since carried with it its own curse.

403. The First Poor Law (1601). In Elizabeth's reign the first effective English poor law was passed. It required each parish to make provision for such paupers as were unable to work, while the able-bodied were compelled to labor for their own support. This measure relieved much of the distress which had prevailed during the three previous reigns (§ 354), and forms the basis of the law in force at the present time (§ 607).

404. Elizabeth's Death (1603). The death of the great Queen (1603) was as sad as her life had been brilliant. Her favorite, Essex, Shakespeare's intimate friend, had been beheaded for an attempted rebellion against her power. From that time she grew, as she said, " heavy-hearted." Her old friends and counselors were dead, her people no longer welcomed her with their former enthusiasm. She kept a sword always within reach. Treason had grown so common that Hentzner, a German traveler in England, said that he counted three hundred heads of persons, who had suffered death for this crime, exposed on London Bridge. Elizabeth felt that her sun was nearly set; gradually her strength declined; she ceased to leave her palace, and sat muttering to herself all day long, " Mortua, sed non sepulta!" (Dead, but not buried).

At length she lay propped up on cushions on the floor,[1] "tired," as she said, "of reigning and tired of life." In that sullen mood she departed to join that "silent majority" whose realm under earth is bounded by the sides of the grave. "Four days afterward," says a writer of that time, "she was forgotten."

One sees her tomb, with her full-length, recumbent effigy, in the north aisle of Henry VII's Chapel, Westminster Abbey, while in

LONDON BRIDGE IN ELIZABETH'S TIME

the south aisle he sees the tomb and effigy of her old rival and enemy, Mary Queen of Scots (§ 397). The sculptured features of both look placid. "After life's fitful fever they sleep well."

405. Summary. The Elizabethan period was in every respect remarkable. It was great in its men of thought, great in its literature, and equally great in its men of action. It was greatest, however, in its successful resistance to the armed hand of religious oppression. "Practically the reign of Elizabeth," as Bishop Creighton remarks, "saw England established as a Protestant country."[2]

[1] See in the works of Delaroche his fine picture of "The Death of Queen Elizabeth."
[2] See "The Dictionary of English History" ("The Reformation"), p. 860.

The defeat of the Spanish Armada in 1588 gave renewed courage to the cause of the Reformation, not only in England, but in every Protestant country in Europe. It meant that a movement had begun which, though it might be temporarily hindered, would secure to all civilized countries, which accepted it, the right of private judgment and of liberty of conscience in matters of religion.

GENERAL REFERENCE SUMMARY OF THE TUDOR PERIOD (1485–1603)

(See note in italics on page 43.)

I. Government. II. Religion. III. Military Affairs. IV. Literature, Learning, and Art. V. General Industry and Commerce. VI. Mode of Life, Manners, and Customs

I. Government

406. Absolutism of the Crown ; Free Trade ; the Post Office. During a great part of the Tudor period the power of the Crown was well-nigh absolute. Four causes contributed to this : (1) The destruction of a very large part of the feudal nobility by the Wars of the Roses.[1] (2) The removal of many of the higher clergy from the House of Lords.[2] (3) The creation of a new nobility dependent on the king. (4) The desire of the great body of the people for " peace at any price."

Under Henry VII and Elizabeth the courts of Star Chamber and High Commission exercised arbitrary power, and often inflicted cruel punishments for offenses against the government, and for heresy or the denial of the religious supremacy of the sovereign.

Henry VII established a treaty of free trade, called the " Great Intercourse," between England and the Netherlands. Under Elizabeth the first postmaster-general entered upon his duties, though the post office was not fully established until the reign of her successor.

[1] In the last Parliament before the Wars of the Roses (1454) there were fifty-three temporal peers ; at the beginning of the reign of Henry VII (1485) there were only twenty-nine.

[2] Out of a total of barely ninety peers, Henry VIII, by the suppression of the monasteries, removed upwards of thirty-six abbots and priors. He, however, added five new bishops, which made the House of Lords number about fifty-nine.

II. Religion

407. Establishment of the Protestant Church of England. Henry VIII suppressed the Roman Catholic monasteries, seized their property, and ended by declaring the Church of England independent of the Pope. Thenceforth he assumed the title of Supreme Head of the National Church. Under Edward VI Protestantism was established by law. Mary led a reaction in favor of Roman Catholicism, but her successor, Elizabeth, reinstated the Protestant form of worship. Under Elizabeth the Puritans demanded that the National Church be completely " purified " from all Catholic forms and doctrines. Severe laws were passed under Elizabeth for the punishment of both Catholics and Puritans who failed to conform to the Church of England.

III. Military Affairs

408. Arms and Armor; the Navy. Though gunpowder had been in use for two centuries, yet full suits of armor were still worn during a great part of the period. An improved matchlock gun, with the pistol, an Italian invention, and heavy cannon were introduced. Until the death of Henry VIII foot soldiers continued to be armed with the long bow; but under Edward VI that weapon was superseded by firearms. The principal wars of the period were with Scotland, France, and Spain, the last being by far the most important, and ending with the destruction of the Armada.

Henry VIII established a permanent navy, and built several vessels of upwards of one thousand tons register. The largest men-of-war under Elizabeth carried forty cannon and a crew of several hundred men.

IV. Literature, Learning, and Art

409. Schools. The revival of learning gave a great impetus to education. The money which had once been given to monasteries was now spent in building schools, colleges, and hospitals. Dean Colet established the free grammar school of St. Paul's, several colleges were endowed at Oxford and Cambridge, and Edward VI opened upwards of forty charity schools in different parts of the country, of which the Christ's Hospital or " Blue-Coat School," originally established in London, is one of the best known. Improved textbooks were prepared for the schools, and Lily's " Latin Grammar," first published in 1513 for the use of Dean Colet's school, continued a standard work for over three hundred years.

410. Literature; the Theater. The latter part of the period deserves the name of the " Golden Age of English Literature." More, Sydney,

Hooker, Jewell, and Bacon were the leading prose writers; while Shakespeare, Spenser, Marlowe, and Jonson represented the poets.

In 1574 a public theater was erected in London, in which Shakespeare was a stockholder. Not very long after, a second was opened. At both these, the Globe and the Blackfriars, the great dramatist appeared in his own plays, and in such pieces as " King John," " Richard the Third," and the Henrys, he taught his countrymen more of the true spirit and meaning of the nation's history than they had ever learned before. His historical plays are chiefly based on Holinshed and Hall, two noted chroniclers of the period.

411. Progress of Science ; Superstitions. The discoveries of Columbus, Cabot, Magellan, and other navigators, had proved the earth to be a globe. Copernicus, a Prussian astronomer, now demonstrated the fact that it both turns on its axis and revolves around the sun, but the discovery was not accepted until many years later.

On the other hand, astrology, witchcraft, and the transmutation of copper and lead into gold were generally believed in. In preaching before Queen Elizabeth, Bishop Jewell urged that stringent measures be taken with witches and sorcerers, saying that through their demoniacal acts " your Grace's subjects pine away even unto death, their color fadeth, their flesh rotteth." Lord Bacon and other eminent men held the same belief, and many persons eventually suffered death for the practice of witchcraft.

412. Architecture. The Gothic, or Pointed, style of architecture reached its final stage (the Perpendicular) in the early part of this period. The first examples of it have already been mentioned at the close of the preceding period (§ 324). After the close of Henry VII's reign no attempts were made to build any grand church edifices until St. Paul's Cathedral was rebuilt by Wren, in the seventeenth century, in the Italian, or classical, style.

In the latter part of the Tudor period many stately country houses [1] and grand city mansions were built, ornamented with carved woodwork and bay windows. Castles were no longer constructed, and, as the country was at peace, many of those which had been built were abandoned, though a few castellated mansions like Thornbury, Gloucestershire, were built in Henry VIII's time. The streets of London still continued to be very narrow, and the houses, with their projecting stories, were so near together at the top that neighbors living on opposite sides of the street might almost shake hands from the upper windows.

[1] Such as Hatfield House, Knowle Hall, Hardwick Hall, and part of Haddon Hall; and, in London, Crosby Hall and other noble mansions.

V. General Industry and Commerce

413. Foreign Trade. The geographical discoveries of this period gave a great impulse to foreign trade with Africa, Brazil, and North America. The wool trade continued to increase, and also commerce with the East Indies. In 1600 the East India Company was established, thus laying the foundation of England's Indian empire, and ships now brought cargoes direct to England by way of the Cape of Good Hope.

Sir Francis Drake did a flourishing business in plundering Spanish settlements in America and Spanish treasure ships on the sea, and Sir John Hawkins became wealthy through the slave trade, — kidnaping negroes on the coast of Guinea, and selling them to the Spanish West India colonies. The domestic trade of England was still carried on largely by great annual fairs. Trade, however, was much deranged by the quantities of debased money issued under Henry VIII and Edward VI.

Elizabeth reformed the currency, and ordered the mint to send out coin which no longer had a lie stamped on its face, thereby setting an example to all future governments, whether monarchical or republican.

VI. Mode of Life, Manners, and Customs

414. Life in the Country and the City. In the cities this was an age of luxury; but on the farms the laborer was glad to get a bundle of straw for a bed, and a wooden trencher to eat from. Vegetables were scarcely known, and fresh meat was eaten only by the well to do. The cottages were built of sticks and mud, without chimneys, and were nearly as bare of furniture as the wigwam of an American Indian.

The rich kept several mansions and country houses, but paid little attention to cleanliness; and when the filth and vermin in one became unendurable, they left it " to sweeten," as they said, and went to another of their estates. The dress of the nobles continued to be of the most costly materials and the gayest colors.

At table a great variety of dishes were served on silver plate, but fingers were still used in place of forks. Tea and coffee were unknown, and beer was the usual drink at breakfast and supper.

Carriages were seldom used, except by Queen Elizabeth, and most journeys were performed on horseback. Merchandise was also generally transported on pack horses, the roads rarely being good enough for the passage of wagons. The principal amusements were the theater, dancing, masquerading, bull and bear baiting (worrying a bull or bear with dogs), cockfighting, and gambling.

NINTH PERIOD[1]

"It is the nature of the devil of tyranny to tear and rend the body which he leaves." — MACAULAY

BEGINNING WITH THE DIVINE RIGHT OF KINGS AND ENDING WITH THE DIVINE RIGHT OF THE PEOPLE

KING OR PARLIAMENT?

HOUSE OF STUART (1603–1649, 1660–1714)

JAMES I, 1603–1625
CHARLES I, 1625–1649
"THE COMMONWEALTH AND PROTECTORATE," 1649–1660

CHARLES II, 1660–1685
JAMES II, 1685–1689
WILLIAM AND MARY,[2] 1689–1702
ANNE, 1702–1714

415. Accession of James I. Elizabeth was the last of the Tudor family (§ 376). By birth, James Stuart, only son of Mary Stuart, Queen of Scots, and great-grandson of Margaret, sister of Henry VIII, was the nearest heir to the crown.[3] He was already King of Scotland under the title of James VI. He now, by act of Parliament, became James I of England. By his accession the two countries were united under one sovereign, but each retained its own Parliament, its own National Church, and its own laws.[4]

---

[1] REFERENCE BOOKS on this Period will be found in the CLASSIFIED LIST OF BOOKS in the Appendix. The pronunciation of names will be found in the Index. THE LEADING DATES stand unenclosed; all others are in parentheses.

[2] House of Orange-Stuart.   [3] See Genealogical Table, p. 207.

[4] On his coins and in his proclamations James styled himself King of Great Britain, France, and Ireland. But the term "Great Britain" did not properly come into use until somewhat more than a hundred years later, when, by an act of Parliament under Anne, Scotland and England were legally united.

The English Parliament refused to grant free trade to Scotland and denied to the people of that country, even if born after James I came to the English throne (or "Post Nati," as they were called), the rights and privileges possessed by natives of England.

The new monarch found himself ruler over three kingdoms, each professing a different religion. Puritanism prevailed in Scotland, Catholicism in Ireland, Anglicanism or Episcopacy in England.

416. The King's Appearance and Character. James was unfortunate in his birth. Neither his father, Lord Darnley, nor his mother had high qualities of character. The murder of Mary's Italian secretary in her own palace, and almost in her own presence (§ 395), gave the Queen a shock which left a fatal inheritance of cowardice to her son. Throughout his life he could not endure the sight of a drawn sword. If we can trust common report, his personal appearance was by no means impressive. He had a feeble, rickety body, he could not walk straight, his tongue was too large for his mouth, and he had goggle eyes. Through fear of assassination he habitually wore thickly padded and quilted clothes, usually green in color. He was a man of considerable shrewdness, but of small mind, and of unbounded conceit. His Scotch tutor had crammed him with much ill-digested learning, so that he gave the impression of a man educated beyond his intellect. His favorites used to flatter him by telling him that he was the " British Solomon " ; but the French ambassador came nearer to the mark when he called him " the wisest fool in Christendom."

The King wrote on witchcraft, kingcraft, and theology, and composed numerous commonplace verses. He also wrote a sweeping denunciation of the new plant called tobacco, which Raleigh (§ 392) had brought from America, and whose smoke now began to perfume, or, according to James, to poison, the air of England. His Majesty had all the superstitions of the age, and one of his earliest acts was the passage of a statute punishing witchcraft with death. Under that law many a wretched woman perished on the scaffold, whose only crime was that she was old, ugly, and friendless.

417. The Great Puritan Petition (1603). During the latter part of Elizabeth's reign, the Puritans (§ 378) in England had increased so rapidly that Archbishop Whitgift told James he was amazed to find how " the vipers " had multiplied. The Puritans felt that the Reformation had not been sufficiently thorough.

They complained that many of the forms and ceremonies of the Church of England were by no means in harmony with the

Scriptures. Many of them wished also to change the Episcopal form of Church government, and instead of having bishops appointed by the King, to adopt the more democratic method of having presbyters or elders chosen by the congregation.

While James was on the way from Scotland to London to receive the crown, the Puritans presented the " Millenary Petition " to him. It was so called because it purported to have a thousand signers. The ministers presenting it asked that they might be permitted to preach without wearing the white gown called a surplice, to baptize without making the sign of the cross on the child's forehead, and to perform the marriage ceremony without using the ring. Bishop Hooker and Lord Bacon had pleaded for a certain degree of toleration for the Puritans. They even quoted the words of Christ: " He that is not against us is for us." But the King had no patience with such a plea.

418. Hampton Court Conference (1604). The King convened a conference at Hampton Court, near London, to consider the Petition, or rather to make a pedantic display of his own learning. The probability that he would grant the petitioners' request was small. James had come to England disgusted with the violence of the Scotch Presbyterians or Puritans (§ 378), especially since Andrew Melville, one of their leading ministers in Edinburgh, had seized his sleeve at a public meeting and addressed him, with a somewhat brutal excess of truth, as " God's silly vassal." [1]

But the new sovereign had a still deeper reason for his antipathy to the Puritans. He saw that their doctrine of equality in the Church naturally led to that of equality in the State. If they objected to Episcopal government in the one, might they not presently object to royal government in the other? Hence to all their arguments he answered with his favorite maxim, " No bishop, no king," meaning that the two must stand or fall together.

At the Hampton Court Conference all real freedom of discussion was practically prohibited. The Conference, however, had one good result, for the King ordered a new and revised translation of the Bible to be made (§§ 254, 357). It was published a

[1] Gardiner in the " Dictionary of National (British) Biography," " James I," thinks that by " silly " Melville meant " weak." But that is not much improvement.

few years later (1611). This translation of the Scriptures excels all others in simplicity, dignity, and beauty of language. After more than three hundred years it still remains the version used in the great majority of Protestant churches and Protestant homes wherever English is spoken.

James regarded the Conference as a success. He had refuted the Puritans, as he believed, with much Latin and some Greek. He ended by declaiming against them with such unction that one enthusiastic bishop declared that his Majesty must be specially inspired by the Holy Ghost!

He closed the meeting by imprisoning the ten persons who had presented the petition, on the ground that it tended to sedition and rebellion. Henceforth, the King's attitude toward the Puritans (§ 378) was unmistakable. "I will make them conform," said he, "or I will harry them out of the land" (§ 422).

Accordingly, a law was enacted which required every curate to accept the Thirty-Nine Articles (§ 383) and the Prayer Book of the Church of England (§ 381) without reservation. This act drove several hundred clergymen from the Established Church.

419. The Divine Right of Kings, 1604 ; the Protest of the Commons ; "Favorites." As if with the desire of further alienating his people, James now constantly proclaimed the doctrine of the Divine Right of Kings. This theory, which was unknown to the English constitution, declared that the King derived his power and right to rule directly from God, and in no way from the people.[1] "It is atheism and blasphemy," he said, "to dispute what God can do, . . . so it is presumption and high contempt in a subject to dispute what a king can do."

In making these utterances James seems to have entirely forgotten that he owed his throne to that act of the English Parliament which accepted him as Elizabeth's successor (§ 415). In his exalted position as head of the nation, he boasted of his power much like the dwarf in the story, who, perched on the giant's shoulders, cries out, "See how big I am!"

---

[1] James's favorite saying was, "A Deo rex, a rege lex" (God makes the king, the king makes the law). He boasted that kings might, as he declared, "make what liked them law and gospel."

Acting on this assumption, James levied customs duties on goods without asking the consent of Parliament; violated the privileges of the House of Commons; rejected members who had been legally elected; and imprisoned those who dared to criticize his course. The contest was kept up with bitterness during the whole reign.

Toward its close James truckled meanly to the power of Spain, hoping thereby to marry his son Charles to a Spanish princess. Later, he made a feeble and futile effort to help the Protestant party in the great Thirty Years' War (1618–1648), which had begun between the Catholics and Protestants in Germany. The House of Commons implored the King not to humiliate himself and the nation at the feet of Spain. The King replied by warning the House not to meddle with matters which did not concern them, and denied their right to freedom of speech. The Commons solemnly protested, and James seized their official journal, and with his own hands tore out the record of the protest (1621).

Yet, notwithstanding his arbitrary character, James was easily managed by those who would flatter his vanity. For this reason he was always under the control of worthless favorites like Carr, Earl of Somerset, or Villiers, Duke of Buckingham. These men were the secret power behind the throne, and they often dictated the policy of the Crown.

420. The Gunpowder Plot (1605). The King's arbitrary spirit angered the House of Commons, many of whom were Puritans (§ 378). They believed that the King secretly favored the Roman Catholics; and for this reason they increased the stringency of the laws against persons of that religion. To vindicate himself from this suspicion, the King proceeded to execute the new statutes with rigor. As a rule, the Catholics were loyal subjects. We have seen that when Spain threatened to invade the country, they fought as valiantly in its defense as the Protestants themselves (§§ 399, 400). Many of them were now ruined by enormous fines, while the priests were driven from the realm.

One of the sufferers by these unjust measures was Robert Catesby, a Catholic gentleman of good position. He, with the aid of a Yorkshire man, named Guy Fawkes, and about a dozen more, formed a plot to blow up the Parliament House on the day the King was to open the session (November 5, 1605). Their intention, after they had thus summarily disposed of the government, was to induce the Catholics to rise and proclaim a new sovereign. The plot was discovered, the conspirators were executed, and the Catholics treated with greater severity than ever (§ 382).

421. American Colonies, Virginia, 1607. A London joint-stock company of merchants and adventurers, or speculators, established the first permanent English colony in America, on the coast of Virginia, in 1607, at a place which they called Jamestown, in honor of the King. (See map facing p. 222.) The colony was wholly under the control of the Crown.

The religion was to be that of the Church of England. Most of those who went out were described as "gentlemen," that is, persons not brought up to manual labor. Fortunately the energy and determined courage of Captain John Smith, who was the real soul of the enterprise, saved it from miserable failure.

Negro slavery, which in those days touched no man's conscience, was introduced, and by its means great quantities of tobacco were raised for export. The settlement grew in population and wealth, and at the end of twelve years (1619) it had secured the privilege of making its own local laws, thus becoming practically a self-governing community.

422. The Pilgrims; the New Power. The year after the Virginia legislature was established, another band of emigrants went out from England, not west, but east; not to seek prosperity, but greater religious freedom. James's declaration that he would make all men conform to the Established Church, or drive them out of the land, was having its due effect (§ 418).

Those who continued to refuse to conform were fined, cast into filthy prisons, beaten, and often half starved, so that the old and feeble soon died. Strange to say, this kind of treatment did not win over the Puritans to the side of the bishops and the King. On the contrary, it set many of them to thinking more seriously than ever of the true relations of the government to religion.

The result was that not a few came to the conclusion that each body of Christians had the right to form a religious society of its own, wholly independent of the state. That branch of the

Puritans (§ 378) who held this opinion got the name of Independents, or Separatists, because they were determined to separate from the Established Church of England and conduct their worship and govern their religious societies as they deemed best.

In the little village of Scrooby, Nottinghamshire (see map opposite), Postmaster William Brewster, William Bradford, John Carver, and some others, mostly farmers and poor men of the neighborhood, had organized an independent religious society with John Robinson for its minister. After a time they became convinced that so long as they remained in England they could never be safe from persecution. They therefore resolved to leave their native country. They could not get a royal license to go to America, and for this reason they emigrated to Holland, where all men were free to establish societies for the worship of God in their own manner. With much difficulty and danger they managed to escape to that country.

After remaining in Holland about twelve years, a part of them succeeded in obtaining from King James the privilege of emigrating to America.[1] A London trading company, which was sending out an expedition for fish and furs, agreed to furnish the Pilgrims passage by the *Mayflower*, though on terms so hard that the poor exiles said the "conditions were fitter for thieves and bondslaves than for honest men."

These Pilgrims, or wanderers, set forth in 1620 for that New World beyond the sea, which they hoped would redress the wrongs of the Old. Landing at Plymouth, in Massachusetts, they established a colony on the basis of "equal laws for the general good." Ten years later, John Winthrop, a Puritan gentleman of wealth from Groton, Suffolk (see map opposite), followed with a large number of emigrants and settled Boston (1630). During the next decade no less than twenty thousand Englishmen found a home in America. But to the little band that embarked under Bradford and Brewster in the *Mayflower*, the scene of whose landing at Plymouth is painted on the walls of the Houses of Parliament, belongs the first credit of the great undertaking.

[1] See "Why did the Pilgrim Fathers come to New England?" by Edwin D. Mead, in the *New Englander*, XLI, 711.

THE HOMES OF THE PILGR

SCROOBY CHURCH.

NORTH SEA

RFOLK
Yarmouth•

FFOLK
Groton

N T

BELGIUM

FRANCE

HOLLAND

AMSTERDAM•
• Leyden
Delftshaven•

Meuse R.

HOLLAND

PRUSSIA

ENGLAND AND IN HOLLAND.

Of that enterprise one of their brethren in England wrote in the time of their severest distress, with prophetic foresight, "Let it not be grievous to you that you have been instruments to break the ice for others; the honor shall be yours to the world's end." From this time forward the American coast south of the Bay of Fundy was settled mainly by English emigrants, and in the course of a little more than a century (1620–1733), the total number of colonies had reached thirteen. Thus the nation of Great Britain was beginning to expand into that *greater* Britain which it had discovered and planted beyond the sea.

Meanwhile a new power had arisen in England. It was mightier even than that of kings, because greater for both good and evil. Its influence grew up very gradually. It was part of the fruit of Caxton's work undertaken nearly two centuries earlier (§ 306). This power appeared in the spring of 1622, under the name of the *Weekly News*, — the first regular newspaper.

423. The Colonization of Ireland (1611). While the colonization of America was going on, King James was himself planning a very different kind of colony in the northeast of Ireland. The greater part of the province of Ulster, which had been the scene of the rebellion under Elizabeth (§ 402), had been seized by the Crown. The King now granted these lands to settlers from Scotland and England. The city of London founded a colony which they called Londonderry, and by this means Protestantism was firmly and finally established in the north of the island.

424. The "Addled Parliament"; the New Stand taken by the House of Commons (1610–1614). The House of Commons at this period began to slowly recover the power it had lost under the Tudors (§ 350). James suffered from a chronic lack of money. He was obliged to apply to Parliament to supply his wants (1614), but that body was determined to grant nothing without reforms. It laid down the principle, to which it firmly adhered, that the King should not have the nation's coin unless he would promise to right the nation's wrongs.

After several weeks of angry discussion the King dissolved what was nicknamed the "Addled Parliament," because its enemies accused it of having accomplished nothing. In reality it had accomplished much, for though it had not passed a single bill, it had shown by its determined attitude the growing strength of the people. For the next seven years James ruled without summoning a Parliament. In order to obtain means to support his army in Ireland, the King created a new title of rank, that of baronet,[1] which he granted to any one who would pay liberally for it. As a last resort to get funds he compelled all persons having an income of forty[2] pounds or more a year, derived from landed property, to accept knighthood (thus incurring feudal obligations and payments [§ 150]) or purchase exemption by a heavy fine.

425. Impeachment of Lord Bacon (1621). When James did finally summon a Parliament (1621), it met in a stern mood. The House of Commons impeached Lord Bacon (§ 393) for having taken bribes in lawsuits tried before him as judge. The House of Lords convicted him. He confessed the crime, but pleaded extenuating circumstances, adding, " I beseech your lordships to be merciful unto a broken reed " ; but Bacon had been in every respect a servile tool of James, and no mercy was granted. Parliament imposed a fine of £40,000, with imprisonment. Had the sentence been fully executed, it would have caused his utter ruin. The King, however, interposed, and his favorite escaped with a few days' confinement in the Tower.

426. Execution of Sir Walter Raleigh. Meanwhile Sir Walter Raleigh (§ 392) had been executed on a charge of treason. He had been a prisoner in the Tower for many years (1603–1616), accused of having plotted against the King.[3] Influenced by greed for gain,

---

[1] Baronet: This title (§ 263, note 1) does not confer the right to a seat in the House of Lords. A baronet is designated as " Sir," e.g. Sir John Franklin.

[2] This exaction was ridiculed by the wits of the time in these lines :

> " He that hath forty pounds per annum
> Shall be promoted from the plow ;
> His wife shall take the wall of her grannum *—
> Honor's sold so dog-cheap now."

The distraint of knighthood, as it was called, began at least as far back as Edward I, 1278.

[3] At the beginning of the reign two plots were discovered : one, called the " Main Plot," aimed to change the government and perhaps to place Arabella Stuart, cousin of James, on the throne. The object of the second conspiracy, called the " Bye Plot," was to obtain religious toleration. Raleigh was accused of having been implicated in the Main Plot.

* Take precedence of her grandmother.

James released him to go on an expedition in search of gold to replenish the royal coffers. Raleigh, contrary to the King's orders, came into collision with the Spaniards on the coast of South America.[1] He failed in his enterprise, and brought back nothing. Raleigh was especially hated by Spain, not only on account of the part he had taken in the defeat of the Armada (§ 400), but also for his subsequent attacks on Spanish treasure ships and property.

The King of that country now demanded vengeance, and James, in order to get a pretext for his execution, revived the sentence which had been passed on Raleigh fifteen years before. He doubtless hoped that, by sacrificing Raleigh, he might secure the hand of the daughter of the King of Spain for his son, Prince Charles. Raleigh died as Sir Thomas More did (§ 351), his last words a jest at death. His deeper feelings found expression in the lines which he wrote on the fly leaf of his Bible the night before his judicial murder:

> " Even such is Time, that takes in trust
> 　　Our youth, our joys, our all we have,
> And pays us but with age and dust;
> 　　Who in the dark and silent grave,
> When we have wandered all our ways,
> Shuts up the story of our days.
> But from this earth, this grave, this dust,
> My God shall raise me up, I trust!"

427. Death of James. James died suddenly a few years later, a victim of sloth, drunkenness, and gluttony. He had taught his son, Prince Charles, to believe that the highest power on earth was the royal will. It was a terrible inheritance for the young man, for just as he was coming to the throne, the people were beginning to insist that their will should be respected.

428. Summary. Three chief events demand our attention in this reign. First, the increased power and determined attitude of the House of Commons. Secondly, the growth of the Puritan and

---

1 It is said that James had treacherously informed the Spanish ambassador of Raleigh's voyage, so that the collision was inevitable.

Independent parties in religion. Thirdly, the establishment of permanent, self-governing colonies in Virginia and New England, destined in time to unite with others and become a new and independent nation, — the American Republic.

CHARLES I — 1625–1649

429. Accession of Charles ; Result of the Doctrine of the Divine Right of Kings. The doctrine of the Divine Right of Kings, which had been so zealously put forth by James (§ 419), bore its full and fatal fruit in the career of his son. Unlike his father, Charles was by nature a gentleman. In his private and personal relations he was conscientious and irreproachable ; in public matters he was exactly the reverse.

This singular contrast — this double character, as it were — arose from the fact that, as a man, Charles felt himself bound by truth and honor, but, as a sovereign, he considered himself superior to such obligations. In all his dealings with the nation he seems to have acted on the principle that the people had no rights which kings were bound to respect.

430. The King's Two Mistakes at the Outset. Charles I began his reign with two mistakes. First, he insisted on retaining the Duke of Buckingham, his father's favorite (§ 419), as his chief adviser, though the Duke was, for good reasons, generally distrusted and disliked. Next, shortly after his accession, Charles married Henrietta Maria, a French Catholic princess. The majority of the English people hated her religion, and her extravagant habits soon got the King into trouble.

To meet her incessant demands for money, and to carry on a petty war with Spain, and later with France, he was obliged to ask Parliament for funds. Parliament declined to grant him the supply he demanded unless he would redress certain grievances of long standing. Charles refused and dissolved that body.

431. The Second Parliament (1626) ; the King extorts Loans. Necessity, however, compelled the King to call a new Parliament. When it met, the Commons, under the lead of Sir John Eliot and other eminent men, proceeded to draw up articles of impeachment, accusing the Duke of Buckingham of mismanagement (§§ 243, 425). To save his favorite from being brought to trial, the King dissolved Parliament (1626), and as no supplies of money had been voted, Charles now proceeded to levy illegal taxes and to extort illegal loans. Sir John Eliot, Sir Edmund Hampden, cousin of the famous John Hampden (§ 436), and Thomas Wentworth refused (1627) to lend his Majesty the sum asked for. For this refusal they were thrown into prison. This led to increased agitation and discontent. At length the King found himself again forced to summon Parliament; to this Parliament, Eliot and Wentworth, with others who sympathized with them, were elected.

432. The Petition of Right, 1628. Shortly after assembling, the House of Commons, led by Sir Thomas Wentworth and John Pym, drew up the Petition of Right, which passed the Lords and was presented to the King for his signature. The Petition was a law reaffirming some of the chief provisions of the Great Charter, which the nation, more than four centuries earlier, had extorted from King John (§ 199). It stipulated in particular, that no taxes whatever should be levied without the consent of Parliament, and that no one should be unlawfully imprisoned for refusing to pay such taxes. In the petition there was not an angry word, but as a member of the Commons declared, " We say no more than what a worm trodden upon would say if he could speak : I pray thee tread on me no more."

433. Charles signs the Petition of Right, 1628 ; but he revives Monopolies. Charles refused to sign the Petition ; but finding that money could be got on no other terms, he at length gave his signature, 1628.[1] But for Charles to pledge his royal word to the nation meant its direct and open violation. The King now revived the " monopolies," which had been abolished under Elizabeth (§ 388).

By these grants certain persons bought the sole right of dealing in nearly every article of food, drink, fuel, and clothing. The Commons denounced this outrage. One member said : " The ' monopolists ' have seized everything. They sip in our cup, they sup in our dish, they sit by our fire."

---

[1] Petition of Right : See Summary of Constitutional History in the Appendix, p. xvi, § 17, and p. xxix.

434. Eliot's Remonstrance (1629). Sir John Eliot (§ 431) drew up a remonstrance against these new acts of royal tyranny, but the Speaker of the House of Commons, acting under the King's order, refused to put the measure to vote, and endeavored to adjourn.

Several members sprang forward and held him in his chair until the resolutions were passed, which declared that whoever levied or paid any taxes not voted by Parliament, or attempted to make any change in religion, was an enemy to the kingdom. In revenge Charles sent Eliot to close confinement in the Tower. He died there three years later, a martyr in the cause of liberty.

435. The King rules without Parliament; "Thorough." For the next eleven years (1629-1640) the King ruled without a Parliament. The obnoxious Buckingham (§ 431) had led an expedition against France which resulted in miserable failure. He was about setting out on a second expedition to aid the Huguenots, who had rebelled against the French King, when he was assassinated (1628). His successor was Sir Thomas Wentworth, who later (1640) became Earl of Strafford. Wentworth had signed the Petition of Right (§ 432), but he was now a renegade to liberty, and wholly devoted to the King. By means of the Court of Star Chamber (§ 330) and his scheme called "Thorough," which meant that he would stop at nothing to make Charles absolute, Strafford labored to establish a complete despotism.

Archbishop Laud worked with Strafford through the High Commission Court (§ 382). Together, the two exercised a crushing and merciless system of political and religious tyranny; the Star Chamber fining and imprisoning those who refused the illegal demands for money made upon them, the High Commission Court showing itself equally zealous in punishing those who could not conscientiously conform to the Established Church of England.[1]

Charles exasperated the Puritans (§ 378) still further by reissuing (1633) his father's Declaration of Sunday Sports, which had never really been enforced. This Declaration encouraged parishioners to

[1] To strengthen the hands of Archbishop Laud and to secure absolute uniformity of faith, Charles issued (1628) a Declaration (still found in the English editions of the Book of Common Prayer), which forbade any one to understand or explain the Thirty-Nine Articles (§ 383) in any sense except that established by the bishops and the King.

dance, play games, and practice archery in the churchyards after divine service. Laud used it as a test, and turned all clergymen out of their livings who refused to read it from their pulpits. When the Puritans finally got the upper hand (1644) they publicly burned the Declaration.

436. " Ship Money " ; John Hampden refuses to pay it, 1637. To obtain means with which to equip a standing army, the King forced the whole country to pay a tax known as " ship money," on the pretext that it was needed to free the English coast from the depredations of Algerine pirates. During previous reigns an impost of this kind on the coast towns in time of war might have been considered legitimate, since its original object was to provide ships for the national defense.

In time of peace, however, such a demand could not be rightfully made, especially on the inland towns, as the Petition of Right (§ 432) expressly provided that no money should be demanded from the country without the consent of its representatives in Parliament. John Hampden, a wealthy farmer in Buckinghamshire, refused to pay the twenty shillings required from him. He did not grudge the money, but he would not tamely submit to have even that trifling sum taken from him contrary to law. The case was brought to trial (1637), and the corrupt judges decided for the King.

437. Hampden and Cromwell endeavor to leave the Country. Meanwhile John Winthrop with many other Puritans emigrated to America to escape oppression. According to tradition John Hampden (§ 436) and his cousin, Oliver Cromwell, who was a member of the last Parliament, embarked on a vessel in the Thames for New England. But it is said that they were prevented from sailing by the King's order. The two friends remained to teach the despotic sovereign a lesson which neither he nor England ever forgot.[1]

438. The Difficulty with the Scottish Church (1637). The King determined to force the use of a prayer book, similar to that used

[1] Macaulay's " Essay on Hampden," Guizot's " English Revolution," and other well-known authorities, relate the proposed sailing of Hampden and Cromwell, but several recent writers question its truth.

in the English Church (§ 381), on the Scotch Puritans. But no sooner had the Dean of Edinburgh opened the book than a general cry arose in the church, "A Pope, a Pope! Antichrist! Stone him!" When the bishops endeavored to appease the tumult, the enraged congregation clapped, stamped, and yelled.

Again the dean tried to read a prayer from the hated book, when an old woman hurled her stool at his head, shouting, "D'ye mean to say mass [1] at my lug [ear]?" Riots ensued, and eventually the Scotch solemnly bound themselves by a Covenant to resist all attempts to change their religion. The King resolved to force his prayer book on the Covenanters [2] at the point of the bayonet.

But he had no money to pay his army, and the "Short Parliament," which he summoned in the spring of 1640, refused to grant any unless the King would redress the nation's grievances.

439. The "Long Parliament," 1640; Impeachment of Strafford and Laud; the "Grand Remonstrance." In the autumn Charles summoned that memorable Parliament which met in November of 1640. It sat almost continuously for thirteen years, and so got the name of the "Long Parliament." [3] This new Parliament was made up of three parties: the Church of England party, the Presbyterian party, and the Independents (§ 422). The spirit of this body soon showed itself. John Pym (§ 432), the leader of the House of Commons, demanded the impeachment of Strafford (§ 435) for high treason and despotic oppression. He was tried and sentenced to execution. The King refused to sign the death warrant, but Strafford himself urged him to do so in order to appease the people. Charles, frightened at the tumult that had arisen, and entreated by his wife, finally put his hand to the paper, and thus sent his most faithful servant to the block.

Parliament next charged Archbishop Laud (§ 435) with attempting to overthrow the Protestant religion. It condemned him to

[1] Mass: here used for the Roman Catholic church service.

[2] The first Covenanters were the Scottish leaders, who, in 1557, bound themselves by a solemn covenant to overthrow all attempts to reëstablish the Catholic religion in Scotland; when Charles I undertook to force the Scotch to accept Episcopacy the Puritan party in Scotland drew up a new covenant (1638) to resist it.

[3] Long Parliament: It was not finally dissolved until 1660, twenty years from its first meeting.

prison, and ultimately to death. Next, it abolished the Star Chamber and the High Commission Court (§ 435). It next passed the Triennial Act,[1] a bill requiring Parliament to be summoned once in three years, and also a statute forbidding the collection of " ship money " unless authorized by Parliament.

Under the leadership of Pym, it followed this by drawing up the " Grand Remonstrance," [2] which was printed and circulated throughout the country. The " Remonstrance " set forth the faults of the King's government, while it declared utter distrust of his policy. Cromwell did not hesitate to say that if the House of Commons had failed to adopt and print the " Remonstrance," he would have left England never to return. The radicals in the House next made an ineffectual attempt to pass the " Root and Branch Bill," for the complete destruction — " root and branch " — of the Established Church of England. Finally, the House enacted a law forbidding the dissolution of the present Parliament except by its own consent.

440. The King attempts to arrest Five Members (1642). The parliamentary leaders had entered into communication with the Scots and so laid themselves open to a charge of treason. It was rumored, too, that they were about to take a still bolder step and impeach the Queen for having conspired with the Catholics and the Irish to destroy the liberties of the country. No one knew better than Charles how strong a case could be made out against his frivolous and unprincipled consort.

Driven to extremities, Charles determined to seize the five members, John Pym, John Hampden (§§ 432, 436), and three others, who headed the opposition.[3] The King commanded the House of Commons to give them up for trial. The request was not complied with and the Queen urged Charles to take them by force, saying, " Go along, you coward, and pull those rascals out by the ears!" Thus taunted, the King went on the next day to the House

---

[1] The Triennial Act was repealed (in form only) in 1664 ; it was reënacted in 1694 ; in 1716 it was superseded by the Septennial Act (§ 535).

[2] See Summary of Constitutional History in the Appendix, p. xvii, § 19.

[3] The full list was Hampden, Pym, Hollis, Haselrig, and Strode, to which a sixth, Mandeville, was added later. Copley's fine painting of the " Attempted Arrest " is in the Boston Public Library.

of Parliament with a company of soldiers to seize the members. They had been forewarned, and had left the House, taking refuge in the "city," which showed itself then, as always, on the side of liberty (§ 34, note 1). Leaving his soldiers at the door, the King entered the House of Commons. Seeing that the five members

CHARLES I ATTEMPTS TO ARREST FIVE MEMBERS

were absent, the King turned to the Speaker and asked where they were. The Speaker, kneeling before the King, answered, "May it please your Majesty, I have neither eyes to see nor tongue to speak in this place but as this House is pleased to direct me." Vexed that he could learn nothing further, Charles left the hall amid ominous cries of "Privilege! privilege!"[1]

1 Privilege: the privilege of Parliament to debate all questions exempt from royal interference.

441. The Great Civil War, 1642–1649, between the King and Parliament. The King, baffled in his purpose, resolved to coerce Parliament by military force. He left London in 1642, never to return until he came as a prisoner, and was delivered into the custody of that legislative body that he had insulted and defied. Parliament now attempted to come to an understanding with the King.

There was then no standing army in England, but each county and large town had a body of militia, formed of citizens who were occasionally mustered for drill. This militia was under the control of the King. Parliament insisted on his resigning that control to them. Charles refused to give up his undoubted constitutional right in the matter, and raised the royal flag at Nottingham, August, 1642. Parliament then organized an army of its own, and the war began.

442. Cavaliers and Roundheads. It opened in the autumn of that year (1642) with the battle of Edgehill, Warwickshire, and was at first favorable to the King. On his side were a majority of the nobility, the clergy, and the country gentlemen. They were mainly members of the Church of England and were known collectively as Cavaliers, from their dashing and daring horsemanship. Their leader was Prince Rupert, a nephew of Charles.[1]

On the side of Parliament were the shopkeepers, small farmers and landowners, with a considerable number of men of high rank ; as a rule they were Puritans (§ 378). The King's party nicknamed them " Roundheads," because, despising the long locks and effeminate ringlets worn by the Cavaliers, they cut their hair short so that it showed the shape of the head.[2] Essex and Fairfax were the first leaders of the " Roundheads " ; later, Cromwell became their commander.

443. How the Country was divided ; Rise of Political Newspapers. Taking England as a whole, we may say that the southeastern half, that is, what was then the richest part of England, with London and most of the other large towns, was against the King, and that the southwestern half, with most of the North,

---

[1] See " A Charge with Prince Rupert," *Atlantic Monthly*, III, 725.
[2] " Those roundheaded dogs that bawled against bishops," said the Cavaliers.

was for him. (See map opposite.) Each side made great sacrifices in carrying on the war. The Queen sold her crown jewels, and the Cavaliers melted down their silver plate to provide money to pay the King's troops.

On behalf of the People's army Parliament imposed heavy taxes, and levied now for the first time a duty on domestic products, especially on ales and liquors, known as the "Excise Tax." Furthermore, it required each household to fast once a week, and to give the price of a dinner to support the soldiers who were fighting against the King.

Parliament also passed what was called the "Self-denying Ordinance" (1644) (repeated in 1645). It required all members who had any civil or military office to resign, and, as Cromwell said, "deny themselves and their private interests for the public good." The real object of this measure was to get rid of incompetent commanders, and give the People's army (soon to be remodeled) the vigorous men that the times demanded.

With the outbreak of the war great numbers of little local newspapers sprang into short-lived existence in imitation of the first publication of that sort, the *Weekly News*, which was issued not quite twenty years before in the reign of James I (§ 422). Each of the rival armies, it is said, carried a printing press with it, and waged furious battles in type against the other. The whole country was inundated with floods of pamphlets discussing every conceivable religious and political question.

444. The "New Model"; Death of John Hampden; the Solemn League and Covenant (1642–1645). At the first battle fought, at Edgehill, Warwickshire (1642), Cromwell saw that the Cavaliers (§ 442) had the advantage, and told John Hampden (§§ 436, 440) that "a set of poor tapsters [drawers of liquor] and town apprentices would never fight against men of honor." He forthwith proceeded to organize his regiment of "Ironsides," a "lovely company," he said, none of whom swore or gambled.

After the first Self-denying Ordinance was passed (§ 443), Cromwell and Fairfax formed a new People's army of "God-fearing men" on the same pattern, almost all of whom were Independents (§ 439). This was called the "New Model" (1645) and was

CHIEF BATTLEFIELDS OF
THE CIVIL WAR
OF THE 17TH CENTURY

Edinburgh
Glasgow
R. Clyde
R. Forth
Dunbar
1650
Berwick
R. Tweed
SCOTLAND
Philiphaugh
1645

NORTH

Newcastle
R. Tyne
Carlisle
Durham
ENGLAND
R. Tees

SEA

ISLE OF MAN

Marston Moor
1644
R. Ouse
IRISH SEA
Preston
1648
Hull
R. Humber
Liverpool
Sheffield
R. Mersey
ANGLESEA
Warrington
1648
Lincoln
Chester
Newark
R. Trent
Rowton Heath
1645
WALES
Nottingham

*Cardigan
Bay*
The Wash
R.
Naseby
1645
R. Nen
Worcester
1651
R. Severn
R. Gt. Ouse
Newmarket
R. Wye
Cambridge
R. Usk
Edgehill
1642
Rye House
Oxford
Chalgrove
1643
Milford Haven
Cardiff
Bristol
R. Avon
Newbury
1643 & 1644
R. Thames
LONDON
Bristol Channel
ENGLAND
Sedgemoor
1685
R. Tone
R. Itchen
Brighton
Exeter
Carisbrooke   ISLE OF WIGHT

ENGLISH CHANNEL

The country west of the broad dotted line supported the cause of Charles I;
that on the east supported Parliament.

placed under the joint command of the men who organized it. Very many of its officers were kinsmen of Cromwell's, and it speedily became the most formidable body of soldiers of its size in the world, — always ready to preach, pray, exhort, or fight.[1]

Meanwhile John Hampden (§§ 436, 440) had been mortally wounded in a skirmish at Chalgrove Field, Oxfordshire. His death was a terrible blow to the parliamentary army fighting in behalf of the rights of the people.[2]

Parliament endeavored to persuade the Scotch to give their aid in the war against the King. The latter finally agreed to do so (1643) on condition that Parliament would sign the Solemn League and Covenant (§ 438). Parliament signed it, and so made the Scotch Presbyterian worship the state religion of England and Ireland (1647). In reality only a small part of the English people accepted it; but the change forced a large number of Episcopal clergymen to leave their parishes.

445. Marston Moor and Naseby, 1644, 1645. On the field of Marston Moor, Yorkshire, 1644, the north of England was conquered by Cromwell with his invincible little army. The following year Cromwell's " Ironsides," who " trusted in God and kept their powder dry," gained the decisive victory of Naseby, 1645, in the Midlands. (See map facing p. 252.) After the fight papers belonging to the King were picked up on the battlefield. They proved that Charles intended betraying those who were negotiating with him for peace, and that he was planning to bring foreign troops to England. The discovery of these papers, which were published by Parliament, was more damaging to the royal cause than the defeat itself.

446. The King and Parliament. Standing on the walls of the ancient city of Chester, Charles saw his last army utterly routed (1645). Shortly afterwards he fled to the Scots. Oxford, the King's chief city in the Midlands, surrendered to Fairfax (1646). The first

---

[1] " The common soldiers, as well as the officers, did not only pray and preach among themselves, but went up into the pulpits in all churches and preached to the people." — CLARENDON, " History of the Rebellion," Book X, 79.

[2] See Macaulay's " Essay on Hampden." Clarendon says that Hampden's death produced as great consternation in his party " as if their whole army had been cut off."

civil war was now practically over. The Scots gave up the King (1647) to the parliamentary commissioners, and he was taken to Holmby House, Northamptonshire. There Cromwell and the army made overtures to him, but without effect. He was then brought by the Parliamentary or People's army to Hampton Court, near London.

Here, and elsewhere, the army again attempted to come to some definite understanding with the King, but all to no purpose. Politically speaking, Charles was his own worst enemy. He was false to the core, and, as Carlyle has said: "A man whose word will not inform you at all what he means, or will do, is not a man you can bargain with. You must get out of that man's way, or put him out of yours."

447. The Second Civil War (1648); Pride's Purge (1648); the "Rump Parliament." After two years spent in fruitless negotiations, Charles, who had fled to Carisbrooke Castle in the Isle of Wight, made a secret treaty with the Scots (1648), promising to sanction the establishment of the Scotch Presbyterian Church in England (§ 444), if they would send an army into the country to restore him to the throne.[1]

The Scots marched into England, the Royalists rose to aid them, and the second civil war began. It speedily ended in the utter defeat of the King's forces. The People's army now vowed that they would bring the King to justice. To this neither the Presbyterians in the House of Commons nor the members of the House of Lords would agree.

Colonel Pride then proceeded (1648), as he said, to purge the "Long Parliament" (§ 439) by driving out all who were opposed to this measure. Cromwell had no part in Pride's expulsion of members, though he afterwards expressed his approval of it. Those who remained were a small body of Independents only (§§ 422, 439). They did not number sixty; they became the mere tool of the Parliamentary or People's army and were called in derision the "Rump Parliament."

[1] When Cromwell found out that Charles had resolved to destroy him and the Independent army, he apparently made up his mind to put the King to death. See Lord Broghill's story in S. R. Gardiner's "History of the Great Civil War," III, 259.

WINDSOR CASTLE FROM THE THAMES

448. Execution of King Charles, 1649. This so-called "Rump Parliament" named one hundred and thirty-five persons to constitute a high court of justice to try the King on a charge of treason against the nation; the chief judge or presiding officer was John Bradshaw. Less than half of these judges were present throughout the trial. Of those who signed the death warrant Oliver Cromwell was one. Prince Charles, the King's son, then a refugee in France, made every effort to save his father. He sent a blank paper, bearing his signature and seal, to the judges, offering to bind himself to any conditions they might insert, provided they would spare his father's life; but no answer was returned.

The King was brought into court in Westminster Hall, London; a week later the trial was over. The judges pronounced sentence of death on "Charles Stuart, King of England," as a "tyrant, traitor, murderer, and public enemy."

Throughout the trial Charles bore himself with dignity and self-possession. The crisis had brought out the best elements of his nature. He was beheaded January 30, 1649, in London in front of the royal palace of Whitehall. "A great shudder ran through the crowd that saw the deed, then came a shriek, and all immediately dispersed." Tradition declares that Cromwell went secretly that night to see the beheaded corpse. He looked steadfastly at it, shook his head, sighed out the words "Cruel necessity!" and departed.[1]

449. Summary. The whole of Charles I's reign must be regarded as a prolonged struggle between the King and the nation. Under the Tudors and James I the royal power had been growing more and more despotic, while at the same time the progress of the Protestant Reformation and of Puritanism had encouraged freedom of thought.

Between these opposite forces a collision was inevitable, since religious liberty always favors political liberty. Had Charles known how to yield in time, or been sincere in the concessions which he did make, all might have gone well. His duplicity was his ruin. Though his death did not absolutely destroy the theory of the Divine Right of Kings, yet it gave it a blow from which it never recovered.

[1] S. R. Gardiner's "Great Civil War," III, 604; and see in Delaroche's works the picture of Cromwell looking at the King's corpse.

THE COMMONWEALTH AND PROTECTORATE — 1649–1660

450. Establishment of the Commonwealth, or Republic, 1649.
While the crowd that had witnessed the execution of Charles I was
leaving the spot (§ 448), the remnant of the House of Commons
met. This "Rump Parliament" (§ 447), composed of only about fifty
members, claimed the right to act for the whole nation. A few days
later it abolished the House of Lords as " useless and dangerous."
Next, for similar reasons, it abolished the office of king, and declared
that " The People are, under God, the origin of all just power."

England was now a commonwealth or republic, governed, in
name at least, by a Council of State. Of this Council John Bradshaw (§ 448) was president, and the poet Milton was foreign secretary, while General Fairfax with Oliver Cromwell had command of
the army. The real power was in the army, and the true head
of the army was Cromwell. Without him the so-called republic
could not have stood a day.

451. Radical Changes. All members of the House of Commons,
with those who held any civil or military office, were required to swear
allegiance to the Commonwealth " without King, or House of Lords."
The use of the English church service was forbidden, and the statues
of Charles I in London were pulled down and demolished.

The Great Seal of England (§ 145) had already been cast aside,
and a new one adopted, having on one side a map of England and
Ireland, on the other a representation of the House of Commons
in session, with the words, " In the first year of freedom, by God's
blessing restored 1648." [1]

452. Difficulties of the New Republic. Shortly after the establishment of the Commonwealth, General Fairfax (§ 442) resigned
his command, and Cromwell became the sole leader of the military
forces of the country. But the new government, even with his
aid, had no easy task before it.

It had enemies in the Royalists, who, since the King's execution, had grown stronger ; in the Presbyterians, who hated both
the " Rump Parliament " (§ 450) and the Parliamentary army ;
finally, it had enemies in its own ranks, for there were half-crazy

---

[1] 1648 Old Style would here correspond to 1649 New Style. (See § 545, note 2.)

fanatics, " Levelers," [1] " Come-outers," [2] and other " cattle and creeping things," who would be satisfied with nothing but destruction and confusion.

Among these there were socialists, or communists, who, like those of the present day, wished to abolish private property, and establish " an equal division of unequal earnings," while others declared and acted out their belief in the coming end of the world. Eventually Cromwell had to deal with these crack-brained enthusiasts in a decided way, especially as some of them threatened to assassinate him in order to hasten the advent of the personal reign of Christ and his saints on earth.

453. The Late King's Son proclaimed King in Ireland and Scotland; Dunbar; Worcester (1649–1651). An attempt of the English Puritan party (§ 378) to root out Catholicism in Ireland (1641) had caused a horrible insurrection. The Royalist party in Ireland now proclaimed Prince Charles, son of the late Charles I, King. Parliament deputed Cromwell to reduce that country to order, and to destroy the Royalists. Nothing could have been more congenial to his " Ironsides " (§ 445) than such a crusade. They descended upon the unhappy island (1649), and wiped out the rebellion in such a whirlwind of fire and slaughter that the horror of the visitation has never been forgotten. To this day the direst imprecation a southern Irishman can utter is, " The curse of Cromwell on ye!" [3]

Several years later (1653–1654), Cromwell determined to put in practice a still more drastic policy. He resolved to repeople a very large section of southern Ireland by driving out the Roman Catholic inhabitants and giving their lands to English and Scotch Protestants. It seemed to him the only effectual way of overcoming the resistance which that island made to English rule. By the use of military power, backed up by an Act of Parliament, his generals forced the people to leave their houses and emigrate to the

---

[1] " Levelers " : a name given to certain radical republicans who wished to reduce all ranks and classes to the same level with respect to political power and privileges.

[2] " Come-outers " : those who abandoned all established ways in government and religion.

[3] At Drogheda and Wexford, Cromwell, acting in accordance with the laws of war of that day, massacred the garrisons that refused to surrender.

province of Connaught on the west coast. Part of that district was so barren and desolate that it was said, "it had not water enough to drown a man, trees enough to hang him, or earth enough to bury him." Thousands were compelled to go into this dreary exile, and hundreds of families who refused were shipped to the West Indies and sold to the planters as slaves for a term of years, — a thing often done in that day with prisoners of war.

In Scotland also Prince Charles was looked upon as the legitimate sovereign by a strong and influential party. He found in the brave Montrose,[1] who was hanged for treason at Edinburgh, and in other loyal supporters far better friends than he deserved. The Prince came to Scotland (1650); while there, he was crowned and took the oath of the Covenant (§ 438). It must have been a bitter pill for a man of his free and easy temperament. But worse was to come, for the Scottish Puritans made him sign a paper declaring that his father had been a tyrant and that his mother was an idolater. No wonder the caricatures of the day represented the Scots as holding the Prince's nose to a grindstone. Later, Prince Charles rallied a small force to fight for him, but it was utterly defeated at Dunbar (1650).

Twelve months afterward, on the anniversary of his defeat at Dunbar, the Prince made a second attempt to obtain the crown. At the battle of Worcester Cromwell again routed his forces and brought the war to an end. Charles escaped into Shropshire, where he hid for a day in an oak at Boscobel. After many narrow escapes he at length succeeded in getting out of the country.

454. Cromwell expels Parliament. Cromwell now urged the necessity of dissolving the "Rump Parliament" (§ 450) and of electing a Parliament which should really represent the nation, reform the laws, and pass a general act of pardon. In his despatch to the House of Commons after the victory of Worcester, he called the battle a "crowning mercy." Some of the republicans in that body took alarm at this phrase, and thought that Cromwell used it to foreshadow a design to place the crown on his own head. For this reason, perhaps, they hesitated to dissolve.

---

[1] See "The Execution of Montrose," in Aytoun's "Lays of the Scottish Cavaliers." Prince Charles basely abandoned Montrose to his fate.

But at last they could not withstand the pressure, and a bill was introduced (1653) for summoning a new Parliament of four hundred members, but with the provision that all members of the present House were to keep their seats, and have the right to reject newly elected members.

Cromwell, with the army, believed this provision a trick on the part of the " Rump " (§ 450) to keep themselves in perpetual power.

Sir Harry Vane, who was a leading member of the House of Commons, and who had been governor of the colony of Massachusetts, feared that the country was in danger of falling into the hands of Cromwell as military dictator. He therefore urged the immediate passage of the bill as it stood. Cromwell heard that a vote was about to be taken. Putting himself at the head of a squad of soldiers, he suddenly entered the House (1653). After listening to the debate for some time, he rose from his seat and charged the Commons with injustice and misgovernment. A member remonstrated. Cromwell grew excited, saying: " You are no Parliament! I say you are no Parliament ! " Then he called in the musketeers. They dragged the Speaker from his chair, and drove the members after him.

As they passed out, Cromwell shouted "drunkard," "glutton," "extortioner," with other opprobrious names. When all were gone, he locked the door and put the key in his pocket. During the night some Royalist wag nailed a placard on the door, bearing the inscription in large letters, " This House to let, unfurnished ! "

455. Cromwell becomes Protector ; the " Instrument of Government " (1653). Cromwell summoned a new Parliament, which was practically of his own choosing. It consisted of one hundred and thirty-nine members, and was known as the " Little Parliament." [1] The Royalists nicknamed it " Barebone's Parliament " from one of its members, a London leather dealer named Praise-God Barebone. Notwithstanding the irregularity of its organization and the ridicule cast upon it, the " Barebone's Parliament " proposed several reforms of great value, which the country afterwards adopted.

---

[1] A regularly summoned Parliament, elected by the people, would have been much larger. This one was chosen from a list furnished by the ministers of the various Independent churches (§ 422). It was in no true sense a representative body.

By Charles Lucy, R.A.

Oliver Cromwell

Cromwell resolving to refuse the crown (see § 455)

A council of Cromwell's leading men now secured the adoption of a constitution entitled the " Instrument of Government." [1] It made Cromwell Lord Protector of England, Ireland, and Scotland.

Up to this time the Commonwealth had been a republic, nominally under the control of the House of Commons, but as a matter of fact governed by Cromwell and the army. Now it became a republic under a Protector, or President, who was to hold his office for life.

A few years later (1657), Parliament offered the title of King to Cromwell, and with it a new constitution called the " Humble Petition and Advice." The new constitution provided that Parliament should consist of two Houses, since the majority of influential men felt the need of the restoration of the Lords (§ 450). For, said a member of " Barebone's Parliament," " the nation has been hopping on one leg " altogether too long. Cromwell had the same feeling, and endeavored to put an end to the " hopping " by trying to restore the House of Lords, but he could not get the Peers to meet. He accepted the new constitution, but the army objected to his wearing the crown, so he simply remained Lord Protector.

456. Emigration of Royalists to America. Under the tyranny of the Stuart Kings, John Winthrop and many other noted Puritans had emigrated to Massachusetts and other parts of New England. During the Commonwealth the case was reversed, and numbers of Royalists fled to Virginia. Among them were John Washington, the great-grandfather of George Washington, and the ancestors of Jefferson, Patrick Henry, the Lees, Randolphs, and other prominent families, destined in time to take part in founding a republic in the New World much more democratic than anything the Old World had ever seen.

457. Cromwell as a Ruler ; Puritan Fanaticism. When Cromwell's new Parliament (§ 455) ventured to criticize his course, he

[1] " Instrument of Government ": The principal provisions of this constitution were : (1) the government was vested in the Protector and a council appointed for life ; (2) Parliament, consisting of the House of Commons only, was to be summoned every three years, and not to be dissolved under five months ; (3) a standing army of thirty thousand was to be maintained ; (4) all taxes were to be levied by Parliament ; (5) the system of representation was reformed, so that many large places hitherto without representation in Parliament now obtained it ; (6) all Roman Catholics, and those concerned in the Irish rebellion, were disfranchised forever.

dissolved it (1654) quite as peremptorily as the late King had done (§ 431). Soon afterwards, fear of a Royalist rebellion led him to divide the country into eleven military districts (1655), each governed by a major general, who ruled by martial law and with despotic power. All Royalist families were heavily taxed to support Cromwell's standing army, all Catholic priests were banished, and no books or papers could be published without permission of the government.

Cromwell, however, though compelled to resort to severe measures to secure peace, was, in spirit, no oppressor. On the contrary, he proved himself the Protector not only of the realm but of the Protestants of Europe. When they were threatened with persecution, his influence saved them. He showed, too, that in an age of bigotry he was no bigot. Puritan fanaticism, exasperated by the persecution it had endured under James and Charles, often went to the utmost extremes, even as " Hudibras "[1] said, to " killing of a cat on Monday for catching of a rat on Sunday."

It treated the most innocent customs, if they were in any way associated with Catholicism or Episcopacy, as serious offenses. It closed all places of amusement; it condemned mirth as ungodly; it made it a sin to dance round a Maypole, or to eat mince pie at Christmas. Fox-hunting and horse-racing were forbidden, and bear-baiting prohibited, " not because it gave pain to the bear, but because it gave pleasure to the spectators."

In such an age, when a man could hardly claim to be religious unless he wore sad-colored raiment, talked through his nose, and quoted Scripture with great frequency, Cromwell showed exceptional moderation and good sense.

458. Cromwell's Religious Toleration. He favored the toleration of all forms of worship not directly opposed to the government as then constituted. He befriended the Quakers, who were looked upon as the enemies of every form of worship, and who were treated with cruel severity both in England and America. He was instrumental in sending the first Protestant missionaries to Massachusetts to convert the Indians, then supposed by many to

---

[1] " Hudibras ": a burlesque poem by Samuel Butler (1663). It satirized the leading persons and parties of the Commonwealth, but especially the Puritans.

be a remnant of the lost tribes of Israel; and after an exclusion of many centuries (§ 222), he permitted the Jews to return to England, and even to build a synagogue in London.

On the other hand, there are few of the cathedral or parish churches of England which do not continue to testify to the Puritan army's destructive hatred of everything savoring of the rule of either Pope or bishop.[1] The empty niches, where some gracious image of the Virgin or the figure of some saint once looked down; the patched remnants of brilliant stained glass, once part of a picture telling some Scripture story; the mutilated statues of noted men; the tombs, hacked and hewed by pike and sword, because they bore some emblem or expression of the old faith, — all these still bear witness to the fury of the Puritan soldiers, who did not respect even the graves of their ancestors, if those ancestors had once thought differently from themselves.

459. Victories by Land and Sea; the Navigation Act (1651). Yet during Cromwell's rule the country, notwithstanding all the restrictions imposed by a stern military government, grew and prospered. The English forces gained victories by land and sea, and made the name of the Protector respected as that of Charles I had never been.

At this period the carrying trade of the world, by sea, had fallen into the hands of the Dutch, and Amsterdam had become a more important center of exchange than London. The Commonwealth passed a measure called the "Navigation Act"[2] (1651) to encourage British commerce. It prohibited the importation or exportation of any goods into England or its colonies in Dutch or other foreign vessels.

Later, war with the Dutch broke out partly on account of questions of trade, and partly because Royalist plotters found protection in Holland. Then Cromwell created such a navy as the country had never before possessed. Under the command of Admiral Blake, "the sea king," and Admiral Monk, the Dutch were finally

---

[1] But part of this destruction occurred under Henry VIII and Edward VI (§§ 352, 364).

[2] The Navigation Act was renewed later. Though aimed at the Dutch, this measure damaged the export trade of the American colonies for a time.

beaten so thoroughly (1653) that they bound themselves to ever after salute the English flag wherever they should meet it on the seas. A war undertaken in alliance with France against Spain was equally successful. Jamaica was taken as a permanent possession by the British fleet, and France, in return for Cromwell's assistance, reluctantly gave the town of Dunkirk to England (1658), and the flag of the English Commonwealth was planted on the French coast. But a few years later (1662), the selfish and profligate Charles II sold Dunkirk back to Louis XIV in order to get money to waste on his pleasures.

460. Cromwell's Death; his Character (1658). After being King in everything but name for five years, Cromwell died (September 3, 1658) on the anniversary of the victories of Dunbar and Worcester (§ 453). During the latter part of his career he had lived in constant dread of assassination, and wore concealed armor. At the hour of his death one of the most fearful storms was raging that had ever swept over England. To many it seemed a fit accompaniment to the close of such a life.

In one sense, Cromwell was a usurper and a tyrant; but, at heart, his object was his country's welfare. In such cases the motive is all in all. He was a lonely man of rough exterior and hard manner.[1] He cared little for the smooth proprieties of life, yet he had that dignity of bearing which high moral purpose gives. In all that he did he was eminently practical. In an age of isms, theories, and experiments, he was never confused and never faltered in his course. To-day a colossal bronze statue of the great soldier and ruler stands in the shadow of the Houses of Parliament, where the English people, more than two hundred and forty years after his burial, voted to erect it.

461. The Times needed Such a Man. There are emergencies when an ounce of decision is worth a pound of deliberation. When the ship is foundering or on fire, or when the crew have mutinied, it will not avail to sit in the cabin and discuss how it happened.

---

[1] Cromwell was always a lonely man, and had so few real friends that Walter Scott may have expressed his true feeling when he makes him say in his novel of "Woodstock": "I would *I* had any creature, were it but a dog, that followed me because it loved me, not for what it could make of me."

Something must be done, and that promptly. Cromwell was the man for such a juncture. He saw clearly that if the country was to be kept together, it must be by decided measures, which no precedent, law, or constitution justified, but which stood justified none the less by exigencies of the crisis, by his own conscious rectitude of purpose, and by the result.

. If there is any truth in Napoleon's maxim, that "The tools belong to him that can use them," then Cromwell had a God-given right to rule ; for, first, he had the ability ; and, next, though he used his power in his campaign in Ireland (§ 453) with merciless severity, yet the great purpose of his life was to establish order and justice on what seemed to him the only practical basis.

462. Summary. Cromwell's original object appears to have been to organize a government representing the will of the nation more completely than it had ever been represented before. He strongly favored the restoration of the House of Lords, he endeavored to reform the laws, and he sought to secure religious toleration for the great body of Protestants. One who knew Cromwell intimately said, "A larger soul, I think, hath seldom dwelt in a house of clay, than his was."

Circumstances, however, were often against him ; he had many enemies, and in order to secure peace he was obliged to resort to the exercise of absolute power. Yet the difference in this respect between Cromwell and Charles I was immense : the latter was despotic on his own account, the former for the advantage of those he governed.

RICHARD CROMWELL — September 3, 1658–April 22, 1659

463. Richard Cromwell's Incompetency. Richard Cromwell, Oliver's eldest son, now succeeded to the Protectorate (§ 455). He was an amiable individual, as negative in character as his father had been positive. With the extreme Puritans (§ 457), known as the "godly party," he had no sympathy whatever. "Here," said he to one of them, pointing to a friend of his who stood by, "is a man who can neither preach nor pray, yet I would trust him before you all." Such frankness was not likely to make the new ruler popular with the army, made up of men who never lacked a Scripture text to justify either a murder or a massacre. Moreover, the times were perilous, and called for a decided hand at the helm. After a brief reign of less than eight months the military leaders requested Richard to resign, and soon afterwards recalled the "Rump Parliament" (§ 447).

464. Richard retires. The Protector retired not only without remonstrance, but apparently with a sense of relief at being so soon eased of a burden too heavy for his weak shoulders to carry. To the people he was hereafter familiarly known as "Tumble-down-Dick," and was caricatured as such on tavern signboards.

The nation pensioned him off with a moderate allowance, and he lived in obscurity to an advanced age, carrying about with him to the last a trunk filled with the congratulatory addresses and oaths of allegiance which he had received when he became Protector.

Years after his abdication it is reported that he visited Westminster, and when the attendant, who did not recognize him, showed him the throne, he said, "Yes; I have not seen that chair since I sat in it myself in 1659."

465. The "Convention Parliament." The year following Richard Cromwell's withdrawal was full of anxiety and confusion. The army of the Commonwealth had turned Parliament out of doors (1659). There was no longer any regularly organized government, and the country drifted helplessly like a ship without a pilot.

General Monk, then commander in chief in Scotland, now marched into England (1660) with the determination of calling a new Parliament, which should be full, free, and representative of the real political feeling of the nation. When he reached London with his army, the members of the "Rump Parliament" (§ 447) had resumed their sessions.

At Monk's invitation the Presbyterian members, whom Colonel Pride had driven from their seats eleven years before (§ 447), now went back. This assembly issued writs for the summoning of a "Convention Parliament" (so styled because called without royal authority), and then dissolved by their own consent. Thus ended that memorable "Long Parliament" (§ 439), which had existed nearly twenty years. About a month later the Convention, including

ten members of the House of Lords, met, and at once invited
Charles Stuart, then in Holland, to return to his kingdom. He
had made certain promises, called the "Declaration of Breda,"[1]
which were intended to smooth the way for his return.

466. Summary. Richard Cromwell's government existed in
name only, never in fact. During his so-called Protectorate the
country was under the control of the army of the Commonwealth
or of that "Rump Parliament" which represented nothing but
itself.

The period which elapsed after Oliver Cromwell's death was
one of waiting and preparation. It ended in the meeting of the
free national Parliament, which put an end to the republic, and
restored royalty in the person of Charles II.

CHARLES II — 1660–1685

**467. The Restoration of Monarchy ; Accession of Charles ; a New
Standing Army, 1660.** The English army heard that Charles was
coming, with sullen silence ; the ex-members of the "Rump Parliament" (§ 465), with sullen dread ; the rest of the nation, with a
feeling of relief. However much they had hated the despotism of
the two Stuart Kings, James I and Charles I, four fifths of the
people stood ready to welcome any change which promised to do
away with a government maintained by bayonets.

Charles II was received at Dover with the wildest demonstrations
of joy. Bells pealed, flags waved, bonfires blazed all the way to
London, and the King said, with characteristic irony, "It must
have been my own fault that I did not come before, for I find no
one but declares that he is glad to see me."

The existence of the late Republic and the Protectorate (§§ 450,
455) was as far as possible ignored. The House of Lords was
restored (§§ 450, 455). The new reign was dated, not when it
actually began, but from the day of Charles I's execution twelve
years before. The troops of the Commonwealth were speedily

---

[1] The Declaration of Breda, made by Charles in Holland (1660), promised :
(1) free pardon to all those not excepted by Parliament ; (2) liberty of conscience to
all whose views did not disturb the peace of the realm ; (3) the settlement by Parliament of all claims to landed property ; (4) the payment of arrears to Monk's army.

disbanded, but the King retained a picked guard of five thousand men, which became the nucleus of a new standing army.

468. The King's Character. The sovereign who now ascended the throne was in every respect the opposite of Cromwell. Charles II had no love of country, no sense of duty, no belief in man, no respect for woman. Evil circumstances and evil companions had made him "a good-humored but hard-hearted voluptuary." For twelve years he had been a wanderer, and at times almost a beggar. Now the sole aim of his life was enjoyment. He desired to be King because he would then be able to accomplish that aim.

469. Reaction from Puritanism. In this purpose Charles had the sympathy of a considerable part of the people. The Puritan faith (§ 378), represented by such men as Hampden (§ 436) and Milton (§ 450), was noble indeed ; but unfortunately there were many in its ranks who had no like grandeur of soul, but who pushed Puritanism to its most injurious and offensive extreme. That attempt to reduce the whole of life to a narrow system of sour self-denial had at last broken down.

Now, under the Restoration, the reaction set in, and the lower and earthly side of human nature — none the less human because it is at the bottom and not at the top — seemed determined to take its full revenge. Butler ridiculed religious zeal in his poem of "Hudibras" (§ 457), which every courtier had by heart. Society was smitten with an epidemic of immorality. Profligacy became the fashion in both speech and action, and much of the popular literature of that day will not bear the light.

470. The Royal Favorites. The King surrounded himself with men like himself. This merry gang of revelers vied with each other in dissipation and in jests on each other. Charles's two chief favorites were the Earl of Rochester, a gifted but ribald poet, and Lord Shaftesbury, who became Lord Chancellor. Both have left on record their estimate of their royal master. The first wrote on the door of the King's bedchamber :

> "Here lies our sovereign lord, the King,
>   Whose word no man relies on ;
> He never says a foolish thing,
>   Nor ever does a wise one."

To which Charles, on reading it, retorted, "'T is true! because while my words are my own, my acts are my ministers'."

A bright repartee tells us what the second favorite thought. "Ah! Shaftesbury," said the King to him one day, "I verily believe you are the wickedest dog in my dominions." "Yes, your Majesty," replied Shaftesbury, "for a *subject* I think perhaps I may be."

471. The Clarendon Ministry; Punishment of the Regicides. From a political point of view, the new reign began decently and ably under the direction of the Earl of Clarendon as leading minister or adviser to the King. The first act of Charles's first Parliament was to proclaim a pardon to all who had fought against his father in the civil war. The only persons excepted were the members of that high court of justice (§ 448) which had sent Charles I to the block. Of these, ten were executed and nineteen imprisoned for life. Most of the other regicide judges were either already out of the country or managed to escape soon after.

Among these, William Goffe, Edward Whalley, and Colonel John Dixwell took refuge in Connecticut, where they remained concealed for several years. Eventually the first two went to Hadley, Massachusetts, where they lived in seclusion in the house of a clergyman until their death.

The bodies of Oliver Cromwell, Ireton, Bradshaw, and Pride, all of whom had served as judges in the trial and condemnation of Charles (§ 448), were dug up from their graves in Westminster Abbey and hanged in chains at Tyburn.[1] They were then buried at the foot of the gallows along with the moldering remains of highway robbers and criminals of the lowest sort, but Cromwell's head was cut off and set up on a pinnacle of Westminster Hall.[2]

472. Religious Persecution; Covenanters; Bunyan. The first Parliament that met (1661) commanded the common hangman to publicly burn the Solemn League and Covenant (§ 444); it restored the Episcopal form of worship and enacted four very severe

---

[1] Tyburn: near the northeast entrance to Hyde Park, London. It was for several centuries the chief place for the public execution of felons.

[2] It has since been questioned whether Cromwell's body was disposed of in this manner or whether another body, supposed at that time to be his, was dealt with as here described. See the "Dictionary of National (British) Biography," under "Oliver Cromwell."

laws, called the "Clarendon Code," against those Nonconformists or Dissenters who had ejected the Episcopal clergy (§ 444).[1]

The first of these new laws was entitled the "Corporation Act" (1661). It ordered all holders of municipal offices to renounce the Covenant[2] which had been put in force in 1647, and to take the sacrament of the Church of England. Next, a new Act of Uniformity (1662) (§ 382) enforced the use of the Episcopal Prayer Book upon all clergymen and congregations. This was followed by the Conventicle Act[3] (1664), which forbade the meeting of any religious assemblies except such as worshiped according to the Established Church of England. Lastly, the Five-Mile Act (1665) forbade all dissenting ministers to teach in schools, or to settle within five miles of an incorporated town.

The second of these stringent retaliatory statutes, the Act of Uniformity, drove two thousand Presbyterian ministers from their parishes in a single day, and reduced them to the direst distress. The able-bodied among them might indeed pick up a precarious livelihood by hard labor, but the old and the weak soon found their refuge in the grave.

Those who dared to resist these intolerant and inhuman laws were punished with fines, imprisonment, or slavery. The Scottish Parliament abolished Presbyterianism and restored Episcopacy. It vied with the Cavalier or King's party in England in persecution of the Dissenters,[4] and especially of the Covenanters (§ 438).

---

[1] The chief Nonconformists then were: (1) the Presbyterians; (2) the Independents, or Congregationalists; (3) the Baptists; (4) the Society of Friends, or Quakers. Originally the name "Nonconformist" was given to those who refused to conform to the worship of the Church of England, and who attempted to change it to suit their views or else to set up their own form of faith as an independent church. The name "Nonconformist" (or Dissenter) now applies to any Protestant outside the Established Church of England (§§ 496, 498).

[2] Covenant: the oath or agreement to maintain the Presbyterian faith and worship. It originated in Scotland (§ 438).

[3] See, too, on these acts, the Summary of Constitutional History in the Appendix, p. xix, § 20.

[4] The Scottish Parliament granted what was called the "Indulgence" to Presbyterian ministers who held moderate views. The extreme Covenanters regarded these "indulged Presbyterians" as deserters and traitors who were both weak and wicked. For this reason they hated them worse than they did the Episcopalians. See Burton's "Scotland," VII, 457–468.

Claverhouse, who figures as the "Bonny Dundee" of Sir Walter Scott, hunted the Covenanters with bugle and bloodhound, like so many deer; and his men hanged and drowned those who gathered secretly in glens and caves to worship God.[1] The father of a family would be dragged from his cottage by the soldiers, asked if he would take the test of conformity to the Church of England and the oath of allegiance to King Charles II; if he refused, the officer in command gave the order, "Make ready — take aim — fire!" — and there lay the corpse of the rebel.

Among the multitudes who suffered in England for religion's sake was a poor tinker and day laborer named John Bunyan. He had served against the King in the civil wars, and later had become converted to Puritanism, and turned exhorter and itinerant preacher. He was arrested, while preaching in a farmhouse, and convicted of having "devilishly and perniciously abstained from coming to church."

The judge sentenced him to the Bedford county jail, where he remained a prisoner for twelve years (1660-1672). Later on, he was again arrested (1675) and sent to the town jail on Bedford Bridge. It was, he says, a squalid "Denn."[2] But in his marvelous dream of "A Pilgrimage from this World to the Next," which he wrote while shut up within the narrow limits of that filthy prison house, he forgot the misery of his surroundings. Like Milton in his blindness, loneliness, and poverty, he looked within and found that

> "The mind is its own place, and in itself
> Can make a heaven of hell." [3]

473. Seizure of a Dutch Colony in America (1664). While these things were going on in England, a strange event took place abroad. The Dutch had established a colony on the Hudson River. It was on territory which the English claimed (§ 335), but which they had never explored or settled. The Dutch had built a town at the mouth

---

[1] See the historical poem of the "Maiden Martyr of Scotland," in the collection of "Heroic Ballads," Ginn and Company.

[2] "As I walk'd through the wilderness of this world, I lighted on a certain place where there was a Denn, and I laid me down in that place to sleep: and as I slept I dreamed a dream." — "The Pilgrim's Progress," 1678.

[3] "Paradise Lost," Book I, 253.

of the Hudson, which they called New Amsterdam. They held the place undisturbed for fifty years, and if "Possession is nine points of the law," they seem to have acquired it. Furthermore, during the period of Cromwell's Protectorate (§ 455), England had made a treaty with Holland and had recognized the claims of the Dutch in the New World.

Charles had found shelter and generous treatment in Holland when he needed it most. But he now coolly repudiated the treaty, and, though the two nations were at peace, he treacherously sent out a secret expedition to capture the Dutch colony for his brother James, Duke of York, to whom he had granted it.

One day a small English fleet suddenly appeared (1664) in the harbor of the Dutch town, and demanded its immediate and unconditional surrender. The governor was unprepared to make any defense, and the place was given up. Thus, without so much as the firing of a gun, New Amsterdam got the name of New York in honor of the man who had now become its owner. The acquisition of this territory, which had separated the northern English colonies from the southern, gave England complete control of the Atlantic coast from Maine to northern Florida.

474. The Plague and the Fire, 1665, 1666. The next year a terrible outbreak of the plague occurred in London, 1665, which spread throughout the kingdom (§ 244). All who could, fled from the city. Hundreds of houses were left vacant, while on hundreds more a cross marked on the doors in red chalk, with the words "Lord have mercy on us," written underneath, told where the work of death was going on.[1]

This pestilence swept off over a hundred thousand victims within six months. Among the few brave men who voluntarily remained in the stricken city were the Puritan ministers, who stayed to comfort and console the sick and dying. After the plague was over, they received their reward through the enforcement of those

---

[1] Pepys writes in his "Diary," describing the beginning of the plague: "The 7th of June, 1665, was the hottest day I ever felt in my life. This day, much against my will, I did in Drury Lane see two or three houses with a red cross upon the door, and 'Lord have mercy upon us' writ there, which was a sad sight."— PEPYS, "Diary," 1660-1669. Defoe wrote a journal of the plague in 1722, based, probably, on the reports of eyewitnesses. It gives a vivid and truthful account of its horrors.

acts of persecution which drove them homeless and helpless from their parishes and friends (§ 472).

The dead cart had hardly ceased to go its rounds, when a fire broke out, 1666, of which Evelyn, a courtier who witnessed it, wrote that it "was not to be outdone until the final conflagration of the world."[1] By it the city of London proper was reduced to ruins, little more being left than a fringe of houses on the northeast.

Great as the calamity was, yet from a sanitary point of view it did immense good. Nothing short of fire could have effectually

LONDONERS FLEEING FROM THE PLAGUE

From an old print

cleansed the London of that day, and so put a stop to the periodical ravages of the plague. By sweeping away miles of narrow streets crowded with miserable buildings black with the encrusted filth of ages, the conflagration in the end proved friendly to health and life.

A monument near London Bridge still marks the spot where the flames first burst out. For many years it bore an inscription affirming that the Catholics kindled them in order to be revenged on their persecutors. The poet Pope, at a later period, exposed the falsehood in the lines:

"Where London's column pointing toward the skies
Like a tall bully lifts its head and lies."[2]

[1] Evelyn's "Diary," 1641–1705; also compare Dryden's poem "Annus Mirabilis."
[2] "Moral Essays," Epistle III.

Sir Christopher Wren, the most famous architect of the period, rebuilt the city. The greater part of it had been of wood, but it rose from the ashes brick and stone. One irreparable loss was the old Gothic church of St. Paul. Wren erected the present cathedral on the foundations of the ancient structure. He lies buried under the grand dome of his own grandest work. On a tablet near the tomb of the great master builder one reads the inscription in Latin, "Reader, if you seek his monument, look around." [1]

475. Invasion by the Dutch (1667). The new city had not risen from the ruins of the old, when a third calamity overtook it. Charles was at war with France and Holland. The contest with the latter nation grew out of the rivalry of the English and the Dutch to get the exclusive possession of foreign trade (§ 459). Parliament granted the King large sums of money to build and equip a navy, but the pleasure-loving monarch wasted it in dissipation. The few ships he had were rotten old hulks, but half provisioned, with crews ready to mutiny because they could not get their pay.

A Dutch fleet sailed up the Thames. It was manned in part by English sailors who had deserted in disgust because when they asked for cash to support their families they got only worthless government tickets. There was no force to oppose them. They burned some half-built men-of-war, blockaded London for several weeks, and then made their own terms of peace.

476. The "Cabal" (1667–1673); Treaty of Dover, 1670; the King robs the Exchequer (1672). Shortly after this humiliating event the enemies of Clarendon drove him from office (§ 471). The fallen minister was accused of high treason. He had been guilty of certain arbitrary acts, and, rather than stand trial, he fled to France, and was banished for life. He sent a humble petition to the Lords, but they promptly ordered the hangman to burn it. Six years later the old man begged piteously that he might "come back and die in his own country and among his own children." Charles refused to let him return, for Clarendon had committed the unpardonable offense of daring to look "sourly" at the vices of the King and his shameless companions flushed "with insolence

---

[1] "Lector, si monumentum requiris, circumspice."

and wine." Charles now formed a new ministry or "Cabal," [1] consisting of five of his most intimate friends. Several of its members were notorious for their depravity, and Macaulay calls it the "most profligate administration ever known." [2] The chief object of its leaders was to serve their own private interests by making the King's power supreme. The "Cabal's" true spirit was not unlike that of the council of the "infernal peers" which Milton portrays in "Paradise Lost," first published at that time. There he shows us the five princes of evil, Moloch, Belial, Mammon, Beelzebub, and Satan, meeting in the palace of Pandemonium to plot the ruin of the world. [3] The chief ambition of Charles was to rule without a Parliament ; he did not like to have that body inquire too closely how he spent the money which the taxpayers granted him. But his lavish outlays on his favorites made it more and more difficult for him to avoid summoning a Parliament in order to get supplies of cash. At length he hit on a plan for securing the funds he wanted without begging help from Parliament.

Louis XIV of France, then the most powerful monarch in Europe, wished to conquer Holland, with the double object of extending his own kingdom and the power of Catholicism. He saw in Charles the tool he wanted to gain this end. With the aid of two members of the "Cabal," Charles negotiated the secret Treaty of Dover, 1670. Thereby Louis bribed the English King with a gift of £300,000 to help him carry out his scheme. Thus, without the knowledge of Parliament, Charles deliberately sold

---

[1] This word was originally used to designate the confidential members of the King's private council, and meant perhaps no more than the word "cabinet" does to-day. In 1667 it happened, however, by a singular coincidence, that the initial letters of the five persons comprising it, namely, (C)lifford, (A)shley-Cooper [Lord Shaftesbury], (B)uckingham, (A)rlington, and (L)auderdale, formed the word "CABAL," which henceforth came to have the odious meaning of secret and unscrupulous intrigue that it has ever since retained. It was to Charles II's time what the political "ring" is to our own.

[2] Macaulay's "Essay on Sir William Temple."

[3] Milton's "Paradise Lost," Book II. The first edition was published in 1667, the year the "Cabal" came into power, though its members had long been favorites with the King. It has been supposed by some that the great Puritan poet had them in his mind when he represented the Pandemonic debate. Shaftesbury and Buckingham are also two of the most prominent characters in Dryden's noted political satire of "Absalom and Achitophel," published in 1681 ; and compare Butler's "Hudibras."

ST. PAUL'S CATHEDRAL

277

himself to the French sovereign, who was plotting to destroy the political liberty and Protestant faith of Holland.

In addition to the above sum, it was furthermore agreed that Louis should pay Charles a pension of £200,000 a year from the date when the latter should openly avow himself a Roman Catholic. Later (1671), Charles made a sham treaty with Louis XIV in which the article about his avowing himself a Catholic was omitted in order to deceive Parliament.[1]

True to his infamous contract, Charles provoked a new war with the Dutch, but found that he needed more money to prosecute it successfully. Not knowing where to borrow, he determined to steal it. Various London merchants, bankers, and also persons of moderate means had lent to the government sums of money on promise of repayment from the taxes.

A part of the national revenue amounting to about £1,300,000, a sum equal to at least $10,000,000 now, had been deposited in the exchequer, or government treasury, to meet the obligation. The King seized this money,[2] partly for his needs, but chiefly to squander on his vices, and to satisfy the insatiate demands of his favorites, — of whom a single one, the Duchess of Portsmouth, had spent £136,000 within the space of a twelvemonth! The King's treacherous act caused a financial panic which shook London to its foundations and ruined great numbers of people.

477. More Money Schemes; Declaration of Indulgence; Test Act, 1673. By declaring war against Holland Charles had now fulfilled the first part of his secret treaty with Louis (§ 476), but he was afraid to undertake the second part and openly declare himself a convert to the Church of Rome. He, however, did the next thing to it, by issuing a cautiously worded Declaration of Indulgence, 1673, suspending all penal laws affecting the religious liberty of Protestant Dissenters (§§ 382, 472) and Roman Catholics. Under cover of this act the King could show especial favor to the Catholics. Parliament issued such a vigorous protest, however, that the King withdrew the Declaration.

---

[1] See Summary of Constitutional History in the Appendix, p. xix, § 21.

[2] "'Rob me the Exchequer, Hal,' said the King to his favorite minister in the 'Cabal'; then 'all went merry as a marriage bell.'" — Evelyn's "Diary."

Parliament next passed the Test Act,[1] 1673, requiring every government officer to acknowledge himself a Protestant according to the rites of the Church of England. Charles became alarmed at this decided stand, and now tried to conciliate Parliament, and coax from it another grant of money by marrying his niece, the Princess Mary, to William of Orange, President of the Dutch republic, and head of the Protestant party on the Continent.

478. The So-Called "Popish Plot"; the Exclusion Bill, and Disabling Act, 1678. While the King was playing this double part, a scoundrel, named Titus Oates, whose hideous face was but the counterpart of a still more hideous character, pretended that he had discovered a terrible plot. He declared that the Catholics had formed a conspiracy to burn London, massacre the inhabitants, kill the King, and restore the religion of Rome.

The news of this alleged discovery caused an excitement which soon grew into a sort of popular madness. The memory of the great fire (§ 474) was still fresh in people's minds. In their imagination they now saw those scenes of horror repeated, with wholesale murder added. Great numbers of innocent persons were thrown into prison, and many executed.

As time went on, the terror seemed to increase. With its increase, Oates grew bolder in his accusations. Chief Justice Scroggs showed himself an eager abettor of the miserable wretch who swore away men's lives for the sake of the notoriety it gave him. In the extravagance of his presumption Oates even dared to accuse the Queen of an attempt to poison Charles. The craze, however, had at last begun to abate somewhat, no action was taken, and in the next reign Oates got the punishment he deserved — or at least a part of it (§ 485).

An attempt was now made (1679) to pass a law called the "Exclusion Bill," debarring Charles's brother James, the Catholic Duke of York, from succeeding to the crown; but though voted by the Commons, it was defeated by the Lords. Meanwhile a second measure, called the "Disabling Act," had received the sanction of both Houses, 1678. It declared Catholics incapable of sitting in either House of Parliament (§ 382); and from this

[1] See Summary of Constitutional History in the Appendix, p. xix, § 21.

date they remained shut out from all legislative power and from all civil and corporate offices until 1829, a period of over a century and a half (§ 573).

479. Rise of Permanent Political Parties, 1678 ; the King revokes City Charters. It was about this time that the names "Whig" and "Tory" (changed after 1832 to Liberal and Conservative) (§ 582) began to be given to two political parties, which soon became very powerful, and which practically have ever since divided the government of the country between them.

The term "Whig" was originally given by way of reproach to the Scotch Puritans, or Covenanters, who refused to accept the Episcopacy which Charles I endeavored to impose upon them (§ 438). "Tory," on the other hand, was a nickname which appears to have first been applied to the Roman Catholic outlaws of Ireland, who were regarded by Elizabeth and by Cromwell as both robbers and rebels (§ 453).

The name of "Tory" was now given to those who supported the claims of the King's brother James, the Roman Catholic Duke of York, as successor to the throne ; while that of "Whig" (or "Country Party") was borne by those who were endeavoring to exclude him (§ 478), and secure a Protestant successor.[1]

The excitement over this Exclusion Bill (§ 478) threatened at one period to bring on another civil war. In his fury against the Whigs, Charles revoked the charters of London and many other cities, which were regranted only on terms agreeable to the Tories. An actual outbreak against the government would probably have occurred had it not been for the discovery of a new conspiracy, which resulted in a reaction favorable to the Crown.

[1] Politically, the Whigs and Tories may perhaps be considered as the successors of the Roundheads and Cavaliers of the civil war, the former seeking to limit the power of the Crown, the latter to extend it. At the Restoration (1660), the Cavaliers were all-powerful; but at the time of the dispute on the Exclusion Bill (1679), the Roundhead, or People's party, had revived. On account of their petitioning the King to summon a new Parliament, by means of which they hoped to carry the bill shutting out the Catholic Duke of York from the throne, they were called "Petitioners," and later, "Whigs"; while those who expressed their abhorrence of their efforts were called "Abhorrers," and afterwards, "Tories." The more radical Whigs came to be known as the "Country Party," and at least one of their most prominent leaders, Algernon Sidney, was in favor of restoring the republican form of government in England.

480. The Rye-House Plot (1683). This conspiracy, known as the " Rye-House Plot," had for its object the murder of Charles and his brother James at a place called the Rye House in Hertfordshire, not far from London. It was concocted by a number of violent Whigs, who, in their disappointment at their failure to secure the passage of the Exclusion Bill (§ 478), took this method of gaining their ends.

It is said that they intended placing on the throne James, Duke of Monmouth, a natural son of Charles, who was popularly known as the " Protestant Duke." Algernon Sidney, Lord Russell, and the Earl of Essex, who were prominent advocates of the Exclusion Bill (§ 478), were arrested for participating in the plot. Essex committed suicide in the Tower; Sidney and Russell were tried, convicted, and sentenced to death on insufficient evidence. They died martyrs to the cause of liberty, — Russell, with the fortitude of a Christian; Sidney, with the calmness of a philosopher. The Duke of Monmouth, who was supposed to be implicated in the plot, was banished to Holland (§ 486).

481. The Royal Society (1662). Early in this reign the Royal Society was established for purposes of scientific research. In an age when thousands of well-informed people still cherished a lingering belief that lead might be changed into gold; that some medicine might be discovered which would cure every disease, (including old age, that worst disease of all); when every cross-grained old woman was suspected of witchcraft, and was liable to be tortured and hanged on that suspicion, — the formation of an association to study physical facts was most significant.

It showed that the time had come when, instead of guessing what might be, men were at last beginning to resolve to know what actually is. In 1684 an English mathematician and philosopher demonstrated the unity of the universe by proving that the same law which governs the falling of an apple also governs the movements of the planets in their orbits. He published his great work on this subject a few years later.

It was with reference to that wonderful discovery of the all-pervading power of gravitation, which shapes and holds in its control the drop of dew before our eyes, and the farthest star shining in the heavens, that the poet Pope suggested the epitaph which should be graven on the tomb of the great thinker in Westminster Abbey :

> " Nature and Nature's laws lay hid in night ;
> God said, ' Let Newton be ! ' and all was light."

482. Chief Political Reforms ; Abolition of Feudal Dues, 1660 ; the Habeas Corpus Act, 1679. As the age did not stand still with respect to progress in knowledge, so it was not wholly unsuccessful in political progress. A great reform inaugurated in the outset of Charles's reign was the abolition, 1660, of the King's right to feudal dues and service, by which he was accustomed to extort as much as possible from his subjects [1] (§ 150), and the substitution of a fixed yearly allowance, raised by tax, of £1,200,000 on beer and liquor.[2] This change may be considered to have practically abolished the feudal system in England, so far as the Crown is concerned, though the law still retains some remnants of that system with respect to the relation of landlord and tenant.[3]

The second great reform measure was the Habeas Corpus Act,[4] 1679, which provided that no subject should be detained in prison except by due process of law, thus putting an end to the arbitrary confinement of men for months, and years even, without conviction of guilt or even form of trial.

483. Death of Charles. The reign came suddenly to an end (1685). Evelyn, one of the courtiers of the day, tells us in his " Diary " that he was present at the palace of Whitehall on Sunday morning, the last of January of that year. There he saw the King sitting in the grand banqueting room, chatting gayly with three famous court beauties, — his special favorites, — while a

---

[1] See Blackstone's " Commentaries," II, 76.

[2] This tax should have been levied on the landed proprietors who had been subject to the feudal dues, but they managed to put it on beer and spirits ; this compelled the body of the people to bear the burden for them.

[3] See Summary of Constitutional History in the Appendix, p. xviii, § 20.

[4] *Habeas Corpus* (1679) (you may have the body) : This writ is addressed by the judge to him who detains another in custody, commanding him to bring him into court and show why he is restrained of his liberty. The right of Habeas Corpus was contained in germ in the Great Charter (§ 199, Article 2) ; and see Summary of Constitutional History in the Appendix, p. xix, § 21, and p. xxxii.

crowd of richly dressed nobles were gathered around a gambling table heaped with gold. Six days after, as he expresses it, all was " in the dust."

Charles died a Roman Catholic, his Catholic brother James (§ 478) having quietly brought a priest into the King's chamber in time to hear his confession and grant him absolution. Certainly few English rulers ever stood in greater need of both.

484. Summary. The chief events of the period were the persecution of the Puritans, the Plague and Great Fire of London, the Secret Treaty of Dover, the Test Act, the Disabling Act, the so-called " Popish Plot," the Rye-House Plot, the Dutch Wars, the Abolition of Feudal Dues, the Habeas Corpus Act, the rise of permanent Political Parties, and Newton's Discovery of the Law of Gravitation. Aside from these, the reign presents two leading points : (1) the policy of the King ; (2) that of the nation.

Charles II, as we have seen, lived solely to gratify his inordinate love of pleasure. For that, he wasted the revenue, robbed the exchequer, and cheated the navy ; for that, he secretly sold himself to France, made war on Holland, and shamefully deceived both Parliament and people.

In so far, then, as Charles II had an object, it began and ended with himself. Therein he stood lower than his father, who at least conscientiously believed in the Divine Right of Kings (§ 429) and their accountability to the Almighty.

The policy of the nation, on the other hand, was divided. The Whigs were determined to limit the power of the Crown, and secure at all hazards a Protestant successor to the throne. The Tories were equally resolved to check the growing power of the people, and preserve the hereditary order of succession (then in the Stuart family) without any immediate regard to the religious question involved in the Exclusion Bill (§ 478).

Beneath these issues both parties had a common object, which was to maintain the National Episcopal Church and the monarchical system of government. Whigs and Tories alike detested the principles of the late Commonwealth period. They preferred to cherish patriotism through loyalty to a personal sovereign rather than patriotism through devotion to a democratic republic.

JAMES II — 1685-1689

485. James II ; his Proclamation ; his Two Objects ; Titus Oates again. James, Duke of York, brother of the late Charles II, now came to the throne. He at once issued a Proclamation pledging himself to " preserve the government in both Church and State as it is now by law established." This solemn declaration was welcomed as " the word of a king," but unfortunately that king did not keep his word. His first great ambition was to rule independently of Parliament, so that he might have his own way in everything ; his second, which was, if possible, still nearer his heart, was to restore the Roman Catholic religion in England (§§ 370, 382, 477).

He began that restoration at once ; and on the Easter Sunday preceding his coronation, " the worship of the Church of Rome was once more, after an interval of a hundred and twenty-seven years, performed at Westminster with royal splendor." [1]

Not long afterwards James brought the miscreant Oates to trial for the perjuries he had committed in connection with the so-called " Popish Plot " (§ 478). He was found guilty and sentenced to imprisonment for life ; in addition he was publicly whipped through London with such terrible severity that a few more strokes of the lash would have ended his worthless life (1685). But in the next reign Oates was liberated and a pension was granted him.

486. Monmouth's Rebellion ; Sedgemoor, 1685. At the time of the discovery of the Rye-House Plot (§ 480) a number of Whigs (§ 479) who were implicated in the conspiracy fled to Holland, where the Duke of Monmouth had gone when banished. Four months after the accession of James, the Duke, aided by these refugees and by a small force which he had gathered in the Netherlands, resolved to invade England and demand the crown. He believed that a large part of the nation would look upon him as representing the cause of Protestantism, and would therefore rally to his support. He landed at Lyme on the coast of Dorsetshire (1685), and there issued an absurd proclamation declaring James to be a usurper, tyrant, and murderer, who had set the great fire of London (§ 474), cut the throat of Essex (§ 480), and poisoned Charles II !

1 Macaulay's " England."

At Taunton, in Somersetshire, a procession of welcome, headed by a lady carrying a Bible, met the Duke, and presented him with the book in behalf of the Protestant faith. He received it, saying, " I come to defend the truths contained in this volume, and to seal them, if it must be so, with my blood." Shortly afterwards he proclaimed himself sovereign of Great Britain. He was popularly known as " King Monmouth." Many of the country people now joined him, but the Whig nobles (§ 479), on whose help he had counted, stood aloof, alienated doubtless by the ridiculous charges he had made against James.

At the battle of Sedgemoor, in Somersetshire (1685), " King Monmouth," with his hastily gathered forces, was utterly routed. He himself was soon afterwards captured, hiding in a ditch. He desired to be taken to the King. His request was granted. When he entered his uncle's presence, he threw himself down and crawled to his feet, weeping and begging piteously for life — only life — on any terms, however hard.

He denied that he had issued the lying proclamation published at Lyme ; he denied that he had sought the crown of his own free will ; finally, in an agony of supplication, he hinted that he would even renounce Protestantism if thereby he might escape death. James told him that he should have the service of a Catholic priest, but would promise nothing more. Monmouth groveled and pleaded, but the King's heart was like marble, and he turned away in silence. Then the Duke, seeing that all his efforts were vain, rose to his feet and regained his manhood.

He was forthwith sent to the Tower, and shortly afterwards to execution. His headless body was buried under the communion table of that little chapel of St. Peter within the Tower grounds, where the remains of Anne Boleyn, Lady Jane Grey, Sir Thomas More, and many other royal victims, are gathered. No sadder spot exists on earth, " since there death is associated with whatever is darkest in human nature and human destiny." [1]

After Monmouth's death there were no further attempts at insurrection, and the struggle at Sedgemoor remains the last encounter worthy of the name of battle fought on English soil.

[1] Macaulay's " England."

487. The " Bloody Assizes " (1685). The defeat of the insurgents who had rallied under Monmouth's flag was followed by a series of trials known, from their results, as the " Bloody Assizes " (1685). They were conducted by Judge Jeffreys, assisted by a band of soldiers under Colonel Kirke, ironically called, from their ferocity, " Kirke's Lambs." Jeffreys was by nature cruel, and enjoyed the spectacle of mental as well as bodily anguish. As he himself said, he delighted to give those who had the misfortune to appear before him " a lick with the rough side of his tongue," preparatory to roaring out the sentence of torture or death, in which he delighted still more.

All who were in the remotest way implicated in the late rebellion were now hunted down and brought to a trial which was but a mockery of justice. No one was permitted to defend himself. In fact, defense would have been useless against the blind fury of such a judge. The threshold of the court was to most that crossed it the threshold of the grave. A gentleman present at one of these scenes of slaughter, touched with pity at the condition of a trembling old man called up for sentence, ventured to put in a word in his behalf. " My Lord," said he to Jeffreys, " this poor creature is dependent on the parish." " Don't trouble yourself," cried the judge; " I will soon ease the parish of the burden," and ordered the officers to execute him at once.

Those who escaped death were often still more to be pitied. A young man was sentenced to be imprisoned for seven years, and to be whipped once a year through every market town in the county. In his despair, he petitioned the King to grant him the favor of being hanged. The petition was refused, but a partial remission of the punishment was at length gained by bribing the court; for Jeffreys, though his heart was shut against mercy, always had his pockets open for gain. Alice Lisle, an aged woman, who, out of pity, had concealed two men flying from the King's vengeance, was condemned to be burned alive ; and it was with the greatest difficulty that the clergy of Winchester Cathedral succeeded in getting the sentence commuted to beheading.

As the work went on, the spirits of Jeffreys rose higher and higher. He laughed, shouted, joked, and swore like a drunken man. When the court had finished its sittings, more than a thousand persons had been brutally scourged, sold as slaves, hanged, or beheaded. The guideposts of the highways were converted into gibbets, from which blackened corpses swung in chains, and from every church tower in Somersetshire ghastly heads looked down on those who gathered there to worship God; in fact, so many bodies were exposed that the whole air was ." tainted with corruption and death."

Not satisfied with vengeance alone, Jeffreys and his friends made these trials a means of speculation. Batches of rebels were given as presents to courtiers, who sold them for a period of ten years to be worked to death or flogged to death on West India plantations; and the Queen's maids of honor extorted large sums of money for the pardon of a number of country schoolgirls who had been convicted of presenting Monmouth with a royal flag at Taunton.

On the return of Jeffreys to London after this carnival of blood, his father was so horrified at his cruelty that he forbade him to enter his house. James, on the contrary, testified his approval by making Jeffreys Lord Chancellor of the realm, at the same time mildly censuring him for not having shown greater severity!

The new Lord Chancellor testified his gratitude to his royal master by procuring the murder, by means of a packed jury, of Alderman Cornish, a prominent London Whig (§ 479), who was especially hated by the King on account of his support of that Exclusion Bill (§ 478) which was intended to shut James out from the throne. On the same day on which Cornish was executed, Jeffreys also had the satisfaction of knowing that Elizabeth Gaunt was burned alive at Tyburn, London, for having assisted one of the Rye-House conspirators, who had fought for Monmouth at Sedgemoor, to escape.

488. The King makes Further Attempts to reëstablish Catholicism; Second Declaration of Indulgence (1687); Oxford. An event occurred about this time which encouraged James to make a more decided attempt to restore Catholicism. Henry IV of France had granted the Protestants of his kingdom liberty of worship, by the Edict of Nantes (1598). Louis XIV deliberately revoked it (1685).

By that shortsighted act the Huguenots, or French Protestants, were exposed to cruel persecution, and thousands of them fled to England and America.

James, who, like his late brother Charles II, was "the pensioned slave of the French King" (§ 476), resolved to profit by the example set him by Louis. He did not expect to drive the Protestants out of Great Britain as Louis had driven them from France, but he hoped to restore the country to its allegiance to Rome (§§ 370, 382, 477). He began by suspending the Test Act (§ 477) and putting Catholics into important offices in both Church and State.[1] He furthermore established an army of 13,000 men on Hounslow Heath, just outside London (1686), to hold the city in subjection in case it should rebel.

He next recalled the Protestant Duke of Ormonde, governor of Ireland, and put in his place Talbot, Earl of Tyrconnel, a Catholic. Tyrconnel had orders to recruit an Irish Roman Catholic army to aid the King in carrying out his designs (1687). He raised some soldiers, but he also raised that famous song of "Lilli Burlero," by which, as its author boasted, James was eventually "sung out of his kingdom."[2]

Having got the courts completely under his control through the appointment of judges in sympathy with Jeffreys (§ 487) and with himself, the King issued a Declaration of Indulgence similar to that

[1] The Dispensing Power and the Suspending Power were prerogatives by which the King claimed the right of preventing the enforcement of such laws as he deemed contrary to public good. A packed bench of judges sustained the King in this position, but the power so to act was finally abolished by the Bill of Rights (1689). See § 497 and top of page xxxii, Article XII.

[2] Lord Wharton, a prominent English Whig (§ 479), was the author of this satirical political ballad, which, it is said, was sung and whistled from one end of England to the other, in derision of the King's policy. It undoubtedly had a powerful popular influence in bringing on the Revolution of 1688.

The ballad began:

> "Ho, Brother Teague, dost hear de decree?
> Lilli Burlero, bullen a-la,
> Dat we shall have a new deputie,
> Lilli Burlero, bullen a-la."

The refrain, "Lilli Burlero," etc. (also written "Lillibullero"), is said to have been the watchword used by the Irish Catholics when they rose against the Protestants of Ulster in 1641. See Wilkins's "Political Songs," Vol I.

which his brother Charles II had issued (§ 477).[1] It suspended all penal laws against both the Roman Catholics on the one hand, and the Protestant Dissenters (§ 472) on the other. The latter, however, suspecting that this apparently liberal measure was simply a trick to establish Catholicism, refused to avail themselves of it, and denounced it as an open violation of the Constitution.

James next proceeded, by means of the tyrannical High Commission Court, which he had revived (§ 382), to bring Magdalen College, Oxford, under Catholic control. The President of that college having died, the Fellows were considering the choice of a successor. The King ordered them to elect a Catholic. The Fellows refused to obey, and elected a Protestant. James ejected the new President, and drove out the Fellows, leaving them to depend on the charity of the neighboring country gentlemen for their support.

But the King, in attacking the rights of the college, had "run his head against a wall,"[2] as he soon discovered to his sorrow. His temporary success, however, emboldened him to reissue the Declaration of Indulgence (1688). Its real object, like that of the first Declaration (§ 477), was to put Roman Catholics into still higher positions of trust and power.

489. The Petition of the Seven Bishops, 1688. James commanded the clergy throughout the realm to read this Declaration (§ 488) on a given Sunday from their pulpits. The clergy were by nature conservative. They still generally upheld the theory of the "Divine Right of Kings" and of "Passive Obedience." A majority of them taught the doctrine which James I had proclaimed: "God makes the King; the King makes the law; his subjects are bound to obey that law" (§§ 419, 429). Now, however, nearly all of them revolted. They felt that to comply with the mandate of the King would be to strike a blow at the supremacy of the Church of England. In this crisis the Archbishop of Canterbury, accompanied by six bishops, petitioned the King to be excused from reading it from their pulpits. The King refused to consider

---

[1] See Summary of Constitutional History in the Appendix, p. xxi, § 23.

[2] "What building is that?" asked the Duke of Wellington of his companion, Mr. Croker, pointing, as he spoke, to Magdalen College wall, just as they entered Oxford in 1834. "That is the wall which James II ran his head against," was the reply.

the petition. When the day came, hardly a clergyman read the paper, and in Westminster Abbey the entire congregation rose in a body and left rather than listen to it. Furious at such an unexpected result, James ordered the refractory bishops to be sent to the Tower and kept prisoners there.

The whole country now seemed to turn against the King. By his obstinate folly James had succeeded in making enemies of all

THE SEVEN BISHOPS GOING TO THE TOWER

classes, not only of the Whig Roundheads (§ 479) who had fought against his father in the civil war, but also of the Tory Cavaliers (§ 479) who had fought for him, and of the clergy who had taught the duty of obedience to him.

One of the bishops sent to the Tower was Trelawney of Bristol. He was a native of Cornwall. The news of his imprisonment roused the rough, independent population of that country. From one end of it to the other the people were now heard singing:

" And shall Trelawney die, and shall Trelawney die?
   There 's thirty thousand Cornishmen will know the reason why."

Then the miners took up the words, and beneath the hills and fields the ominous echo was heard:

" And shall Trelawney die, and shall Trelawney die?
  There's twenty thousand underground will know the reason why."

When the seven bishops were brought to trial the popular feeling in their favor was so strong that not even James's servile judges dared use their influence to convict them. After the case was given to the jury, the largest and most robust man of the twelve rose and said to the rest: "Look at me! I am bigger than any of you, but before I will bring in a verdict of guilty, I will stay here until I am no thicker than a tobacco pipe." That decided the matter, and the bishops were acquitted (1688). The news was received in London like the tidings of some great victory, with shouts of joy, illuminations, and bonfires.

490. Birth of a Prince ; Invitation to William of Orange (1688). But just before the acquittal an event took place which changed everything and brought on the " Glorious Revolution " of 1688, — for such was the title which was solemnly given to it after William and Mary had come to the throne (§§ 491, 494).

Up to this time the succession to the throne after James rested with his two daughters, — Mary, who had married William, Prince of Orange (§ 477), President of the Dutch republic, and resided in Holland ; and her younger sister Anne, who had married George, Prince of Denmark, and was then living in London. Both of the daughters were zealous Protestants, and the expectation that one of them would receive the English crown on the King's death had kept the people quiet while James was endeavoring to restore Catholicism.

But while the seven bishops were in prison awaiting trial (§ 489) the alarming intelligence was spread that a son had been born to the King (1688). If true, he would now be the next heir to the crown, and would in all probability be educated and come to power a Catholic. This prospect brought matters to a crisis.

Many people, especially the Whigs (§ 479), believed the whole matter an imposition, and it was reported that the young Prince was not the true son of the King and Queen, but a child that had been smuggled into the palace to deceive the nation. For this report there was absolutely no foundation in fact.

On the very day that the bishops were set at liberty (§ 489) seven of the leading nobility and gentry, representing both the Whigs and the Tories (§ 479),[1] seconded by the city of London, secretly sent a formal invitation to William, Prince of Orange, " the champion of Protestantism on the Continent and the deadly foe of James's ally, the King of France." Admiral Herbert, disguised as a common sailor, set out on the perilous errand to the Prince. The invitation he carried implored William to come over with an army to defend his wife Mary's claim to the English throne, and to ensure " the restoration of English liberties and the protection of the Protestant religion."

William decided to accept the invitation, which was probably not unexpected on his part. He was confirmed in his decision not only by the cordial approval of the leading Catholic princes of Europe, except, of course, Louis XIV of France, but also by the Pope himself, who had more than once expressed his emphatic disgust at the foolish rashness of King James.[2]

491. The " Glorious Revolution " of 1688; William comes, James goes. William's ship, which led his fleet, displayed this flag.

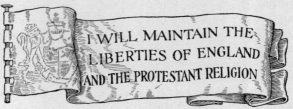

He landed with 14,000 troops on the shore of Torbay, Devonshire. (See map facing p. 334.) It was the fifth and last great

---

[1] The seven gentlemen who signed in cipher the secret letter to William, Prince of Orange, were Henry Sidney, brother of Algernon Sidney (§ 480); Edward Russell, a kinsman of Lord Russell, beheaded by Charles II (§ 480); the Earl of Devonshire, chief of the Whig party; Lord Shrewsbury; Danby, the old Tory minister of Charles II; Compton, Bishop of London, whom James II had tyrannically suspended; and Lord Lumley. See the letter in J. Dalrymple's " Memoirs of Great Britain," II, Appendix, p. 228.

[2] Bright's, Guizot's, Lingard's, and Von Ranke's Histories of England.

landing in the history of England.[1] He declared that he came in the interest of his wife Mary, the heir to the throne (§ 477), and in the interest of the English nation, to secure a free and legal Parliament which should decide the question of the succession. James endeavored to rally a force to resist him, but Baron Churchill, afterwards Duke of Marlborough (§ 509), and the King's son-in-law, Prince George, both secretly went over to William's side.

His troops likewise deserted, and finally even his daughter Anne went over to the enemy. " Now God help me!" exclaimed James, in despair; " for my own children forsake me ! " The Queen had already fled to France, taking with her her infant son, the unfortunate Prince James Edward, whose birth (§ 490) had caused the revolution. Instead of a kingdom, he inherited nothing but the nickname of " Pretender," which he in turn transmitted to his son.[2] King James soon followed his wife.

As he crossed the Thames in a boat by night, James threw the Great Seal of State into the river, in the vain hope that without it a Parliament could not be legally summoned to decide the question which his adversary had raised.[3] The King got as far as the coast, but was discovered by some fishermen and brought back. William reluctantly received him, and purposely allowed him to escape a second time. He reached France, and Louis XIV, who had long had the treacherous King in his secret pay, received him at the court of Versailles. There could be now no reasonable doubt that James's daughter Mary (§ 477) would receive the English crown.

492. Character of the Revolution of 1688. Never was a revolution of such magnitude and meaning accomplished more peacefully. Not a drop of blood had been shed. There was hardly any excitement or uproar. Even the bronze statue of the runaway King was permitted to stand undisturbed in the rear of the palace of Whitehall, London, where it remains to this day.

---

[1] The first being that of the Romans, the next that of the Saxons, the third that of St. Augustine, the fourth that of William the Conqueror, the fifth that of the Prince of Orange.

[2] Prince James Edward Stuart, the so-called " Old Pretender," and his son, Prince Charles Edward Stuart, the so-called " Young Pretender." See, too, Genealogical Table, p. 323.

[3] On the Great Seal of State (§ 145).

The great change had taken place thus quietly because men's minds were ripe for it. England had entered upon another period of history, in which old institutions, laws, and customs were passing away and all was becoming new.

Feudalism had vanished under Charles II (§ 482), but political and religious persecution had continued. In future, however, we shall hear no more of the revocation of city charters or of other punishments inflicted because of political opinion (§§ 479, 487), and rarely of any punishment for religious dissent.

Courts of justice will undergo reform. They will cease to be " little better than caverns of murderers," [1] where judges like Scroggs and Jeffreys (§§ 478, 487) browbeat the prisoners, took their guilt for granted, insulted and silenced witnesses for their defense, and even cast juries into prison under penalties of heavy fines, for venturing to bring in verdicts contrary to their wishes. [2]

The day, too, had gone by when an English sovereign could cast his subjects into fetid dungeons in the Tower and leave them to die there of lingering disease, in darkness, solitude, and despair. No future king like the marble-hearted James II would sit in the court room at Edinburgh, and watch with curious delight the agony inflicted by the Scotch instruments of torture, the " boot " and the thumbscrew, or like his grandfather, James I, burn Unitarian heretics at the stake in Smithfield market place in London (§ 518).

For the future, thought and discussion in England were to be in great measure free, as in time they would be wholly so. Perhaps the coward King's heaviest retribution in his secure retreat in the royal French palace of Versailles was the knowledge that all his efforts, and all the efforts of his friend Louis XIV, to prevent the coming of this liberty had absolutely failed.

493. Summary. The reign of James must be regarded as mainly taken up with the attempt of the King to rule independently of Parliament and of law, and, apparently, he sought to restore the Roman Catholic faith as the Established Church of England.

---

[1] Hallam's " Constitutional History of England," p. 138. Hallam also says that the behavior of the Stuart judges covered them " with infamy," p. 597.

[2] See Hallam, and also the introduction to Professor Adams's " Manual of Historical Literature." For a graphic picture of the times, see, in Bunyan's " Pilgrim's Progress," Christian's trial before Lord Hategood.

THE PRINCE OF ORANGE LANDING IN ENGLAND

Monmouth's rebellion, though without real justification, since he could not legitimately claim the crown, was a forerunner of that memorable Revolution which invited William of Orange to come to the support of Parliament, and which placed a Protestant King and Queen on the throne.

WILLIAM AND MARY (HOUSE OF ORANGE-STUART) — 1689–1702

494. The " Convention Parliament "; the Declaration of Right. 1689. After the flight of James II, a " Convention Parliament " met, and declared that, James having broken " the original contract between king and people," the throne was therefore vacant. The Convention next issued a formal statement of principles under the name of the " Declaration of Right," 1689.[1]

That document recited the illegal and arbitrary acts of the late King James II, proclaimed him no longer sovereign, and resolved that the crown should be tendered to William and Mary.[2] The Declaration having been read to them and having received their assent, they were formally invited to accept the joint sovereignty of the realm, with the understanding that the actual administration should be vested in William alone.

495. Jacobites and Nonjurors (1689). At the accession of the new sovereigns the extreme Tories (§ 479), who believed the action of the Convention unconstitutional, continued to adhere to James II as their lawful King. Henceforth this class became known as " Jacobites," from *Jacobus*, the Latin name for James. They were especially numerous and determined in the Highlands of Scotland and the south of Ireland. They kept up a secret correspondence with the refugee monarch, and were constantly plotting for his restoration.

About four hundred of the clergy of the Church of England, including the Archbishop of Canterbury and four more of the

[1] It was called a " Convention Parliament " because it had not been summoned by the King (§ 491). Declaration of Right : see Summary of Constitutional History in the Appendix, p. xxii, § 24. On the coronation oath see § 380, note 1.

[2] William of Orange stood next in order of succession to Mary and Anne (provided the claim of the newly born Prince James, the so-called " Pretender," was set aside [§§ 490, 491]). See Genealogical Table, p. 323.

famous seven bishops (§ 489), with some members of the universities and also some Scotch Presbyterians, refused to take the oath of allegiance to William and Mary. They became known on this account as the "Nonjurors," and although they were never harshly treated, they were compelled to resign their positions.

496. The Mutiny Act and the Toleration Act, 1689. We have seen that one of the chief means of despotism on which James II relied was the organization of a powerful standing army (§ 488), such as was unknown in England until Cromwell was compelled to rule by military force (§ 457). Charles II had perpetuated such an army (§ 467), but it was so small that it was no longer formidable.

It was now evident that owing to the abolition of the feudal levies (§§ 150, 482) a standing army under the King's command must be maintained, especially as war was impending with Louis XIV, who threatened by force of arms and with the help of the Jacobites (§ 495) to restore James II to the English throne. To prevent the sovereign from making bad use of such a power, Parliament passed a law called the "Mutiny Act," 1689, which practically put the army under the control of the nation,[1] as it has since remained. Thus all danger from that source was taken away.

James's next method for bringing the country under the control of Rome had been to issue Declarations of Indulgence (§ 488). It was generally believed that his object in granting these measures of toleration, which promised freedom to all religious beliefs, was that he might place Roman Catholics in power.

As an offset to these Declarations, Parliament now passed the Toleration Act, 1689, which secured freedom of worship to all religious believers except "Papists and such as·deny the Trinity." This measure, though one-sided and utterly inconsistent with the broader and juster ideas of toleration which have since prevailed, was nevertheless a most important reform. It put an end at once and forever to the persecution which had disgraced the reigns of

---

[1] The Mutiny Act provides : (1) that the standing army shall be at the King's command — subject to certain rules — for one year only ; (2) that no pay shall be issued to troops except by special acts of Parliament ; (3) that no act of mutiny can be punished except by the annual reënactment of the Mutiny Bill.

the Stuarts, though unfortunately it still left the Catholics, the Unitarians, and the Jews subject to the heavy hand of tyrannical oppression,[1] and they remained so for many years (§§ 573, 599).

497. The Bill of Rights, 1689, and Act of Settlement, 1701. Not many months later, Parliament embodied the Declaration of Right (§ 494), with some slight changes, in the Bill of Rights, 1689,[2] which received the signature of the King and became law. It constitutes the third and last great step which England has taken in making anything like a formal *written* Constitution,[3] — the first being Magna Carta, or the Great Charter (§ 199), and the second the Petition of Right (§ 432). The Habeas Corpus Act (§ 482) was contained, in germ at least, in Magna Carta (§ 199 (2)); hence these three measures, namely, Magna Carta, 1215; the Petition of Right, 1628; and the Bill of Rights, 1689 (including the Act of Settlement to be mentioned presently), sum up the written safeguards of the nation, and constitute, as Lord Chatham said, " *The Bible of English Liberty.*"

With the passage of the Bill of Rights,[4] the doctrine of the Divine Right of Kings to govern without being accountable to their subjects (§§ 419, 429), which James I and his descendants had tried so hard to reduce to practice, came to an end forever.

The chief provisions of the Bill of Rights were :

(1) That the King should not maintain a standing army in time of peace, except by consent of Parliament.

(2) That no money should be taken from the people save by the consent of Parliament.

(3) That every subject has the right to petition the Crown for the redress of any grievance.

(4) That the election of members of Parliament ought to be free from interference.

---

[1] In 1663 Charles granted a charter to Rhode Island which secured religious liberty to that colony. It was the first royal charter recognizing the principle of toleration.

[2] See Summary of Constitutional History in the Appendix, p. xxii, § 25, and p. xxxi.

[3] It should be borne in mind that a large part of the English Constitution is based on ancient customs or unwritten laws, and another part on acts of Parliament passed for specific purposes.

[4] For summary of the bill, see Constitutional Documents in the Appendix, p. xxxi. For the complete text, see Taswell-Langmead's " Constitutional History of England " or Lee's " Source Book of English History."

(5) That Parliament should frequently assemble and enjoy entire freedom of debate.

(6) That the King be debarred from interfering in any way with the proper execution of the laws.

(7) That a Roman Catholic or a person marrying a Roman Catholic be henceforth incapable of receiving the crown of England.

Late in the reign (1701) Parliament reaffirmed and still further extended the provisions of the Bill of Rights by the Act of Settlement, which established a new royal line of sovereigns confined exclusively to Protestants.[1] This Act with the preceding one may be said to have introduced that principle of the British Constitution which has been called "The Reign of Law." It practically abolished the principle of a fixed hereditary succession and reëstablished in the clearest and most decided manner the right of the nation to choose its own rulers.

According to that measure, "an English sovereign is now as much the creature of an act of Parliament as the pettiest taxgatherer in his realm";[2] and he is dependent for his office and power on the will of the people as really, though of course not as directly as the President of the United States.

Finally, the Bill of Rights and the Act of Settlement, by restricting the royal succession to Protestants, made it henceforth unconstitutional for the Crown to permit or invite the Papal Power to take any recognized part in the government of England. The enactment of these two measures, therefore, effectually put an end to that great conflict between England and Rome which had been going on, in some form, for more than six hundred years (§ 349, note 2).

To-day entire harmony exists. Catholics and Protestants "work together for good" in Parliament, in the Cabinet, in the Courts

---

[1] Compare § 349, note 2. The Act of Settlement (see p. xxxii of Appendix) provided that after Princess Anne (in default of issue by William or Anne) the crown should descend to the Electress Sophia of Hanover, Germany, and her *Protestant descendants*. The Electress Sophia was the granddaughter of James I. She married Ernest Augustus, Elector (or ruler) of Hanover. As Hallam says, she was "very far removed from any hereditary title," as, aside from James II's son (§ 490), whose legitimacy no one now doubted, there were several who stood nearer in right of succession.

[2] Green's "Short History of the English People" and Bryce's "American Commonwealth."

of Justice, in the Universities, in the Army and Navy, in the service of the Press, and in private life.[1]

498. Further Benefits of the Revolution. Foremost in the list of other benefits which England gained by the Revolution of 1688 should be placed: 1. The Toleration Act already mentioned (§ 496), which gave a very large number of people the right of worshiping God according to the dictates of conscience, and which was the stepping-stone to later measures that completed the good work of extending religious liberty in England (§§ 573, 599).

2. Parliament now established the salutary rule that no money should be voted to the King except for specific purposes, and it also limited the royal revenue to a few years' supply instead of granting it for life, as had been done in the case of Charles II and James. Later the supply was limited to an annual grant. As the Mutiny Act (§ 496) made the army dependent for its existence on the annual meeting and action of the House of Commons, these two measures practically gave the people full control of the two great powers, — the purse and the sword, — which they have ever since retained.

3. Parliament next enacted that judges should hold office not as heretofore, at his Majesty's pleasure, but during good behavior (or until the death of the reigning sovereign vacated their commissions). This took away that dangerous authority of the King over the courts of justice, which had caused so much oppression and cruelty.

4. But, as Macaulay remarks, of all the reforms produced by the change of government, perhaps none proved more extensively useful than the establishment of the liberty of the press. Up to this time no book or newspaper could be published in England without a license.[2] In the period of the Commonwealth John Milton, the great Puritan poet, had earnestly labored to get this severe law repealed, declaring that "while he who kills a man kills a reasonable creature, . . . he who destroys a good book [by refusing to let it appear in print] kills reason itself."[3] But under James II,

[1] The names of many eminent Catholics might be cited, such as Professor Lingard, the historian (1851), the late Lord Chief Justice Russell, the late Lord Acton, Professor of History at Cambridge, and the late Sir Francis Burnand, editor of *Punch.*

[2] See Summary of Constitutional History in the Appendix, p. xxiii, § 26.

[3] Milton's "Areopagitica," or "Speech for the Liberty of Unlicensed Printing."

Chief Justice Scroggs had declared it a crime to publish anything whatever concerning the government, whether true or false, without a license. During that reign there were only four places in England — namely, London, Oxford, Cambridge, and York — where any book, pamphlet, or newspaper could be legally issued, and then only with the sanction of a rigid inspector.

Under William and Mary this restriction was removed. Henceforth men were free not only to think, but to print and circulate their thought (subject, of course, to the law of libel and sedition). They could thus bring the government more directly before that bar of public opinion which judges all men and all institutions.

499. James II lands in Ireland (1689); Act of Attainder; Siege of Londonderry. But though William was King of England, and had been accepted as King of Scotland, yet the Irish, like the Scotch Highlanders, refused to recognize him as their lawful sovereign. The great body of Irish population was then, as now, Roman Catholic. But they had been gradually dispossessed of their hold on the land (§§ 159, 402, 453), and the larger part of the most desirable portion of the island was owned by a few hundred thousand Protestant colonists.

On the other hand, James II had, during his reign, put the civil government and the military power in the hands of the Catholics. The Earl of Tyrconnel (§ 488) now raised the standard of rebellion in Ireland in the interest of the Catholics, and invited James II to come over from France (§ 491) and regain his throne. The Protestants of the north stood by William of Orange (§ 491), and thus got that name of Orangemen which they have ever since retained. James landed in Ireland in the spring (1689) with a small French force lent him by Louis XIV (§ 491).

He established his headquarters at Dublin. Not long afterwards he issued that great Act of Attainder (1689) which summoned all who were in rebellion against his authority to appear for trial on a given day, or be declared traitors, hanged, drawn, and quartered, and their property confiscated.[1] Next, the Protestant city of

---

[1] Attainder (§ 351): This act contained between two and three thousand names. It embraced all classes, from half the peerage of Ireland to tradesmen, women, and children. If they failed to appear, they could be put to death without trial.

Londonderry (§ 423) was besieged (1689). For more than three months it held out against shot and shell, famine and fever.

The starving inhabitants, exceeding thirty thousand in number, were finally reduced to the last extremities. Nothing was left to eat but a few miserable horses and some salted hides. As they looked into each other's hollow eyes, the question came, Must we surrender? Then it was that an aged clergyman, the venerable George Walker, one of the governors of the city, pleaded with them, Bible in hand, to remain firm.

That appeal carried the day. They declared that rather than open the gates to the enemy, they would perish of hunger, or, as some voice whispered, that they would fall " first on the horses and the hides, — *then on the prisoners*, — then — *on each other !*" But at this moment, when all hope seemed lost, a shout of triumph was heard. An English force had sailed up the river, broken through all obstructions, and the valiant city was saved.

500. Battle of the Boyne, 1690 ; Treaty of Limerick. A year later occurred the decisive battle of the Boyne,[1] 1690, at which King William commanded in person on one side, while James II was present on the opposite side. William had a somewhat larger force and by far the greater number of well-armed, veteran troops. The contest ended with the utter defeat of James. He stood on a hill at a safe distance, and when he saw that the battle was going against him, turned and fled to France. William, on the other hand, though suffering from a wound, led his own men. The cowardly behavior of James excited the disgust and scorn of both the French and Irish. " Change kings with us," shouted an Irish officer later, to one of William's men, " change kings with us, and we 'll fight you over again."

The war was brought to an end by the treaty of Limerick (1691), when about ten thousand Irish soldiers who had fought for James, and who no longer cared to remain in their own country after their defeat, were permitted to go to France. " When the wild cry of the women, who stood watching their departure, was hushed, the silence of death settled down upon Ireland. For a

[1] Fought in the east of Ireland, on the banks of the river of that name. (See map facing p. 358.)

hundred years the country remained at peace, but the peace was that of despair."[1] In violation of that treaty, a severe act was passed against Roman Catholics; they were hunted like wild beasts, and terrible vengeance was now taken for that Act of Attainder (§ 499) which James had issued. Furthermore, England selfishly closed her own ports and those of her colonies against Irish products; this policy starved the industry of that unfortunate island.

501. Massacre of Glencoe (1692). Fighting against William and Mary had also been going on in Scotland; for Claverhouse, or " Bonny Dundee " (§ 472), was an ardent adherent of James II and vowed, " Ere the King's crown shall fall, there are crowns to be broke."[2] But the Jacobites, or adherents of James (§ 495), had been conquered, and a proclamation was sent out commanding all the Highland clans to take the oath of allegiance before the beginning of the new year (1692).

A chief of the clan of the Macdonalds of Glencoe, through no fault of his own, failed to make submission within the appointed time. Scotch enemies of the clan told the King that the chief had refused to take the oath, and urged William " to extirpate that set of thieves." The King signed an order to that effect, without clearly understanding what was intended.

Thereupon the Scotch authorities sent a body of soldiers to Glencoe, who were hospitably received by the Macdonalds. After stopping with them a number of days, they rose before light one winter morning, and, suddenly attacking their friendly hosts, murdered all the men who did not escape, and drove the women and children out into the snowdrifts to perish of cold and hunger.

They finished their work of destruction by burning the cabins and driving away the cattle. By this act, Glencoe, or the " Glen of Weeping," was changed into the Valley of the Shadow of Death. The blame which attaches to William is that he did nothing toward punishing those who planned and carried out the horrible massacre.

502. La Hogue; the Peace of Ryswick, 1697. The English naval commander, Admiral Russell, like many of William's pretended friends and supporters, had been engaged in treasonable

---

[1] Green's " Short History of the English People."
[2] Scott's Poems, " Bonny Dundee."

correspondence with James II. If the latter succeeded in recovering his crown, the Admiral hoped to bask in the sunshine of royal favor; but he later changed his mind and fought so bravely in the sea fight off La Hogue that the French supporters of James were utterly beaten.

King William, however, continued his Continental wars for the next five years, until, by the Peace of Ryswick, in Holland, 1697, Louis XIV bound himself to recognize William as King of England, the Princess Anne [1] as his successor, to withdraw all support from James, and to place the chief fortresses of the Netherlands, or Low Countries, in the hands of the Dutch garrisons. The Peace of Ryswick marked the end of the conspiracy between Louis and the Stuarts to turn England into a Roman Catholic country dependent on France (§§ 477, 488). When William went in solemn state to return thanks for the conclusion of the war, it was to the new cathedral of St. Paul's, which Wren had nearly completed (§ 474), and which was then first used for public worship.

503. The National Debt, 1693; the Bank of England, 1694. William had now gained, at least temporarily, the object that he had in view when he accepted the English crown. He had succeeded in drawing the English into a close defensive alliance against Louis XIV,[2] who, as we have seen, was bent on destroying both the political and the religious liberty of the Dutch as a Protestant people (§ 476).

William's wars had compelled him to borrow large sums from the London merchants. Out of these loans sprang the permanent National Debt. That debt was destined to grow from less than a million of pounds to so many hundred millions that all thought of ever paying it has long since been given up. Furthermore, it became necessary to organize a Banking Company, 1694, for the management of this colossal debt; together the two were destined to become more widely known than any of William's victories.

The building erected by that Company covers not far from four acres of land in the very heart of London. In the first room which one enters stands a statue of the King, bearing this inscription:

[1] The second (Protestant) daughter of James II. See Genealogical Table, p. 323.
[2] Guizot's " History of Civilization," chap. xiii.

" To the memory of the best of Princes, William of Orange, founder of the Bank of England,"— the largest and most important financial institution in the world.

504. William's Death. King William had a brave soul in a feeble body. All his life he was an invalid, but he learned to conquer disease, or at least to hold it in check, as he conquered his enemies. He was worn out with overwork, sickness, and the cares of office. If he could have been assured of the safety of his beloved Holland, death would have been welcome to one who had so long been stretched " upon the hard rack of this tough world." He was never popular in England, and at one time was kept from returning to his native country only through the earnest protestation of the Lord Chancellor, who refused to stamp the King's resignation with the Great Seal (§ 145).

There were plots to assassinate him, and many who pretended to be friends were treacherous, and only wanted a good opportunity to go over to the side of James II. Others were eager to hear of his death, and when it occurred, through the stumbling of his horse over a molehill, they drank to " the little gentleman in black velvet," whose work underground caused the fatal accident.

505. Summary. William's reign was a prolonged struggle for the great Protestant cause and for the maintenance of political liberty in both England and Holland. Invalid as he was, he was yet a man of indomitable resolution as well as indomitable courage.

Though a foreigner by birth, and caring more for Holland than for any other country in the world, yet, through his Irish and Continental wars with James II and Louis XIV, he helped more than any other man of the seventeenth century, Cromwell alone excepted, to make England free.

ANNE — 1702–1714

506. Accession and Character of Anne. William (§ 504) left no children, and according to the provisions of the Bill of Rights (§ 497) [1] the Princess Anne, younger sister of the late Queen Mary, now came to the throne. She was a negative character, with kindly impulses and little intelligence. " When in good humor

[1] See the Bill of Rights (third paragraph) on page xxxi of the Appendix.

she was meekly stupid, and when in ill humor, sulkily stupid."[1] But if there was any person duller than her Majesty, that person was her Majesty's husband, Prince George of Denmark. Charles II, who knew him well, said, " I have tried Prince George sober, and I have tried him drunk, and drunk or sober, there is nothing in him."

Along with the amiable qualities which gained for the new ruler the title of " Good Queen Anne " her Majesty inherited the obstinacy, the prejudices, and the superstitions of the Stuart sovereigns. Though a most zealous Protestant and an ardent upholder of the Church of England, she declared her faith in the Divine Right of Kings (§§ 419, 429), which had cost her grandfather, Charles I, his head, and she was the last English sovereign who believed that the touch of the royal hand could dispel disease.

The first theory she never openly proclaimed in any offensive way, but the harmless delusion that she could relieve the sick was a favorite notion with her; and we find in the London *Gazette* (March 12, 1712) an official announcement, stating that on certain days the Queen would "touch" for the cure of "king's evil," or scrofula.

Among the multitudes who went to test her power was a poor Lichfield bookseller. He carried to her his little half-blind, sickly boy, who, by virtue either of her Majesty's beneficent fingers or from some other and better reason, grew up to be known as the famous author and lexicographer, Dr. Samuel Johnson.[2]

507. Whig and Tory ; High Church and Low.

Politically, the government of the country was divided between the two great parties of the Whigs and the Tories (§ 479), since succeeded by the Liberals and Conservatives. Though mutually hostile, each believing that its rival's success meant national ruin, yet both were sincerely opposed to despotism on the one hand, and to anarchy on the other. The Whigs (§ 479), setting Parliament above the throne, were pledged to maintain the Act of Settlement (§ 497) and the Protestant succession ; while the Tories (§ 479), insisting

---

[1] Macaulay's " England " ; and compare Stanhope's " Reign of Anne."

[2] Johnson told Boswell, his biographer, that he remembered the incident, and that " he had a confused, but somehow a sort of solemn recollection of a lady in diamonds and a long black hood." — BOSWELL'S " Johnson."

on a strict, unbroken line of hereditary sovereigns, were anxious to set aside that act and restore the excluded Stuarts (§ 494).

The Church of England was likewise divided into two parties, known as High Church and Low Church. The first, who were generally Tories, wished to exalt the power of the bishops and were opposed to the toleration of Dissenters (§ 472); the second, who were Whigs as a rule, believed it best to curtail the authority of the bishops, and to secure to all Trinitarian Protestants entire liberty of worship and all civil and political rights and privileges. Thus to the bitterness of heated political controversy there was added the still more acrid bitterness of theological dispute.

Addison illustrates the feeling that then prevailed by an amusing story of an earlier occurrence. A boy who had lost his way in London was called a " popish cur " by a Whig because he ventured to inquire for Saint Anne's Lane, while he was cuffed for irreverence by a Tory when, correcting himself, he asked bluntly for Anne's Lane.

The Queen, although she owed her crown mainly to the Whigs (§ 479), sympathized with the Tories (§ 479) and the High Church, and did all in her power to strengthen both. As for the leaders of the two parties, they seem to have looked out first for themselves, and afterwards — often a long way afterwards — for their country. During the whole reign they were plotting and counterplotting, mining and undermining. Their subtle schemes to secure office and destroy each other become as incomprehensible and as fathomless as those of the fallen angels in Milton's vision of the bottomless pit.

508. The War of the Spanish Succession, 1702. Anne had no sooner come to the throne than war broke out with France. It had its origin in the previous reign. William III had cared little for England compared with his native Holland, whose interests always had the first place in his heart. He had spent his life battling to preserve the independence of the Dutch republic and fighting Louis XIV of France, who was determined, if possible, to annex the Netherlands, including Holland, to his own dominions (§ 502).

During the latter part of William's reign the French King seemed likely to be able to accomplish his purpose. The King of Spain, who had no children, was in feeble health, and at his death it was probable that Louis XIV's grandson, Philip of Anjou, would receive the crown. If that happened, Louis XIV, who was then the most powerful prince in Europe, would obtain the control of the Spanish dominions, which, besides Spain, comprised a large part of the Netherlands,[1] parts of Italy, and immense provinces in North and South America. The possession of such an empire would make Louis irresistible in Europe, and the little, free Protestant states of Holland could not hope to stand before him.

Not long afterwards, the King of Spain died and bequeathed the crown to Philip of Anjou. When Philip left Paris for Madrid, Louis XIV exultingly exclaimed, "The Pyrenees no longer exist." That was simply his short way of saying, Now France and Spain are made one, and *France* is that one.[2]

Louis at once put French garrisons in the border towns of the Spanish Netherlands, and he thus had a force ready at any moment to march across the frontier into Holland. Finally, on the death of the royal refugee, James II (§ 491), which occurred shortly before King William's death, Louis XIV publicly acknowledged the exiled monarch's son, James Edward, the so-called "Old Pretender" (§§ 490, 491), as rightful sovereign of England, Scotland, and Ireland.

This effectually roused the English people; they were preparing for hostilities when William's sudden death occurred (§ 504). Immediately after Anne came to the throne (1702) war with France was declared, and since it had grown out of Louis's designs on the crown of Spain, it was called the "War of the Spanish Succession."

The contest was begun by England, mainly to prevent the French King from carrying out his threat of placing the so-called "Pretender," son of the late James II, on the English throne and so

---

[1] The whole of the Netherlands at one time belonged to Spain, but the northern part, or Holland, had succeeded in establishing its independence, and was protected on the southern frontier by a line of fortified towns.

[2] When Philip of Anjou went to Spain, Louis XIV, by letters patent, conditionally reserved the succession to the Spanish throne to France, thus virtually uniting the two countries, so that the Pyrenees Mountains would no longer have any political meaning as a boundary between the two countries.

overturning the Bill of Rights (§ 497) and the Act of Settlement (§ 497), and thereby restoring the country to the Roman Catholic Stuarts. Later, the war came to have two other important objects. The first of these was to defend Holland, now a most valuable ally; the second was to protect the colonies of Virginia and New England against the power of France, which threatened, through its own American colonies and through the extensive Spanish possessions it expected to acquire, to get control of the whole of the New World.[1]

Thus England had three objects at stake:

(1) The maintenance of Protestant government at home.

(2) The maintenance of the Protestant power of Holland.

(3) The retention of a large part of the American continent. For this reason the War of the Spanish Succession may be regarded as the beginning of a second Hundred Years' War between England and France (§ 237),[2] one destined to decide which was to build up the great empire of the future in the western hemisphere.[3]

509. Marlborough; Blenheim, Gibraltar, and Other Victories (1702–1709). John Churchill, Duke of Marlborough (§ 491), commanded the English and Dutch forces, and had for his ally Prince Eugene of Savoy, who led the German armies. The Duke, who was known in the enemy's camps by the flattering name of "the handsome Englishman," had risen from obscurity. He owed the beginning of his success to his good looks and a court intrigue. In politics he sympathized chiefly with the Tories (§ 479), but his interests in the war led him to support the Whigs (§ 479).

He was avaricious, unscrupulous, and treacherous. James II trusted him, and he deceived him and went over to William (§ 491); William trusted him, and he deceived him and opened a treasonable correspondence with the dethroned James; Anne trusted him, and he would undoubtedly have betrayed her if the so-called

---

[1] At this time England had twelve American colonies extending from New England to South Carolina, inclusive, with part of Newfoundland. France and Spain claimed all the rest of the continent.

[2] During the next eighty years fighting was going on between England and France, directly or indirectly, for a great part of the time.

[3] Seeley's "Expansion of England."

"Pretender" (§§ 490, 491) had been able to bid high enough, or if he could have shown him that his cause was likely to be successful. In his greed for money the Duke hesitated at nothing; he took bribes from army contractors, and robbed his soldiers of their pay.[1]

As a soldier, Marlborough had no equal. Voltaire says of him with truth that "he never besieged a fortress which he did not take, nor fought a battle which he did not win." This man, at once so able and so false, to whom war was a private speculation rather than a contest for right or principle, now opened the campaign. He captured those fortresses in the Spanish Netherlands which Louis XIV had garrisoned with French troops to menace Holland, but he could not induce the enemy to risk a battle in the open field.

At length, Marlborough, by a brilliant movement (1704), changed the scene of the war from the Netherlands to Bavaria in southern Germany. There, at the little village of Blenheim,[2] he, with Prince Eugene, gained a victory over the French which saved Germany from the power of Louis XIV. (See map opposite.) England, out of gratitude for the humiliation of her powerful enemy, presented the Duke with the ancient royal Park of Woodstock, near Oxford, and built for him the palace of Blenheim, which the architect called "the biggest house for the biggest man in England." It is still occupied by descendants of the Duke's family. A few days before the battle of Blenheim, a powerful English fleet had attacked and taken Gibraltar (1704). England thus gained and still holds the command of the great inland sea of the Mediterranean. In the course of the next five years Marlborough fought three great battles,[3] by which he drove the French out of the Netherlands once for all, and finally beat them on a hotly contested field in northern France. The power of Louis XIV was now so far broken that England no longer felt any fear that he would overcome her colonies in America (§ 508).

[1] See Hallam, Macaulay; and Thackeray's "Henry Esmond."

[2] Blenheim: The palace grounds are nearly twelve miles in circumference. The Marlborough family hold Blenheim on condition that they present a flag every year (August 2) to the English sovereign at Windsor Castle.

[3] Ramillies (1706); Oudenarde (1708); Malplaquet (1709).

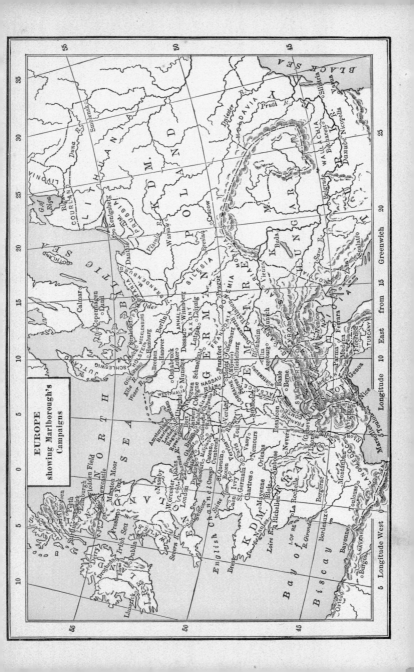

510. The Powers behind the Throne; Jennings against Masham.
But if the Duke of Marlborough was remarkable, so too was his
wife. While the war was going on, the real power of the Crown,
though it stood in Anne's name, was practically in the hands of
Sarah Jennings, Duchess of Marlborough, who held the office of
Mistress of the Robes. She and the Queen had long been inseparable, and it was her influence that caused Anne to desert her
father (§ 491) and espouse the cause of William of Orange.

The imperious temper of the Duchess carried all before it, and
in her department she won victories which might well be compared with those the Duke, her husband, gained on the field of
battle. In time her sway over her royal companion grew to be
so absolute that she seemed to decide everything, from questions
of state to the cut of a gown or the color of a ribbon. Finally, it
became a common saying that " Queen Anne reigns, but Queen
Sarah governs." [1]

While the Duchess continued in power, she used her influence
to urge forward the war with France undertaken by England to
check the designs of Louis XIV on Spain and Holland, and also
to punish him for his recognition of the claim of the Pretender to
the English crown (§ 491). Her object was to advance her husband, who, as commander in chief of the English and Dutch forces
on the Continent, had won fame and fortune, — the first by his
splendid ability, the second by his unscrupulous greed (§ 509).

After a number of years, the Queen and the Duchess quarreled,
and the latter was superseded by her cousin, a Mrs. Masham
(1711), who soon got as complete control of Anne as the former
favorite had possessed. Mrs. Masham was as sly and supple as
the Duchess had been dictatorial and violent. She was cousin to
Robert Harley, a prominent Tory politician (§ 479). Through
her influence Harley now became Prime Minister in everything
but name. He succeeded in putting a stop to further fighting, and
Marlborough was ordered home in disgrace on a charge of having robbed the government. Thus it was, as Hallam remarks, that

[1] For years the Queen and the Duchess corresponded almost daily under the names
of " Mrs. Morley " (the Queen) and " Mrs. Freeman " (the Duchess), the latter taking
that name because, she said, it suited the frank and bold character of her letters.

" the fortunes of Europe were changed by the insolence of one waiting woman and the cunning of another." [1]

511. Dr. Sacheverell (1710). An incident occurred about this time which greatly helped the Tories (§ 479) in their schemes. Dr. Sacheverell, a violent Tory and High Churchman (§ 507), began preaching a series of vehement sermons in London condemning the Whig policy which called for the reopening of the war. He also endeavored to revive the exploded theory of the Divine Right of Kings (§§ 419, 429), and declared that no tyranny on the part of a sovereign could by any possibility justify a subject in resisting the royal will. The Whig leaders brought the preacher to trial for alleged treasonable utterances (1710). He was suspended from his office for three years, and his book of sermons was publicly burned by the common hangman.

This created intense popular excitement; Sacheverell was regarded as a political martyr by all who wished the war ended. A reaction against the Government set in; the Whigs (§ 479) were driven from power, and the Tories passed two very harsh laws [2] against Dissenters (§ 472), though they were repealed a few years later. The Duchess of Marlborough had to leave her apartments in the palace of St. James, and in her spite broke down marble mantels and tore off the locks from doors. Mrs. Masham's friends, the Tories (§ 479), or peace party, who had now triumphed, prepared to put a complete end to the fighting.

512. The Peace of Utrecht, 1713. Not long after this change a messenger was privately dispatched to Louis XIV to ask if he wished for peace. "It was," says the French minister, "like asking a dying man whether he would wish to be cured." [2] Later, terms were secretly agreed upon between the Tories (§ 479) and the French, and in 1713, in the quaint Dutch city of Utrecht, the allies, together with France and Spain, signed the treaty bearing that name.

By it Louis XIV bound himself:

(1) To acknowledge the right of England to limit the succession to the crown to Protestant sovereigns (§ 497).

---

[1] Hallam's "Constitutional History of England."
[2] These were the Occasional Conformity Act and the Schism Act (§ 518).
[3] Morris's "The Age of Anne."

(2) To compel Prince James Edward, the so-called "Pretender" (§§ 490, 491) to quit France.

(3) To renounce the union of the crowns of France and Spain; but Philip was to retain the Spanish throne (§ 508).

(4) To cede to England all claims to Newfoundland, Acadia, or Nova Scotia, and that vast region known as the Hudson Bay Company's Possessions.

Next, Spain was to give up:

(1) The Spanish Netherlands to Austria, an ally of Holland, and grant to the Dutch a line of forts to defend their frontier against France.

(2) England was to have the exclusive right for thirty-three years of supplying the Spanish-American colonists with negro slaves.[1]

This trade had long been coveted by the English, and had been carried on to some extent by them ever since Sir John Hawkins entered upon it in Queen Elizabeth's reign. Sir John grew very rich through his traffic in human flesh, and he set up a coat of arms emblazoned with a slave in fetters, so that all might see how he had won wealth and distinction.

513. Union of England and Scotland, 1707. Since the accession of James I (1603), England and Scotland had been ruled by one sovereign, but each country retained its own Parliament and its own forms of worship. In 1707 the two countries were finally united under the name of Great Britain.

The Established (Presbyterian) Church of Scotland and the Scottish laws were to be preserved. The independent Parliament of Scotland was given up, and the Scotch were henceforth represented in the English Parliament by sixteen peers chosen by members of the Scottish peerage at the summoning of every Parliament; and by forty-five (now seventy-two) members returned by Scotland to the House of Commons.

With the consummation of the union between the two countries Great Britain adopted a new flag, the Union Jack, which

---

[1] This right (called the "Assiento," or Contract) had formerly belonged to France. By its transfer England got the privilege of furnishing 4800 "sound, merchantable negroes" annually, "two thirds to be males" between ten and forty years of age.

was formed by the junction of the red cross of St. George of England and the white cross of St. Andrew of Scotland.[1]

514. Literature of the Period; the First Daily Paper. The reign of Anne has been characterized as one of corruption in high places and of brutality in low, but in literature it takes rank next to that of Elizabeth (§ 393). There was indeed no great central luminary like Shakespeare, but a constellation of lesser ones, — such as Addison, Defoe, and Pope. They shone with a splendor of their own. The lurid brilliancy of the half-mad satirist Dean Swift was beginning to command attention; he was the greatest political writer of the times; on the other hand, the calm, clear light of the philosopher John Locke was near its setting.

Aside from these great names in letters, it was an age generally of contented dullness, well represented in the good-natured mediocrity of Queen Anne herself. During her reign the first daily newspaper (§§ 422, 443) appeared in England, — the *Daily Courant* (1703); it was a dingy, badly printed little sheet, not much bigger than a man's hand. The publisher said he made it so small " to save the Publick at least one half the Impertinences of Ordinary News-Papers."

Perhaps it was well this journal set up no greater pretensions, for it had to compete with swarms of abusive political pamphlets, such as Swift wrote for the Tories and Defoe for the Whigs (§ 479). It had also to compete with the gossip and scandal of the coffeehouses and the clubs; for this reason the proprietor found it no easy matter either to fill it or to sell it.

A few years later (1711) a periodical appeared, called the *Spectator*. It was published daily, and Addison, its chief contributor, soon made it famous. Each number consisted of an essay hitting off the follies and foibles of the age, and it was regularly served at the breakfast tables of people of fashion along with their tea and toast.

One of the greatest merits of the *Spectator* was its happy way of showing that wit and virtue are after all better friends than wit

---

[1] After Ireland was united to Great Britain (1800) the red cross of St. Patrick was added to the flag (1801). The first Union Jack was the work of James I, whose usual signature was *Jacques* (hence " Jack "), French for James.

and vice. Neither this little magazine nor the newspapers of that time dared to publish a single line of parliamentary debate. But they mark the humble beginning of that vast organized power, represented by the daily press of London, which discusses everything of interest throughout the world.

515. Death of the Queen. The ingratitude of public men and the furious quarrels of politicians so teased and vexed the Queen that she at last fell into a fatal illness. Her physician wrote to Dean Swift, " I believe sleep was never more welcome to a weary traveler than death was to her." When she laid down the scepter (1714) she left no heir to the throne, and so the power of the Stuarts (§ 415) came to an end.

According to the terms of the Act of Settlement (§ 497) the crown now passed to George, Elector of Hanover, a Protestant descendant of James I of England. (See Table, p. 323.) James Edward, son of James II, believed to the last that his half-sister, Queen Anne, would name him her successor;[1] instead of that it was she who first dubbed him the " Pretender " (§ 491).

516. Summary. The whole reign of Anne was taken up with the strife of political parties at home, and the War of the Spanish Succession abroad. The Whigs (§ 479) were always intriguing through the Duchess of Marlborough and other leaders to keep up the war and to keep out the so-called " Pretender "; the Tories (§ 479), on the other hand, were just as busy through Mrs. Masham and her coadjutors in endeavoring to establish peace, and with it the Divine Right of Kings (§§ 419, 429).

The extreme Tories hoped for the restoration of the Roman Catholic Stuarts in the person of James Edward, the so-called " Pretender." The War of the Spanish Succession resulted in the defeat of Louis XIV and the confirmation of that Act of Settlement (§ 497) which secured the English crown to a Protestant prince.

---

[1] Anne and the so-called " Pretender " were children of James II by different mothers.

GENERAL REFERENCE SUMMARY OF THE STUART PERIOD

(See note in italics on page 43.)

1603-1714 (COMMONWEALTH, 1649-1660)

I. GOVERNMENT. II. RELIGION. III. MILITARY AFFAIRS. IV. LIT-
ERATURE, LEARNING, AND ART. V. GENERAL INDUSTRY AND COM-
MERCE. VI. MODE OF LIFE, MANNERS, AND CUSTOMS

I. GOVERNMENT

517. The Divine Right of Kings; the Civil War; the "Glorious Revolution" of 1688. The period began with the attempt of James I to carry out his theory that the King derives his right to rule directly from God, and in no wise from the people. Charles I adopted this disastrous theory, and was supported in it by Manwaring and other clergymen, who declared that the King represents God on earth, and that the subject who resists his will, or refuses a tax or loan to him, does so at the everlasting peril of his soul.

Charles I's arbitrary methods of government and levies of illegal taxes, with the imprisonment of those who refused to pay them, led to the meeting of the Long Parliament and the enactment in 1628 of the statute of the Petition of Right, or second great charter of English liberties.

The same Parliament abolished the despotic courts of Star Chamber and High Commission, which had been used by Strafford and Laud to carry out their tyrannical scheme called "Thorough."

Charles I's renewed acts of oppression and open violation of the laws, with his levies of "ship money," led to the Grand Remonstrance, an appeal to the nation to support Parliament in its struggle with the King. The attempt of the King to arrest five members who had taken a prominent part in drawing up the Remonstrance brought on the Civil War and the establishment of the Commonwealth. The new republic was utterly opposed to the doctrine of the Divine Right of Kings. It declared "the People are, under God, the origin of all just power." Eventually Cromwell became Protector of the nation, and ruled by means of a strong military force.

On the restoration of the Stuarts, Feudal Tenure and the Right of Purveyance were abolished by Parliament (1660). Charles II endeavored to rule without Parliament by selling his influence to Louis XIV, by the secret Treaty of Dover. During his reign, the Habeas Corpus Act was passed and feudalism was practically abolished.

James II endeavored to restore the Roman Catholic religion. His treatment of the University of Oxford, and imprisonment of the Seven Bishops, with the birth of a son who would be educated as a Roman Catholic, caused the Revolution of 1688, and placed William and Mary on the throne.

Parliament now, 1689, passed the Bill of Rights, the third great charter for the protection of the English people, and later confirmed it, 1701, by the Act of Settlement, which secured the crown to a line of Protestant sovereigns. The Mutiny Bill, passed at the beginning of William III's reign, made the army dependent on Parliament. These measures practically put the government in the hands of the House of Commons, where it has ever since remained. The Long Parliament had passed a Triennial Act (1641) requiring a new Parliament to be summoned within three years from the dissolution of the last Parliament, which was to sit not longer than three years. This law was repealed in 1664 and reënacted under William III in 1694. William's wars caused the beginning of the National Debt and the establishment of the Bank of England.

In the reign of Anne, 1707, Scotland and England were united under the name of Great Britain. During her sovereignty the permanent Whig and Tory parties, which came into existence in the time of Charles II, became especially prominent. They have since continued to divide the parliamentary government between them, — the Whigs seeking to extend the power of the people; the Tories, that of the Crown and the Church. After the passage of the Reform Bill in 1832 (§ 582) the Whigs took the name of Liberals and the Tories that of Conservatives. The system of Cabinet Government, which now prevails, took its rise in 1721 under Robert Walpole, seven years after Anne's death (§ 534).

II. Religion

518. Religious Parties and Religious Legislation. At the beginning of this period we find four religious parties in England: (1) the Roman Catholics; (2) the Episcopalians, or supporters of the National Church of England; (3) the Puritans, who wished to remain members of that Church, but who sought to " purify " it from certain Roman Catholic customs and modes of worship; (4) the Independents, who were endeavoring to establish independent congregational societies. In Scotland the Puritans established their religion in a Church governed by

elders, or presbyters, instead of bishops, which on that account got
the name of Presbyterian.

James I persecuted all who dissented from the Church of England;
and after the Gunpowder Plot the Roman Catholics were practically
deprived of the protection of the law, and subject to terrible oppression.
In James's reign Bartholomew Legate, a Unitarian, was burned at West
Smithfield Market, London (1612), for denying the doctrine of the
Trinity. He was the last English martyr. Charles I greatly exasperated
the Puritans in the English Church by his Declaration of Sports,
which recommended games in the churchyards after service on Sunday.
Clergymen who refused to read the Declaration to their congregations
were dismissed from their places.

During the period of the Civil War and the Commonwealth, Presbyterianism was established as the national worship of England and Scotland by the Solemn League and Covenant. A great many Episcopal
clergymen were deprived of their parishes. At the Restoration severe
laws against the Scotch Covenanters and other Dissenters were enforced,
and retaliatory legislation drove two thousand clergymen from their
parishes to starve. On the other hand, the pretended Popish Plot
caused the exclusion of Roman Catholics from both houses of Parliament, and all persons holding office were obliged to partake of the
sacrament according to the Church of England. James II's futile attempt to restore Catholicism ended in the Revolution and the passage
of the Toleration Act, granting liberty of worship to all Protestant
Trinitarians. Stringent laws were passed against Catholics (1700), but
they were not regularly enforced. Under Anne the Occasional Conformity Act (1711) and the Schism Act (1714) were aimed at Dissenters.
The first of these laws punished officeholders who, during their term of
office, should attend any dissenting place of worship; the second forbade
any person's keeping a public or private school unless he was a member of the Church of England. Both laws were repealed a few years
later (1718).

III. MILITARY AFFAIRS

519. Armor and Arms. Armor still continued to be worn in some
degree during this period, but it consisted chiefly of the helmet with
breastplates and backplates. Firearms of various kinds were in general
use; also hand grenades, or small bombs, and the bayonet. The chief
wars of the period were the Civil War, the wars with the Dutch,
William's war with France, which extended to America, and the War of
the Spanish Succession.

IV. LITERATURE, LEARNING, AND ART

520. Great Writers. The most eminent prose writers of this period were Sir Walter Raleigh, Lord Bacon, Sir Isaac Newton, John Bunyan, Bishop Hooker, Jeremy Taylor, John Locke, Hobbes, Dean Swift, Defoe, and Addison ; the chief poets, Shakespeare and Jonson (mentioned under the preceding period), Milton, Dryden, Pope, Butler, and Beaumont and Fletcher, with a class of writers known as the " Comic Dramatists of the Restoration," whose works, though not lacking in genius, exhibit many of the worst features of the licentious age in which they were produced. Three other great writers were born in the latter part of this period, — Fielding, the novelist, Hume, the historian, and Butler,[1] the ablest thinker of his time in the English Church, — but their productions belong to the time of the Georges.

521. Progress in Science and Invention. Sir Isaac Newton revolutionized natural philosophy by his discovery and demonstration of the law of gravitation, and Dr. William Harvey accomplished as great a change in physiological science by his discovery of the circulation of the blood. The most remarkable invention of the age was a rude steam engine, patented in 1698 by Captain Savery, and so far improved by Thomas Newcomen in 1712 that it was used for pumping water in coal mines for many years. Both were destined to be superseded by James Watt's engine, which belongs to a later period (1765).

522. Architecture. The Gothic style of the preceding periods was followed by the Italian, or classical, represented in the works of Inigo Jones and Sir Christopher Wren. It was a revival, in modified form, of the ancient Greek and Roman architecture. St. Paul's Cathedral, the grandest church ever built in England for Protestant worship, is the best example of this style. Many beautiful manor houses were built in the early part of this period, which, like the churches of the time, were often ornamented with the exquisite wood carving of Grinling Gibbons. There were no great artists in England in this age, though Charles I employed Rubens and other foreign painters to decorate the palace of Whitehall and Windsor Castle.

523. Education. The higher education of the period was confined almost wholly to the study of Latin and Greek. The discipline of all schools was extremely harsh. Nearly every lesson was emphasized by a liberal application of the rod, and the highest recommendation a teacher could have was that he was known as " a learned and lashing master."

[1] Bishop Butler, author of " The Analogy of Religion " (1736), a work which gained for him the title of " The Bacon of Theology."

V. General Industry and Commerce

524. Manufactures. Woolen goods continued to be a chief article of manufacture. Silks were also produced by thousands of Huguenot weavers, who fled from France to England in order to escape the persecutions of Louis XIV. Coal was·now extensively mined, and iron and pottery works were giving industrial importance to Birmingham and other growing towns in the Midlands.

525. Commerce. A permanent English colony was established in America in 1607, and by 1714 the number of such colonies had increased to twelve. During a great part of this period intense commercial rivalry existed between England and Holland, each of which was anxious to get the monopoly of the colonial import and export trade. Parliament passed stringent navigation laws, under Cromwell and later, to prevent the Dutch from competing with English merchants and shippers. The East India and South Sea companies were means of greatly extending English commercial enterprise, as was also the tobacco culture of Virginia.

526. Roads and Travel. Good roads were still unknown in England. Stagecoaches carried a few passengers at exorbitant rates, requiring an entire day to go a distance which an express train now travels in less than an hour. Goods were carried on pack horses or in cumbrous wagons, and so great was the expense of transportation that farmers often let their produce rot on the ground rather than attempt to get it to the nearest market town.

In London a few coaches were in use, but covered chairs, carried on poles by two men and called "sedan chairs," were the favorite vehicles. They continued to be used for a century after this period closes. Although London had been in great part rebuilt since the Great Fire (1666), the streets were still very narrow, without sidewalks, heaped with filth, and miserably lighted.

527. Agriculture; Pauperism. Agriculture generally made no marked improvement, but gardening did, and many vegetables and fruits were introduced which had not before been cultivated.

Pauperism remained a problem which the government had not yet found a practical method of dealing with. There was little freedom of movement; the poor man's parish was virtually his prison, and if he left it to seek work elsewhere, and required help on the way, he was certain to be sent back to the place where he was legally settled.

VI. MODE OF LIFE, MANNERS, AND CUSTOMS

528. Dress. In the time of Charles II and his successors the dress of the wealthy and fashionable classes was most elaborate and costly. Gentlemen wore their hair long, in ringlets, with an abundance of gold lace and ruffles, and carried long, slender swords, known as rapiers. Sometimes indeed they outshone the ladies in the splendor of their costume, and in one instance the bride at a wedding burst into tears because her gorgeously dressed husband looked so much handsomer than she did that all eyes were fixed on him alone. Later on, large flowing wigs came into fashion, and no man of any social standing thought of appearing without one.

In Queen Anne's reign both ladies and gentlemen powdered their hair. The ladies also painted their faces and ornamented them with minute black patches, which served not only for "beauty spots," but showed, by their arrangement, with which political party they sympathized.

529. Coffeehouses. Up to the middle of the seventeenth century ale and beer were the common drink of all classes; but about that time coffee was introduced, and coffeehouses became fashionable resorts for gentlemen and for all who wished to learn the news of the day. Tea had not yet come into use; but, in 1660, Pepys says in his diary: "Sept. 25. I did send for a cup of tee, a China drink, of which I never had drank before."

530. The Streets of London. No efficient police existed in London; at night the streets were infested with brutal ruffians, and, as late as Queen Anne's time, by bands of "fine gentlemen" not less brutal, who amused themselves by overturning sedan chairs, rolling women downhill in barrels, and compelling men to dance jigs, under the stimulus of repeated pricks from a circle of sword points, until the victims fell fainting from exhaustion. Duels were frequent, on the slightest provocation. Highwaymen abounded both in the city and without, and, unless one went well armed, it was often dangerous to travel any distance in the country.

531. Brutal Laws. Hanging was the common punishment for theft and many other crimes. The public whipping of both men and women through the streets was frequent. Debtors were shut up in prison, and left to beg from the passers-by or starve; and ordinary offenders were fastened in a wooden frame called the "pillory" and exposed on a high platform, where they were pelted by the mob with mud, rotten eggs, and other unsavory missiles. In some cases their bones were broken with clubs and brickbats. The pillory continued in use until the accession of Victoria in 1837.

TENTH PERIOD[1]

"The history of England is emphatically the history of progress. It is the history of a constant movement of the public mind, of a constant change in the institutions of a great society." — MACAULAY.

INDIA GAINED; AMERICA LOST — PARLIAMENTARY REFORM — GOVERNMENT BY THE PEOPLE

THE HOUSE OF HANOVER (1714) TO THE PRESENT TIME

GEORGE I,	1714–1727	WILLIAM IV,	1830–1837
GEORGE II,	1727–1760	VICTORIA,	1837–1901
GEORGE III,	1760–1820	EDWARD VII,	1901–1910
GEORGE IV,	1820–1830	GEORGE V,	1910–

532. Accession of George I. As Queen Anne died without leaving an heir to the throne (§ 515), George, Elector of Hanover, in accordance with the Act of Settlement (§ 497), now came into possession of the English crown. (See Genealogical Table opposite.) The new King had no desire whatever to go to England.

As he owed his new position to Whig legislation (§ 479), he naturally favored that party and turned his back on the Tories (§ 479), who, deprived of the sunshine of royal favor, were as unhappy as their rivals were jubilant. The triumphant Whigs denounced "the shameful Peace of Utrecht" (§ 512). Next, they impeached the three fallen Tory leaders,[2] of whom Harley was the

---

[1] REFERENCE BOOKS on this Period will be found in the CLASSIFIED LIST OF BOOKS in the Appendix. The pronunciation of names will be found in the Index. THE LEADING DATES stand unenclosed; all others are in parentheses.

[2] The three Tory leaders were Harley, now Earl of Oxford (§ 510), St. John (Viscount Bolingbroke), and Butler (Duke of Ormonde). Bolingbroke and Ormonde fled to France, where the first entered the service of the "Pretender," but he was ultimately permitted to return to England. Ormonde never came back. Harley, as stated above, was sent to the Tower; while there he secretly wrote to the "Pretender" (§ 490), and offered him his services.

chief (§ 510), on a charge of treason. The indictment accused them of having given back to Louis XIV, in the late war, more captured territory than was necessary. Furthermore, they were said to be guilty of having intrigued to restore the House of Stuart with the design of making the "Pretender" King (§§ 490, 491). Harley was sent to the Tower of London for a time; he was then acquitted and released. Meanwhile his two indicted associates had fled to France.

Later, the Whigs repealed two harsh religious statutes (§ 511) directed against Dissenters (§ 472), which the Tories and the High Churchmen had enacted in the previous reign for the purpose of keeping themselves in power.

533. Character of the New King. The new sovereign was a selfish, coarse old man, who in private life would, as Lady Montagu said, have passed for an honest blockhead. He neither knew anything about England, nor did he desire to know anything of it. He could not speak a word of the language of the country he was

THE HOUSE OF HANOVER, also called BRUNSWICK AND GUELF

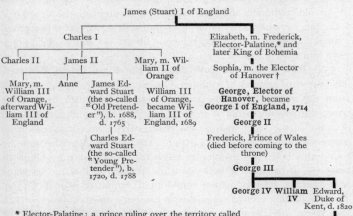

* Elector-Palatine: a prince ruling over the territory called the Palatinate in western Germany, on the Rhine.
† Elector of Hanover: a prince ruling over the province of Hanover, a part of the German Empire, lying on the North Sea. The elector received his title from the fact that he was one of a certain number of princes who had the right of electing the German Emperor.

called to govern, and he made no attempt to learn it; even the coronation service had to be explained to him as best it might, in such broken Latin as the ministers could muster.

Laboring under these disadvantages he wisely declined to take any active part in the affairs of the nation. He trusted everything to his Whig friends (§ 532) and let them, with Sir Robert Walpole at their head, manage the country in their own way.

Fortunately, the great body of the English people were abundantly able to take care of themselves. A noted French writer said of them that they resembled a barrel of their own beer, froth at the top, dregs at the bottom, but thoroughly sound and wholesome in the middle. It was this middle class, with their solid, practical good sense, that kept the nation right.

They were by no means enthusiastic worshipers of the German King who had come to reign over them, but they saw that he had three good qualities: he was no hypocrite, he did not waste the people's money, and he was a man of unquestioned courage. But they also saw more than this, for they realized that though George I might be as heavy, dull, and wooden as the figurehead of an old-fashioned ship, yet, like that figurehead, he stood for something greater and better than himself, — for he represented Protestantism, with civil and religious liberty, — and so the people gave him their allegiance.

534. Rise of Cabinet Government; the First Prime Minister.
The present method of Cabinet Government dates in great part from this reign. From the earliest period of English history the sovereign was accustomed to have a permanent council composed of some of the chief men of the realm, whom he consulted on all matters of importance (§§ 144, 145). Charles II, either because he found this body inconveniently large for the rapid transaction of business, or because he believed it inexpedient to discuss his plans with so many, selected a small confidential committee from it (§ 476). This committee met to consult with the King in his cabinet, or private room, and so came to be called " the Cabinet Council," or briefly, " the Cabinet," a name which it has ever since retained.

During Charles II's reign and that of his immediate successors the King continued to choose this special council from those whom he believed to be friendly to his measures, often without much regard to party lines, and he was always present at their meetings. With the accession of George I, however, a great change took place. His want of acquaintance with prominent men made it difficult for him to select a Cabinet himself, and his ignorance of English rendered his presence at its meetings wholly useless. For these reasons the new King adopted the expedient of appointing a chief adviser, or Prime Minister, who personally chose his own Cabinet from men of the political party to which he belonged.

Sir Robert Walpole, who held this office of chief adviser for more than twenty years (1721–1742), is commonly considered to have been the first actual Prime Minister, and the founder of that system of Cabinet Government which prevails in England to-day. He was a master hand at managing his fellow ministers in the Cabinet, and when one of them, named Townshend, aspired to share the leadership, Walpole said to him, " The firm must be Walpole and Townshend, not Townshend and Walpole." But later (1741) a minority in the Lords protested " that a sole or even First Minister is an officer unknown to the law of Britain, inconsistent with the Constitution of this country, and destructive of liberty in any government whatsover." Then Walpole thought it expedient to disclaim the title ; but many years later the younger Pitt declared (1803) that there ought to be " an avowed minister possessing the chief weight in the Council " or Cabinet, and that view eventually prevailed.[1] The Cabinet, or "Government," as it is usually called,[2] generally consists of twelve or fifteen persons chosen by the Prime Minister, or Premier,[3] from the leading members of both houses of Parliament, but whose political views agree in the main with the majority of the House of Commons.[4]

[1] Feilden's " Constitutional History of England," Taswell-Langmead's " English Constitutional History," and A. L. Lowell's " The Government of England," 2 vols.

[2] "The Cabinet, the body to which, in common use, we have latterly come to give the name of *Government*." Encyclopædia Britannica (10th edition, VIII, 297).

[3] " Premier " : from the French *premier*, first or chief.

[4] The existence of the Cabinet depends on custom, not law. Its three essential characteristics are generally considered to be : (1) Practical unanimity of party ; (2) Practical unity of action under the leadership of the Prime Minister; (3) Collective responsibility to the party in the House of Commons which represents the political majority of the nation. Its members are never *officially* made known

But this system, as it now stands, was gradually developed. It had advanced to such a point under the dictatorial rule of Sir Robert Walpole that George II, chafing under the restriction of his power, said bitterly, "In England the ministers are King." George III, however, succeeded, for a time, in making himself practically supreme, but Cabinet Government soon came to the front again, and, under William IV, the Prime Minister, with his Cabinet, ceased to look to the sovereign for guidance and support, and became responsible to the House of Commons alone (§§ 582, 587). Since then, that House has become the true King of England; for no Cabinet can now hope to stand which does not have the confidence of a majority of the Commons (provided that body reflects the public opinion of the nation).

535. The "Pretender"; "The Fifteen" (1715); the Septennial Act (1716). The fact that George I exclusively favored the Whigs exasperated the opposite, or Tory, party. The Jacobites, or extreme members of that party (§ 495), in Scotland, with the

to the public, nor its proceedings recorded. Its meetings, which take place at irregular intervals, according to pressure of business, are entirely secret, and the sovereign is never present. As the Cabinet agrees in its composition with the majority of the House of Commons, it follows that if the Commons are Conservative, the Cabinet will be so likewise; and if Liberal, the reverse. Theoretically, the sovereign chooses the Cabinet; but practically the selection is now always made by the Prime Minister. If at any time the Prime Minister, with his Cabinet, finds that his political policy no longer agrees with that of the House of Commons, he and the other members of the Cabinet resign, and the sovereign chooses a new Prime Minister from the opposite party, who forms a new Cabinet in harmony with himself and the Commons. If, however, the Prime Minister has good reason for believing that a different House of Commons would support him, the sovereign may, by his advice, dissolve Parliament. A new election then takes place, and according to the political character of the members returned, the Cabinet remains in or goes out of power. The Cabinet, or Government, now invariably includes the following officers:

1. The First Lord of the Treasury (usually the Prime Minister).
2. The Lord Chancellor.
3. The Lord President of the Council.
4. The Lord Privy Seal.
5. The Chancellor of the Exchequer.
6. The Secretary of State for Home Affairs.
7. The Secretary of State for Foreign Affairs.
8. The Secretary of State for the Colonies.
9. The Secretary of State for India.
10. The Secretary of State for War.
11. The First Lord of the Admiralty.

In addition, a certain number of other officers are frequently included, making the whole number about twelve or fifteen.

secret aid of many in England, now rose, in the hope of placing on the throne James Edward Stuart, the son of James II. He was called the "Chevalier"[1] by his friends, but the "Pretender" by his enemies (§§ 490, 491, 512). The insurrection was led by John, Earl of Mar, who, from his frequent change of politics, had got the nickname of "Bobbing John." Mar encountered the royal forces at Sheriffmuir, in Perthshire, Scotland (1715), where an indecisive battle was fought, which the old ballad thus describes:

> "There's some say that we won, and some say that they won,
>   And some say that none won at a', man;
>   But one thing is sure, that at Sheriffmuir
>   A battle there was, which I saw, man."

On the same day of the fight at Sheriffmuir, the English Jacobites (§ 495), with a body of Scotch allies, marched into Preston, Lancashire, and there surrendered, almost without striking a blow.

The leaders of the movement, except the Earl of Mar, who, with one or two others, escaped to the Continent, were beheaded or hanged, and about a thousand of the rank and file were sold as slaves to the West India and Virginia plantations (§ 487). The "Pretender" himself landed in Scotland a few weeks after the defeat of his friends; but finding no encouragement, he hurried back to the Continent again. Thus ended the rebellion known from the year of its outbreak (1715) as "The Fifteen."

One result of this rising was the passage of the Septennial Act (1716), extending the duration of Parliament from three years, which was the longest time that body could sit (§§ 439, 517), to seven years (since reduced to five years).[2] The object of this change was

---

[1] The Chevalier de St. George: After the birth of the "Chevalier's" son Charles in 1720, the father was known by the nickname of the "Old Pretender," and the son as the "Young Pretender." So far as birth could entitle them to the crown, they held the legal right of succession; but the Revolution of 1688 and the Act of Settlement barred them out (§ 497).

[2] The Triennial Act (§§ 439, 517) provided that at the end of three years Parliament must be dissolved and a new election held. This was to prevent the sovereign from keeping that body in power indefinitely, contrary, perhaps, to the political feeling of the country, which might prefer a different set of representatives. Under the Septennial Act the time was extended four years, making seven in all, but the sovereign may, of course, dissolve Parliament at any time. In 1911 the Parliament Act (§ 631) limited the duration of Parliament to five years.

to do away with the excitement and tendency to rebellion at that time, resulting from frequent elections, in which party feeling ran to dangerous extremes.

536. The South Sea Bubble, 1720. A few years later a gigantic enterprise was undertaken by the South Sea Company, a body of merchants originally organized as a company trading in the southern Atlantic and Pacific oceans. A Scotchman named Law had started a similar project in France, known as the "Mississippi Company," which proposed to pay off the national debt of France from the profits of its commerce with the West Indies and the country bordering on the Mississippi River.

Following his example, the South Sea Company now undertook to pay off the English National Debt (§ 503), mainly, it is said, from the profits of the slave trade between Africa and Brazil.[1] Sir Robert Walpole (§ 534) had no faith in the scheme, and attacked it vigorously; but other influential members of the Government gave it their encouragement. The directors came out with prospectuses promising dividends of fifty per cent on all money invested. Everybody rushed to buy stock, and the shares rapidly advanced from £100 to £1000 a share.

A speculative craze followed, the like of which has never since been known. Bubble companies sprang into existence with objects almost as absurd as those of the philosophers whom Swift ridiculed in "Gulliver's Travels," where one man was trying to make gunpowder out of ice, and another to extract sunbeams from cucumbers.

A mere list of these companies would fill several pages. One was to give instruction in astrology, by which every man might be able to foretell his own destiny by examining the stars; a second was to manufacture butter out of beech trees; a third was for a wheel for driving machinery, which once started would go on forever, thereby furnishing a cheap perpetual motion.

A fourth projector, going beyond all the rest in audacity, had the impudence to offer stock for sale in an enterprise "which shall be revealed hereafter." He found the public so gullible and so greedy that he sold £2000 worth of the new stock in the course

[1] Loftie's "History of London"; and see § 512.

of a single morning. He then prudently disappeared with the cash, and the unfortunate investors found that where he went with their money was not among the things to "be revealed hereafter."

The narrow passage leading to the London stock exchange was crowded all day long with struggling fortune hunters, both men and women. Suddenly, when the excitement was at its height, the bubble burst, as Law's scheme in France had a little earlier.

Great numbers of people were hopelessly ruined, and the cry for vengeance was as loud as the bids for stocks had once been. One prominent government official who had helped to blow the bubble was sent to the Tower. Another committed suicide rather than face a parliamentary committee of investigation, one of whose members had suggested that it would be an excellent plan to sew the South Sea directors up in sacks and throw them into the Thames.

537. How a Terrible Disease was conquered, 1721, 1796. But among the new things which the people were to try in that century was one which led to most beneficent results. For many generations the great scourge of Europe was the smallpox. Often the disease was as violent as the plague (§ 474), and carried off nearly as many victims. Medical art seemed powerless to deal with it, and even in years of ordinary health in England about one person out of ten died of this loathsome pestilence. In the early part of George I's reign, Lady Mary Montagu, then traveling in Turkey, wrote that the Turks were in the habit of inoculating their children for the disease, which rendered it much milder and less fatal, and that she was about to try the experiment on her own son.

Later, Lady Montagu returned to England, and through her influence and example the practice was introduced there, 1721. It was tried first on five criminals in Newgate who had been sentenced to the gallows, but were promised their freedom if they would consent to the operation. As it proved a complete success, the Princess of Wales, with the King's consent, caused it to be tried on her daughter, with equally good results.

The medical profession, however, generally refused to sanction the practice, and the clergy in many cases preached against it as an "invention of Satan, intended to counteract the purposes of an all-wise Providence." But through the perseverance and good sense of Lady Montagu, with a few others, the new practice gradually gained ground. Subsequently Dr. Jenner began to make experiments of a different kind, which led, late in the century (1796–1798), to the discovery of vaccination, by which millions of lives have been saved; this, and the discovery of the use of ether in our own time (§ 615), may justly be called two of the greatest triumphs of the art of medicine.

538. How Sir Robert Walpole governed. We have seen that Sir Robert Walpole (§ 534) became the first Prime Minister in 1721, and that he continued in office as head of the Cabinet, or Government, until near the middle of the next reign. He was an able financier, and succeeded in reducing the National Debt (§ 503). He believed in keeping the country out of war, and also, as we have seen, out of "bubble speculation" (§ 536). Finally, he was determined at all cost to maintain the Whig party in power, and the Protestant Hanoverian sovereigns on the throne (§§ 515, 532).

In order to accomplish these objects, he openly bribed members of Parliament to support his party; he bought votes and carried elections by gifts of titles, honors, and bank notes. He thus proved to his own satisfaction the truth of his theory that most men "have their price," and that an appeal to the pocketbook is both quicker and surer than an appeal to principle. But before the end of his ministry he had to confess that he had found in the House of Commons a "boy patriot," as he sneeringly called him, named William Pitt (afterward Earl of Chatham), whom neither his money could buy nor his ridicule move (§§ 549, 550).

Bad as Walpole's policy was in its corrupting influence on the nation, it was an admission that the time had come when the King could no longer venture to rule by force, as in the days of the Stuarts. It meant that the Crown no longer possessed the arbitrary power it once wielded. Walpole was a fox, not a lion; and "foxes," as Emerson tells us, "are so cunning because they are not strong."

539. Summary. Though George I did little for England except keep the "Pretender" (§ 535) from the throne by occupying it himself, yet that was no small advantage, since it gave the country peace. The establishment of Cabinet Government under Sir Robert

BRIBING A VOTER

By Hogarth

Walpole as the first Prime Minister, the suppression of the Jacobite insurrection, the disastrous collapse of the South Sea Bubble, and the introduction of vaccination are the principal events.

GEORGE II—1727–1760

540. Accession and Character. The second King George, who was also of German birth, was much like his father, though he had the advantage of being able to speak English readily, but with a strong German accent. His tastes were far from being refined and he bluntly declared, " I don't like Boetry, and I don't like Bainting." His wife, Queen Caroline, was an able woman. She possessed the happy art of ruling her husband without his suspecting it, while she, on the other hand, was ruled by Sir Robert Walpole, whom the King hated, but whom he had to keep as Prime Minister (§§ 534, 538). George II was a good soldier, and decidedly preferred war to peace ; but Walpole saw clearly that the peace policy was best for the nation, and he and the Queen managed to persuade the King not to draw the sword.

541. The War of Jenkins's Ear (1739). At the end of twelve years, however, trouble arose with Spain. According to the London newspapers of that day, a certain Captain Jenkins, while cruising, or, more probably, smuggling, in the West Indies, had been seized by the Spaniards and barbarously maltreated. They, if we accept his story, accused him of attempting to land English goods contrary to law, and searched his ship. Finding nothing against him, they vented their rage and disappointment by hanging him to the yardarm of his vessel until he was nearly dead.

They then tore off one of his ears, and bade him take it to the King of England with their compliments. Jenkins, it is said, carefully wrapped up his ear and put it in his pocket. When he reached England, he went straight to the House of Commons, drew out the mutilated ear, showed it to the House, and demanded justice.

The Spanish restrictions on English trade with the Indies and South America [1] had long been a source of ill feeling. The sight

---

[1] By the Treaty of Utrecht one English ship was allowed to carry slaves once a year to the colonies of Spanish America (§ 512, note 1).

of Jenkins's ear brought matters to a climax; even Sir Robert Walpole, the Prime Minister, could not resist the clamor for vengeance, and contrary to his own judgment he had to vote for war (§ 538).

Though Jenkins was the occasion, the real object of the war was to compel Spain to permit the English to get a larger share in the lucrative commerce, especially the slave trade, with the New World. It was another proof that America was now rapidly becoming an important factor in the politics of Great Britain (§§ 421, 422).

The announcement of hostilities with Spain was received in London with delight, and bells pealed from every steeple. "Yes," said Walpole, "they may ring the bells now, but before long they will be wringing their hands." This prediction was verified by the heavy losses the English suffered in an expedition against the Spanish settlement of Carthagena, South America. But later the British commander, Commodore Anson, inflicted great damage on the Spanish colonies, and returned to England with vessels laden with large amounts of captured silver.

542. War of the Austrian Succession, 1741 ; Treaty of Aix-la-Chapelle, 1748. On the death of Charles VI, of the House of Austria, Emperor of Germany, his daughter Maria Theresa succeeded to the Austrian dominions. France now united with Spain, Prussia, and other European powers to overturn this arrangement, partly out of jealousy of the Austrian power, and partly from desire to get control of portions of the Austrian possessions. England and Holland, however, both desired to maintain Austria as a check against their old enemy France, and declared war, 1741.

During this war George II went over to the Continent to lead the English forces in person. He was not a man of commanding appearance, but he was every inch a soldier, and nothing exhilarated him like the smell of gunpowder. At the battle of Dettingen, in Bavaria, he got down from his horse, and drawing his sword, cried: "Come, boys, now behave like men, and the French will soon run."

With that, followed by his troops, he rushed upon the enemy with such impetuosity that they turned and fled. This was the last battle in which an English king took part in person. It was followed by that of Fontenoy, in the Netherlands (Belgium), in which the French gained the victory. After nearly eight years' fighting the treaty of Aix-la-Chapelle, 1748, secured a peace advantageous for England.

543. Invasion by the " Young Pretender "; " The Forty-Five." [1] While the War of the Austrian Succession was in progress, the French encouraged James II's grandson, Prince Charles Edward, the " Young Pretender" (§ 535), to make an attempt on the English crown. He landed (1745) on the northern coast of Scotland with only seven followers, but with the aid of the Scotch Jacobites (§§ 495, 535) of the Highlands he gained a battle over the English at Prestonpans, near Edinburgh. Emboldened by his success, he now marched into Derbyshire, England, on his way to London. He hoped that as he advanced the country would rise in his favor; but finding no support, he retreated to Scotland.

The next year he and his adherents were defeated with great slaughter by " Butcher " Cumberland, as the Scotch called him, at Culloden, near Inverness (1746). (See map facing p. 120.) The " Young Pretender" fled from the battlefield to the Hebrides. After wandering in those islands for many months he escaped to France through the devotion and courage of the Scottish heroine, Flora Macdonald. When he left the country his Highland sympathizers lost all hope. There were no more ringing Jacobite songs, sung over bowls of steaming punch, of " Wha 'll be king but Charlie ? " " Over the Water to Charlie," and "Wae 's me for Prince Charlie"; and when (1788) Prince Charles Edward died in Rome, the unfortunate House of Stuart, which began with James I (1603), disappeared from English history.[2]

[1] " The Forty-Five " : so called from the Scotch rising of 1745.
[2] Devoted loyalty to a hopeless cause was never more truly or pathetically expressed than in some of these Jacobite songs, notably in those of Scotland, in honor of Prince Charles Edward, the "Young Pretender," of which the following lines from " Over the Water to Charlie " are an example :

> " Over the water, and over the sea,
>   And over the water to Charlie ;
>   Come weal, come woe, we 'll gather and go,
>   And live or die with Charlie."
>
> SCOTT, " Redgauntlet "

544. War in the East; the Black Hole of Calcutta; Clive's Victories; English Empire of India, 1751–1757. The English acquired Madras, their first trading post in India, in the reign of Charles I (1639). Later, they obtained possession of Bombay, Calcutta, and other points, but they had not got control of the country, which was still governed by native princes. The French also had established an important trading post at Pondicherry, south of Madras, and were now secretly planning through alliance with the native rulers to get possession of the entire country. They had met with some success in their efforts, and the times seemed to favor their gaining still greater influence unless some decided measures should be taken to prevent them.

At this juncture Robert Clive, a young man who had been employed as clerk in the service of the English East India Company, but who had obtained a humble position in the army, obtained permission to try his hand at driving back the enemy. It was the very work for which he was fitted. He met with success from the first, and he followed it up by the splendid victory of Arcot, 1751, which practically gave the English control of southern India. Shortly after that, Clive returned to England.

During his absence the native prince of Bengal undertook an expedition against Calcutta, a wealthy British trading post. He captured the fort which protected it (1756), and seizing the principal English residents, one hundred and forty-six in number, drove them at the point of the sword into a prison called the "Black Hole," a dungeon less than twenty feet square, and having but two small windows.

In such a climate, in the fierce heat of midsummer, that dungeon would have been too close for a single European captive; to crowd it with more than sevenscore persons for a night meant death by all the agonies of heat, thirst, and suffocation. In vain they endeavored to bribe the guard to transfer part of them to another room, in vain they begged for mercy, in vain they tried to burst the door. Their jailers only mocked them and would do nothing.

When daylight came the floor was heaped with corpses. Out of the hundred and forty-six prisoners only twenty-three were alive and they were so changed "that their own mothers would not have known them." [1]

When Clive returned he was met with a cry for vengeance. He gathered his troops, recovered Calcutta, and ended by fighting that great battle of Plassey, 1757, which was the means of permanently establishing the English empire in India on a firm foundation. (See map opposite.)

545. The Seven Years' War in Europe and America, 1756-1763. Before the contest had closed by which England won her Asiatic dominions, a new war had broken out. In the fifth year, 1756, of the New Style [2] of reckoning time, the aggressive designs of Frederick the Great of Prussia caused such alarm that a grand alliance was formed by France, Russia, Austria, and Poland to check his further advance. Great Britain, however, gave her support to Frederick, in the hope of humbling her old enemy France, who, in addition to her attempts to oust the English from India, was also making preparations on a grand scale to get possession of America.

Every victory, therefore, which the British forces could gain in Europe would, by crippling the French, make the ultimate victory of the English in America so much the more certain; for this reason we may look upon the alliance with Frederick as an indirect means employed by England to protect her colonies on the other side of the Atlantic. These colonies now extended along the entire coast, from the Kennebec River, in Maine, to the borders of Florida.

The French, on the other hand, had planted colonies at Quebec and Montreal, on the St. Lawrence; at Detroit, on the Great Lakes; at New Orleans and other points on the Mississippi. They

---

[1] Macaulay's "Essay on Clive."

[2] The New Style was introduced into Great Britain in 1752. Owing to a slight error in the calendar, the year had, in the course of centuries, been gradually losing, so that in 1752 it was eleven days short of what the true computation would make it. Pope Gregory corrected the error in 1582, and his calendar was adopted in nearly every country of Europe except Great Britain and Russia, both of which regarded the change as a "popish measure." But in 1751, notwithstanding the popular outcry, September 3, 1752, was made September 14, by an act of Parliament, and by the same act the beginning of the legal year was altered from March 25 to January 1. The popular clamor against the reform is illustrated in Hogarth's picture of an Election Feast, in which the People's party carry a banner, with the inscription, "Give us back our eleven days."

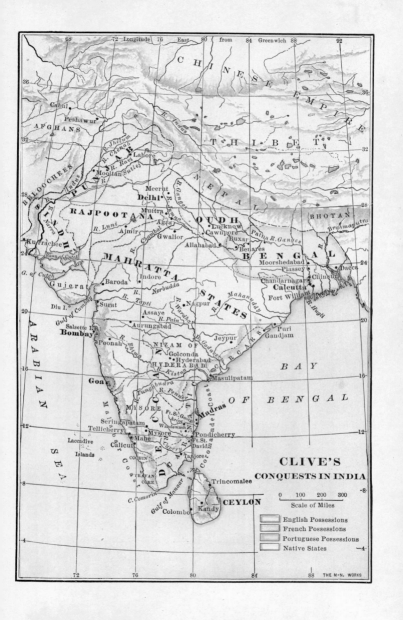

CLIVE'S
CONQUESTS IN INDIA

Scale of Miles
0   100   200   300

English Possessions
French Possessions
Portuguese Possessions
Native States

THE M-N. WORKS

had also begun to build a line of forts along the Ohio River, which, when completed, would connect their northern and southern colonies, and thus secure to them the whole country west of the Alleghenies. They expected to conquer the East as well, to erase Virginia, New England, and all other English colonial titles from the map, and in their place to put the name New France.

During the first part of the war, the English were unsuccessful. In an attempt to take Fort Duquesne, General Braddock met with a crushing defeat (1756) from the combined French and Indian forces, which would indeed have proved his utter destruction had not a young Virginian named George Washington saved a remnant of Braddock's troops by his calmness and courage. Not long afterwards, a second expedition was sent out against the French fort, in which Washington led the advance. The garrison fled at his approach, the English colors were run up, and the place was named Pittsburg, in honor of William Pitt, later, Lord Chatham, Secretary of State, but virtually Prime Minister (§ 534) of England.

About the same time, the English took the forts on the Bay of Fundy, and drove out several thousand French settlers from Acadia, or Nova Scotia. Other successes followed, by which they obtained possession of important points. Finally, Canada was won from the French by Wolfe's victory over Montcalm, at Quebec, 1759,[1] where both gallant soldiers verified the truth of the words, "The paths of glory lead but to the grave,"[2] which the English general had quoted to some brother officers the evening before the attack. This ended the war.

Spain now ceded Florida to Great Britain, so that, when peace was made in 1763, the English flag waved over the whole eastern half of the American continent, from the Atlantic to the Mississippi.

---

[1] See "Leading Facts of American History," in this series, § 142.

> [2] "The boast of heraldry, the pomp of power,
> And all that beauty, all that wealth e'er gave,
> Await alike the inevitable hour ;
> The paths of glory lead but to the grave."
>
>   GRAY, "Elegy" (1750)

"I would rather be the author of that poem," said Wolfe, "than to have the glory of beating the French to-morrow." Wolfe and Montcalm were both mortally wounded and died within a few hours of each other.

Thus, within a comparatively few years, England had gained an empire in the east (India) (§ 544) and another in the west (America).

Six years later (1769) Captain Cook explored and mapped the coast of New Zealand, and next the eastern coast of the island continent of Australia. Before the middle of the following century both these countries were added to the possessions of Great Britain. Then, as Daniel Webster said, her "morning drum beat, following the sun and keeping company with the hours," literally circled "the earth with one continuous and unbroken strain of the martial airs of England."

546. Moral Condition of England; Intemperance; Rise of the Methodists, 1738. But grand as were the military successes of the British arms, the reign of George II was morally torpid. With the exception of a few public men like Pitt, the majority of the Whig party (§ 479) seemed animated by no higher motive than self-interest. It was an age whose want of faith, coarseness, and brutality were well portrayed by Hogarth's pencil and Fielding's pen.

For a long time intemperance had been steadily on the increase; strong drink had taken the place of beer, and every attempt to restrict the traffic was met at the elections by the popular cry, "No gin, no king." The London taverns were thronged day and night, and in the windows of those frequented by the lowest class, placards were exhibited with the tempting announcement, "Drunk for a penny; dead drunk for twopence; clean straw for nothing." On the straw lay men and women in beastly helplessness.

Among the upper classes matters were hardly better. It was a common thing for great statesmen to drink at public dinners until one by one they slid out of their seats and disappeared under the table; and Sir Robert Walpole, the late Prime Minister of England (§§ 534, 538), said that when he was a young man his father would say to him as he poured out the wine, "Come, Robert, you shall drink twice while I drink once, for I will not permit the son in his sober senses to be witness of the intoxication of his father." [1]

Such was the condition of England when a great religious revival began, 1738. Its leader was John Wesley. A number of years

[1] Coxe's "Memoirs of Walpole" and Lecky's "England."

earlier, while a tutor at Oxford, he and his brother Charles, with a few others, were accustomed to meet at certain hours for devotional exercises. The regularity of their meetings, and of their habits generally, got for them the name of " Methodists," which, like " Quaker " and many another nickname of the kind, was destined to become a title of respect and honor.

At first Wesley had no intention of separating from the Church of England, but labored only to quicken it to new life; eventually, however, he found it best to begin a more extended and independent movement. The revival swept over England with its regenerating influence, and was carried by Whitefield, Wesley's lifelong friend, across the sea to America. It was especially powerful among those who had hitherto scoffed at both Church and Bible. Rough and hardened men were touched and melted to tears of repentance by the fervor of this Oxford graduate, whom neither threats nor ridicule could turn aside from his one great purpose of saving souls.

Unlike the Church, Wesley did not ask the multitude to come to him; he went to them. In this respect his work recalls that of the " Begging Friars " of the thirteenth century (§ 208), and of Wycliffe's " Poor Priests " in the fourteenth (§ 254). For more than thirty years he rode on horseback from one end of England to the other, making known the glad tidings of Christian hope. He preached in the fields, under trees which are still known by the expressive name of " Gospel Oaks "; he spoke in the abandoned mining pits of Cornwall, at the corners of the streets in cities, on the docks, in the slums; in fact, wherever he could find listening ears and responsive hearts.

The power of Wesley's appeal was like that of the great Puritan movement of the seventeenth century (§§ 378, 417). Nothing more effective had been heard since the days when Augustine and his band of monks set forth on their mission among the barbarous Saxons (§ 42). The results answered fully to the zeal that awakened them. Better than the growing prosperity of extending commerce, better than all the conquests made by the British flag in the east or west, was the new religious spirit which stirred the people of both England and America. It provoked the National Church to emulation in good works; it planted schools, checked intemperance, and brought into vigorous activity whatever was best and bravest in a race that when true to itself is excelled by none.

547. Summary. The history of the reign may be summed up in the great Religious Movement begun by John Wesley, which has just been described, and in the Asiatic, Continental, and American wars with France, which ended in the extension of the power of Great Britain in both hemispheres, — in India in the Old World and in North America in the New.

GEORGE III — 1760-1820

548. Accession and Character; the King's Struggle with the Whigs. By the death of George II his grandson,[1] George III, now came to the throne. The new King was a man of excellent character, who prided himself on having been born an Englishman. He had the best interests of his country at heart, but he lacked many of the qualities necessary to a great ruler. He was thoroughly conscientious, but he was narrow and stubborn to the last degree and he was at times insane.

His mother, who had seen how ministers and parties ruled in England (§ 534), resolved that her son should have the control. Her constant injunction to the young Prince was, "Be King, George, be King!" so that when he came to power George was determined to be King if self-will could make him one.[2]

But beneath this spirit of self-will there was moral principle. In being King, George III intended to carry out a reform such as neither George I nor George II could have accomplished, supposing that either one had possessed the desire to undertake it.

The great Whig (§§ 479, 507) families of rank and wealth had now held uninterrupted possession of the government for nearly half a century. Their influence was so supreme that the sovereign had practically become a mere cipher, dependent for his authority on the political support which he received. The King was resolved

---

[1] Frederick, Prince of Wales, George II's son, died before his father, leaving his son George heir to the throne. See Genealogical Table, p. 323.

[2] See Summary of Constitutional History in the Appendix, p. xxv, § 28.

that this state of things should continue no longer. He was determined to reassert the royal authority, secure a government which should reflect his principles, and have a ministry to whom he could dictate, instead of one that dictated to him.

For a long time he struggled in vain, but at last succeeded, and found in Lord North a Prime Minister (§ 534) who bowed to the royal will, and endeavored to carry out George III's favorite policy of "governing for, but never by, the people." That policy finally called forth Mr. Dunning's famous resolution in the House of Commons (1780). It boldly declared the King's influence "had increased, was increasing, and ought to be diminished." But his Majesty's measures had other consequences, which were more far-reaching and disastrous than any one in the House of Commons then imagined.

549. Taxation of the American Colonies. The wars of the two preceding reigns had largely increased the National Debt (§ 503), and the Government resolved to compel the American colonies to share in a more direct degree than they had yet done the constantly increasing burden of taxation. England then, like all other European countries, regarded her colonies in a totally different way from that in which she considers the colonies she now holds.

It was an open question at that time whether colonial legislative rights existed save as a matter of concession or favor on the part of the Home Government. It is true that the Government had found it expedient to grant or recognize such rights, but it had seldom defined them clearly, and in many important respects no one knew just what the settlers of Virginia or Massachusetts might or might not lawfully do.[1]

The mother country, however, was perfectly clear on three points:

1. That the American colonies were convenient receptacles for the surplus population, good or bad, of the British Islands.

2. That they were valuable as sources of revenue and profit, politically and commercially.

3. That, finally, they furnished excellent opportunities for the King's friends to get office and make fortunes.

[1] Story's "Constitution of the United States."

Such had long been the feeling about India, and such too was the feeling, modified by difference of circumstances, about America.

Politically the English colonists in America enjoyed a large measure of liberty. So far as local legislation was concerned, they were in most cases practically self-governing and independent. So, too, their personal rights were carefully safeguarded. On the other hand, the commercial policy of England toward her colonies, though severely restrictive, was far less so than that of Spain or France toward theirs. The Navigation Laws (§ 459) compelled the Americans to confine their trade to England alone, or to such foreign ports as she directed. If they sent a hogshead of tobacco or a barrel of salt fish to another country by any but an English or a colonial built vessel, they were legally liable to forfeit their goods. On the other hand, they enjoyed the complete monopoly of the English tobacco market, and in certain cases they received bounties on some of their products. Furthermore, the Navigation Laws had not been rigidly enforced for a long time, and the New England colonists generally treated them as a dead letter.

When George III came to the throne he resolved to revive the enforcement of the Navigation Laws, to build up the British West Indies, and to restrict the colonial trade with the Spanish and French West Indies. This was done, not for the purpose of crippling American commerce, but either to increase English revenue or to inflict injury on foreign rivals or enemies.

Furthermore, British manufacturers had at an earlier period induced the English Government to restrict certain American home manufactures. In accordance with that policy, Parliament had enacted statutes which virtually forbade the colonists making their own woolen cloth, or their own beaver hats, except on a very limited scale. They had a few ironworks, but they were forbidden to erect another furnace, or another mill for manufacturing iron rods or plates, and such industries were declared to be a nuisance.

William Pitt, who later became Lord Chatham (§ 538), was one of the warmest friends that America had; but he openly advocated this narrow policy, saying that if British interests demanded it he would not permit the colonists to make so much as a " horseshoe nail." Adam Smith, an eminent English political economist of that day, vehemently condemned the British Government's colonial mercantile system as suicidal; but his condemnation came too late to have any effect. The fact was that the world was not ready then — if indeed it is yet — to receive the gospel of "Live and let live."

550. The Stamp Act, 1765. In accordance with these theories about the colonies, and to meet the pressing needs of the Home Government, the English ministry proceeded to levy a tax on the colonies (1764) in return for the protection they granted them against the French and the Indians. The colonists, however, had paid their full proportion of the expense of the French and Indian wars out of their own pockets, and they now felt abundantly able to protect themselves.

But notwithstanding this plea, a form of direct tax on the American colonies, called the stamp tax, was brought forward in 1765. The proposed law required that a multitude of legal documents, such as deeds, wills, notes, receipts, and the like, should be written upon paper bearing stamps, purchased from the agents of the Home Government. The colonists, generally, protested against the passage of the law, and Benjamin Franklin, with other agents, was sent to England to sustain their protests by argument and remonstrance. But in spite of their efforts the law was passed, and the stamps were sent over to America. The people, however, refused to use them, and serious riots ensued.

In England strong sympathy with the colonists was expressed by William Pitt (Lord Chatham), Burke, Fox, and generally by what was well called "the brains of Parliament." Pitt in particular was extremely indignant. He urged the immediate repeal of the act, saying, "I rejoice that America has resisted."

Pitt further declared that any taxation of the colonies without their representation in Parliament was tyranny, and that opposition to such taxation was a duty. He vehemently insisted that the spirit shown by the Americans was the same that had withstood the despotism of the Stuarts in England (§ 436), and established the principle once for all that the King cannot take his subject's money without that subject's consent (§ 436). So, too, Fox ardently defended the American colonists, and boldly maintained that the stand they had taken helped " to preserve the liberties of mankind." [1]

Against such opposition the law could not stand. The act was accordingly repealed (1766), amid great rejoicing in London; the church bells rang out in triumph, and the shipping in the Thames was illuminated. But the good effect on America was lost by the passage of another act which maintained the unconditional right of Parliament to legislate for the colonies, and to tax them, if it saw fit, without their consent.

551. The Tea Tax and the " Boston Tea Party," 1773, with its Results. Another plan was now devised for getting money from the colonies. Parliament enacted a law (1767) compelling the Americans to pay taxes on a number of imports, such as glass, paper, and tea. In opposition to this law, the colonists formed leagues refusing to use these taxed articles, while at the same time they encouraged smugglers to land them secretly, and the regular trade suffered accordingly.

Parliament, finding that this was bad both for the government and for commerce, now abolished all of these duties except that on tea (1770). That duty was retained for a double purpose: first, and chiefly, to maintain the principle of the right of Great Britain to tax the colonies; and, next, to aid the East India Company, which was pleading piteously for help.

In consequence mainly of the refusal of the American colonists to buy tea, the London warehouses of the East India Company were full to overflowing with surplus stock, and the company itself was in a half-bankrupt condition. The custom had been for the company to bring the tea to England, pay a tax on it, and then sell it to be reshipped to America. To aid the company in its embarrassment, the Government now agreed to remit this first duty altogether, and to impose a tax of only threepence (six cents) a pound on the consumers in America.

In itself the threepenny tax was a trifle, as the ship-money tax of twenty shillings was to John Hampden (§ 436); but underlying

---

[1] See Bancroft's " United States," III, 107–108; " Columbia University Studies," III, No. 2, " The Commercial Policy of England toward the American Colonies "; Lecky's ' American Revolution "; and C. K. Adams's " British Orations."

it was a principle which seemed to the Americans, as it had seemed to Hampden, no trifle; for such principles revolutions had been fought in the past; for such they would be fought in the future.

The colonists resolved not to have the tea at any price. A number of ships laden with the taxed herb arrived at the port of Boston. The tea was seized by a band of men disguised as Indians, and thrown into the harbor, 1773. The news of that action made the King and his ministry furious. Parliament sympathized with the Government, and in retaliation passed four laws of such severity that the colonists nicknamed them the " Intolerable Acts."

The first law was the " Boston Port Act," which closed the harbor to all trade; the second was the "Regulating Act," which virtually annulled the charter of Massachusetts, took the government away from the people, and gave it to the King; the third was the " Administration of Justice Act," which ordered that Americans who committed murder in resistance to oppression should be sent to England for trial; the fourth was the " Quebec Act," which declared the country north of the Ohio and east of the Mississippi a part of Canada.[1] The object of this last act was to conciliate the French Canadians, and secure their help against the colonists in case of rebellion.

Even after Parliament had enacted these four drastic measures a compromise might have been effected, and peace maintained, if the counsels of the best men had been followed; but George III would listen to no policy short of coercion. He meant well, but his brain was not well balanced, he was subject to attacks of mental derangement, and his one idea of *being King* at all hazards had become a kind of monomania (§ 548). Pitt condemned such oppression as morally wrong, Burke denounced it as inexpedient, and Fox, another prominent member of Parliament, wrote, " It is intolerable to think that it should be in the power of one blockhead to do so much mischief."

For the time, at least, the King was as unreasonable as any of the Stuarts. The obstinacy of Charles I cost him his head, that

---

[1] Embracing territory now divided into the five states of Ohio, Indiana, Illinois, Michigan, and Wisconsin, with eastern Minnesota.

of James II his kingdom, that of George III resulted in a war which saddled the English taxpayer with an additional debt of £120,000,000, and forever detached from Great Britain the fairest and richest dominions that she ever possessed.

552. The American Revolution; Independence declared, 1776. In 1775 war began, and the stand made by the patriots at Lexington and the fighting which followed at Concord and Bunker Hill showed that the Americans were in earnest. The cry of the colonists had been, " No taxation without representation "; now they had got beyond that, and demanded, " No legislation without representation." But events moved so fast that even this did not long suffice, and on July 4, 1776, the colonies, in Congress assembled, solemnly declared themselves free and independent.[1]

As far back as the French war there was at least one man who foresaw this declaration. After the English had taken Quebec (§ 545), an eminent French statesman said of the American colonies with respect to Great Britain, " They stand no longer in need of her protection; she will call on them to contribute toward supporting the burdens they have helped to bring on her; and they will answer by striking off all dependence." [2]

This prophecy was now fulfilled. After the Americans had defeated Burgoyne in 1777 the English ministry became alarmed; they declared themselves ready to make terms; they offered to grant everything but independence; [3] but they had opened their eyes to the facts too late, and nothing short of independence would now satisfy the colonists. Attempts were made to open negotiations with General Washington, but the commander in chief declined to receive a letter from the English Government addressed to him, not in his official capacity, but as " George Washington, Esq.," and so the matter came to nothing.

553. The Battle of Yorktown; the King acknowledges American Independence, 1782. The war against the rebellious states was never really popular in England. From the outset great numbers refused to enlist to fight the Americans, and spoke of the contest

---

[1] See Summary of Constitutional History in the Appendix, p. xxv, § 29.
[2] This was Vergennes; see Bancroft's " History of the United States."
[3] This was after France had recognized the independence of the United States, 1778.

GEORGE III ACKNOWLEDGING THE INDEPENDENCE OF THE
UNITED STATES

347

as the "King's War" to show that the bulk of the English people did not encourage it. The struggle went on with varying success through seven heavy years, until, with the aid of the French, the Americans defeated Lord Cornwallis at Yorktown in 1781.[1] By that battle France got her revenge for the loss of Quebec in 1759 (§ 545), and America finally won the cause for which she had spent so much life and treasure.

George III could hold out no longer; on a foggy December morning in 1782, he entered the House of Lords, and with a faltering voice read a paper in which he acknowledged the independence of the United States of America. He closed his reading with the prayer that neither Great Britain nor America might suffer from the separation; and he expressed the hope that religion, language, interest, and affection might prove an effectual bond of union between the two countries.

Eventually the separation proved "a mutual advantage, since it removed to a great extent the arbitrary restrictions on trade, gave a new impetus to commerce, and immensely increased the wealth of both nations."[2]

554. The Lord George Gordon Riots (1780). While the American war was in progress, England had not been entirely quiet at home. A prominent Whig leader in Parliament had moved the repeal of some of the most severe laws against the Roman Catholics.[3] The greater part of these measures had been enacted under William III, "when England was in mortal terror" of the restoration of James II (§ 491). The Solicitor-General said, in seconding the motion for repeal, that these laws were "a disgrace to humanity." Parliament agreed with him in this matter. Because these unjust acts were stricken from the Statute Book,

---

[1] It is pleasant to know that a hundred years later, in the autumn of 1881, a number of English gentlemen were present at the centennial celebration of the taking of Yorktown, to express their hearty good will toward the nation which their ancestors had tried in vain to keep a part of Great Britain.

[2] Goldwin Smith's lectures on "The Foundation of the American Colonies." In general see "Lecky's American Revolution," and the "Leading Facts of American History" or the "Student's American History," in this series.

[3] The worst of these laws was that which punished a priest who should celebrate mass, with imprisonment for life. See Taswell-Langmead's "English Constitutional History," p. 627, and compare J. F. Bright's "History of England," III, 1087.

Lord George Gordon, a half-crazed fanatic,[1] who was in Parliament, led an attack upon the government (1780).

For six days London was at the mercy of a furious mob of 50,000 people, who set fire to Catholic chapels, pillaged many dwellings, and committed every species of outrage. Newgate prison was broken into, the prisoners were released, and the prison was burned. No one was safe from attack who did not wear a blue cockade to show that he was a Protestant, and no man's house was secure unless he chalked " No Popery " on the door in conspicuous letters. In fact, one individual, in order to make doubly sure, wrote over the entrance to his residence : " No Religion Whatever." Before the riot was subdued a large amount of property had been destroyed and many lives sacrificed.

555. Impeachment of Warren Hastings (1788). Six years after the American Revolution came to an end Warren Hastings, Governor-General of India, was impeached for corrupt and cruel government in that distant province. He was tried before the House of Lords, gathered in Westminster Hall. On the side of Hastings was the powerful East India Company, ruling over a territory many times larger than the whole of Great Britain. Against him were arrayed the three ablest and most eloquent men in England, — Burke, Fox, and Sheridan.

" Raising his voice until the oak ceiling resounded, Burke exclaimed at the close of his fourth great speech, ' I impeach Warren Hastings of high crimes and misdemeanors. I impeach him in the name of the Commons of Great Britain, whose trust he has betrayed. I impeach him in the name of the English nation, whose ancient honor he has sullied. I impeach him in the name of the people of India, whose rights he has trodden under foot, and whose country he has turned into a desert. Lastly, in the name of human nature itself, in the name of both sexes, in the name of every age, in the name of every rank, I impeach the common enemy and oppressor of all ! ' "

The trial was continued at intervals for over seven years. It resulted in the acquittal of the accused (1795); but it was proved

---

[1] Gordon seems to have been of unsound mind. He used to attack both political parties with such fury that it was jocosely said there were " three parties in Parliament — the ministry, the opposition, and Lord George Gordon."

that the chief business of those who went out to India was to wring fortunes from the natives, and then go back to England to live like "nabobs," and spend their ill-gotten money in a life of luxury. This fact, and the stupendous corruption that was shown to exist, eventually broke down the gigantic monopoly, and British India was thrown open to the trade of all nations.[1]

556. Liberty of the Press ; Law and Prison Reforms ; Abolition of the Slave Trade. Since the discontinuance of the censorship of the press (§ 498), though newspapers were nominally free to discuss public affairs, yet the Government had no intention of permitting any severe criticism. On the other hand, there were men who were determined to speak their minds through the press on political as on all other matters. In the early part of the reign, John Wilkes, an able but scurrilous writer, attacked the policy of the Crown in violent terms (1763). Some years later (1769), a writer, who signed himself " Junius," began a series of letters in a daily paper, in which he handled the King and the " King's friends " still more roughly. An attempt was made by the Government to punish Wilkes and the publisher of the " Junius " letters, but it signally failed in both cases. Public feeling was plainly in favor of the right of the freest political expression,[2] which was eventually conceded.

Up to this time parliamentary debates had rarely been reported. In fact, under the Tudors and the Stuarts, members of Parliament would have run the risk of imprisonment if their criticisms of royalty had been made public; but now, 1771, the papers began to contain the speeches and votes of both Houses on important questions. Every effort was made to suppress these reports, but again the press gained the day. Henceforth the nation could learn how far its representatives really represented the will of the people, and so could hold them strictly accountable, — a matter of vital importance in every free government.[3]

Another field of reform was also found. The times were brutal. The pillory still stood in the center of London;[4] and if the

---

1 See Macaulay's " Essay on Warren Hastings " ; also Burke's " Speeches."

2 Later, during the excitement caused by the French Revolution, there was a reaction from this feeling, but it was only temporary.

3 See Summary of Constitutional History in the Appendix, p. xxvi, § 30.

4 The pillory (§ 531) was not abolished until the accession of Queen Victoria.

unfortunate offender who was put in it escaped with a shower of mud and other unsavory missiles, instead of clubs and brickbats, he was lucky indeed. Gentlemen of fashion arranged pleasure parties to visit the penitentiaries for women to see the wretched inmates whipped. The whole code of criminal law was savagely vindictive. Capital punishment was inflicted for about two hundred offenses, many of which would now be thought to be sufficiently punished by one or two months' imprisonment in the house of correction.

Not only men, but women and children even, were hanged for pilfering goods or food worth a few shillings.[1] The jails were crowded with poor wretches whom want had driven to theft, and who were " worked off " on the gallows every Monday morning in batches of a dozen or twenty, in sight of the jeering, drunken crowds who gathered to witness their death agonies.

Through the efforts of Sir Samuel Romilly, Jeremy Bentham, and others, a reform was effected in this bloody code. Next, the labors of the philanthropic John Howard, and later of Elizabeth Fry, purified the jails of abuses which had made them not only dens of suffering and disease, but schools of crime as well.

The laws respecting punishment for debt were also changed for the better, and thousands of miserable beings who were without means to satisfy their creditors were set free, instead of being kept in useless lifelong imprisonment. At the same time Clarkson, Wilberforce, Fox, and Pitt were endeavoring to abolish that relic of barbarism, the African slave trade. After twenty years of persistent effort both in Parliament and out, they at last accomplished that great and beneficent work in 1807.

557. War with France (1793-1805); Battle of the Nile; Trafalgar, 1805. Near the close of the century (1789) the French Revolution broke out. It was a violent and successful attempt to destroy those feudal institutions which France had outgrown, and which had, as we have seen, disappeared gradually in England after the rebellion of Wat Tyler (§§ 250, 252). At first the revolutionists received the hearty sympathy of many of the Whig party

---

[1] Five shillings, or $1.25, was the hanging limit; anything stolen above that sum in money or goods might send the thief to the gallows.

(§ 479), but after the execution of Louis XVI and Queen Marie Antoinette,[1] England became alarmed not only at the horrible scenes of the Reign of Terror but at the establishment of the French democratic republic which seemed to justify them, and joined an alliance of the principal European powers for the purpose of restoring monarchy in France.

Napoleon had now become the real head of the French nation, and seemed bent on making himself master of all Europe. He undertook an expedition against Egypt and the East, which was intended as a stepping-stone toward the ultimate conquest of the English empire in India, but his plans were frustrated by Nelson, who completely defeated the French fleet at the battle of the Nile (1798).

With the assistance of Spain, Napoleon next prepared to invade England, and was so confident of success that he caused a gold medal to be struck, bearing the inscription, "Descent upon England." "Struck at London, 1804." But the English warships drove the French and Spanish fleets into the harbor of Cadiz, and Napoleon had to postpone his great expedition for another year.[2] In the autumn of 1805, the French and Spanish fleets sallied forth determined to win. But Lord Nelson, that frail little man who had lost his right arm and the sight of his right eye fighting his country's battles, lay waiting for them off Cape Trafalgar,[3] near by.

Two days later he descried the enemy at daybreak. Both sides felt that the decisive struggle was at hand. With the exception of a long, heavy swell the sea was calm, with a light breeze, but sufficient to bring the two fleets gradually within range.

> "As they drifted on their path
> There was silence deep as death;
> And the boldest held his breath
> For a time." [4]

---

[1] See "Death of Marie Antoinette," in Burke's "Reflections on the French Revolution."

[2] In 1801 Robert Fulton, of Pennsylvania, proposed to Napoleon that he should build warships to be propelled by steam. The proposal was submitted to a committee of French scientists, who reported that it was absurd. Had Napoleon acted on Fulton's suggestion, his descent on England might have been successful.

[3] Cape Trafalgar, on the southern coast of Spain.

[4] Campbell's "Battle of the Baltic," but applicable as well to Trafalgar.

NELSON RECEIVING THE SURRENDER OF A FLEET

Just before the action Nelson ran up this signal to the masthead of his ship, where all might see it: "ENGLAND EXPECTS EVERY MAN TO DO HIS DUTY." The answer to it was three ringing cheers from the entire fleet, and the fight began. When it ended, Napoleon's boasted navy was no more. Trafalgar Square, in the heart of London, with its tall column bearing aloft a statue of Nelson, commemorates the decisive victory, which was dearly bought with the life of the great admiral.

The battle of Trafalgar snuffed out Napoleon's projected invasion of England. He had lost his ships, and their commander, in his despair, committed suicide. The French Emperor could no longer hope to bridge "the ditch," as he derisively called the boisterous Channel, whose waves rose like a wall between him and the island which he hated (§ 14). A few years later, Napoleon, who had taken possession of Spain and placed his brother on the throne, was driven from that country by Sir Arthur Wellesley, destined to be better known as the Duke of Wellington, and the crown was restored to the Spanish nation.

558. Second War with the United States, 1812–1815. The United States waged its first war with Great Britain to gain an independent national existence; in 1812 it declared a second war to secure its rights upon the sea. During the long and desperate struggle between England and France, each nation had prohibited neutral powers from commercial intercourse with the other, or with any country friendly to the other.

Furthermore, the English Government had laid down the principle that a person born on British soil could not become a citizen of another nation, but that "once an Englishman always an Englishman" was the only true doctrine. In accordance with that theory, it claimed the right to search American ships and take from them and force into their own service any seaman supposed to be of British birth. In this way Great Britain had seized more than six thousand men, and notwithstanding their protest that they were American citizens, either by birth or by naturalization, had compelled them to enter the English navy.

Other points in dispute between the two countries were in a fair way of being settled amicably, but there appeared to be no

THE NELSON MONUMENT, TRAFALGAR SQUARE, LONDON

355

method of coming to terms in regard to the question of search and impressment, which was the most important of all, since, though the demand of the United States was, in the popular phrase of the day, for "Free Trade and Sailors' Rights," it was the last which was especially emphasized.

In 1812 war against Great Britain was declared, and an attack made on Canada which resulted in the American forces being driven back. During the war British troops landed in Maryland, burned the Capitol and other public buildings in Washington, and destroyed the Congressional Library.

On the other hand, the American navy had unexpected and extraordinary successes on the ocean and the lakes. Out of fifteen sea combats with approximately equal forces, the Americans gained twelve. The contest closed with the signal defeat of the English at New Orleans, when General Andrew Jackson (1815) completely routed the forces led by Sir Edward Pakenham, brother-in-law of the Duke of Wellington. The right of search was thenceforth dropped, although it was not formally abandoned by Great Britain until more than forty years later (1856).

559. Battle of Waterloo, 1815. In the summer of 1815, the English war against Napoleon (§ 557), which had been carried on almost constantly since his accession to power, culminated in the decisive battle of Waterloo.[1] Napoleon had crossed the Belgian frontier in order that he might come up with the British before they could form a junction with their Prussian allies. All the previous night the rain had fallen in torrents, and when the soldiers rose from their cheerless and broken sleep in the trampled and muddy fields of rye, a drizzling rain was still falling.

Napoleon planned the battle for the purpose of destroying first the English and then the Prussian forces, but Wellington held his own against the furious attacks of the French. It was evident, however, that even the " Iron Duke," as he was called, could not continue to withstand the terrible assaults many hours longer.

As time passed on, and he saw his solid squares melting away under the murderous French fire, as line after line of his soldiers coming forward silently stepped into the places of their fallen

[1] Waterloo, near Brussels, Belgium.

comrades, while the expected Prussian reënforcements still delayed their appearance, the English commander exclaimed, "O that night or Blücher would come!" At last Blücher with his Prussians did come, and as Grouchy, the leader of a division on which Napoleon was counting, did not, Waterloo was finally won by the combined strength of the allies. Not long afterwards Napoleon was sent to die a prisoner on the desolate rock of St. Helena.

When all was over, Wellington said to Blücher, as he stood by him on a little eminence looking down upon the field covered with the dead and dying, "A great victory is the saddest thing on earth, except a great defeat."

With that victory ended the second Hundred Years' War of England with France, which began (1704) under Marlborough (§ 508). The object of that war was, first, to humble the power of Louis XIV that threatened the independence of England; and, secondly, to protect the American colonies, destined to become the republic of the United States. At Waterloo the forces representing English constitutional liberty triumphed over Napoleonic despotism. That triumph helped forward the world's peace.

560. Increase of the National Debt; Taxation. Owing to these hundred years and more of war (§ 559) the National Debt of Great Britain and Ireland (§ 503), which in 1688 was much less than a million of pounds, had now reached the enormous amount of over nine hundred millions (or $4,500,000,000), bearing yearly interest at the rate of more than $160,000,000.[1] So great had been the strain on the finances of the country, that the Bank of England (§ 503) suspended payment, and many heavy failures occurred. In addition to this, a succession of bad harvests sent up the price of wheat to such a point that at one time an ordinary-sized loaf of bread cost the farm laborer more than half a day's wages.

Taxes had gone on increasing until it seemed as though the people could no longer endure the burden. As Sydney Smith declared, with entire truth, there were duties on everything. They began, he said, in childhood, with "the boy's taxed top"; they followed to old age, until at last "the dying Englishman, pouring his taxed medicine into a taxed spoon, flung himself back

[1] Encyclopædia Britannica, under "National Debt."

on a taxed bed, and died in the arms of an apothecary who had paid a tax of a hundred pounds for the privilege of putting him to death." [1]

561. The Irish Parliament; the Irish Rebellion (1798). For a century after the battle of the Boyne (§ 500) Ireland can hardly be said to have had a history. The iron hand of English despotism had crushed the spirit out of the inhabitants, and they suffered in silence. During the first part of the eighteenth century the destitution of the people was so great that Dean Swift, in bitter mockery of the government's neglect, published what he called his " Modest Proposal." He suggested that the misery of the half-starved peasants might be relieved by allowing them to eat their own children or else sell them to the butchers.

But a new attempt was now made to improve the political condition of the wretched country. That distinguished statesman, Edmund Burke (§ 550), had already tried to secure a fair measure of commercial liberty for the island, but without success. Since the reign of Henry VII the so-called " free Parliament " of Ireland had been bound hand and foot by Poynings's Act (§ 329, note 1). The eminent Protestant Irish orator, Henry Grattan, now urged the repeal of that law with all his impassioned eloquence. He was seconded in his efforts by the powerful influence of Fox in the English House of Commons. Finally, the obnoxious act was repealed (1782), and a, so-called, independent Irish Parliament, to which Grattan was elected, met in Dublin.

But although more than three quarters of the Irish people were Catholics, no person of that faith was permitted to sit in the new Parliament or to vote for the election of a member. This was not the only injustice, for many Protestants in Belfast and the north of Ireland had no right to be represented in it. Such a state of things could not fail to excite angry protest, and Grattan, with other Protestants in Parliament, labored for reform. The discontent finally led to the organization of an association called the " Society of United Irishmen." The leaders of that movement hoped to secure the coöperation of Catholics and Protestants, and to obtain fair and full representation for both in the Irish

[1] Sydney Smith's Essays, " Review of Seybert's Annals of the United States."

Parliament. A measure of political reform was secured (1793), but it did not go far enough to give the relief desired.

Eventually the Society of United Irishmen became a revolutionary organization which sought, by the help of the French, to make Ireland an independent republic. The sprigs of shamrock or the shamrock-colored badges displayed by these men gave a new significance to "the wearing of the green."[1] By this time many Protestants had withdrawn from the organization, and many Catholics refused to ask help from the French revolutionary party, who were hostile to all churches and to all religion.

Then a devoted band of Catholics in the south of Ireland resolved to rise and, trusting to their own right arms, to strike for independence. A frightful rebellion broke out (1798), marked by all the intense hatred springing from rival races and rival creeds, and aggravated by the peasants' hatred of oppressive landlords. Both sides perpetrated horrible atrocities. The government employed a large force of Orangemen,[2] or extreme Protestants, to help suppress the insurrection. They did their work with remorseless cruelty.

562. Union of Great Britain and Ireland, 1800; Emmet. Matters now came to a crisis. William Pitt, son of the late Earl of Chatham (§ 550), was Prime Minister. He believed that the best interests of both Ireland and England demanded their political union. He devoted all his energies to accomplishing the work. The result was that in the last year of the eighteenth century the English Government succeeded, by the most unscrupulous use of money, in gaining the desired end. Lord Cornwallis, acting as Pitt's agent, confessed with shame that he bought up a sufficient number of members of the Irish Parliament to secure a vote in favor of union with Great Britain. In 1800 the two countries were joined — in name at least — under the title of the "United Kingdom of Great Britain and Ireland."[3]

[1] See a quotation from the famous Irish song, "The Wearin' o' the Green," in the "Shan Van Vocht," in the "Heroic Ballads," published by Ginn and Company.

[2] Orangemen: the Protestants of the north of Ireland, who had taken the side of William of Orange in the Revolution of 1688–1689 (§ 499). They wore an orange ribbon as their badge, to distinguish them from the Catholic party, who wore green badges.

[3] The first Parliament of the United Kingdom met in 1801.

Pitt used all his powerful influence to obtain for Ireland a full and fair representation in the united Parliament (1801). He urged that Catholics as well as Protestants should be eligible for election to that body. But the King positively refused to listen to his Prime Minister. He even declared that it would be a violation of his coronation oath for him to grant such a request. The consequence was that not a single Catholic was admitted to the Imperial Parliament until nearly thirty years later (§ 573).

Two years after the first Imperial Parliament met in London the Irish patriot, Robert Emmet, made a desperate effort to free his country (1803). To his mind the union of England with Ireland was simply " the union of the shark with its prey." He staked his life on the cause of independence; he lost, and paid the forfeit on the scaffold.

But notwithstanding Emmet's hatred of the union, it resulted advantageously to Ireland in at least two respects. First, more permanent peace was secured to that distracted and long-suffering country. Secondly, the Irish people made decided gains commercially. The duties on their farm products were removed, at least in large degree, and the English ports hitherto closed against them were thrown open. The duties on their manufactured goods seem to have been taken off at that time only in part.[1] Later, absolute freedom of trade was secured.

563. " The Industrial Revolution " of the Eighteenth Century; Material Progress; Canals; the Steam Engine, 1785. The reign of George III was in several directions one of marked progress, especially in England. Just after the King's accession the Duke of Bridgewater constructed a canal from his coal mine in Worsley to Manchester, a distance of seven miles. Later, he extended it to Liverpool; eventually it was widened and deepened and became the " Manchester and Liverpool Ship Canal." The Duke of Bridgewater's work was practically the commencement of a system which has since developed to such a degree that the canals of England now extend nearly 5000 miles, and exceed in length its navigable

---

[1] See May's " Constitutional History of England," Lecky's " England in the Eighteenth Century"; but compare O'Connor Morris's work on " Ireland, from 1798 to 1898," p. 58.

rivers. The two form such a complete network of water communication that it is said no place in the realm is more than fifteen miles distant from this means of transportation, which connects all the large towns with each other and with the chief ports.

In the last half of the eighteenth century James Watt obtained the first patent (1769) for his improved steam engine (§ 521), but did not succeed in making it a business success until 1785. The story is told [1] that he took a working model of it to show to the King. His Majesty patronizingly asked him, " Well, my man, what have you to sell ? " The inventor promptly answered, " What kings covet, may it please your Majesty, — *power !* " The story is perhaps too good to be true, but the fact of the " power " could not be denied, — power, too, not simply mechanical, but, in its results, moral and political as well.

Such was the increase of machinery driven by steam, and such were the improvements made by Hargreaves, Arkwright, and Crompton in machinery for spinning and weaving cotton, that much distress arose among the hand spinners and hand weavers. The price of bread was growing higher and higher, while in many districts skilled operatives working at home could not earn by their utmost efforts eight shillings a week. They saw their hand labor supplanted by great cotton mills filled with machinery driven by " monsters of iron and fire," which never grew weary, which subsisted on water and coal, and never asked for wages.

Led by a man named Ludd (1811), the starving workmen attacked a number of these mills, broke the machinery to pieces, and sometimes burned the buildings. The riots were at length suppressed, and a number of the leaders executed ; but a great change for the better was at hand, and improved machinery driven by steam was soon to remedy the evils it had seemingly created. It led to an enormous demand for cotton. This helped to stimulate

[1] This story is told also of Boulton, Watt's partner. See Smiles's " Lives of Boulton and Watt," p. 1. Newcomen had invented a rude steam engine in 1705, which in 1712 came into use to some extent for pumping water out of coal mines. But his engine was too clumsy and too wasteful of fuel to be used by manufacturers. Boulton and Watt built the first steam-engine works in England at Soho, a suburb of Birmingham, in 1775 ; but it was not until 1785 that they began to do sufficient business to make it evident that they were on their way to success.

cotton growing in the United States of America as well as to encourage the manufacture of cotton in Great Britain.

Up to this period the north of England had remained the poorest part of the country. The population was sparse, ignorant, and unprosperous. It was in the south that improvements originated. In the reign of Henry VIII, the North fought against the dissolution of the monasteries (§§ 352, 357); in Elizabeth's reign it resisted Protestantism; in that of George I it sided with the so-called " Pretender " (§ 535).

But steam transformed an immense area. Factories were built, population increased, cities sprang up, and wealth grew apace. Birmingham, Manchester, Leeds, Nottingham, Leicester, Sheffield, and Liverpool made the North a new country. (See Industrial Map of England, p. 10.) Lancashire is the busiest cotton-manufacturing district in Great Britain, and the saying runs that " what Lancashire thinks to-day, England will think to-morrow." So much for James Watt's *power* and its results.

564. Discovery of Oxygen (1774); Introduction of Gas (1815). Notwithstanding the progress that had been made in many departments of knowledge, the science of chemistry remained almost stationary until (1774) Dr. Joseph Priestley discovered oxygen, the most abundant, as well as the most important, element in nature.

That discovery "laid the foundation of modern chemical science." It enlarged our knowledge of the composition of the atmosphere, of the solid crust of the earth, and of water. Furthermore, it revealed the interesting fact that oxygen not only enters into the structure of all forms of animal and vegetable life, but that no kind of life can exist without it. Finally, Priestley's great discovery proved to be of direct practical utility, since the successful pursuit of innumerable trades and manufactures, with the profitable separation of metals from their ores, stands in close connection with the facts which his experiments with oxygen made known.

As intellectual light spread, so also did material light. In London, up to near the close of the reign of George III, only a few feeble oil lamps were in use. Many miles of streets were dark and dangerous, and highway robberies were frequent. At length (1815) a company was formed to light the city with gas. After much opposition from those who were in the whale-oil interest the enterprise succeeded. The new light, as Miss Martineau said, did more to prevent crime than all that the Government had accomplished since the days of Alfred. It changed, too, the whole aspect of the English capital, though it was only the forerunner of the electric light, which has since changed it even more.

The sight of the great city now, when viewed at night from Highgate archway on the north, or looking down the Thames from Westminster Bridge, is something never to be forgotten. It gives one a realizing sense of the immensity of "this province covered with houses," which cannot be got so well in any other way. It brings to mind, too, those lines expressive of the contrasts of wealth and poverty, success and failure, inevitable in such a place :

> " O gleaming lamps of London, that gem the city's crown,
> What fortunes lie within you, O lights of London town !
> .　.　.　.　.　.　.　.　.　.
> O cruel lamps of London, if tears your light could drown,
> Your victims' eyes would weep them, O lights of London town." [1]

The same year in which gas was introduced, Sir Humphry Davy invented the miner's safety lamp. Without seeking a patent, he generously gave his invention to the world, finding his reward in the knowledge that it would be the means of saving thousands of lives wherever men are called to work underground.

565. Steam Navigation, 1807, 1819, and 1840. Since Watt had demonstrated the value of steam for driving machinery (§ 563), a number of inventors had been experimenting with the new power, in the hope that they might apply it to propelling vessels. In 1807 Robert Fulton, an American, built the first successful steamboat, and made the voyage from New York to Albany in it. Shortly afterwards his vessel began to make regular trips on the Hudson. A number of years later a similar boat began to carry passengers on the Clyde, in Scotland. Finally, in 1819, the bold undertaking was made of crossing the Atlantic by steam. An American steamship, the *Savannah*, of about three hundred tons, set the example by a voyage from the United States to Liverpool. Dr. Lardner, an English scientist, had proved to his own satisfaction that ocean

---

[1] From the play, "The Lights of London."

steam navigation was impracticable. The book containing the doctor's demonstration was brought to America by the *Savannah* on her return.

Twenty-one years afterward, in 1840, the Cunard Company established the first regular line of ocean steamers. They sailed between England and the United States. Since then fleets of steamers ranging from two thousand to more than forty thousand tons each have been built. They now make passages from continent to continent with the regularity of clockwork, and in fewer

A TWENTIETH-CENTURY OCEAN STEAMER

days than the ordinary sailing vessels formerly required weeks. The fact that during a period of more than seventy years one of these lines has never lost a passenger is conclusive proof that Providence is on the side of steam, when steam has men that know how to handle it.

566. Literature ; Art ; Education ; Travel ; Dress. The reign of George III is marked by a long list of names eminent in letters and art. First in point of time among these stands Dr. Samuel Johnson, the compiler of the first English dictionary worthy of the name, and that on which those of our own day are based to a considerable extent. He was also the author of the story of " Rasselas,"— that notable satire on discontent and the search after happiness. Next stands Johnson's friend, Oliver Goldsmith, famous for his genius, his wit, and his improvidence, — which was always getting him into trouble, — but still more famous for his poems, and his novel, " The Vicar of Wakefield."

Edward Gibbon, David Hume, author of the well-known " History of England," and Adam Smith come next in time. In 1776 Gibbon published his " Decline and Fall of the Roman Empire," which after more than a hundred years still stands the ablest history of the subject in our language. In the same year Adam Smith issued " An Inquiry into the Nature and Causes of the Wealth of Nations," which had a great effect on legislation respecting commerce, trade, and finance. During this period, also, Sir William Blackstone became prominent as a writer on law, and Edmund Burke, the distinguished orator and statesman, wrote his " Reflections on the French Revolution."

The poets, Burns, Byron, Shelley, and Keats, with Sheridan, the orator and dramatist, and Sterne, the humorist, belong to this reign; so, too, does the witty satirist, Sydney Smith, and Sir Walter Scott, whose works, like those of Shakespeare, have " made the dead past live again." Then again, Maria Edgeworth and Jane Austen have left admirable pictures of the age in their stories of Irish and English life. Coleridge and Wordsworth began to attract attention toward the last of this period, and to be much read by those who loved the poetry of thought and the poetry of nature; while, early in the next reign, Charles Lamb published his delightful " Essays of Elia."

In art we have the first English painters and engravers. Hogarth, who died a few years after the beginning of the reign, was celebrated for his coarse but perfect representations of low life and street scenes; and his series of Election pictures with his " Beer Lane " and " Gin Alley " are valuable for the insight they give into the history of the times.

The chief portrait painters were Reynolds, Lawrence, and Gainsborough, the last of whom afterwards became noted for his landscapes. They were followed by Wilkie, whose pictures of " The Rent Day," " The Reading of the Will," and many others, tell a story of interest to every one who looks at them.

Last came Turner, who in some respects surpassed all former artists in his power of reproducing scenes in nature. At the same time, Bewick, whose cuts used to be the delight of every child that read "Æsop's Fables," gave a new impulse to wood engraving, while Flaxman rose to be the leading English sculptor, and Wedgwood introduced useful and beautiful articles of pottery.

A SEDAN CHAIR

In common-school education little advance had been made for many generations. In the country the great mass of the people were nearly as ignorant as they were in the darkest part of the Middle Ages. Hardly a peasant over forty years of age could be found who could read a verse in the Bible, and not one in ten could write his name.

There were no cheap books or newspapers, and no proper system of public instruction. The poor seldom left the counties in which they were born. They knew nothing of what was going on in the world. Their education was wholly of that practical kind which comes from work and things, not from books and teachers; yet many of them with only these simple helps found out two secrets which the highest culture sometimes misses, — how to be useful and how to be happy.[1]

The ordinary means of travel were still very imperfect. Stagecoaches had been in use for more than a hundred and fifty years. They crawled along at the rate of about three miles an hour. Mail coaches began to run in 1784. They attained a speed of six miles an hour, and later of ten. This was considered entirely satisfactory.

[1] See Wordsworth's poem "Resolution and Independence."

The close of George III's reign marks the beginning of the present age. It was indicated in many ways, and among others by the declining use of sedan chairs, which had been the fashion for upwards of a century, and by the change in dress. Gentlemen were leaving off the picturesque costumes of the past, — the cocked hats, elaborate wigs, silk stockings, ruffles, velvet coats, and swords, — and gradually putting on the plain democratic garb, sober in cut and color, by which we know them to-day.

567. Last Days of George III. George III died (1820) at the age of eighty-two. During ten years he had been blind, deaf, and crazy, having lost his reason not very long after the jubilee, which celebrated the fiftieth year of his reign (1809). Once, in a lucid interval, he was found by the Queen singing a hymn and playing an accompaniment on the harpsichord.

He then knelt and prayed aloud for her, for his family, and for the nation; and in closing, for himself, that it might please God to avert his heavy calamity, or grant him resignation to bear it. Then he burst into tears, and his reason again fled.[1] In consequence of the incapacity of the King, his eldest son, the Prince of Wales, was appointed regent (1811), and on the King's death came to the throne as George IV.

568. Summary. The long reign of George III covered sixty very eventful years. During that time England lost her possessions in America, but gained India and prepared the way for getting possession of New Zealand and Australia. During that period, also, Ireland was united to Great Britain. The wars with France, which lasted more than twenty years, ended in the great naval victory of Trafalgar and the still greater victory on the battlefield of Waterloo. In consequence of these wars, with that of the American Revolution, the National Debt of Great Britain rose to a height which rendered the burden of taxation well-nigh insupportable.

The second war with the United States in 1812 made America independent on the sea, and eventually compelled England to give up her assumed right to search American vessels. The two greatest reforms of the period were the abolition of the slave trade and the mitigation of the laws against debt and crime; the

---

[1] See Thackeray's " Four Georges."

chief material improvement was the extension of canals and the application of steam to manufacturing and to navigation. The "Industrial Revolution" transformed the North of England.

GEORGE IV — 1820-1830

here

569. Accession and Character of George IV. George IV, eldest son of the late King, came to the throne in his fifty-eighth year; but, owing to his father's insanity, he had virtually been King for nearly ten years (§ 567). His habits of life had made him a selfish, dissolute spendthrift, who, like Charles II, cared only for pleasure. Though while Prince of Wales he had received for many years an income of upwards of £100,000, which was largely increased at a later period, yet he was always hopelessly in debt.

Parliament (1795) appropriated over £600,000 to relieve him from his most pressing creditors, but his wild extravagance soon involved him in difficulties again, so that had it not been for help given by the long-suffering taxpayers, His Royal Highness must have become as bankrupt in purse as he was in character.

After his accession matters became worse rather than better. At his coronation, which cost the nation over £200,000, he appeared in hired jewels, which he forgot to return, and which Parliament had to pay for. Not only did he waste the nation's money more recklessly than ever, but he used whatever political influence he had to oppose such measures of reform as the times demanded.

570. Discontent; the "Manchester Massacre" (1819). When (1811) George, then Prince of Wales, became regent (§ 567), he desired to form a Whig ministry, not because he cared for Whig principles (§ 479), but solely because he would thereby be acting in opposition to his father's wishes. Finding his purpose impracticable, he accepted Tory rule (§ 479), and a Cabinet (§ 534) was formed with Lord Liverpool as Prime Minister. It had for its main object the continued exclusion of Catholics from representation in Parliament (§ 478).

Lord Liverpool was a dull, well-meaning man, who utterly failed to comprehend the real tendency of the age. He was the son of a commoner who had been raised to the peerage. He had always had a reputation for honest obstinacy, and for little else. After he became Premier, a prominent French lady, who was visiting England, asked him one day, " What has become of that *very* stupid man, Mr. Jenkinson ? " " Madame," answered the unfortunate Prime Minister, " he is now Lord Liverpool." [1]

From such a Cabinet or Government, which continued in power for fifteen years, nothing but trouble could be expected. The misery of the country was great. Food was selling at famine prices. Thousands were on the verge of starvation, and tens of thousands did not get enough to eat. Trade was seriously depressed, and multitudes were unable to obtain work. Under these circumstances, the suffering masses undertook to hold public meetings to discuss the cause and cure of these evils; but as violent speeches against the Government were often made at the meetings, the authorities dispersed them on the ground that they were seditious and tended to riot and rebellion.

Many large towns at this period had no voice in legislation. At Birmingham, which was one of this class, the citizens had met and chosen, though without legal authority, a representative to Parliament. Manchester, another important manufacturing town, now determined to do the same thing. The people were warned not to assemble, but they persisted in doing so, on the ground that peaceful discussion, with the election of a representative, was no violation of law. The meeting was held in St. Peter's Fields, and, through the blundering of a magistrate, it ended in an attack by a body of troops, by which many people were wounded and a number killed (1819).

571. The Six Acts (1819); the Conspiracy. The bitter feeling caused by the " Manchester Massacre," or " Peterloo," as it was called, was still further aggravated by the passage of the Six Acts (1819). The object of these severe coercive measures was to make it impossible for men to take any public action demanding political reform. They restricted freedom of speech, freedom of the press, and the right of the people to assemble for the purpose of open discussion of the course taken by the Government. These harsh

[1] Earl's " English Premiers," Vol. II.

laws coupled with other repressive measures taken by the Tories
(§ 479), who were still in power, led to the "Cato Street Conspiracy." Shortly after the accession of George IV a few desperate men banded together, and meeting in a stable in Cato Street,
London, formed a plot to murder Lord Liverpool and his entire
Cabinet at a dinner at which all the ministers were to be present.

The plot was discovered, and the conspirators were speedily disposed of by the gallows or transportation, but nothing was done to
relieve the suffering which had provoked the intended crime. No
new conspiracy was attempted, but in the course of the next ten
years a silent revolution took place, which, as we shall see later,
obtained for the people that fuller representation in Parliament
which they had hitherto vainly attempted to get (§ 582).

572. Queen Caroline. While he was Prince of Wales, George IV
had, contrary to law, privately married Mrs. Fitzherbert (1785),[1]
a Roman Catholic lady of excellent character, and possessed of
great beauty. Ten years later, partly through royal compulsion
and partly to get money to pay off some of his numerous debts,
the Prince married his cousin, the Princess Caroline of Brunswick.
The union proved a source of unhappiness to both. The Princess
lacked both discretion and delicacy, and her husband, who disliked
her from the first, was reckless and brutal toward her.

He separated from her in a year's time, and as soon as she
could, she withdrew to the Continent. When he became King he
excluded Queen Caroline's name from the Prayer Book, and next
applied to Parliament for a divorce on the ground of the Queen's
unfaithfulness to her marriage vows.

Henry Brougham, afterwards Lord Brougham, acted as the
Queen's counsel. No sufficient evidence was brought against her,
and the ministry declined to take further action. It was decided,
however, that she could not claim the honor of coronation, to
which, as Queen Consort, she had a right sanctioned by custom
but not secured by law. When the King was crowned (1821), no
place was provided for her. By the advice of her counsel, she

[1] By the Royal Marriage Act of 1772, no descendant of George II could make a
legal marriage without the consent of the reigning sovereign, unless twenty-five
years of age, and unless the marriage was not objected to by Parliament.

presented herself at the entrance of Westminster Abbey as the coronation ceremony was about to begin; but, by order of her husband, admission was refused, and she retired to die, heartbroken, a few days after.

573. Three Great Reforms. Seven years later (1828) the Duke of Wellington, a Tory (§ 479) in politics, became Prime Minister. His sympathies in all matters of legislation were with the King, but he made a virtue of necessity, and for the time acted with those who demanded reform. The Corporation Act (§ 472), which was originally passed in the reign of Charles II, and had for its object the exclusion of Dissenters (§ 472) from all town or corporate offices, was now repealed; henceforth a man might become a mayor, alderman, or town officer, without belonging to the Church of England. At the same time the Test Act (§ 477), which had also been passed in Charles II's reign to keep both Catholics and Dissenters out of government offices, whether civil or military, was repealed. As a matter of fact " the teeth of both acts had long been drawn " by an annual Indemnity Act (1727).[1]

In 1829 a still greater reform was carried. For a long period the Catholic Association had been laboring to obtain the abolition of the laws which had been on the statute books for over a century and a half, by which Catholics were excluded from the right to sit in Parliament. These laws, it will be remembered, were enacted at the time of the alleged Popish Plot, and in consequence of the perjured evidence given by Titus Oates (§ 478).[2] The King, and the Tory party marshaled by the Duke of Wellington, strenuously resisted the repeal of these statutes; but finally the Duke became convinced that further opposition was useless. He therefore suddenly changed about and solely, as he declared, to avert civil war, took the lead in securing the success of a measure which he heartily hated.

But at the same time that Catholics were admitted to both Houses of Parliament, an act was passed raising the property

---

[1] This act virtually suspended the operation of the Corporation Act (§ 472) and the Test Act against Dissenters so that they could obtain civil offices from which these two acts had excluded them.

[2] See Sydney Smith's " Peter Plymley's Letters."

qualification of a very large class of small Irish landholders from £2 to £10. This measure deprived many thousands of their right to vote. The law was enacted on the pretext that the small Irish landholders would be influenced by their landlord or their priest.

Under the new order of things, Daniel O'Connell, an Irish gentleman of an old and honorable family, and a man of distinguished ability, came forward as leader of the Catholics. After much difficulty he succeeded in taking his seat in the House of Commons (1829). He henceforth devoted himself, though without avail, to the repeal of the act uniting Ireland with England (§ 562), and to the restoration of an independent Irish Parliament.

574. The New Police (1829). Although London had now a population of a million and a half, it still had no effective police. The guardians of the peace at that date were infirm old men, who spent their time dozing in sentry boxes, and had neither the strength nor energy to be of service in any emergency. The young fellows of fashion considered these venerable constables as legitimate game. They often amused themselves by upsetting the sentry boxes with their occupants, leaving the latter helpless in the street, kicking and struggling like turtles turned on their backs, and as powerless to get on their feet again.

During the last year of the reign Sir Robert Peel got a bill passed (1829) which organized a new and thoroughly efficient police force, properly equipped and uniformed. Great was the outcry against this innovation, and the "men in blue" were hooted at, not only by London "roughs," but by respectable citizens, as "Bobbies" or "Peelers," in derisive allusion to their founder. But the "Bobbies," who carry no visible club, were not to be jeered out of existence. They did their duty like men, and have continued to do it in a way which long since gained for them the good will of all who care for the preservation of law and order.

575. Death of the King (1830). George IV died soon after the passage of the new Police Bill (1830). Of him it may well be said, though in a very different sense from that in which the expression was originally used, that "nothing in his life became him like the leaving it." During his ten years' reign he had squandered enormous sums of money in gambling and dissipation, and had done his utmost to block the wheels of political progress.

How far this son of an insane father (§ 567) was responsible, it may not be for us to judge. Walter Scott, who had a kind word for almost every one, and especially for any one of the Tory party (§ 479), did not fail to say something in praise of the generous good nature of his friend George IV. The sad thing is that his voice seems to have been the only one. In a whole nation the rest were silent; or, if they spoke, it was neither to commend nor to defend, but to condemn.

576. Summary. The legislative reforms of George IV's reign are its chief features. The repeal of the Test and Corporation acts and the grant to Catholics of the right to reënter Parliament were tardy measures of justice. Neither the King nor his ministers deserve any credit for them, but, none the less, they accomplished great and permanent good.

WILLIAM IV — 1830–1837

577. Accession and Character of William IV. As George IV left no heir, his brother William, a man of sixty-five, now came to the throne. He had passed most of his life on shipboard, having been placed in the navy when a mere lad. He was somewhat rough in his manner, and cared nothing for the ceremony and etiquette that were so dear to both George III and George IV. His faults, however, were on the surface. He was frank, hearty, and a friend to the people, to whom he was familiarly known as the " Sailor King."

578. Need of Reform in Parliamentary Representation. From the beginning of this reign it was evident that the great question which must soon come up for settlement was that of parliamentary representation. Large numbers of the people of England had now no voice in the government. This unfortunate state of things was chiefly the result of the great changes which had taken place in the growth of the population of the Midlands (or the central portion of England) and the North (§ 563).

Since the introduction of steam (§ 563) the rapid increase of manufactures and commerce had built up Birmingham, Leeds, Sheffield, Manchester, and other large towns in the iron, coal, pottery and manufacturing districts. (See Industrial Map of England, p. 10.) These important towns could not send a member to Parliament; while, on the other hand, many places in the south of England which did send members had long since ceased to be of any importance. Furthermore, the representation was of the most haphazard description. In one section no one could vote except substantial property holders, in another none but town officers, while in a third every man who had a tenement big enough to boil a pot in, and hence called a " Pot-walloper," possessed the right.

To this singular state of things the nation had long been indifferent. During the Middle Ages the inhabitants often had no desire either to go to Parliament themselves or to send others. The expense of the journey was great, the compensation was small, and unless some important matter of special interest to the people was at stake, they preferred to stay at home. On this account it was often almost as difficult for the sheriff to get a distant county member up to the House of Commons in London as it would have been to carry him there a prisoner to be tried for his life.

Now, however, everything was changed; the rise of political parties (§ 479), the constant and heavy taxation, the jealousy of the increase of royal authority, the influence and honor of the position of a Parliamentary representative, all conspired to make men eager to obtain their full share in the management of the government.

This new interest had begun as far back as the civil wars of the seventeenth century, and when Cromwell came to power he effected many much-needed reforms. But after the restoration of the Stuarts (§ 467), the Protector's wise measures were repealed or neglected. Then the old order, or rather disorder, again asserted itself, and in many cases matters became worse than ever.

579. " Rotten Boroughs." For instance, the borough or city of Old Sarum, in Wiltshire, which had once been an important place, had, at an early period, gradually declined through the growth of New Sarum, or Salisbury, near by. (See map, p. 436.) In the sixteenth century the parent city had so completely decayed that not a single habitation was left on the desolate hilltop where the castle and cathedral once stood. At the foot of the hill was an old tree. The owner of that tree and of the field where it grew sent (1830) two members to Parliament, — that action represented what had been regularly going on for something like three hundred years!

In Bath, on the other hand, none of the citizens, out of a large population, might vote except the mayor, alderman, and common council. These places now got the significant name of "rotten boroughs" from the fact that whether large or small there was no longer any sound political life existing in them. Many towns were so completely in the hands of the squire or some other local "political

"OLD SARUM HILL"

boss" that, on one occasion when a successful candidate for Parliament thanked the voters for what they had done, a man replied that he need not take the trouble to thank them; for, said he, "if the squire had zent his great dog we should have chosen him all one as if it were you, zur."[1]

580. The Great Reform Bill. For fifty years after the coming in of the Georges the country had been ruled by a powerful Whig (§§ 479, 548) monopoly. Under George III that monopoly was broken (§ 548), and the Tories (§ 479) got possession of the government. But whichever party ruled, Parliament, owing to the

[1] See Hindon, in Murray's "Wiltshire."

"rotten-borough" system, no longer represented the nation, but simply stood for the will of certain wealthy landholders and town corporations. A loud and determined demand was now made for reform. In this movement no one was more active or influential among the common people than William Cobbett. He was a vigorous and fearless writer, who for years published a small newspaper called the *Political Register*, which was especially devoted to securing a just and uniform system of representation.

On the accession of William IV the pressure for reform became so great that Parliament was forced to act. Lord John Russell brought in a bill (1831) providing for the abolition of the "rotten boroughs" and for a fair system of elections. But those who owned or controlled those boroughs had no intention of giving them up. Their opponents, however, were equally determined, and they knew that they had the support of the nation.

In a speech which the Reverend Sydney Smith made at Taunton, he compared the futile resistance of the House of Lords to the proposed reform, to Mrs. Partington's attempt to drive back the rising tide of the Atlantic with her mop. The ocean rose, and Mrs. Partington, seizing her mop, rose against it; yet, notwithstanding the good lady's efforts, the Atlantic got the best of it; so the speaker prophesied that in this case the people, like the Atlantic, would in the end carry the day.[1]

When the bill came up, the greater part of the Lords and the bishops, who, so far as they were concerned personally, had all the rights and privileges they wanted, opposed it; so too did the Tories (§ 479), in the House of Commons. They thought that the proposed law threatened the stability of the government. The Duke of Wellington (§ 573) was particularly hostile to it, and wrote, "I don't generally take a gloomy view of things, but I confess that, knowing all that I do, I cannot see what is to save the Church, or property, or colonies, or union with Ireland, or, eventually, monarchy, if the Reform Bill passes." [2]

581. The Lords reject the Bill ; Serious Riots (1831). The King dissolved Parliament (§ 534, note 2) ; a new one was elected, and

[1] Sydney Smith's " Essays and Speeches."
[2] Wellington's " Despatches and Letters," II, 451.

THE BRISTOL RIOT

the Reform Bill was passed by the House of Commons; but the upper House rejected it. Then a period of wild excitement ensued. The people in many of the towns collected in the public squares, tolled the church bells, built bonfires in which they burned the bishops in effigy, with other leading opponents of the bill, and cried out for the abolition of the House of Lords.

In London the rabble smashed the windows of Apsley House, the residence of the Duke of Wellington. At Nottingham the mob fired and destroyed the castle of the Duke of Newcastle because he was opposed to reform. In Derby a serious riot broke out. In Bristol matters were still worse. A mob got possession of the city, and burned the Bishop's Palace and a number of public buildings. The mayor was obliged to call for troops to restore order. Many persons were killed, and four of the ringleaders of the insurrection were hanged. All over the country shouts were heard, " The Bill, the whole Bill, and nothing but the Bill!"

582. Passage of the Great Reform Bill, 1832 ; Results. In the spring of 1832 the battle began again more fiercely than ever. Again the House of Commons voted the bill, and once again the House of Lords defeated it.

Earl Grey, the Whig Prime Minister (§ 479), had set his heart on carrying the measure. In this crisis he appealed to the King for help. If the Tory Lords would not pass the bill, the King had the power to create a sufficient number of new Whig Lords who would. William refused to exercise this power. Thereupon Earl Grey, with his Cabinet (§ 534), resigned, but in a week the King had to recall them. Then William, much against his will, gave the following document to his Prime Minister:

" *The King grants permission to Earl Grey, and to his Chancellor, Lord Brougham, to create such a number of Peers as will be sufficient to insure the passing of the Reform Bill — first calling up Peers' eldest sons.*

 " WILLIAM R., Windsor, May 17, 1832 "[1]

---

[1] " First calling up Peers' eldest sons " : that is, in creating new Lords, the eldest sons of Peers were to have the preference. William R. (*Rex*, King) : this is the customary royal signature. Earl Grey was the leader of that branch of the Whig party known as the " Aristocratic Whigs," yet to him and his associate Cabinet ministers the people were indebted for the great extension of the suffrage in 1832.

But there was no occasion to make use of this permission. As soon as the Lords found that the Cabinet (§ 534), with Earl Grey at the head, had actually compelled the King to bow to the demands of the people, they withdrew their opposition. The " Great Charter of 1832 " was carried, received the royal signature, and became law.

The passage of this memorable act brought about these beneficent changes :

(1) It abolished nearly sixty "rotten boroughs " (§ 579).

(2) It gave every householder who paid a rent of ten pounds in any town a vote, and largely extended the list of county voters as well.

(3) It granted two representatives to Birmingham, Leeds, Manchester, and nineteen other large towns, and one representative each to twenty-one other places, all of which had hitherto been unrepresented, besides granting fifteen additional members to the counties.

(4) It added, in all, half a million voters to the list, mostly men of the middle class, and it helped to purify the elections from the violence which had disgraced them.[1]

Before the passing of the Reform Bill, and the legislation which supplemented it, the election of a member of Parliament was a kind of local reign of terror. The smaller towns were sometimes under the control of drunken ruffians for several weeks. During that time they paraded the streets in bands, assaulting voters of the opposite party with clubs, kidnaping prominent men and confining them until after the election, and perpetrating other outrages, which so frightened peaceable citizens that often they did not dare attempt to vote at all.

Finally, the passage of the Reform Bill of 1832 effected, in its own way, a change which was perhaps as momentous as that which the Revolution of 1688 had accomplished.[2] That, as we have seen (§ 497), made the King dependent for his crown on his election to office by Parliament. On the other hand, the Reform Bill

---

[1] See Summary of Constitutional History in the Appendix, p. xxvi, § 31.

[2] Compare the three previous Revolutions represented by (1) Magna Carta (§ 199) ; (2) De Montfort's House of Commons (§ 213) ; (3) the Civil War and its effects (§§ 441, 450, 451).

practically took the last vestige of real political authority from the King and transferred it to the Cabinet (§ 534), who had now become responsible to the House of Commons, and hence to the direct will of the majority of the nation. But though the Sovereign had laid down his political scepter, never to resume it, he would yet, by virtue of his exalted position, continue to wield great power, — that of social and diplomatic influence, which is capable of accomplishing most important results both at home and abroad. To-day then, though the King still reigns, the People, and the People alone, govern.

583. Abolition of Slavery, 1833 ; Factory Reform, 1833-1841. With the new Parliament that came into power the names of Liberal and Conservative began to supplant those of Whig and Tory (§ 479), for it was felt that a new political era needed new party names. Again, the passage of the Reform Bill (§ 582) changed the policy of both these great political parties. It made Liberals and Conservatives bid against each other for the support of the large number of new voters (§ 582 (4)), and it acted as an entering wedge to prepare the way for the further extension of suffrage in 1867 and 1884 (§ 600). Meanwhile the House of Commons reflected the will of the people better than ever before ; the authority of the Cabinet ministers (§ 534), representing the Commons, had gained a most significant victory ; and further reforms were accordingly carried against the strenuous opposition of the King.

Buxton, Wilberforce, Brougham, and other noted philanthropists secured the passage through Parliament of a bill, 1833, for which they, with the younger Pitt, had labored in vain for half a century. By this act all negro slaves in the British West India colonies, numbering about eight hundred thousand, were set free, and the sum of £20,000,000 was appropriated to compensate the owners.

It was a grand deed grandly done. Could America have followed that noble example, she might thereby have saved a million of human lives and many thousand millions of dollars which were cast into the gulf of civil war, while the corrupting influence of five years of waste and discord would have been avoided.

But negro slaves were not the only slaves in those days. There were white slaves as well, — women and children born in England, but condemned by their necessities to work underground in the coal mines, or to exhaust their strength in the cotton mills. They were driven by brutal masters who cared as little for the welfare of those under them as the overseer of a West India plantation did for his gangs of black toilers in the sugar-cane fields. On investigation it was found that children only six and seven years of age were compelled to labor for twelve and thirteen hours continuously in the factories. In the coal mines their case was even worse. All day long these poor creatures sat in absolute darkness, opening and shutting doors for the passage of coal cars. If, overcome with fatigue, they fell asleep, they were cruelly beaten with a strap.[1]

Parliament at length turned its attention to these abuses, and passed acts, 1833, forbidding the employment of women and young children in such work; a later act put an end to the barbarous practice of forcing children to sweep chimneys.

584. The First Steam Railway, 1830; the Railway Craze; the Friction Match, 1834. Ever since the application of steam to machinery, inventors had been discussing plans for placing the steam engine on wheels and using it as a propelling power in place of horses. Macadam, a Scotch surveyor, had constructed a number of very superior roads made of gravel and broken stone in the south of England, which soon made the name of "macadamized turnpike" celebrated.

The question then arose, Might not a still further advance be made by employing steam to draw cars on these roads, or, better still, on iron rails? The first locomotives built were used in hauling coal at the mines in the North of England. *Puffing Billy*, the pioneer machine (1813), worked for many years near Newcastle. At length George Stephenson, an inventor and engineer, together with certain capitalists, succeeded in getting Parliament to pass an act for constructing a passenger railway between Liverpool and Manchester, a distance of about thirty miles.

When the line was completed by Stephenson, he had great difficulty in getting permission to use an engine instead of horse power on it. Finally, Stephenson's new locomotive, *The Rocket*, —

---

[1] See Gibbin's "Industrial History of England," E. F. Cheyney's "Industrial History of England," and Mrs. E. B. Browning's poem, "The Cry of the Children."

which first introduced the tubular boiler, and employed the exhaust, or escaping, steam to increase the draft of the fire, — was tried with entire success.[1]

The Liverpool and Manchester Railway was formally opened in the autumn of 1830, and the Duke of Wellington, then Prime Minister, was one of the few passengers who ventured on the trial trip. The growth of this new mode of transportation was so rapid that in five years from that time London and the principal seaports were connected with the great manufacturing towns,

ONE OF THE FIRST PASSENGER TRAINS IN ENGLAND

while local steam navigation had also nearly doubled its vessels and its tonnage.

Later on (1844–1847), Stephenson might easily have made himself "rich beyond the dreams of avarice," — or at least of the avarice of that day. All he had to do was to lend the use of his name to new and doubtful railway projects ; but he refused on the ground that he did not care " to make money without labor or honor." Meanwhile the whole country became involved in a speculative craze for building railways. Scores of millions of pounds were invested ; for a time Hudson, the so-called " Railway King,"

[1] Stephenson's *Rocket* and Watt's stationary steam engine (§ 563) are both preserved in the South Kensington Museum, London. The boiler of the *Rocket* was traversed by a number of tubes communicating with the smoke pipe. The heat passing through these tubes generated steam very rapidly. The steam, after it had done its work in the cylinders of the engine, escaped with great force through the smoke pipe and so created a very powerful draft. Without these two important improvements the locomotive would probably never have made an average speed of more than six or seven miles an hour.

ruled supreme, and Dukes and Duchesses, and members of Parliament generally, did homage to the man whose schemes promised to cover the whole island with a network of iron roads, every one of which was expected to be as profitable as a gold mine. These projects ended in a panic, second only to that of the South Sea Bubble (§ 536), and thousands found that steam could destroy fortunes even faster than it made them.

Toward the close of William's reign (1834–1835) a humble invention was perfected of which little was said at the time,

RECEPTION BY HUDSON, THE "RAILWAY KING," 1845
By special permission of the proprietors of *Punch*

but which contributed in no small degree to the comfort and convenience of every one. Up to this date two of the most important of all civilizing agents — fire and light — could be produced only with much difficulty and at considerable expense.

Various devices had been contrived to obtain them, but the common method continued to be the primitive one of striking a bit of flint and steel sharply together until a falling spark ignited a piece of tinder or half-burned rag, which, when it caught, had, with no little expense of breath, to be blown into a flame. The progress of chemistry suggested the use of phosphorus, and after years of experiments the friction match was invented by an English apothecary, who thus gave to the world what is now the commonest, and perhaps at the same time the most useful, domestic article in existence.

585. Summary. William IV's short reign of seven years was marked (1) by the great Reform Bill of 1832, which, to a great extent, took Parliament out of the hands of rich men and " rotten boroughs " and put it under the control of the people ; (2) by the abolition of slavery in the British colonies, and factory reform ; (3) by the introduction of the friction match, and by the building of the first successful line of steam railway.

VICTORIA — 1837–1901

586. The Queen's Descent ; Stability of the Government. As William IV left no child to inherit the crown, he was succeeded by his niece, the Princess Victoria, daughter of his brother Edward, Duke of Kent. (See Genealogical Table, p. 323.) In her lineage the Queen represented nearly the whole past sovereignty of the land over which she reigned.[1] The blood of both Cerdic, the first Saxon king, and of William the Conqueror,[2] flowed in her veins, — a fact which strikingly illustrates the vitality of the hereditary and conservative principles in the history of the English Crown.

This fact stands out in stronger relief if we call to mind what England had passed through in that intervening period of time.

In 1066 the Normans crossed the Channel, invaded the island, conquered its inhabitants, and seized the throne. In the course of the next five centuries two kings were deposed, one died a captive in the Tower of London,[3] and the Catholic religion, as an established Church, was supplanted in England by the Protestant faith of Luther.

Somewhat less than a hundred years after that event, Civil War broke out in 1642 ; the King was dethroned and beheaded, and in 1648 a republic established. The monarchy was restored in 1660, only to be followed by the Revolution of 1688, which changed the order of royal succession, drove one line of sovereigns from the land, and called in another from Germany to take its place. Meanwhile the House of Commons had gained enormously in political

[1] The only exceptions are the four Danish sovereigns and Harold II.
[2] See Genealogical Table of the Descent of English Sovereigns in the Appendix.
[3] Namely, Edward II (§ 233), Richard II (§ 257), and Henry VI (§ 305).

power, and Cabinet Government had been fully and finally established (§ 534). In 1832 the Reform Bill was passed, by which the power of the people was largely extended in Parliament; the two great political parties had been reorganized; yet after all these events, at the end of more than ten centuries from the date when Egbert first became Overlord of all the English, in 829 (§ 49), we find England governed by a descendant of her earliest rulers!

587. The Power of the House of Commons and of the Cabinet fully and finally recognized, 1837. Queen Victoria was but little over eighteen when called to the throne. At her accession a new order of things began. The Georges had insisted on dismissing their Cabinet ministers, or chief political advisers, when they pleased, without condescending to give Parliament any reason for the change. We have seen too that William IV tried to do the same thing, but had to acknowledge that he was beaten (§ 582). William's unsuccessful attempt was never repeated. The last vestige of "personal government," [1] that is, of the determination of the Crown to act contrary to the will of the majority of the nation, as expressed by the Cabinet, died with the late King.

With the coronation of Victoria the principle was established, once for all, that henceforth the Sovereign of the British Empire cannot remove the Prime Minister or his Cabinet (§ 582) without the consent of the House of Commons; nor, on the other hand, would the Sovereign now venture to retain a ministry which the Commons refused to support.[2] This limitation of the prerogatives of royalty emphasized the fact that the House of Commons had practically become the ruling power in England; and since that

---

[1] See the reign of Victoria in McCarthy's "History of Our Own Times."

[2] In order to guard herself against any political influence adverse to that of the Cabinet (§ 582), and hence of the majority of the House of Commons, the Queen was compelled to consent (1841) that the Mistress of the Robes, or head of her Majesty's household, should change at the demand of the incoming Prime Minister; and it was furthermore agreed that any ladies under her whose presence might be politically inconvenient to the Prime Minister, should retire "of their own accord." In other words, the incoming Prime Minister, with his Cabinet, has the right to remodel the Sovereign's household — or any other body of offices — in whatever degree he may think requisite, and the late Prince Albert could not even appoint his own private secretary, but much to his chagrin had to accept one appointed for him by the Prime Minister. See May's "Constitutional History of England" and Martin's "Life of the Prince Consort."

House is freely elected by the great body of the people, in order that it may declare and enforce their will, it follows that the government of the realm is essentially democratic. In fact, so far as reflecting public opinion is concerned, no republic in the world is more democratic.

Custom, too, has decided that the Sovereign must sanction every bill which Parliament approves and resolves to make law. Queen Anne was the last occupant of the English throne who ventured to veto a bill, by refusing to assent to it. That was in 1707, or more than two hundred years ago, and there is little probability that any wearer of the crown will ever attempt to do what she did. In fact, an able and authoritative English writer has not hesitated to declare that if the two Houses of Parliament should agree to send the reigning Sovereign his own death warrant, he would be obliged to sign it, or abdicate.[1]

An English sovereign's real position to-day is that of a person who has much indirect influence and but little direct power, — far less in fact than that of the President of the United States; for the latter can veto a bill, and can remove any or all of his cabinet officers at pleasure.

588. The House of Lords in the Past and To-day. A change equally great was taking place with respect to the Peers, or Lords.[2] As that body has played a most important part in the government of England and still retains considerable influence, it may be well to consider its history and present condition.

It will be remembered that the peerage originated with the Norman Conquest. William rewarded the barons, or chief men, who fought under him at Hastings[3] with grants of immense estates, which were given on two conditions: one of military

---

[1] See Bagehot's "The English Constitution."

[2] Peers (from the Latin *pares*, equals): The word first occurs in an act of Parliament, 1321, — "Pares et proceres regni Angliae spirituales et temporales." The name Peers, referring to the House of Lords, is here limited, as it has been ever since, to the higher clergy (now consisting of certain bishops) and to the hereditary nobility.

[3] The names of the great barons have been preserved in Domesday Book (see § 120), in the roll of Battle Abbey (though that was tampered with by the monks), and on the wall of the twelfth-century church at Dives, Normandy, where the Conqueror built his ships.

" YOUR MAJESTY "

Announcement to the Princess Victoria of her accession to the crown,
June 20, 1837

service at the call of the Sovereign (§ 150); the other their attendance, when required, at the Great or Royal Council (§ 144), an advisory and legislative body which contained the germ of what later came to be called Parliament.

It will thus be seen that the Conqueror made the possession of landed property directly dependent on the discharge of public duties. So that if, on the one hand, the Conquest carried out the principle

> " That they should take who have the power,
> And they should keep who can," [1]

on the other, it insisted on the higher principle that in return for such *taking* and *keeping* the victors should bind themselves by oath to help defend the kingdom, and to help govern it.

In later reigns the King summoned other influential men to attend Parliament. To distinguish them from the original barons by land tenure, they were called "barons by writ" (§ 263). Subsequently it became customary for the Sovereign to create barons by letters patent, as is the method at present (§ 263).

Edward I, 1295, is generally considered to have been the "Creator of the House of Lords" in the form in which it has since stood.[2] From his time the right to sit in the House of Lords was limited to those whom the King summoned, namely, the hereditary Peers (save in the case of a very limited number of life Peers), and to the upper clergy.

The original baronage continued predominant until the Wars of the Roses (§ 316) destroyed so many of the ancient nobility that, as Lord Beaconsfield says, "A Norman baron was almost as rare a being in England then as a wolf is now." With the coming in of the Tudors a new nobility was created (§ 352). Even this has become in great measure extinct. Perhaps not more than a fourth of those who now sit in the House of Lords can trace their titles further back than the Georges, who created great numbers of Peers in return for political services either rendered or expected.

Politically speaking, the nobility of England, unlike the old nobility of France, is strictly confined and strictly descends to but one

[1] Wordsworth's "Rob Roy's Grave."
[2] W. Stubbs's "English Constitutional History," II, 184, 203; also Feilden's "Short Constitutional History of England," pp. 121–122.

member of the family, — the eldest son receiving the preference. None of the children of the most powerful Duke or Lord has, during his father's life, any civil or legal rights or privileges above that of the poorest and most obscure native-born day laborer in Great Britain.[1]

The whole number of Peers is about six hundred.[2] They own a very large part of the land of England[3] and possess all the social and political influence naturally belonging to such a body. Yet notwithstanding the exclusive and aristocratic spirit of this long-established class, it has always been ready to receive recruits from the ranks of the people. For just as any boy in America feels himself a possible senator or President, so any one born or naturalized in England, like Pitt, Disraeli, Churchill, Nelson, Wellesley, Brougham, Tennyson, Macaulay, Lord Lyndhurst,[4] and many others, may win his way to a title, and also to a seat in the House of Lords, since brains and character go to the front in England just as surely as they do everywhere else.

In their legislative action the Lords are, with very rare exceptions, extremely conservative. It is a "galling fact"[5] that they have seldom granted their assent to any liberal measure except from pressure of the most unmistakable kind. They opposed the Habeas Corpus Act under Charles II, Catholic Emancipation in 1829, the Great Reform Bill of 1832, the Education Bill of 1834, the repeal of the Corn Laws in 1846, the admission of the Jews to Parliament in 1858, and they very reluctantly consented to the necessity of granting later extensions of the elective franchise.

[1] Even the younger children of the Sovereign are no exception to this rule. The only one born with a title is the eldest, who is Duke of Cornwall by birth, and is created Prince of Wales. The others are simply commoners. See E. A. Freeman's "Growth of the English Constitution."

[2] The full assembly of the House of Lords would consist of five hundred and sixty-two temporal Peers and twenty-six spiritual Peers (archbishops and bishops).

[3] So strictly is property entailed that there are proprietors of large estates who cannot so much as cut down a tree without permission of the heir. See Badeau's "English Aristocracy."

[4] J. S. Copley (Lord Lyndhurst), son of the famous artist, was born in Boston in 1772. He became Lord Chancellor. All of the eminent men named above rose from the ranks of the people and were made Peers of the realm, either for life or as a hereditary right; and in a number of cases, as the elder Pitt (Earl of Chatham), Wellesley (Duke of Wellington), Disraeli (Earl of Beaconsfield), Copley (Lord Lyndhurst), they received seats in the House of Lords.

[5] See A. L. Lowell's "The Government of England," I, 414, 422.

But, on the other hand, it was their influence which compelled John to sign Magna Carta in 1215 ; it was one of their number — Simon de Montfort, Earl of Leicester — who called the House of Commons into being in 1265 ; and it was the Lords as leaders who inaugurated the Revolution of 1688, and established constitutional sovereignty under William and Mary in the place of the despotic self-will of James II. Again, it was Lord Derby, the Prime Minister, and Mr. Disraeli, later known as Lord Beaconsfield, who, as leaders of the Tory, or Conservative, Party, felt obliged to carry the Reform Bill of 1867, by which the right to vote was greatly extended among the people (§ 600).

Seven hundred years ago the House of Lords was the only legislative and executive body in the country ; now, nearly all the most important business of Parliament is done in the House of Commons (consisting of some six hundred and seventy members), and the Lords cannot vote a penny of money for any purpose whatever unless the Commons first passes a bill to that effect (§ 281). Thus taxation, which is generally regarded as the most important of all measures, has passed from the Lords to the direct representatives of the people.

At one time certain impatient Radicals in the House of Commons denounced the Peers as " titled obstructionists." In fact, late in the nineteenth century (1894) a resolution to put an end to their obstructive power was carried in the Commons (when half the members were absent) by a majority of two. But the vote was not taken seriously, and the Lords were not called upon to go out of business. The upper House has continued, on occasion, to exercise its constitutional right of vetoing bills sent up to it by the House of Commons, though since 1860 it has rejected but one " Money Bill " (1909), and that only temporarily (§§ 629, 631).[1]

---

[1] As far back as 1671, the House of Commons resolved " that in all aids given to the King by the Commons, the rate or tax ought not to be altered by the Lords." In 1678 they emphatically repeated this resolution. In 1860 when the Lords rejected a " Money Bill " (for the repeal of paper duties) the Commons vigorously protested, declaring that they regarded the exercise of that power by the upper House with " particular jealousy." From that time the Commons were careful to include all the financial measures of the year in one bill, which the Lords "were forced to accept or reject as a whole." See H. S. Feilden's " Short Constitutional History of England," pp. 114-115, and A. L. Lowell's " The Government of England," I, 400-401.

Later, the Liberal Party demanded more strenuously than ever that the veto power of the Lords should be limited. In 1911 they succeeded in accomplishing that great work (§ 633).

The House of Lords always includes a number of members eminent for their judicial ability, some of whom have been created Peers for that reason. This section acts as the National Court of Appeal and sits to decide the highest questions of constitutional law. In this respect it corresponds to the Supreme Court of the United States.

589. The Queen's Marriage (1840). In her twenty-first year, Queen Victoria married her cousin, Prince Albert of Saxe-Coburg-Gotha, a duchy of Central Germany. The Prince was about her own age, of fine personal appearance, and had just graduated from one of the German universities. He was particularly interested in art and education, and throughout his life used his influence to raise the standard of both.

590. Sir Rowland Hill's Postal Reforms, 1839. The preceding year Sir Rowland Hill introduced a uniform system of cheap postage. The rate had been as high as a shilling for a single letter.[1] Such a charge was practically prohibitive, and, as a rule, no one wrote in those days if he could possibly avoid it. Sir Rowland reduced it to a penny (paid by stamp) to any part of the United Kingdom.[2] Since then the government has taken over all the telegraph lines, and cheap telegrams and the cheap transportation of parcels by mail (a kind of government express known as " parcels post ") have followed. They are all improvements of immense practical benefit.

591. Rise of the Chartists (1838–1848). The feeling attending the passage of the Reform Bill of 1832 (§ 582) had passed away;

---

[1] An illustration of the effects of such high charges for postage is related by Coleridge. He says that he met a poor woman at Keswick just as she was returning a letter from her son to the postman, saying she could not afford to pay for it. Coleridge gave the postman the shilling, and the woman then told the poet that the letter was really nothing more than a blank sheet which her son had agreed to send her every three months to let her know he was well; as she always declined to take this dummy letter, it of course cost her nothing. See G. B. Hill's " Life of Sir Rowland Hill," I, 239, note.

[2] The London papers made no end of fun of the first envelopes and the first postage stamps (1840). See the facsimile of the ridiculous " Mulready Envelope " in Hill's " Life of Sir Rowland Hill," I, 393.

but now a popular agitation began which produced even greater excitement. Although the act of 1832 had equalized parliamentary representation and had enlarged the elective franchise to a very considerable degree, yet the great body of workingmen were still shut out from the right to vote. A Radical Party called the "Chartists" now arose, which undertook to secure further measures of reform.

They embodied their measures in a document called the "People's Charter," which demanded :

1. Universal male suffrage.

2. That the voting at elections should be by ballot.

3. Annual Parliaments.

4. The payment of members of Parliament.

5. The abolition of the property qualification for parliamentary candidates.[1]

6. The division of the whole country into equal electoral districts.

The Chartists held public meetings, organized clubs, and published newspapers to disseminate their principles, but for many years made very little visible progress. The French revolution which dethroned King Louis Philippe (1848) imparted fresh impetus to the Chartist movement. The leader of that movement was Feargus O'Connor. He formed the plan of sending a monster petition to Parliament, containing, it was claimed, nearly five million signatures, praying for the passage of the People's Charter.

A procession of a million or more signers was to act as an escort to the document, which made a wagonload in itself. The Government became alarmed at the threatened demonstration, forbade it, on the ground that it was an attempt to coerce legislation, and organized a body of 250,000 special policemen to preserve order.

The Duke of Wellington took command of a large body of troops held in reserve to defend the city ; and the Bank of England, the

[1] Property qualification : In 1711 an act was passed requiring candidates for election to the House of Commons to have an income of not less than £300 derived from landed property. The object of this law was to secure members who would be comparatively free from the temptation of receiving bribes from the Crown, and also to keep the landed proprietors in power to the exclusion of rich merchants. This law was repealed in 1858.

THE HOUSES OF PARLIAMENT, WITH WESTMINSTER ABBEY

From the Thames

393

Houses of Parliament, the British Museum, and other public buildings were made ready to withstand a siege.

It was now the Chartists' turn to be frightened. When they assembled (1848) on Kennington Common in south London, they numbered less than thirty thousand, and the procession of a million which was to march across Westminster Bridge, to the Houses of Parliament, dwindled to half a dozen. When the huge petition was unrolled it was found to contain only about a third of the boasted number of names. Further examination showed that many of the signatures were spurious, having been put down in jest, or copied from gravestones and old London directories. With that discovery the whole movement collapsed, and the House of Commons rang with "inextinguishable laughter" over the national scare.

Still the demands of the Chartists had a solid foundation of good sense, which the blustering bravado of the leaders of the movement could not wholly destroy. Most, if not all, of the reforms asked for were needed. Since then, the steady, quiet influence of reason and of time has compelled Parliament to grant the greater part of them.[1]

The printed or written ballot has been substituted for the old method of electing candidates by a show of hands or by shouting yes or no, — a method by which it was easy to make blunders, and equally easy to commit frauds. Every voter must now have his name and address registered in a printed list. Every voter, too, casts a secret ballot and so safeguards his political independence (§ 609). The property qualification has been abolished (§ 591, note 1), so that the day laborer may now run for Parliament. He is sure, too, of being well paid, for Parliament voted (1911) to give £400 a year to every member of the House of Commons. The right of "manhood suffrage" has been greatly extended, and before the twentieth century has advanced much farther every man in England will probably have a voice in the elections.

---

[1] Sir Thomas Erskine May, in his "Constitutional History of England," says: "Not a measure has been forced upon Parliament which the calm judgment of a later time has not since approved; not an agitation has failed which posterity has not condemned."

592. The Corn Laws (1841). At the accession of the Queen protective duties or taxes existed in Great Britain on all imported breadstuffs and on many manufactured articles. Sir Robert Peel, the Conservative Prime Minister (1841), favored a reduction in the last class of duties, but believed it necessary to maintain the former in order to keep up the price of grain and thus encourage the English farmers. The result of this policy was great distress among the poorly paid, half-fed workingmen, who could not afford to buy dear bread. A number of philanthropists led by Richard Cobden and John Bright organized an Anti-Corn Law League[1] to obtain the repeal of the grain duties.

At the same time, Ebenezer Elliott, the " Corn-Law Rhymer," gave voice to the sufferings of the poor in rude but vigorous verse, which appealed to the excited feelings of thousands in such words as these:

> " England ! what for mine and me,
>   What hath bread tax done for thee ?
>   .   .   .   .   .   .
>   Cursed thy harvest, cursed thy land,
>   Hunger-stung thy skill'd right hand."

When, however, session after session of Parliament passed and nothing was done for the relief of the perishing multitudes, many began to despair, and great numbers joined in singing Elliott's new national anthem:

> " When wilt Thou save the people ?
>   O God of mercy ! when ?
>   Not kings and lords, but nations !
>   Not thrones and crowns, but men !
>   Flowers of thy heart, O God, are they !
>   Let them not pass, like weeds, away !
>   Their heritage a sunless day !
>   God save the people ! "

Still the Government was not convinced; the Corn Laws were enforced, the price of bread showed no signs of falling, and the situation grew daily more desperate and more threatening.

---

[1] Corn is the name given in England to wheat or other grain used for food. Indian corn or maize cannot be grown in that climate, and is seldom eaten there.

593. The Irish Famine, 1845–1846. At last the Irish famine opened the Prime Minister's eyes (§ 592). When in Elizabeth's reign Sir Walter Raleigh brought over the cheap but precarious potato from America and planted it in Ireland, his motive was one of pure good will. He could not foresee that it would in time become in that country an almost universal food, that through its very abundance the population would rapidly increase, and that then, by the sudden failure of the crop, terrible destitution would ensue. Such was the case in the summer of 1845. It is said by eyewitnesses that in a single night the entire potato crop was smitten with disease, and the healthy plants were transformed into a mass of putrefying vegetation. Thus at one fell stroke the food of nearly a whole nation was cut off.[1]

In the years that followed, the famine became appalling. The starving peasants left their miserable huts and streamed into the towns for relief, only to die of hunger in the streets.

Parliament responded nobly to the piteous calls for help, and voted in all no less than £10,000,000 to relieve the distress.[2] Subscriptions were also taken up in London and the chief towns, by which large sums were obtained, and America contributed shiploads of provisions and a good deal of money ; but the misery was so great that even these measures failed to accomplish what was hoped. When the famine was over, it was found that Ireland had lost about two million (or one fourth) of her population.[3] This was the combined effect of starvation, of the various diseases that followed in its path, and of emigration.[4]

594. Repeal of the Corn Laws, 1846–1849 ; Free Trade established, 1869. In the face of such appalling facts, and of the bad harvests and distress in England, Sir Robert Peel (§ 592) could hold out no longer, and by a gradual process, extending from 1846 to 1849, the obnoxious Corn Laws were repealed, with the exception of a trifling duty, which was finally removed in 1869.

[1] O'Connor's "The Parnell Movement."

[2] Molesworth's "History of England from 1830."

[3] The actual number of deaths from starvation, or fever caused by insufficient food, was estimated at from two hundred thousand to three hundred thousand. See the Encyclopædia Britannica under "Ireland."

[4] McCarthy's "History of Our Own Times," Vol. I.

The beginning once made, free trade in nearly everything, except wine, spirits, and tobacco, followed. They were, and still are, subject to a heavy duty, perhaps because the government believes, as Napoleon did, that the vices have broad backs and can comfortably carry the heaviest taxes. A few years later (1849) the old Navigation Laws (§ 459) were totally repealed. This completed the English free-trade measures. But, by a singular contrast, while nearly all goods and products now enter England free, yet Australia, Canada, New Zealand, and the Union of South Africa — in a word, all the great self-governing English colonies — continue to impose duties on imports from the mother country (§ 625).

595. The World's Fair (1851); Repeal of the Window and the Newspaper Tax ; the Atlantic Cable, 1866. The great industrial exhibition known as the " World's Fair " was opened in Hyde Park, London (1851). The original plan of it was conceived by Prince Albert. It proved to be not only a complete success in itself, but it led to many similar fairs on the part of different nations. For the first time in history the products and inventions of all the countries of the globe were brought together under one roof, in a gigantic structure of glass and iron called the " Crystal Palace," which is still in use for exhibition purposes at Sydenham, a suburb of London.

The same year (1851) the barbarous tax on light and air, known as the " Window Tax," [1] was repealed and the House Tax (which is still in force) was substituted for it. From that date the Englishman, whether in London or out, might enjoy his sunshine, when he could get it, without having to pay for every beam, — a luxury which only the rich could afford.

A little later (1855) a stamp tax on newspapers, which had been devised in Queen Anne's time in the avowed hope of crushing them out, was repealed. The result was that henceforth cheap papers could be published, and the workingman, as he sat by his fireside, could inform himself of what the world was doing and thinking, — two things of which he had before known almost nothing, and cared, perhaps, even less.

[1] This tax, which took the place of the ancient Hearth Tax (1663-1689), was first imposed in 1695.

To get this news of the world's life more speedily, England had established the first line of Atlantic steamers (§ 565); next, the first Atlantic cable, connecting England with America, was laid (1858). It soon gave out, but was permanently relaid not long afterwards, in 1866. Since then a large part of the globe has been joined in like manner,[1] and the great cities of every civilized land are practically one in their knowledge of all important events. So many improvements have also been made in the use of electricity, not only for the transmission of intelligence, but as an illuminator, and more recently still as a motive power, that it now seems probable that "the age of steam" will be superseded by the higher "age of electricity."

596. The Opium War (1839); the War in the Crimea (1854). For nearly twenty years after Victoria's accession no wars occurred in her reign worthy of mention, with the exception of that with China (1839). At that time the Chinese Emperor, either from a desire to put a stop to the consumption of opium in his dominions, or because he wished to encourage the home production of the drug, prohibited its importation. As the English in India were largely engaged in the production of opium for the Chinese market, — the people of that country smoking it instead of tobacco, — the British government insisted that the Emperor should not interfere with so lucrative a trade. War ensued.

The Chinese, being unable to contend against English gunboats, were soon forced to withdraw their prohibition of the foreign opium traffic. The English government, with the planters of India, reaped a golden reward of many millions for their deliberate violation of the rights of a heathen and half-civilized people. The war opened five important ports to British trade, and subsequent wars opened a number more on the rivers in the interior. This action, with the later aggressions of other European powers, roused an intensely bitter feeling among large numbers of the Chinese. Their hatred of foreigners finally led to a desperate but unsuccessful attempt (1900) to drive all Europeans and Americans, including missionaries, out of the country.

[1] There are now over 250,000 miles of submarine electric cables in operation in the world.

Eventually, the pressure of the great powers of Europe and the diplomatic influence of the United States induced China to grant the "Open Door" to the demands of foreign trade. Later, England and China made an agreement (1911) which bids fair to stop the exportation of opium to that country.

Next, Turkey declared war against Russia (1853). The latter Power had insisted on protecting all Christians in the Turkish dominions against the oppression of the Sultan. England and France considered the Czar's championship of the Christians as a mere pretext for occupying Turkish territory. To prevent this aggression they formed an alliance with the Sultan, which resulted in the Russo-Turkish war, and ended in the taking of Sebastopol by the allied forces. Russia was obliged to retract her demands, and peace was declared (1856).

597. The Great Rebellion in India, 1857. The following year, 1857, was memorable for the outbreak of rebellion in India. The real cause of the revolt was probably a long-smothered feeling of resentment on the part of the Sepoy, or native, troops against English rule, — a feeling that dates back to the extortion and misgovernment of Warren Hastings (§ 555). The immediate cause of the uprising was the introduction of an improved rifle using a greased cartridge, which had to be bitten off before being rammed down.

To the Hindu the fat of cattle or swine is an abomination, and his religion forbids his tasting it. An attempt on the part of the British Government to enforce the use of the new cartridge brought on a general mutiny among three hundred thousand Sepoys. During the revolt the native troops perpetrated the most horrible atrocities on the English women and children who fell into their hands. When the insurrection was finally quelled under Havelock and Campbell, the English soldiers retaliated by binding numbers of prisoners to the mouths of cannon and blowing them to shreds. At the close of the rebellion, the government of India was wholly transferred to the Crown, and later the Queen received the title of " Empress of India " (1876).

598. Death of Prince Albert; the American Civil War, 1861. Not long after the Sepoy rebellion was quelled, Prince Albert (§ 589) died suddenly (1861). In him the nation lost an earnest promoter of social, educational, and industrial reforms, and the United States a true and judicious friend, who, at a most critical period in the Civil War, used his influence to maintain peace between the two countries.

After his death the Queen held no court for many years, and so complete was her seclusion that Sir Charles Dilke, a well-known Radical, suggested in Parliament (1868) that her Majesty be invited to abdicate or choose a regent. The suggestion was indignantly rejected; but it revealed the feeling, which quite generally existed, that "the real Queen died with her husband," and that only her shadow remained.

In the spring of the year 1861, in which Prince Albert died, the American Civil War broke out between the Northern and Southern States. Lord Palmerston, the Liberal Prime Minister, preferred to be considered the minister of the nation rather than the head of a political party. At the beginning of the war he was in favor of the North. As the conflict threatened to be bitter the Queen issued a proclamation declaring her " determination to maintain a strict and impartial neutrality in the contest between the said contending parties." The rights of belligerents — in other words, all the rights of war according to the law of nations — were granted to the South equally with the North; and her Majesty's subjects were warned against aiding either side in the conflict.

The progress of the war caused terrible distress in Lancashire, owing to the cutting off of supplies of cotton for the mills through the blockade of the ports of the Confederate States. The starving weavers, however, gave their moral support to the North, and continued steadfast to the cause of the Union even in the sorest period of their suffering. The great majority of the manufacturers and business classes generally, and the nobility, with a few exceptions, sympathized with the efforts of the South to establish an independent Confederacy. Most of the distinguished political and social leaders, in Parliament and out, with nearly all the influential journals, were on the same side, and were openly hostile to the Union.[1]

---

[1] Lord John Russell (Foreign Secretary), Lord Brougham, Sir John Bowring, Carlyle, Ruskin, and the London *Times* and *Punch* espoused the cause of the South more or less openly; while others, like Mr. Gladstone, declared their full belief in

Late in the autumn (1861) Captain Wilkes, of the United States Navy, boarded the British mail steamer *Trent*, and seized two Confederate commissioners (Mason and Slidell) who were on their way to England. When intelligence of the act was conveyed to President Lincoln, he expressed his unqualified disapproval of it, saying: "This is the very thing the British captains used to do. They claimed the right of searching American ships, and taking men out of them. That was the cause of the War of 1812. Now, we cannot abandon our own principles; we shall have to give up these men, and apologize for what we have done."

The British Government made a formal demand that the commissioners should be given up. Through the influence of Prince Albert, and with the approval of the Queen, this demand was couched in most conciliatory language. Slidell and Mason were handed over to Great Britain, and an apology was made by Secretary Seward.

During the progress of the Civil War a number of fast-sailing vessels were fitted out in England, and employed in running the blockade of the Southern ports, to supply them with arms, ammunition, and manufactured goods of various kinds. Later, several gunboats were built in British shipyards by agents of the Confederate government, for the purpose of attacking the commerce of the United States. The most famous of these vessels was the *Alabama*, built expressly for the Confederate service by the Lairds, of Birkenhead, armed with British cannon, and manned chiefly by British sailors.

Charles Francis Adams, the American Minister at London, notified Lord Palmerston, the Prime Minister, of her true character. But Palmerston permitted the *Alabama* to leave port (1862), satisfied with the pretext that she was going on a trial trip.[1] She set

the ultimate success of the Confederacy. On the other hand, Prince Albert, the Duke of Argyll, John Bright, John Stuart Mill, Professor Newman, Lord Palmerston, at least for a time, and the London *Daily News* defended the cause of the North. After the death of President Lincoln, *Punch* manfully acknowledged (see issue of May 6, 1865) that it had been altogether wrong in its estimate of him and his measures; and Mr. Gladstone, in an essay on "Kin beyond Sea" in his "Gleanings of Past Years," paid a noble tribute to the course pursued by America since the close of the war.

[1] The Queen's advocate gave his opinion that the *Alabama* should be detained, but it reached the Foreign Secretary (Lord Russell) just after she had put out to sea.

sail on her career of destruction, and soon drove nearly every American merchant vessel from the seas. Two years later (1864) she was defeated and sunk by the United States gunboat *Kearsarge*. After the war the Government of the United States demanded damages from Great Britain for losses caused by the *Alabama* and other English-built privateers.

A treaty was agreed to by the two nations; and by its provisions an international court was held at Geneva, Switzerland (1872), to deal with the demands made by the United States on Great Britain. The court awarded $15,500,000 in gold as compensation to the United States, which was duly paid. One very important result of this decision was that it established a precedent for settling by arbitration on equitable and amicable terms whatever questions might arise in future between the two nations.[1]

599. Municipal Reform (1835); Woman Suffrage; the Jews. Excellent as was the Reform Bill of 1832 (§ 582), it did not go far enough. There was also great need of municipal reform, since in many cities the taxpayers had no voice in the management of local affairs, and the city officers sometimes spent the income of large charitable funds in feasting and merrymaking while the poor got little or nothing.

A law was passed (1835) giving taxpayers in cities (except London) control of municipal elections. By a subsequent amendment, the ballot in such cases was extended to women,[2] and for the first time perhaps in modern history partial woman suffrage was formally granted by supreme legislative act. A number of years later the political restrictions imposed on the Jews were removed.

There was a considerable number of Jews in London and in other large cities who were men of wealth and influence. They

---

[1] This treaty imposed duties on neutral governments of a far more stringent sort than Great Britain had hitherto been willing to concede. It resulted, furthermore, in the passage of an act of Parliament, punishing with severe penalties such illegal shipbuilding as that of the *Alabama*. See Sheldon Amos's "Fifty Years of the English Constitution, 1830-1880."

[2] Woman suffrage in municipal elections was granted to single women and widows (householders) in 1869. In 1870 an act was passed enabling them to vote at school-board elections, and also to become members of such boards. By act of 1894 women were made eligible to sit and vote in district and parish councils (or local-government elections).

were entitled to vote and hold municipal office, but they were
debarred from election to Parliament by a law which required
them to make oath "on the faith of a Christian." The law was
now so modified (1858) that a very prominent Jew, Baron Roths-
child, took his seat in Parliament. Finally the Oaths Act (1888)
abolished all religious tests in Parliament.

**600. Second and Third Reform Acts, 1867, 1884 ; County and
Parish Councils (1884, 1894).** In 1867 the pressure of public
opinion moved Mr. Disraeli (later Lord Beaconsfield), a member of Lord Derby's Conservative Cabinet (§ 479), to bring in a
second Reform Bill (§ 582), which became law. This bill provided
"household suffrage." It gave the right to vote to all male householders in the English parliamentary boroughs (that is, towns having the right to elect one or more members to Parliament), who
paid a tax for the support of the poor, and to all lodgers paying
a rental of £10 yearly; it also increased the number of voters
among small property holders in counties.[1]

There still remained, however, a large class in the country districts for whom nothing had been done. The men employed by
the farmers to till the soil were wretchedly poor and deplorably
ignorant. Joseph Arch, a Warwickshire farm laborer, who had been
educated by hunger and toil, succeeded in establishing a national
union among men of his class (1872). In 1884 Mr. Gladstone, the
Liberal Prime Minister, secured the ballot for agricultural laborers
by the passage of the third Reform Act, which gave all residents of
counties throughout the United Kingdom the right to vote on the
same liberal conditions as the residents of towns.

It is estimated that this last law added about two and a half
millions of voters ; this gave one voter to every six persons of the
total population, whereas, before the passing of the first Reform
Bill in 1832, there was not over one in fifty. When the new or
so-called "People's Parliament" convened (1886), Joseph Arch
and several other successful candidates took their seats in the
House of Commons as representatives of classes of the population
who, up to that date, had no voice in the legislation of the country.

[1] See Summary of Constitutional History in the Appendix, p. xxvi, § 31. Lord
Derby held the office, but Mr. Disraeli was really Prime Minister.

The next step may bring universal "manhood suffrage." The County Council and Parish Council acts (1888, 1894) greatly extended the power of the people in all matters of local government, so that now every village in England controls its own affairs.

601. Compulsory Church Rates abolished; Disestablishment in Ireland (1869). While these reforms were taking place with respect to elections, others of great importance were also being effected. From its origin in 1549 the established Protestant Church of England (§ 362) had compelled persons of all religious beliefs to pay rates or taxes for the maintenance of the Established Church in the parish where they resided. Methodists, Baptists, and other Dissenters (§§ 472, 496, 507) objected to this law as unjust, since, in addition to the expense of supporting their own form of worship, they were obliged to contribute toward maintaining one with which they had no sympathy. So great had the opposition become to paying these "church rates," that in over fifteen hundred parishes in England (1859) the authorities could not collect them. After long debate Mr. Gladstone carried through a bill (1868) which abolished this mode of taxation and made the payment of these rates purely voluntary.[1]

A similar act of justice was soon after granted to Ireland (1869).[2] At the time of the union of the two countries in 1800 (§ 562), the maintenance of the Protestant Episcopal Church continued to remain obligatory upon the Irish people, although only a small part of them were of that faith. Mr. Gladstone, now Liberal Prime Minister, succeeded in getting Parliament to enact a law which disestablished this branch of the National Church and left all religious denominations in Ireland to the voluntary support of those who belonged to them. Henceforth the English Protestant residing in that country could no longer claim the privilege of worshiping God at the expense of his Roman Catholic neighbor.

602. The Elementary Education Act, 1870. In 1870 Mr. Forster, a member of Mr. Gladstone's Liberal Cabinet (§§ 534, 601),

---

[1] Church rates were levied on all occupiers of land or houses within the parish. The Church of England is now supported by a tax on landowners, by its endowments, and by voluntary gifts.

[2] The Disestablishment Bill was passed in 1869 and took effect in 1871.

succeeded in passing a measure of the highest importance, entitled The Elementary Education Act. This act did not undertake to establish a new system of instruction, but to aid and improve that which was then in use. In the course of time, however, it effected such changes for the better in the common schools that it practically re-created most of them.

It will be remembered that before the Reformation the Catholic monasteries took the leading part in educating the children of the country (§§ 45, 60). The destruction of the monasteries by Henry VIII (§ 352) put a stop to their work; but after Henry's death, his son, Edward VI, established many Protestant schools (§§ 364, 365), while others were founded by men who had grown suddenly rich through getting possession of the monastic lands. These new schools did good work, and are still doing it; but they seldom reached the children of the poor. Later on, many wealthy persons founded Charity Schools to help the class who could not afford to pay anything for their tuition. The pupils who lived in these institutions (of which a number still exist) were generally obliged to wear a dress which, by its peculiarity of cut and color, always reminded them that they were "objects of public or private benevolence." Furthermore, while the boys in these institutions were often encouraged to go on and enter Grammar Schools, the girls were informed that a very little learning would be all that they would ever need in the humble station in life to which Providence had seen fit to call them.

Meanwhile, the Church of England, and other religious denominations, both Catholic and Protestant, established many common schools (1781–1811) for the benefit of the poor. The cost of carrying them on was usually met by private contributions. All of these schools gave some form of denominational religious instruction. As the population increased many more schools were required. At length Parliament began (1833) to grant money to help the different religious societies in maintaining their systems of instruction. When able, the parents of the children were also called on to pay a small sum weekly. In 1870 the Liberal Government took hold of the education question with great vigor. It provided that in all cases where the existing Church of England or other denominational schools were not able to accommodate the children of a given district, School Boards should be established to open new schools, which, if necessary, should be maintained entirely at the public expense. In these " Board Schools," as they were called, no denominational religious instruction whatever could be given.

This very important act "placed a school within the reach of every child," but, except in very poor districts, these schools were not made free schools ; in fact, free schools, in the American sense, cannot be said to exist in Great Britain. Later on (1880) compulsory attendance was required, and subsequent acts of Parliament (1902, 1904) transferred the management of these schools from the School Boards to the Town and County Councils.[1] Again, these new measures make it practicable for a boy or girl, who has done well in the primary course, to secure assistance which will open opportunities for obtaining a higher education. Thus, as a recent writer declares, " There is now a path leading from the workman's home even to the University." [2]

Meanwhile (1871) the universities and colleges, with most of the offices and professorships connected with them, were thrown open to all persons without regard to religious belief ; whereas, formerly, no one could graduate from Oxford or Cambridge without subscribing to the doctrines of the Church of England.

603. The First Irish Land Act, 1870. In 1870, the same year that the Government undertook to provide for the education of the masses (§ 602), Mr. Gladstone, who was still Prime Minister and head of the Liberal Party (§ 601), brought in a bill for the relief of small Irish farmers, those who had to support themselves and their families from the little they could get from a few hired acres. Since the union (§ 562) much of the general policy of England toward Ireland had been described as " a quick alternation of kicks and

---

[1] But many men and women who belong to the Dissenting Denominations complain that the Educational Acts of 1870–1904 compel them to pay taxes for the support of a great number of public elementary schools which are under the control of the English Church, and furthermore, that teachers who are members of Dissenting societies, such as the Presbyterians, Methodists, Baptists, etc., can seldom, if ever, get appointments in the class of schools mentioned. Quite a number of these Dissenters who call themselves " Passive Resisters " have refused to pay the school tax and have had their property seized or have been sent to jail year after year.

[2] A. L. Lowell's " The Government of England," II, 323.

kindness." Mr. Gladstone did not hesitate to say that he believed
the misery of the island sprang mainly from its misgovernment.
He thought that the small farmer needed immediate help and that
it was the duty of the Liberal Party to grant it.

The circumstances under which land was held in Ireland were
peculiar. A very large part of it was owned by Englishmen whose
ancestors obtained it through the wholesale confiscations of James I,
Cromwell, and later rulers (§§ 423, 453). Very few of these English landlords cared to reside in the country or to do anything for
its improvement. Their agents or overseers generally forced the
farm tenants to pay the largest amount of rent that could be wrung
from them, and they could dispossess a tenant of his land whenever
they saw fit, without giving a reason for the act. If, by his labor,
the tenant made the land more fertile, he seldom reaped any additional profit from his industry, for the rent was usually increased,
and swallowed up all that he raised. Such a system of extortion
was destructive to those who tilled the soil, and if it brought in
more money for the landlord, it produced nothing but misery and
discontent for his tenant.

Mr. Gladstone's new law endeavored to remedy these evils by
the following provisions :

1. In case a landlord ejected a rent-paying tenant, he was to
pay him damages, and allow him a fair sum for whatever improvements he had made.

2. It secured a ready means of arbitration between landlord
and tenant, and if a tenant failed to pay an exorbitant rate he could
not be hastily or unjustly driven from his farm.

3. It made it possible for the tenant to borrow a certain sum
from the government for the purpose of purchasing the land in
case the owner was willing to sell.

604. Distress in Ireland ; the Land League (1879). The friends
of the new Irish land law hoped that it would be found satisfactory ;
but the potato crop again failed in Ireland (1876-1879), and the
country seemed threatened with another great famine (§ 593).
Thousands who could not get the means to pay even a moderate
rent were now forced to leave their cabins and seek shelter in the
bogs, with the prospect of dying there of starvation.

The wretched condition of the people led a number of influential Irishmen to form a Land League (1879). This organization sought to abolish the entire landlord system in Ireland and to secure legislation which should eventually give the Irish peasantry possession of the soil they cultivated.

In time the League grew to have a membership of several hundred thousand persons, extending over the greater part of Ireland. Finding it difficult to get parliamentary help for their grievances, the League resolved to try a different kind of tactics. Its members refused to work for, buy from, sell to, or have any intercourse with landlords, or their agents, who extorted exorbitant rent, ejected tenants unable to pay, or took possession of land from which tenants had been unjustly driven. This process of social excommunication was first tried on an English agent, or overseer, named Boycott, and soon became famous under the name of " boycotting."

As the struggle went on, many of the suffering poor became desperate. Farm buildings belonging to landlords and their agents were burned, many of their cattle were horribly mutilated, and a number of the agents shot. At the same time the cry rose of " No Rent, Death to the Landlords ! " Hundreds of Irish tenants now refused to pay anything for the use of the land they cultivated, and attacked those who did.

Eventually the lawlessness of the country compelled the Government to take severe measures. It suppressed the Land League (1881), which was believed to be responsible for the refusal to pay rent, and for the accompanying outrages ; but it could not extinguish the feeling which gave rise to that organization, and the angry discontent soon burst forth more violently than ever.

605. The Second Irish Land Act (1881); Fenian and Communist Outrages. Mr. Gladstone (§ 603) now succeeded in carrying through a second Irish Land Law (1881) (§ 603), which he hoped might be more effective in relieving the Irish peasants than the first had been. This measure was familiarly known as the " Three F's,"— meaning Fair rent, Fixity of tenure, and Free sale. By the provisions of this act the tenant could appeal to a board of land commissioners appointed to fix the rate of his rent in case the demands made by the landlord seemed to him excessive.

Next, he could continue to hold his farm, provided he paid the rate determined on, for a period of fifteen years, during which time the rent could not be raised nor the tenant evicted except for violation of agreement or persistent neglect or waste of the land. Finally, he could sell his tenancy whenever he saw fit to the highest bidder. This law was later amended and extended in the interest of the peasant farmer (1887).

The year following the passage of this second Land Act, Lord Frederick Cavendish, chief secretary of Ireland, and Mr. Burke, a prominent government official, were murdered in Phœnix Park, Dublin (1882). Later, members of the Fenian society, and of other secret organizations sympathizing with the small Irish farmers, perpetrated dynamite outrages in London and other parts of England for the purpose of intimidating the Government. These acts were denounced with horror by the leaders of the Irish National Party. They declared that " the cause of Ireland was not to be served by the knife of the assassin or by the infernal machine."

Notwithstanding the vindictive feeling caused by these rash deeds, despite also the passage of the Coercion Bill (1887), the majority of the more intelligent and thoughtful of the Irish people had faith in the progress of events. They believed that the time would come when their country would obtain the enjoyment of all the political rights which England so fully possesses. It will be seen (§ 620) that about ten years later they did gain a very important extension of the right of local self-government.[1]

606. The Darwinian Theory of Evolution, 1859 ; the Persistence of Force. In the progress of science the Victorian period surpassed all previous records in England except that made by Sir Isaac Newton's discovery of the law of gravitation (§ 481). That great thinker demonstrated in 1684 that all forms of matter, great or small, near or distant, are governed by one universal force of attraction. In like manner the researches and investigations of the nineteenth century led to the conviction that all forms of life upon the earth obey a universal law of development. By this law the higher are evolved from the lower through a succession of gradual but progressive changes.

[1] See Summary of Constitutional History in the Appendix, p. xxvii, § 33.

This conception originated long before the beginning of the Victorian era, but it lacked the support of carefully examined facts, and most sensible men regarded it as nothing more than a plausible conjecture. The thinker who did more than any other to supply the facts, and to put the theory, so far as it relates to natural history, on a solid and lasting foundation, was the distinguished English naturalist, Charles Darwin.[1]

On his return (1837) from a voyage of scientific discovery round the world, Darwin began to examine and classify the facts which he had collected, and continued to collect, relating to certain forms of animal life. After twenty-two years of uninterrupted labor he published a work in 1859, entitled "The Origin of Species," in which he aimed to show that life generally owes it course of development to the struggle for existence and to "the survival of the fittest."

Darwin's work may truthfully be said to have wrought a revolution in the study of nature as great as that accomplished by Newton in the seventeenth century. Though it excited heated and prolonged discussion, the Darwinian theory gradually made its way, and is now generally received, though sometimes in a modified form, by practically every eminent man of science throughout the world.

After Mr. Darwin began his researches, but before he completed them, Sir William Grove, an eminent electrician, commenced a series of experiments which resulted in his publishing his remarkable book[2] on the connection of the physical forces of nature. He showed that heat, light, and electricity are mutually convertible; that they must be regarded as modes of motion; and, finally, that all force is persistent and indestructible, thus proving, as Professor Tyndall says, that "to nature, nothing can be added; from nature, nothing can be taken away." Together, the work of Darwin and Grove, with kindred discoveries, resulted in the theory of evolution, or development. Later on, Herbert Spencer and other students of

[1] Alfred Russel Wallace, also noted as a naturalist, worked out the theory of evolution by "natural selection" about the same time, though not so fully, with respect to details, as Darwin; as each of these investigators arrived at his conclusions independently of the other, the theory was thus doubly confirmed.

[2] "The Correlation of the Physical Forces" (1846).

evolution endeavored to make it the basis of a system of philosophy embracing the whole field of nature and life.

The Victorian period was also noted for many other great names in science, philosophy, literature, and art. The number was so great that it would manifestly be impracticable to devote any adequate space to them here.[1]

607. The Queen's Two Jubilees ; Review of Sixty Years of English History (1837–1897). Queen Victoria celebrated the fiftieth year of her reign (1887); ten years later (1897) the nation spontaneously rose to do honor to her " Diamond Jubilee." The splendid military pageant which marked that event in London was far more than a brilliant show, for it demonstrated the enthusiastic loyalty of the English people and of the English colonies.

The real meaning of the occasion is best sought in a review of the record of those threescore years. They were, in large degree, a period of progress ; perhaps, in fact, no similar period in European history has been so " crowded with benefit to humanity."

When Victoria came to the throne in her nineteenth year (1837) she found the kingdom seething with discontent, and the province of Canada approaching rebellion. In business circles reckless speculation and the bursting of " Bubble Companies " had been followed by " tight money " and " hard times." Among the poor matters were far worse. Wages were low, work was scarce, bread was dear. In the cities half-fed multitudes lived in cellars ; in the country the same class occupied wretched cottages hardly better than cellars.[2]

The " New Poor Law " (§ 403),[3] which went into effect in 1834, or shortly before the Queen's accession, eventually accomplished

[1] It will be sufficient to mention the novelists, Dickens, Thackeray, Brontë, and " George Eliot " ; the historians, Stubbs, Hallam, Arnold, Grote, Macaulay. Alison, Buckle, Froude, Freeman, and Gardiner ; the essayists, Carlyle, Landor, and De Quincey ; the poets, Browning and Tennyson ; the philosophical writers, Hamilton, Mill, and Spencer ; with Lyell, Faraday, Carpenter, Tyndall, Huxley, Darwin, Wallace, and Lord Kelvin in science ; John Ruskin, the eminent art critic ; and, in addition, the chief artists of the period, Millais, Rossetti, Burne-Jones, Watts, and Hunt.

[2] See Cobbett's " Rural Rides, 1821–1832."

[3] The " New Poor Law " : Between 1691 and 1834 the administration of relief for the poor was in the hands of justices of the peace, who gave aid indiscriminately to those who begged for it. In 1795 wages for ordinary laborers were so low that the justices resolved to grant an allowance to every poor family in accordance with

much good; but for a time it forced many laborers into the work-house. This result aggravated the suffering and discontent, and the predominant feeling of the day may be seen reflected in the pages of Dickens, Carlyle, and Kingsley.[1]

Notwithstanding the passage of the Reform Bill of 1832 (§ 582), political power was still held chiefly by men of property who distrusted the masses of the people. They feared that the widespread distress would culminate in riots, if not in open insurrection.

The Chartist movement (§ 591), which speedily began (1838), seemed to justify their apprehension. But the dreaded revolt never came; the evils of the times were gradually alleviated and, in some cases, cured. Confidence slowly took the place of distrust and fear. When, in June (1897), the Queen's "Diamond Jubilee" procession moved from Buckingham Palace to St. Paul's, and thence through some of the poorest quarters of London, none of the dense mass that filled the streets cheered more lustily than those who must always earn their daily bread by their daily toil.

The explanation of that change was to be found in the progress of good government, the extension of popular rights, and the advance of material improvements. Let us consider these changes in their natural order.

608. Further Extension of the Right to Vote, 1832–1894.[2] We have already described the far-reaching effects of the Reform Bill (§ 582) of 1832, which, on the one hand, put an end to many "rotten boroughs," and on the other, granted representation in

---

its numbers. The result of this mistaken kindness was speedily seen; employers cut down wages to the starvation point, knowing that the magistrates would give help out of the poor fund. The consequence was that the tax rate for relief of the poor rose to a degree that became unbearable.

The "New Law" of 1834 effected a sweeping reform: (1) it forbade outdoor relief to the able-bodied poor, and thus, in the end, compelled the employer to give better wages (but outdoor relief is now frequently granted); (2) it restricted aid to that given in workhouses, where the recipient, if in good health, was obliged to labor in return for what he received; (3) it greatly reduced the expense of supporting the poor by uniting parishes in workhouse "unions"; (4) it modified the old rigid Law of Settlement, thereby making it possible for those seeking employment to take their labor to the best market.

[1] See Dickens's "Oliver Twist" (1838), Carlyle's "Chartism" (1839), and Kingsley's "Yeast" and "Alton Locke" (1849).

[2] See Summary of Constitutional History in the Appendix, p. xxvi, § 31.

Parliament to a number of large towns hitherto without a voice in that body. Three years later (1835) came the Municipal Reform Act. It placed the government of towns, with the exception of London,[1] in the hands of the taxpayers who lived in them.

This radical measure put a stop to the arbitrary and corrupt management which had existed when the town officers elected themselves and held their positions for life (§ 599). Furthermore, it prevented parliamentary candidates from buying up the entire municipal vote, — a thing which frequently happened so long as the towns were under the absolute control of a few individuals.

A generation passed before the next important step was taken. Then, as we have seen, the enactment of the Second Reform Bill (1867) (§ 600) doubled the number of voters in England. The next year an act reduced the property qualification for the right to vote in Scotland and Ireland; thus the ballot was largely increased throughout the United Kingdom.

The Third Reform Act (1884) (§ 600) granted the right to vote for members of Parliament to more than two million persons, chiefly to the farm laborers and other workingmen. Since that date, whether the Liberals or the Conservatives[2] have been in power, "the country," as Professor Gardiner says, "has been under democratic influence."

But though these acts wrought an immense change by transferring political power from the hands of the few to the greater part of the nation, further progress in this direction was destined to come soon. Originally the government of the shires, or counties, was in the hands of the people; they gradually lost it, and the wealthy landed proprietors obtained control. The Local Government, or County Councils, Act (1888) restored the power in great measure to those who had parted with it, by putting the

[1] The ancient city of London, or London proper, is a district covering about a square mile, and was once enclosed by walls; it is still governed by a lord mayor, court of aldermen, and a common council elected mainly by members of the "city" companies, representing the medieval trade guilds (§ 274). The metropolis outside the "city" is governed by the London County Council and a number of associate bodies, among which are the councils of twenty-eight metropolitan boroughs.

[2] The Whigs (§ 479) included two elements, one aristocratic and the other radical. After the passage of the Reform Bill of 1832 they took the name of Liberals; and the Tories (§ 479), who found their old name unpopular, adopted that of Conservatives.

management of county affairs under the direction of the County Councils elected by the householders of the counties or shires. These Councils look after the highways, the sanitary condition of towns, the education of children, and the care of the poor.

Six years later (1894) the principle of self-government was carried almost to the farthest point by the passage of the Parish Councils Bill.[1] This measure did for country villages and other small places what the Local Government Act did for the counties. It gave back to the inhabitants of the parishes certain rights which they had once possessed, but which had gradually come under the control of the squire, the parson,[2] and a few privileged families.

Now every man and woman who has resided in the parish for a twelvemonth has the right not only to vote for the members of the Parish Council but to run as candidate for election to that body. This village parliament discusses all questions which are of public interest to the parish. It is in some respects more democratic even than a New England town meeting, since it gives women a voice, a vote, and opportunity to hold office. Its work supplements that of the County Councils and of Parliament.

609. Overthrow of the "Spoils System"; the Army; the "Secret Ballot," 1870-1872. Meanwhile reforms not less important had been effected in the management of the civil service. The ancient power of the Crown to give fat pensions to its favorites had been pared down to very modest proportions, but another great abuse still flourished like an evil weed in rich soil.

For generations, public offices had been regarded as public plunder, and the watchword of the politicians was, "Every man for himself, and the National Treasury for us all." Under this system of pillage the successful party in an election came down like a flock of vultures after a battle. They secured all the "spoils," from petty clerkships worth £100 a year up to places worth thousands.

About the middle of the last century (1855) an effort was made to break up this corrupt and corrupting custom, but the real work

---

[1] Parish : This name was given originally to a district assigned to a bishop or priest; at present it generally refers simply to the area which was formerly contained in such a district.

[2] The squire was the chief landholder in a village or parish; the parson, the minister of the parish church.

was not accomplished until 1870. In that year England threw open the majority of the positions in the civil service to competitive examination. Henceforth the poorest day laborer, whether man or woman, might, if competent, ask for any one of many places which formerly some influential man or political "boss" reserved as gifts for those who obeyed his commands.

The next year (1871) the purchase of commissions in the army was abolished.[1] This established the merit system in the ranks, and now military honors and military offices are open to all who can earn them.

The Registration Act of 1843 required every voter to have his name and residence recorded on a public list. This did away with election frauds to a large extent. It was supplemented in 1872 by the introduction of the "secret ballot" (§ 591). This put an end to the intimidation of voters and to the free fights and riots which had so frequently made the polls a political pandemonium. The Bribery Act of 1883 was another important measure which did much toward stopping the wholesale purchase of votes by wealthy candidates or by powerful corporations.

610. Reforms in Law Procedures. During Queen Victoria's reign great changes for the better were effected in simplifying the laws and in the administration of justice. When she came to the throne the Parliamentary Statutes at Large filled fifty-five huge folio volumes, and the Common Law, as contained in judicial decisions dating from the time of Edward II (1307), filled about twelve hundred more. The work of examining, digesting, and consolidating this enormous mass of legislative and legal lore was taken in hand (1863) and has been slowly progressing ever since.

The Judicature Acts (1873, 1877) united the chief courts in a single High Court of Justice. This reform did away with much confusion and expense. But the most striking changes for the better were those made in the Court of Chancery (§ 147) and the criminal courts.

---

[1] Up to 1871 an officer retiring from the army could sell his commission to any officer next below him in rank who had the money to buy the position; whereas under the present system the vacancy would necessarily fall to senior officers in the line of promotion. In the year following this salutary change the entire British army was reorganized.

In 1825 the property belonging to suitors in the former court amounted to nearly forty millions of pounds.[1] The simplest case might require a dozen years for its settlement, while difficult ones consumed a lifetime, or more, and were handed down from father to son, — a legacy of baffled hopes, of increasing expense, of mental suffering worse than that of hereditary disease.

Much has been done to remedy these evils, which Dickens set forth with such power in his novel of " Bleak House." At one time the prospect of reform seemed so utterly hopeless that it was customary for a prize fighter, when he had got his opponent's neck twisted under his arm, and held him absolutely helpless, to declare that he had his head " in chancery " !

611. Reforms in Criminal Courts and in the Treatment of the Insane. In criminal courts an equal reform was effected, and men accused of burglary and murder are now allowed to have counsel to defend them, and the right of appeal is secured; whereas, up to the era of the coronation of Victoria, they were obliged to plead their own cases as best they might against skilled public prosecutors, who used every resource known to the law to convict them.

Great changes for the better have also taken place in the treatment of the insane. Until near the close of the eighteenth century this unfortunate class was quite generally regarded as possessed by demons, and dealt with accordingly. William Tuke, a member of the Society of Friends, inaugurated a better system (1792); but the old method continued for many years longer. In fact, we have the highest authority for saying that down to a pretty late period in the nineteenth century the inmates of many asylums were worse off than the most desperate criminals.

They were shut up in dark, and often filthy, cells, where " they were chained to the wall, flogged, starved, and not infrequently killed." [2] Since then, mechanical restraints have, as a rule, been abolished, and the patients are generally treated with the care and kindness which their condition demands.

612. Progress in the Education of the Masses. We have seen that since 1837 the advance in popular education equaled that

---

[1] See Walpole's " History of England," Vol. III.

[2] Encyclopædia Britannica (10th and 11th editions) under " Insanity."

made in the extension of suffrage and in civil service reform. When Victoria began her reign a very large proportion of the children of the poor were growing up in a state bordering on barbarism. Many of them knew little more of books or schools than the young Hottentots in Africa.

The marriage register shows that as late as 1840 forty per cent of the Queen's adult subjects could not write their names in the book; by the close of her reign (1901) the number who had to " make their mark " in that interesting volume was only about one in ten. This proves, as Lord Brougham said, that " the school-master " has been " abroad " in the land.

The national system of education began, as we have already seen, in 1870 (§ 602). Later, the Assisted Education Act (1891) made provision for those who had not means to pay even a few pence a week for instruction. That law practically put the key of knowledge within reach of every child in England.

613. Religious Toleration in the Universities ; Payment of Church Rates abolished. The universities felt the new impulse. The abolition of religious tests for degrees at Oxford and Cambridge (1871) threw open the doors of those venerable seats of learning to students of every faith. Since then colleges for women have been established at Oxford and in the vicinity of Cambridge, and the " university-extension " examinations, with " college settlements " in London and other large cities, have long been doing excellent work.

The religious toleration granted in the universities was in accord with the general movement of the age. It will be remembered that the Catholics were readmitted to sit in Parliament (§ 573) late in the reign of George IV (1829), and that under Victoria the Jews were admitted (1858) to the same right (§ 599). Finally Mr. Brad-laugh got his Oaths Bill passed (1888), and so opened Parliament to persons not only of all religious beliefs but of none.

In the meantime the compulsory payment of rates for the support of the Church of England had been abolished (1868) (§ 601); and the next year (1869) was made memorable by the just and generous act by which Mr. Gladstone disestablished the Irish branch of the English Church (§ 601).

614. Transportation and Communication. When the Queen ascended the throne (1837), the locomotive (§ 584) was threatening to supersede the stagecoach; but the progress of steam as a motor power on land had not been rapid, and England then had

less than 200 miles of railway open;[1] but before the end of her reign there were nearly 22,000 miles in operation, and there are now about 24,000. At first, the passenger accommodations were limited. Those who could indulge in such luxuries sometimes preferred to travel in their own private carriages placed on platform cars for transportation. For those who took first-class tickets there were excellent and roomy compartments at very high prices. The second class fared tolerably well on uncushioned seats, but the unfortunate third class were crowded like cattle into open trucks, without seats, and with no roofs to keep the rain out. But time remedied this. Long before the Queen celebrated her first Jubilee (§ 607) the workingman could fly through the country at the rate of from thirty to fifty miles an hour, for a penny a

REDUCED COPY OF TELEGRAPH POSTER

Announcing the opening of the first line, from London to Slough, January, 1845

mile, and could have all the comforts that a reasonable being should ask for.

Cheap postage (§ 590) came in (1840) with the extension of railways, and in a few years the amount of mail carried increased enormously. Every letter, for the first time, carried on it a stamp bearing

[1] A part of what is now the London and Northwestern Railway.

a portrait of the young Queen, and in this way the English people came to know her better than they had ever known any preceding sovereign. The London papers now reached the country by train.

The Telegraph began to come into use in January, 1845, between the railway station at Paddington, a western district of London, and Slough, near Windsor. The government eventually purchased all the lines, and reduced the charge on a despatch of twelve words to sixpence to any part of the United Kingdom. The Telephone followed (1876), and then Wireless Telegraphy (1899).

615. Light in Dark Places ; Photography ; the New Surgery (1834–1895). The invention of the friction match, 1834 (§ 584), the abolition of the tax on windows (1851) (§ 595), with the introduction of American petroleum, speedily dispelled the almost subterraneous gloom of the laborer's cottage. Meanwhile photography, which began to be used in 1839, revealed the astonishing fact that the sun is always ready not only to make a picture but to take one, and that nothing is so humble as to be beneath his notice.

News came across the Atlantic from Boston, 1846, that Dr. Morton had rendered surgery painless by the use of ether. Before a year passed the English hospitals were employing it. Sir James Y. Simpson of Edinburgh introduced chloroform (1847). These two agents have abolished the terror of the surgeon's knife, and have lengthened life by making it possible to perform a class of operations which formerly very few patients had been able to bear.

A score of years later Sir Joseph Lister called attention to the important results obtained by antiseptic methods in surgery ; next came (1895) the introduction from Germany of the marvelous X ray, by whose help the operator can photograph and locate a bullet or other foreign substance which he is endeavoring to extract. Together, these discoveries have saved multitudes of lives.

616. Progress of the Laboring Classes ; Free Trade, 1846. At the date of the Queen's accession a number of laws existed restricting the free action of workingmen. Only three years before Victoria's coronation six poor agricultural laborers in Dorsetshire were transported (1834) to penal servitude at Botany Bay, Australia, for seven years, for peacefully combining to secure an increase of their wages, which at that time were only six shillings a week. In fact, the so-called "Conspiracy Laws," which made Labor Unions liable to prosecution as unlawful, if not actually criminal organizations, were not wholly repealed until after the opening of the twentieth century.

Meanwhile Parliament passed the Trade Union Acts, in 1871 and 1876, which recognized the right of workingmen to form associations to protect their interests by the use of all measures not forbidden by the Common Law.[1] In 1906 the persistent political pressure of organized labor induced a Liberal Cabinet (of which Sir Henry Campbell-Bannerman was Prime Minister) and the invariably Conservative House of Lords to pass a still more important act. That measure exempted Trades Unions from liability to pay damages for a certain class of injuries which they might commit in carrying on a strike.[2] During the above period of more than thirty years the unions have gained very largely in numbers and in financial as well as political strength. On the other hand they now have to contend with the radical Socialists who are seeking to convert England into a republic in which the government would carry on all industries and would prohibit private individuals from conducting any business whatever.

The unions will accomplish more still if they succeed in teaching their members to study the condition of industry in England, to respect the action of those workers who do not join associations, and to see clearly that "if men have a right to combine," they must also "have an equal right to refuse to combine."

In 1837 the English Corn Laws (§ 592) virtually shut out the importation of grain from foreign countries. The population had outgrown its food supply, and bread was so dear that even the agricultural laborer cried out. "I be protected," said he, "but I be starving." The long and bitter fight against the Corn Laws resulted not only in their gradual abolition, 1846, but in the opening of English ports to the products and manufactures of the

---

[1] One result of the organization of Trades or Labor Unions has been the shortening of the hours of labor. In 1894 the Government established an eight-hour day for workingmen in dockyards and in ordnance factories.

[2] The Trade Disputes Act of 1906. This forbids any suit for tort against a Trade Union. See A. L. Lowell's "The Government of England," II, 534; and S. Gompers in *The Outlook* for February, 1911, p. 269.

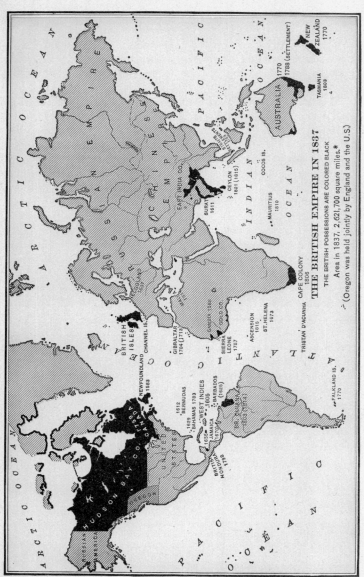

THE BRITISH EMPIRE IN 1837

THE BRITISH POSSESSIONS ARE COLORED BLACK

Area in 1837, 2,621,700 square miles.*

∴ (Oregon was held jointly by England and the U.S.)

NEW ZEALAND 1770

AUSTRALIA 1770
1788 (SETTLEMENT)

TASMANIA 1803

EAST INDIA CO.

SURAT 1611

CEYLON 1801 (1815)

COCOS IS.

MAURITIUS 1810

CAPE COLONY 1806

ST. HELENA 1673

ASCENSION 1815.

TRISTAN D'ACUNHA

FALKLAND IS. 1770

BRITISH ISLES

CHANNEL IS.

GIBRALTAR 1704 (1713)

GAMBIA 1686

SIERRA LEONE 1787

GOLD CO.

NEWFOUNDLAND 1583

BERMUDAS 1612

BAHAMAS 1783

WEST INDIES 1605

1629

JAMAICA 1670

BARBADOS 1625

BRITISH HONDURAS 1739

BR. GUIANA 1803 (1814)

HUDSON BAY CO. 1670

CANADA 1759

RUSSIAN AMERICA

UNITED STATES

ARCTIC OCEAN

PACIFIC OCEAN

ATLANTIC OCEAN

INDIAN OCEAN

CHINESE EMPIRE

RUSSIAN EMPIRE

* This area is given by J. Scott Keltie in the *English Illustrated Magazine*, July, 1897.

world. With the exception of tobacco, wines, spirits, and a few other articles, all imports enter the kingdom free.

But though Great Britain carries out the theory that it is better to make things cheap for the sake of those who buy them, than it is to make them dear for the sake of those who produce them, yet all of the great self-governing English colonies impose protective duties [1] even against British products (§ 625). One of the interesting questions suggested by the Queen's "Diamond Jubilee" (1897) (§ 607) was whether England's children in Australia, New Zealand, and Canada would take any steps toward forming a commercial free-trade union with the mother country. More than ten years later that point still remained under discussion (§ 625).

617. The Small Agricultural Holdings Act ; the Agricultural Outlook. Through the influence of the greatly increased popular vote, which resulted from the Third Reform Act (§ 600), the farm laborers made themselves felt in the House of Commons. They secured the passage of the Small Agricultural Holdings Act (1892). This gave those who worked on the land the privilege of purchasing from one to fifty acres, or of taking it on lease if they preferred.[2] But, notwithstanding the relief granted by this measure, the agricultural problem is to-day one of the most serious England has to solve. Just as New England now depends in large measure on the West for its food supply, so the British Isles depend in great measure on America for breadstuffs. Thousands of acres of fertile soil have gone out of cultivation in the eastern half of the island, mainly because the farmers cannot compete with foreign wheat.

The Royal Agricultural Commission, in a report made a number of years ago (1897), could suggest no remedy, and believed matters must grow worse. A leading English journal,[3] in commenting on the report, said, " The sad and sober fact is that the English farmer's occupation is gone, or nearly gone, never to return."

1 Except in certain cases, where the colonies, e.g. Canada, grant preferential duties, or practical free trade, in certain articles exported to the British Isles.

2 The Small Agricultural Holdings Act enables the County Council (§ 600) to acquire, by voluntary arrangement, suitable land for the purpose of reletting or reselling it to agricultural laborers and men of small means. Under certain safeguards the Council may advance up to three fourths of the purchase money.

3 The Bristol *Times and Mirror*, August 5, 1897.

The continued agricultural depression ruined many tillers of the soil, and drove the rural population more and more into the already overcrowded towns. There they bid against the laboring men for work, and so reduced wages to the lowest point. If they failed to get work, they became an added burden on the poor rates, and taxes rose accordingly.

Should no remedy be found, and should land in England continue to go out of cultivation, it is difficult to see how the majority of proprietors can resist the temptation to break up and sell their estates. The tendency of an important act of Parliament (1894) is believed by many to work in the same direction.[1] It imposes an inheritance tax on the heirs to landed property, which they find it hard to meet, especially when their tenants have abandoned their farms rather than try to pay the rent.

To-day a few thousand wealthy families hold the title deeds to a large part of the soil on which more than forty millions live. Generally speaking, the rent they demand does not seem to be excessive.[2] It is an open question whether England would be the gainer if, as in France, the land should be cut up into small holdings, worked by men without capital, and hence without power to make improvements.

618. The Colonial Expansion of England. Meanwhile, whether from an economic point of view England is gaining or losing at home, there can be no question as to her colonial expansion. A glance at the accompanying maps of the world (see double map opposite and map facing p. 420) in 1837 and in 1911 shows the marvelous territorial growth of the British Empire.

When Victoria was crowned it had an area of less than three million square miles ; to-day it has over eleven million, or more than one fifth of the entire land surface of the globe. England added to her dominions, on the average, more than one hundred and forty-five thousand square miles of territory every year of Victoria's reign.

Canada's wonderful growth in population and wealth is but one example. Australia began its career (1837) as a penal colony

[1] The Consolidated Death Duties Act.
[2] This is the opinion of the Royal Commission; but Gibbins's " Industry in England " (1896), p. 441, takes the opposite view.

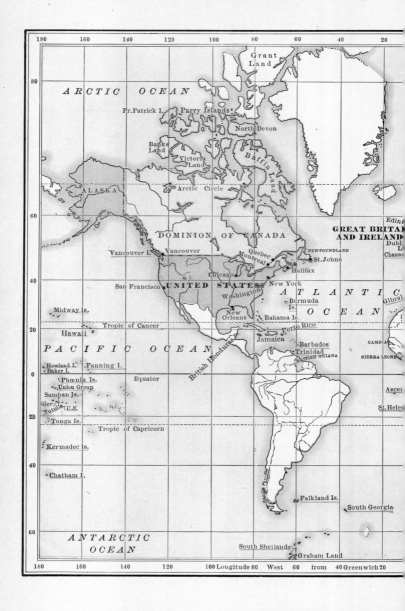

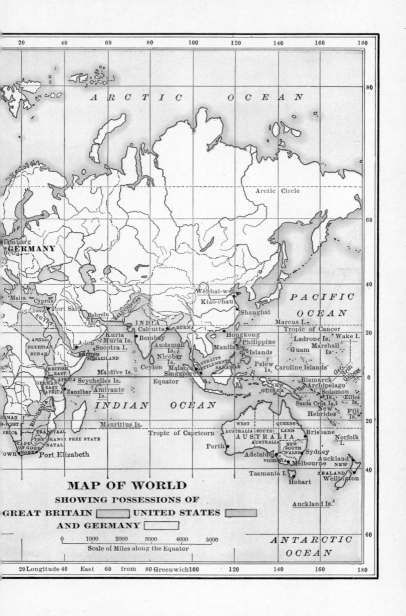

MAP OF WORLD

SHOWING POSSESSIONS OF

GREAT BRITAIN ☐ UNITED STATES ☐

AND GERMANY ☐

0   1000   2000   3000   4000   5000
Scale of Miles along the Equator

with a few shiploads of convicts; now it is a prosperous, powerful, and loyal part of the Empire (§ 545). Later than the middle
of the nineteenth century, New Zealand was a mission field where
cannibalism still existed (1857); now it is one of the leaders in
English civilization.

Again, when Victoria came to the throne (1837) the greater
part of Africa was simply a geographical expression; the coast
had been explored, but scarcely anything was known of the country back of it. Through the efforts of Livingstone and those who
followed him (1840–1890), the interior was explored and the
source of the Nile was discovered (1863). Stanley undertook
his great work on the Congo River, and the "dark continent"
ceased to be dark. Trade was opened with the interior, and the discovery of diamond mines and gold mines in South Africa (1867,
1884) stimulated emigration. Railways have been pushed forward
in many directions (§ 622), new markets are springing up, and
Africa, once the puzzle of the world, seems destined to become
one of the great fields which the Anglo-Saxon race is determined
to control, if not to possess.

On the other hand, the British West Indies have of late years
greatly declined from their former prosperity. The English demand
for cheap sugar has encouraged the importation of beet-root sugar
from Germany and France. This has reduced the market for cane
sugar to so low a point that there has been but little, if any, profit
in raising it in the West Indies;[1] but fruit is a success.

619. England's Change of Feeling toward her Colonies. One of
the most striking features of the "Diamond Jubilee" celebration
(§ 607) was the prominence given to the Colonial Prime Ministers.
There was a time, indeed, when the men who governed England
regarded Canada and Australia as "a source of weakness," and
the Colonial Office in London knew so little of the latter country
that it made ridiculous blunders in attempting to address official
despatches to Melbourne, Australia.[2] Even as late as the middle of
the last century Disraeli, then Chancellor of the Exchequer, wrote
to Lord Malmesbury in regard to the Newfoundland fisheries,

---

[1] See Brooks Adams's "America's Economic Supremacy."
[2] See Traill's "Social England," VI, 684.

" These wretched colonies will all be independent, too, in a few years, and are a millstone around our necks."

Twenty years afterwards Disraeli, later Lord Beaconsfield, declared that one of the great objects he and his party had in view was to uphold the British Empire and to do everything to maintain its unity. That feeling has steadily gained in power and was never stronger than it is to-day. Canada, Australia, and the other self-governing colonies (§ 625) have since responded by actions as well as words, and " Imperial Federation " has become something more than a high-sounding phrase (§§ 625, 626).

620. The Condition of Ireland ; International Arbitration. But to make such federation harmonious and complete, the support of Ireland must be obtained. That country is the only member of the United Kingdom whose representatives in Parliament refused, as a rule, to take part in the celebration of the Queen's reign. They felt that their island had never been placed on a true equality with its stronger and more prosperous neighbor. In fact, the Royal Commission, appointed to inquire into the relative taxation of England and Ireland, reported (1897) nearly unanimously that " for a great many years Ireland had paid annually more than £2,000,000 beyond her just proportion of taxation." [1] It has been estimated that the total excess obtained during the Queen's reign amounted to nearly £100,000,000.

Mr. Gladstone, the Liberal Prime Minister (1893), made a vigorous effort to secure " Home Rule " for Ireland. His bill granting that country an independent Parliament passed the House of Commons by a very large majority, but was utterly defeated in the House of Lords. Five years later (1898) Lord Salisbury, the Conservative Prime Minister, passed a bill which, though it did not give Ireland " Home Rule," did give it local self-government on the same popular foundation on which it rests in England (§ 608) and Scotland. Mr. Bryce, the British Ambassador at Washington, said (1911) the condition of the people of Ireland had greatly improved and was " still advancing," and that " before long nearly all the land would belong to the cultivators " (§ 605). In 1914 an Irish Home Rule Bill was passed over the Lords' veto (§ 633).

[1] McCarthy's " History of Our Own Times," V, 487.

GLADSTONE SPEAKING IN THE HOUSE OF COMMONS
On his introduction of the Home Rule Bill for Ireland, February 13, 1893

425

The recognition of the principle of international arbitration by England in the *Alabama* case (§ 598), in the Bering Sea Seal Fisheries dispute (1893), in the Venezuela boundary controversy (1896), and in the Newfoundland Fisheries case (1910) proved that the English people saw that the victories of peace are worth as much to a nation as the victories of war. The Hague Peace Conference Treaty, ratified by Great Britain with the United States and the leading nations of Europe and the Far East (1899), provided for the establishment of a permanent Court of Arbitration at The Hague between all of the great powers which signed it. All appeals to it, however, are entirely voluntary.

Ten years earlier, a proposition to establish such a court for the purpose of strengthening the cause of international peace would have been looked upon as "a splendid but delusive dream." To-day many of the ablest men on both sides of the Atlantic believe that the time is not far off when England and America will agree to settle by arbitration all questions which diplomacy cannot deal with, which may arise between them. Sir Edward Grey, Secretary for Foreign Affairs in Mr. Asquith's Liberal Cabinet, fears that the continued expenditure on larger and larger armaments " will end in international revolution." On the other hand, those who are constantly advocating the building of more and bigger battleships admit that the Peace Party presents strong arguments in support of its views, and that " the war against war " is making progress.

621. Death of Gladstone ; the Cabot Tower ; Centennial of the First Savings Bank, 1899. Meanwhile, Mr. Gladstone, the great Liberal leader, died, full of years and honors, at his residence, Hawarden Castle, in North Wales (1898). The "Grand Old Man" — as his friends delighted to call him — was buried in that Abbey at Westminster which holds so much of England's most precious dust. His grave is not far from the memorial to Lord Beaconsfield, the eminent Conservative leader, who was his lifelong rival and political opponent.

In the autumn (1898) the Cabot monument was opened at Bristol. It is a commanding tower, overlooking the ancient city and port from which John Cabot (§ 335) sailed in the spring of 1497. The monument commemorates that explorer's discovery of the mainland of the New World. An inscription on the face of the tower expresses " the earnest hope that Peace and Friendship may ever continue between the kindred peoples " of England and America.

In May of the next year, 1899, the one hundredth anniversary of the establishment of savings banks in Great Britain was celebrated. Near the closing year of the eighteenth century, 1799, Reverend Joseph Smith, Vicar of Wendover in Buckinghamshire, invited the laborers of his parish to deposit their savings with him on interest. " Upon the first day of the week," said he, quoting St. Paul's injunction, " let every one of you lay by him in store." [1] He offered to receive sums as small as twopence. Before the end of the year he had sixty depositors. Eventually the government took up the scheme and established the present system of national postal savings banks.

They have done and are doing incalculable good. At present there are over eleven million depositors in the United Kingdom. Most of them belong to the wage-earning class, and they hold more than £212,000,000. In this case certainly the grain of mustard seed, sown a few generations ago, has produced a mighty harvest.

622. England in Egypt; Progress in Africa. While busy at home, the English had been busy outside of their island. Five years after the opening of the Suez Canal (1869), Lord Beaconsfield, then the Conservative Prime Minister, bought nearly half of the canal property from the Governor of Egypt. Since then England has kept her hand on the country of the Pharaohs and the pyramids, and kept it there greatly to the advantage of the laboring class.

About ten years later (1881), Arabi Pasha, an ambitious colonel in the native army, raised the cry, " Down with all foreigners — Egypt for the Egyptians ! " Lord Wolseley defeated Arabi's forces, and the colonel was banished from the country.

Two years afterwards (1883) a still more formidable rebellion broke out in the Sudan, — a province held by Egypt. (See map facing p. 428.) The leader of the insurrection styled himself the Mahdi, or great Mohammedan Prophet. Then (1884) Gladstone sent General Gordon to withdraw the Egyptian troops from

[1] The quotation is from 1 Corinthians xvi, 2.

Khartoum, the capital of the Sudan. The Mahdi's forces shut up the heroic soldier in that city, and before help could reach him, he and all his Egyptian troops were massacred. No braver or truer man ever died at the post of duty, for in him was fulfilled Wordsworth's eloquent tribute to the " Happy Warrior." [1]

Many years later, Lord Kitchener advanced against the new Mahdi, and at Omdurman his terrible machine guns scattered the fanatical Dervishes, or Mohammedan monks, like chaff before the whirlwind. The next autumn (1899) the British overtook the fugitive leader of the Dervishes and annihilated his army.

Since then British enterprise, British capital, and American inventive skill have transformed Egypt. The completion of the great dam across the Nile, at Assouan (1902), regulates the water supply for lower Egypt. The creation of this enormous reservoir promises to make the Nile valley one of the richest cotton-producing regions in the world.

The " Cape to Cairo " railway, which is more than half finished, is another British undertaking of immense importance. (See map opposite.) When ready for traffic, through its whole length of nearly six thousand miles, besides its branch lines, it will open all Eastern Africa, from the Cape of Good Hope to the Mediterranean, to the spread of commerce and civilization.

623. The Boers ; the Boer War, 1899 ; Death of Queen Victoria (1901). The history of the British in South Africa has been even more tragic than their progress in Egypt (§ 622).

In the middle of the seventeenth century (1652) the Dutch took possession of Cape Colony. (See map opposite.) Many Boers, or Dutch farmers, and cattle raisers emigrated to that far distant land. There they were joined by Huguenots, or French Protestants, who had been driven out of France. All of them became slaveholders. Early in the nineteenth century (1814) England purchased the Cape from Holland. Twenty years later the English Parliament bought all the negroes held by the Boers and set them free.

Eight thousand Boers, disgusted with the loss of their slaves and with the small price they had received for them, left the Cape (1836) and pushed far northward into the wilderness. Crossing

---

[1] See Wordsworth's poems " The Happy Warrior."

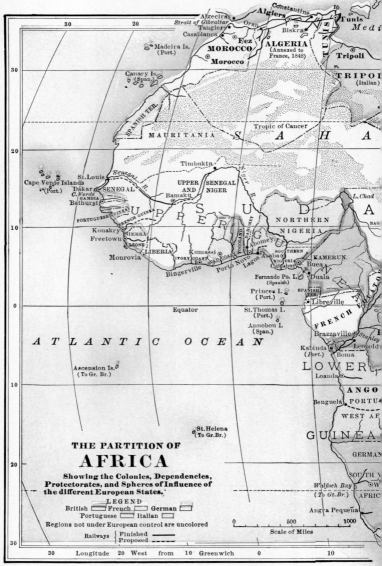

THE PARTITION OF
AFRICA

**Showing the Colonies, Dependencies,
Protectorates, and Spheres of Influence of
the different European States.**

LEGEND
British ⬚ French ⬚ German ⬚
Portuguese ⬚ Italian ⬚
Regions not under European control are uncolored

Railways ⎰ Finished
⎱ Proposed ----

0   500   1000
Scale of Miles

30   Longitude   20 West   from   10 Greenwich   0   10

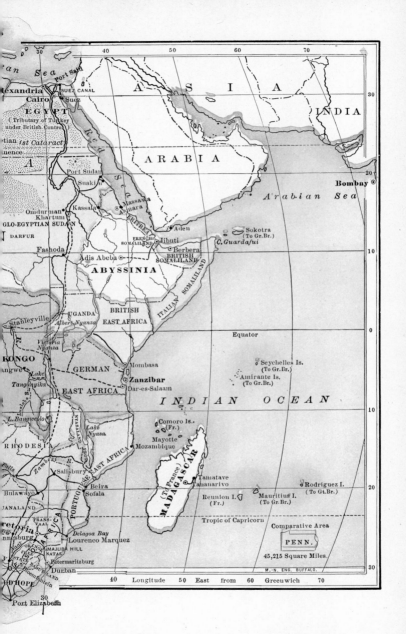

the Orange River, they founded the "Orange Free State." Another party of Boers, going still further north, crossed the Vaal River (a tributary of the Orange) and set up the Transvaal, or "South African Republic," on what was practically a slaveholding foundation. Later (1852), England, by a treaty known as the Sand River Convention, virtually recognized the independence of the settlers in the Transvaal, and two years afterwards made a still more explicit recognition of the independence of the Orange Free State.

The Zulus and other fierce native tribes bordering on the Transvaal hated the Boers and threatened to "eat them up." Later (1877), England thought it for her interest, and for that of the Boers as well, to annex the Transvaal. The English Governor did not grant the Boers the measure of political liberty which he had promised; this led to a revolt, and a small body of English soldiers was beaten at Majuba Hill (1881).

Mr. Gladstone, the Liberal Prime Minister, did not think that the conquest of the Transvaal, supposing it to be justifiable, would pay for its cost, and he accordingly made a treaty with the people of that country (1881). Lord Beaconsfield thought this policy a serious mistake, and that it would lead to trouble later on. He said, "We have failed to whip the boy, and we shall have to fight the man." The Gladstone Treaty acknowledged the right of the Boers to govern themselves, but subject to English control. Three years later (1884) that treaty was modified. The Boers declared that the English then gave up all control over them, except with regard to the power to make treaties which might conflict with the interests of Great Britain. But this statement the English Government emphatically denied.[1]

The discovery of diamond fields in Cape Colony (1867) and of the richest gold mines in the world (1884) in the Transvaal stimulated a great emigration of English to South Africa. In a few

[1] The preamble of the Convention or agreement made between England and the Boers in 1881 at Pretoria, the capital of the Transvaal, secured to the Boers "complete self-government, subject to the suzerainty of her Majesty," Queen Victoria. In the Convention of 1884, made at London, the word "suzerainty" was dropped; but Mr. Chamberlain, Colonial Secretary of Great Britain, contended that it was implied or understood. This interpretation of the agreement President Kruger of the South African or Boer Republic absolutely rejected.

years the " Outlanders " — as the Boers called all foreigners — outnumbered the Boers themselves. The " Outlanders," who worked the gold mines and paid nearly all the taxes, complained that the laws made by the Boers were unjust and oppressive. They demanded the right to vote. The Boers, on the other hand, refused to give them that right, except under arduous restrictions, lest the foreigners should get the upper hand in the Transvaal Republic, and then manage it to suit themselves.

Things went on from bad to worse. At length (1895) a prominent Englishman of Cape Colony, Dr. Jameson, armed a small body of " Outlanders," who undertook to get by force what they could not get by persuasion. The Boers captured the Revolutionists and compelled some of the leaders to pay, in all, about a million dollars in fines. Dr. Jameson was sent to England and imprisoned for a short time. A committee appointed by Parliament investigated the invasion of the Transvaal and charged Cecil J. Rhodes, then Prime Minister of Cape Colony, with having helped on the raid. From this time the feeling of hatred between the Boers and the " Outlanders " grew more and more intense. Lord Salisbury, the Conservative Prime Minister, believed, with his party, that the time had come for decisive action on the part of the Government. The fires so long smoldering now burst into flame, and England resolved to fight to maintain her authority in the Transvaal.

War began in the autumn of 1899, and the Orange Free State united with the Transvaal against Great Britain. (See map facing p. 428.) The Boers took up arms for independence. The English forces under Lord Roberts began fighting, first in behalf of the " Outlanders," next to keep the British Empire together, and, finally, " to extend English law, liberty, and civilization."

Mr. Chamberlain, who was in Lord Salisbury's Cabinet (§ 534), agreed with his chief that the sword must settle the question, but he said that the contest in South Africa would be " a long war, a bitter war, and a costly war." Events proved the truth of part of his prediction. The contest was certainly " bitter," for it carried sorrow and death into many thousand homes. It was " costly," too, for the total expense to England amounted to nearly £200,000,000.

England finally overthrew and formally annexed (1901) the two Boer republics, aggregating over one hundred and sixty-seven thousand square miles. But to accomplish that work she was forced to send two hundred and fifty thousand men to South Africa, — the largest army she ever put into the field in the whole course of her history. The great majority of the English people believed that the war was inevitable. But there was an active minority who insisted that it was really undertaken in behalf of the South African mine owners. They did not hesitate to condemn the " Jingo " policy [1] of the Government as disastrous to the best interests of the country. In the midst of the discussion Queen Victoria died (January 22, 1901). The Prince of Wales succeeded to the crown under the title of King Edward VII.

624. Summary. Queen Victoria's reign of sixty-three years — the longest in English history — was remarkable in many ways.

The chief political events were :

1. The establishment of the practical supremacy of the House of Commons, shown by the fact that the Sovereign was now obliged to give up the power of removing the Prime Minister or members of his Cabinet without the consent of the House, or of retaining them contrary to its desire.

2. The broadening of the basis of suffrage and the extension of the principle of local self-government.

3. The abolition of the requirement of property qualification for Parliamentary candidates ; the admission of Jews to Parliament ; and the overthrow of the Spoils System.

4. The repeal of the Corn Laws ; the adoption of the Free-Trade policy ; and the Emancipation of Labor.

5. The Small Agricultural Holdings Act ; the Irish Land Acts ; the abolition of Church rates ; and the disestablishment of the Irish branch of the Church of England.

6. The arbitration of the *Alabama* case.

---

[1] Lord Beaconsfield, the Conservative Prime Minister (1874-1880), made several petty wars in South Africa and in Afghanistan. A popular music-hall song glorified his work, declaring :

> " We don't want to fight, but by Jingo, if we do,
> We 've got the ships, we 've got the men,
> We 've got the money, too."

7. The progress of transportation and of the rapid transmission of intelligence was marked by the extension of railways to all parts of the British Isles and to many other parts of the Empire; the introduction of the telegraph and the telephone; the laying of the Atlantic cable; the establishment of the first regular line of Atlantic steamers; the introduction of penny postage; the rise of cheap newspapers, of photography, of wireless telegraphy, and of the use of electricity to drive street cars and machinery.

8. The progress of education was marked by the establishment of practically free elementary schools, free libraries, and the abolition of religious tests in the universities.

9. The progress of science and philosophy was shown by the introduction of painless and also of antiseptic surgery, the use of the German X ray, and the rise and spread of the Darwinian theory of Evolution.

10. Other events having far-reaching results were the terrible Irish famine, the Opium War, the Crimean War, the rebellion in India, the *Trent* affair, the war in the Sudan, and the great Boer War.

11. Finally, we see the important work accomplished in India, Egypt, and other parts of Africa; the acquisition of the control of the Suez Canal; and the great expansion of the power of the Empire in Canada, Australia, and New Zealand.

EDWARD VII — 1901–1910

625. End of the Boer War (1902); Completion of Imperial Federation, 1910. Not long after Edward VII came to the throne the Boers (§ 623) laid down their arms (1902) and recognized the King as their true and lawful Sovereign. The announcement set the " joy bells " ringing all over Great Britain.

Under Edward VII the Crown became the center of a great movement for more complete Imperial Unity. We have seen that the process of forming a federation of Great Britain and her widely scattered colonies had made good progress under Victoria (§§ 618, 619). She had seen the creation of the Dominion of Canada (1867), the Dominion of New Zealand (1875), and the consolidation of the six Australian colonies into the Commonwealth of Australia (1901). Nine years later (1910) the four states which had been the scene of the Boer War (§ 623) were consolidated in like manner and received the name of the Union of South Africa.[1] Boer and Briton seem now to have made up their minds to live together as one family, and, as farmers and stock raisers, they will work out their destiny on the land. Speaking of the political significance of this event, a prominent official in South Africa said, "Without the influence of King Edward, I do not think the union could have been effected."

The establishment of the Union of South Africa completed the framework of the Imperial Federation (§§ 618, 619). Admiral Mahan, of the American navy, classes the expansion of the British Empire with that of the expansion of the United States, and declares that it ranks as one of the foremost facts of "contemporaneous history." The Commonwealth of Australia and the Union of South Africa (with the Dominion of New Zealand) mark the southern limit of the Imperial Federation. The Dominion of Canada marks its northern limit. (See map facing p. 422.)

All these British possessions enjoy a degree of self-government which falls but little short of entire independence. In fact, commercially they are independent, for, as we have seen (§ 616), while England maintains free trade, her colonies still keep up a strict protective tariff and impose duties even on British imports. Notwithstanding this difference, all the colonies are loyal subjects of the English Crown, and all stand ready to defend the English flag.

626. The League of Empire. While this successful movement toward Imperial Federation was going on, the organization called the League of Empire had been formed (1901) to coöperate with it and strengthen it.

The League is nonpolitical and nonsectarian. It aims to unite the different parts of the Imperial Federation by intellectual and moral bonds. It appeals to the whole body of the people of the

[1] The Union of South Africa is formed of the states of the Cape of Good Hope, Natal, the Transvaal, and the Orange Free State. Lord Gladstone, son of the late W. E. Gladstone, was appointed Governor of the new Commonwealth, and General Botha, who had commanded in the Boer army, was made Prime Minister.

Empire, but it deals especially with the children in the schools. It endeavors to educate them in the duties of citizenship, and it calls on them to salute the national flag as the symbol of patriotism, of unity, and of loyalty. A little later, Empire Day was established (1904) as a public holiday to help forward the work of the League. King Edward gave it his hearty encouragement, and it is celebrated throughout the British Isles and the self-governing colonies of the Imperial Federation.

627. The King's Influence in Behalf of Peace. While seeking to make all England and English dominions one in spirit, King Edward constantly used his influence to maintain peace both at home and abroad. He was a man whose natural kindliness of heart endowed him with the double power of making and of keeping friends. Furthermore, he was a born diplomatist. He saw at once the best method of handling the most difficult questions. Those who knew him intimately said that " he always did the right thing, at the right time, in the right way."

To a great extent he was a creator of international confidence. In his short reign he succeeded in overcoming the old race feeling which made England and France regard each other as enemies. Again, Russia and England had been on unfriendly terms for nearly two generations, but the King, by his strong personal influence, brought the two countries to understand each other better.

He saw that Europe needed peace. He saw that the outbreak of a general war would strike the laboring man a terrible blow, and would destroy the fruits of his toil. When he ascended the throne (1901) the contest with the Boers in South Africa was still going on. General Botha, one of the Boer leaders, publicly stated that the King did everything in his power to secure the establishment of an honorable and permanent peace between the combatants. More than that, even, he was in favor of granting a large measure of self-government to the very people who had only just laid down the arms with which they had been fighting him.

But the King's influence for good was not limited to the Old World. It extended across the Atlantic. Mr. Choate, who was formerly our ambassador to England, said that Edward VII endeavored to remove every cause of friction between Great Britain and America. While he lay on a sick bed he signed a treaty relating to the Panama Canal, which made " it possible for the United States to construct the waterway and to protect it forever." [1]

It is the remembrance of these things which has gained for the late Sovereign the title of " Edward the Peacemaker."

628. The Political Battle in England ; Labor gets into Parliament, 1906. But the King's success in international politics did not secure peace in the field of home politics. Organized labor had long been bent on pushing its way into Parliament. In a few cases, like that of Joseph Arch (§ 600), it had elected a representative,[2] but these were scattered victories which made no great impression.

The real upheaval came in the General Election of 1906. That contest wrought a silent revolution. Up to that date, with very few exceptions, the wealthy class was the only one which had been represented in the House of Commons. Furthermore, it cost a good deal of money for any candidate to get into the House, and as members drew no pay, it cost a good deal more money to remain there.

In 1906 the Liberal Party and the Labor Party gained a sweeping victory over the Conservative Party, and Sir Henry Campbell-Bannerman, the Liberal Prime Minister, came into power, 1906–1908. Out of the six hundred and seventy members who had been elected to the House of Commons, fifty-four came from the ranks of the workingmen, — those to whom life means an unending struggle to live.[3] The combined Labor voters sent these men to represent them in Parliament, and then raised a fund to meet the expense of keeping them there.[4]

These " Laborites," as they are popularly called, claim that their influence secured the passage of the Old Age Pensions Act (1908),

[1] This was the treaty repealing the Clayton-Bulwer Treaty of 1850. See the address of Honorable Joseph H. Choate before the New York Chamber of Commerce, June 2, 1910.

[2] Besides Joseph Arch, such men as John Burns and J. Keir Hardie.

[3] John Burns, who was one of the earliest workingmen to enter Parliament as a Labor leader, said of himself, " Came into the world with a struggle, struggling now, with prospects of continuing it."

[4] But later, the Court of Appeal (§ 588) decided that the Labor Party could not legally compel any member of the Labor Union to contribute to this fund against his will. Now (1911) Parliament pays all members of the Commons (see § 591).

for the relief of the aged and deserving poor; the Act for Feeding Destitute School Children; and the Act establishing Labor Exchanges (1909) throughout the country to help those who are looking for work.

The entrance of the working class and of the Socialists into Parliament marks the transference of power from the House of Commons directly to the mass of the people. Public opinion is now the real active force in legislation, and the lawmakers are eager to know what "the man in the street" and the "man with the hoe" are thinking.

This closeness of touch between Parliament and People has evident advantages, but it also has at least one serious drawback. In times of great public excitement it might lead to hasty legislation, unless the House of Lords should be able to interpose and procure the further consideration of questions of vital importance which it would be dangerous to attempt to settle offhand (§ 631).

629. The Budget; Woman Suffrage; the Contest with the Lords. Mr. Asquith, the Liberal Prime Minister,[1] found that the Government must raise a very large amount of money to defray the heavy cost of the old-age pensions (§ 628) and the far heavier cost of eight new battleships. Mr. Lloyd George, the Chancellor of the Exchequer, or Secretary of the Treasury, brought in a Budget[2] which roused excited and long-continued debate. The Chancellor's measure called for a great increase of taxes on real estate in towns and cities where the land had risen in value, and on land containing coal, iron, or other valuable minerals.[3]

The House of Commons passed the Budget (1909), but the House of Lords, which includes the wealthiest landowners in the British Isles, rejected it. They declared that it was not only unjust and oppressive, but that it was a long step toward the establishment

[1] Mr. Asquith succeeded Sir Henry Campbell-Bannerman, the Liberal Minister (§ 628), who died in the spring of 1908.

[2] The official estimate of the amount of money which the Government must raise by taxation to meet its expenses for the year, together with the scheme of taxation proposed, are called the Budget.

[3] In all cases where the owner of the land had himself done nothing to produce the rise in value, the Chancellor called that rise the "unearned increment," and held that the owner should be taxed for it accordingly. Most great landowners and many small ones execrate the man who made a practical application of this unpalatable phrase.

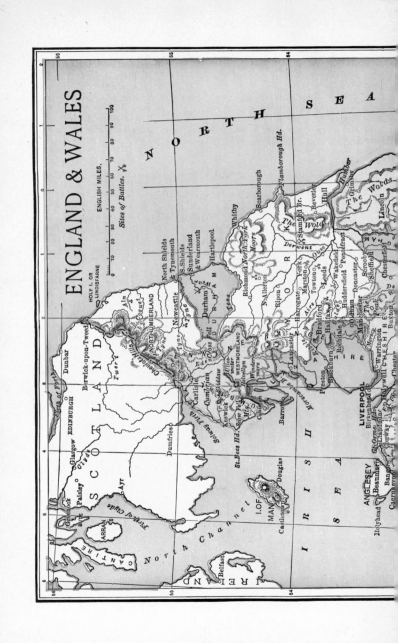

ENGLAND & WALES

HOLY I. OR
LINDISFARNE

ENGLISH MILES.

Sites of Battles. ✗

0   10   20   30   40   50   60   70   80   90   100

N O R T H   S E A

A

SCOTLAND

Firth of Forth
EDINBURGH
Glasgow
Paisley
Greenock
BUTE
ARRAN
Ayr
CANTIRE
Firth of Clyde
Dunbar
Berwick-upon-Tweed
Cheviot Hills
NORTHUMBERLAND
Tweed
Aln
Coquet
Tyne
Newcastle
N. Tyne
S. Tyne
North Shields & Tynemouth
S. Shields
Sunderland & Wearmouth
Hartlepool
Whitby
Scarborough
Flamborough Hd.
DURHAM
Wear
Tees
Cleveland
Richmond
NORTH YORK Moors
N. Allerton
Ripon
Harrogate
York
Derwent
Stamford Br.
Beverley
Hull
The Wolds
Grimsby
Lincoln
LINCOLN
The Wolds
K.

Dumfries
Solway Firth
Carlisle
CUMBERLAND
Cross Fell
Eden
Keswick
Derwent
Skiddaw
Penrith
Ullswater
WESTMORELAND
Helvellyn
Windermere
Appleby

St.Bees Hd.
Barrow
Morecambe B.
Lancaster
LANCASHIRE
Preston
Blackburn
Ribble
Rochdale
Bolton
Manchester
Liverpool
Birkenhead
Warrington
CHESHIRE
Chester
Oldham
Huddersfield
Halifax
Bradford
Leeds
Wakefield
Pontefract
Aire
Doncaster
Don
Sheffield
Chesterfield
Buxton
Towton
Marston
Ouse

IRISH
SEA

I. OF MAN
Douglas
Castletown

North Channel

IRELAND
Belfast

ANGLESEY
Holyhead
Beaumaris
Gt. Orme's Hd.
Llandudno
Conway
Bangor
Llanrwst
Caernarvon
Denbigh
Flint
Holywell
Mold

54
55
55½
56
2
1
0

54
55
55½
56
2
3
4
5
6

of socialism, and that it threatened to lead to the confiscation of
private property in land. A bitter conflict ensued between the two
branches of Parliament.

This contest was rendered harder by the actions of a small
number of turbulent women, who demanded complete suffrage but
failed to get it (§§ 599, 608).[1] Adopting the methods of a football
team, they endeavored to force their way into the House of Commons. Later, they assaulted members of the Cabinet, burned
churches, and destroyed works of art. When sent to prison for
these crimes, they refused to eat, but as soon as they had gained
their liberty by "hunger striking," they began to commit fresh
outrages. On the outbreak of the great European War, in 1914,
these "wild women" resolved that during the awful contest they
would refrain from all acts of violence (§ 633).

**630. A New Parliamentary Election; the Lords accept the
Budget.** The rejection of the Budget by the House of Lords
(§ 629) caused a new Parliamentary election (1910). The Liberal
Party with the Labor Party again won the victory, but with a
decidedly diminished majority. Mr. Asquith, the Liberal Prime
Minister, declared that the policy of the Liberal Government forbade any concessions whatever to the Lords. The Lords thought it
unwise to carry the contest further, and when the new Parliament
met they bowed to the inevitable and reluctantly voted to accept
the Budget, — land taxes and all.[2]

**631. New Warships; a New Domesday Book; Death of King
Edward.** This acceptance of the Budget made the Government
feel reasonably sure that it would get the £16,000,000 required to
pay for eight new battleships (§ 629). It also encouraged the War
Department to spend a considerable sum in experimenting with
military airships as a means of defense against invasion. Great
Britain, like Germany, believes that such vessels have become a
necessity; for since a foreigner flew across the Channel and landed
at Dover (1909), England has felt that her navy on the sea must

---

[1] The great majority of woman suffragists refused to adopt these violent methods.

[2] The Liberal Party in power threatened, in case the Lords continued to refuse
to accept the Budget, that they would either request the King to create a sufficient
number of new Liberal Peers to carry it (§ 582), or that they would make the country
go through another election.

be supplemented by a navy above the sea. Two of these government airships are now frequently seen circling at express speed
around the great dome of St. Paul's.

The Government also began preparations for the compilation of
a new Domesday Book (§ 120), which should revalue all the land
in the British Isles, in order to establish a permanent basis for
increased taxation.[1] The House of Commons furthermore took up
the debate on adopting measures for limiting the power of the
Lords to veto bills passed by the Commons. While they were so
engaged King Edward died (May 6, 1910); his son was crowned
in 1911, with the title of George V.

632. Summary. The most important events in the reign of
Edward VII were (1) the completion of the Imperial Federation
by which all of the leading British colonies were brought into closer
union with the " mother country "; (2) the excellent work accomplished by the King for the maintenance of the peace of Europe,
and for the furtherance of the project for constructing the American Panama Canal; (3) the great change in the composition of
the House of Commons by the entrance of the working class into
Parliament.

GEORGE V — 1910-

633. Parliament Act; Compulsory Insurance; Home Rule, 1914.
For many years the Liberal Party in England had been endeavoring to pass a Home Rule Bill which would enable the people of
Ireland to establish a local Parliament or Legislature. When (1893)
Gladstone finally failed to get through such a bill (§ 620), he declared that before it could be done the absolute power of veto
possessed by the House of Lords must be properly restricted.

In 1911 the Liberals in the Imperial Parliament, sitting in
London, succeeded, by the help of some eighty Irish Nationalist
members in the House of Commons, in passing the Parliament
Bill embodying the desired restriction. Mr. Asquith, the Liberal

---

[1] The last general valuation of the land was made in 1692; it was then fixed at
£9,000,000. The land tax, based on this valuation, has yielded about £2,000,000
annually. The Government expects that the new valuation will yield much more.

Prime Minister, then forced the Lords to accept the measure. He accomplished that seemingly impossible undertaking by doing exactly what Earl Grey did when he " jammed through " the great Reform Bill of 1832 (§ 582). In other words, he threatened the Lords that if they continued to resist the will of the Commons, he would advise King George to create a large number of peers pledged to vote for the proposed law. Rather than see their conservative House swamped, the peers ceased to fight and the Parliament Act was put on the statute books. That Act deprives the House of Lords of the power to defeat any Public Bill which the House of Commons has passed for three successive sessions, extending over a period of not less than two years. (See Constitutional Documents, in Appendix, p. xxxiii.)

The momentous Act was passed at a time when the great Dockers Strike had practically closed the port of London and had cut off the chief food supply of the city. A little later, the Prime Minister passed the Salary Bill, which pays the members of the House of Commons £400 annually (§ 591). Next, the Government passed the Workmen's Compulsory Insurance Bill (1911) against sickness and unemployment. The worker and his employer contribute small sums weekly; the Government gives the rest by a tax levied on the whole community. The motive of the law is excellent, though it has created considerable friction in working.

In the meantime the Liberal Government, helped by the same Irish Nationalists in Parliament, were hurrying forward a new Home Rule Bill for Ireland (§ 620). The Unionist, or Conservative, Party obstinately opposed it; but as the Lords' veto power had now been limited by the Parliament Act, mentioned above, the bill was carried in the spring of 1914 by a large majority. It gave Ireland the right to elect a local Parliament, subject, however, to the control of the Imperial Parliament in London on all questions of supreme importance.[1]

---

[1] The Irish Parliament is prohibited from legislating (1) on peace or war; (2) on the army or navy; (3) on coinage; (4) on foreign commerce; (5) on the collection, at least for the present, of all taxes; (6) on endowing any religion, or granting any special privilege to any religion, or making any religious ceremony a necessity for a valid marriage.

The avowed object of this very important measure was the belief, on the part of its friends, that it would make Ireland a loyal and contented member of the United Kingdom. Unfortunately it not only failed to accomplish that laudable purpose, but it split the island into two warring factions. These two factions were the Catholics and the Protestants. The Catholics, who constitute by far the greater part of the population, were eager to set up the local Parliament; the Protestants, who are a powerful minority, bitterly opposed such an institution.[1]

The largest proportion of Protestants in any one section are inhabitants of Ulster, which comprises the whole northern extremity of Ireland (see map facing page 358). This territory was originally peopled by Irish, but in the seventeenth century the English and Scotch planted Protestant colonies there.[2]

Ulster is not only the largest and most populous province of Ireland, but it claims to be the richest and to pay two-thirds of all the taxes of Ireland. It also includes Belfast, the greatest commercial and manufacturing city in the island. When the Unionists, or Conservative Party, of Ulster found that they could not induce the House of Commons to permanently exempt that province from the jurisdiction of the new law, they took extreme measures — measures, in fact, which their opponents termed "treasonable." Under the leadership of Sir Edward Carson, a member of the Imperial Parliament, a powerful armed force was raised to resist the authority of the Irish Parliament. This was done on the ground that it would consist of an overwhelming majority of Catholic members, and that in all legislative action the Protestants would be practically helpless. The provisions of the law seem, on the surface, to be ample for safeguarding the interests of non-Catholics (see note 1, p. 439), but Sir Edward and his followers had no faith in their efficacy and preferred powder and ball instead.

On the other hand, the Irish Nationalists did not stand idle. Under the leadership of Mr. John E. Redmond, who was also a

---

[1] The total population of Ireland is officially estimated at 3,242,670 Catholics and 1,147,549 Protestants, or non-Catholics.

[2] The total population of the province of Ulster is estimated, in round numbers, at 1,580,000, of which 890,000 are Protestants and 690,000 are Catholics.

member of the Imperial Parliament, they proceeded to raise and equip a Catholic army to compel the Ulster "rebels" to obey the law.

Alarmed at the threatening aspect of affairs the English Government carried an Amending Bill [1] through the House of Commons, which it hoped would be acceptable to both parties in Ireland. But all compromise was rejected. Civil war seemed to be well-nigh inevitable. In view of that ominous fact the London *Times* declared that "the country is now confronted with one of the greatest crises in the history of the British race."

634. Outbreak of the Great European War, 1914. Just at this critical juncture all Europe was startled, as by a fire bell in the night, by the cry, "International War!" We do not know the real cause of the war. Perhaps the Emperor of Austria or the German Kaiser or the Czar of Russia could tell; but all we now know is the fatal event that brought on the war.

A student of Servia — who was apparently connected with a band of anarchists — assassinated the Crown Prince of Austria, heir to the Emperor's throne. The Emperor charged the Servian Government with being in sympathy with these anarchists and made a long list of demands on the King of Servia, which he was ordered to return, with his reply, within forty-eight hours. He conceded all of them but one; that one he declined to grant because it gave Austria power to interfere in the free action of the Servian courts of justice. The King proposed that this particular article should be submitted to a board of international arbitrators. England was most urgent in her efforts to secure an amicable settlement of this momentous question, on which the peace of Europe depended; but all of her suggestions were rejected. Germany had already assured Austria that she would approve "any action" she might

---

[1] The Amending Bill offered to exempt the four counties of Ulster which have the largest percentage of Protestants from the control of the Irish Parliament for the space of six years (or the normal life of two Imperial Parliaments), after which date the jurisdiction of the Irish Parliament would extend over all parts of Ulster.

The radical Unionists, under the leadership of Sir Edward Carson, rejected any time limit whatever; they also rejected the proposed limit of area. They declared that the whole of Ulster must remain subject to the Imperial Parliament and to that Parliament only.

take in this matter.[1] The Emperor Francis Joseph would not grant even an hour's delay. He at once pronounced Servia's answer "unsatisfactory," and forthwith declared war.

Russia came forward to defend the Servians, because they have Russian blood in their veins. Germany took sides with Austria, for both countries had a kindred origin. France felt bound to act as an ally of Russia — not for any race reasons, but because she would thereby derive powerful military support. Furthermore she hoped that the opportunity would come for her to recover the provinces of Alsace and Lorraine, which Germany had seized in the Franco-Prussian War of 1870. German troops at once set out to move across the neutral territory of Belgium[2] in order to reach France. Belgium made fierce resistance to the violation of her soil. Then England entered the great contest, to uphold the treaty rights of the Belgians against invasion by the forces of Germany.[3]

In his war speech in the House of Commons Mr. Asquith, the Prime Minister, was very careful to define clearly the position taken by Great Britain. He said, "We are fighting to fulfil a solemn international obligation, which if it had been entered into between private persons, in the ordinary concerns of life, would have been regarded as an obligation, not only of law but of honor, which no self-respecting man could possibly have repudiated."

[1] "We were able to assure our ally [Austria] most heartily," says the German official statement, "of our agreement with her view of the situation, and to assure her that any action that she might consider it necessary to take in order to put an end to the movement in Servia directed against the existence of the Austro-Hungarian Monarchy would receive our approval." The New York *Nation*, August 27, 1914, p. 239, "The Heart of the 'White Papers.'"

[2] The neutrality of Belgium was guaranteed in 1830 by international treaty. That treaty was regarded by all the Great Powers as a part of "the permanent system of Europe." In speaking of it, Sir Edward Grey, the English Minister of Foreign Affairs, said that Belgium's independence as a sovereign nation was bound up with her neutrality, so that if that went, her independence would go with it.

Furthermore the Hague Convention of 1907, to which Germany, among other nations, was a signatory, contained this explicit provision, "Belligerents are forbidden to move troops or convoys of either munitions of war or supplies across the territory of a neutral Power."

[3] Later, Japan declared war against Germany, because that Power refused to withdraw her warships from Japanese and Chinese waters, and, at the same time, to deliver to Japan the territory of Kiao-chau which the German government held, by lease, on the northeastern coast of China.

England's movement had an instantaneous effect on the Irish question. Catholics and Protestants mingled. They cried, "We are no longer enemies, we are sons of Britain and we will fight under her flag for her defence." Later, after the Home Rule Bill had become law (§ 633), Parliament promptly suspended its operation for "a year, or during the war."

The effect of the declaration of war on the violent suffragettes (§ 629) was likewise noteworthy. They had vowed that nothing should pacify them; but suddenly they became converts to peace. They quenched the torch, they threw away the hatchet, and gave their long-suffering country a much-needed rest. It was time, for the British nation was arming to fight for its life.

What will come of this terrible conflict? That is the question every man is asking, but no one dares reply. Never before in modern history has the world seen preparations for war on so vast a scale as this. It is a death-grapple of millions with millions. Of course it is possible that an overwhelming victory or an overwhelming defeat of one or more of the Great Powers may open the way for mediation and for peace. But if this should not happen and the awful contest should go on, it would seem as though it must sooner or later exhaust the resources of all who are engaged in it. The destruction of hundreds of thousands of lives will simply precede or accompany financial ruin and universal distress. In that case the war may come to an end through a general upheaval or revolution of the forces of society. If this occurs, the map of Continental Europe, and the great autocratic monarchies now represented on it, may undergo radical reconstruction, and it is possible that these monarchies, as they are now constituted, may even disappear forever.

635. General Summary of the Development of the English Nation. Let us pause here, and consider, by way of review, the general condition of the English nation in the twentieth century and in the reign of King George V. Looking back to the time when Cæsar landed in Britain, we see that since that period an island which then had a population of a few thousand "barbarians" (§§ 4, 18) has gradually become the center of a great and powerful empire (§§ 14, 15).

The true history of the country began, however, not with Cæsar's landing, but with the Saxon invasion in 449, about five centuries later. Then the fierce blue-eyed German and Scandinavian races living on the shores of the Baltic and the North Seas took possession of Britain. They, with the help of the primitive British, or Celtic, stock, laid the foundation of a new nation. Their speech in a modified form, their laws, and their customs became in large degree permanent.

Later, missionaries from Rome converted this mixed population to the Christian faith. They baptized Britain with the name England, which it has ever since retained (§ 50).

In the eleventh century the Normans, who sprang originally from the same stock as the Northmen and Saxons, conquered the island. They grafted onto the civilization which they found there certain elements of Continental civilization (§ 126). Eventually the Saxon yeoman and the Norman knight joined hands and fortunes, and became one people (§ 192).

This union was first unmistakably recognized in the provisions of Magna Carta (§ 199). When in 1215 the barons forced King John to grant that memorable document they found it expedient to protect the rights of every class of the population. Then nobles, clergy, farmers, townsmen, and laborers whether bond or free, stood, as it were, shoulder to shoulder.

The rise of free towns marked another long step forward (§ 183). That movement secured to their inhabitants many precious privileges of self-government. Then the Wat Tyler insurrection of a subsequent period (§ 251) led gradually to the emancipation of that numerous class which had long been in partial bondage (§ 252).

Meanwhile the real unity of the people clearly showed itself at the time when the Crown began to tax the poor as well as the rich. The moment the King laid hands on the tradesman's and the laborer's pockets they demanded to have their share in making the laws. Out of that demand, made in 1265, rose the House of Commons (§§ 213, 217). It was a body, as its name implies, composed of representatives chosen mainly from the people and by the people.

Next, after generations of arduous struggle, followed by the King's grant of the Petition of Right (§ 432) and then by the great

Civil War (§§ 441, 450), it was finally settled that the House of Commons, and the House of Commons alone, had complete power over the nation's purse. From that time the King knew, once for all, that he could not take the people's money unless it was granted by the people's vote (§ 588).

After the flight of James II Parliament passed the Bill of Rights in 1689 and in 1701 the Act of Settlement (§ 497). These two revolutionary measures wrought a radical change in the government of England. They deliberately set aside the old order of hereditary royal succession and established a new order which made the King directly dependent on the people for his title and his power to rule (§ 497). About the same time, Parliament passed the Toleration Act, which granted a larger degree of religious liberty (§ 496), and in 1695 the House of Commons took action which secured the freedom of the press (§ 498).

Less than thirty years afterwards another radical change took place. Hitherto the King had appointed his own private Council, or Cabinet (§ 476), but when George I came to the throne from Germany he could speak no English. One of the members of the Cabinet became Prime Minister in 1721, and the King left the management of the government to him and to his associates (§ 534).

Two generations later another great change occurred. Watt's invention of a really practical steam engine in 1785, together with the rapid growth of manufacturing towns in the Midlands and the North of England, brought on an " Industrial Revolution " (§ 563). A factory population grew up, which found itself without any representation in Parliament. The people of that section demanded that this serious inequality should be righted. Their persistent efforts compelled the passage of the great Reform Bill of 1832. That measure (§ 582) broke up the political monopoly hitherto enjoyed in large degree by the landholders, and distributed much of the power among the middle classes.

The next important change took place at the accession of Victoria (1837). The principle was then finally established that the ruling power of the government does not center in the Crown but in the Cabinet (§ 534). Furthermore, it was settled that the Prime Minister and his Cabinet are responsible solely to the House of

Commons, which in its turn is responsible only to the expressed will of the majority of the nation (§ 587).

In the course of the next half century the Reform Bills of 1867 and 1884 extended the suffrage to the great majority of the population (§ 600). A little more than twenty years later, in 1906, the combined Liberal and Labor parties gained an overwhelming victory at the polls. This secured the workingmen fifty-four seats in Parliament (§ 628), whereas, up to that time, they had never had more than three or four. It then became evident that a new power had entered the House of Commons. From that date the nation has fully realized that although England is a monarchy in name, yet it is a republic in fact. The slow progress of time has at length given to the British people — English, Scotch, Welsh, and Irish — the great gift of practical political liberty; but along with it, it has imposed that political responsibility which is always the price which must be paid for the maintenance of liberty.

636. Characteristics of English History; the Unity of the English-Speaking Race; Conclusion. This rapid and imperfect sketch shows what has been accomplished by the people of Britain. Other European peoples may have developed earlier, and made, perhaps, more rapid advances in certain forms of civilization, but none have surpassed, nay, none have equaled, the English-speaking race in the practical character and permanence of its progress.

Guizot says [1] that the true order of national development in free government is, first, to convert the natural liberties of man into clearly defined political rights; and, next, to guarantee the security of those rights by the establishment of forces capable of maintaining them.

Nowhere do we find better illustrations of this truth than in the history of England, and of the colonies which England has planted. For the fact cannot be too strongly emphasized that *in European history England stands as the leader in the development of constitutional government* (§§ 199, 497). Trial by jury (§ 176), the legal right to resist oppression (§ 261), legislative representation (§§ 213, 217), religious freedom (§ 496), the freedom of the press (§ 498), and, finally, the principle that all political power is a

[1] Guizot's " History of Representative Government," lect. vi.

trust held for the public good,[1] — these are the assured results of Anglo-Saxon growth, and the legitimate heritage of every nation of Anglo-Saxon descent.

It is no exaggeration to say that the best men and the best minds in England, without distinction of rank or class, are now laboring for the advancement of the people. They see, what has never been so clearly seen before, that the nation is a unit, that the welfare of each depends ultimately on the welfare of all, and that the higher a man stands and the greater his wealth and privileges, so much the more is he bound to extend a helping hand to those less favored than himself.

The Socialists, it is true, demand the abolition of private property in land and the nationalizing not only of the soil but of all mines, railways, waterworks, and docks in the kingdom. Thus far, however, they have shown no disposition to attain their objects by violent action. England, by nature conservative, is slow to break the bond of historic continuity which connects her present with her past.

" Do you think we shall ever have a second revolution ? " the Duke of Wellington was once asked. " We may," answered the great general, " but if we do, it will come by act of Parliament." That reply probably expresses the general temper of the people, who believe that they can gain by the ballot more than they can by an appeal to force, knowing that theirs is

> " A land of settled government,
> A land of just and old renown,
> Where freedom broadens slowly down,
> From precedent to precedent." [2]

It is impossible for the great majority of Americans not to take a deep interest in this movement, for we can never forget that English history is in a very large degree our history, and that England is, as Hawthorne liked to call it, " our old home."

In fact, if we go back less than three centuries, the record of America becomes one with that of the mother country, which first discovered (§§ 335, 421) and first permanently settled this, and which gave us for leaders and educators Washington, Franklin,

---

[1] Macaulay's " Essay on Sir Robert Walpole."
[2] Tennyson's " You Ask Me Why."

the Adamses, and John Harvard. In descent by far the greater part of us are of English blood or of blood akin to it.[1] We owe to England — that is, to the British Isles and to the different races which have met and mingled there — much of our language, literature, law, legislative forms of government, and the essential features of our civilization. In fact, without a knowledge of her history, we cannot rightly understand our own.

Standing on her soil, we possess practically the same personal rights that we do in America ; we speak the same tongue, we meet with the same familiar names. We feel that whatever is glorious in her past is ours also ; that Westminster Abbey belongs as much to us as to her, for our ancestors helped to build its walls and their dust is gathered in its tombs ; that Shakespeare and Milton belong to us in like manner, for they wrote in the language we speak, for the instruction and delight of our fathers' fathers, who beat back the Spanish Armada and gave their lives for liberty on the fields of Marston Moor and Naseby.

Let it be granted that grave issues have arisen in the past to separate us ; yet, after all, our interests and our sympathies, like our national histories, have more in common than they have apart. The progress of each country now reacts for good on the other.[2]

---

[1] In 1840 the population of the United States, in round numbers, was 17,000,000, of whom the greater part were probably of English descent. Since then there has been an enormous immigration, 40 per cent of which was from the British Isles ; but it is perhaps safe to say that three quarters of our present population are those who were living here in 1840, with their descendants. Of the immigrants (up to 1890) coming from non-English-speaking races, the Germans and Scandinavians predominated, and it is to them, as we have seen, that the English, in large measure, owe their origin (§§ 37-39, 126). It should be noted here that the word "English" is used so as to include the people of the United Kingdom and their descendants on both sides of the Atlantic.

[2] In this connection the testimony of Captain Alfred T. Mahan, in his recent work, "The Problem of Asia," is worth quoting here. He says (p. 187), speaking of our late war with Spain : "The writer has been assured, by an authority in which he entirely trusts, that to a proposition made to Great Britain to enter into a combination to constrain the use of our [United States] power, — as Japan was five years ago constrained by the joint action of Russia, France, and Germany, — the reply [of Great Britain] was not only a positive refusal to enter into such a combination [against the United States], but an assurance of active resistance to it if attempted. . . . Call such an attitude [on the part of England toward the United States] friendship, or policy, as you will, — the name is immaterial ; the fact is the essential thing and will endure, because it rests upon solid interest."

If we consider the total combined population of the United States and of the British Empire, we find that to-day upwards of 150,000,000 people speak the English tongue and are governed by the fundamental principles of that Common Law which has its root in English soil. This population holds possession of more than 15,000,000 square miles of the earth's surface, — an area much larger than that of the united continents of North America and Europe. By far the greater part of the wealth and power of the globe is theirs.

They have expanded by their territorial and colonial growth as no other people have. They have absorbed and assimilated the multitudes of emigrants from every quarter of the globe that have poured into their dominions.

The result is that the inhabitants of the British Isles, of Australia, of New Zealand, of a part of South Africa, of the United States, and of Canada practically form one great Anglo-Saxon race,[1] diverse in origin, separated by distance, but everywhere exhibiting the same spirit of intelligent enterprise and of steady, resistless growth. Thus considered, America and England are necessary one to the other. Their interests now and in the future are essentially the same. Both countries are virtually pledged to make every effort to maintain liberty and self-government, and also to maintain mutual peace by arbitration. The crisis of the great European War of 1914 gives still greater emphasis to these vitally important principles.

In view of these facts let us say, with an eminent thinker[2] whose intellectual home was on both sides of the Atlantic : " Whatever there be between the two nations to forget and forgive, is forgotten and forgiven. If the two peoples, which are one, be true to their duty, who can doubt that the destinies of the world must be in large measure committed to their hands ? "

---

[1] Such apparent exceptions as the Dutch in South Africa, the French in Canada, and the Negroes in the United States do not essentially affect the truth of this statement, since in practice the people of these races uphold the great fundamental principles on which all Anglo-Saxon government rests.

[2] Dean Farrar, Address on General Grant, Westminster Abbey, 1885.

GENERAL SUMMARY OF ENGLISH CONSTITUTIONAL HISTORY [1]

1. Origin and Primitive Government of the English People. The main body of the English people did not originate in Britain, but in Northwestern Germany. The Jutes, Saxons, and Angles were independent, kindred tribes living on the banks of the Elbe and its vicinity.

They had no written laws, but obeyed time-honored customs which had all the force of laws. All matters of public importance were decided by each tribe at meetings held in the open air. There every freeman had an equal voice in the decision. There the people chose their rulers and military leaders; they discussed questions of peace and war; finally, acting as a high court of justice, they tried criminals and settled disputes about property.

In these rude methods we see the beginning of the English Constitution. Its growth has been the slow work of centuries, but the great principles underlying it have never changed. At every stage of their progress the English people and their descendants throughout the globe have claimed the right of self-government; and, if we except the period of the Norman Conquest, whenever that right has been persistently withheld or denied, the people have risen in arms and regained it.

2. Conquest of Britain; Origin and Power of the King. After the Romans abandoned Britain the English invaded the island 449 (?), and in the course of a hundred and fifty years conquered it and established a number of rival settlements. The native Britons were, in great part, killed off or driven to take refuge in Wales and Cornwall.

The conquerors brought to their new home the methods of government and modes of life to which they had been accustomed in Germany. A cluster of towns — that is, a small number of enclosed habitations (§ 103) — formed a hundred (a district having either a hundred families or able to furnish a hundred warriors); a cluster of hundreds formed a shire or county. Each of these divisions had its public meeting, composed of all its freemen or their representatives, for the management of

---

[1] **This Summary** is inserted for the benefit of those who desire a compact, connected view of the development of the English Constitution, such as may be conveniently used either for reference, for a general review of the subject, or for purposes of special study. — D. H. M.

For authorities, see Stubbs (449–1485); Hallam (1485–1760); May (1760–1870); Amos (1870–1880); see also Hansard and Cobbett's "Parliamentary History," the works of Freeman, Taswell-Langmead (the best one-volume Constitutional History), Feilden's Manual, and A. L. Lowell's "The Government of England," 2 vols., in the CLASSIFIED LIST OF BOOKS beginning on page xxxvi.

The references inserted in parentheses are to sections in the body of the history.

its own affairs. But a state of war — for the English tribes fought each other as well as fought the Britons — made a strong central government necessary. For this reason the leader of each tribe was made king. At first he was chosen, at large, by the entire tribe; later, unless there was some good reason for a different choice, the King's eldest son was selected as his successor. Thus the right to rule was practically fixed in the line of a certain family descent.

The ruler of each of these petty kingdoms acted as commander-in-chief in war, and as supreme judge in law.

3. The Witenagemot, or General Council. In all other respects the King's authority was limited — except when he was strong enough to get his own way — by the Witenagemot, or General Council. This body consisted of the chief men of each kingdom acting in behalf of its people.[1] It exercised the following powers: (1) It elected the King, and if the people confirmed the choice, he was crowned. (2) If the King proved unsatisfactory, the Council might depose him and choose a successor. (3) The King, with the consent of the Council, made the laws, — that is, he declared the customs of the tribe. (4) The King, with the Council, appointed the chief officers of the kingdom (after the introduction of Christianity this included the bishops); but the King alone appointed the sheriff, to represent him and collect the revenue in each shire. (5) The Council confirmed or denied grants of portions of the public lands made by the King to private persons. (6) The Council acted as the high court of justice, the King sitting as supreme judge. (7) The Council, with the King, discussed all questions of importance, — such as the levying of taxes, and the making of treaties; smaller matters were left to the towns, hundreds, and shires to settle for themselves. After the consolidation of the different English kingdoms into one, the Witenagemot expanded into the National Council. In it we see " the true beginning of the Parliament of England."

4. How England became a United Kingdom; Influence of the Church and of the Danish Invasions. For a number of centuries Britain consisted of a number of little rival kingdoms, almost constantly at war with each other. Meanwhile missionaries from Rome had introduced Christianity, 597. Through the influence of Theodore of Tarsus, Archbishop of Canterbury (668), the clergy of the different hostile kingdoms met in general Church councils.[2] This religious unity of action prepared the way for political unity. The Catholic Church — the only Christian Church (except the Greek Church) then existing — made men feel that their highest interests were one; it " created the nation " (§ 48).

This was the first cause of the union of the kingdoms. The second was the invasion of the Danes. These fierce marauders forced the people

---

[1] The Witenagemot (i.e. the Meeting of the Witan, or Wise Men, § 80), says Stubbs ("Select Charters"), represented the people, although it was not a collection of representatives.

[2] This movement began several years earlier (§ 48), but Theodore of Tarsus was its first great organizer.

south of the Thames to join in common defense, under the leadership of Alfred, King of the West Saxons. By the Treaty of Wedmore, 878, the Danes were compelled to give up Southwestern England, but they retained the whole of the Northeast. About the middle of the tenth century, one of Alfred's grandsons conquered the Danes, and took the title of " King of England." [1] Later, the Danes, reënforced by fresh invasions of their countrymen, made themselves masters of the land; yet Canute, the most powerful of these Danish kings, ruled according to English methods. At length the great body of the people united in choosing Edward the Confessor king (1042–1066). He was English by birth, but Norman by education. Under him the unity of the English kingdom was, in name at least, fully restored.

5. Beginning of the Feudal System; its Results. Meantime a great change had taken place in England with respect to holding land (§§ 86, 150). We shall see clearly to what that change was tending if we look at the condition of France. There a system of government and of land tenure existed known as the Feudal System. Under it the King was regarded as the owner of the entire realm. He granted, with his royal protection, the use of portions of the land to his chief men or nobles, with the privilege of building castles and of establishing courts of justice on these estates. Such grants were made on two conditions: (1) that the tenants should take part in the King's Council; (2) that they should do military service in the King's behalf, and furnish besides a certain number of fully armed horsemen in proportion to the amount of land they had received. So long as they fulfilled these conditions — made under oath — they could retain their estates, and hand them down to their children; but if they failed to keep their oath, they forfeited the land to the King.

These great military barons or lords let out parts of their immense manors,[2] or estates, on similar conditions, — namely (1) that their vassals or tenants should pay rent to them by doing military or other service; and (2) that they should agree that all questions concerning their rights and duties should be tried in the lord's private court.[3] On the other hand, the lord of the manor pledged himself to protect his vassals.

On every manor there were usually three classes of these tenants: (1) those who discharged their rent by doing military duty; (2) those

---

[1] Some authorities consider Edgar (959) as the first " King of all England." In 829 Egbert, King of the West Saxons, forced all the other Saxon Kings of Britain to acknowledge him as their " Overlord " (§ 49).

[2] Manor (măn'or): see plan of a manor (Old French *manoir*, "a mansion") on page 75, the estate of a feudal lord. Every manor had two courts. The most important of these was the "*court baron*." It was composed of all the free tenants of the manor, with the lord (or his representative) presiding. It dealt with civil cases only. The second court was the "*court customary*," which dealt with cases connected with villeinage. The manors held by the greater barons had a third court, the "*court leet*," which dealt with criminal cases, and could inflict the death penalty. In all cases the decisions of the manorial courts would be pretty sure to be in the lord's favor. In England, however, these courts never acquired the degree of power which they did on the Continent.

[3] See note above, on the manor.

who paid by a certain fixed amount of labor — or, if they preferred, in produce or in money; (3) the villeins, or common laborers, who were bound to remain on the estate and work for the lord, and whose condition, although they were not wholly destitute of legal rights, was practically not very much above that of slaves (§ 113).

But there was another way by which men might enter the Feudal System; for while it was growing up there were many small free land-holders, who owned their farms and owed no man any service whatever. In those times of constant civil war such men would be almost in daily peril of losing, not only their property, but their lives. To escape this danger, they would hasten to "commend" themselves to some powerful neighboring lord. To do this, they pledged themselves to become "his men," surrendered their farms to him, and received them again as feudal vassals. That is, the lord bound himself to protect them against their enemies, and they bound themselves to do "suit and service"[1] like the other tenants of the manor; *for "suit and service" on the one side, and "protection" on the other, made up the threefold foundation of the Feudal System.*

Thus in time all classes of society became bound together. At the top stood the King, who was no man's tenant, but, in name at least, every man's master; at the bottom crouched the villein, who was no man's master, but was, in fact, the most servile and helpless of tenants.

Such was the condition of things in France. In England, however, this system of land tenure was not completely established until after the Norman Conquest, 1066; for in England the tie which bound men to the King and to each other was originally one of pure choice, and had nothing directly to do with land. Gradually, however, this changed; and by the time of Edward the Confessor land in England had come to be held on conditions so closely resembling those of France that one step more — and that a very short one — would have made England a kingdom exhibiting all the most dangerous features of French feudalism.

For, notwithstanding certain advantages,[2] feudalism had this great evil: that the chief nobles often became in time more powerful than the King. This danger now menaced England. For convenience Canute the Dane had divided the realm into four earldoms. The holders of these vast estates had grown so mighty that they scorned royal authority. Edward the Confessor did not dare resist them. The ambition of each earl was to get the supreme mastery. This threatened to bring on civil war, and to split the kingdom into fragments. Fortunately for the welfare of the nation, William, Duke of Normandy, by his invasion and conquest of England, 1066, put an effectual stop to the selfish schemes of these four rival nobles.

---

[1] That is, they pledged themselves to do suit in the lord's private court, and to do service in his army.

[2] On the Advantages of Feudalism, see § 87.

6. William the Conqueror and his Work. After William's victory at Hastings and march on London (§§ 74, 107), the National Council chose him sovereign, — they would not have dared to refuse, — and he was crowned by the Archbishop of York in Westminster Abbey. This coronation made him the legal successor of the line of English kings. In form, therefore, there was no break in the order of government; for though William had forced himself upon the throne, he had done so according to law and custom, and not directly by the sword.

Great changes followed the conquest, but they were not violent. The King abolished the four great earldoms (§ 64), and restored national unity. He gradually dispossessed the chief English landholders of their lands, and bestowed them, under strict feudal laws, on his Norman followers. He likewise gave all the highest positions in the Church to Norman bishops and abbots. The National Council now changed its character. It became simply a body of Norman barons, who were bound by feudal custom to meet with the King. But they did not restrain his authority; for William would brook no interference with his will from any one, not even from the Pope himself (§ 118).

But though the Conqueror had a tyrant's power, he rarely used it like a tyrant. We have seen [1] that the great excellence of the early English government lay in the fact that the towns, hundreds, and shires were self-governing in all local matters; the drawback to this system was its lack of unity and of a strong central power that could make itself respected and obeyed. William supplied this power, — without which there could be no true national strength, — yet at the same time he was careful to encourage the local system of self-government. He gave London a liberal charter to protect its rights and liberties (§ 107). He began the organization of a royal court of justice; he checked the rapacious Norman barons in their efforts to get control of the people's courts.

Furthermore, side by side with the feudal cavalry army, he maintained the old English county militia of foot soldiers, in which every freeman was bound to serve. He used this militia, when necessary, to prevent the barons from getting the upper hand, and so destroying those liberties which were protected by the Crown as its own best safeguard against the plots of the nobles.

Next, William had a census, survey, and valuation made of all the estates in the kingdom outside London which were worth examination. The result of this great work was recorded in Domesday Book (§ 120). By means of that book — still preserved — the King knew what no English ruler had known before him; that was, the property-holding population and resources of the kingdom. Thus a solid foundation was laid on which to establish the feudal revenue and the military power of the Crown.

---

[1] See §§ 2, 3 of this Summary.

Finally, just before his death, the Conqueror completed the organization of his government. Hitherto the vassals of the great barons had been bound to them alone. They were sworn to fight for their masters, even if those masters rose in open rebellion against the sovereign. William changed all that. At a meeting held at Salisbury, 1086, he compelled every landholder in England, from the greatest to the smallest, — sixty thousand, it is said, — to swear to be "faithful to him against all others" (§ 121). By that oath he "broke the neck of the Feudal System" *as a form of government*, though he retained and developed the principle of feudal land tenure. Thus at one stroke he made the Crown the supreme power in England; had he not done so, the nation would soon have fallen a prey to civil war.

7. William's Norman Successors. William Rufus has a bad name in history, and he fully deserves it. But he had this merit: he held the Norman barons in check with a stiff hand, and so, in one way, gave the country comparative peace.

His successor, Henry I, granted, 1100, a Charter of Liberties (§ 135, note 1) to his people, by which he recognized the sacredness of the old English laws for the protection of life and property. Somewhat more than a century later this document became, as we shall see, the basis of the most celebrated charter known in English history. Henry attempted important reforms in the administration of the laws, and laid the foundation of that system which his grandson, Henry II, was to develop and establish. By these measures he gained the title of the "Lion of Justice," who "made peace for both man and beast." Furthermore, in an important controversy with the Pope respecting the appointment of bishops (§ 136), Henry obtained the right (1107) to require that both bishops and abbots, after taking possession of their Church estates, should be obliged like the baron to furnish troops for the defense of the kingdom.

But in the next reign — that of Stephen — the barons got the upper hand, and the King was powerless to control them. They built castles without royal license, and from these private fortresses they sallied forth to ravage, rob, and murder in all directions. Had that period of terror continued much longer, England would have been torn to pieces by a multitude of greedy tyrants.

8. Reforms of Henry II; Scutage; Assize of Clarendon; Juries; Constitutions of Clarendon. With Henry II the true reign of law begins. To carry out the reforms begun by his grandfather, Henry I, the King fought both barons and clergy. Over the first he won a complete and final victory; over the second he gained a partial one.

Henry began his work by pulling down the unlicensed castles built by the "robber barons" in Stephen's reign. But, according to feudal usage, the King was dependent on these very barons for his cavalry, — his chief armed force. He resolved to make himself independent of their reluctant aid. To do this he offered to release them from military service, providing they would pay a tax, called "scutage," or "shield money" (1159).[1] The barons gladly accepted the offer. With the money Henry was able to hire "mercenaries," or foreign troops, to fight for him abroad, and, if need be, in England as well. Thus he struck a great blow at the power of the barons, since they, through disuse of arms, grew weaker, while the King grew steadily stronger. To complete the work, Henry, many years later (1181), reorganized the old English national militia,[2] and made it thoroughly effective for the defense of the royal authority. For just a hundred years (1074–1174) the barons had been trying to overthrow the government; under Henry II the long struggle came to an end, and the royal power triumphed.

But in getting the military control of the kingdom Henry had won only half of the victory he was seeking; to complete his supremacy over the powerful nobles, the King must obtain control of the administration of justice.

In order to do this more effectually, Henry issued the Assize of Clarendon (1166). It was the first true national code of law ever put forth by an English king, since previous codes had been little more than summaries of old "customs." The realm had already been divided into six circuits, having three judges for each circuit. The Assize of Clarendon gave these judges power not only to enter and preside over every county court, but also over every court held by a baron on his manor. This put a pretty decisive check to the hitherto uncontrolled baronial system of justice — or injustice — with its private dungeons and its private gibbets. It brought everything under the eye of the King's judges, so that those who wished to appeal to them could now do so without the expense, trouble, and danger of a journey to the royal palace.

Again, it had been the practice among the Norman barons to settle disputes about land by the barbarous method of Trial by Battle (§ 148); Henry gave tenants the right to have the case decided by a body of twelve knights acquainted with the facts.

In criminal cases a great change was likewise effected. Henceforth twelve men from each hundred, with four from each township, — sixteen at least, — acting as a grand jury, were to present all suspected criminals to the circuit judges.[3] The judges sent them to the Ordeal (§ 91); if they failed to pass it, they were then punished by law as convicted felons; if they did pass it, they were banished from the kingdom as persons of evil repute. After the abolition of the Ordeal (1215), a petty jury of witnesses was allowed to testify in favor of the accused, and clear them if they could from the charges brought by the grand jury. If their testimony was not decisive, more witnesses were added until twelve were

---

[1] Scutage : see § 161. The demand for scutage seems to show that the feudal tenure was now fully organized, and that the whole realm was by this time divided into knights' fees, — that is, into portions of land yielding £20 annually, — each of which was obliged to furnish one fully armed, well-mounted knight to serve the King (if called on) for forty days annually.

[2] National militia : see §§ 96, 150.

[3] See the Assize of Clarendon (1166) in Stubbs's " Select Charters."

obtained who could unanimously decide one way or the other. In the course of time [1] this smaller body became judges of the evidence for or against the accused, and thus the modern system of Trial by Jury was established about 1350.

These reforms had three important results : (1) they greatly diminished the power of the barons by taking the administration of justice, in large measure, out of their hands ; (2) they established a more uniform system of law ; (3) they brought large sums of money, in the way of court fees and fines, into the King's treasury, and so made him stronger than ever.

But meanwhile Henry was carrying on a still sharper battle in his attempt to bring the Church courts — which William I had separated from the ordinary courts — under control of the same system of justice. In these Church courts any person claiming to belong to the clergy had a right to be tried. Such courts had no power to inflict death, even for murder. In Stephen's reign many notorious criminals had managed to get themselves enrolled among the clergy, and had thus escaped the hanging they deserved. Henry was determined to have all men — in the circle of clergy or out of it — stand equal before the law. Instead of two kinds of justice, he would have but one ; this would not only secure a still higher uniformity of law, but it would sweep into the King's treasury many fat fees and fines which the Church courts were then getting for themselves.

By the laws entitled the "Constitutions of Clarendon," 1164 (§ 165), the common courts were empowered to decide whether a man claiming to belong to the clergy should be tried by the Church courts or not. If they granted him the privilege of a Church-court trial, they kept a sharp watch on the progress of the case ; if the accused was convicted, he must then be handed over to the judges of the ordinary courts, and they took especial pains to convince him of the Bible truth, that "the way of the transgressor is hard." For a time the Constitutions were rigidly enforced, but in the end Henry was forced to renounce them. Later, however, the principle he had endeavored to set up was fully established.[2]

The greatest result springing from Henry's efforts was the training of the people in public affairs, and the definitive establishment of that system of Common Law which regards the people as the supreme source of both law and government, and which is directly and vitally connected with the principle of representation and of trial by jury.[3]

9. Rise of Free Towns. While these important changes were taking place, the towns were growing in population and wealth (§ 183). But as

---

[1] The date usually given is 1350 ; but as late as the reign of George I juries were accustomed to bring in verdicts determined partly by their own personal knowledge of the facts. See Taswell-Langmead (revised edition), p. 179.

[2] Edward I limited the jurisdiction of the Church courts to purely spiritual cases, such as heresy and the like ; but the work which he, following the example of Henry II, had undertaken was not fully accomplished until the fifteenth century.

[3] See Green's "Henry II," in the English Statesmen Series.

these towns occupied land belonging either directly to the King or to some baron, they were subject to the authority of one or the other, and so possessed no real freedom. In the reign of Richard I many towns purchased certain rights of self-government from the King.[1] This power of controlling their own affairs greatly increased their prosperity, and in time, as we shall see, secured them a voice in the management of the affairs of the nation.

10. John's Loss of Normandy; Magna Carta. Up to John's reign many barons continued to hold large estates in Normandy, in addition to those they had acquired in England; hence their interests were divided between the two countries. Through war John lost his French possessions (§ 191). Henceforth the barons shut out from Normandy came to look upon England as their true home. From Henry II's reign the Normans and the English had been gradually mingling; from this time they became practically one people. John's tyranny and cruelty brought their union into sharp, decisive action. The result of his greed for money, and his defiance of all law, was a tremendous insurrection. Before this time the people had always taken the side of the King against the barons; now, with equal reason, they turned about and rose with the barons against the King.

Under the guidance of Archbishop Langton, barons, clergy, and people demanded reform. The Archbishop brought out the half-forgotten charter of Henry I (§ 135, note 1). This now furnished a model for Magna Carta, or the " Great Charter of the Liberties of England." [2]

It contained nothing that was new in principle. It was simply a clearer, fuller, stronger statement of those " rights of Englishmen which were already old."

John, though wild with rage, did not dare refuse to affix his royal seal to the Great Charter of 1215. By doing so he solemnly guaranteed: (1) the rights of the Church; (2) those of the barons; (3) those of all freemen; (4) those of the villeins, or farm laborers. The value of this charter to the people at large is shown by the fact that nearly one third of its sixty-three articles were inserted in their behalf. Of these articles the most important was that which declared that no man should be deprived of liberty or property, or injured in body or estate, save by the judgment of his equals or by the law of the land.

In regard to taxation, the Charter provided that, except the customary feudal " aids," [3] none should be levied unless by the consent of the National Council. Finally, the Charter expressly provided that twenty-five barons — one of whom was mayor of London — should be appointed to compel the King to carry out his agreement.

11. Henry III and the Great Charter; the Forest Charter; Provisions of Oxford; Rise of the House of Commons; Important Land Laws. Under Henry III the Great Charter was reissued. But the important

---

[1] See § 183.   [2] Magna Carta: see §§ 195–202; and see Constitutional Documents, p. xxix.
[3] For the three customary feudal aids, see § 150.

articles which forbade the King to levy taxes except by consent of the National Council, together with some others restricting his power to increase his revenue, were dropped, and never again restored.[1]

On the other hand, Henry was obliged to issue a Forest Charter, based on certain articles of Magna Carta, which declared that no man should lose life or limb for hunting in the royal forests.

Though the Great Charter was now shorn of some of its safeguards to liberty, yet it was still so highly prized that its confirmation was purchased at a high price from successive sovereigns. Down to the second year of Henry VI's reign (1423) we find that it had been confirmed no less than thirty-seven times.

Notwithstanding his solemn oath (§ 210), the vain and worthless Henry III deliberately violated the provisions of the Charter, in order to raise money to waste in his foolish foreign wars or on his court circle of French favorites.

Finally (1258), a body of armed barons, led by Simon de Montfort, Earl of Leicester, forced the King to summon a Parliament at Oxford. There a scheme of reform, called the "Provisions of Oxford," was adopted (§ 209). By these Provisions, which Henry swore to observe, the government was practically taken out of the King's hands, — at least as far as he had power to do mischief, — and entrusted to certain councils or committees of state.

A few years later, Henry refused to abide by the Provisions of Oxford, and civil war broke out. De Montfort, Earl of Leicester, gained a decisive victory at Lewes, and captured the King. The Earl then summoned a National Council, made up of those who favored his policy of reform (§ 213). This was the famous Parliament of 1265. To it De Montfort summoned: (1) a small number of barons; (2) a large number of the higher clergy; (3) two knights, or country gentlemen, from each shire; (4) two burghers, or citizens, from every town.

The knights of the shire had been summoned to Parliament before;[2] but this was the first time that the towns had been invited to send representatives. By that act the Earl set the example of giving the people at large a fuller share in the government than they had yet had. To De Montfort, therefore, justly belongs the glory of being "the founder of the House of Commons." His work, however, was defective (§ 213); and owing, perhaps, to his death shortly afterwards at the battle of Evesham (1265), the regular and continuous representation of the towns did not begin until thirty years later.

Meanwhile, 1279–1290, three land laws of great importance were enacted. The first limited the acquisition of landed property by the Church;[3] the second encouraged the transmission of land by will to the

---

[1] See Stubbs's "Select Charters" (Edward I), p. 484; but compare note 1, p. 443.

[2] They were first summoned by John in 1213.

[3] Statute of Mortmain (1279): see § 226; it was especially directed against the acquisition of land by monasteries.

eldest son, thus keeping estates together instead of breaking them up among several heirs;[1] the third made purchasers of estates the direct feudal tenants of the King.[2] The object of these three laws was to prevent landholders from evading their feudal obligations; hence they decidedly strengthened the royal power.[3]

12. Edward I's "Model Parliament"; Confirmation of the Charters. In 1295 Edward I, one of the ablest men that ever sat on the English throne, adopted De Montfort's scheme of representation. The King was greatly pressed for money, and his object was to get the help of the towns, and thus secure a system of taxation which should include all classes. With the significant words, "That which toucheth all should be approved by all," he summoned to Westminster the first really complete or "Model Parliament" (§ 217),[4] consisting of King, Lords (temporal and spiritual), and Commons.[5] The form Parliament then received it has kept substantially ever since. We shall see how from this time the Commons gradually grew in influence, — though with periods of relapse, — until at length they have become the controlling power in legislation.

Two years after the meeting of the "Model Parliament," in order to get money to carry on a war with France, Edward levied a tax on the barons, and seized a large quantity of wool belonging to the merchants. So determined was the resistance to these acts that civil war was threatened. In order to avert it, the King was obliged to summon a Parliament, 1297, and to sign a confirmation of all previous charters of liberties, including the Great Charter (§ 202). He furthermore bound himself in the most solemn manner not to tax his subjects or seize their goods without their consent. Henceforth Parliament alone was considered to hold control of the nation's purse; and although this principle was afterwards evaded, no king openly denied its binding force. Furthermore, in Edward's reign the House of Commons gained (1322), for the first time, a direct share in legislation. This step had results of supreme constitutional importance.

13. Division of Parliament into Two Houses; Growth of the Power of the Commons; Legislation by Statute; Impeachment; Power over the Purse. In Edward III's reign a great change occurred in Parliament. The knights of the shire (about 1343) joined the representatives

---

[1] Statute De Donis Conditionalibus or Entail (Westminster II) (1285): see § 225.

[2] Statute of Quia Emptores (1290): see § 225.

[3] During the same period the Statute of Winchester (1285) reorganized the national militia and the police system (§ 224).

[4] De Montfort's Parliament was not wholly lawful and regular, because not voluntarily summoned by the King himself. Parliament must be summoned by the sovereign, opened by the sovereign (in person or by commission); all laws require the sovereign's signature to complete them; and, finally, Parliament can be suspended or dissolved by the sovereign only.

[5] The lower clergy were summoned to send representatives to the Commons; but they came very irregularly, and in the fourteenth century ceased coming altogether. From that time they voted their supplies for the Crown in Convocation, until 1663, when Convocation ceased to meet. The higher clergy — bishops and abbots — met with the House of Lords.

from the towns, and began to sit apart from the Lords as a distinct House of Commons. This union gave that House a new character, and invested it with a power in Parliament which the representation from the towns alone could not have exerted. But though thus strengthened, the Commons did not venture to claim an equal part with the Lords in framing laws. Their attitude was that of humble petitioners. When they had voted the supplies of money which the King asked for, the Commons might then meekly beg for legislation. Even when the King and the Lords assented to their petitions, the Commons often found to their disappointment that the laws which had been promised did not correspond to those for which they had asked. Henry V pledged his word (1414) that the petitions, when accepted, should be made into laws without any alteration. But, as a matter of fact, this was not effectually done until near the close of the reign of Henry VI (about 1461). Then the Commons succeeded in obtaining the right to present proposed laws in the form of regular bills instead of petitions. These bills when enacted became statutes or acts of Parliament, as we know them to-day. This change was a most important one, since it made it impossible for the King with the Lords to fraudulently defeat the expressed will of the Commons after they had once assented to the legislation the Commons desired.

Meanwhile the Commons gained, for the first time (1376), the right of impeaching such ministers of the Crown as they had reason to believe were unfaithful to the interests of the people. This, of course, put an immense restraining power in their hands, since they could now make the ministers responsible, in great measure, for the King.[1]

Next (1406), the Commons insisted on having an account rendered of the money spent by the King; and at times they even limited[2] their appropriations of money to particular purposes. Finally, in 1407, the Commons took the most decided step of all. They boldly demanded and obtained *the exclusive right of making all grants of money* required by the Crown.[3]

In future the King, unless he violated the law, had to look to the Commons — that is, to the direct representation of the mass of the people — for his chief supplies. This made the will of the Commons more powerful than it had ever been.

14. Religious Legislation; Emancipation of the Villeins; Disfranchisement of County Electors. The Parliament of Merton had already (1236) refused to introduce the canon or ecclesiastical law (§ 265). In the next century two very important statutes relating to the Church were enacted, — that of Provisors (1350)[4] and the Great Act of Præmunire,

---

[1] But after 1450 the Commons ceased to exercise the right of impeachment until 1621, when they impeached Lord Bacon and others.

[2] The Commons dropped the right of appropriating money for specific objects, — except in a single instance under Henry VI, — and did not revive it until 1624.

[3] This right the Commons never surrendered.

[4] Provisors: this was a law forbidding the Pope to provide any person (by anticipation) with a position in the English Church until the death of the incumbent.

1393,[1] — limiting the power of the Pope over the English Church. On the other hand, the rise of the Lollards had caused a statute to be passed (1401) against heretics, and under it the first martyr had been burned in England. During this period the villeins had risen in insurrection (1381) (§§ 250–252), and were gradually gaining their liberty. Thus a very large body of people who had been practically excluded from political rights now began to slowly acquire them.[2] But, on the other hand, a statute was enacted (1430) which prohibited all persons having an income of less than forty shillings a year — or what would be equal to forty pounds at the present value of money — from voting for knights of the shire (§ 297). The consequence was that the poorer and humbler classes in the country were no longer directly represented in the House of Commons.

15. Wars of the Roses; Decline of Parliament; Partial Revival of its Power under Elizabeth. The Civil Wars of the Roses (1455–1485) gave a decided check to the further development of parliamentary power. Many noble families were ruined by the protracted struggle, and the new nobles created by the King were pledged to uphold the interests of the Crown. Furthermore, numerous towns absorbed in their own local affairs ceased to elect members to the Commons. Thus, with a House of Lords on the side of royal authority, and with a House of Commons diminished in numbers and in influence, the decline of the independent attitude of Parliament was inevitable.

The result of these changes was very marked. From the reign of Henry VI to that of Elizabeth, a period of nearly a hundred and forty years, "the voice of Parliament was rarely heard." The Tudors practically set up a new or "personal monarchy," in which their will rose above both Parliament and the constitution;[3] and Henry VII, instead of asking the Commons for money, extorted it by fines enforced by his Court of Star Chamber, or compelled his wealthy subjects to grant it to him in "benevolences" (§ 330), — those "loving contributions," as the King called them, "lovingly advanced"!

During this period England laid claim to a new continent, and Henry VIII, repudiating the authority of the Pope, declared himself the "supreme head" (1535) of the English Catholic Church. In the next reign (Edward VI) the Catholic worship, which had existed in England for nearly a thousand years, was abolished (1540), and the Protestant faith became henceforth — except during Mary's short reign — the established religion of the kingdom. It was enforced by two Acts of Uniformity (1549, 1552). One effect of the overthrow of Catholicism

---

[1] Præmunire: see Constitutional Documents, p. xxxii. Neither the law of Provisors nor of Præmunire was strictly enforced until Henry VIII's reign.

[2] Villeins appear, however, to have had the right of voting for knights of the shire until the statute of 1430 disfranchised them.

[3] Theoretically Henry VII's power was restrained by certain checks (see § 328, note 1), and even Henry VIII generally ruled according to the letter of the law, however much he may have violated its spirit. It is noticeable, too, that it was under Henry VIII (1541) that Parliament first formally claimed freedom of speech as one of its "undoubted privileges."

was to change the character of the House of Lords, by reducing the number of spiritual lords from a majority to a minority, as they have ever since remained (§ 406, note 2).

At the beginning of Elizabeth's reign the Second Act of Supremacy (1559) shut out all Catholics from the House of Commons (§ 382), Protestantism was fully and finally established as the state religion,[1] embodied in the creed known as the Thirty-Nine Articles (1563); and by the Third Act of Uniformity (1559) very severe measures were taken against all — whether Catholics or Puritans — who refused to conform to the Episcopal mode of worship. The High Commission Court was organized (1583) to try and to punish heretics — whether Catholics or Puritans. The great number of paupers caused by the destruction of the monasteries under Henry VIII and the gradual decay of relations of feudal service caused the passage of the first Poor Law (1601) (§ 403), and so brought the Government face to face with a problem which has never yet been satisfactorily settled; namely, what to do with habitual paupers and tramps.

The closing part of Elizabeth's reign marks the revival of parliamentary power. The House of Commons now had many Puritan members, and they did not hesitate to assert their right to advise the Queen on all questions of national importance. Elizabeth sharply rebuked them for presuming to meddle with questions of religion, or for urging her either to take a husband or to name a successor to the throne; but even she did not venture to run directly counter to the will of the people. When the Commons demanded (1601) that she should put a stop to the pernicious practice of granting trading monopolies (§ 388) to her favorites, she was obliged to yield her assent.

16. James I; the Divine Right of Kings; Struggle with Parliament. James began his reign by declaring that kings rule not by the will of the people, but by "divine right." "God makes the King," said he, "and the King makes the law" (§ 419). For this reason he demanded that his proclamations should have all the force of acts of Parliament. Furthermore, since he appointed the judges, he could generally get their decisions to support him; thus he made even the courts of justice serve as instruments of his will. In his arrogance he declared that neither Parliament nor the people had any right to discuss matters of state, whether foreign or domestic, since he was resolved to reserve such questions for the royal intellect to deal with. By his religious intolerance he maddened both Puritans and Catholics, and the Pilgrim Fathers fled from England to escape his tyranny.

But there was a limit set to his overbearing conceit. When he dictated to the Commons (1604) what persons should sit in that body, they indignantly refused to submit to any interference on his part, and their refusal was so emphatic that James never brought the matter up again.

[1] By the Third Act of Uniformity and the establishment of the High Commission Court (§ 382). The First and Second Acts of Uniformity were enacted under Edward VI (§ 362).

The King, however, was so determined to shut out members whom he did not like that he attempted to gain his ends by having such persons seized on charges of debt and thrown into prison. The Commons, on the other hand, not only insisted that their ancient privilege of exemption from arrest in such cases should be respected, but they passed a special law (1604) to clinch the privilege.

Ten years later (1614) James, pressed for money, called a Parliament to get supplies. He had taken precautions to get a majority of members elected who would, he hoped, vote him what he wanted. But to his dismay the Commons declined to grant him a penny unless he would promise to cease imposing illegal duties on merchandise. The King angrily refused, and dissolved the so-called " Addled Parliament." [1]

Finally, in order to show James that it would not be trifled with, a later Parliament (1621) revived the right of impeachment, which had not been resorted to since 1450. [2] The Commons now charged Lord Chancellor Bacon, judge of the High Court of Chancery, and " keeper of the King's conscience," with accepting bribes. Bacon held the highest office in the gift of the Crown, and the real object of the impeachment was to strike the King through the person of his chief official and supporter. Bacon confessed his crime, saying, " I was the justest judge that was in England these fifty years, but it was the justest censure in Parliament that was these two hundred years."

James tried his best to save his servile favorite, but it was useless, and Bacon was convicted, disgraced, and partially punished (§ 425).

The Commons of the same Parliament petitioned the King against the alleged growth of the Catholic religion in the kingdom, and especially against the proposed marriage of the Prince of Wales to a Spanish Catholic princess. James ordered the Commons to let mysteries of state alone. They claimed liberty of speech. The King asserted that they had no liberties except such as the royal power saw fit to grant. Then the Commons drew up their famous Protest, in which they declared that their liberties were not derived from the King, but were " the ancient and undoubted birthright and inheritance of the people of England." In his rage James ordered the journal of the Commons to be brought to him, tore out the Protest with his own hand, and sent five of the members of the House to prison (§ 419). This rash act made the Commons more determined than ever not to yield to arbitrary power. James died three years later, leaving his unfortunate son Charles to settle the angry controversy he had raised. Macaulay remarks that James seems to have been sent to hasten the coming of Civil War.

17. Charles I ; Forced Loans ; the Petition of Right. Charles I came to the throne full of his father's lofty ideas of the Divine Right of Kings

---

[1] This Parliament was nicknamed the " Addled Parliament," because it did not enact a single law, though it most effectually " addled " the King's plans (§ 424).

[2] See § 13 of this Summary.

to govern as they pleased. In private life he was conscientious, but in his public policy he was a man "of dark and crooked ways."

He had married a French Catholic princess, and the Puritans, who were now very strong in the House of Commons, suspected that the King secretly sympathized with the Queen's religion. This was not the case; for Charles, after his peculiar fashion, was a sincere Protestant, though he favored the introduction into the English Church of some of the ceremonies peculiar to Catholic worship.

The Commons showed their distrust of the King by voting him the tax of tonnage and poundage (certain duties levied on wine and merchandise), for a single year only, instead of for life, as had been their custom. The Lords refused to assent to such a limited grant,[1] and Charles deliberately collected the tax without the authority of Parliament. Failing, however, to get a sufficient supply in that way, the King forced men of property to grant him "benevolences," and to loan him large sums of money with no hope of its return. Those who dared to refuse were thrown into prison on some pretended charge, or had squads of brutal soldiers quartered in their houses.

When even these measures failed to supply his wants, Charles was forced to summon a Parliament, and ask for help. Instead of granting it, the Commons drew up the Petition of Right[2] of 1628, as an indignant remonstrance, and as a safeguard against further acts of tyranny. This Petition has been called the "Second Great Charter of the Liberties of England." It declared: (1) That no one should be compelled to pay any tax or to supply the King with money, except by order of act of Parliament. (2) That neither soldiers nor sailors should be quartered in private houses.[3] (3) That no one should be imprisoned or punished contrary to law. Charles was forced by his need of money to assent to this Petition, which thus became a most important part of the English constitution. But the King did not keep his word. When Parliament next met (1629), it refused to grant money unless Charles would renew his pledge not to violate the law. The King made some concessions, but finally resolved to adjourn Parliament. Several members of the Commons held the Speaker in the chair by force, — thus preventing the adjournment of the House, — until resolutions offered by Sir John Eliot were passed (§ 434). These resolutions were aimed directly at the King. They declared: (1) that he is a traitor who attempts any change in the established religion of the kingdom;[4] (2) who levies any tax not voted by Parliament; (3) or who voluntarily pays such a tax. Parliament then adjourned.

18. "Thorough"; Ship Money; the "Short Parliament." The King swore that "the vipers" who opposed him should have their

---

[1] See Taswell-Langmead (revised edition), p. 557, note.

[2] Petition of Right: see § 432, and Constitutional Documents, p. xxx.

[3] The King was also deprived of the power to press citizens into the army and navy.

[4] The Puritans had come to believe that the King wished to restore the Catholic religion as the Established Church of England, but in this idea they were mistaken.

reward. Eliot was thrown into prison and kept there till he died. Charles made up his mind that, with the help of Archbishop Laud in Church matters, and of Lord Strafford in affairs of state, he would rule without Parliaments. Strafford urged the King to adopt the policy of " Thorough " [1] (§ 435); in other words, to follow the bent of his own will without consulting the will of the nation. This, of course, practically meant the overthrow of parliamentary and constitutional government. Charles heartily approved of this plan for setting up what he called a " beneficent despotism " based on " Divine Right."

The King now resorted to various unconstitutional means to obtain supplies. The last device he hit upon was that of raising ship money. To do this, he levied a tax on all the counties of England, — inland as well as seaboard, — on the pretext that he purposed building a navy for the defense of the kingdom. John Hampden refused to pay the tax, but Charles's servile judges decided against him, when the case was brought into court (§ 436).

Charles ruled without a Parliament for eleven years. He might, perhaps, have gone on in this way for as many more, had he not provoked the Scots to rebel by attempting to force a modified form of the English Prayer Book on the Church of that country (§ 438). The necessities of the war with the Scots compelled the King to call a Parliament. It declined to grant the King money to carry on the war unless he would give some satisfactory guarantee of governing according to the will of the people. Charles refused to do this, and after a three weeks' session he dissolved what was known as the " Short Parliament."

19. The "Long Parliament"; the Civil War. But the war gave Charles no choice, and before the year was out he was obliged to call the famous " Long Parliament " of 1640.[2] That body met with the firm determination to restore the liberties of Englishmen or to perish in the attempt. (1) It impeached Strafford and Laud, and sent them to the scaffold as traitors.[3] (2) It swept away those instruments of royal oppression, the Court of Star Chamber and the High Commission Court (§§ 330, 382). (3) It expelled the bishops from the House of Lords. (4) It passed the Triennial Bill, compelling the King to summon a Parliament at least once in three years.[4] (5) It also passed a law declaring that the King could not suspend or dissolve Parliament without its

---

[1] "Thorough": Strafford wrote to Laud, " You may govern as you please. . . . I am confident that the King is able to carry any just and honorable action thorough [i.e. through or against] all imaginable opposition." Both Strafford and Laud used this word "thorough," in this sense, to designate their tyrannical policy.

[2] The "Long Parliament": it sat from 1640 to 1653, and was not finally dissolved until 1660.

[3] Charles assured Strafford that Parliament should not touch "a hair of his head"; but to save himself the King signed the Bill of Attainder (see p. xxxii), which sent his ablest and most faithful servant to the block. Well might Strafford exclaim, " Put not your trust in princes."

[4] The Triennial Act was repealed in 1664 and reënacted in 1694. In 1716 the Septennial Act increased the limit of three years to seven. This act is still in force.

consent. (6) Last of all, the Commons drew up the Grand Remonstrance (§ 439), enunciating at great length the grievances of the last sixteen years, and vehemently appealing to the people to support them in their attempts at reform. The Remonstrance was printed and distributed throughout England.[1]

About a month later (1642) the King, at the head of an armed force, undertook to seize Hampden, Pym, and three other of the most active members of the Commons on a charge of treason (§ 449). The attempt failed. Soon afterwards the Commons passed the Militia Bill, and thus took the command of the national militia and of the chief fortresses of the realm, " to hold," as they said, " for King and Parliament." The act was unconstitutional; but, after the attempted seizure of the five members, the Commons felt certain that if they left the command of the militia in the King's hands, they would simply sign their own death warrant.

In resentment of this action, Charles now (1642) began the great Civil War. It resulted in the execution of the King, and in the temporary overthrow of the monarchy, the House of Lords, and the Established Episcopal Church (§§ 450, 451). In place of the monarchy, the party in power set up a short-lived Puritan Republic. This was followed by the Protectorate of Oliver Cromwell (which claimed to be republican in spirit) and by that of his son Richard (§§ 455, 463).

20. Charles II ; Abolition of Feudal Tenure ; Establishment of a Standing Army. In 1660 the people, weary of the Protectorate form of government, welcomed the return of Charles II. His coming marks the restoration of the monarchy, of the House of Lords, and of the National Episcopal Church.

A great change was now effected in the source of the King's revenue. Hitherto it had sprung largely from feudal dues. These had long been difficult to collect, because the Feudal System had practically died out. The feudal land tenure with its dues was now abolished, — a reform, says Blackstone, greater even than that of Magna Carta, — and in their place a tax was levied for a fixed sum (§ 482). This tax should in justice have fallen on the landowners, who profited by the change; but they managed to evade it in great measure, and by getting it levied on beer and some other liquors, they forced the working classes to shoulder the chief part of the burden, which they carried until very recently.[2]

Parliament now restored the command of the militia to the King;[3] and, for the first time in English history, it also gave him the command of a standing army of five thousand men, — thus, in one way, making him more powerful than ever before (§ 467).

On the other hand, Parliament revived the practice of limiting its appropriations of money to specific purposes.[4] It furthermore began to

---

[1] The press soon became, for the first time, a most active agent of political agitation, both for and against the King (§ 443).

[2] See § 34 of this Summary.

[3] See Militia Bill, § 19 of this Summary.

[4] See § 13 of this Summary.

require an exact account of how the King spent the money, — a most embarrassing question for a man like Charles II to answer. Again, Parliament did not hesitate to impeach and remove the King's ministers whenever they forfeited the confidence of that body.[1]

The religious legislation of this period marks the strong reaction from Puritanism which had set in. (1) The Corporation Act (1661) excluded all persons who did not renounce the Puritan Covenant and partake of the Sacrament according to the Church of England, from holding municipal or other corporate offices (§ 472). (2) The Fourth Act of Uniformity (1662)[2] required all clergymen to accept the Book of Common Prayer of the Church of England (§ 472). The result of this law was that no less than two thousand Puritan ministers were driven from their pulpits in a single day. (3) The Conventicle Act (§ 472) followed (1664). It forbade the preaching or hearing of Puritan doctrines, under severe penalties. (4) The Five-Mile Act (1665) (§ 472)[3] prohibited nonconforming clergymen from teaching, or from coming within five miles of any corporate town (except when traveling).

21. Charles II's Cabinet; the Secret Treaty of Dover; the Test Act; the Habeas Corpus Act; Rise of Cabinet Government. Charles II made a great and most important change with respect to the Privy Council. Instead of consulting the entire Council on matters of state, he established the custom of inviting only a few to meet with him in his cabinet, or private room. This limited body of confidential advisers was called the " Cabal," or secret council (§ 476).

Charles's great ambition was to increase his standing army, to rule independently of Parliament, and to get an abundance of money to spend on his extravagant pleasures and vices.

In order to accomplish these three ends he made a secret and shameful treaty with Louis XIV of France, 1670 (§ 476). Louis wished to crush the Dutch Protestant Republic of Holland, to get possession of Spain, and to secure, if possible, the ascendancy of Catholicism in England as well as throughout Europe. Charles, who was destitute of any religious principle, — or, in fact, of any sense of honor, — agreed to publicly declare himself a Catholic, to favor the propagation of that faith in England, and to make war on Holland in return for very liberal grants of money, and for the loan of six thousand French troops by Louis, to help him put down any opposition in England. Two members of the " Cabal " were acquainted with the terms of this secret Treaty of Dover. Charles made a second secret treaty with Louis XIV in 1678.

Charles did not dare to openly avow himself a convert — or pretended convert — to the Catholic religion; but he issued a Declaration

[1] See § 13 of this Summary (Impeachment).

[2] The First and Second Acts of Uniformity date from Edward VI (1549, 1552), the Third from Elizabeth (1559) (§§ 362, 382, 472).

[3] The Five-Mile Act (1665) excepted those clergymen who took the oath of nonresistance to the King, and who swore not to attempt to alter the constitution of Church or State. See Hallam's " Constitutional History of England."

of Indulgence, 1672, suspending the harsh statutes against the English Catholics (§ 477).

Parliament took the alarm and passed the Test Act, 1673, by which all Catholics were shut out from holding any government office or position (§ 477). This act broke up the "Cabal," by compelling a Catholic nobleman, who was one of its leading members, to resign. Later, Parliament further showed its power by compelling the King to sign the Act of Habeas Corpus, 1679 (§ 482), which put an end to his arbitrarily throwing men into prison, and keeping them there, in order to stop their free discussion of his plots against the constitution.[1]

But though the "Cabal" had been broken up, the principle of a limited private council survived, and long after the Revolution of 1688 it was revived and the Cabinet, under the lead of Sir Robert Walpole, the first Prime Minister,[2] in 1721, became responsible for the policy of the sovereign.[3] At present, if the Commons decidedly oppose that policy, the Prime Minister, with his Cabinet, either resigns, and a new Cabinet is chosen, or the Minister appeals to the people for support, and the sovereign dissolves Parliament and orders a new parliamentary election, by which the nation decides the question. This method renders the old, and never desirable, remedy of the impeachment of the ministers of the sovereign no longer necessary. The Prime Minister — who answers for the acts of the sovereign and for his policy — is more directly responsible to the people than is the President of the United States.

22. The Pretended "Popish Plot"; Rise of the Whigs and the Tories; Revocation of Town Charters. The pretended "Popish Plot" (1678) (§ 478) to kill the King, in order to place his brother James — a Catholic convert — on the throne, caused the rise of a strong movement (1680) to exclude James from the right of succession. The Exclusion Bill failed; but the Disabling Act was passed, 1678, excluding Catholics from sitting in either House of Parliament; but an exception was made in favor of the Duke of York (§ 478). Henceforward two prominent political parties appear in Parliament, — one, that of the Whigs or Liberals, bent on extending the power of the people; the other, that of the Tories or Conservatives, resolved to maintain the power of the Crown.

Charles II, of course, did all in his power to encourage the latter party. In order to strengthen their numbers in the Commons, he found pretexts for revoking the charters of many Whig towns (§ 479). He then issued new charters to these towns, giving the power of election to the Tories.[4] While engaged in this congenial work the King died, and his brother James II came to the throne.

---

[1] See Habeas Corpus Act in Constitutional Documents, p. xxxii.

[2] See § 27 of this Summary.

[3] The real efficiency of the Cabinet system of government was not fully developed until after the Reform Act of 1832 had widely extended the right of suffrage, and thus made the government more directly responsible to the people (§ 582).

[4] The right of election in many towns was then confined to the town officers or to a few influential inhabitants. This continued to be the case until the passage of the Reform Bill in 1832.

23. James II; the Dispensing Power; Declaration of Indulgence; the Revolution of 1688. James II was a zealous Catholic, and therefore naturally desired to secure freedom of worship in England for people of his own faith. In his zeal he went too far, and the Pope expressed his disgust at the King's foolish rashness. By the exercise of the Dispensing Power [1] he suspended the Test Act and the Act of Uniformity, in order that Catholics might be relieved from the penalties imposed by these laws, and also for the purpose of giving them civil and military offices, from which the Test Act excluded them (§ 477). James also established a new High Commission Court [2] (§ 488), and made the infamous Judge Jeffreys the head of this despotic tribunal. This court had the supervision of all churches and institutions of education. Its main object was to further the spread of Catholicism, and to silence those clergymen who preached against that faith. The King appointed a Catholic president of Magdalen College, Oxford, and expelled from the college all who opposed the appointment. Later, he issued two Declarations of Indulgence, 1687, 1688, in which he proclaimed universal religious toleration (§ 488). It was generally believed that under cover of these Declarations the King intended to favor the ascendancy of Catholicism. Seven bishops, who petitioned for the privilege of declining to read the Declarations from their pulpits, were imprisoned, but on their trial were acquitted by a jury in full sympathy with them (§ 489).

These acts of the King, together with the fact that he had greatly increased the standing army, and had stationed it just outside of London, caused great alarm throughout England (§ 488). The majority of the people of both political parties (§ 489) believed that James was plotting to "subvert and extirpate the Protestant religion and the laws and liberties of the kingdom." [3]

Still, so long as the King remained childless, the nation was encouraged by the hope that James's daughter Mary might succeed him. She was known to be a decided Protestant, and she had married William, Prince of Orange, the head of the Protestant Republic of Holland. But the birth of a son to James (1688) put an end to that hope. Immediately a number of leading Whigs and Tories (§§ 479, 490) united in sending an invitation to the Prince of Orange to come over to England with an army to protect Parliament against the King backed by his standing army.

24. William and Mary; Declaration of Right; Results of the Revolution. William came; James fled to France. A Convention Parliament [4] drew up a Declaration of Right which declared that the King had vacated

---

[1] This was the exercise of the right, claimed by the King as one of his prerogatives, of exempting individuals from the penalty of certain laws. The King also claimed the right of suspending entirely (as in the case of the Declaration of Indulgence) one or more statutes. Both these rights had been exercised, at times, from a very early date.

[2] New High Commission Court: see § 19 of this Summary.

[3] See the language of the Bill of Rights (Constitutional Documents), p. xxxi.

[4] Convention Parliament: it was so called because it was not regularly summoned by the King, — he having fled the country.

the throne, and the crown was therefore offered to William and Mary
(§ 494). They accepted. Thus by the bloodless Revolution of 1688 the
English nation transferred the sovereignty to those who had no direct
legal claim to it so long as James and his son were living (§ 490). Hence
by this act the people deliberately set aside hereditary succession, as a
binding rule, and revived the primitive English custom of choosing such
a sovereign as they deemed best. In this sense the uprising of 1688 was
most emphatically a revolution (§ 491, 492). It made, as Green has said,
an English monarch as much the creature of an act of Parliament as the
pettiest taxgatherer in his realm (§ 497). But it was a still greater revolution in another way, since it gave a deathblow to the direct "personal
monarchy," which began with the Tudors two hundred years before.
It is true that in George III's reign we shall see that power temporarily
revived, but we shall never hear anything more of that Divine Right of
Kings, for which one Stuart "lost his head, and another his crown."
Henceforth the House of Commons will govern England, although, as
we shall see, it will be nearly a hundred and fifty years before that House
will be able to free itself entirely from the control of either a few powerful families on the one hand, or that of the Crown on the other.

**25. Bill of Rights; the Commons by the Revenue and the Mutiny
Act obtain Complete Control over the Purse and the Sword.** In order to
make the constitutional rights of the people unmistakably clear, the Bill
of Rights, 1689, — an expansion of the Declaration of Right — was
drawn up (§ 497). The Bill of Rights [1] declared: (1) That there should
be no suspension or change in the laws, and no taxation except by act of
Parliament. (2) That there should be freedom of election to Parliament
and freedom of speech in Parliament (both rights that the Stuarts had
attempted to control). (3) That the sovereign should not keep a standing army, in time of peace, except by consent of Parliament. (4) That in
future no Roman Catholic should sit on the English throne. This last
clause was reaffirmed by the Act of Settlement, 1701 (§ 497).[2]

This most important bill, having received the signature of William
and Mary, became law. It constitutes the third great written charter or
safeguard of English liberty. Taken in connection with Magna Carta
and the Petition of Right, it forms, according to Lord Chatham, *the
Bible of English liberty* (§ 497).

But Parliament had not yet finished the work of reform it had taken
in hand. The executive strength of every government depends on its
control of two powers, — the purse and the sword. Parliament had, as
we have seen, got a tight grasp on the first, for the Commons, and the
Commons alone, could levy taxes; but within certain very wide limits the
personal expenditure of the sovereign still practically remained unchecked.
Parliament now, 1689, took the decisive step of voting by the Revenue
Act (1) a specific sum for the maintenance of the Crown; and (2) of voting

---

[1] Bill of Rights: see Constitutional Documents, p. xxxi.
[2] See, too, Constitutional Documents, p. xxxii.

this supply, not for the life of the sovereign, as had been the custom, but for four years (§ 498). A little later this supply was fixed for a single year only. This action gave to the Commons final and complete control of the purse (§§ 498, 588).

Next, Parliament passed the Mutiny Act (1689) (§ 496), which granted the King power to enforce martial law — in other words, to maintain a standing army — for one year at a time, and no longer, save by renewal of the law. This act gave Parliament complete control of the sword, and thus finished the great work; for without the annual meeting and the annual vote of that body, an English sovereign would at the end of a twelvemonth stand penniless and helpless.

26. Reforms in the Courts; the Toleration Act; the Press made Free. The same year (1689) Parliament effected great and sorely needed reforms in the administration of justice (§ 492).

Next, Parliament passed the Toleration Act, 1689 (§ 496). This measure granted liberty of worship to all Protestant Dissenters except those who denied the doctrine of the Trinity.[1] The Toleration Act, however, did not abolish the Corporation Act or the Test Act[2] (§§ 472, 477), and it granted no religious freedom to Catholics.[3] Still, the Toleration Act was a step forward, and it prepared the way for that absolute liberty of worship and of religious belief which now exists in England.

In finance, the reign of William and Mary was marked by the practical beginning of the permanent National Debt in 1693 and by the establishment in 1694 of the Bank of England (§ 503).

Now, too, 1695, the English press, for the first time in its history, became, in large measure, free (§§ 498, 556), though hampered by a very severe law of libel and by stamp duties.[4] From this period the influence of newspapers continued to increase, until the final abolition of the stamp duty (1855) made it possible to issue penny and even halfpenny papers at a profit. These cheap newspapers sprang at once into an immense circulation among all classes, and thus they became the power for good or evil, according to their character, which they are to-day; so that it would be no exaggeration to say that back of the power of Parliament now stands the greater power of the press.

27. The House of Commons no longer a Representative Body; the First Two Georges and their Ministers. But now that the Revolution of 1688 had done its work, and transferred the power of the Crown to the House of Commons, a new difficulty arose. This was the fact that the Commons did not represent the people, but stood simply as the

[1] Freedom of worship was granted to Unitarians in 1812.

[2] The Act of Indemnity of 1727, and passed from year to year, suspended the penalties of the Test and the Corporation Acts; they were both repealed in 1828.

[3] Later, the fear that James II might be invited to return led to the enactment of very severe laws against the Catholics; and in the next reign (Anne's) the Act of Occasional Conformity and the Schism Act were directed against Protestant Dissenters.

[4] Debates in Parliament could not be reported until 1771 (§ 556), and certain Acts (1793, 1799) checked the freedom of the press for a time. See May's " History of England."

representative of a small number of rich Whig landowners.[1] In many towns the right to vote was confined to the town officers or to the well-to-do citizens. In other cases, towns which had dwindled in population to a very few inhabitants continued to have the right to send two members to Parliament, while, on the other hand, large and flourishing cities had grown up which had no power to send even a single member (§ 578). The result of this state of things was that the wealthy Whig families bought up the votes of electors, and so regularly controlled the elections (§ 538).

Under the first two Georges, both of whom were foreigners, the ministers — especially Sir Robert Walpole, who was the first real Prime Minister of England, and who held his place for twenty years (1721–1742) — naturally stood in the foreground.[2] They understood the ins and outs of English politics, while the two German sovereigns, the first of whom never learned to speak English, neither knew nor cared anything about them. When men wanted favors or offices, they went to the ministers for them (§ 538). This made men like Walpole so powerful that George II said bitterly, " In England the ministers are king " (§ 534).

28. George III's Revival of "Personal Monarchy"; the "King's Friends." George III was born in England, and prided himself on being an Englishman. He came to the throne fully resolved, as Walpole said, " to make his power shine out," and to carry out his mother's constant injunction of, " George, be King! " (§ 548). To do this, he set himself to work to trample on the power of the ministers, to take the distribution of offices and honors out of their hands, and furthermore to break down the influence of the great Whig families in Parliament. He had no intention of reforming the House of Commons, or of securing the representation of the people in it; his purpose was to gain the control of the House, and use it for his own ends. In this he was thoroughly conscientious, according to his idea of right, — for he believed with all his heart in promoting the welfare of England, — but he thought that welfare depended on the will of the King much more than on that of the nation. His maxim was " everything for, but nothing by, the people." By liberal gifts of money, — he spent £25,000 in a single day (1762) in bribes,[3] — by gifts of offices and of honors to those who favored him, and by taking away offices, honors, and pensions from those who opposed him, George III succeeded in his purpose. He raised up a body of men in Parliament, known by the significant name of the " King's Friends," who stood ready at all times to vote for his measures. In this way he actually revived " personal monarchy "[4] for a

---

[1] The influence of the Whigs had secured the passage of the Act of Settlement which brought in the Georges; for this reason the Whigs had gained the chief political power.

[2] See § 21 of this Summary.

[3] Pitt (Lord Chatham) was one of the few public men of that day who would neither give nor take a bribe; Walpole declared with entire truth that the great majority of politicians could be bought, — it was only a question of price. The King appears to have economized in his living, in order to get more money to use as a corruption fund. See May's " Constitutional History."

[4] " Personal monarchy ": see § 15 of this Summary.

time, and by using his " Friends " in the House of Commons and in the Lords as his tools, he made himself quite independent of the checks imposed by the Constitution.

29. The American Revolution. The King's power reached its greatest height between 1770 and 1782. He made most disastrous use of it, not only at home but abroad. He insisted that the English colonists in America should pay taxes, without representation in Parliament, even of that imperfect kind which then existed in Great Britain. This determination brought on the American Revolution — called in England the " King's War " (§§ 549–552). The war, in spite of its ardent support by the " King's Friends," roused a powerful opposition in Parliament. Chatham, Burke, Fox, and other able men protested against the King's arbitrary course. Finally, Dunning moved and carried this resolution (1780) in the Commons : " Resolved, that the power of the Crown has increased, is increasing, and ought to be diminished " (§ 548). This vigorous proposition came too late to affect the conduct of the war, and England lost the most valuable of her colonial possessions. The struggle, which ended successfully for the patriots in America, was in reality part of the same battle fought in England by other patriots in the halls of Parliament. On the western side of the Atlantic it resulted in the establishment of national independence; on the eastern side, in the final overthrow of royal tyranny and the triumph of the constitution. It furthermore laid the foundation of that just and generous policy on the part of England toward Canada and her other colonies which has made her mistress of the largest and most prosperous empire on the globe.[1]

30. John Wilkes and the Middlesex Elections ; Publication of Parliamentary Debates. Meanwhile John Wilkes (§ 556), a member of the House of Commons, had gained the recognition of a most important principle. He was a coarse and violent opponent of the royal policy, and had been expelled from the House on account of his bitter personal attack on the King.[2] Several years later (1768) he was reëlected to Parliament, but was again expelled for seditious libel;[3] he was three times reëlected by the people of London and Middlesex, who looked upon him as the champion of their cause; each time the House refused to permit him to take his seat, but at the fourth election he was successful. A few years later (1782) he induced the House to strike out from its journal the resolution there recorded against him.[4] Thus Wilkes, by his indomitable persistency, succeeded in establishing the right of the people to elect the candidate of their choice to Parliament. During the same period the people gained another great victory over Parliament. That body had utterly refused to permit the debates to be reported in

[1] The area of the British Empire in 1911 was nearly 12,000,000 square miles.

[2] In No. 45 of the *North Briton* (1763) Wilkes rudely accused the King of having deliberately uttered a falsehood in his speech to Parliament.

[3] The libel was contained in a letter written to the newspapers by Wilkes.

[4] The resolution was finally stricken out, on the ground that it was " subversive of the rights of the whole body of electors."

the newspapers. But the redoubtable Wilkes was determined to obtain and publish such reports; rather than have another prolonged battle with him, Parliament conceded the privilege (1771) (§ 556). The result was that the public then, for the first time, began to know what business Parliament actually transacted, and how it was done. This fact, of course, rendered the members of both Houses far more directly responsible to the will of the people than they had ever been before.[1]

31. The Reform Bills of 1832, 1867, 1884; Demand for "Manhood Suffrage." But notwithstanding this decided political progress, still the greatest reform of all — that of the system of electing members of Parliament — still remained to be accomplished. Cromwell had attempted it (1654), but the Restoration put an end to the work which the Protector had so wisely begun. Lord Chatham felt the necessity so strongly that he had not hesitated to declare (1766) that the system of representation — or rather misrepresentation — which then existed was the "rotten part of the constitution." "If it does not drop," said he, "it must be amputated." Later (1770), he became so alarmed at the prospect that he declared that "before the end of the century either the Parliament will reform itself from within, or be reformed from without with a vengeance" (§ 578).

But the excitement caused by the French Revolution and the wars with Napoleon not only prevented any general movement of reform, but made it possible to enact the Six Acts and other stringent laws against agitation in that direction (§ 571). Finally, however, the unrepresented classes rose in their might (§§ 580–582), and by terrible riots made it evident that it would be dangerous for Parliament to postpone action on their demands. The Reform Bill — the "Great Charter of 1832" — swept away the "rotten boroughs," which had disgraced the country. It granted the right of election to many large towns which had hitherto been unable to send members to Parliament, and it placed representation on a broader, healthier, and more equitable basis than had ever existed before (§ 582). It was a significant fact that when the first reformed Parliament met, composed largely of Liberals, it showed its true spirit by abolishing slavery in the West Indies. It was followed by the Municipal Reform Act of 1835 (§ 599). Later (1848), the Chartists advocated further reforms (§ 591), most of which have since been adopted.

In 1867 an act (§ 599), scarcely less important than that of 1832, broadened representation still further; and in 1884 the franchise was again extended (§ 599). A little later (1888) the County Council Act reconstructed the local self-government of the country in great measure.[2] It was supplemented in 1894 by the Parish Council Act (§ 600). The

[1] The publication of Division Lists (equivalent to Yeas and Nays) by the House of Commons in 1836 and by the Lords in 1857 completed this work. Since then the public have known how each member of Parliament votes on every important question.

[2] The "Local Government" Act: this gives to counties the management of their local affairs and secures uniformity of method and of administration.

cry is now for unrestricted " manhood suffrage," on the principle of
" one man one vote "; [1] woman suffrage in a limited degree has existed
since 1869 (§ 599).

**32. Extension of Religious Liberty ; Admission of Catholics and Jews
to Parliament ; Free Trade.** Meanwhile immense progress was made in
extending the principles of religious liberty to all bodies of believers.
After nearly three hundred years (or since the Second Act of Supremacy,
1559), Catholics were admitted in 1829 to the House of Commons (§ 573);
and in the next generation, 1858, Jews were likewise admitted (§ 599).
The Oaths Act of 1888 makes it impossible to exclude any one on
account of his religious belief or unbelief (§ 599).

Commercially the nation has made equal progress. The barbarous
Corn Laws (§§ 592, 594) were repealed in 1848, the narrow protective
policy of centuries abandoned ; and since that period England has practically taken its stand on unlimited free trade with all countries.

**33. Condition of Ireland ; Reform in the Land and the Church
Laws ; Civil-Service Reform ; Education.** In one direction, however,
there had been no advance. Following the example of Scotland (§ 513),
Ireland was politically united to Great Britain (§ 562); at the beginning of the century when the first Imperial Parliament met (1801), but
long after the Irish Catholics had obtained the right of representation
in Parliament, they were compelled to submit to unjust land laws,
and also to contribute to the support of the Established (Protestant)
Church in Ireland. Finally, through the efforts of Mr. Gladstone and
others, this branch of the Church was disestablished (1869) (§ 601) ; later
(1870, 1881, 1903), important reforms were effected in the Irish land
laws (§§ 603, 605, 620). Irish Home Rule came in 1914 (§ 633).

To supplement the great electoral reforms which had so widely extended the power of the popular vote, two other measures were now
carried. One was that of Civil-Service Reform, 1870, which opened all
clerkships and similar positions in the gift of the government to the free
competition of candidates, without regard to their political opinions
(§ 609). This did away with most of that demoralizing system of favoritism which makes government offices the spoils by which successful
political parties reward " little men for little services." The " secret
ballot," another measure of great importance, followed (1872) (§ 609).

The same year, 1870, England, chiefly through Mr. Forster's efforts,
took up the second measure, the question of national education. The
conviction gained ground that if the working classes are to vote, then
they must not be allowed to remain in ignorance ; the nation declared
" we must educate our future masters." In this spirit a system of elementary government schools was established, which gives instruction
to tens of thousands of children who hitherto were forced to grow up

---

[1] That is, the abolition of certain franchise privileges springing from the possession of
landed property in different counties or parliamentary districts by which the owner of such
property is entitled to cast more than one vote for a candidate for Parliament.

without its advantages (§ 602). These schools are not yet entirely free, although the legislation of 1891–1894 practically puts most of them on that basis.

England now has a strong and broad foundation of national education and of political suffrage.

34. Imperial Federation; Labor enters Parliament; Old Age Pensions; Budget of 1910; Veto Power of the Lords. The defeat of the Boers in the Great Boer War (1899–1902) led to the completion of the scheme of Imperial Federation, by the establishment of the Union of South Africa (1910) as the fourth of the self-governing colonies, of which Australia, New Zealand, and Canada are the other three.

In 1906, in the reign of Edward VII, organized Labor secured for the first time adequate representation in Parliament, through the overwhelming victory gained at the elections by the combined Liberal and Labor parties (§ 628). The "Laborites," as they are popularly called, claim that their influence obtained the passage of the Old Age Pensions Act of 1908.

Two years later the Liberal Government compelled the Lords to accept a Budget calling for an enormous increase of taxes imposed in large measure on land and incomes and levied partly for the purpose of paying the new pensions (§§ 629, 630).

The death of Edward VII, in the spring of 1910, brought George V to the throne. He came at a critical time. Mr. Asquith, the Liberal Prime Minister, was then demanding that the veto power of the House of Lords should be limited or practically abolished so that in future the House of Commons should be distinctly recognized as the dominant factor in the government (§ 631).

In the summer of 1911 Mr. Asquith passed his Parliament Bill restricting the veto power of the House of Lords and making it impossible for that body to resist any measures the Commons should resolutely resolve to carry. He also passed the Salary Bill, by which members of the House of Commons are paid £400 annually. Later, in 1911, he passed the Workmen's Compulsory Insurance Bill against sickness and unemployment. The worker contributes a small sum weekly, his employer does the same, and the Government gives the rest. The law applies to many millions of people, and it is expected to do great good. In 1914 the Liberal Government, with the help of a large number of Irish votes, carried through the Irish Home Rule Bill establishing a local Parliament in Ireland (§ 633).

These facts show that while England remains a monarchy in name, it has now become a republic in fact. A sovereign reigns, but the People rule. The future is in their hands.

CONSTITUTIONAL DOCUMENTS

Abstract of the Articles of Magna Carta, 1215. 1. "The Church of England shall be free, and have her whole rights, and her liberties inviolable." The freedom of elections of ecclesiastics by the Church is confirmed. 2–8. Feudal rights guaranteed, and abuses remedied. 9–11. Treatment of debtors alleviated. 12. "*No scutage or aid [except the three customary feudal aids] shall be imposed in our kingdom, unless by the Common Council of the realm.*"[1] 13. London, and all towns, to have their ancient liberties. 14. *The King binds himself to summon the Common Council of the realm respecting the assessing of an aid (except as provided in 12) or a scutage.*[1] 15, 16. Guarantee of feudal rights to tenants. 17–19. Provisions respecting holding certain courts. 20, 21. *Of amercements. They are to be proportionate to the offence, and imposed according to the oath of honest men in the neighborhood. No amercement to touch the necessary means of subsistence of a free man, the merchandise of a merchant, or the agricultural tools of a villein; earls and barons to be amerced by their equals.* 23–34. Miscellaneous, minor articles. 35. Weights and measures to be uniform. 36. *Nothing shall be given or taken, for the future, for the Writ of Inquisition of life or limb, but it shall be freely granted, and not denied.*[2] 37, 38. Provisions respecting land-tenure and trials at law. 39. "NO FREEMAN SHALL BE TAKEN OR IMPRISONED, OR DISSEIZED, OR OUT-LAWED, OR BANISHED, OR ANY WAYS DESTROYED, NOR WILL WE PASS UPON HIM, NOR WILL WE SEND UPON HIM, UNLESS BY THE LAWFUL JUDGMENT OF HIS PEERS, OR BY THE LAW OF THE LAND." 40. "WE WILL SELL TO NO MAN, WE WILL NOT DENY TO ANY MAN, EITHER JUSTICE OR RIGHT." 41, 42. Provisions respecting merchants, and freedom of entering and quitting the realm, except in war time. 43–46. Minor provisions. 47, 48. Provisions disafforesting all forests seized by John, and guaranteeing forest rights to subjects. 49–60. Various minor provisions. 62. Provision for carrying out the charter by the barons in case the King fails in the performance of his agreement. 63. The freedom of the Church reaffirmed. Every one in the kingdom to have and hold his liberties and rights.

"Given under our hand, in the presence of the witnesses above named, and many others, in the meadow called Runnymede between Windsor and Stains, the 15th day of June, in the 17th of our reign." [Here is appended the King's seal.]

Confirmation of the Charters by Edward I, 1297. In 1297 Edward I confirmed Magna Carta and the Forest Charter granted by Henry III in 1217 by letters patent. The document consists of seven articles, of which the following, namely, the sixth and seventh, are the most important.

6. Moreover we have granted for us and our heirs, as well to archbishops, bishops, abbots, priors, and other folk of holy Church, as also to earls, barons, and to all the commonalty of the land, that *for no business from henceforth will we take such manner of aids, tasks, nor prises but by the common consent of the realm*, and for the common profit thereof, saving the ancient aids and prises due and accustomed.

7. And for so much as the more part of the commonalty of the realm find themselves sore grieved with the maletote [*i.e.* an unjust tax or duty] of wools, that is to wit, a toll of forty shillings for every sack of wool, and have made petition to us to release the same; we, at their requests, have clearly released it, and have granted for us and our heirs that we shall not take such thing nor any other without their common assent and good will; saving to us and our heirs the custom of wools, skins, and leather, granted before by the commonalty aforesaid. In witness of which things we have caused these our letters to be made patents. Witness Edward our son, at London, the 10th day of October, the five-and-twentieth of our reign.

And be it remembered that this same Charter, in the same terms, word for word, was sealed in Flanders under the King's Great Seal, that is to say, at Ghent, the 5th day of November, in the 25th year of the reign of our aforesaid Lord the King, and sent into England.

---

[1] These important articles were omitted when Magna Carta was reissued in 1216 by Henry III. Stubbs says they were never restored; but Edward I, in his Confirmation of the Charters, seems to reaffirm them. See the Confirmation; see also Gneist's "English Constitution," II, 9.

[2] This article is regarded by some authorities as the prototype of the statute of Habeas Corpus; others consider that it is implied in Articles 39–40.

THE PETITION OF RIGHT

JUNE 7, 1628

The Petition exhibited to His Majesty by the Lords Spiritual and Temporal, and Commons in this present Parliament assembled, concerning divers Rights and Liberties of the Subjects, with the King's Majesty's Royal Answer thereunto in full Parliament.

TO THE KING'S MOST EXCELLENT MAJESTY: Humbly show unto our Sovereign Lord the King, the Lords Spiritual and Temporal, and Commons in Parliament assembled, that whereas it is declared and enacted by a statute made in the time of the reign of King Edward the First, commonly called *Statutum de Tallagio non concedendo*,[1] that no tallage [here, a tax levied by the King upon the lands of the crown, and upon all royal towns] or aid shall be laid or levied by the King or his heirs in this realm, without the goodwill and assent of the Archbishops, Bishops, Earls, Barons, Knights, Burgesses, and other the freemen of the commonalty of this realm : and by authority of Parliament holden in the five and twentieth year of the reign of King Edward the Third, it is declared and enacted, that from henceforth no person shall be compelled to make any loans to the King against his will, because such loans were against reason and the franchise of the land ; and by other laws of this realm it is provided, that none should be charged by any charge or imposition, called a Benevolence, or by such like charge, by which the statutes before-mentioned, and other the good laws and statutes of this realm, your subjects have inherited this freedom, that they should not be compelled to contribute to any tax, tallage, aid, or other like charge, not set by common consent in Parliament.

Yet nevertheless, of late divers commissions directed to sundry Commissioners in several counties with instructions have issued ; by means whereof your people have been in divers places assembled, and required to lend certain sums of money unto your Majesty, and many of them upon their refusal so to do, have had an oath administered unto them, not warrantable by the laws or statutes of this realm, and have been constrained to become bound to make appearance and give attendance before your Privy Council, and in other places, and others of them have been therefore imprisoned, confined, and sundry other ways molested and disquieted : and divers other charges have been laid and levied upon your people in several counties, by Lords Lieutenants, Deputy Lieutenants, Commissioners for Musters, Justices of Peace and others, by command or direction from your Majesty or your Privy Council, against the laws and free customs of this realm :

And where also by the statute called, "The Great Charter of the Liberties of England," it is declared and enacted, that no freeman may be taken or imprisoned or be disseized of his freeholds or liberties, or his free customs, or be outlawed or exiled ; or in any manner destroyed, but by the lawful judgment of his peers, or by the law of the land :

And in the eighth and twentieth year of the reign of King Edward the Third, it was declared and enacted by authority of Parliament, that no man of what estate or condition that he be, should be put out of his lands or tenements, nor taken, nor imprisoned, nor disinherited, nor put to death, without being brought to answer by due process of law :

Nevertheless, against the tenor of the said statutes, and other the good laws and statutes of your realm, to that end provided, divers of your subjects have of late been imprisoned without any cause showed, and when for their deliverance they were brought before your Justices, by your Majesty's writs of Habeas Corpus, there to undergo and receive as the Court should order, and their keepers commanded to certify the causes of their detainer ; no cause was certified, but that they were detained by your Majesty's special command, signified by the Lords of your Privy Council, and yet were returned back to several prisons, without being charged with anything to which they might make answer according to law :

And whereas of late great companies of soldiers and mariners have been dispersed into divers counties of the realm, and the inhabitants against their wills have been compelled to receive them into their houses, and there to suffer them to sojourn, against the laws and customs of this realm, and to the great grievance and vexation of the people :

And whereas also by authority of Parliament, in the 25th year of the reign of King Edward the Third, it is declared and enacted, that no man shall be forejudged of life or limb against the form of the Great Charter, and the law of the land : and by the said Great Charter and other the laws and statutes of this your realm, no man ought to be adjudged to death ; but by the laws established in this your realm, either by the customs of the same realm or by Acts of Parliament : and whereas no offender of what kind soever is exempted from the proceedings to be used, and punishments to be inflicted by the laws and statutes of this your realm ; nevertheless of late divers commissions under your Majesty's Great Seal have issued forth, by which certain persons have been assigned and appointed Commissioners with power and

---

[1] A statute concerning tallage not granted by Parliament. This is now held not to have been a statute. See Gardiner's "Documents of the Puritan Revolution," p. 1. It is considered by Stubbs an unauthorized and imperfect abstract of Edward I's Confirmation of the Charters — which see.

authority to proceed within the land, according to the justice of martial law against such soldiers and mariners, or other dissolute persons joining with them, as should commit any murder, robbery, felony, mutiny, or other outrage or misdemeanour whatsoever, and by such summary course and order, as is agreeable to martial law, and is used in armies in time of war, to proceed to the trial and condemnation of such offenders, and them to cause to be executed and put to death, according to the law martial :

By pretext whereof, some of your Majesty's subjects have been by some of the said Commissioners put to death, when and where, if by the laws and statutes of the land they had deserved death, by the same laws and statutes also they might, and by no other ought to have been, adjudged and executed.

And also sundry grievous offenders by colour thereof, claiming 'an exemption, have escaped the punishments due to them by the laws and statutes of this your realm, by reason that divers of your officers and ministers of justice have unjustly refused, or forborne to proceed against such offenders according to the same laws and statutes, upon pretence that the said offenders were punishable only by martial law, and by authority of such commissions as aforesaid, which commissions, and all other of like nature, are wholly and directly contrary to the said laws and statutes of this your realm :

They do therefore humbly pray your Most Excellent Majesty, that no man hereafter be compelled to make or yield any gift, loan, benevolence, tax, or such like charge, without common consent by Act of Parliament; and that none be called to make answer, or take such oath, or to give attendance, or be confined, or otherwise molested or disquieted concerning the same, or for refusal thereof; and that no freeman, in any such manner as is beforementioned, be imprisoned or detained; and that your Majesty will be pleased to remove the said soldiers and mariners, and that your people may not be so burdened in time to come; and that the foresaid commissions for proceeding by martial law may be revoked and annulled; and that hereafter no commissions of like nature may issue forth to any person or persons whatsoever, to be executed as aforesaid, lest by colour of them any of your Majesty's subjects be destroyed or put to death, contrary to the laws and franchise of the land.

All which they most humbly pray your Most Excellent Majesty, as their rights and liberties according to the laws and statutes of this realm : and that your Majesty would also vouchsafe to declare, that the awards, doings, and proceedings to the prejudice of your people, in any of the premises, shall not be drawn hereafter into consequence or example : and that your Majesty would be also graciously pleased, for the further comfort and safety of your people, to declare your royal will and pleasure, that in the things aforesaid all your officers and ministers shall serve you, according to the laws and statutes of this realm, as they tender the honour of your Majesty, and the prosperity of this kingdom.

[Which Petition being read the 2d of June, 1628, the King gave the following evasive and unsatisfactory answer, instead of the usual one, given below.]

The King willeth that right be done according to the laws and customs of the realm : and that the statutes be put in due execution, that his subjects may have no cause to complain of any wrong or oppressions, contrary to their just rights and liberties, to the preservation whereof he holds himself as well obliged as of his prerogative.

On June 7 the King decided to make answer in the accustomed form, *Soit droit fait comme est désiré.* [Equivalent to the form of royal assent, " Le roi (*or* la reine) le veult," meaning " the King grants it." On the Petition of Right, see Hallam and compare Gardiner's " England " ; and his " Documents of the Puritan Revolution."]

The Bill of Rights, 1689. This Bill consists of thirteen Articles, of which the following is an abstract. It begins by stating that " *Whereas the late King James II, by the advice of divers evil counsellors, judges, and ministers employed by him, did endeavor to subvert and extirpate the Protestant religion, and the laws and liberties of this Kingdom:* " 1. By dispensing with and suspending the laws without consent of Parliament. 2. By prosecuting worthy bishops for humbly petitioning him to be excused for concurring in the same assumed power. 3. By erecting a High Commission Court. 4. By levying money without consent of Parliament. 5. By keeping a standing army in time of peace without consent of Parliament. 6. By disarming Protestants and arming Papists. 7. By violating the freedom of elections. 8. By arbitrary and illegal prosecutions. 9. By putting corrupt and unqualified persons on juries. 10. By requiring excessive bail. 11. By imposing excessive fines and cruel punishments. 12. By granting fines and forfeiture against persons before their conviction.

It is then declared that " the late King James the Second having abdicated the government, and the throne being thereby vacant," therefore the Prince of Orange (" whom it hath pleased Almighty God to make the glorious instrument of delivering their kingdom from Popery and arbitrary power ") did by the advice of " the Lords Spiritual and Temporal, and divers principal persons of the Commons " summon a Convention Parliament.

This Convention Parliament declares, that the acts above enumerated are contrary to law. They then bestow the Crown on William and Mary — the sole regal power to be vested only in the Prince of Orange — and provide that after the decease of William and Mary the Crown shall descend "to the heirs of the body of the said Princess; and, for default of such issue, to the Princess Anne of Denmark[1] and the heirs of her body; and for default of such issue, to the heirs of the body of the said Prince of Orange."

Here follow new oaths of allegiance and supremacy in lieu of those formerly required.

The subsequent articles are as follows: IV. Recites the acceptance of the Crown by William and Mary. V. The Convention Parliament to provide for "the settlement of the religion, laws, and liberties of the Kingdom." VI. All the clauses in the Bill of Rights are "the true, ancient, and indubitable rights and liberties of the people of this Kingdom." VII. Recognition and declaration of William and Mary as King and Queen. VIII. Repetition of the settlement of the Crown and limitations of the succession. IX. Exclusion from the Crown of all persons holding communion with the "Church of Rome" or who "profess the Popish religion" or who "shall marry a Papist." X. Every King or Queen hereafter succeeding to the Crown to assent to the Act [*i.e.* Disabling Act of 1678 (§ 478)] "disabling Papists from sitting in either House of Parliament." XI. The King and Queen assent to all the articles of the Bill of Rights. XII. The Dispensing Power (§ 488, note 1) abolished. XIII. Exception made in favor of charters, grants, and pardons made before October 23, 1689.

The Act of Settlement, 1700-1701.[2] Excludes Roman Catholics from succession to the Crown; and declares that if a Roman Catholic obtains the Crown, "the people of these realms shall be and are thereby absolved of their allegiance." Settles the Crown on the Electress Sophia,[3] and "the heirs of her body being Protestants." Requires the sovereign to join in communion with the Church of England. No war to be undertaken in defence of any territories not belonging to the English Crown except with the consent of Parliament. Judges to hold their office during good behaviour. No pardon by the Crown to be pleadable against an impeachment by the House of Commons (§ 488).

MISCELLANEOUS ACTS AND LAWS

I. The Constitutions of Clarendon, 1164. These measures (§ 165), says Bishop Stubbs, were "really a part of a great scheme of administrative reform." They were drawn up by a committee of bishops and barons, with the Justiciar or Chief Minister at the head. The object of the Constitutions was "to assert the supremacy of the State over clergy and laity alike." They limited the jurisdiction of the ecclesiastical courts; they established a more uniform system of justice; and, in certain cases, they provided for a kind of jury trial (see Stubbs's "Constitutional History," I, 525; or, for a brief abstract of the Constitutions, see Acland and Ransome's "Political History," p. 24).

II. Bill of Attainder, 1321. This was a bill (first used apparently in 1321) passed by Parliament, which might in itself decree sentence of death (§§ 351, 356). Originally, the blood of a person held to be convicted of treason or felony was declared to be *attainted* or corrupted so that his power to inherit, transmit, or hold property was destroyed. After Henry VIII's reign the law was modified so as not to work "corruption of blood" in the case of new felonies. Under the Stuarts, Bills of Attainder were generally brought only in cases where the Commons believed that impeachment would fail, — as in the cases of Strafford and Laud. It should be noticed that in an Impeachment the Commons bring the accusation, and the Lords act as judges; but that in a Bill of Attainder the Commons — that is, the accusers — themselves act as judges, as well as the Lords.

III. The Great Statute of Præmunire, 1393. This statute (first passed in 1353) was reënacted in 1393 to check the power claimed by the Pope in England in cases which interfered with power claimed by the King, as in appeals made to the Court of Rome respecting Church matters, over which the King's court had jurisdiction. The statute received its name from the writ served on the party who had broken the law: "*Præmunire facias*, A. B.";that is, "Cause A. B. to be forewarned" that he appear before us to answer the contempt with which he stands charged. Henry VIII made use of this statute in order to compel the clergy to accept his supremacy over the English Church (§§ 265, 346, 348).

---

[1] The Princess Anne, sister of the Princess Mary, married Prince George of Denmark in 1683; hence she is here styled "the Princess of Denmark."

[2] This act, says Taswell-Langmead, is "the Title Deed of the reigning Dynasty, and a veritable original contract between the Crown and the People."

[3] The Electress Sophia was the granddaughter of James I: she married the Elector of Hanover, and became mother of George I. See genealogical table of Descent of the English Sovereigns in the Appendix.

IV. Habeas Corpus Act, 1679. The name of this celebrated statute is derived from its referring to the opening words of the writ: "*Habeas Corpus ad subjiciendum.*" Sir James Mackintosh declares that the essence of the statute is contained in clauses 39, 40 of Magna Carta—which see. The right to Habeas Corpus was conceded by the Petition of Right and also by the Statute of 1640. But in order to better secure the liberty of the subject and for prevention of imprisonments beyond the seas, the Habeas Corpus Act of 1679 was enacted, regulating the issue and return of writs of Habeas Corpus.

The principal provisions of the Act are: 1. Jailers (except in cases of commitment for treason or felony) must within three days of the reception of the writ produce the prisoner in court, unless the court is at a distance, when the time may be extended to twenty days at the most. 2. A jailer, refusing to do this, forfeits £100 for the first offense, and £200 for the second. 3. No one set at liberty upon any Habeas Corpus to be recommitted for the same offense except by the court having jurisdiction of the case. 4. The Act not to apply to cases of debt.

V. Abstract of the Parliament Act (or Veto Act, § 631), 18th August, 1911. The Preamble states that "it is intended to substitute for the House of Lords, as it at present exists, a Second Chamber *constituted on a popular instead of hereditary basis*, but such substitution cannot be immediately brought into operation": therefore "it is expedient to make such provision as in this Act appears for restricting the existing powers of the House of Lords" (i.e. the power of the Lords to veto bills sent them by the Commons).

1. If a Money Bill—that is, a Public Bill concerning taxation or the appropriation of money or the raising of a loan, etc.—shall be passed by the House of Commons, but shall not be passed by the House of Lords, within one month, then it shall become law without the consent of the Lords.

2. If any Public Bill (other than a Money Bill or a Bill providing for the extension of the maximum duration of Parliament beyond five years) shall be passed by the House of Commons in three successive sessions (whether of the same Parliament or not) and shall be rejected by the House of Lords in each of those sessions, "that Bill shall on its rejection for the third time by the House of Lords, unless the House of Commons direct to the contrary, become an Act of Parliament, without the consent of the Lords, provided that two years have elapsed since the Bill was introduced and passed by the House of Commons."

7. Five years shall be substituted for seven years as the time fixed for the maximum duration of Parliament under the Septennial Act of 1715[1] (§ 535).

See "The Public General Statutes," of Great Britain and Ireland, for 1911; Chapter 13, pp. 38–40.

VI. William the Conqueror's Charter to London (§ 107). "William, the King, greets William the Bishop, and Gosfrith the Port-reeve [or chief officer of the city] and all the burghers [or citizens] within London, French and English, friendly: and I do you to wit that I will that ye twain be worthy of all the law that ye were worthy of in King Edward's day. And I will not endure that any man offer any wrong to you. God keep you."

Taswell-Langmead's "English Constitutional History," Chapter 1, p. 18. E. A. Freeman, in his "Norman Conquest," IV, 29, says that William signed this charter with a cross (in addition to his seal, which was attached to the document), but Dr. R. R. Sharpe, in his "History of London and the Kingdom," I, 34, note 1, states that "this appears to be a mistake." Dr. Sharpe is the "Records Clerk" of the City, and he shows that there is no trace of any cross on the charter, which is now preserved in the Guildhall Library, London.

---

[1] This date is usually given 1716.

DESCENT OF THE ENGLISH SOVEREIGNS FROM EGBERT TO GEORGE V *

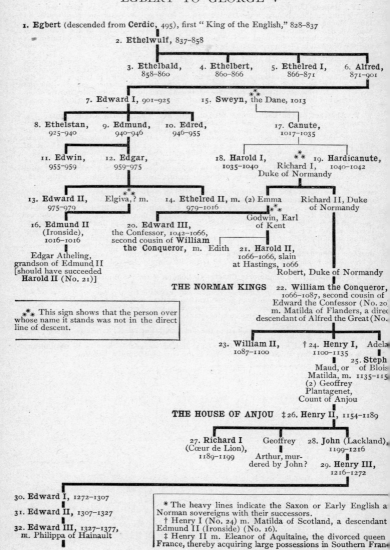

1. Egbert (descended from Cerdic, 495), first " King of the English," 828–837

2. Ethelwulf, 837–858

3. Ethelbald, 858–860   **4. Ethelbert,** 860–866   **5. Ethelred I,** 866–871   **6. Alfred,** 871–901

7. Edward I, 901–925   **15. Sweyn,** the Dane, 1013

8. Ethelstan, 925–940   **9. Edmund,** 940–946   **10. Edred,** 946–955   **17. Canute,** 1017–1035

11. Edwin, 955–959   **12. Edgar,** 959–975   **18. Harold I,** 1035–1040   Richard I,   **19. Hardicanute,** 1040–1042 Duke of Normandy

13. Edward II, 975–979   Elgiva,? m.   **14. Ethelred II,** m. (2) Emma 979–1016   Richard II, Duke of Normandy

Godwin, Earl of Kent

16. Edmund II (Ironside), 1016–1016

20. Edward III, the Confessor, 1042–1066, second cousin of **William the Conqueror,** m. Edith

21. Harold II, 1066–1066, slain at Hastings, 1066

Edgar Atheling, grandson of Edmund II [should have succeeded **Harold II** (No. 21)]

Robert, Duke of Normandy

THE NORMAN KINGS   **22. William the Conqueror,** 1066–1087, second cousin of Edward the Confessor (No. 20 m. Matilda of Flanders, a direc descendant of Alfred the Great (No.

✳ This sign shows that the person over whose name it stands was not in the direct line of descent.

23. William II, 1087–1100   †**24. Henry I,** 1100–1135   Adela

Maud, or Matilda, m. (2) Geoffrey Plantagenet, Count of Anjou

25. Steph of Blois 1135–115

THE HOUSE OF ANJOU ‡**26. Henry II,** 1154–1189

27. Richard I (Cœur de Lion), 1189–1199   Geoffrey   **28. John** (Lackland), 1199–1216

Arthur, murdered by John?

29. Henry III, 1216–1272

30. Edward I, 1272–1307

31. Edward II, 1307–1327

32. Edward III, 1327–1377, m. Philippa of Hainault

* The heavy lines indicate the Saxon or Early English a Norman sovereigns with their successors.
† Henry I (No. 24) m. Matilda of Scotland, a descendant Edmund II (Ironside) (No. 16).
‡ Henry II m. Eleanor of Aquitaine, the divorced queen France, thereby acquiring large possessions in Southern Fran

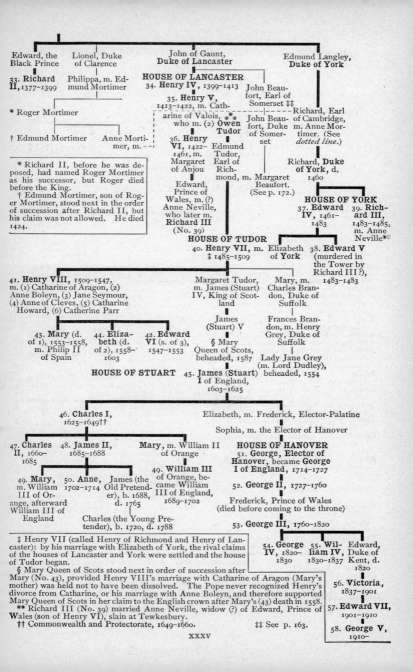

Edward, the Black Prince — Lionel, Duke of Clarence — John of Gaunt, **Duke of Lancaster** — Edmund Langley, **Duke of York**

HOUSE OF LANCASTER

33. **Richard II,** 1377–1399

Philippa, m. Edmund Mortimer

34. **Henry IV,** 1399–1413

John Beaufort, Earl of Somerset ‡‡

* Roger Mortimer

35. **Henry V,** 1413–1422, m. Catharine of Valois, ** who m. (2) **Owen Tudor**

John Beaufort, Duke of Somerset

Richard, Earl of Cambridge, m. Anne Mortimer. (See *dotted line*.)

† Edmund Mortimer   Anne Mortimer, m.

36. **Henry VI,** 1422–1461, m. Margaret of Anjou

Edmund Tudor, Earl of Richmond, m. Margaret Beaufort. (See p. 172.)

Richard, **Duke of York,** d. 1460

> * Richard II, before he was deposed, had named Roger Mortimer as his successor, but Roger died before the King.
> † Edmund Mortimer, son of Roger Mortimer, stood next in the order of succession after Richard II, but his claim was not allowed. He died 1424.

Edward, Prince of Wales, m. (?) Anne Neville, who later m. **Richard III** (No. 39)

HOUSE OF YORK

37. **Edward IV,** 1461–1483

39. **Richard III,** 1483–1485, m. Anne Neville**

HOUSE OF TUDOR

40. **Henry VII,** m. Elizabeth of York ‡ 1485–1509

38. **Edward V** (murdered in the Tower by Richard III ?), 1483–1483

41. **Henry VIII,** 1509–1547, m. (1) Catharine of Aragon, (2) Anne Boleyn, (3) Jane Seymour, (4) Anne of Cleves, (5) Catharine Howard, (6) Catherine Parr

Margaret Tudor, m. James (Stuart) IV, King of Scotland

Mary, m. Charles Brandon, Duke of Suffolk

43. **Mary** (d. of 1), 1553–1558, m. Philip II of Spain

44. **Elizabeth** (d. of 2), 1558–1603

42. **Edward VI** (s. of 3), 1547–1553

James (Stuart) V

Frances Brandon, m. Henry Grey, Duke of Suffolk

§ **Mary** Queen of Scots, beheaded, 1587

Lady Jane Grey (m. Lord Dudley), beheaded, 1554

HOUSE OF STUART

45. **James (Stuart)** I of England, 1603–1625

46. **Charles I,** 1625–1649††

Elizabeth, m. Frederick, Elector-Palatine

Sophia, m. the Elector of Hanover

47. **Charles II,** 1660–1685

48. **James II,** 1685–1688

Mary, m. William II of Orange

HOUSE OF HANOVER

51. **George,** Elector of Hanover, became **George I** of England, 1714–1727

49. **Mary,** m. William III of Orange, afterward William III of England

50. **Anne,** 1702–1714

James (the Old Pretender), b. 1688, d. 1765

49. **William III** of Orange, became William III of England, 1689–1702

52. **George II,** 1727–1760

Charles (the Young Pretender), b. 1720, d. 1788

Frederick, Prince of Wales (died before coming to the throne)

53. **George III,** 1760–1820

> ‡ Henry VII (called Henry of Richmond and Henry of Lancaster): by his marriage with Elizabeth of York, the rival claims of the houses of Lancaster and York were settled and the house of Tudor began.
> § Mary Queen of Scots stood next in order of succession after Mary (No. 43), provided Henry VIII's marriage with Catharine of Aragon (Mary's mother) was held not to have been dissolved. The Pope never recognized Henry's divorce from Catharine, or his marriage with Anne Boleyn, and therefore supported Mary Queen of Scots in her claim to the English crown after Mary's (43) death in 1558.
> ** Richard III (No. 39) married Anne Neville, widow (?) of Edward, Prince of Wales (son of Henry VI), slain at Tewkesbury.
> †† Commonwealth and Protectorate, 1649–1660.   ‡‡ See p. 163.

54. **George IV,** 1820–1830

55. **William IV,** 1830–1837

Edward, Duke of Kent, d. 1820

56. **Victoria,** 1837–1901

57. **Edward VII,** 1901–1910

58. **George V,** 1910–

A CLASSIFIED LIST OF BOOKS OF ENGLISH HISTORY

[The * marks contemporary or early history]

N.B. A selected list of twenty-eight works, especially adapted to the use of teachers and pupils for reference and collateral reading, is given on this first page. It includes the names of publishers with prices.

General Histories

Oman, C. History of England (earliest times to the present). 7 vols. Putnam's Sons, N.Y. ($3.00 per vol.).

Gardiner, S. R. A Student's History of England, illustrated, 3 vols. Longmans, N.Y. ($3.50); or bound in one very thick volume ($3.00).

Tout, T. F. History of England, 1 vol. Longmans, N.Y. ($1.50).

Gardiner, S. R. English History. Holt, N.Y. (80 cents). (For young folks.)

Smith, Goldwin. The United Kingdom, a Political History, 2 vols. The Macmillan Company, N.Y. ($4.00).

Bright, J. F. History of England, 4 vols. Longmans, N.Y. ($6.75).

Green, J. R. A Short History of the English People, 1 vol. Harper & Bros., N.Y. ($2.00); the same beautifully illustrated, 4 vols. ($20.00).

Brewer, J. S. The Student's Hume, 1 vol. Murray, London (7s 6d).

Creighton, M. Epochs of English History, 6 small vols. in one. Longmans, N.Y. ($1.25).

Knight, C. The Popular History of England, 9 vols., illustrated. Warne, London (£3 3s.).

English Constitutional History

Ransome, C. Rise of Constitutional Government in England, 1 vol. Longmans, N.Y. ($2.00). (An excellent short constitutional history.)

Taswell-Langmead, T. P. English Constitutional History, new and revised edition, 1 vol. Stevens & Haynes, London ($3.12). (This is the best complete constitutional history of England.)

Feilden, H. St. C. A Short Constitutional History of England (revised edition), 1 vol. Ginn and Company, Boston ($1.25). (This is a reference manual of exceptional value.)

General Works of Reference

Cannon, H. L. Reading References for English History, 1 vol. Ginn and Company, Boston ($2.50). (This is a work practically indispensable to both teachers and students. See further, p. xl.)

Low and Pulling. Dictionary of English History (revised edition), 1 vol. Cassell, N.Y. ($3.50).

Gardiner, S. R. A School Atlas of English History, 1 vol. Longmans, N.Y. ($1.50).

Lee, G. C. Source-Book of English History (giving leading documents, etc.), 1 vol. Holt & Co., N.Y. ($2.00).

Cheyney, E. P. Readings in English History, 1 vol. Ginn and Company, Boston ($1.80).

Kendall, E. K. Source-Book of English History, 1 vol. The Macmillan Company, N.Y. (80 cents).

Acland and Ransome. English Political History in Outline. Longmans, N.Y. ($1.25). (Excellent for reference.)

Powell, J. York. English History from Contemporary Writers, 16 vols. Nutt & Co., London (1s. per vol.) (A series of great value.)

Cheyney, E. P. Industrial and Social History of England, 1 vol. The Macmillan Company, N.Y. ($1.40).

Gibbins, H. de B. An Industrial History of England, 1 vol. Scribner's, N.Y. ($1.20).

Cunningham and MacArthur. Outlines of English Industrial History. The Macmillan Company, N.Y. ($1.50).

Church, A. J. Early Britain. (Story of the Nations Series.) Putnams, N.Y. ($1.50).

Story, A. T. The Building of the British Empire, 2 vols. Putnams, N.Y. ($3.00).

McCarthy, J. The Story of the People of England in the XIXth Century, 2 vols. Putnams, N.Y. ($3.00).

Works of Reference to be found in Libraries

Hunt, W., and Poole, R. L. Political History of England (earliest times to the present). 12 vols.
Traill, H. D. Social England, 6 vols.
The New Encyclopædia Britannica, 29 vols.
Chambers's Encyclopædia, 10 vols.
Nelson's Encyclopædia, 12 vols.
The International Encyclopædia, 17 vols.
The New Encyclopædia Americana, 15 vols.
The Catholic Encyclopædia, 15 vols.
The Jewish Encyclopædia, 12 vols.
Stephen, L. Dictionary of National [British] Biography, 66 vols. (A work of the highest rank.)
Adams's Manual of Historical Literature.
Mullinger's Authorities on English History.
Bailey's Succession to the Crown (with full genealogical tables).
Henderson's Side Lights on English History.
Poole's Index to Reviews.

I. The Prehistoric Period

Dawkins's Early Man in Britain.
Wright's The Celt, the Roman, and the Saxon.
Elton's Origins of English History.
Rhys's Celtic Britain.
Geoffrey of Monmouth's Chronicle (legendary).
Geike's Influence of Geology on English History, in *Macmillan's Magazine*, 1882.

II. The Roman Period, 55, 54 B.C.; A.D. 43–410

*Cæsar's Commentaries on the Gallic War (Books IV and V, chiefly 55, 54 B.C.).
*Tacitus' Agricola and Annals (chiefly from 78–84).
*Gildas' History of Britain (whole period).
*Bede's Ecclesiastical History of Britain (whole period).
Wright's The Celt, the Roman, and the Saxon.
Elton's Origins of English History.
Pearson's England during the Early and Middle Ages.
Scarth's Roman Britain.[1]

III. The Saxon or Early English Period, 449–1066

*The Anglo-Saxon Chronicle (whole period).
*Gildas' History of Britain (Roman Conquest to 560).
*Bede's Ecclesiastical History of Britain (earliest times to 731).
*Nennius' History of Britain (earliest times to 642).

*Geoffrey of Monmouth's Chronicle (legendary) (earliest times to 689).
*Asser's Life of Alfred the Great.
Elton's Origins of English History.
Pauli's Life of Alfred.
Green's Making of England.
Green's Conquest of England.
Freeman's Norman Conquest, Vols. I–II.
Pearson's History of England during the Early and Middle Ages.
Freeman's Origin of the English Nation.
Stubbs's Constitutional History of England.
Taine's History of English Literature.
Church's Beginning of the Middle Ages.
Armitage's Childhood of the English Nation.[2]
Freeman's Early English History.[2]

IV. The Norman Period 1066–1154

*The Anglo-Saxon Chronicle (Peterborough continuation) (whole period).
*Ordericus Vitalis' Ecclesiastical History (to 1141).
*Wace's Roman de Rou (Taylor's translation) (to 1106).
*Bruce's Bayeux Tapestry Elucidated (with plates).
*William of Malmesbury's Chronicle (to 1142).
*Roger of Hoveden's Chronicle (whole period).
Freeman's Norman Conquest.
Church's Life of Anselm.
Taine's History of English Literature.
Stubbs's Constitutional History of England.
Freeman's Short History of the Norman Conquest.[3]
Armitage's Childhood of the English Nation.[3]
Johnson's Normans in Europe.[3]
Creighton's England a Continental Power.[3]

V. The Angevin Period, 1154–1399

*Matthew Paris's Chronicle (1067–1253).
*Richard of Devizes's Chronicle (1189–1192).
*Froissart's Chronicles (1325–1400).
*Jocelin of Brakelonde's Chronicle (1173–1102) (see Carlyle's Past and Present, Book II).
Norgate's Angevin Kings.
Taine's History of English Literature.
Anstey's William of Wykeham.
Pearson's England in the Early and Middle Ages.
Maurice's Stephen Langton.
Creighton's Life of Simon de Montfort.
Stubbs's Constitutional History of England.
Gairdner and Spedding's Studies in English History (the Lollards).
Blade's Life of Caxton.
Seebohm's Essay on the Black Death, in *Fortnightly Review*, 1865.
Maurice's Wat Tyler, Ball, and Oldcastle.

---

[1] The best short history.   [2] The two best short histories.   [3] The four best short histories.

Gibbins's English Social Reformers (Langland and John Ball).
Buddensieg's Life of Wiclif.
J. York Powell's History of England.
Burrows's Wicklif's Place in History.
Pauli's Pictures of Old England.
Stubbs's Early Plantagenets.[1]
Rowley's Rise of the People.[1]
Warburton's Edward III.[1]
Shakespeare's John and Richard (Hudson's edition).
Scott's Ivanhoe and The Talisman (Richard I and John).

VI. The Lancastrian Period, 1399-1461

*The Paston Letters (Gairdner's edition) (1424-1506).
*Fortescue's Governance of England (Plummer's edition) (1460?).
*Hall's Chronicle (1398-1509).
Brougham's England under the House of Lancaster.
Besant's Life of Sir Richard Whittington.
Taine's English Literature.
Rand's Chaucer's England.
Stubbs's Constitutional History of England.
Strickland's Queens of England (Margaret of Anjou).
Reed's English History in Shakespeare.
Gairdner's Houses of Lancaster and York.[2]
Rowley's Rise of the People.[2]
Shakespeare's Henry IV, V, and VI (Hudson's edition).

VII. The Yorkist Period, 1461-1485

*The Paston Letters (Gairdner's edition) (1424-1506).
*Sir Thomas More's Edward V and Richard III
*Hall's Chronicle (1398-1509).
Hallam's Middle Ages.
Gairdner's Richard III.
Taine's English Literature.
Stubbs's Constitutional History of England.
Gairdner's Houses of Lancaster and York.[2]
Rowley's Rise of the People.[2]
Shakespeare's Richard III (Hudson's edition).

VIII. The Tudor Period, 1485-1603

*Holinshed's History of England (from earliest times to 1577).
*Lord Bacon's Life of Henry VII.
*Latimer's 1st and 6th Sermons before Edward VI and "The Ploughers" (1549).
*Hall's Chronicle (1398-1509).
Hallam's Constitutional History of England.
Lingard's History of England (Catholic) 13 vols.
Brewer's Reign of Henry VIII.

Creighton's Cardinal Wolsey.
Gibbins's Social Reformers (Sir Thomas More).
Froude's History of England.
Strickland's Queens of England (Catharine of Aragon, Anne Boleyn, Mary, Elizabeth).
Demaus's Life of Latimer.
Froude's Short Studies.
Nicholls's Life of Cabot.
Dixon's History of the Church of England.
Hall's Society in the Age of Elizabeth.
Thornbury's Shakespeare's England.
Macaulay's Essay on Lord Burleigh.
Barrows's Life of Drake.
Creighton's Life of Raleigh.
Taine's English Literature.
Creighton's The Tudors and the Reformation.[3]
Seebohm's Era of the Protestant Revolution.[3]
Moberly's Early Tudors.[3]
Creighton's Age of Elizabeth.[3]
Shakespeare's Henry VIII (Hudson's edition).
Scott's Kenilworth, Abbot, Monastery (Elizabeth and Mary Queen of Scots).

IX. The Stuart Period (First Part), 1603-1649

*The Prose Works of James I (1599-1625).
Jesse's Memoirs of the Court of England.
*Fuller's Church History of Britain (earliest times to 1648).
*Clarendon's History of the Rebellion (1625-1660).
*Memoirs of Col. Hutchinson (1616-1664).
*May's History of the Long Parliament (1640-1643).
Carlyle's Historical Sketches of Reigns of James I and Charles I.
Taine's History of English Literature.
Spedding's Lord Bacon and his Times.
Gardiner's History of England (1603-1649).
Church's Life of Lord Bacon.
Hallam's Constitutional History of England.
Hume's History of England (Tory).
Macaulay's History of England (Whig).
Lingard's History of England (Catholic). 13 vols.
Strickland's Queens of England. 10 vols.
Ranke's History of England in the Seventeenth Century. 5 vols.
Macaulay's Essays (Bacon, Hampden, Hallam's History).
Goldwin Smith's Three English Statesmen (Cromwell, Pym, Hampden).
Cordery's Struggle against Absolute Monarchy.[1]
Cordery and Phillpott's King and Commonwealth.[1]
Gardiner's Puritan Revolution.[1]
Scott's Fortunes of Nigel (James I).

---

[1] The three best short histories.   [2] The two best short histories.   [3] The four best short histories.

X. The Commonwealth and Protectorate, 1649-1660 (see Preceding Period)

Gardiner's History of England (1649-1660).
*Ludlow's Memoirs (1640-1668).
*Carlyle's Life and Letters of Oliver Cromwell.
Carlyle's Hero Worship (Cromwell).
Guizot's Cromwell and the Commonwealth.
Morley's Cromwell.
Roosevelt's Cromwell.
Guizot's Richard Cromwell.
Guizot's Life of Monk.
Masson's Life and Times of Milton.
Bisset's Omitted Chapters in the History of England.
Pattison's Life of Milton.
Scott's Woodstock (Cromwell).

XI. Stuart Period (Second Part), 1660-1714

*Evelyn's Diary (1641-1706).
*Pepys's Diary (1659-1669).
*Burnet's History of his Own Time (1660-1713).
Macaulay's History of England (Whig).
Hallam's Constitutional History of England.
Taine's History of English Literature.
Strickland's Queens of England.
Ranke's History of England in the Seventeenth Century.
Hume's History of England (Tory).
Brewster's Life of Newton.
Lingard's History of England (Catholic). 13 vols.
Green's History of the English People.
Stanhope's History of England.
Lecky's History of England in the Eighteenth Century.
Macaulay's Essays (Milton, Mackintosh's History, War of the Spanish Succession, and The Comic Dramatists of the Restoration).
Creighton's Life of Marlborough.
Guizot's History of Civilization (Chapter XIII).
Morris's Age of Anne.[1]
Hale's Fall of the Stuarts.[1]
Cordery's Struggle against Absolute Monarchy.[1]
Scott's Peveril of the Peak and Old Mortality (Charles II).
Thackeray's Henry Esmond (Anne).

XII. The Hanoverian Period, 1714 to the Present time

*Memoirs of Robert Walpole.
*Horace Walpole's Memoirs and Journals.
Hallam's Constitutional History of England (to death of George II, 1760).

May's Constitutional History (1760-1870).
Amos's English Constitution (1830-1880).
Bagehot's English Constitution.
Lecky's History of England in the Eighteenth Century.
Walpole's History of England (1815-1816).
Molesworth's History of England (1830-1870).
Martineau's History of England (1816-1846).
Taine's History of English Literature.
Gibbins's Social Reformers (Wesley and Wilberforce; and the Factory Reformers).
Lecky's American Revolution (edited by Professor J. A. Woodburn).
Bancroft's History of the United States.
Bryant's History of the United States.
Stanhope's History of England (1713-1783).
Green's Causes of the Revolution.
Seeley's Expansion of England.
Frothingham's Rise of the Republic.
Southey's Life of Wesley.
Southey's Life of Nelson.
Wharton's Wits and Beaux of Society.
Waite's Life of Wellington.
Massey's Life of George III.
Smith's, Goldwin, Lectures (Foundation of the American Colonies).
Macaulay's Essays (Warren Hastings, Clive, Pitt, Walpole, Chatham, Johnson, Madame D'Arblay).
Scott's Rob Roy, Waverley, and Redgauntlet (the Old and the Young Pretender, 1715, 1735-1753).
Thackeray's Virginians (Washington).
Dickens's Barnaby Rudge (1780).
Smiles's Life of James Watt.
Smith's, Sydney, Peter Plymley's Letters.
Smiles's Life of Stephenson.
Thackeray's Four Georges.
McCarthy's Four Georges.
Smiles's Industrial Biography.
Allen's, Grant, Life of Darwin.
Ashton's Dawn of the XIXth Century in England.
Ludlow's American Revolution.[1]
Rowley's Settlement of the Constitution (1689-1784).[1]
Morris's Early Hanoverians (George I and II).[1]
McCarthy's Epoch of Reform (1830-1850).[1]
Tancock's England during the American and European Wars (1765-1820).[1]
Browning's Modern England (1820-1874).[1]
McCarthy's History of Our Own Times (1837-1897).
McCarthy's England under Gladstone (1880-1884).
Ward's Reign of Victoria (1837-1887).
Bolton's Famous English Statesmen of Queen Victoria's Reign.
Hinton's English Radical Leaders.
Gibbins's Social Reformers (Kingsley, Carlyle, and Ruskin).
Traill's Social England, Vol. VI.
Adams's, Brooks, America's Economic Supremacy.

[1] The nine best short histories.

Escott's Victorian Age.
The article on Victoria in the Diction-
  ary of National [British] Biography, Vol.
  LX.
The English Illustrated Magazine for July,
  1897.[1]

The Contemporary Review for June, 1897.[1]
The Fortnightly Review for June, 1897.[1]
King Edward VII. See Poole's Index to
  Reviews for 1910.
McCarthy's History of Our Own Times (to
  accession of George V).

[1] Contain valuable articles on the Victorian Era, giving general view of the reign.

SPECIAL READING REFERENCES ON TOPICS
OF ENGLISH HISTORY [1]

I. See, on this whole subject, Professor H. L. Cannon's Reading
References for English History referred to in the Short List of Books
on page xxxvi. Professor Cannon's volume contains "exact references
to some two thousand of the most useful and accessible works on English history." No other single volume can compare with it for usefulness
in this department.

II. See E. K. Kendall's Source-Book of English History; G. C. Lee's
Source-Book of English History; and Professor E. P. Cheyney's Read-
ings of English History (1 vol.); A. H. D. Acland, and C. Ransome,
Outline of the Political History of England, 1 vol.

III. See, for brief but carefully written biographical and historical
articles relating to English history, Chambers's Encyclopædia, 10 vols.
For fuller treatment see the New Encyclopædia Britannica (29 vols.),
The Dictionary of National [British] Biography (66 vols.), and the
International Encyclopædia (17 vols.).

IV. For recent events in English history, see Whitaker's Almanack,
Hazell's Annual, the Annual Register, the Statesman's Year-Book, and
other publications of this class.

[1] In connection with the investigation of topics it will be found that the five questions,
1. *When did the event occur?* 2. *Where did it occur?* 3. *How did it occur?* 4. *What caused
it?* 5. *What came of it?* (see Suggestions to Teachers, at the beginning of the book), can often
be used to good advantage. By slightly modifying their form they can be used equally well
respecting persons who have taken a leading part in originating or controlling events.

INDEX

ANNOUNCEMENTS

OUTLINES OF EUROPEAN HISTORY

By JAMES HARVEY ROBINSON, Columbia University, CHARLES A.
BEARD, Columbia University, and JAMES HENRY
BREASTED, The University of Chicago

PART I, $1.50   PART II, $1.50

THIS new series of textbooks offers the most noteworthy solution of the present-day high-school history problem yet attempted. With the two volumes of " Outlines of European History " in hand the teacher can cover general European history, beginning with ancient history, satisfactorily in two years, leaving the third year for American history. Moreover, the series is fully in accord with the new spirit in the teaching of history. Emphasis throughout is placed on conditions and institutions rather than on unrelated events, while by devoting Part II to the history of the last two hundred years, the course directs the pupil's attention especially to the problems and developments that are of present-day import. In short, both volumes of " Outlines of European History " are designed primarily to furnish the pupil the needed background for the intelligent interpretation of contemporary events.

The authors' reputation for sound scholarship and historical insight is international, while their style has an incisiveness and an imaginative freshness that make as attractive reading for the high-school pupil as any romance. The success of previous textbooks by the same authors is guaranty of the teachability of these new texts and of their entire fitness at every point for class use.

PART I 728 pages By JAMES HARVEY ROBINSON and JAMES HENRY BREASTED

THIS volume covers oriental, classical, and medieval history to the beginning of the eighteenth century, setting forth vividly those fundamental notions most essential to an understanding of subsequent developments. In style, in illustration, in organization, this book sets a new standard of achievement for high-school histories. The abundance and excellence of the illustrations are particularly notable. These, with their detailed legends, form a sort of parallel narrative of immense value to a proper understanding of the text. Several full-page illustrations in color and a number of "pen etchings," designed especially for this volume, add to the artistic excellence.

PART II 555 pages By JAMES HARVEY ROBINSON and CHARLES A. BEARD

THIS volume offers an illuminating treatment of European history from the eighteenth century to the present time. It includes the best and most comprehensive treatment of European developments of the first decade of the twentieth century available in any high-school history. The text is a rewriting and condensation for high schools of the authors' two-volume " Development of Modern Europe," the standard college text in the subject.

AMERICAN HISTORY

By DAVID SAVILLE MUZZEY
Barnard College, Columbia University, New York

12mo, cloth, 662 pages, illustrated, $1.50

THE object of this book is to present a lively and continuous narrative of the political development of our country, by a clear statement of the social and economic problems which have determined that development. These problems are treated topically, and the temptation merely to mention or allude to a vast number of facts not vitally connected with them has been resolutely resisted. Details such as the circumstances attending each colonial plantation, the tactics and casualties of military campaigns, the careers of men of slight influence in high office, have been excluded in order that the topics of first-rate importance in our history might receive a clear and ample treatment.

Special features of the book are its vivid literary style, its development of each topic regardless of such artificial chronological categories as presidential administrations, its full discussion of the federal power in connection with the Constitution, its emphasis on the westward-moving frontier as the most constant and potent force in our history, and its recognition of the influence of economic factors on our sectional rivalries and political theories. Over one third of the text is devoted to the political and economic history of the United States since the Civil War. The book is designed especially for the upper grades of the high school.

110a

GINN AND COMPANY PUBLISHERS

TEXT-BOOKS ON HISTORY

FOR HIGHER SCHOOLS AND COLLEGES

By D. H. MONTGOMERY
Author of the " Leading Facts of History Series "

THE STUDENT'S AMERICAN HISTORY. (Revised Edition.) A text book for high schools and colleges. 12mo. Cloth. 612 + lvii pages. With maps and illustrations. $1.40.

THE LEADING FACTS OF ENGLISH HISTORY. (Revised Edition.) 12mo. Cloth. xviii + 444 + lxix pages. Illustrated. $1.20.

THE LEADING FACTS OF FRENCH HISTORY. 12mo. Cloth. 328 + xxvii pages. Illustrated. $1.12.

IN the " Student's American History " the attractive and enduring qualities of Mr. Montgomery's other histories are found in an even higher degree. It follows the same general lines as the "Leading Facts of American History." It differs, however, from that manual in several important respects. It is much fuller in its treatment of political and constitutional history and of all the chief events in the nation's development. In this thorough revision particular attention has been given to the leading political features, to questions of constitutional history, and to the opening and settlement of the West and its influence on the development of the nation.

In Montgomery's " English History " the important events of that country are treated with great fullness, and their relation to that of Europe and the world is carefully shown.

No pains has been spared to make the execution of the work equal to its plan. Vivid touches here and there betray the author's mastery of details.

The object of Montgomery's " French History " is to present, within a moderate compass, the most important events of the history of France, selected, arranged, and treated according to the soundest principles of historical study and set forth in a clear and attractive narrative.

GINN & COMPANY PUBLISHERS

REFERENCE BOOKS IN HISTORY

Abbott: History and Description of Roman Political Institutions (Third Edition) $1.50

Brigham: Geographic Influences in American History 1.25

Callender: Selections from the Economic History of the United States, 1765–1860 . . . . 2.75

Cannon: Reading References for English History 2.50

Channing, Hart, and Turner: Guide to the Study and Reading of American History (Revised and Augmented Edition) . . 2.50

Cheyney: Readings in English History 1.80

Emerton: Introduction to the Middle Ages 1.12

Emerton: Mediæval Europe 1.50

Fess: History of Political Theory and Party Organization in the United States 1.50

Hayes: British Social Politics 1.75

Keller: Colonization 3.00

Myers: History as Past Ethics 1.50

Reinsch: Readings on American Federal Government 2.75

Reinsch: Readings on American State Government 2.25

Richardson, Ford, and Durfee: Syllabus of Continental European History 75

Riggs: Studies in United States History 60

Robinson: Readings in European History

Volume I 1.50

Volume II 1.50

Abridged Edition 1.50

Robinson and Beard: Readings in Modern European History

Volume I 1.40

Volume II 1.50

Thallon: Readings in Greek History 2.00

Tuell and Hatch: Selected Readings in English History 1.40

Webster: General History of Commerce 1.40

GINN AND COMPANY PUBLISHERS